PAUL SELIGSON
NICOLA MELDRUM
EDUARDO TRINDADE

English ID

2nd edition

Teacher's Book 1

Richmond

58 St Aldates
Oxford
OX1 1ST
United Kingdom

ISBN: 978-84-668-3051-5
Third reprint: 2024
CP: 944336

Publishing Director: Deborah Tricker
Publishers: Luke Baxter, Laura Miranda
Media Publisher: Luke Baxter
Editor: Sian Williams
Proofreaders: Glenys Davis, Lily Khambata, Diyan Leake
Design Manager: Lorna Heaslip
Cover Design: Lorna Heaslip
Design & Layout: Dave Kuzmicki
Photo Researcher: Magdalena Mayo
Audio Production: John Marshall Media Inc.

We would like to thank all those who have given their kind permission to reproduce material for this book:

Illustrators: Alexandra Barbarozza, Alexandre Matos, Beach-o-matic, Bernardo Franca, Bill Brown, Guillaume Gennet, Diego Loza, Gus Morais, Alvaro Nuñez, Klayton Luz, Leonardo Teixeira, Martins CG Studio, Rico

Photos:
V. Atmán; 123RF/Juan Bauitista Cofreces, Antonio Balaguer Soler, Tatjana Baibakova, oleksiy, Gerold Grotelueschen, ALFREDO COSENTINO, Julian Peters, Cathy Yeulet; ALAMYAKP Photos, Peter Forsberg/People, WENN Ltd, Pictorial Press Ltd, Simon Grosset, Ilene MacDonald, Collection Christophel, Stefan Sollfors, Inner Vision Pro, dennizn, Granger Historical Archive, Don Douglas, Michael Wheatley, Everett Collection Inc, Wm. Baker/GhostWorx, dcphoto, Martin Thomas Photography, carlos cardetas, AF Archive; GETTY IMAGES SALES SPAIN/Fuse, Enjoynz, FOX, E+, Anna Frajitova, Stockbyte, Amarita, AJ_Watt, Londoneye, tBoyan, Tomazl, Xavier Arnau, TriggerPhoto, CJ Rivera, Nikada, Maskot, Zxvisual, Lisafx, Caziopeia, Onston, Drbimages, Vostok, Klaus Vedfelt, wakila, Phive2015, Alvarez, AntonioGuillem, Andresr, Byrdyak, DimaChe, CSA Images, Eyewave, Gerenme, Kaantes, Jabiru, Klasu Tiedge, Stockcam, Ipopba, CaronB, Jeff Kravitz, Dragonimages, Bill Baptist, Win McNamee, Nazar_ab, Pingebat, Serts, Leeser87, JoKMedia, Pekic, Jaromila, Mr.nutnuchit Phutsawagung/EyeEm, NurPhoto, Bas Vermolen, Boston Globe, Erik Isakson, Image Source, Robynmac, Scanrail, Klaus Tiedge, Totororo, WPA Pool, Wsfurlan, PaoloGaetano, Adie Bush, Alan Graf, Ansonimao, Ricky Vigil, bowdenimages, Chalabala, Cindy Ord, Designalldone, FatCamera, Heshphoto, LJM Photo, Luis Cataneda, Martin-dm, Mixdabass, Nancy Ney, Rafael Fabres, Polka Dot, Ridofranz, StockFood, Janoka82, Tuan Tran, Westend61, icarmen13, karandaev, Adam Gault, Ajr_images, Buyenlarge, Eric McCandless, Dreamnikon, Drewhadley, EnolaBrain, Eri Morita, FSTOPLIGHT, Grandriver, Hillwoman2, Maica, Gkrphoto, Flavijus, Kali9, Flashpop, Harold Stiver/EyeEm, Georgeclerk, Dmitry_7, JackF, Filadendron, Bettmann, Eva-Katalin, Don Farrall, Yvdavyd, Fudio, Futureimage, TangMan Photography, Hero Images, Ildo Frazao, Jay's Photo, Jesse Grant, Karinsasaki, Karwai Tang, Lovelypeace, Arnab Guha Photography, Rose_Carson, Ryan MacVay, Sam Edwards, Shapecharge, Simoningate, Svariophoto, The_burtons, Igor Kisselev - www.close-up.biz, 10'000 Hours, Photo by Ivan Dmitri/Michael Ochs Archives, BamBamImages, Tom Werner, spooh, Pixelfit, Recep-bg,

© Richmond / Santillana Global S.L. 2019

All rights reserved. No part of this book may be reproduced, stored in a retrieval system or transmitted in any form by any means, electronic, mechanical, photocopying, recording or otherwise, without the prior permission in writing of the Publisher.

Tom Merton, Gpointstudio, BraunS, RichLegg, Juice Images, Karin Dreyer, Karl Tapales, Kevin Winter, YinYang, Thinkstock, Ligia Botero, Michael Tran, Mike Cameron, Momentimages, Morsa Images, Oneinchpunch, Brian Cullen/EyeEm, PeopleImages, Raymond Hall, Rustemgurler, South_agency, Stocksnapper, Tim Robberts, Travis Payne, Theo Wargo, Spinkle, Ayzek, AlasdairJames, Andersen Ross, Ariel Skelley, Carsten Koall, Dan Bannister, Thatpichai, Gabriel Bouys, Inti St Clair, Istanbulimage, Jamie Garbutt, Johner Images, Joseph Okpako, Jupiterimages, Ryan McVay, Merinka, Mikkelwilliam, Mitchell Funk, Mlsfotografia, Pacific Press, Paul Bradbury, Peathegee Inc, Peter Cade, Samir Hussein, Serhil Brovko, Stephen Marks, Steve Granitz, Ullstein Bild, _human/iStock, Anadolu Agency, OJO images, Marcaux, Caracterdesign, David De Lossy, Digital Vision, Dzphotogallery, FS Productions, Image_By_Kenny, Kryssia Campos, LauriPatterson, Martin Barraud, Shannon Finney, SinghaphanAllB, Zero Creatives, franckreporter, Axel Bernstorff, Aonip, Fabrice LEROUGE, JGI/Jamie Grill, Lutsina Tatiana, MakiEni's Photo, Mario Gutierrez, Michael Dunning, Philippe Regard, Philippe TURPIN, Piotr Pawelczyk, Adam Lunde/EyeEm, Aurelien Maunier, Crady Von Pawlak, Education Images, Kansas City Star, MangoStar_Studio, Asia Images Group, Mike Prior, Alexander Tamargo, Abel Halasz/EyeEm, MiguelMalo, Lawcain, Yulia_Davidovich, C Squared Studios, ColorBlind Images, ElenaNichizhenova, Jonathan Paciullo, Malcolm P Chapman, Maya Karkalicheva, PeterHermesFurian, Vi Ngoc Minh Khue, AleksandarGeorgiev, Richard E. Aaron, Buena Vista Images, Enrique Diaz/7cero, Jason Merritt/TERM, Jonas Hafner/EyeEm, Julie Moquet/EyeEm, Katra Toplak/EyeEm, Larry Busacca/PW18, Oksana Vejus/EyeEm, PamelaJoeMcFarlane, Razvan Chisu/EyeEm, Tim Clayton-Corbis, Burcu Atalay Tankut, Dan Thornberg/EyeEm, Dave and Les Jacobs, Elizabeth Fernandez, Lars Baron, Quynh Anh Nguyen, Teresa Recena/EyeEm, The Washington Post, Axelle/Bauer-Griffin, Classen Rafael/EyeEm, Color Day Production, Fabiano Santos/EyeEm, Jose Luis Pelaez Inc, Monkeybusinessimages, Nils Hendrik Mueller, Santiago Bluguermann, Aaron Fortunato/EyeEm, Andriy Mykhalchevskyy, Sara Herrlander/EyeEm, Science Photo Library, Peter Macdiarmid, Athletea Widjaja/EyeEm, Cynthia Lafrance/EyeEm, Hinterhaus Productions, James Haliburton/EyeEm, Gallo Images-Stuart Fox, chokkicx/Digital Vision, Benedetta Barbanti/EyeEm, Caiaimage/Agnieszka Olek, Szabo Ervin-Edward/EyeEm, Jules Frazier Photography, Thomas Roetting/LOOK-foto, Paul Mansfield Photography, De Agostini Picture Library, Jon Feingersh Photography Inc, John Fenigersh Photography Inc, JB Lacroix, LIU JIN, Michael Rheault - madfire@gmail.com, Compassionate Eye Foundation/Gary Burchell, Poba, ANDREYGUDKOV; ISTOCKPHOTO/Getty Images Sales Spain, Susan Chiang, Juanmonino, Chmiel; NASA; SHUTTERSTOCK/ Arts Illustrated Studios, Moviestore Collection, ESB Professional, Swan Gallet/WWD, ParrySuwanitch, Happy Together, Ken McKay, AlexLMX; Louisville Convention & Visitor Bureau; Tumbleweed Tiny House Company; Kaitlyn Schlicht; Kelly Bruno; Dotta; Helen Chelton López de Haro; Jorge Cueto; United Nations; ARCHIVO SANTILLANA

The Publisher has made every effort to trace the owner of copyright material; however, the Publisher will correct any involuntary omission at the earliest opportunity.

Printed in Brazil by Forma Certa Grafica Digital
Lote: 799669
Código: 290530515

Contents

ID SB Language Map	**4**
Introduction	**6**
Features Presentation	
Unit 1	**24**
Unit 2	**48**
Review 1	**72**
Unit 3	**76**
Unit 4	**100**
Review 2	**124**
Unit 5	**128**
Mid-term Review	**152**
Unit 6	**156**
Review 3	**180**
Unit 7	**184**
Unit 8	**208**
Review 4	**232**
Unit 9	**236**
Unit 10	**260**
Review 5	**284**
SB1 Grammar	**288**
Sounds & Usual Spellings	**308**
Audioscript	**310**
Songs	**324**

ID SB Language map

	Question syllabus	Vocabulary	Grammar	Speaking & Skills
1	1.1 Are you Canadian?	Countries & nationalities Adjectives and a / an + noun	Verb be – ➕ ➖ Yes / No ❓ Subject pronouns	Introduce yourself & greetings Ask & answer about countries & nationalities Give opinions about people and places
	1.2 How do you spell your last name?	The alphabet Numbers 11–100		Spell words & your name Say your age & where you're from
	1.3 What's your email address?	Personal objects / plurals	Verb be – Wh- ❓ Demonstrative pronouns	Ask for & give personal information Ask about & identify objects
	1.4 Are these your glasses?	Adjectives & colors	Possessive adjectives	Talk about possessions Describe objects
	1.5 What's your full name?			Complete a form
	How are you?	Greetings & responses		Meeting people & social interaction
	Writing 1: A social media profile	ID Café 1: Role-play a class reunion		
2	2.1 When do you get up?	Activities & days of the week Time expressions	go activities	Describe routine Ask & answer about routine Ask & answer about sleeping habits
	2.2 What do you do in the mornings?	Morning routine	Simple present ➕ ➖ Prepositions of time	Talk about & compare morning routines
	2.3 Who do you live with?	Family	Simple present ❓	Describe family Question intonation Ask and answer simple present questions
	2.4 When do you check your phone?	Cell phone expressions	Frequency adverbs	Talk about cell phone habits Do a survey about phone use
	2.5 How old are you?			Role-play an interview
	How do you celebrate your birthday?	Special occasions		Use celebratory expressions
	Writing 2: A personal email	ID Café 2: Talk about reviews and reports		Review 1 p. 30
3	3.1 What's the weather like?	Weather	It's + adjective	Describe weather Ask & answer about weather
	3.2 Are you busy at the moment?	Everyday actions (1) Months & seasons	Present continuous ➕ ➖	Talk about what's happening now Talk about months & seasons
	3.3 What are you doing these days?	Technology problems	Present continuous ❓	Ask & answer about what's happening now Discuss technology problems
	3.4 What do you do after school / work?	Everyday actions (2) Verbs for emotion, senses or mental states Future time expressions	Simple present vs. present continuous	Talk about what people are doing now and what they usually do Talk about celebrity activists
	3.5 Why are you learning English?		need to / have to	Analyze your English
	Are you thirsty?	Adjectives (feelings)	Informal English	Make offers
	Writing 3: A language profile	ID Café 3: Discuss photography		
4	4.1 Do you like tennis?	Sports	Definite article the	Talk about sports Pronunciation of the
	4.2 Can you drive a tractor?	Abilities	Can: Yes / No ❓ / short answers	Ask and answer about ability Rank items that can change the world
	4.3 What languages can you speak?	Talents	Can: ➕ ➖ and Wh- ❓ Adverbs	Ask and answer about ability & talents Role-play a job interview
	4.4 Are you an organized person?	Clothes	Possessive pronouns Possessive s	Talk about what people are wearing Talk about ownership Talk about being messy / tidy
	4.5 Do you like spas?	Spa facilities		Read for details Describe a perfect spa day
	What shoe size are you?	Shopping expressions	Punctuation	Shop for clothes
	Writing 4: A job application	ID Café 4: Design and present a superhero		Review 2 p. 56
5	5.1 Is there a mall in your area?	Public places	There is / there are ➕ ➖ ❓	Describe a town / neighborhood
	5.2 What are your likes and dislikes?	Free-time activities Household chores	like / love / hate / enjoy / not mind + verb + -ing	Talk about likes and dislikes Sentence stress
	5.3 What do you like doing on vacation?	Vacation	Comparative adjectives	Talk about vacations and vacation activities Describe a perfect vacation
	5.4 How often do you leave voice messages?	House sitting	Object pronouns Imperatives Comparatives / superlatives	Talk about house sitting Give instructions
	5.5 What's a staycation?			Give and understand instructions
	Do you live near here?	Giving directions		Give and follow directions
	Writing 5: A city brochure	ID Café 5: Talk about personal technology		Mid-term review p. 70

	Question syllabus		Vocabulary	Grammar	Speaking & Skills
6	6.1	What's in your refrigerator?	Food & drink	Countable vs. uncountable nouns	Talk about food & drink Describe what's in your refrigerator
	6.2	What do you eat for lunch and dinner?	Food portions & containers	Quantifiers: *some* and *any*	Talk about morning food & healthy eating
	6.3	How often do you eat chocolate?	Food and nutrition	Quantifiers: *a little, a few, a lot of*	Use quantifiers to talk about activities you like / don't like
	6.4	How many meals do you cook a week?	Food Cognates	*How much* vs. *how many*	Talk about food and nutrition Take a class survey
	6.5	Are you hungry?	Menu food		Scan a menu Order food from a menu
		What would you like for lunch?	Restaurant phrases		Order food in a restaurant
	Writing 6: A food diary		ID Café 6: Role-play a restaurant situation		Review 3 *p. 84*
7	7.1	Do you live in a house?	Rooms & furniture	Past of *be*: *there was / there were*	Describe your home Compare a home then and now
	7.2	Where were you last night?	Party items Past time expressions	Past of *be*: ⊕⊖❓ / short answers	Talk about a party Ask & answer about last week
	7.3	Where were you last New Year's Eve?	New Year's Eve celebrations	Prepositions of place	Describe New Year's Eve celebrations Describe positions of objects
	7.4	Was your hometown different 10 years ago?	Dates Places in a city	*there is / there are* & *there was / there were*	Talk about changes to cities Compare your hometown in the past and now
	7.5	Do you enjoy weddings?			Predict from context Describe a special event
		How about a barbecue on Sunday?			Make invitations
	Writing 7: An online review		ID Café 7: Describe a party		
8	8.1	When did you start school?	Life events Past time expressions	Simple past regular verbs ⊕⊖	Talk about past events Write a biography Pronunciation of past tense verbs
	8.2	Did you go out last weekend?	Ordinal numbers & dates Simple past irregular verbs	Simple past irregular verbs ⊕⊖	Talk about what you did yesterday / last birthday Pronunciation of past irregular verbs
	8.3	Where did you go on your last vacation?	Vacations	Simple past ❓ / short answers	Ask and answer about your last vacation / Pronunciation of *Did you*
	8.4	When do you listen to music?	Everyday activity verbs	Subject questions vs. object questions	Do a pop quiz Write questions for a class quiz
	8.5	Can I use your phone?	Phone phrases		Understand a story Tell a story
		Could you help me, please?	Phrases to make requests		Ask for favors and respond
	Writing 8: A vacation message		ID Café 8: Call a friend for help		Review 4 *p. 110*
9	9.1	How did you get here today?	Transportation	*How do / did you get to …?*	Ask & answer about personal transportation Describe transportation problems
	9.2	What do you do?	Jobs	Articles + jobs	Talk about occupations & dream jobs Talk about commuting & keeping in shape
	9.3	Where are you going to be in 2025?	Future plans	*going to* for future	Talk about future plans Make predictions Pronunciation of *going to / gonna*
	9.4	What are you going to do next year?	Life changes	Present continuous for future *going to* vs. present continuous	Talk about intentions and plans Write New Year's resolutions
	9.5	Would you like to be a nurse?	Jobs		Make connections Discuss occupations in the future
		Could I borrow your pen?			Ask for permission
	Writing 9: A reply to a blog post		ID Café 9: Speculate about life in the future		
10	10.1	Do you look like your mom?	The body & face Adjectives (appearance)		Talk about parts of the body Describe physical appearance
	10.2	Are you like your dad?	Adjectives (character)	Comparatives with *-er* & *more* *Like* as verb & preposition	Talk about a timeline Make comparisons
	10.3	Who's the most generous person in your family?	Personality types Adjectives (character)	Superlatives with *-est* & *most*	Describe personality and places
	10.4	What's the best place in the world?	Geographical features	Comparatives & superlatives	Sentence stress Talk about surprising facts
	10.5	What's your blood type?	Parts of the body		Understand facts
		Is your English better than a year ago?			Make choices
	Writing 10: A family profile		ID Café 10: Talk about making changes to physical appearance		Review 5 *p. 136*

Grammar *p. 138*   Sounds and Usual Spellings *p. 158*   Audioscript *p. 160*

Introduction

This is the 2nd edition of Richmond's four-level American English course for monolingual adult and young adult learners whose mother tongue is Spanish or Portuguese. Together with iDentities 1 and 2, it forms the first six-level course purpose-built for Latin America, taking learners from Beginner to a strong C1 level.

With the right focus, embracing and celebrating familiar language while anticipating inevitable transfer errors, speakers of Spanish and Portuguese ought to learn to be both fluent and accurate in English more quickly than most.

This unique, highly original course, with a brand-new eye-catching design, motivating topics and constant opportunities for personalization, helps learners to express who they are—their personality, culture, their identity—in English. English iD helps you learn to be yourself in English.

What do Romance-language speakers most expect and need from an English course?

You might want to note down your own answers before you read on.

Our research suggests that, above all, learners expect:

- to become fluent listeners and speakers as quickly as possible;
- confidence building—to know the L1 equivalent of new language items quickly so that they can overcome their fears and speak meaningfully in class;
- quick results, and a strong sense of progress;
- contemporary, locally pertinent, interesting content, tailored to their likely interests and linguistic needs. Real-life, adult, local relevance, with lots of personalization;
- overt teaching of grammar and vocabulary, a systematic approach to pronunciation, plenty of skills practice;
- specific help with writing and spelling;
- an appropriate, adult teaching style combined with strong self-study elements, including autonomous learning tools to speed up their learning: we provide keys to most of the material, audio for all longer texts, and all the listening and video activities are available on the Richmond Learning Platform for self-study;
- value—both for the time they invest and the money they spend.

Methodology

English iD is in every sense a communicative course, teaching learners to speak in as short a time as possible and focusing on both fluency and accuracy.

Fluency: notice the multiple exchanges modeled throughout lessons in speech bubbles, or the number of Latinate cognates included in every text, with word stress marked in pink to give sts confidence to try to say them.

Accuracy: via the 110 **Common mistakes** (anticipating likely L1 transfer errors that should be avoided) presented in each lesson, or the 84 Notice tasks in the **Audioscript** to provide genuine contextualized help with pronunciation and spelling.

Learners need to be given opportunities to express their thoughts. English iD and, later, iDentities progressively adapt as the series evolves to reflect the best learning practices at each of the learner's advancing levels. Initially, English iD Starter relies on lots of short question-and-answer exchanges supported by lots of drilling in the Students' Book, to be done in class. Then, at subsequent levels, such drills become more discretionary, moving into both Workbook and Teacher's Book. At advanced levels, there is an increased focus on levels of formality, as a student's need to master various registers gradually increases.

The same goes for the lexis—where the initial simple task of matching vocabulary to pictures in the early levels of English iD becomes more abstract and contextualized—and grammar, where spoon-feeding is reduced and inductive learning increased, as learners' confidence and foreign language learning experience grow.

English iD provides the tools to allow you, the teacher, to incorporate your own pedagogical identity into the course, as well as to emphasize what you think will be more relevant for your learners.

Advantaging Monolingual Classes

Globally, most classes are monolingual. English iD was conceived to facilitate monolingual classroom learning. The frequent lack of opportunity to speak English locally means teachers need to maximize fluency practice, getting the students to use the language as much as possible in class.

In monolingual classes, learners share the same L1 and most aspects of a culture, which a teacher can exploit. They share similar advantages / difficulties with English too, which should be a unifying "strength" for anticipating problems and errors. Accelerating through what is easier for learners, and spending more time on what is difficult, "sharpens" classes to maximize the learning potential.

Adults need a radically different approach from children, whose mother tongue is not yet established, and who learn like sponges, absorbing all the English you throw at them. Young adults' and adults' minds are different: they cannot help but translate—mentally at least—and immediately

Introduction

resort to the mother tongue when they cannot find the words to express their thoughts in English. Rather than running against nature, English ID avoids this trap by gently embracing similar items when appropriate, but without ever forcing active use of L1, leaving that option up to you.

Paraphrasing Ur (2011), "teachers should choose procedures that lead to best learning by whichever students they're teaching" (extracted from *Vocabulary Activities*, Penny Ur, Cambridge University Press, 2011). We believe English ID's formula can really help native speakers of Spanish and Portuguese learn both more comfortably and more efficiently.

English ID embraces students' linguistic strengths. It helps students to use what they know and helps you, the teacher, to foresee these automatic transfers and focus appropriately on them. With English ID, students can easily enjoy what is easy and, at the same time, the more complex issues can be made clearer for them.

Flexi-lessons

Each English ID lesson is linear, and can be taught directly from the page, with our interleaved *Teacher's Book* lesson plans reflecting and fully supporting this.

However, as we appreciate that all teachers and classes are different, English ID also provides multiple entry points for each lesson for you to choose from.

You can begin with:

- the suggested **warm-up** activity in every *Teacher's Book* lesson plan;
- the *Teacher's Book* books-closed presentation (either of main lexis or grammar);
- the **lesson title question**. Return to it at the end of class for sts to answer it better—a "test–teach–test" route through the lesson;
- a **Make it personal** from the page in the same test-teach-test way;
- the lesson's **song line**;
- the **Common mistakes** —board them corrected or focus on them on the page at the start of class to highlight what to avoid and thus maximize opportunities to get things right throughout the class;
- the **Grammar** pages for a more traditional, deductive presentation.

In addition, you can choose from these lesson routes for monolingual Spanish / Portuguese learners as monolingual classes allow you to be more proactive, and offer opportunities for more tailored, accelerated pedagogy:

- Divide lexical presentations into two phases: first, focus on cognates, then the other words. Have sts guess the pronunciation of the words they recognize.
- Read the lesson text (on-page reading or listening from the **Audioscript** section). In pairs, sts try to pronounce the pink-stressed words. Teach the class as usual, then come back to the words at the end of the class, and have sts pronounce them better.
- Underline the words which look the same (or similar) in Spanish or Portuguese, then check as the lesson evolves whether they are or are not true cognates, and how to pronounce them. This is especially good for weaker learners, as it helps them get familiar with texts in a non-threatening way.
- Do the same as above with suffixes.
- Speed up or avoid inductive presentations, by, e.g., the **Common mistakes** route above.
- Compare word stress, as in the presentation of the months in *Student's Book 1* on p. 35, ex. 3A.

Key concepts

English ID promotes the three "friendlies": It is language-friendly, learner-friendly, and teacher-friendly.

1. Language-friendly

English ID is not just another international series. It is a language-friendly series, which embraces sts' existing language knowledge—a fundamental pillar of all foreign language learning through, e.g., exploiting cognates, familiar structures, famous song lines, and local cultural background—to help them better understand how English works.

2. Learner-friendly

English ID respects the learner's need to be spoken to as an adult, so sts explore a full range of topics requiring critical thinking. It also helps sts to negotiate and build their own new identity in English.

In addition, English ID:

- supports sts, helping them avoid obvious errors in form, word order, and pronunciation;
- motivates sts, as they discover they can recognize a lot of English, which they already have "inside themselves";
- offers a vast range of activities, resources and recycling in order to ensure sts have enough practice to finally learn to speak English.

Introduction

3. Teacher-friendly

English ID respects each teacher's need to teach as he or she wants to. Some wish to teach off the page with minimal preparation, others dip in and out, while others largely follow the *Teacher's Book*. All these options have been built into English ID from the start.

The flexi-lesson structure helps teachers to individualize, personalize and vary classes, as well as focus on what is important for them.

Key features

1. A 60-question syllabus

Every lesson begins with a question as the title, which serves as a natural warm-up activity to introduce and later review each lesson topic.

These questions offer:

- an introduction to the lesson topic, an essential component for a good lesson, as, in some cases, topics may be new to sts;
- a ready-made short lead-in to create interest, paving the way for the integration of skills, grammar, and content;
- an opportunity for sts to get to know and feel comfortable with each other before the lesson begins, facilitating pair and group work;
- an instant review or speaking activity, whenever you need one: sts in pairs can look back at the map of the book and ask and answer questions;
- a wonderful expression of syllabus;
- a useful placement test. Asking some of the 60 questions when sts are being level-tested is a good way to help place them appropriately.

2. A balanced approach to grammar

Our rich grammar syllabus offers an eclectic approach to meet the needs of all sts. It offers an innovative combination of:

- inductive grammar, with students discovering patterns and completing rules for themselves in and around the lesson-page grammar boxes;
- deductive grammar—the 20-page "Grammar" section, which regularly encourages sts to contrast English with their L1 and notice where English is easier, in order to motivate. This can be done in class for quick diagnostic work if sts are making lots of mistakes, or assigned as homework as a form of "flipping"—sts complete the grammar exercises before the forthcoming lesson, in order to speed up input and give more time for practice;
- implicit, contrastive grammar analysis, by showing what not to say via **Common mistakes**;
- a wide variety of extra grammar practice in Reviews, the *Workbook*, and on the Richmond Learning Platform, as well as suggestions for extra contextualized writing in the Teacher's Book.

3. It has to be personal

Not only the 60 lesson question titles, but each phase of every lesson (and most *Workbook* lessons) ends with **Make it personal** activities: real, extended personalization—the key stage in any language practice activity. Sts expand all topics and main language items into their own lives, opinions, contexts, and experiences. This is how sts continue to construct and consolidate their English identity. Successfully "making it personal" is what makes sts believe that they can be themselves in English.

4. Avoid common mistakes to speak better, more quickly

Most lessons include **Common mistakes**, a flexible resource to foster accuracy. We highlight what to avoid before, during, and / or after any lesson. **Common mistakes** helps maximize self- and peer-correction too. Sts are enabled to help and teach themselves, by anticipating and therefore more quickly avoiding, reviewing, and remembering typical learner errors.

If short of time, as teachers so often are, **Common mistakes** can help you cut through a longer, more inductive presentation and get to the practice activity more quickly. They are flexible, too: you can refer to them at any time in the lesson, usually the earlier the better.

5. Integrated skills

The fifth lesson in each unit is an integrated skills page, which gives sts the opportunity to immerse themselves in a highly engaging, contemporary topic and practice all four skills in real-world activities.

6. Classic song lines to "hook" language

English ID uses music in exercises, cultural references, images, and, most obviously, the authentic song lines in each lesson. In addition, music as a theme features prominently in several lessons.

Why music? Songs are often the most popular source of authentic listening practice in and out of class. Most sts have picked up a lot of English words through songs, ads, TV theme tunes, movie soundtracks, etc. But often they don't realize they know them or the exact meaning of what they're singing.

Introduction

The song lines empower both teachers and sts by offering useful language references and pronunciation models; and an authentic source of student-friendly input to elicit, present, practice, personalize, extend, and "hook" almost anything.

Unique to English iD and iDentities, the song lines have a direct link to each lesson, whether to illustrate grammar, lexis, or the lesson topic, and are designed to provide an authentic hook to help sts remember the lesson and the language studied. Looking for the link provides an additional fun, puzzle-like element to every lesson.

English iD *Teacher's Book* offers a highly original useful **Songs** bank of cultural, background, and procedural notes for every song line, including the artist's name, suggestions on exactly where and how to exploit it, and optional activities. You can find this useful resource on pages 324–336.

Tip Of course, we don't suggest you use these songs in full, just the extract we've chosen. Besides, many aren't actually appropriate when you look at the complete lyrics, but the lines we've chosen are globally famous and should be easy to identify, find on the Internet, and be sung by at least some sts. Obviously, with your own classes you can exploit the song lines in a variety of ways.

Some ways to use song lines in English iD:

- play / show (part of) the song as sts come into class;
- sing / hum the song line and / or look for links to the song at an appropriate time during the class to help sts remember the lesson later;
- read and guess the artist's gender, message, etc.;
- analyze the song for pronunciation: rhyme, repeated sounds, alliteration;
- expand. *What comes before / after this line? What's the whole song about?*;
- change the tense or some words to make it more or less formal and see how it sounds. *Why did the artist choose this tense?*;
- provoke discussion around a theme / issue;
- ask *What do you associate the song with?*, e.g., a moment, vacation, dance, movie;
- search online for other songs that connect to the lesson in some way;
- use sections of the song as a class warm-up, review, listening for pleasure, an end of the lesson sing-along, etc.;
- board or dictate the line but add, subtract, or change some words for sts to correct it (similar to **Common mistakes**).

Course structure and components

English coursebooks have often been too long, too repetitive, or inflexible, meaning teachers have either to rush to get through them—denying sts the practice they need to achieve an adequate degree of fluency—or start omitting sections, often leaving sts feeling frustrated. English iD was designed to be flexible, so you can tailor it to fit your schedule.

English iD has ...

- ten core units, each comprised of five approximately one-hour lessons, followed by an integrated **Writing** lesson and an iD **Café** video lesson;
- 20 pages of grammar reference with corresponding exercises;
- selected audioscripts that encourage sts to focus on specific listening points;
- *Workbook*: one page of review and extra practice material per lesson;
- Richmond Learning Platform for English iD, which can be accessed using the code on the inside front cover of the *Student's Book*;
- *Digital Book for Teachers*: IWB version of the Student's Book.

Vocabulary

Vocabulary teaching is a particularly strong feature of English iD because of the variety of input and review options.

1. Picture Dictionary

The most popular way to teach / learn vocabulary is through some kind of "picture + key" approach, where students can work out the meaning from the visual, without the need to translate, and then cover and test themselves.

Every English iD unit begins with a contextualized, lesson-integrated picture dictionary. Core vocabulary is presented through various combinations of this basic four-step approach:

1. Match words / phrases to pictures.
2. Guess pronunciation (from the pink stress / sts' own linguistic experience, and growing knowledge of English).
3. Listen to the words in context and check / repeat as necessary.
4. Cover and test yourself / a partner, either immediately or any time later for review.

Introduction

All **Reviews** begin by sending sts back to the picture dictionary elements in each unit to review and remember words. Almost all of the images in English ID are contextualized and used to present, review, and test vocabulary.

2. A cognate-friendly approach

Thousands of words with cognate relationships are common to English and most Latin languages. Over 1,500 of these are very common. There are also thousands of recognizable cognate-rooted words. By systematically building them into English ID, we feel we have created a unique opportunity for students to progress more quickly and more comfortably with English. Put simply, they can both understand and produce more language—and more interesting adult language—faster.

Throughout their learning process, students make cross-linguistic connections, so we have chosen to nurture this strategy systematically throughout English ID. It enhances both their language awareness and their English lexical knowledge, and makes learning more efficient.

English ID prides itself on helping students to expand their vocabulary quickly. Lexical presentations often separate what is "known / easy"—whether from "international" English, words already seen in the course, or near cognates—from "what is new / unfamiliar," to help students focus better.

Familiar words mainly require attention for pronunciation and spelling, whereas the unfamiliar require a lot more effort to learn meaning too. This provides a valuable additional "hook" into the student's memory.

Significant stress or word-formation patterns are regularly highlighted to enable "learning leaps."

English ID consciously works on developing the confidence the students need to begin to guess how words might be pronounced or spelled in English. Guessing—being willing to take a shot, bringing in words that you already know which might work well in English—is a key learning strategy, often ignored elsewhere.

Embracing cognates also allows much more interesting, more adult speaking, and listening tasks too, e.g., asking *Any coincidences / similarities / pronunciation surprises? What do you have in common? Who is more assertive?*, etc.

> **Tip** We do not suggest you drill all these words nor try to make them all into active vocabulary. In most cases, cognates are there just as passive vocabulary, actually helping sts understand more. We see no point in hiding words from sts when they can cope with them, and indeed usually enjoy doing so. The words which become active differ greatly from group to group and will always be your choice, not ours. We are simply trying to give sts access to more adult language more quickly.

Skills

Speaking

English ID teaches spoken English and prioritizes oral fluency. Fluency naturally precedes accuracy, and this is why English ID gives sts plenty of cognates to express themselves quickly, leading to accuracy sooner.

In order to learn both quickly and well, sts should be given every opportunity to try to express their ideas and opinions in comprehensible English at every stage of every lesson. After all, practice and personalization are the best way to improve and self-correct, and whatever method you use, accuracy will always be the last element of competence learners will acquire. In English ID, every lesson, be it a listening, vocabulary, grammar, reading, or writing focus, is full of controlled oral practice and personalized speaking opportunities, clearly marked and modeled by multiple speech bubbles on every page.

Listening

English ID has a huge amount of recorded material, in both the *Student's Book* and the *Workbook*, which are all available on the Richmond Learning Platform.

Listening homework should be set as often as possible, as what sts most need is to spend the maximum time in the company of English in order to become truly confident when expressing themselves in English. These days this is relatively easy—they can listen while doing other things, at home, traveling, at the gym, etc.

In addition to the material included in the course itself, teachers may find some of the following suggestions helpful, either in or out of class:

- have sts create their own listening practice at this level—listening to music or podcasts, watching TV or movies, using bilingual websites to figure out what words mean, sending each other recordings in English via, e.g., WhatsApp;
- dictogloss short sections of any listening activity—listen and remember (or write down) all you can, then compare in pairs;
- pause at any time in any listening to check comprehension: *What do you think was said?* after any short section is a key question in trying to teach rather than keep testing listening.

If time permits …

- sensitize sts to how words blur and have a variety of sound shapes in connected speech and elicit / explain how pronunciation changes;

Introduction

- expose sts to "the difficult," e.g., phoneme variations in connected speech; dictate multiple examples of phrases containing the same weak forms;
- model processes used by L1 listeners: decoding sounds into words / clauses and building larger scale meaning;
- transcribe elision as they hear it: old people = *ole people*, a blind man = *a bly man*, etc;
- study and interpret, e.g. pairs: *He said he called* vs. *He said he'd call*.

The following are some ideas for listening homework that you could set your sts:

- listening to recordings of the class itself (flipped)—instructions, stories, pair work, role-play, etc.;
- web-based listening: songs, podcasts, searching online for the huge number of online lessons available now, YouTube, radio, audiobooks, TV (with subtitles in L1 & L2);
- homework partners—call / record messages, check answers with partner, dub favorite movie scene, etc.

Reading

English ID provides substantial reading practice in terms of the amount available, and the complexity of cognate-rich texts, building on sts' existing language knowledge to gain fluency more quickly. We strongly suggest you break up longer texts, giving short tasks.

- Keep tasks to 2 or 3 minutes, then have sts share what they remember, and predict what comes next before reading on.
- Sts in pairs each read a different paragraph to create an information gap, then tell each other what they read.
- Give sts (via the digital board, cut up slips, or let them choose) random samples of the texts—a couple of lines from different paragraphs, or the first and last line of each paragraph, etc., to share what they understood and speculate about what else they will read.
- With any text, you can get sts to cover it with a sheet of paper, read one line at a time, guess what comes next in pairs, then unveil the next line to see if they were right. They then do the same with the next line, and so on.
- Make each st in a group responsible for finding the answer to one of the questions, then share with the group.
- Help sts experience different reading skills: skimming, scanning, etc., even within the same text, by setting different tasks, and perhaps giving them reading role-cards for different paragraphs or columns of text: *A) Read and translate the text word by word.; B) Read the text in order to memorize as much of the information as you can.; C) Read the text for the general idea.; D) Read the text aloud quietly to yourself at a comfortable speed.*

These ideas and many more you will find expanded in the *Teacher's Book* notes.

Writing

Our writing syllabus is primarily covered by the integrated **Writing** lesson at the end of each unit. Here sts are given a clear written model, a variety of tasks to analyze it, specific writing tips and a structured model to draft, check, then share with a classmate, before finally submitting it to you or posting on the class learning platform / wiki. The intention is to protect you, the busy teacher, from having to dedicate time to excessive marking of avoidable mistakes, as well as to help sts be more in control of their own writing.

Pronunciation

The English ID "Audioscript" section is not just a script to be read or listened to with no clear focus. It's designed to provide real training with listening and pronunciation.

It aims to help sts learn to listen better as the course progresses by focusing on features of pronunciation:

- noticing sounds, stress, aspects of connected speech, intonation and spelling relationships;
- spoken language (e.g., noticing discourse signals such as fillers, pauses, repetition, self-correction, and interruptions);
- sub-skills of listening, like inferring, predicting, identifying main points in discourse, understanding attitudinal meaning and all aspects of listening.

Again, it is flexible and both teacher- and learner-friendly. All the tasks are "noticing" tasks. The tasks are always "highlighted," making them all free-standing, to avoid the need for teacher intervention, unless, of course, you wish to spend time here. So, you can choose to do them in class, or sts can do them on their own.

It is a good idea for sts to listen, read, and notice the "Audioscript" tasks as extra preparation before a role-play. Rather than just listening (and reading) again and again, trying to memorize dialogues before role-playing them, these tasks give a clear focus for additional listening and pre-role-play pronunciation practice.

All new polysyllabic words are introduced in context, with the stress highlighted for students in pink. Regularly marking stress on new words (in the book and on the board) means you progress from just teaching form and spelling, on to really prioritizing teaching, modeling, and recording spoken language. Word stress is shown in pink only the first time a word appears. To include it each time would give no sense of syllabus or progress to sts.

The "Sounds and Usual Spellings" chart is another excellent resource. This gives two illustrated model words for each of the 40 sounds in U.S. English, and access to the phonetic symbol.

Introduction

Knowing all the potential sounds in a language sets a ceiling on their guesses and builds confidence. If sts can learn those two words per sound, they should be able to have a reasonable guess at the pronunciation of words in a dictionary and begin to get comfortable with using phonetics. Remember, learning to guess pronunciation of new words is a key skill.

The table also provides model words to illustrate the usual spelling patterns for each sound. Sensitizing sts to sound–spelling combinations is a key part of learning to read, write, and pronounce with confidence.

To the extent that you choose to work on pronunciation, any of the following ideas may be helpful.

- Emphasize the relevance of the pronunciation tasks to improve listening comprehension and increasingly natural-sounding English.
- Make sure sts understand that their pronunciation does not need to be "perfect" or "near native," but it does need to be clear and facilitate communication. To that end, focus on features that most impinge on international communication with your particular learners.
- Explore what sts already know, e.g., from song lines, TV, their travels, etc., and have them record and listen to themselves imitating texts they like or wish to deliver better.
- Model new words in context rather than in isolation, e.g., in a phrase: *the environment* not just *environment*, so they get used to stressing and reducing. In this way, the focus on intonation, phrase or sentence stress, word boundaries, etc. increases.
- Respond naturally to incorrect models or effects of "wrong" intonation and encourage repetition to say it better, e.g., say *Excuse me?* in response to incorrect pronunciation or flat intonation.
- Highlight linking (a line between words: *an_orange*), pauses (/ = short pause, // = longer pause) and sentence stress shift (eliciting different meanings according to which words are stressed).
- Work on transcripts, e.g., shadow read text and sub-vocalize to self; notice and underline most stressed words / pauses / links. Turn any audioscript into a proper listening / pronunciation teaching vehicle.
- Spot the "music", e.g., help them hear changes of pitch.
- Have sts track, shadow, rehearse, imitate, repeat, and record themselves.

Reviews

There is ample opportunity for review and recycling throughout the book via the six review lessons. These include many additional activities focusing on speaking, grammar, listening, reading, writing, self-test (error-correction), and point of view (debate). Some skills alternate across the review units, but all are thoroughly covered. Don't forget, you can always look back at the song lines and re-use the lesson question titles, too!

Learner autonomy

English ID offers a clear layout, lessons that progress transparently, and many language explanations. While these features greatly facilitate classroom teaching, they also allow for easy review and autonomous learning. Depending on the classroom hours available, many activities in the course (e.g. selected vocabulary, grammar, reading, and writing tasks) could be assigned for homework. The student-friendly grammar boxes, with additional explanation in the "Grammar" section, also allow for easy review. The Reviews themselves can be assigned for homework also.

If it seems feasible, you may wish to consider "flipping" more of your classes, too. Before any major presentation or review activity, have sts search online for material to support the next lesson. This is especially useful for weaker sts, who might be struggling to keep up, but also works for stronger sts, who might even be able to lead the next class themselves.

Sts who regularly have to miss classes should be trained to use these routes to catch up. For example, how to:

- use the picture dictionary pages to cover the words and test themselves;
- listen again to texts which they have read in class via the audio on the Richmond Learning Platform;
- work on their own pronunciation using the pink word stress for all new polysyllabic words;
- do the "Audioscript" tasks and use the "Sounds and Usual Spellings" chart;
- use the word list and phrase bank from the Richmond Learning Platform for constant review, e.g. by recording, listening to, and repeating the phrase bank on their phones, in their cars, etc.;
- ask and answer the question titles, plus follow-up questions;
- look at and avoid the **Common mistakes**;
- investigate and sing the song lines via the Internet, etc.;
- enjoy all the features of the Richmond Learning Platform. We suggest you spend some class time taking them through each of these features, and regularly reminding them how much they can do with on their own.

Introduction

Richmond Learning Platform for English ID

This extremely useful and user-friendly blended learning tool has been developed in parallel with the series and combines the best of formal and informal learning to extend, review and test core lesson content. The full range of resources is available to teachers and sts who adopt any of the levels of English ID.

The Richmond Learning Platform content for English ID includes:

- Extra Practice Activities that cover all language points in the *Student's Books*. New activities have been added to accompany the 2nd edition. Sts can now record themselves interacting with the characters from ID **Café**, practice their pronunciation using the "Sounds and Usual Spellings" chart, and identify **Common mistakes**;
- Richmond Test Manager contains tests specifically created to review the content of English ID. Teachers can choose what to include in their tests and can choose between digital versions of the tests or printable versions;
- Skills Boost: extra reading and listening practice available in both interactive and PDF format;
- Resources for teachers, including sets of photocopiables for practice and reference;
- Complete downloadable audio and video.

The Richmond Learning Platform's key features and tools include:

- Class Materials, where teachers and sts can find all content related to the level of English ID they are using in class;
- Assignments—a tool that allows teachers to assign digital and non digital content for sts to complete by a specified date;
- Test Manager, where teachers can find all the test content for English ID, and build their own tests to be delivered in the format that suits their teaching. Once generated, tests can be assigned to the whole class or specific sts, to be completed by a specific date and time;
- Markbook allows sts to access their own scores, while teachers can view the scores of the whole class and have a number of options to view the details of their sts' progress;
- Forum is a tool for communication between members of the class and can be used to bring writing activities to life.

Workbook

In the *Workbook*, a single page corresponds to each *Student's Book* lesson, designed to consolidate and reinforce all the main language. Exercises can be used in class, e.g. for fast finishers, or extra practice of specific areas.

The *Workbook* includes:

- a variety of exercises, texts, and puzzles to scaffold, continue practicing, and extend the main grammar and vocabulary of each lesson;
- Skills Practice: several listening activities per unit to continue practicing the most important skill outside class, plus plenty of short, enjoyable reading texts.

Interleaved Teacher's Book

English ID offers a rich, complete, teacher-friendly, lesson plan for every left- and right-hand page of each lesson. It provides a complete step-by-step lesson plan from beginning to end, offering:

- lesson overviews and aims;
- an optional books-closed warm-up for every lesson;
- an alternative books-open warm-up based around the question title;
- step-by-step notes and suggestions for each on-page activity, including background information and language notes where appropriate;
- help with identifying the focus of each activity and any new language being presented, including additional help (where relevant) on presenting increasingly complicated grammar;
- language tips specifically highlighting areas that may be problematic for Spanish / Portuguese speakers;
- teaching tips to vary and hone your teaching skills;
- suggestions for multi-level classes (ideas for both stronger and weaker sts);
- a complete answer key and audioscript;
- a bank of original ideas for exploiting each song line in a different way, as well as background information and step-by-step teaching notes for the song lines.

Digital Book for Teachers / IWB

The *Digital Book for Teachers* is a separate medium containing all the pages of the *Student's Book*. Teachers can use this resource to promote variety in their classes, at all stages of any lesson, so that sts can see the images on the IWB instead of looking at the book. It's particularly useful for operating the audio, zooming images, and adding zest and color to your classes!

On the next pages, you will find detailed information about all the features of English ID.

Welcome to English ID!

Finally, an English course you can understand!

Lesson titles are questions to help you engage with the content.

Famous **song lines** illustrate language from lessons.

Contextualized picture dictionary to present and review vocabulary.

Word stress in pink on new words.

Focus on **Common mistakes** accelerates accuracy.

Introduction

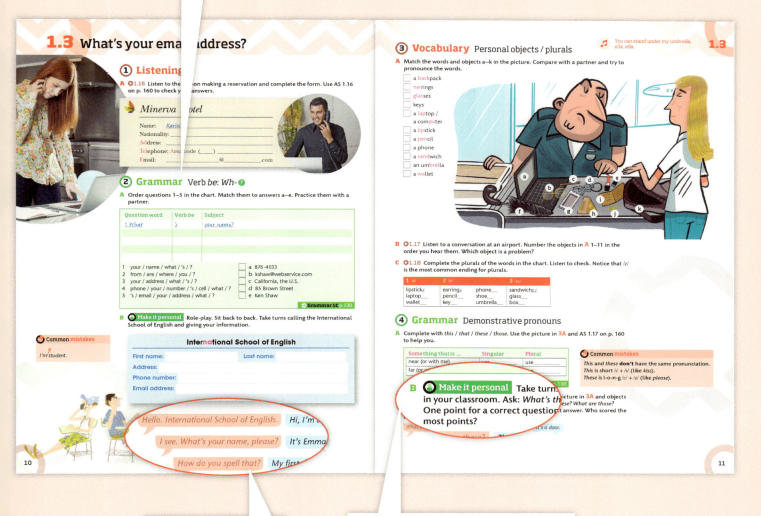

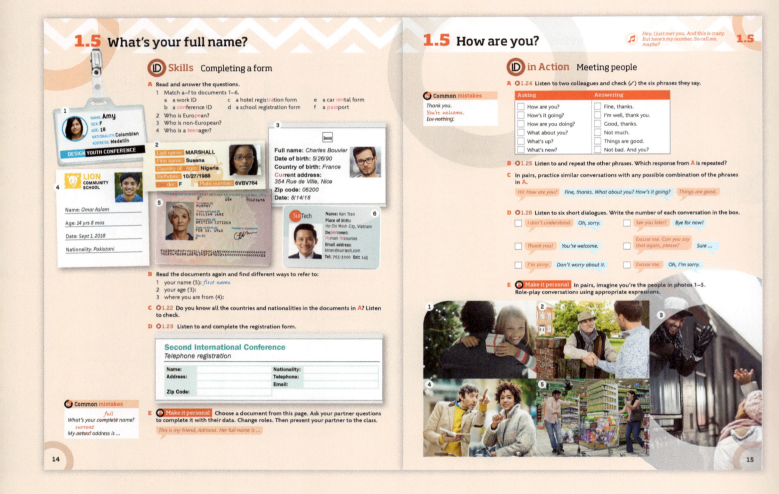

Introduction

Writing lessons integrated into each unit, with clear models and careful scaffolding to increase writing confidence.

ID Café: sitcom videos to consolidate language.

Reviews systematically recycle language.

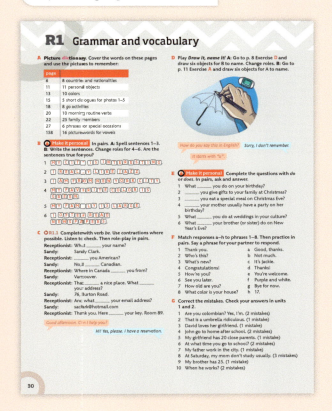

Authentic videos present topics in real contexts.

A complete **Grammar** reference with exercises. A full answer key can be found on the Richmond Learning Platform.

Grammar Unit 1

1A Verb be ⊕ ⊖ and Yes / No ❓

The verb *be* only has three forms: *am, is, are*.
Use contractions when you speak or write informally.

⊕		Contractions	
I *am*		I'm	a student.
You (singular) *are*		You're	Latin American.
He / She / It *is*		He's / She's / It's	Panamanian.
We *are*		We're	from Brazil.
You (plural) *are*		You're	students.
They *are*		They're	British.

⊖	
I'm not	Colombian.
You're *not* or *aren't*	Asian.
He's / She's / It's *not* or *isn't*	Spanish.
We / You / They're *not* or *aren't*	Canadian.

	Short answers	
❓	Yes	No
Are you from the U.S.?	Yes, I am.	
Are you American?	Yes, I'm Texan.	No, I'm not.
Is he a great player?	Yes, he is.	No, he's not. / isn't.
Is she an OK actor?	Yes, she is.	No, she's not. / isn't.
Is it a Chinese phone?	Yes, it is.	No, it's not. / isn't.
Are you students?	Yes, we are.	No, we're not. / aren't.
Are they actors?	Yes, they are.	No, they're not. / aren't.

We usually answer *Yes / No* questions with a short answer.
Are you Spanish? Yes, I am. NOT *Yes, I'm.*
Do not use contractions with ⊕ short answers.

1B Adjectives and a / an + noun

a	an
She's **a** good person.	He's **an** interesting person.

Use *a* before a consonant sound / *an* before a vowel sound.

Adjectives

article adjective noun	article adjective noun
Neymar's **a** Brazilian soccer player.	Jennifer Lawrence is **a** fantastic actor.
Buenos Aires is **a** great city.	This is **a** green book. Those are green books.

In English, the adjective comes *before* a noun, and doesn't have a plural form.

1C Verb be: Wh- ❓

- What's your address?
- Where are you from?
- Why are they here?
- When's your birthday?
- Who's he?
- How are you?

Wh- question words come before the verb *be*.
Remember to invert in questions.
Where are you from? NOT *Where you are from?*

1D Demonstrative pronouns

Use *this* / *these* for things or people that are with you or near you (here).
- **This** is my pen. (It's with me.)
- **These** are my keys. (They're here.)

Use *that* / *those* for things or people that are with other people or distant from you (there).
- **That's** my pen. (It's on the table.)
- **Those** are my keys. (They're there.)

Remember to invert in questions.
Is this your book? NOT *This is your book?*
Use pronouns in answers.
Yes, it is. NOT *Yes, this is.*

1E Possessive adjectives

Subject pronoun	Possessive adjective
I	**My** car is blue.
You	**Your** green glasses are on the table.
He	**His** new laptop is fantastic.
She	That's **her** teacher.
It	This is my dog. Oh, what's **its** name?
We	**Our** friends are here.
You	Please turn off **your** cell phones.
They	**Their** city is really cool.

Possessive adjectives only have one form.
Possessive adjectives go before a noun or an adjective + noun.
My new shoes. NOT *Mys shoes news.*

Hi, I'm your teacher. My name's Bruno.

Unit 1

1A

1 Complete 1–5 with verb *be*. Use contractions when possible.
1 He _____ not from the U.S. He _____ Canadian.
2 We _____ not Hawaiian, we _____ Mexican.
3 It _____ not an Irish flag, it _____ an Italian flag.
4 They _____ from NY, but the statue _____ from France!
5 Her name _____ not Emma. It _____ Emily.

2 Complete 1–5 with verb *be*. In pairs, ask and answer. Remember to use short answers when possible.
1 _____ you Chilean?
2 _____ Christ the Redeemer statue in Spain?
3 _____ Justin Bieber American?
4 _____ you and Neymar friends?
5 _____ Idris Elba and Emily Blunt British?

1B

1 Correct the mistakes.
1 She's a girl cool.
2 They're not actors terrible.
3 Rio de Janeiro is a city excellent.
4 You're a player fantastic.
5 Is it a car Korean?

2 Order the words to make sentences.
1 interesting / is / San Francisco / an / city / .
2 actor / intelligent / an / Antonio Banderas / is / .
3 players / are / they / important / soccer / .
4 is / a / ridiculous / it / movie / .
5 excellent / I / student / an / am / .

1C

1 Order the words to make *Wh-* questions.
1 the name of / what / in Mexico / 's / that place / ?
2 are / when / home / you / ?
3 who / your / 's / friend / best / ?
4 you / why / are / here / ?
5 email / 's / what / address / your / ?

2 Correct the mistakes.
1 How's her name?
2 What's your favorite actor?
3 Is where his laptop?
4 Why you're in this class?
5 What's your favorite cities?

1D

1 Look at the examples and write questions and answers.
What are those? Those are ...
What's this? This is ...

2 Complete with the correct demonstrative pronoun.
1 _____ is a blue bookbag.
2 Is _____ your friend Tina?
3 _____ are my friends, Dan and Mary.
4 _____ is not my homework. _____ is my homework.
5 _____ is my email address.

1E

1 Correct two mistakes in each.
1 Her name is josé and she's from Spain.
2 I think his name is Mary. She's american.
3 Is we in the same English class?
4 These is our teacher, Ms. Jones. We are in his class.
5 That not my phone. The my phone is black.

2 Complete with the correct possessive adjectives.
1 _____ name is Daniel and I'm from Mexico.
2 This is my friend. _____ name is Karina.
3 We are in English class together. _____ school is in California.
4 This is our new teacher. _____ name is Bruno.
5 These are my parents. _____ names are David and Marcia.

Introduction

Pictures to present and practice **pronunciation** with audio to accompany it on the Richmond Learning Platform.

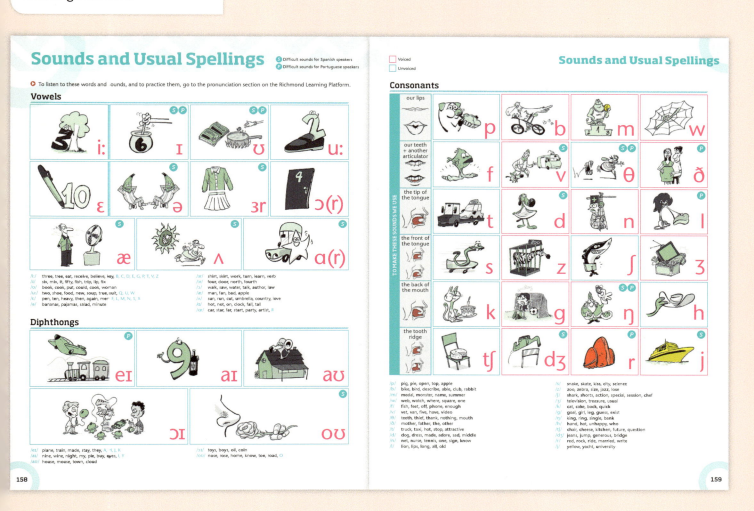

Audioscript activities to consolidate pronunciation.

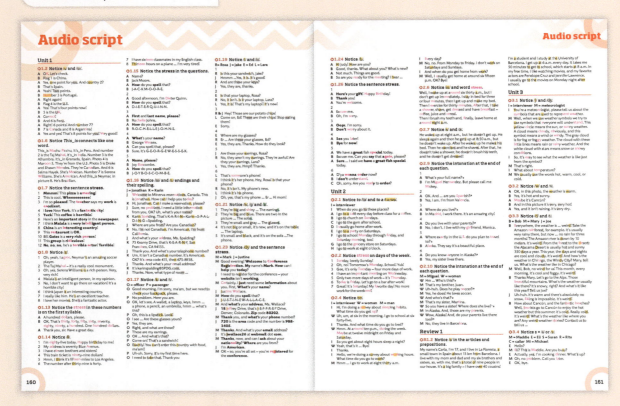

Workbook to practice and consolidate lessons with complete audio on the Richmond Learning Platform.

Phrase Bank to practice common expressions.

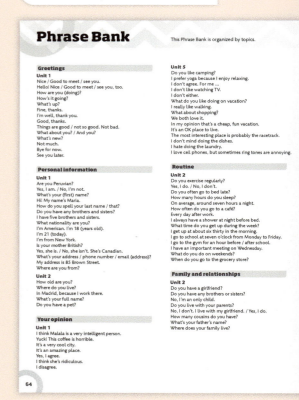

English ID 2nd Edition Digital

 Richmond *Learning* **Platform**

- Teachers and students can find all their resources in one place.
- **Richmond Test Manager** with interactive and printable tests.
- Activity types including pronunciation, common mistakes, and speaking.

New look

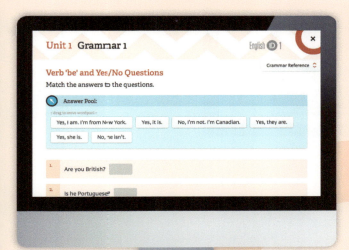

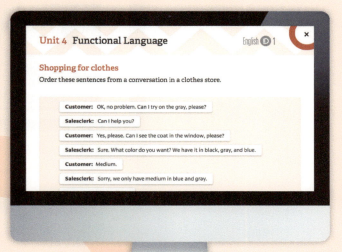

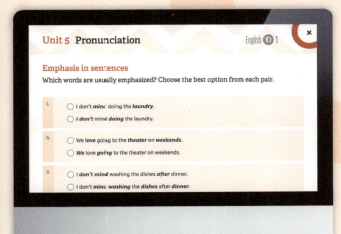

New activities

iD Café: Students watch the videos, do a language activity, and then record themselves taking part in a conversation with one of the characters from the video. Students can then download their conversation and share it with their teacher.

Introduction

Common mistakes: In order to revise this key feature of English ID, we have added a correct-the-mistakes activity for each unit.

Sounds and Usual Spellings: For the 2nd edition, we have brought the famous ID chart to life with a new activity for each sound in the chart. Students can listen to the sounds and the example words and then record themselves and compare their recordings to the examples. These recordings can then be downloaded and shared with their teacher.

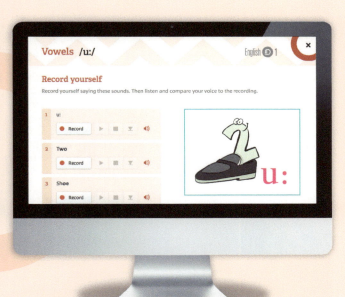

1

1.1 Are you Canadian?

1 Vocabulary Countries and nationalities

A ▶1.1 Listen and circle the correct words. Introduce yourself to the class.

Hello / Hi! My name's Marty / Judy and I'm Brazilian / Mexican / American. I'm from New York / Mexico City / Brasilia. Nice / Good to see / meet you.

B ▶1.2 Match flags 1–8 to the countries. Listen to the quiz to check. What's your score?

- ☐ The U.S.
- ☐ Argentina
- ☐ The UK
- ☐ Peru
- ☐ China
- ☐ Canada
- ☐ Portugal
- ☐ Spain

C ▶1.3 Match the nationalities to countries 1–8 in **B**. Guess the pronunciation. Listen to check. Notice the unstressed suffixes.

- ☐ Peru**vian**
- ☐ Spa**nish**
- ☐ A**mer**ican
- ☐ Chi**nese**
- ☐ Argen**tin**ian
- ☐ Bri**tish**
- ☐ Cana**dian**
- ☐ Portu**guese**

D 🔴 Make it personal Say the names of countries and nationalities near your country.

Bolivia – Bolivian

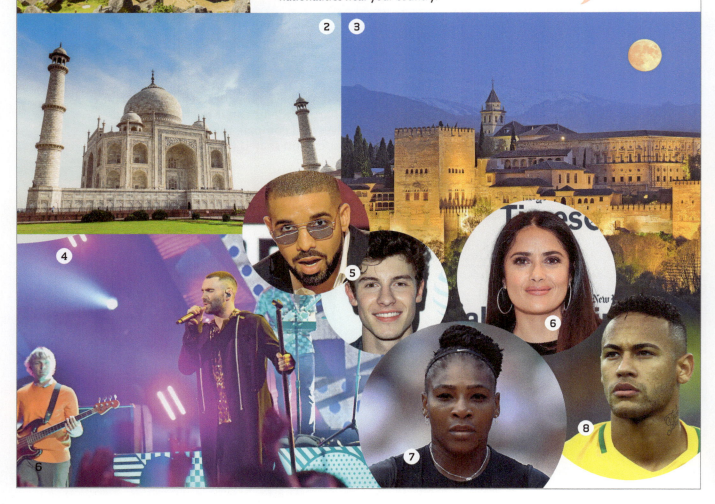

Unit overview: The main topics of unit 1 are the verb *be* in the simple present (positive / negative and interrogative forms in *Yes / No* and *Wh-* questions), countries and nationalities, opinion adjectives, the alphabet, numbers, possessive adjectives, colors and nouns (singular and plural forms).

1.1 Are you Canadian?

Lesson Aims: Sts learn to use the verb *be* through the context of introducing themselves and asking and answering questions about nationalities. Sts also learn adjectives for describing people and places and describe famous people.

Function
Introducing yourself.
Asking and answering questions about countries and nationalities.
Giving opinions about places and people.

Language
Hi! My name's Marty.
I'm (Peruvian), from (Lima).
Are you / Is he / she / it (Mexican)?
Yes, I am / he / she / it is. No, I'm not / he / she / it isn't.
I think she's a great actress. Brazil is an interesting country. She's a cool girl.

Vocabulary: Countries and nationalities (Argentina, Argentinian; the U.S., American; the UK, British, etc.). Adjectives and the indefinite article (cool, fantastic, amazing, etc.).

Grammar: Verb *be* (I, you, he, she, it, we, they) and *Yes / No* questions. The definite article *a / an* (He's an amazing soccer player. It's a horrible city.).

Warm-up Books closed. Introduce yourself to the whole class: *Hi! My name's _____. I'm (nationality), from (city / town)*. Drill *Hi, my name's _____.* for pronunciation and do a quick substitution drill. *I'm (Brazilian / American / Mexican), from (São Paulo / New York / Mexico City)*. Elicit the model and write it on the board, but don't let sts copy at this stage.

Get sts to introduce themselves to each other in pairs.

After pairwork, ask sts to stand up, mingle and introduce themselves to as many people as possible.

1 Vocabulary Countries and nationalities

A Books open. Read the title out loud then ask sts: *Are you Latin American?* Point to the short text. Start to read it: *Hi! My name's ...* (pause and ask) *Marty? Judy?* Say: *I don't know!* Listen. Play ▶1.1 and pause after *Marty*. Elicit the correct answer and demonstrate a circle. Sts circle *Marty*. Play the rest of the recording and ask sts to circle the correct answers. Paircheck (use L1 to explain paircheck if necessary or use a cognate, *compare*). Classcheck.

> Hi!, Judy, Brazilian, Brasilia, Nice, meet

Tip In pairs, sts role-play Marty and Judy introducing themselves to each other.

B Pre-teach *country*, e.g. *New York is a city. The United States is a country.* Check for any sts whose countries are not represented by the flags and make sure the countries and nationalities of all sts are mentioned. Highlight initial capital letter for countries and nationalities in English.

Point to flag number 4 and elicit *the U.S.* Tell sts to match the other flags to the correct countries. Sts paircheck. Sts listen to ▶1.2 to check their answers. Play again. Sts listen and repeat. Draw sts' attention to pink syllables and show them they are stressed. Tell sts to cover the names of the countries and test each other in pairs. *What's number 4? It's _____.* Write a model on the board if necessary.

> 1 China 2 Spain 3 Portugal 4 the U.S. 5 the UK
> 6 Peru 7 Canada 8 Argentina

C Sts match the nationalities to the countries 1–8. Using the pink word stress, get them to guess the pronunciation in pairs. Do the first one with them as an example. Play ▶1.3. Use the audio to confirm.

After the listening, elicit the correct pronunciation of each country individually.

> 1 Chinese 2 Spanish 3 Portuguese 4 American
> 5 British 6 Peruvian 7 Canadian 8 Argentinian

D Make it personal Draw a map of the country you are in on the board and elicit what countries are near or next to it. Write example sentences on the board. *(Name of country) is next to / near our country. They are (nationality).* Refer to the speech bubble and tell sts to say other examples in pairs. Encourage sts to use suffixes *-an*, *-ian*, and *-ean* and have them say the nationalities of three countries which are near your own country (e.g. in the case of Mexico it would be American, Guatemalan, Honduran, Belizean). Correct on spot, write the correct guesses on the board, and drill pronunciation.

Tip Ask sts: *What is the most common suffix for nationalities in our continent?* Guide sts to notice that the most common suffix in South, Central and North America is *-an* (over 30 nationalities). Encourage sts to find out which are the only two nationalities in the Americas that are not formed with this suffix (Guianese and Surinamese). Point out that *-ese* is a stressed suffix, unlike *-an*, *-ian* and *-ean*. **Note:** Remind sts that citizens from Argentina might be called Argentinian or Argentine.

2 Grammar Verb *be* ➕➖ and *Yes / No* ❓

🎵 *When I see your face, There's not a thing that I would change, 'Cause you're amazing, Just the way you are.*

A ▶1.4 Listen to the questions and answers. Complete the grammar box. Use contractions where possible. Listen again to check.

➕	❓	➕➖ Short answers
I'm Chinese.	<u>Am</u> I Chinese?	Yes, you *are*. / No, you're *not*.
You're Argentinian.	_____ you Argentinian?	No, I _____. / Yes, I _____.
She's Brazilian.	_____ she Brazilian?	No, she _____. / Yes, she _____.
He's Colombian.	_____ he Colombian?	No, he _____. / Yes, he _____.
It's Indian.	_____ it Indian?	No, it _____. / Yes, it _____.
We're Chilean.	<u>Are</u> we Chilean?	Yes, we *are*. / No, we *aren't*.
They're Ecuadorian.	<u>Are</u> they Ecuadorian?	Yes, they *are*. / No, they *aren't*.

➡ Grammar 1A p.138

Common mistakes
~~Are you~~ You are Latin American?
~~we are.~~ Yes, we're.
~~Chinese Are you chineses?~~

B 🗣 **Make it personal** ▶1.5 Listen to the example dialogue. Look at the photos on p. 6. In pairs, ask and answer about the people, countries, and nationalities to identify the photos.

> Photo 5 ... Shawn Mendes and Drake. Are they American?   No, they aren't. They're Canadian.

C ▶1.6 Listen to check. Did you identify all of the photos correctly?

3 Vocabulary Adjectives and *a / an* + noun

A ▶1.7 Listen and put the positive and negative adjectives in the right place.

amazing
cool
excellent
fantastic
horrible
important
intelligent
interesting
~~OK~~
rich
ridiculous
terrible

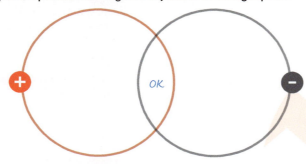

Common mistakes
He's an interesting person.
~~He's a person interesting.~~
It's a very cool city.
~~It's a city very cool.~~

B ▶1.8 Listen to the opinions about people and places. Complete 1–8 with *a / an*.

1 He's _____ amazing player.
2 It's _____ cool monument.
3 She's _____ rich person.
4 She's _____ intelligent person.
5 It's _____ horrible city.
6 It's _____ interesting country.
7 He's _____ excellent teacher.
8 She's _____ fantastic actor.

C Complete the rules with the correct word.

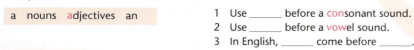

1 Use _____ before a consonant sound.
2 Use _____ before a vowel sound.
3 In English, _____ come before _____.

D 🗣 **Make it personal** Think of five different countries and a famous person / place in each one. In pairs, give your opinions about them.

> Chichén Itzá is a Mayan city in Mexico. It's an amazing place!   Yes, I agree.

> Lady Gaga is an American musician. I think she's ridiculous!   I disagree. She's amazing!

1.1

🎵 **Song line:** Turn to p. 324 for notes about this song and an accompanying task.

2 Grammar Verb be ⊕ ⊖ and Yes / No ❓

A Point to photo 5 on p. 6 and ask: *What's her name?* (Salma Hayek.) Point to photo 2 and ask: *Is that Indian?* (Yes, it is.)

Books closed. Write the 🔑 **Common mistakes** on the board and elicit errors as a class.

Play ▶ 1.4 and ask sts to complete the grammar box. Monitor closely. Paircheck. Classcheck. Write the answers on the board. You could include more examples here that relate directly to the sts, perhaps adding vocabulary that will help with activity 3. Write them on the board and elicit the responses, e.g. *You're Latin American. Are you Colombian? (Yes, you are. / No, you aren't.). She's an actor. Is she from Brazil? (Yes, she is. / No, she isn't.) You are students. Are you Australian? (No, we aren't).* Point out the differences for *you* in singular and plural. Ask: *Is this the same or similar in your language?*

> Questions: Are, Is, Is, Is
> Short answers: 'm not / am, isn't / is, isn't / is

➡ **Grammar 1A p. 138** This could be set as homework or done in class if sts need guided practice before completing oral practice in **B**. As this is the first lesson, take sts there to show the different sections of English.

B Drill. Ask sts: *Are you teachers/students/doctors, actors, etc. …?* to elicit *Yes, we are / No, we aren't. Are the Golden State Warriors from Spain? No, they aren't. Are they from the U.S? Yes, they are.*

👤 **Make it personal** Sts listen to ▶ 1.5 and follow the example dialogue, then do the same for the other photos on p. 6 in pairs. Try to avoid telling sts all the names at this stage. The answers will be confirmed in **C**.

Tip Bring in extra pictures of famous people and places to extend this activity.

C Sts listen to ▶ 1.6 to check if all their guesses are correct. Ask: *Any pronunciation surprises?*

> 1 Machu Picchu, Peru 2 the Taj Mahal, India
> 3 the Alhambra, Spain 4 Maroon 5, the U.S.
> 5 Drake and Shawn Mendes, Canada
> 6 Salma Hayek, Mexico 7 Serena Williams, the U.S.
> 8 Neymar, Brazil

Tip Ask sts to turn to the AS on p. 160. Sts listen again and notice how *This_is* and *It's_in* sound like one word.

Extra activity In pairs, A: Pretend to be a person on this page. B: Guess who A is. Count your guesses.
e.g. B: *Are you a man?*

3 Vocabulary Adjectives and a / an + noun

A Play ▶ 1.7 and pause after sentence 1. Ask: *Is it positive or negative?*

Elicit the adjective and show how *cool* goes in the positive group, *OK* in the middle group as it can be positive and negative, and *horrible* in the negative one. Sts listen to 2–11 to identify and repeat the adjective they hear each time. Drill pronunciation as necessary. Replay it and tell sts to write the adjectives under + or −. Paircheck. Ask sts which words are similar / the same in L1. *Note:* Almost all these adjectives are cognates (except *amazing*). The idea is to get sts using words they "know".

> + amazing, cool, excellent, fantastic, important, intelligent, interesting, rich
> − horrible, ridiculous, terrible

B **Books closed.** Say sentence 1 and ask: *Is it a positive or negative opinion?* Repeat procedure with 2–8. Pause after each sentence. (1–4 positive, 5 negative, 6–8 positive).

Books open. Point to the sentences. Sts listen to ▶ 1.8 and complete with *a* or *an*. Do not explain the grammar rule. Drill answers. Drill several exchanges and elicit more examples.

> 1 an 2 a 3 a 4 an 5 a 6 an 7 an 8 a

Tip Ask sts to turn to the AS on p. 160. Sts listen again and notice how the letter *s* is often pronounced /z/.

C Point to the gaps and ask sts to complete the rules. Monitor and check progress. You may need to clarify *consonant* and *vowel* by writing some sounds on the board.

> 1 a 2 an 3 adjectives, nouns

D 👤 **Make it personal** Write a country on the board and elicit famous people and places.

Ask: *What's your opinion of (Brazil / Neymar)?* Add their opinions onto the board and do not erase them.

🔑 **Common mistakes** Say: *In English, we don't say, "He's a person interesting." The adjectives go before the person or place.*

Tip Do a quick substitution drill:
T: *I think Neymar is a fantastic player.*
Sts: *I think Neymar is a fantastic player.*
T: *Great.*
Sts: *I think Neymar is a great player.*

Focus on the speech bubbles and have sts prepare their examples. Sts work in pairs or groups of three and give opinions about five people and places. Refer to the model on the board.

Extra writing Get sts to write *Yes / No* questions about people and places on strips of paper for other sts to read and write answers to them. All sts should write one or two and stick them on the wall for the class to mingle in pairs and answer verbally, or in writing.

➡ **Workbook** p. 4

1.2 How do you spell your last name?

1 Pronunciation The alphabet

A ▶1.9 Match the pairs of words to the pictures in **B**. Listen, check, and repeat.

- [ ] a shoe • two
- [ ] a car • a star
- [ ] a pen • ten
- [ ] a nose • a rose
- [1] a plane • a train
- [ ] three • a tree
- [ ] nine • wine

B ▶1.10 Listen to the words and letters in the chart and notice the vowel sounds.

1	2	3	4	5	6	7
eɪ	iː	ɛ	aɪ	oʊ	uː	ɑr
A	B	F	I	O	Q	R
H	C	L	__	__	U	__
J	D	M			__	
__	E					

Common mistakes

~~How can I write?~~
How do you spell that?

C ▶1.11 Listen to these letters and put them in the correct column in **B**.

G K N P S T V W X Y Z

D 🟠 **Make it personal** Point to a picture. Ask your partner to say it. Which vowel sound is it? Try to spell the word. Use a dictionary if necessary.

What's that?   It's rain.   How do you spell "rain"?   R-A-I-N   Correct!

1.2 How do you spell your last name?

Lesson Aims: Sts learn the alphabet and numbers 11–100 through the context of saying prices and playing bingo, and short dialogues spelling their names.

Function	Language
Saying the alphabet.	A-H-J-K, plane, a train.
Saying prices in dollars / cents / euros.	20 cents.
Spelling words and names.	13 dollars.
	I think it's 15 miles to Los Angeles.
	My address is 70 Blue Avenue.
	How do you spell ...?

Vocabulary: The alphabet. Numbers 11–100.
Pronunciation: The alphabet.

Warm-up Review lesson 1.1. Hand out a card to each st with the name of a well-known celebrity on it. Say: *This is your new identity.* Ask sts to stand up and mingle, introducing themselves as the celebrity on their cards.

> **Weaker classes** For real beginners, write prompts on the board: *Hi. I'm (Madonna). I'm (American). What about you?*

Books closed. Divide the class into two groups and play *Hangman* on the board. Choose adjectives from lesson 1.1 **3A** (e.g. *excellent, horrible*). In groups, sts take turns guessing letters. Keep track of wrong guesses as well. This game will allow you to see which letters sts have problems pronouncing.

1 Pronunciation The alphabet

A Go over each pair of words and quickly demonstrate meaning, e.g. point to a shoe, your nose, and a pen in the classroom. Quickly draw a bottle of wine and a rose to elicit meaning. Drill pronunciation, making sure sts notice the similarity of vowel sounds in each pair, even though the spelling is very different.

Point to picture 1 and ask: *What's this?* Elicit *a train* and *a plane.* Show sts sound 1 has been done for them. Do the same for sound 2, /iː/, and let sts match the rest of the pairs in **A** to the sounds in **B** on their own. Paircheck. Play ▶ 1.9 to check answers.

In pairs. Sts race their partner to say all the words in **A**.

> **Stronger classes** Add more rhyming pairs: game / flame; beach / peach; bed / head; clothes / toes; pool / school; guitar / chart. Ask: *Which words take an article?* (All except *clothes / toes*.)

Point out that *clothes* has only one syllable, /kloʊðz/.

> 2 three, a tree   3 a pen, ten   4 nine, wine
> 5 a nose, a rose   6 a shoe, two   7 a car, a star

B Play ▶ 1.10. Sts check their answers and repeat the seven vowel sounds and letters.

C Play ▶ 1.11 and repeat the letters and words (pause to make space for repetition).

> 1 K   2 G, P, T, V, Z   3 N, S, X   4 Y   6 W

Tip Portuguese L1 speakers tend to produce the letter *d* as *g* because this is how it is commonly used when not combined with *a, o* or *u*. This also leads to errors when pronouncing *g* because sts tend not to use the affricate /dʒ/ and just reproduce as the fricative /ʒ/. For example, they may pronounce the profession DJ as /'dʒi: dʒeɪ/. Help sts to realize that *g* is the same sound that they use incorrectly for d in DJ. Refer to the Sounds and Usual Spellings chart on p. 158.

🎵 **Song line:** Turn to p. 324 for notes about this song and an accompanying task.

D **Make it personal**   Point to the speech bubbles and then to one of the photos and ask: *What's that?* Elicit a response from the sts. Ask: *How do you spell ...?* Again, elicit a response. Then, pairs do the same taking turns to point and ask questions.

Monitor and make a note of pronunciation errors. Go over problem sounds and letters after they have finished.

Tip Show the position of the tongue, lips, and jaw to help sts make the sounds. For example, /iː/ has the lips smiling and the tongue high in the mouth. For /ɑː/ the mouth is open and the tongue low in the mouth. If you have a phonemic chart you could refer to that to show how the vowel section relates to the position of the mouth.

Tip To increase the challenge, put the alphabet, A–Z, on the board and get sts to try to do it without the groups. It will make them keep looking back at the chart and understand how useful the seven columns are.

♪ It's fun to stay at the Y.M.C.A.

2 Vocabulary Numbers 11–100

A ▶1.12 Complete the numbers under the prices. Listen, check, and repeat with the correct stress.

12¢	14¢	16¢	€18	20¢
$11	tw_lv_	$13	f___rt___n	€15	s_xt___n	$17	e_ght___n	$19	tw___nty
eleven		th__rteen		f__ft__n		s_v_nt__n		n_n_t__n	

B ▶1.13 How do you say these numbers? Listen, check, and repeat with the correct stress.

30 40 50 60 70 80 90 100   *Thirty, forty …*

C ▶1.14 Listen to sentences 1–8 and circle the number you hear.

| 1 | 18 80 85 | 3 | 20 11 12 | 5 | 15 50 55 | 7 | 06 60 16 |
| 2 | 17 70 73 | 4 | 19 90 99 | 6 | 14 40 43 | 8 | 13 30 33 |

D 🔵 **Make it personal** Play *Bingo*. Write numbers from 1 to 20 on the card.
One student: Call numbers from 1 to 20 in any order.
Winner: Shout *Bingo!* when you complete a line.

Play again with numbers from 21 to 40, 41 to 60, etc.

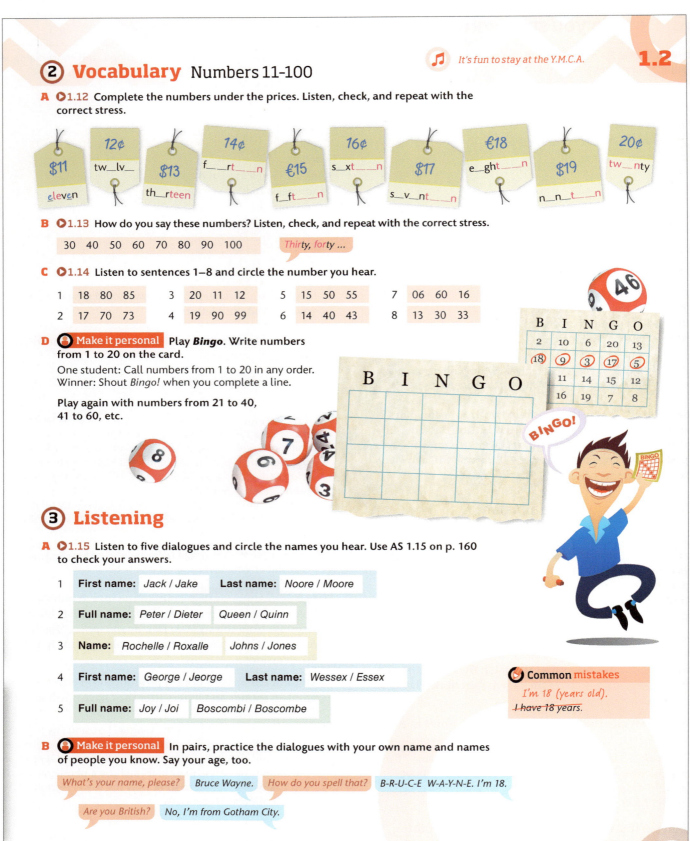

3 Listening

A ▶1.15 Listen to five dialogues and circle the names you hear. Use AS 1.15 on p. 160 to check your answers.

1 **First name:** Jack / Jake   **Last name:** Noore / Moore
2 **Full name:** Peter / Dieter   Queen / Quinn
3 **Name:** Rochelle / Roxalle   Johns / Jones
4 **First name:** George / Jeorge   **Last name:** Wessex / Essex
5 **Full name:** Joy / Joi   Boscombi / Boscombe

🔴 **Common mistakes**
I'm 18 (years old).
~~I have 18 years.~~

B 🔵 **Make it personal** In pairs, practice the dialogues with your own name and names of people you know. Say your age, too.

What's your name, please? Bruce Wayne. How do you spell that? B-R-U-C-E W-A-Y-N-E. I'm 18.

Are you British? No, I'm from Gotham City.

② Vocabulary Numbers 11–100

A Elicit numbers 1–10. Write them on the board. Elicit the sequence on the board up to 20. Drill pronunciation.

Focus on the numbers and currency symbols and tell sts these are price tags. Check if they know the symbols and drill the currencies: $ = dollar, c = cent, € = euro. Tell sts to complete the numbers with the missing letters.

Weaker classes Sts might need prompts on the board— write *e, i, o, u* and say those are the letters they'll need.

Play ▶1.12 and tell sts to check their answers. Play it again and ask them to listen and repeat.

> twelve, thirteen, fourteen, fifteen, sixteen, seventeen, eighteen, nineteen, twenty

B Write *thirty* on the board and ask: *How many syllables?* (two) Say *thirty* and ask: *Which syllable is louder / stronger?* Mark the correct stress.

Tip Help sts see the number of syllables when you mark stress. You can do this these ways:
Thir / ty *or* Oo *or* Thir- ty

Play ▶1.13 and ask sts to mark the stressed syllables. Check answers (all stressed on the first syllable). Play the audio again and ask sts to listen and repeat.

Write *13 / 30* and *14 / 40* on the board. Elicit and mark the correct word stress of each: *thirteen / thirty, fourteen / forty*. Do the same for *15 / 50* and *16 / 60*.

Tip Make it clear for sts that there is contrastive stress (*ty* vs. *teen*) when we pronounce them individually. In connected speech it can be less clear. Say *thirteen dollars* quickly to demonstrate this. In many cases the context helps us figure out what number was said.

For an extra challenge, write 101 and 122 on the board and elicit or teach *a hundred one* and *a hundred twenty-two*.

C Write *18 80 85* on the board. Play ▶1.14 and do number 1 with the class, circling the number on the board (85). Do the same for number 2 (70). Say: *Now listen to sentences 3–8 and circle the correct number.* Classcheck answers.

> 1 85   2 70   3 11   4 99   5 15   6 40   7 16   8 13

D 🔴 **Make it personal**   Say: *Bingo time!* and show sts the example card on p. 9. Tell them to complete their own cards with 1–20 in a different order. Have sts take turns and pick a strip of paper from the bag / envelope and call out numbers to class. Sts circle called numbers and say *Bingo!* when one line is complete. If time allows, or another day, play again with numbers 20–40, 50–60, 1–100, or 120–140.

③ Listening

A This exercise helps sts to hear and practice pronunciation of letters in short dialogues. **Books closed.** Tell sts you are going to dictate two names to them. Dictate *Jack* and *Jake*. Check answers. Ask: *What's the pronunciation?* Elicit the differences /æ/ and /eɪ/. **Books open.** Direct sts to the exercise and play ▶1.15. Do number 1 and classcheck. Sts do 2–5. Paircheck and classcheck. Ask sts what they thought of the listening, e.g. *Was this easy or difficult?*

> 1 Jack Moore   2 Dieter Quinn   3 Rochelle Johns
> 4 George Wessex   5 Joy Boscombe

Tip Ask sts to turn to the AS on p. 160. Sts listen again and notice the stress in the questions.

B 🔴 **Make it personal**   Point to the speech bubbles and ask a st to act it out with you using the example. Then, nominate another st to act out the dialogue with their real name. Write other names of sts or people you know on the board and ask volunteer sts to act out the same dialogue. Then, write ages next to one or two of the names and write *How old are you?* Ask a st to act out the mini conversation with you. Then sts do the same in pairs.

Weaker classes Leave the question and examples on the board. Tell them to refer to the alphabet chart.

Tip Some sts might have very long full names; in that case, ask them to focus on their first and last names only.

When they have finished, ask sts to report back about their partners. Ask: *What's his / her last name? How do you spell that?*

➔ **Workbook** p. 5

1.2

31

1.3 What's your email address?

1 Listening

A ▶ 1.16 Listen to the person making a reservation and complete the form. Use AS 1.16 on p. 160 to check your answers.

Minerva Hotel

Name: Karin
Nationality: _____
Address: _____
Telephone: Area code (____) _____
Email: _____@_____.com

2 Grammar Verb *be*: Wh-

A Order questions 1–5 in the chart. Match them to answers a–e. Practice them with a partner.

Question word	Verb *be*	Subject
1 What	's	your name?

1 your / name / what / 's / ?
2 from / are / where / you / ?
3 your / address / what / 's / ?
4 phone / your / number / 's / cell / what / ?
5 's / email / your / address / what / ?

a 876-4033
b kshaw@webservice.com
c California, the U.S.
d 85 Brown Street
e Ken Shaw

→ Grammar 1C p.138

B 🔴 **Make it personal** Role-play. Sit back to back. Take turns calling the International School of English and giving your information.

Common mistakes

I'm a student.

International School of English

First name: _____ Last name: _____
Address: _____
Phone number: _____
Email address: _____

Hello. International School of English. — Hi, I'm a student.
I see. What's your name, please? — It's Emma Miranda.
How do you spell that? — My first name is E-double M-A …

10

1.3 What's your email address?

Lesson Aims: Sts continue to practice the verb *be* through the context of asking for / giving personal information and asking / answering about personal objects.

Function
Asking for and giving personal information.
Spelling your name.
Asking about personal objects.

Language
What's your address / email address / phone number?
What's this / that? It's a bag.
What are these / those? They're earrings.
How do you spell your (last) name / that?

Vocabulary: First, last, and full name, address, email address, phone, cell phone, personal objects.
Grammar: *Wh-* questions with verb *be*, demonstrative pronouns singular and plural forms.
Pronunciation: *This* /ɪs/ vs. *These* /iːz/.

Before the lesson Bring to class some objects which appear in activity 3A.

Warm-up Books closed. Recycle giving opinions. Hand out strips of paper with names of famous people, countries, and cities which your sts didn't talk about in lesson 1.1. If technology is available, display photos on an IWB. In small groups, sts take turns giving opinions. Write a prompt on the board if necessary: *I think _____ is a fantastic (city).*

1 Listening

A Books open. Point to the first photo and say: *Karin is phoning the Minerva Hotel to make a reservation.* Ask: *What information is necessary for a hotel reservation?* (Full name, credit card number, phone number, etc.). Focus on the hotel form and point to the address, phone number, and email boxes. Elicit an example of area code. Elicit pronunciation of the symbol @. Say: *Listen and complete with information about Karin.* Play ●1.16. Paircheck. Classcheck with answers on the board. Ask sts: *Which parts were easier to understand? Which parts were harder to understand?*

Name: Karin Spalding
Nationality: American
Address: 75 Kearny Drive, San Francisco, CA 94133
Telephone: (415) 675-8938
Email: karinspalding@SPDG.com

Follow-up Draw sts' attention to the symbol @ and write on the board @ = at. Say *My email address is* (e.g. julia.souza@getmail.com). Pre-teach symbols . (dot), _ (underscore). Ask a stronger st: *What's your email address?* If it is not clear, ask: *How do you spell that?* Sts then dictate their email addresses to each other.

2 Grammar Verb *be*: *Wh-*

A Ask: *What questions do you remember from Karin's phone call?* (*What's your name? What's your address?*, etc.). Show sts the correct order for number 1 and elicit the answer. Sts do the same for the other sentences. Give *the USA* as an alternative to *the U.S.* in c. Paircheck and classcheck.

1 e What's your name?
2 c Where are you from?
3 d What's your address?
4 a What's your cell phone number?
5 b What's your email address?

➡ **Grammar 1C** p. 138

Tip We can start teaching sts sentence stress at lower levels with simple exercises. Draw these patterns on the board and hum or clap to show the stronger and weaker sounds.

OoO   OooO

Say: *Where are you from?* (OooO) Drill the pronunciation showing that stress falls on the content words *where* and *from*. Then do the same for *What's your name?* (OoO) In pairs, sts ask each other questions 1–5. Ask a pair to demonstrate the dialogue for the whole class.

B Make it personal Display the chart on the IWB if you can or point to it in the book. Point to *first name* and ask a st: *What's your first name? What's your last name?*, etc. Write their answers on the board. Pretend you don't know the spelling and ask: *How do you spell that?*

Point to the speech bubbles and ask sts to practice the conversation quickly. Say: *Now, it's your turn to call.* Sitting back to back, they ask questions in pairs to fill out the school form. Remind sts to ask *Could you repeat, please?, Sorry?,* and *How do you spell that?* for clarification. Encourage sts to pretend to be using cell phones while performing the task.

3 Vocabulary Personal objects / plurals

🎵 *You can stand under my umbrella, ella, ella.*

A Match the words and objects a–k in the picture. Compare with a partner and try to pronounce the words.

- ☐ a **back**pack
- ☐ **ear**rings
- ☐ **glas**ses
- ☐ **keys**
- ☐ a **lap**top / a com**pu**ter
- ☐ a **lip**stick
- ☐ a **pen**cil
- ☐ a **phone**
- ☐ a **sand**wich
- ☐ an um**brel**la
- ☐ a **wal**let

B ▶1.17 Listen to a conversation at an airport. Number the objects in **A** 1–11 in the order you hear them. Which object is a problem?

C ▶1.18 Complete the plurals of the words in the chart. Listen to check. Notice that /z/ is the most common ending for plurals.

1 /s/	2 /z/		3 /ɪz/
lipstick**s**	earring**s**	phone___	sandwich**es**
laptop___	pencil___	shoe___	glass___
wallet___	key___	umbrella___	box___

4 Grammar Demonstrative pronouns

A Complete with *this / that / these / those*. Use the picture in **3A** and AS 1.17 on p. 160 to help you.

Something that is …	Singular	Plural
near (or with me)	use _____	use _____
far (or with another person)	use _____	use _____

→ **Grammar 1D** p. 138

⚠ Common mistakes
This and *these* **don't** have the same pronunciation.
This is short /ɪ/ + /s/ (like *kiss*).
These is l-o-n-g /iː/ + /z/ (like *please*).

B 🔵 **Make it personal** Take turns to test a partner with the picture in **3A** and objects in your classroom. Ask: *What's this? What's that? What are these? What are those?* One point for a correct question and one point for a correct answer. Who scored the most points?

🟠 *What are these?* 🔵 *They're windows.* 🟠 *What's that?* 🔵 *It's a door.*

1.3

🎵 **Song line:** Turn to p. 324 for notes about this song and an accompanying task.

③ Vocabulary Personal objects / plurals

Language tip The words *laptop*, *phone*, and *sandwich* are either cognates or easily recognizable words for both Portuguese and Spanish speakers. Before starting **3A**, work separately on the meaning and pronunciation of these words, and then move on to the matching and pronunciation of the whole batch.

A **Books closed.** Use objects in class or your bag (glasses, wallet, keys) as realia to present some of the words. Show sts one object at a time and ask: *How do you say this in English?* Provide answers for what they don't know. Encourage sts to ask: *How do you say this in English?* Drill pronunciation of the question and all the objects.

Books open. Point to the picture and elicit where / who they are (a passenger and a customs officer at the airport). Ask: *What's letter j?* (earrings). Sts match objects with correct vocabulary items. Paircheck. Classcheck.

> a a laptop / a computer   b glasses   c a pencil
> d keys   e a lipstick   f an umbrella   g a phone
> h a sandwich   i a wallet   j earrings   k a backpack

Language tip Remind sts that the word *glasses* in **A** refers to the object that we use to see better. Make sure they understand that, although it refers to one single object, the word is still in the plural. We say *These are your glasses* not *This is your glasses*. (This is an issue particularly for Brazilian speakers.)

B Focus on the picture. Ask: *What's the problem?* (The customs officer wants to see the things in her backpack.) Play ▶ 1.17 and pause after you hear *a backpack*. Ask sts: *What object did he say?* Point to the box next to *a backpack* and tell sts to write *1*. Say: *Now listen and number the objects in order.* Paircheck. Play it again if necessary. Classcheck.

> 1 a backpack   2 a wallet   3 a laptop   4 keys
> 5 a phone   6 a pencil   7 an umbrella   8 a lipstick
> 9 glasses   10 earrings   11 a sandwich
> The sandwich is a problem.

Tip Whenever sts have matched a set of pictures to a list of words in the book, do a quick review. Sts cover the words and test each other in pairs. St A points and asks: *What's letter (g)?* St B: *A phone.*

▶ 1.17 Turn to page 310 for the complete audioscript.

C Put plurals that sts have already seen from the first two lessons on the board in three columns and review how to form plurals in English. (Adding *s*, *es*, or *ies*.) Write /s/ /z/ /ɪz/ on the board and drill the pronunciation. Refer to these sounds in the Sounds Chart on p. 158. Then, ask sts to complete the words with the correct plural ending. Play ▶ 1.18 so sts can listen and check. Ask sts to practice, with one st saying the singular and their partner saying the plural. For weaker sts you could say: *If this is too hard for now, just say /z/ as best you can.*

> 1 -s   2 -s   3 -es

Tip /s/ is unvoiced and /z/ is voiced. They are produced in the same part of the mouth but with /z/ we add vibration using our voice box. Help sts do this by saying the sounds so they can hear the difference. Then ask them put their hand on their throat, say /z/ and /s/, and notice the difference.

④ Grammar Demonstrative pronouns

A Tell sts to read the AS on p. 160 and look for examples of *this / that / these / those*. Elicit the rules, encourage sts to draw their own conclusions. For each case, ask *Is it singular? Is it plural? Why **this** and not **that**?*, etc. Sts complete the rules in pairs. Classcheck.

⚠️ **Common mistakes** Show the different pronunciation. Write the symbols on the board and again show the mouth position and drill *this* and *these* exaggerating the mouth position and vowel length. Point out that for /iː/ that: signals a longer vowel sound.

Tip Some learners tend to mistake *that* for *very far*. Show them an example of *that* referring to an object which is near you but not with you and clear up any doubts.

Ask sts to form small groups and ask and answer questions using their own belongings. For real beginners, have prompts on the board: *What's this / that? It's a …* or *What are these / those? They're … .* Monitor closely and provide any new words sts may need to name their objects. After the activity, ask: *Is this similar or different in your language?*

> near: this, these   far: that, those

➡️ **Grammar 1D** p. 138

B 🎯 **Make it personal** Point to the speech bubbles and read out the dialogue with a st pointing to something in the class. Perform several examples with other sts. Encourage a st to ask you the question. If they get the pronoun correct say: *Good! One point for you!* Sts take turns saying the questions and try to get points. Monitor and make a note of good language and errors. After, ask: *Who's the winner?* Go over errors and good language.

Follow-up **Books closed.** St A points to an object and asks st B: *What is / are this / that / these / those?* St B answers. Then change roles and repeat.

➡️ **Workbook** p. 6

1.4 Are these your glasses?

1 Listening

A ▶ 1.19 Listen to conversations 1–6 and match them to the pictures.

B ▶ 1.19 Complete the sentences in pictures 1–6 with the correct word. Listen again and use AS 1.19 on p. 160 to check.

her   his   my   our   their   your

2 Grammar Possessive adjectives

A ▶ 1.19 Match the item from **1A** to the owner. Listen to check.

1 potato chips — Ed
2 earrings — Lara
3 glasses — Rosa
4 sandwich — Jake
5 phone — Jake and Rosa
6 laptop

B Complete the grammar box.

Subject	Possessive adjective + noun
I	*my* phone
you	_____ keys
_____	her friend
he	_____ shoes
_____	our house
they	_____ breakfast

→ Grammar 1E p. 138

Common mistakes
Are these your glasses?
~~Is this your glasses?~~

Common mistakes
                         her
Lisa's online with ~~your~~ boyfriend.
                      his
John loves ~~your~~ girlfriend.

C 🗣 **Make it personal** In groups, each person puts one item in a bag. Take the items out in turn. Point and say what the things are using different possessive adjectives.

1.4 Are these your glasses?

Lesson Aims: Sts continue to practice the verb *be* by asking and answering about possessions. Sts also learn colors, and more adjectives, and practice describing objects and giving their opinion.

Function
Talking and asking about possessions.
Describing objects and giving opinions.

Language
Are these your glasses?
Is this your sandwich?
Hey! Those are my chips!
They're small and black, and they're cool.

Vocabulary: Colors (red, white, blue, black, green, yellow, purple, pink, brown, orange) and opposite adjectives (good / bad, pretty / ugly, light / heavy, new / old).
Grammar: Possessive adjectives (my, her, his, your, our, their). Recycling the verb *be* interrogative form and demonstrative pronouns.

Before the lesson Prepare about six photos of objects which sts learned in lesson 1.3, **3A**, p. 11. You'll also need a photo of an old, heavy cell phone.

Warm-up Recycle personal objects and demonstrative pronouns. **Books closed.** Display about six photos on the IWB, or use flashcards or realia of objects in lesson 1.3. When selecting your photos, choose a variety of singular and plural nouns. Sts should point to the board (or flashcards / realia on the teacher's table) and use *that* or *those* to test each other in pairs, asking *What is that? / What are those?* and answering *It's a ... / They're ...* Drill pronunciation briefly and model with a st.

Books open to p. 11. Sts now test each other by pointing to the items in **3A**. Make sure they switch to *this* and *these* and ask *What's this? / What are these?*

1 Listening

A Focus on the pictures and elicit / pre-teach objects sts can see in each of them. Establish the context (after a party).

Ask: *What's this? / What are these?* (earrings, chips, a sandwich, a laptop, etc.) If you have time, for each object they identify, review the alphabet and ask the whole class: *How do you spell that?*, writing on the board as sts spell objects for you. Say: *Listen to six dialogues and match them to the correct picture / situation.* Point to the dialogues and pictures. Highlight the small box in each dialogue where they should write the correct number. Play ▶ 1.19. Paircheck. Classcheck.

From top to bottom, then left to right: 1, 3, 2, 4, 5, 6

B Sts look at possessive adjectives in the box. Listen again and complete with the sentences in **A**. Pause after each dialogue if necessary. Classcheck with board answers. Focus on answers on the board and elicit rules / use of each possessive adjective. Associate them with personal pronouns *I, you, he, she*, etc.

1 your, your   2 my   3 our, their   4 your   5 my   6 her, his

2 Grammar Possessive adjectives

A Sts look at the objects. Ask: *Does Rosa own the earrings?* (No, she doesn't). Sts then do the matching. Play ▶ 1.19 and ask them to listen and check. Classcheck.

1 Jake and Rosa   2 Lara   3 Ed   4 Jake   5 Jake   6 Lara

B Tell sts to complete the grammar box.

→ **Grammar 1E** p. 138

Common mistakes Focus on the first sentence with the mistake and respond accordingly: *What?! With **my** boyfriend?!* (Look angry. Make sure sts see the misunderstanding caused by *your*.) Write *your* on the board and highlight the word *you* in it. Say: *I only use **your** when I talk to you and refer to your objects, things, etc.* Exemplify with objects. Hold a pen and say: *This is **your** pen.* (Talking to the pen owner.) Elicit the correct sentence from another st *This is (her / his) pen.*

Subject: she, we
Possessive adjective: your, his, their

Language tip In Portuguese and Spanish, the possessive adjective for *he* and *she* can be the same as the one for *you* (seu / sua / su). This can cause confusion when sts learn about possessive adjectives in English. Make sure they understand that there is one possessive adjective for *you* (*your*) both singular and plural, and two more for *he* and *she* (*his* and *her*).

C **Make it personal** Ask sts to bring personal objects and put them on your table. Cover your eyes or turn around. When they are finished, open your eyes and pick up each object and say, pointing to different sts: *This is your pen. This is her phone. These are her keys.* etc. Sts say yes or no. Sts then do the same by first putting things in a bag while one person in each group closes their eyes. Monitor and make a note of good use of the target language and errors. Go over this after they have finished.

1.4

3 Vocabulary Adjectives and colors

Purple rain, purple rain, I only want to see you bathing in the purple rain.

A ▶1.20 In pairs, take the quiz. Match the answers to questions a–j and photos 1–10. Listen, check, and repeat the colors.

Can you name …

a the color of ba**na**nas and the Simpson family?
b the color of snow?
c a **common** fruit that is also a color?
d a car**toon** a**ni**mal?
e a **small** cartoon cha**ra**cter with a dog called Snoopy?
f Jay-Z and Beyoncé's **young** **daugh**ter?
g a **fictional** character from a **fa**mous **sto**ry?
h a Californian rock group who sing "American Idiot"?
i the day after Thanksgiving when **e**verything is **cheap**?
j a po**pu**lar Prince song?

☐ **Blue** Ivy Carter
☐ **Black** Friday
☐ **Red** Riding Hood
☐ **Green** Day
J 9 **Purple** Rain
☐ Orange
☐ White
☐ Yellow
☐ Charlie **Brown**
☐ The **Pink** Panther

B Underline all the adjectives in the quiz. Circle the correct rules.
Adjectives go **before** / **after** the noun.
Adjectives have **a** / **no** plural form.

C Match the **bold** adjectives in the quiz to their opposites. Test your partner.
1 rare _____   3 big _____   5 unpopular _____
2 expensive _____ 4 real _____   6 old _____
What's the opposite of "rare"? common

▶ **Common mistakes**
blue eyes
My brother has ~~eyes blues~~.

D ▶1.21 Listen to descriptions of five items in the pictures in **1A** on p. 12. Name them after the beep. Then listen to the answer.

E 🔴 **Make it personal** In small groups.
A: Describe an object in the room and give an opinion about it.
B and C: Ask questions and guess what the object is.
They're small and black, and they're really cool! Are they my glasses? Yes, they are!

1.4

🎵 **Song line:** Turn to p. 324 for notes about this song and an accompanying task.

3 Vocabulary Adjectives and colors

A **Books closed.** Point to different colors in the classroom and ask: *What color is it / are they?* Teach and drill pronunciation of *red, white, blue, black, green, yellow, purple, pink, brown,* and *orange.* Play a quick game: call out a color and sts have to find / point to it in the classroom. Have sts call out colors as well and take part in the game with the whole class.

Sts look at photos 1–10. See if they can identify what some of them are about. Elicit / Pre-teach vocabulary from some of the photos. Start the quiz with the whole class (j 9) as an example. In pairs, sts match questions a–i plus photos 1–10 to the second column of the quiz. Sts listen to ▶ 1.20 and check their answers. Classcheck. Promote chorus repetition of the colors at the end of each sentence in the audio track.

Extra activity Say: *I think Black Panther is a good movie.* Ask: *What about you?* Elicit opinions, e.g. *Yes, it's cool. No, it's boring.* Sts then take turns making comments about the songs, characters, and movies. Sts reply with opinions using adjectives from lesson 1.1.

> a 7 Yellow   b 5 White   c 3 Orange
> d 8 The Pink Panther   e 6 Charlie Brown
> f 1 Blue Ivy Carter   g 4 Red Riding Hood
> h 2 Green Day   i 10 Black Friday   j 9 Purple Rain

B Show (a photo of) an old cell phone and contrast it to a new one to teach *new and light* vs. *old and heavy.* Use gestures to convey meaning. Sts look at the quiz in **A** again and notice the adjectives in bold. Individually, they write opposites to the adjectives. Paircheck. Classcheck. Drill pronunciation.

> Adjectives: common, small, young, fictional, famous, Californian, American, cheap, popular
> Rules: before, no

> **Tip** Write the phrase *What's the opposite of …?* on a large sheet of paper and add it to your list of helpful phrases on the classroom wall.

C Have sts test each other briefly. St A closes his / her book. St B asks: *What's the opposite of good? / new?* for 30 seconds. Then sts change roles. Sts match adjectives to their opposites. Paircheck.

> 1 common   2 cheap   3 small   4 fictional   5 popular
> 6 young

D Tell sts to listen to descriptions of five items on p. 12. They should name the objects after they hear a beep. Play ▶ 1.21. Classcheck.

> **Tip** Ask sts to turn to the AS on page 161. Sts listen again and notice the pronunciation of /b/, /g/, and /z/.

E 🎧 **Make it personal**   Model the activity yourself. Choose a singular object in the classroom, but don't tell sts what it is. Choose something they will easily guess. Describe and give your opinion. Say: *It's big, red, and cool.* Ask: *What is it?* (e.g. a st's bag). Encourage / Prompt questions like: *Is it my / his bag?* Repeat procedure for a plural object. Invite a st to describe and give his / her opinion of an object in the room, and you and the rest of the group try to guess it by asking *Is it / Are they his / her (wallet / glasses)?* Drill *be* + possessive adjectives questions to foster fluency. In groups of three, sts play the game on their own. Monitor closely.

➡ **Workbook** p. 7

1.5 What's your full name?

Skills Completing a form

A Read and answer the questions.
1 Match a–f to documents 1–6.
  a a work ID   c a hotel registration form   e a car rental form
  b a conference ID   d a school registration form   f a passport
2 Who is European?
3 Who is non-European?
4 Who is a teenager?

1
NAME: Amy
SEX: F
AGE: 18
NATIONALITY: Colombian
ADDRESS: Medellín
DESIGN YOUTH CONFERENCE

2
Last name: MARSHALL
First name: Susana
Country of origin: Nigeria
Birthdate: 10/27/1988
Gender: F   Plate number: 6VBV764

3
Full name: Charles Bouvier
Date of birth: 5/26/90
Country of birth: France
Current address:
354 Rue de Ville, Nice
Zip code: 06200
Date: 8/14/18

4
LION COMMUNITY SCHOOL
Name: Omar Aslam
Age: 14 yrs 8 mos
Date: Sept 1, 2018
Nationality: Pakistani

5
UNITED KINGDOM OF GREAT BRITAIN AND NORTHERN IRELAND
Type: P   Code: GBR   No: 70125698
Surname (1): MURPHY
Given name(s) (2): GILLIAN JANE
Nationality (3): BRITISH CITIZEN
Date of Birth (4): FEB 15, 1965
Sex (5): F
P<GBRMURPHY<<GILLIAN<<JANE<<<<<<<<<<<<<<<<<<
70125698GBR12896345F18900245<<<<<<<<<<<<<<05

6
SunTech
Name: Ken Tran
Place of birth: Ho Chi Minh City, Vietnam
Department: Human Resources
Email address: ktran@suntech.com
Tel: 765-3000   Ext: 145

B Read the documents again and find different ways to refer to:
1 your name (5): *first name*
2 your age (3):
3 where you are from (4):

C ▶1.22 Do you know all the countries and nationalities in the documents in **A**? Listen to check.

D ▶1.23 Listen to and complete the registration form.

Second International Conference
Telephone registration

Name:		Nationality:	
Address:		Telephone:	
		Email:	
Zip Code:			

Common mistakes
What's your ~~complete~~ *full* name?
My ~~actual~~ *current* address is …

E Make it personal Choose a document from this page. Ask your partner questions to complete it with their data. Change roles. Then present your partner to the class.
This is my friend, Adriana. Her full name is …

1.5 What's your full name?

Lesson Aims: Sts continue to practice the verb *be* through the context of reading / completing documents and forms.

Function	Skills	Language
Reading documents and forms. Listening to phone banking registration instructions. Asking and answering personal questions.	Completing a form.	Country of birth: France. Surname: Murphy. What's your address? Where are you from? What's your phone number? How are you?

Vocabulary: Personal information (address, name, last name, etc.).
Grammar: Review personal information questions.

Warm-up Books closed. Recycle colors, the alphabet, and *How do you spell that?* Hand out slips of paper with different colors written on them. In pairs, sts test each other and ask *How do you spell (blue)? How do you spell (green)?*, etc.

ID Skills Completing a form

A Books open. Focus on the six images of identification. Ask: *Do you have identification like this? What information is on your ID?* Ask sts to show each other their ID cards if they have them. Sts read and answer the four questions. Classcheck. Highlight *plate number* in ID number 2 and check meaning. Elicit and drill pronunciation and stress on *rental, conference, gender, registration, passport, European,* and *teenager*.

> 1 a 6 b 1 c 3 d 4 e 2 f 5
> 2 Charles Bouvier, Gillian Jane Murphy
> 3 Amy, Susana Marshall, Omar Aslam, Ken Tran
> 4 Amy, Omar Aslam

B Focus on the documents in **A** and draw sts' attention to the various ways to refer to name, age, and nationality. Do number 1 together with the group. Sts complete 2–3 by themselves. Paircheck. Classcheck.

> 1 Name, Last name, Full name, Given name(s)
> 2 Age, Birthdate, Date of birth
> 3 Nationality, Country of origin, Country of birth, Place of birth

Tip Make sure sts understand the ways names, ages, and nationalities are usually referred to in written forms (passports, hotel check-in, etc.). In spoken English, people often ask *Where are you from? How old are you?* rather than *What's your nationality / age?* Transforming each form field into a natural-sounding question is the skill sts learn in this part of the lesson.

C Write *Colombian* on the board, point to Amy's ID, and say *Amy is Colombian. Where is Amy from?* Elicit the country. Sts look at the other IDs with a partner and try to remember the countries and nationalities. Play ▶1.22 and ask sts to say if they were correct. Test sts by saying one of the countries and eliciting the nationality. Sts can then do this in pairs saying countries or nationalities to each other.

D Refer to **Common mistakes** here. Ask: *What is this form for?* (a conference). Check understanding of *conference*. Play ▶1.23 and sts complete the form. Play the audio again.

Weaker students Pause the audio to allow more time to understand and follow the information.

Paircheck. Classcheck.

> Name: Justine Wallace
> Address: 18 Jeffrey Drive, Denver, Colorado
> Zip Code: 80202
> Nationality: American
> Telephone: (720) 988-3405
> Email: jwallace26@webmail.com

▶1.23 Turn to page 311 for the complete audioscript.

E Make it personal Sts choose a form from p. 14 or, alternatively, create a form together with the whole class. It could be a school registration form, a passport request, etc. Ask sts what information they would like to include (name, age, nationality, sex, etc.) and draw the sts' form on the board. Sts copy their form into their notebooks / sheets of paper. Elicit what questions they'll need to ask to complete each field. In pairs, sts ask and give information about themselves and complete the forms about each other.

When they have finished, ask some sts to introduce their friends to the whole class. For real beginners, you'll need to prompt language. Write a model on the board: *This is my friend … He's (nationality). He's (age).*, etc.

Extra activity Say: *Some words with the same pronunciation have different spellings and meanings in English.*

Write the following words on the board and ask sts to say each word as a class. In pairs, ask sts to write a short sentence using each word. Elicit an example or provide one. e.g. *I have four brothers. / This rose is for you.*

Four, for   Right, write
Hi, high   See, sea
I, eye   They're, their, there
No, know   Two, to, too

1.5 How are you?

Hey, I just met you, And this is crazy, But here's my number, So call me, maybe?

ID in Action Meeting people

A ▶1.24 Listen to two colleagues and check (✓) the six phrases they say.

Asking	Answering
☐ How are you?	☐ Fine, thanks.
☐ How's it going?	☐ I'm well, thank you.
☐ How are you doing?	☐ Good, thanks.
☐ What about you?	☐ Not much.
☐ What's up?	☐ Things are good.
☐ What's new?	☐ Not bad. And you?

Common mistakes
Thank you.
You're welcome.
~~For nothing.~~

B ▶1.25 Listen to and repeat the other phrases. Which response from **A** is repeated?

C In pairs, practice similar conversations with any possible combination of the phrases in **A**.

> Hi! How are you?   Fine, thanks. What about you? How's it going?   Things are good.

D ▶1.26 Listen to six short dialogues. Write the number of each conversation in the box.

☐ I don't understand.   Oh, sorry.   ☐ See you later!   Bye for now!

☐ Thank you!   You're welcome.   ☐ Excuse me. Can you say that again, please?   Sure …

☐ I'm sorry.   Don't worry about it.   ☐ Excuse me.   Oh, I'm sorry.

E **Make it personal** In pairs, imagine you're the people in photos 1–5. Role-play conversations using appropriate expressions.

1.5 How are you?

Lesson Aims: Sts learn a range of greetings / short exchanges when meeting.

Function
Listening to colleagues meet at work.
Talking to / Meeting people.

Language
Hi! How's it going?
Chunks (Thank you, You're welcome, Excuse me?, etc.).

Vocabulary: Greetings phrases.
Grammar: Practice simple present and the verb *be*.

♪ **Song line:** Turn to p. 324 for notes about this song and an accompanying task.

ID in Action Meeting people

A Books closed. Review / Elicit greetings (*good morning / afternoon / evening*) and ways of introducing yourself (*Hi / Hello / I'm / My name's … Nice to meet you (too)*). Introduce *How are you?* and elicit possible answers. Prompt by asking *How are you? Are you OK?* Ask for a volunteer in class to act out a dialogue with you. Pair up with the volunteer and introduce yourself. Ask: *How are you? I'm fine, what about you?* Do the same with other sts, alternate, asking *How is it going? How are you doing?*

Books open. Sts read the questions and possible answers chart. Sts listen to ▶1.24 and check the six questions and answers they hear.

> How are you? Good, thanks. What about you? What's new? Not much. Things are good.

▶1.24 Turn to page 311 for the complete audioscript.

B Play ▶1.25 and ask sts to repeat / imitate the pronunciation of the other phrases and identify the repeated response from **A**. The repeated response is *Not much*.

C Ask two sts to read the speech bubbles. Tell sts to work in pairs and create two mini-dialogues using the questions and possible answers from **A**. In Dialogue 1, st A starts. Dialogue 2, st B starts. When pairs have finished, ask some to act out their dialogues to the group.

D Use the example to model what they have to do. Play ▶1.26. Sts listen to six dialogues and write numbers 1–6 in the correct boxes.

> From top to bottom, then left to right: 6, 1, 3, 4, 5, 2

> **Tip** Ask sts to turn to the AS on p. 161. Sts listen again and notice the sentence stress.

E 🔴 **Make it personal** Display the photos on an IWB if you can. Demonstrate the task by pointing to the photos and asking a confident st to come to the front of the class and act out a dialogue with you. Ask: *Which photo?* Secretly show the st which photo you want to act out. Role-play the situation for the class and elicit which photo you are acting out.

Ask sts to look at photos 1–5. In pairs, sts act out each situation and use expressions from **A** and **D**. Assign different pairs / partners.

Round off the activity by putting pairs together to make groups of four or six. Tell them to act out the situations as you did with the st earlier and the others watch, listen, and guess the situation.

➔ **Workbook** p. 8

➔ ⓘ **Richmond Learning Platform**

➔ **Writing** p. 16

➔ ⓘ **Café** p. 17

Writing 1   A social media profile

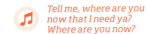
Tell me, where are you now that I need ya? Where are you now?

A Read Cristina's personal profile and complete the form.

e-pals.net

Cristina González
@cristina0330

My name's Cristina González, and I'm 18 years old. I'm Bolivian, from Santa Cruz, but now I live in Toronto, Canada, and I'm a student at Great Lakes High School five days a week. I also work in a local café on weekends. It's popular with students and artists, and the customers are really interesting. Sometimes I don't understand what people say to me, but I'm a fast learner! I don't have a boyfriend at the moment, but I have an amazing best friend called Anya. We go to the gym together. We also go to parties and clubs! Toronto's a fantastic city with an excellent baseball team, the Blue Jays. Anya doesn't like baseball, but I love it. I go alone or with my dad. Please message me: **@cristina0330**.

Profile

Last name:	
First name:	
Age:	
Nationality:	
Country of residence:	
Occupation:	
Username:	

B Read **Write it right!**, then underline the contractions and the connectors in **A**.

> ✓ **Write it right!**
>
> In informal writing, use contractions: *I'm, I don't.*
> Use a variety of connectors: *and, but, or.*

C Find and correct 10 more mistakes in Luís' reply to Cristina.

Messages
LU_PORT:

Hi, Cristina, my name is Luís, I'm ~~portuguese~~ [P]ortuguese and I have 19 years. Wow! You live in Toronto – that is excelent. I live in Porto with my mother and father, and I have a lot of parents here. I too study english, but its very dificult! My brother play baseball, maybe you can meet him, ha-ha! Me, I like the soccer. Pleas email me at **luisporto94@e-mates.com** and tell me much about Toronto.

D From the texts in **A** and **C**, which questions can we answer about Cristina (C), Luís (L), or both (B)?
1. Where are you from? _B_
2. How old are you? ____
3. What's your full name? ____
4. Where do you live? ____
5. Who do you live with? ____
6. What's your email address? ____
7. Do you go to school? ____
8. Do you have any brothers or sisters? ____
9. Do they play sports? ____
10. Do you have a boyfriend / girlfriend? ____
11. Do you have a best friend? ____
12. What are your interests? ____

E 🎧 **Make it personal** Write a similar profile of yourself. Write 120–150 words.

Before	Answer questions 1–12 in **D**. Think about extra information, e.g., your opinion about people, places, or things.
While	Use contractions and a variety of connectors. Use adjectives to give your opinion.
After	Check your profile carefully. Show it to a partner before giving it to your teacher.

16

Writing 1 A social media profile

Direct sts to the title of the lesson. Ask: *What social media do you use? Have you got an online profile? What information do we write in a profile?* Teach the meaning of *e-mates* (*mates* is a synonym of *friends*).

A Integrated speaking Ask sts to cover the text. Point to the girl in the photo and to the registration form and elicit questions for each blank; e.g., (Last name) *What's her last name?*, (First name) *What's her first name?*, (Age) *How old is she?*, etc. In pairs, sts ask and speculate about the girl.

Sts read Cristina's profile to complete the registration form. Paircheck. Classcheck with answers on the board.

> Last name: González
> First Name: Cristina
> Age: 18
> Nationality: Bolivian
> Country of residence: Canada
> Occupation: Student, café worker
> Username: @cristina0330

To engage students with the context of this lesson, ask: *Do you have anything in common with Cristina? Would you reply to her?*

B Read **Write it right!** with the whole class. Point to the underlined words in the text in **A** (My <u>name's</u> and <u>and</u>) and ask sts to underline more contractions and connectors in Cristina's profile. Paircheck. Classcheck.

> **Tip** If an IWB is available, display the page on the *Digital Book for Teachers* and classcheck by asking sts to go to the board and underline their answers.

> Contractions: name's, I'm (x4), It's, don't (x2), Toronto's, doesn't
> Connectors: and (x3), but (x4), or

C Tell sts that Cristina got one reply. Ask: *What's his name? Where's he from?* and let sts find the answers in Luis's reply. Point to the mistakes corrected in red (capitalization) and ask sts to find and correct 10 more mistakes in the text. Paircheck. Classcheck with answers on the board or on the *Digital Book for Teachers*.

> … and I ~~have~~ *am* 19 years *old*. Wow! You live in Toronto—that is ~~excelent~~ *excellent*. I live in Porto with my mother and father and I have a lot of ~~parents~~ *relatives* here. I ~~too~~ *also* study ~~english~~ *English*, but ~~its~~ *it's* very ~~dificult~~ *difficult*! My brother ~~play~~ *plays* baseball, maybe you can meet him, ha-ha! Me, I like ~~the~~ soccer. ~~Pleas~~ *Please* email me at luisporto94@e-mates.com and tell me ~~much~~ *more* about Toronto.

D Read question 1 with sts and ask: *Can we answer this question about Cristina?* (Yes, she's from Bolivia.) *What about Luis?* (Yes, he's from Portugal.) Teach / Convey meaning of *both*. Sts read questions 2-11 and write if they can find answers in **A** and **C** about Cristina (C), Luis (L) or both (B). Paircheck. Classcheck with answers on the board.

> 2 B 3 C 4 B 5 L 6 L 7 C 8 L 9 L 10 C 11 C
> 12 B

E 🔵 **Make it personal** Read the steps Before, While, and After with sts so as to better guide them in writing their own profiles. Tell them to use Cristina's profile in **A** as a model and draw their attention to the length of the composition – that is, 120–150 words.

1 An excellent reunion

 Café

1 Before watching

A Complete 1–3 with the correct words.
1. This _____ Andrea. She's at _____ class reunion.
2. This _____ her brother. _____ name is August.
3. That's _____ cousin, Genevieve. She _____ Canadian.

B 🔘 **Make it personal** What's your opinion of class, work, family, or old friend reunions? Talk in pairs.

> I think class reunions are fun.   Not me. I think they're boring.

2 While watching

A Watch the video and circle the correct answer.
1. The party is **in an apartment** / **at a school**.
2. On the wall are some **new pictures** / **class photos**.
3. **August** / **Andrea** remembers where Kitty is from.
4. **Andrea** / **Genevieve** isn't happy at first.
5. **Andrea** / **Genevieve** says, "I'm so glad you're just my cousin."

B Where are they from? Listen and complete the chart.

Classmate	Country / city	Nationality
Manny Vasquez	_____	Peruvian
_____	Findley	England	_____
_____	Jones	_____	Irish
_____	Belucci	_____	American
_____	Jones	_____	British

C Watch and check (✓) all Genevieve's nicknames you hear.
☐ Gen ☐ Gertrude ☐ Gigi ☐ Jenny ☐ Vie-Vie

D Watch and check (✓) all August's nicknames you hear.
☐ Auggie ☐ Augustus ☐ Gigi ☐ Guto ☐ Iggy

E 🔘 **Make it personal** Do you have a nickname? What do your family, friends, and classmates usually call you?

> My name's Kathleen, but my friends call me Kathy. What's your nickname?   Please, call me Fred.

3 After watching

A True (T) or False (F)?
1. Mrs. Grandby's an old classmate.
2. With Mrs. Grandby, there's never trouble.
3. Ignatius Dansbury's a great guy.
4. Ignatius is in a class above August and Andrea.
5. Joe Bellucci's a rock star.
6. Johnny's Genevieve's old boyfriend.
7. The cute boys from the band are from Canada.

B In pairs, check your answers to **A**. Correct the false statements.

> I think number 1 is false.   Me, too. I think she's their …

C Complete and match the greetings to speakers 1–5. There's one extra person.

1. Andrea   ☐ Oh, hey! It's Genevieve.
2. August   ☐ _____, Gen. How are you?
3. Ignatius   ☐ Hey, _____, what's up?
4. Genevieve   ☐ I'm so _____ to see you!
5. Joe   ☐ Iggy! What's up?

D In pairs, take turns saying phrases 1–12 with the correct intonation. Who says them, August (A), Andrea (An), Genevieve (G), or Joe (J)?
1. Guess who's over there? ____
2. Isn't that Manny? ____
3. What a horrible guy! ____
4. Forget about it! ____
5. Really? ____
6. Wait, isn't your middle name something with a G? ____
7. That's not the point. ____
8. Don't you say it! ____
9. Get it? ____
10. Stop it, little Guto! ____
11. Don't worry, ladies. ____
12. Geez! Don't drop it! ____

E 🔘 **Make it personal** Role-play a class reunion. Imagine you're old friends. In groups of three, gossip!

> Wow, guess who's here? It's Gloria!
> No way! Really? Incredible.
> That's not Gloria. She's too young. And Gloria's in Mexico.

17

ID Café 1 An excellent reunion

1 Before watching

A Point to the photo and say *These three friends are at a class reunion.* Explain that a class reunion is a party where you meet your ex-classmates from school or college. Have sts read sentences 1–3 and ask: *What are their names?* (Andrea, August, and Genevieve.)

Sts complete sentences 1–3 with a suitable word. Paircheck. Classcheck.

> 1 is, a / our / their   2 is, His   3 my / her / his, is

B 🔘 **Make it personal** Get two sts to read the model dialogue in the speech bubbles. In pairs, sts ask each other: *What's your opinion of class or family reunions?* Have sts report back their partners' opinions.

2 While watching

A Tell sts they are going to watch the video of Andrea's, August's, and Genevieve's class reunion. Ask: *Where's the reunion?* Point to the options in 1 and elicit some predictions, ask: *What do you think?*

Tell sts they have to select the correct option as they watch. Give them time to read the options. Play the video and ask sts to circle the answers. Paircheck. Classcheck.

> 1 at a school   2 class photos   3 August   4 Genevieve
> 5 Genevieve

B Tell sts they are going to hear Andrea, August, and Genevieve talk about five classmates. Point to the chart and ask sts to complete it with the missing information.

Classmate	Country / City	Nationality
Manny Vasquez	Peru	Peruvian
Tommy Findley	England	British
Kitty Jones	Ireland	Irish
Joe Bellucci	U.S. / New York	American
Johnny Jones	London	British

Play **Video 1**. Paircheck all answers. Classcheck. Give instructions to **C** and **D** before you replay the video. Sts complete both tasks as they watch again.

C Ask: *What's a nickname? Do you remember Genevieve's nicknames?* Elicit / Say how each option is pronounced.

> Gen / Gigi / Jenny / Vie-Vie

D Ask: *What about August's nicknames?* Elicit / Say how each option is pronounced. Paircheck. Classcheck.

> Augustus / Guto

E 🔘 **Make it personal** Change partners. In pairs, sts ask and answer questions about their nicknames. Refer to the model dialogue in the speech bubbles. Classcheck.

3 After watching

A Individually, sts decide whether sentences 1–7 are true or false.

> 1 F 2 T 3 F 4 T 5 F 6 T 7 F

B In pairs, sts check answers. Tell sts to refer to the dialogue in the speech bubbles. Tell sts to correct the false statements. Monitor closely for accuracy. Classcheck with answers on the board.

C Ask: *Do you remember the greetings the people in the video used to say hello?* Sts fill in the blanks and match greetings to persons 1–5. Paircheck. Classcheck.

> 1 Andrea: Oh hey! It's Genevieve.
> 2 August: Mrs Grandby, how are you? Iggy! What's up? Oh hey! It's Genevieve.
> 3 Ignatius: Hello, Gen. How are you?
> 4 Genevieve: I'm so happy to see you!
> 5 Joe: He is the extra person.

D Elicit from the whole class the correct intonation – or the intonation sts were exposed to in the video – for numbers 1–3, and briefly conduct choral repetition. In pairs, sts continue saying sentences 4–12 with the appropriate intonation. Monitor closely and correct sts on the spot. At the end, have a different st say each sentence one at a time. Praise whenever possible.

> **Weaker classes** Focus on sentences 1–6 and drill pronunciation (chorus and some individual repetition after you). In pairs, sts practice saying sentences 1–6. Monitor closely and correct. Classcheck by having some sts say each sentence. Then, do the same for sentences 7–12.

Change partners. Ask sts to write A, An, G, or J next to sentences 1–12, according to who says them in the video. Classcheck with answers on the board.

> 1 G   2 A   3 An   4 J   5 An   6 A   7 G   8 G
> 9 A   10 An   11 A   12 An

E 🔘 **Make it personal** Put sts in groups of three. Tell them that they are going to pretend to be old friends at a class reunion and talk about their old teachers and classmates. Replay the video one more time if necessary, and point to the examples in the speech bubbles. Encourage sts to use phrases like those in **C** and **D** above. Have some groups perform their role-plays for the whole class.

2.1 When do you get up?

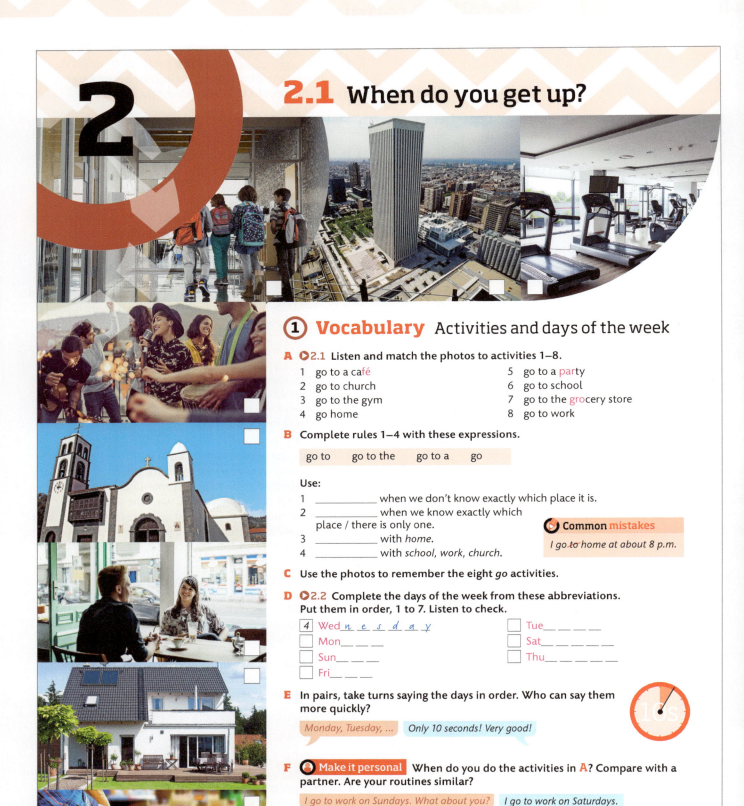

1 Vocabulary Activities and days of the week

A ▶2.1 Listen and match the photos to activities 1–8.
1 go to a café
2 go to church
3 go to the gym
4 go home
5 go to a party
6 go to school
7 go to the grocery store
8 go to work

B Complete rules 1–4 with these expressions.

> go to   go to the   go to a   go

Use:
1 _____ when we don't know exactly which place it is.
2 _____ when we know exactly which place / there is only one.
3 _____ with *home*.
4 _____ with *school*, *work*, *church*.

● **Common mistakes**
I go to home at about 8 p.m.

C Use the photos to remember the eight *go* activities.

D ▶2.2 Complete the days of the week from these abbreviations. Put them in order, 1 to 7. Listen to check.

☐ 4 Wed<u>n e s d a y</u>
☐ Mon__ __ __
☐ Sun__ __ __
☐ Fri__ __ __
☐ Tue__ __ __ __
☐ Sat__ __ __ __
☐ Thu__ __ __ __ __

E In pairs, take turns saying the days in order. Who can say them more quickly?

Monday, Tuesday, …   *Only 10 seconds! Very good!*

F ● **Make it personal** When do you do the activities in **A**? Compare with a partner. Are your routines similar?

I go to work on Sundays. What about you?   *I go to work on Saturdays.*

Unit overview: Through the contexts of routine and habits, family, celebrations, and reading and listening to interviews, sts learn to use and practice the simple present with daily routine verbs, places they visit, frequency adverbs, and common chunks for congratulating people or celebrating holidays and events. The simple present 3rd person singular is introduced. The main theme is asking and answering personal questions.

2.1 When do you get up?

Lesson Aims: Sts learn to use *go* phrases by talking about places they go to and when or what day(s) of the week they do so. Sts also learn how to tell the time.

Function	Language
Talking about places you go.	I go to a café on Mondays.
Talking about when or what day(s) of the week you do activities.	I go to the grocery store on Sundays.
Telling what time you do activities.	I go to the gym from Monday to Friday. What time do you get up?
Telling the time.	I go to bed at 10:30 p.m.
	It's 9:30.

Vocabulary: *go* + places (the gym, the grocery store, a café, etc.). Daily routine verbs: get up, go to bed, go to work. Days of the week.
Grammar: Indefinite articles *a / an* and definite article *the* in *go* + activities. Preposition *on* and days of the week. *What time do you ...?* questions.

Warm-up Write on the board *Where do you ___ every day / every week / every month?* Ask: *What word goes in the space?* (go). Ask one or two different sts the questions to check understanding. Tell sts to work in pairs and ask the questions. Monitor and write relevant vocabulary on the board, e.g. activities from **A**.

1 Vocabulary Activities and days of the week

Books open. Focus on photos 1–8 on p. 18. Elicit places sts can see and teach what is new vocabulary for them (a café, the gym, grocery store, etc.).

A Sts look at the phrases.

> **Tip** Read the first phrase (go to a café) with them and say: *A café is a place where we drink coffee, eat cake, etc.* Give examples: *Starbucks is a café. The drink is called coffee.* Write *café vs. coffee* on the board so sts can see the difference in spelling and practice pronunciation: café /kæˈfeɪ/, coffee /ˈkɒfɪ/

Tell sts they will listen to people talking about places 1–8. Play ▶ 2.1 and tell sts to match the phrases to the correct photos. Paircheck. Classcheck. Monitor closely.

> From top to bottom, then left to right: 6, 5, 2, 1, 4, 7, 8, 3

> **Tip** Ask sts to turn to the AS on p. 161. Sts listen again and notice the pronunciation of *to* /tə/ and *to a* /tuːwə/.

B Tell sts to read rule 1. Ask: *Is it a specific place / always the same place?* (No.) Sts complete with *go to a*. Ask the same question for 2: *Is it a specific ...?* (Yes.) Sts complete with *go to a*. Now sts complete 3 and 4.

> 1 go to a   2 go to the   3 go   4 go to

Common mistakes Read the example and highlight the mistake. Say *home* is an exception and no preposition is used after *go*. Explain that most of these common mistakes happen when sts try to translate directly from L1.

C To demonstrate the activity with the class, point to the book, cover the phrases, and ask: *What's this?* Tell sts to test each other for all eight photos.

D Sts complete the days with the missing letters and number them in the correct order. Sts listen to ▶ 2.2 and check. Paircheck. Classcheck with board answers. Highlight that days of the week are all stressed on the first syllable, and that they do not need an article in English. e.g. *Today is Monday.* (and not *Today is the Monday.*).

> 1 Sunday   2 Monday   3 Tuesday   4 Wednesday
> 5 Thursday   6 Friday   7 Saturday

> **Tip** Elicit the days of the week and associate each day with a well-known local TV program / event. Ask *What's on TV on Monday?* and so on.

E Ask for a volunteer. Ask them to say the days of the week in order as fast as they can. Point to your watch or a clock and time them. Tell sts to do the same in their pairs. Tell them to repeat this a few times so they can say it faster each time. Ask sts to report their results to the group.

F **Make it personal** Focus on the speech bubbles and ask two sts to read the dialogue. Elicit some examples / Encourage them to use other *go* activities from **A**. In pairs, sts tell each other when they go to ... (photos 1–8 in **A**).

> **Tip** For some activities, sts are likely to need help with other time phrases such as *every day* or *from Monday to Friday*. Pre-teach / prompt them while monitoring.

While sts perform the activity, monitor the phrases learned in **B** (*go to / the / a*) and the preposition *on* before days of the week. Correct errors afterwards.

2 Listening

I don't care if Monday's blue. Tuesday's gray and Wednesday too. Thursday I don't care about you.

A ▶ 2.3 Listen to and number the times in the order that you hear them. Then match the times to the correct situations a–f.

- a at a soccer game
- b at a party
- c on TV
- d at school
- e at an airport
- f at home

B Write more times for your partner to practice saying.

What time is it?   *It's 5:15.*

C ▶ 2.4 Listen to two short interviews and write the days and times.
1. The woman gets up at _____ in the morning. She goes to school at _____. She goes to bed at _____ during the week. She gets _____ hours of sleep a night.
2. The man goes to work at _____ from _____ to _____. He gets home at _____ in the evening. He doesn't work at night or on weekends.

D ▶ 2.4 Listen again and complete the rules with *on*, *in*, or *at*.

Use:
1. _____ with times and *night*.
2. _____ with days of the week and *weekends*.
3. _____ with the *morning / afternoon / evening*.

E 🔴 Make it personal   In pairs, take turns asking and answering 1–4.
From Monday to Friday, and on weekends, what time do you ...
1. get up?
2. go to bed?
3. go to school / work / university?
4. get home from work / school?

I get up at 7 a.m. during the week, but at around 9 on weekends!

I get up early on weekends, around 6:30! I go to work.

> **Common mistakes**
>
> ~~in~~ at
> I don't work ~~in~~ the night.
>
> ~~in~~ on
> She doesn't go to bed early ~~in~~ weekends.

3 Reading

A Read the report and complete the chart.

On average, how many hours do people in these countries sleep?			
France		Japan	
The U.S.		South Korea	

B 🔴 Make it personal   Do a class survey. Ask:
1. What time do you get up a) on weekdays b) on weekends?
2. What time do you go to bed a) on weekdays b) on weekends?
3. On average, how many hours do people in your class sleep?

The World Sleeps

The Organization for Economic Cooperation and Development asked 18 countries, "How many hours do you sleep?". The French get an average of 8 hours and 50 minutes of sleep a night compared to the U.S. with 8 hours and 38 minutes. The South Koreans only sleep 7 hours and 49 minutes a night, and the Japanese about 8 hours.

2.1

🎵 **Song line:** Turn to p. 325 for notes on this song and an accompanying task.

2 Listening

A Draw a digital clock on the board with 14:15 and ask: *What time is it?* Write the answer *It's two fifteen* on the board. If sts say *quarter past* tell them we are focusing on digital time in this lesson. Focus on the image, play ▶ 2.3 and pause after each number. Paircheck. Play the audio again if necessary. Classcheck. Point to the image. Ask a st: *What's the time in clock 2?* Tell sts to do the same with a partner. Elicit more examples from faster sts.

> From top to bottom, then left to right:
> 3 e   1 b   6 a   5 d   4 c   2 f

> **Tip** Show sts how the stress changes in numbers thirteen oO / thirty Oo, fourteen oO / forty Oo, etc.

B Direct sts back to the image you drew to lead in to **A** and ask: *What time is it?* Change the time to 02:50, then 02:13, then 04:30, and ask the same question, correcting any errors you hear. Then, tell sts to do the same with a partner. Monitor and check pronunciation.

C Introduce and drill *morning, afternoon, evening, night.* Write these times on the board: *7:00 a.m., 2:00 p.m., 6:30 p.m.,* and *10:00 p.m.* Point to the first and ask: *What time is it?* Elicit *It's seven o'clock in the morning.* Continue for the other examples. Elicit the difference between *evening* and *night.*

Tell sts to listen to two interviews and complete with the times and days they hear. ▶ 2.4 Paircheck. Classcheck with answers on the board.

> 1 6, 6:45, 10 p.m., eight
> 2 8:30, Monday, Friday. 6:15

▶ 2.4 Turn to p. 311 for the complete audioscript.

D Write *on* and *at* on the board and tell sts to complete numbers 1–6 with either word as they listen again. Sts complete rules 1–3. Paircheck. Classcheck. Write *Monday morning* on the board and elicit whether we use *on* or *at*. Refer to the **Common mistakes** to highlight differences between English and L1.

> 1 at   2 on   3 in

E **Make it personal** **Books closed.** Conduct choral and individual repetition of *What time do you ...?* and use prompts 1–4. Teach *around* and refer to the example in the speech bubble below.

Books open. Read the sample dialogue with the whole class. In pairs, sts ask each other: *What time do you ...?* (questions about weekdays and weekends). After they finish, ask a pair to present part of their dialogue (three questions) to the class.

> **Tip** Asking sts to report what their partners said might lead to errors at this stage, as they don't know simple present 3rd person singular. Let them say what they can. Prioritize fluency as much as accuracy. Or you might ask: *What time does he / she ...?* and accept short answers (*at 6 a.m.*) instead of complete sentences (*He gets up at ...*).

3 Reading

A In pairs, ask sts to guess pronunciation of pink highlighted words before reading the text. Ask: *How many hours do you sleep?* Teach the meaning of *average* and ask: *Do you think you sleep more or less than the average person? Do you think people in other countries sleep more hours than (insert your country)?* Say: *Let's find out!* Sts read the report and complete the chart. Ask: *Are you surprised by the numbers? Why? Why not?* Highlight and drill pronunciation of minutes /mɪnɪts/.

> France: 8 hours 50 minutes
> The U.S.: 8 hours 38 minutes
> Japan: 8 hours
> South Korea: 7 hours 49 minutes

B **Make it personal** Drill pronunciation of the questions. Ask sts to stand up and walk around the class asking 1 and 2. Tell them to take notes and interview as many classmates as possible. When they have finished, ask them to sit in small groups and compare their answers. Ask the whole class question 3.

Extra activity Ask sts to write a short report of the lesson using these phrases. They can use the report to help them.
In our class, most people / some / a few people ...
... go to ... go ... go to the ... go to a ...   get up at ... go to bed at ...
On average our class sleeps ...

→ **Workbook** p. 9

2.2 What do you do in the mornings?

1 Vocabulary Morning routine

A Match pictures a–j with phrases 1–10.

1. ☐ brush my teeth
2. ☐ exercise / work out
3. ☐ get dressed
4. ☐ get up
5. ☐ have breakfast
6. ☐ leave home
7. ☐ make the bed
8. ☐ shave
9. ☐ take a shower
10. ☐ wake up

B ▶ 2.5 Listen to 10 sound effects. Say the phrase before the audio. Were you correct?

C ▶ 2.6 Listen to Jake describe his morning routine. Match the time expressions to his actions in **A**.
☐ 6:30
☐ not immediately
☐ for 30 minutes
☐ 8 a.m.

D 🔴 **Make it personal** Write down your morning routine and the time you do each activity. Compare with a partner. Are your routines similar or different?

I wake up at 6 a.m. You wake up at 7:30 a.m. That's very different!

▶ **Common mistakes**
What time *do* you get up?

2.2 What do you do in the mornings?

Lesson Aims: Sts learn to use several verbs of action in the 3rd person singular in the context of describing their daily routine.

Function
Daily sleep patterns.
Telling your daily routine.

Language
How many hours a night do you sleep? I wake up at …
He wakes up at around 8 a.m.

Vocabulary: Morning routine: brush my teeth, exercise, get dressed, get up, have breakfast, leave home, make the bed, shave, sleep, take a shower, wake up.
Time phrases: about, hours, minutes, on weekdays / weekends, a night, how many, at (around) + time, for + time, immediately.
Grammar: Simple present: all persons and forms, simple present 3rd person singular.

Warm-up Play a quick mime or pictionary game with the *go* activities and daily routine from the previous lesson: (*go to the gym, go to the grocery store, get up, go to bed / sleep, go home,* etc.) You could ask sts to choose from p. 18, e.g. *I go to school at 7 a.m.* to mime their phrase for the class to guess.

1 Vocabulary Morning routine

A Focus on the pictures. Elicit as many actions as possible and use the pictures and gestures / mime to convey meaning. Write correct verbs on the board as sts suggest them, checking pronunciation. In pairs, sts match phrases 1–10 to the pictures. Paircheck.

🔑
1 i   2 d   3 h   4 j   5 b   6 g   7 f   8 a   9 e   10 c

Follow-up Ask sts to cover the phrases and test each other in pairs. St A points to the pictures, st B comes up with the correct phrase. After a minute, sts change roles. In pairs, they play a mime game. Sts A and B take turns choosing one action from pictures 1–10 to mime for the other to guess.

B Tell sts they will hear sound effects. Say: *Listen and guess the activity and write it down first, then compare with a partner.* Play ▶ 2.5 and classcheck.

C Sts listen to Jake talking about his morning routine. Tell them to use the numbers from **A** to complete the activity. Look at the times and time expressions and elicit from sts how they are said. Play ▶ 2.6 and sts match correct times to his actions. Paircheck. Classcheck. After listening, ask questions to find out about the sts' experience of listening, e.g. *Was this useful? Easy? Enjoyable? Why? Are there any parts you didn't understand?*

🔑
6:30 (10)   not immediately (4)   for 30 minutes (2)
8 a.m. (6)

▶ 2.6 Turn to p. 311 for the complete audioscript.

Tip Always encourage sts to use language / short dialogues to paircheck, instead of doing it visually / looking at each other's books. E.g.: St A: *Not immediately?* B: *Get up. Number 4. What about for 30 minutes?* A: *(That's) exercise. Number 2.*

Language tip Asking about the time when somebody does something might be tricky for Romance language speakers because of direct translation. They are likely to ask *What **hours** do you work?* instead of *What **time** do you go to work?* Pre-empt this by explaining the correct question for finding out this information.

D 🔴 **Make it personal**   Tell sts to write at least five activities they do each morning using the verbs in **A**. Refer to ✅ **Common mistakes** . In pairs, sts tell each other what they do every morning. Ask them to include the time they do each activity. Monitor and listen for good language and errors and go over this after they have finished.

Weaker classes Learners often feel more confident if they have the chance to write things down before they talk. You could give them 3–5 minutes to write down their morning routine before they speak.

2 Grammar Simple present ⊕ and ⊖

🎵 *Don't forget me, I beg, I remember you said, Sometimes it lasts in love but sometimes it hurts instead.*

A Look at the man in the photo. What is his morning routine? Put the activities in **1A** on p. 20 in the order you think the man does them.

B ▶ 2.7 Listen and check your guesses. Any surprises?

C Study the song line above and **Common mistakes**. Then read and complete the grammar box.

> **a** Complete the sentences with the ⊕ form of the verb in parentheses.
>
> | | Subject | Verb | |
> |---|---|---|---|
> | 1 | I | | home at 7 a.m. (**leave**) |
> | 2 | You | | to school at 7:30 a.m. (**go**) |
> | 3 | My sister | | her bed in the morning. (**make**) |
> | 4 | My dad | | a shower at night. (**take**) |
> | 5 | My brother and I | | up at 6 a.m. (**get**) |
> | 6 | My friends | | breakfast at 10 a.m. (**have**) |
>
> **b** Complete the rules about ⊖ sentences in the simple present.
> I **don't** watch TV when I get home.   She **doesn't** have breakfast.
> 1 We use **does / doesn't** with she / he / it, and we use **doesn't / don't** with all other pronouns.
> 2 **Don't** or **doesn't** goes **before / after** the verb.
>
> **c** Make the sentences in **a** negative.

➡ **Grammar 2A** p. 140

Common mistakes
She / He ~~wake~~ **wakes** up at 6:00 a.m.
She ~~don't~~ **doesn't** wake up before 9:00 a.m.
He ~~have~~ **has** breakfast alone.

I wake up at 7 a.m., but I get up at 7:30. I don't make my bed!

D ▶ 2.7 Complete the paragraph about the man's actions. Then listen to check. Is your morning routine similar?

He _wakes up_ (wake up) at 8 a.m., but he _____ (get up). He sleeps again and then he _____ (get up) at 8:50 a.m., but he _____ (wake up)! After he wakes up, he _____ (make his bed). Then he _____ (exercise) and he _____ (shave). After that, he _____ (take a shower), he _____ (brush his teeth), and he _____ (get dressed)!

E 🟢 **Make it personal** In groups, play the game.
1 Guess and write four ⊕ and ⊖ sentences about the routines and everyday activities of the people in your group.
2 Take turns checking your guesses. Say one of your sentences and ask the other students to raise their hands if the sentence is true for them.

I think three people go to the gym on weekends. Is that true?   *No, it isn't! Only one person goes to the gym on weekends.*

2.2

2 Grammar Simple present ⊕ and ⊖

A Refer sts to the photo and **1A** on p. 20. Ask: *What do you think the man does every morning? What does he do first, second, etc.?*

B Play ▶2.7 and tell sts to check their ideas from **A**. Classcheck.

> 1 wakes up   2 gets up   3 makes his bed   4 exercises
> 5 shaves

▶2.7 Turn to p. 311 for the complete audioscript.

> **Tip** Ask sts to turn to the AS on p. 161. Sts listen again and notice /eɪ/ and word stress.

♪ **Song line:** Turn to p. 325 for notes about this song and an accompanying task.

C For a, elicit the verbs to complete the grammar box. Classcheck with answers on the board. Highlight the *s* for 3rd person. For b, tell sts to choose the correct option. Classcheck. Elicit the negative forms for c.

> a 1 leave   2 go   3 makes   4 takes   5 get   6 have
> b 1 doesn't, don't   2 before
> c 1 I don't leave home at 7 a.m.
>   2 You don't go to school at 7:30 a.m.
>   3 My sister doesn't make her bed in the morning.
>   4 My dad doesn't take a shower at night.
>   5 My brother and I don't get up at 6 a.m.
>   6 My friends don't have breakfast at 10 a.m.

➡ **Grammar 2A** p. 140

D Ask: *What is the first thing the man does in the morning?* (He wakes up.) Sts complete the gap fill. Sts listen again and check their answers.

> doesn't get up, gets up, doesn't wake up, makes his bed, exercises, shaves, doesn't take a shower, doesn't brush his teeth, doesn't get dressed

E **Make it personal** Ask a st to read the speech bubbles to the class. Ask: *Do you think these are true for this class?* Say: *I think X people in this class go to the gym on weekends.* Ask: *Do you agree?* and elicit / teach *Yes, I do. / No, I don't*. Write the common mistake *Are you agree? Yes, I am.* on the board and elicit the error from the class. Elicit one or two similar examples to those in the speech bubbles to describe the class and write them on the board, e.g. *I think two people get up at 7 a.m.* Say: *I think six of you agree with this sentence.* Ask: *Do you agree?* Say: *Ah, I was correct* or *Oh no, I was wrong*. Tell sts to read the task instructions and check they know what to do. Put sts into groups of four or five to complete the task.

Ask sts to share some examples of their group's routines with the class.

➡ **Workbook** p. 10

2.3 Who do you live with?

1 Reading and vocabulary Family

A ▶ 2.8 Who are these characters from an animated TV show? Listen to and read this ad. Then complete their family tree.

Meet the Griffins!

Peter Griffin and his wife, Lois, have three children. Meg is their first child and their only daughter. Chris is their teenage son, and Stewie is his baby brother. He's just one year old. The family is completed by Brian, the talking dog, and Peter's parents, Francis and Thelma. They live in Quahog, Rhode Island, in the U.S.
Watch this show every weeknight at 11:30 p.m. on Channel 44.

Francis and Thelma
_____ and Lois
_____ Chris _____

B ▶ 2.8 Complete the family chart with words from the ad. Then read them aloud to your partner. Listen and check your pronunciation.

Female	Male	Male and female
grandmother	grandfather	grandparent(s)
mother	father	_____(s)
sister	_____	siblings / twin(s)
_____	son	child / children
niece	nephew	
_____	husband	couple
aunt	uncle	
		cousin(s)
girlfriend	boyfriend	partner

Common mistakes
~~parents~~
I have two ~~fathers~~: my mom and dad. The others in my family are my ~~parents~~.
relatives

Lois to Peter? — Lois is his wife.

C In pairs, test each other on the relationships in **A**.

D Repeat **C**, this time using the possessive 's. Who's Francis? Thelma's husband.

E Make it personal In small groups, draw another famous family tree (from TV, movies, literature) and write a short ad. Answer questions 1–4.
1 What are their names?
2 Who is who? What are their relationships?
3 Where do they live?
4 What is different or interesting about them?

F Exchange ads with another group. Do you know the family? Who has the best ad?

2.3 Who do you live with?

Lesson Aims: Sts talk about family relationships and practice word order and intonation in questions.

Function
Reading / Talking about family relationships.
Asking for personal information.

Language
Chris is Lois' son.
Francis is Thelma's husband.
What's your full name? Are you Spanish?
Do you live in an apartment?

Vocabulary: Family words (son, daughter, mother, grandparents, etc.). Possessive 's.
Grammar: Simple present question order. QASI (Question Word + Auxiliary + Subject + Infinitive) vs. ASI (Auxiliary + Subject + Infinitive).

Before the lesson Print out logos of some well-known brands with 's in the name (e.g. Levi's, McDonald's) but remove or cover up the brand name. Stick the pictures on the board before sts arrive for the lesson.

Warm-up Elicit the brand names for the logos you have prepared, and write them beside the pictures. Elicit from sts or introduce the meaning of 's.

1 Reading and vocabulary Family

A Explore the cartoon in A and elicit what sts can see (a dog, a baby, a family, etc.). Ask: *Do you know the Griffins?* Tell them the man in white is the father, Peter Griffin. Ask: *How many children does he have?* (three) Encourage sts to tell the class other things they know about the show. Play ▶2.8 and tell sts to listen and read the text and complete the family tree. Paircheck. Classcheck.

> From top to bottom, left to right: Peter, Meg, Stewie

B Sts complete the family table with words from the TV ad in **A**. Paircheck. Draw sts' attention to the pink syllables. to show that the first syllable is stressed on all the two- and three-syllable nouns in this group. Also, highlight the pronunciation of *ph* /f/ in *nephew*. Give extra help with pronunciation of *child* /tʃaɪld/ and *children* /ˈtʃɪldrən/.

> Female: daughter, wife
> Male: brother
> Male and female: parent

Tip Focus on the vowel sound /ʌ/ in *mother* /ˈmʌðər/, *brother* /ˈbrʌðər/, *uncle* /ˈʌŋkl/, *son* /sʌn/, *couple* /ˈkʌpl/, *husband* /ˈhʌsbənd/, and *cousin* /ˈkʌzn/. This will show its different spellings. To help sts produce this sound, show them the open mouth position. Drill the sound in isolation, then ask: *Which words here have this sound?* Tell sts that two-syllable words that end in *-er* usually have stress on the first syllable (**sis**ter, **bro**ther, etc.).

Common mistakes Draw attention to the false friend (in Spanish) between *fathers* and *parents*.

C Model the activity. Ask sts to look at the family tree in **A** and ask: *Who's Lois's husband?* (Peter). Prompt *Thelma's husband* and elicit the question from sts, *Who's Thelma's husband?* and have a st answer (Francis). In pairs, sts take turns asking and answering about the Griffin family.

D Write the following common mistakes on the board and elicit the errors:

Peter is the Meg's father.

Violet is Mr. Incredible daughter.

Then sts ask and answer questions using the possessive 's.

E **Make it personal** Sts sit together in small groups and pick a well-known family (e.g. the Simpsons) to draw a family tree and write a paragraph. Go over questions 1–4 with sts and tell them they need to include the answers. Monitor and give feedback as you read their texts.

F Sts exchange their paragraphs, read them and answer the questions.

Extra activity For further practice of the possessive 's, you could repeat Ex **2A** on p. 12, and this time ask sts to write their answers using 's. e.g. *They are Jake and Rosa's potato chips. / They are Lara's earrings*. etc.

2.3

We are family, I got all my sisters with me,
We are family, Get up everybody and sing!

2 Grammar Simple present

A Do you know your partner? Guess her / his answers to questions 1–4. Then check.
1 Who does X live with?
   a   a friend / relative
   b   no one
2 Does X study another language?
   a   No, just English.
   b   Yes, X studies _____ (language).
3 Which soccer team does X support?
   a   _____ (soccer team)
   b   X doesn't like soccer / have a team.
4 Does X prefer …
   a   tea / coffee?
   b   juice / water?

I think you live alone.

No, that's wrong. I live with my parents.

B Complete the grammar box. Are the questions in **A** ASI or QASI?

> There are two different types of questions. Match the word order to each type.
> 1 A question that asks for **information**. *Where does she live?*
> 2 A question to which the **answer** is *Yes* or *No*. *Does he play soccer?*
>
> ☐ **A**uxiliary verb + **s**ubject + **i**nfinitive verb? (ASI)
> ☐ **Q**uestion word + **a**uxiliary verb + **s**ubject + **i**nfinitive verb? (QASI)
>
> → Grammar 2B p.140

C Are these *Yes / No* (Y / N) or information (I) questions?
1 ☐ What's your full name?
2 ☐ Are you Spanish?
3 ☐ Where do you live?
4 ☐ Do you live with your parents?
5 ☐ Where exactly in the U.S. do you plan to travel to?
6 ☐ Do you know anyone in Alaska?

D ▶2.9 Match questions 1–6 in **C** to the answers. Listen to check.
☐ Yes, my sister lives there.
☐ Miguel Hernández.
☐ No, I don't. I live with my girlfriend, Monica.
☐ In Madrid. I work there. It's an amazing city!
☐ Yes, I am. I'm from Valencia.
☐ Alaska.

Common mistakes
does
Where ~~your~~ mother lives?
do
~~Do~~ you like soccer? Yes, I ~~like~~.

3 Pronunciation: Question intonation and silent *e*

A ▶2.9 Look at AS 2.9 on p. 161. Then listen again and notice how the intonation in each question goes up (↗) or down (↘) at the end. Complete the rules.
1 If it is a *Yes / No* question, the intonation usually goes _____.
2 If it is an information question, the intonation usually goes _____.

B Complete 1–5. Take turns asking and answering the questions. Use the correct intonation.
1 _____ you have a brother?
2 _____ many cousins do you have?
3 _____'s your mother's name?
4 _____'s your father's name?
5 _____ they live near you?

C 🗣 **Make it personal** Write two more *Yes / No* questions and two more information questions. In pairs, take turns asking and answering them. Use the verbs to help you.

| have | go | like | live | play (sport) | study | travel | visit |

Do you live in an apartment?   *Yes, I do.*   *Where exactly do you live?*

♪ **Song line:** Turn to p. 325 for notes about this song and an accompanying task.

2 Grammar Simple present

A Books open. In pairs, ask sts to guess the correct answers about their partner for questions 1–4. Paircheck. Ask sts to read the speech bubbles. Highlight *wrong* (in speech bubble) as the opposite of *correct*. Ask sts to change partners and follow the model to guess the answers to the questions about their new partner. Monitor, then ask: *How many did you get right?*

B Focus on the grammar box. Refer to the questions sts have just used and tell them to identify which of them are Information questions and which are *Yes / No* questions.

➔ **Grammar 2B** p. 140

1 QASI   2 ASI

Tip Acronyms ASI (Auxiliary + Subject + Infinitive) and QASI (Question Word + Auxiliary + Subject + Infinitive) are a useful mnemonic resource to help sts remember word order in questions. Try to elicit from sts why they usually make the mistakes shown (transferring from mother tongue structure / comparing questions in L1 and L2). Tell them that A in ASI and QASI is the easiest part to get wrong.

C Individually, sts classify sentences into *Yes / No* (ASI) or Information (QASI). Paircheck. Classcheck. Do not drill pronunciation of sentences just yet (or have sts ask the questions) as they work on the intonation in the next section.

1 I   2 Y/N   3 I   4 Y/N   5 I   6 Y/N

D Read one of the answers aloud to sts and elicit which question in **C** could match it. For example, *No, I don't. I live with my girlfriend, Monica.* Ask: *What's the question?* and point to 4. Sts match the rest of the answers to the questions. Play ▶ 2.9. Sts listen to check answers. Classcheck.

6 Yes, my sister lives there.
1 Miguel Hernández.
4 No, I don't. I live with my girlfriend, Monica.
3 In Madrid. I work there. It's an amazing city!
2 Yes, I am. I'm from Valencia.
5 Alaska.

3 Pronunciation Question intonation and silent *e*

A Write *Where do you live?* and *Are you Spanish?* on the board and draw two lines next to each.

Ask sts to listen to you and say if your intonation is going up or down. Model the questions clearly and naturally to show falling (↘) in the information question and rising (↗) in the *Yes / No* question. Don't give them the answer but tell them they are going to do some more practice on intonation in different questions.

Direct sts to the AS on p. 161 while listening to notice falling and rising intonation. Sts complete the sentences. Classcheck answers. Conduct choral and individual repetition of all the questions. Monitor sts' ability to produce rising and falling intonation. Use gestures to help. Correct sts on the spot.

1 up   2 down

Tip Explain to sts that intonation is affected by different situations. An information question such as *How many cousins do you have?* might be said with rising intonation if the speaker is surprised and asking for confirmation. *Yes / No* questions such as *Are you married?* could have falling intonation if the question is asked with disappointment. Praise sts who notice exceptions to the rule.

B Revise possessive *'s* quickly by writing *What is your mother name?* on the board and eliciting the mistake. Sts complete questions 1–5 with either an auxiliary verb or a question word. Paircheck. Classcheck with answers on the board. Now ask sts to work in different pairs. Together, they decide whether sentences 1–5 have rising or falling intonation. Do number 1 as a model. Say: *Do you have a brother?* and ask: *Is the intonation of this question going up or down?* (Up). Classcheck and drill pronunciation. Round off the activity by having sts ask and answer questions 1–5 about themselves. Sts report their partner's answers to the class.

1 Do   2 How   3 What   4 What   5 Do

Language tip Silent *e* is one of the most common pronunciation problems for Portuguese L1 speakers because it is always pronounced in their language. Write a list of common words with a final silent *e* and have sts practice saying them aloud.

C 🔴 **Make it personal** Demonstrate the activity with a confident st using the mini-dialogues in the speech bubbles. Sts then work in pairs and ask and answer questions about their relatives. You could extend this activity by adding more verb prompts, such as *know*, *prefer*, *study*, *understand*. Classcheck. Get individual sts to tell you any interesting information they learned.

Extra activity If sts have access to a mobile device and photos of family, ask them to work with a different partner to show photos of their family. Sts ask each other questions to find out more information. *Where does your brother live?*, *What's your brother's name?*, etc.

➔ **Workbook** p. 11

2.4 When do you check your phone?

1 Listening

A ▶ 2.10 Listen to Miguel talking to a friend about these three photos on his phone. How many questions do you hear? Who are the people?

B 🗣 **Make it personal** In pairs, show photos of your family and say who they are. Ask two questions about your partner's photos.

This is my brother, Carlos. *Where does he live?* *He lives in Canada.*

And who's this woman? *This is Susan, my brother's wife.*

2 Reading

A ▶ 2.11 Read the webposts about cell phone habits and match 1–7 with the correct name. Listen to check.

☐ Ruben
☐ Jan
☐ María's boyfriend
☐ Lucía's friends
☐ Gerry
☐ Milton's son
☐ Greg's mom

1 checks her phone at breakfast.
2 doesn't check his phone at dinner.
3 doesn't check her phone.
4 send messages all day.
5 checks his phone at dinner.
6 checks his phone when they go out.
7 doesn't look at his phone when he eats.

Cell phone habits

I n**e**ver look at my phone when I eat. It's a really bad h**a**bit. Oh, except when I have lunch alone!
Ruben, New York

I s**o**metimes check my phone at breakfast. My dad gets really mad!
Jan, Los Angeles

My boyfriend o**cc**asionally checks his phone when we go out together. I think that's OK.
María, Mexico City

My mom never checks her phone, so I have to call her!
Greg, London

My friends send me WhatsApp messages all day, so I **a**lways check my phone every five minutes – when I'm not b**u**sy.
Lucía, La Paz

My boss always sends me messages late at night, so I **of**ten need to check my phone at dinner.
Gerry, Boston

My son plays games and uses apps on his phone all the time, so he's always on it. I in**s**ist he stops at dinner!
Milton, Rio de Janeiro

B 🗣 **Make it personal** In groups, talk about when you and your family / friends check your / their phones. Who checks it when they eat and why? Who has the best reason?

I check my phone at breakfast because my boss gets up at 5:00 a.m.

My brother checks his phone every two minutes - I think he's addicted to it!

2.4 When do you check your phone?

Lesson Aims: Sts talk about how people use cell phones.

Function
Asking / Answering personal questions about friends and family.
Reading / Talking about using cell phones.
Asking / Answering questions about how often you do activities.

Language
This is my brother, Carlos. Where does he live?
He lives in Mexico.
Ruben checks his phone at breakfast.
Jan sends messages all day.
Do you check your phone at dinner?
I never check my phone at dinner.

Vocabulary: Review family relationships (brothers, cousins, parents, etc.). Phone habits (check messages, send messages, look at your phone).
Grammar: Frequency adverbs and review simple present, all forms.

Warm-up Review *Wh-* questions. Write one or two questions on the board and ask a st to ask another st the questions. Give out slips of paper and have sts write three or four questions each to review the grammar from this unit. Then, take in the papers and mix them up. Put sts into groups of three and give each group 6–10 questions. Sts take turns to pick up questions and interview each other: *Where do you live? How many hours do you study English on weekends / per week?* Ask some sts to report some answers to the whole class.

1 Listening

A Explore the photos and elicit possible relationships between the people. (They're family, but let sts speculate a little and do not provide answers.) Tell sts to listen and check if their guesses were right. Play ▶2.10 once. Classcheck. Ask sts what they thought of the recording: *Was it easy / difficult?*

> There are five questions. The people are Miguel's parents, Juan (brother), and Martina (sister).

▶2.10 Turn to p. 312 for the complete audioscript.

Tip Ask sts to turn to the AS on p. 161. Sts listen again and notice the intonation at the end of each sentence.

B **Make it personal** If you can, project a photo of someone from your family and tell sts to ask you questions. Direct them to the examples in the speech bubbles to give them ideas. Tell sts to use their cell phones and show each other photos of family. Tell them to ask and answer questions.

Tip If sts don't have access to phones, before the lesson you could ask them to bring some photos of family to class.

2 Reading

A Direct sts to the title of the lesson. Ask: *Do you use your cell phone a lot? Do your friends and family check their phone a lot?* Ask sts to read the text quickly and underline cognates. Check pronunciation of the words they underline.

Sts read the web posts and match the names to habits 1–7. Paircheck. Play ▶2.11 and check answers. Clarify any new vocabulary. Teach *doesn't have a smart phone*.

> Ruben 7, Jan 1, Maria's boyfriend 6, Lucia's friends 4, Gerry 5, Milton's son 2, Greg's mom 3

▶2.11 Turn to p. 312 for the complete audioscript.

Tip Highlight the use of possessive *'s* and elicit how the same idea is expressed in sts' mother tongue to encourage comparison of word order between L1 and L2.

B **Make it personal** Ask: *Are you a cell phone addict? Let's check!* Refer to the model in the speech bubbles. Tell sts that the sign of a true cell phone addict is someone who checks their phone when they are eating or speaking with a friend, or family. Put sts into groups and ask them to tell each other about when they check their phone and why. Teach *every time it makes a noise, whenever I get a moment, walking down the street*. After they have finished, ask: *Who has the best reason for using their phone?*

You could expand this activity by adding other good and bad phone-related habits, e.g. *Charge your phone all night, Forget to use silent mode, Use the speakerphone in public,* etc.

3 Grammar Frequency adverbs

A Complete the grammar box.

1 Put the frequency adverbs in the correct place in the chart.

always   never   occasionally   often   sometimes   usually

___ ___ ___ ___ ___ ___

2 Number these statements 1-4 from least to most frequent.
  a My sister sometimes goes to the theater. ☐
  b I never go to the gym. ☐
  c My parents always go to work. ☐
  d My friends often go to parties. ☐

3 Does the frequency adverb go before or after the verb?

→ Grammar 2C p.140

🎵 *I will never say never! (I will fight) I will fight till forever! (make it right)*

Common mistakes
~~I always~~
~~Always I~~ go to the movies on the weekend.

B 🟢 **Make it personal** Do a class survey.
1 Read the questions and put a ✓ in column 1 for you.
2 In pairs, ask and answer. Put your partner's answers in column 2.
3 Report your answers to the class. Which are good / bad habits? Who has the best habits?

Do you …	never		occasionally		sometimes		often		usually		always	
	1	2	1	2	1	2	1	2	1	2	1	2
take selfies every day?												
check your phone every five minutes?												
text during a conversation?												
make voice calls?												
leave voicemail?												
use earphones (to listen to music)?												
use your phone in the bathroom?												
turn off your phone at night?												

Carla always texts during a conversation — even with her teacher!

Eduardo never uses earphones to listen to music. He listens on the bus. That's a bad habit!

2.4

🎵 **Song line:** Turn to p. 325 for notes about this song and an accompanying task.

③ Grammar Frequency adverbs

A Use some information from the last activity to lead in with an example on the board, e.g. *(St's name) always uses his phone when he's eating. He does it every time!* Direct sts to the circles in the box and ask: *Which circle is **always**?* (the green circle).

Tell them to complete part 1. Paircheck. Classcheck. Then, do parts 2 and 3 with the class. Ask if they have words like this in their language. Are any of the words similar?

➡ **Grammar 2C** p. 140

> 1 never, occasionally, sometimes, often, usually, always
> 2 a 2 b 1 c 4 d 3
> 3 before

B 🎧 **Make it personal** Ask: *Who checks their phone most in this class? Who checks their phone least?* Sts respond. Say: *Let's find out!* Point to the chart and tell sts to complete the white column about themselves. Before they start 2, demonstrate the activity with a confident st. Ask the first two questions and pretend you are ticking the green column for the correct adverb. Sts complete the task with their partner. Focus on the first speech bubble below the chart and ask pairs: *Who checks their phone the most in your pair?* Ask: *Can you give me an example?* (Don't insist on accuracy here—just focus on the information to keep sts interested in the result.) Decide as a class who checks their phone the most.

➡ **Workbook** p. 12

2.5 How old are you?

Skills Reading Asking for personal information

A Read the interview with Ginny Lomond and complete questions 1–9 with the correct verb.

fresh faces.com

Pop singer **Ginny Lomond** answers your questions about her life.

1 What _____ your full name?
2 Interesting! And how old _____ you?
3 Don't worry! Do you _____ a pet?
4 Where _____ you live?
5 And where _____ your family live?
6 Great! Do you _____ any brothers or sisters?
7 I see. And what _____ you do on the weekend?
8 OK, and what time do you _____ to bed on weekdays?
9 And our final question! _____ you exercise regularly?

☐ No, I don't exercise. Well, only occasionally (when I walk Boston). I'm a little lazy!
☐ Well, my mom lives in Paris, and my dad lives in L.A.
☐ I sleep a lot and occasionally go for a walk. And I never work on Mondays, so I often go to bed late on Sundays.
☐ I usually go to bed at 11 p.m. from Monday to Thursday, but I sometimes go to parties!
☐ Yes, I do. I have a dog called Boston. I love him!
☐ I live in Paris.
☐ Virginia Marie Lomond.
☐ No. I'm an only child.
☐ Umm … OK, I'm 23.

B ▶ 2.12 Match the questions to the answers in the interview. Listen to check.

C Find and underline five examples of frequency adverbs in the interview.

D In pairs, ask and answer *How often …?* questions with the *go* activities in **1A** on p. 18.

How often do you go to the gym?   I never go to the gym!

E 🔴 **Make it personal** In pairs, role-play the interview.
A: Ask the nine questions.
B: Give your own true answers.
Then change roles.

⚠ **Common mistakes**
How often
~~With what frequency~~ do you …?

2.5 How old are you?

Lesson Aims: Sts continue to practice asking and answering personal questions through the context of an interview with a pop star (Ginny Lomond) and talking about how often they do daily activities.

Function
Reading / Role-playing an interview with a rock star.
Talking about how often you do activities.

Language
Do you have a boyfriend?
No, I don't. People don't want to date a famous person.
How often do you go to the gym?
I never go to the gym!

Vocabulary: Review daily activities.
Grammar: Frequency adverbs. *How often* + simple present questions.

Warm-up Books closed. Ask: *What pop singers do you like?* Write names on the board. Ask: *Is (insert a name)'s daily routine the same or very different to yours? How is it different? What do they do on a typical day?* Write ideas on the board and encourage sts to use actions from lesson 2.1 and correct use of 3rd person. Say: *Let's read an interview with a pop star.*

ID Skills: Reading Asking for personal information

A Explore the photo. Ask: *Who's Ginny Lomond? What does she do?* (She's a pop singer.) Sts look at the interview questions and in pairs fill in the blanks. Classcheck with board answers.

Elicit possible answers for question 2 in **A**. Highlight the fact that the verb *be* is present in the question (*How old are you?*).

> 1 's 2 are 3 have 4 do 5 does 6 have 7 do
> 8 go 9 Do

B Point to the interview / Ginny's answers in **A** and ask sts to match questions to answers. Paircheck. Play ▶2.12 for sts to check their answers. Ask sts what they thought of this activity. Was the text useful? Was it easy to understand? Is this similar to something they might usually read in their first language? Did they enjoy reading?

> 1 Virginia Marie Lomond.
> 2 Umm … OK, I'm 23.
> 3 Yes, I do. I have a dog called Boston. I love him!
> 4 I live in Paris.
> 5 Well, my mom lives in Paris, and my dad lives in L.A.
> 6 No. I'm an only child.
> 7 I sleep a lot and occasionally go for a walk. And I never work on Mondays, so I often go to bed late on Sundays.
> 8 I usually go to bed at 11 p.m. from Monday to Thursday, but I sometimes go to parties!
> 9 No, I don't exercise. Well, only occasionally (when I walk Boston). I'm a little lazy!

C You could do this quickly as a class activity. After sts have found the adverbs, ask a st to come up to the board, and with the help of the class write the examples in order on a line *always* to *never*.

> Five examples from: always, often, usually, regularly, sometimes, occasionally, never

Common mistakes Remind sts that although mental translation can help, it can lead to mistakes and they should not rely on it when asking about the frequency of actions. Make sure they understand there is a fixed expression which does not translate exactly to Portuguese or Spanish (*How often do you …?*). *With what frequency do you …?* would sound unnatural.

D Ask: *What question do we use with these answers?* Write *How often …?* on the board. Draw sts' attention to the speech bubbles and tell them to look at the *go* activities again on p. 18. Demonstrate with a stronger st, then sts do the activity in pairs.

Tip Monitor and correct errors in controlled activities like **D** when you hear them. Try prompting sts to self-correct by repeating an error with rising intonation or by using facial expressions or gestures before giving the correct answer. Before sts perform the next task, elicit whether the questions in **A** have rising or falling intonation. Practice the pronunciation.

E Make it personal Sts interview each other using questions from Ginny's interview, but answer about themselves.

Weaker students Give sts time to prepare their answers. Tell them not to write anything but encourage them to think quietly about their answers and rehearse in their heads what they will say.

Stronger students To add challenge, tell sts to tell one or two lies in their answers. When they have finished, ask: *What do you think your partner's lies are?*

2.5 How do you celebrate your birthday?

Music's got me feeling so free, We're gonna celebrate.

ID in Action — Celebrating

A Match the phrases with photos 1–6.
- ☐ Congratulations!
- ☐ Enjoy your meal!
- ☐ Happy birthday!
- ☐ Happy New Year!
- ☐ Have a good trip!
- ☐ Merry Christmas!

B ▶ 2.13 Listen to check. Try to remember the answers.

C What do you say on occasions 1–6? Practice saying the phrases with a partner.
1. before dinner
2. at a wedding
3. on your mom's birthday
4. before a friend goes on vacation
5. on December 25th
6. on January 1st

D 👤 **Make it personal** Write how often you / other people do the activities in the chart on each special occasion.

| always | never | occasionally | often | sometimes | usually |

	On your birthday	At Christmas	On New Year's Eve	On the Day of the Dead	At Carnival	Another celebration?
have a special meal at home						
go to a restaurant						
drink and eat special food						
have a party						
give and receive gifts						
wear special clothes						
go to bed late						
spend a lot of money						
dance and sing						
go to the cemetery						

E In small groups, compare answers. Find one thing you do differently.

I always have a special meal at home on my birthday.

I never eat at home on my birthday. We usually go to a restaurant.

Common mistakes

~~At~~ **On** Christmas Day = a specific day or date.

~~At / For~~ **On** Christmas = a festive period.

2.5 How do you celebrate your birthday?

Lesson Aims: Sts talk about different celebrations.

Function
Talking about celebrations.
Talking about what you usually do on your birthday.

Language
Happy birthday! / Happy New Year!
I always have a special meal at home.
I sometimes have a party.

Vocabulary: Review *go* activities. Chunks for celebrating special dates and occasions (Merry Christmas!, Congratulations!, Enjoy your meal!, Have a good trip!, etc.).
Grammar: Frequency adverbs. Simple present questions.

🎵 **Song line:** Turn to p. 326 for notes about this song and an accompanying task.

ID in Action Celebrating

A Focus on photos 1–6. Elicit what people might be saying in photo 6. (Happy birthday!) In pairs, sts match the rest of the photos to the phrases. Do not tell them the answers as they will check in **B**.

1 Enjoy your meal!
2 Merry Christmas!
3 Have a good trip!
4 Congratulations!
5 Happy New Year!
6 Happy birthday!

Tip For fun, get sts to suggest what the people might be saying, e.g. *Yum!, Bye!, See you!, Thank you!*, etc. You can do this with most people photos and it helps sts to learn lots of useful exclamations.

B Sts listen to 🔊 2.13 to check their answers to **A**. Classcheck and drill pronunciation of all phrases. In pairs, sts test each other: st A covers the phrases and st B points to the photos in **A**. Sts change roles. Round off by asking all sts to cover the phrases. Point to each photo and test the whole class.

C In pairs, sts look at situations 1–6 and take turns asking each other *What do you usually say …?* Classcheck.

1 Enjoy your meal!
2 Congratulations!
3 Happy birthday!
4 Have a good trip!
5 Merry Christmas!
6 Happy New Year!

Cultural note We use *Merry Christmas*, but we say *Happy Birthday*.

Common mistakes Highlight the different uses of *on* + day / date, but *at* for a festive period. Elicit more examples. In pairs, sts talk as much as they can about their own preferred activities on these festive occasions. Add in any locally relevant ones too, e.g. at Easter, at Ramadan (it's a month long), on Independence Day, etc. Get them to ask you first.

Tip Correct any important mistakes, but otherwise try to see the second phase as fluency as much as accuracy. Encourage sts to use the phrases in the chart and then gesture / mime / draw other things they can't say.

D 🔊 **Make it personal** **Books open.** Focus on the chart to establish meaning. Drill pronunciation of the six adverbs. Elicit some examples from sts. Say: *(Student), tell me something you always do*, etc. Ask: *What do you usually do on your birthday?* and point to the chart. Individually, sts check how they celebrate their birthdays with each suggestion. Sts paircheck by asking *How often do you …?* questions. Classcheck by asking sts to report some of their partner's answers to the class.

E Sts work in groups of three or four to find similarities and differences. Focus on the speech bubbles. Sts compare their information. After they have finished, ask one person from each group: *What is different about your celebrations?*

Extra activity Sts role-play being at a celebration and ask and answer questions to exchange personal information. Give them a few minutes to work in pairs and think of questions they could ask each other. Encourage them to look back over units 1 and 2. Tell them to practice the conversation in pairs to build confidence. Monitor and help weaker sts. Tell sts to walk around and role-play being at a celebration. They pretend they don't know each other and ask questions. Play music if you can so sts feel comfortable and relaxed.

➔ **Workbook** p. 13
➔ 🆔 **Richmond Learning Platform**
➔ **Writing** p. 28
➔ 🆔 **Café** p. 29

Writing 2 A personal email

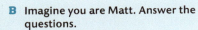
You are not alone, I am here with you, Though we're far apart, You're always in my heart.

A Read the email and number the things that Matt does in order.

- [ ] have breakfast
- [ ] do homework
- [ ] take a shower
- [ ] have dinner
- [ ] go to a café
- [ ] leave home
- [ ] go for a run
- [ ] wake up
- [ ] get up
- [ ] get dressed

To: James
Subject: My typical week
Today at 13:23
All Mail

Hi there,

I live in Hamilton, New Zealand, with my parents and sister. A typical weekday for me starts early. I get up at 6:00 a.m., but I **usually** wake up before that. I **often** go for a run first thing. After my run, I **always** take a shower and have breakfast, then I get dressed and get ready for school. I leave home at 8:00 a.m.

After school, I don't **usually** go straight home. I **sometimes** go to a café to meet my friends, to the park to play football, or I **occasionally** go to the gym. We have dinner at 6:00 p.m., but my dad **doesn't always** get home in time to eat with us. I **usually** do my homework after dinner, between 6:30 p.m. and 8:30 p.m. Then I watch TV, play video games, or message my friends. I **never** go to bed before 10:00 p.m.

On the weekend, I get up late and then go out with my friends. We **usually** go to the beach, or to a party. And we **sometimes** visit my cousins in Auckland. Sunday evenings are **nor**mally very quiet.

That's a typical week for me. What about you?

Matthew James McCarthy (Matt)

B Imagine you are Matt. Answer the questions.
1 What's your full name?
2 Where does your family live?
3 Do you have any brothers or sisters?
4 When do you get up?
5 Do you exercise regularly?
6 What do you do after school?
7 When do you do your homework?
8 What do you usually do on the weekend?

✓ Write it right!

In positive sentences and most questions, put the frequency adverb before the verb. In negatives, put *always*, *usually*, or *often* after the auxiliary (*don't* or *doesn't*).

C Read **Write it right!** Decide where you would put the adverb in the following sentences and questions.
1 Jack goes to the gym on the weekend. (**often**)
2 My brother doesn't remember my birthday. (**always**)
3 Serena checks her phone in class. (**never**)
4 Where do you spend your summer vacation? (**sometimes**)
5 Veronica's friends don't go out on weekday evenings. (**usually**)
6 Do you play games when you should be studying? (**occasionally**)

D Note your own answers to the questions in **B**.

E 🎧 **Make it personal** Write a similar email about your typical week (about 150–180 words).

Before	Use your notes in **D**. Think of some extra information, too.
While	Use frequency adverbs in the correct position.
After	Exchange emails with a partner and give feedback.

Writing 2 A personal email

🎵 **Song line:** Turn to p. 326 for notes about this song and an accompanying task.

Sts could do this in class or as a homework task using their email accounts. If they write emails tell them to copy you in so you can check their work.

A Direct sts to the photo of Matt. Ask: *How old do you think he is? What does he do on a typical day?* Refer sts to the list of daily activities and ask them to quickly order them for their own typical day. Sts compare their order of activities. Tell sts to read the email quickly and order the things 1–10 for Matt. Classcheck. Ask: *Do you have anything in common with Matt?*

> 5 have breakfast
> 10 do homework
> 4 take a shower
> 9 have dinner
> 8 go to a café
> 7 leave home
> 3 go for a run
> 1 wake up
> 2 get up
> 6 get dressed

B Put sts into pairs and ask them to role-play an interview with Matt. Student A is Matt and uses the information in the email to answer student B's questions.

> 1 My name's Matthew James McCarthy
> 2 My family lives in Hamilton, New Zealand.
> 3 I have one sister.
> 4 I get up at 6:00 a.m.
> 5 I occasionally go to the gym, and I sometimes play football.
> 6 After school, I sometimes go to a café to meet my friends, to the park to play football, or to the gym.
> 7 I usually do my homework after dinner.
> 8 On the weekend, I get up late and then go out with my friends. We usually go to the beach, or to a party.

C Read **Write it right!** with the class and ask sts to find two or three examples in the email. Do number 1 with the class and then sts complete 2–6. Remind them to put the adverb after the pronoun in questions, e.g., *Do you **sometimes** go to the gym?* Paircheck. Classcheck.

> 1 Jack often goes …
> 2 My brother doesn't always remember …
> 3 Serena never checks …
> 4 Where do you sometimes spend …
> 5 Veronica's friends don't usually go out …
> 6 Do you occasionally play …

D Sts do this individually. Tell them to make notes of the answers, not to write full sentences.

E 🔵 **Make it personal** Read the steps Before, While, and After with sts so as to guide them to write their own personal emails. Tell them to refer to Matt's email in **A** as a model, and draw their attention to the length of the composition—that is, approximately 150–180 words. As a follow-up activity and before they hand in their texts, ask sts to exchange compositions and answer their partner's questions. They could do this as a speaking or writing activity.

> **Tip** Encourage sts to give feedback on each other's emails. Tell them to find two or three good uses of frequency adverbs and to point out one or two errors if they see any.

2 The critic

Café

1 Before watching

A Complete 1–6 with a word from the box.

critic	guitar	show
record	reviews	voice

1 Genevieve plays the _____ and writes songs.
2 The _____ listens to music and writes about it.
3 The _____ are great.
4 She's a good singer and has a very beautiful _____.
5 Rory has a video camera to _____ the show.
6 Andrea and August are at the café to watch Genevieve's _____.

B Guess and circle the correct answer. Compare in pairs, then watch to check.

1 **Rory uses / The critic uses / Both of them use** a video camera.
2 **Rory wears / The critic wears / Both of them wear** glasses.
3 **Rory listens / The critic listens / Both of them listen** to the music.
4 **Rory sits / The critic sits / Both of them sit** at a table in the café every day.
5 **Rory drinks / The critic drinks / Both of them drink** a cup of coffee.
6 **Rory writes / The critic writes / Both of them write** at a table.

> Who do you think uses a camera?
>
> I guess they both use a camera. Do you agree?

2 While watching

A Watch again. Order the sentences 1–10 as you hear them, then complete them. Who says each one?

- [ ] She plays Monday and Saturday _____ 8 and 9:30.
- [ ] Excuse me. Do you _____?
- [ ] Except he needs _____ give me a good review.
- [ ] Rory _____ you're a great singer anyway.
- [ ] She's not the _____ one that thinks so.
- [ ] She's the _____ there is, for sure.
- [ ] That was _____, cuz. Good job!
- [ ] This is _____ life!
- [ ] You are crazy. He _____ do that.
- [ ] You have _____ amazing voice.

B Order Rory's routine 1–5.

- [ ] He sits down.
- [ ] Rory comes to the café.
- [ ] He orders coffee.
- [ ] He waits for Genevieve to take his order.
- [ ] He drinks his coffee and dreams.

C What's Genevieve's schedule? Check (✓) (M) in the morning, (A) in the afternoon, or (N) at night.

Genevieve …	M	A	N
practices the guitar for two hours.			
takes a class.			
goes to work.			
gets up.			
writes a song.			
sings at the café.			

3 After watching

A How do they feel? Complete 1–4 with the adjectives.

annoyed	excited	nervous	upset

1 Genevieve feels _____ about the show.
2 The critic's very _____ at Rory.
3 Andrea's _____ to hear Genevieve's music.
4 Rory's _____ and leaves the café.

B How many hits does Genevieve's video get online?

- [ ] 9
- [ ] 19
- [ ] 95
- [ ] 99

C 🎤 **Make it personal** Check (✓) the kinds of reviews and reports you read. In pairs, ask and answer about them.

- [ ] books / art / museums
- [ ] movies / TV shows / theater
- [ ] products / online services
- [ ] fashion / music / dance
- [ ] news / weather
- [ ] sports / local events
- [ ] hotels / vacations

> Do you ever read book reviews?
>
> Sometimes, but only online. Never in newspapers.

ID Café 2 The critic

1 Before watching

A Point to the photo of Genevieve singing. Elicit what sts can remember about her (from **ID Café 1**). Ask: *What's her name? / Do you remember her name? / Where's she from?*

In order to raise sts' curiosity, write the questions below on the board and have them guess the answers in pairs. Pre-teach / Clarify any doubts sts might have about the meaning of *voice*, *critics*, and *reviews*.

Is she a good singer? Does she have a good voice?
Does she sing professionally?
What do critics write about her: positive or negative reviews?

Ask some sts to report their predictions but don't say whether their guesses about Genevieve are right or wrong.

Sts complete sentences 1-6 with a word from the box. Paircheck. Classcheck.

1 guitar 2 critic 3 reviews 4 voice 5 record
6 show

B Point to the photo of Rory and the critic and ask sts: *What do you think they do?* Get two sts to read the model dialogue in the speech bubbles. Tell sts not to circle the answers yet, but only to make predictions – they are going to watch the video to check their guesses. In pairs, sts ask each other: *What does Rory / the critic do?*

Classcheck / Elicit predictions from the whole class. Ask: *What does Rory do? What about the critic?*

Play the first part of **Video 2** (the scene with Rory and the critic). Sts circle the correct answers. Get each pair of sts to briefly compare their answers with another pair. Classcheck.

1 Rory uses
2 The critic wears
3 Both of them listen
4 Both of them sit
5 Both of them drink
6 The critic writes

2 While watching

Focus on tasks **A** and **B** first. Read rubrics and options with sts before you replay **Video 2**. It may be useful to ask sts to recall the characters they met in **ID Café 1** (August, Andrea, and Genevieve).

A Tell sts they are going to watch the whole video and put the sentences in order. Play **Video 2** again. Peercheck, then ask sts to complete the sentences and note down who said each phrase (Rory, the critic, Andrea, August, or Genevieve). Classcheck. If necessary, play the video again.

1 She plays Monday and Saturday at 8 and 9:30. Rory
3 Excuse me. Do you mind? Critic
9 Except he needs to give me a good review.
8 Rory thinks you're a great singer anyway. August
6 She's not the only one that thinks so. August
2 She's the best there is, for sure. Rory
4 That was awesome, cuz. Good job! August
10 This is my life!
7 You are crazy. He doesn't do that. Genevieve
5 You have an amazing voice. Andrea

B Point to the sentences and ask: *Do you remember Rory's routine?* Let's watch the video again and check.

2 He sits down at a table.
1 Rory comes to the café.
4 He orders coffee.
3 He waits for Genevieve to take his order.
5 He drinks his coffee and dreams.

Replay **Video 2**. Paircheck and classcheck.

C Ask: *What's Genevieve's schedule?* Have sts complete the table from memory, preferably in pencil. Tell them to check M for morning, A for afternoon, or N for night. Paircheck. Replay **Video 2** for sts to check their answers. Classcheck.

Genevieve...	M	A	N
... practices the guitar for two hours.	✓		
... takes a class.		✓	
... goes to work.	✓		
... gets up.	✓		
... writes a song.		✓	
... sings at the café.			✓

3 After watching

A Drill pronunciation for all four adjectives in the box. Ask the whole class: *How does Genevieve feel in the video about her performance? What about the critic, Andrea and Rory?* Point to sentences 1–4 and ask sts to complete them with the adjectives in the box. Paircheck. Classcheck.

1 nervous 2 annoyed 3 excited 4 upset

B Ask sts to answer the question in pairs and then classcheck.

95

C  **Make it personal** Allow sts a few seconds to check the kinds of reviews they usually read. Get two sts to read the model dialogue in the speech bubbles. In pairs, sts ask and answer: *What kind of reviews do you read?* Classcheck by asking: *What kind of reviews does (partner's name) read? Are the critics usually / always right?*

R1 Grammar and vocabulary

A **Picture dictionary.** Cover the words on these pages and use the pictures to remember:

page	
6	8 countries and nationalities
11	11 personal objects
13	10 colors
15	5 short dialogues for photos 1–5
18	8 *go* activities
20	10 morning routine verbs
22	25 family members
27	6 phrases for special occasions
158	16 picture words for vowels

B 🔴 **Make it personal** In pairs. A: Spell sentences 1–3. B: Write the sentences. Change roles for 4–6. Are the sentences true for you?

1 MY CITY IS INTERESTING.
2 I REALLY LIKE JAZZ.
3 I AM FROM NEW YORK CITY.
4 MY FAVORITE COLOR IS GREEN.
5 MY FAMILY IS LARGE.
6 I OFTEN READ NEWSPAPERS.

C ▶ R1.1 Complete with verb *be*. Use contractions where possible. Listen to check. Then role-play in pairs.

Receptionist: What _____ your name?
Sandy: Sandy Clark.
Receptionist: _____ you American?
Sandy: No, I _____ Canadian.
Receptionist: Where in Canada _____ you from?
Sandy: Vancouver.
Receptionist: That _____ a nice place. What _____ your address?
Sandy: 76, Burton Road.
Receptionist: And what _____ your email address?
Sandy: saclark@hotmail.com
Receptionist: Thank you. Here _____ your key. Room 89.

Good afternoon. Can I help you?

Hi! Yes, please. I have a reservation.

D Play *Draw it, name it!* A: Go to p. 8 Exercise D and draw six objects for B to name. Change roles. B: Go to p. 11 Exercise A and draw six objects for A to name.

How do you say this in English? *Sorry, I don't remember.*

It starts with "u".

E 🔴 **Make it personal** Complete the questions with *do* or *does*. In pairs, ask and answer.

1 What _____ you do on your birthday?
2 _____ you give gifts to your family at Christmas?
3 _____ you eat a special meal on Christmas Eve?
4 _____ your mother usually have a party on her birthday?
5 What _____ you do at weddings in your culture?
6 What _____ your brother (or sister) do on New Year's Eve?

F Match responses a–h to phrases 1–8. Then practice in pairs. Say a phrase for your partner to respond.

1 Thank you.   a Good, thanks.
2 Who's this?   b Not much.
3 What's new?   c It's Jackie.
4 Congratulations!   d Thanks!
5 How're you?   e You're welcome.
6 See you later.   f Purple and white.
7 How old are you?   g Bye for now.
8 What color is your house? h 17.

G Correct the mistakes. Check your answers in units 1 and 2.

1 Are you colombian? Yes, I'm. (2 mistakes)
2 That is a umbrella ridiculous. (1 mistake)
3 David loves her girlfriend. (1 mistake)
4 John go to home after school. (2 mistakes)
5 My girlfriend has 20 close parents. (1 mistake)
6 At what time you go to school? (2 mistakes)
7 My father work in the city. (1 mistake)
8 At Saturday, my mom don't study usually. (3 mistakes)
9 My brother has 25. (1 mistake)
10 When he works? (2 mistakes)

30

Review 1 Units 1-2

Grammar and vocabulary

A Picture dictionary. Pairwork. Sts test each other and review the main vocabulary items learned in units 1 and 2. St A asks: *What's this in English?* and st B answers. There are some possible techniques mentioned on p. 9 of the introduction section on how to work with the Picture Dictionary in order to review vocabulary. You can select whichever of these best suit the needs of your class.

B 🔴 **Make it personal** Pairwork. St B closes their books. Make sure st A covers / does not look at sentences 4–6. St A spells each word in sentences 1–3 for st B to write in a notebook or on a sheet of paper.

> **Tip** Tell sts not to say / signal to their partners where spaces are between words when spelling – the student who listens and writes the letters is supposed to recognize each word / where the spaces are once the sentence is complete. They should say: "Number 1: M-Y-C-I-T-Y-I-S-I-N-T-E-R-E-S-T-I-N-G."

Paircheck. Encourage st A to check if st B's sentences are OK.

Change roles. St A closes the book. St B spells all the letters of sentences 4–6 for st A to write down. Paircheck: St B reads and checks if st A made any mistakes.

Sts take turns saying sentences 1–6 and adapting them to make true sentences about themselves, e.g. *My city is interesting. / I think Jazz isn't great. Jazz is OK. / I'm not from New York City.*, etc. Classcheck by inviting some sts to say their adapted sentences to the whole class.

C Individually, sts complete the dialogue with verb *be*. Paircheck. Play ▶R1.1 for sts to listen and check their answers. Classcheck with answers on the board. Replay the track for the sts to listen and repeat (pause after each line.) In pairs, sts role-play the dialogue, then change roles. Make sure they use contractions whenever possible. Ask one pair to act it out for the whole class.

> 's (is) / Are / 'm (am) / are / 's (is) / 's (is) / 's (is) / 's (is)

D Sts play **Draw it, name it!** on a sheet of paper or notebook. St A draws six objects from p. 8 ex. 4 Pronunciation for st B to guess, e.g. a shoe, a plane, etc. Sts change roles. St B draws six objects from p. 11 ex. 8 Vocabulary for st A to guess, e.g. a lipstick, a sandwich, etc.

> **Tip** If time is available, ask some sts to go to the board and draw objects from p. 8 or p. 11 for the whole class to guess.

E 🔴 **Make it personal** Individually, sts complete questions 1–6 with *do* or *does*. Paircheck. Classcheck with answers on the board.

> **Weaker classes** Drill pronunciation of all questions before sts ask and answer in pairs.

In pairs, sts take turns asking and answering questions 1–6. Monitor closely for accuracy. At the end, ask sts to report some of their partners' answers to the whole class.

> 1 do 2 Do 3 Do 4 Does 5 do 6 does

F Elicit the appropriate response to phrase 1, (You're welcome). Sts match phrases 2–8 to a suitable response in the right column. Paircheck. Classcheck.

> **Tip** In pairs, sts act out short conversations. Monitor for appropriate intonation.

> 1 e 2 c 3 b 4 d 5 a 6 g 7 h 8 f

G Write sentence 1 on the board *Are you colombian? Yes, I'm.* and call sts' attention to the number of mistakes between parentheses (2 mistakes).

Elicit corrections and mark the phrase on the board: *Are you Colombian? Yes, I am.*

In pairs, sts correct sentences 2–10. Encourage them to flip back through and check their answers in units 1 and 2. Classcheck with answers on the board.

> 1 Are you Colombian? Yes, I am.
> 2 That is a ridiculous umbrella.
> 3 David loves his girlfriend.
> 4 John goes home after school.
> 5 My girlfriend has 20 close relatives.
> 6 What time do you go to school?
> 7 My father works in the city.
> 8 On Saturday, my mom doesn't usually study.
> 9 My brother is 25.
> 10 When does he work?

Skills practice

R1

But just because it burns, doesn't mean you're gonna die, You gotta get up and try.

A Match the phone phrases. Read the text to check.

1 send — online
2 make — a meeting
3 take — the dictionary
4 go — a (text) message
5 use — a photo
6 organize — a call

> Everyone has a phone, but people have different attitudes to their phones. Let's take a look at when people check their phones.
>
> 1 "I check it all day all the time. I _____ send messages and post things when I'm at school."
>
> 2 "I don't have a cell phone. I think they ruin conversation! I _____ use my friend's phone to make calls."
>
> 3 "I _____ check my phone for news updates. I _____ read on my phone when I have free time. My parents _____ get annoyed when I look at my phone or go online during meals."
>
> 4 "I _____ check my phone for work. I _____ make calls from the car to talk with clients or organize meetings for the day."
>
> 5 "I _____ use my phone to take photos and to post them on social media all day long! All my friends do the same. I don't want to be different."

B 🎙 **Make it personal** Complete the sentences with the best frequency adverb: *always, usually, often, sometimes, occasionally,* or *never.* Are you similar to any of the people in **A**?

> I'm similar to 5. I don't want to be different from my friends.

C ▶ R1.2 Listen to a student. Circle the correct number.
1 She's **17 / 70** years old.
2 Her town is **13 / 30** km from Barcelona.
3 She has **6 / 9** brothers and sisters.
4 She gets up at **6 / 8** a.m.
5 It takes **15 / 50** minutes to get to school.

D ▶ R1.2 Listen again and answer 1–5.
1 What's her name?
2 Where does she live?
3 Where does she study?
4 When does she go to the movies?
5 Who are her favorite actors?

E In pairs. **A**: Describe family 1. **B**: Describe family 2.

F 🎙 **Make it personal** Complete the chart by checking (✓) the activities you do. Compare with a partner. Any big differences?

How do you spend your weekends?			
	Friday	Saturday	Sunday
get up early			
go shopping			
go to bed late			
meet friends			
play sports			
watch TV			

G 🎙 **Make it personal** Complete 1–6 and compare your answers in pairs. Any unusual choices?
1 _____ is a rich young person.
2 _____ is a great American actor.
3 _____ is an excellent song.
4 _____ is an interesting new movie.
5 _____ is a cool small piece of technology.
6 _____ is a fantastic big city.

H In pairs, role-play this situation.
A: You're a guest at a hotel. You want to leave your bag in their security box. Pay by credit card.
B: You're the receptionist. Ask A for this information: name; ID card number; room number; description of bag; contents of bag; credit card number.

I 🎙 **Make it personal** **Question time**.
In pairs, practice asking and answering the 12 lesson titles in units 1 and 2. Use the book map on p. 2–3. Where possible, ask follow-up questions, too. Can you comfortably ask and answer all the questions?

> Are you Canadian?   No, I'm Peruvian.
>
> Ah, I see. Are you from Lima?

Skills practice

A In pairs, sts match the phone phrases. Sts read the text to find the phone phrases and check their answers. Classcheck. Drill the pronunciation of all the phrases.

> 1 send a (text) message 2 make a call 3 take a photo
> 4 go online 5 use the dictionary 6 organize a meeting

B **Make it personal** Ask sts to complete the blanks with the most appropriate frequency adverbs *always, often, usually, sometimes, occasionally, never*. There may be more than one possible answer. Classcheck. At the end, encourage sts to say which character they are most similar to. Ask: *Are you similar to any of these people? Any surprises in the text?*

C Sts hear a woman talk about herself. Allow sts a few seconds to read sentences 1–5. Play ▶R1.2. Sts circle the numbers they hear. Paircheck. Replay the track if necessary. Classcheck with answers on the board.

> **Weaker classes** Review / Elicit how to say all pairs of numbers in sentences 1–5 before sts perform the activity.

> 1 17 2 13 3 6 4 6 5 50

D Replay ▶R1.2. In pairs, sts answer questions 1–5. Classcheck with answers on the board. Ask: *Any similarities? What do you like doing in your free time? Who are your favorite actors / sportspeople?*

> 1 Carla
> 2 Floresta (near Barcelona)
> 3 at the University of Barcelona
> 4 usually on Monday night after school
> 5 Penelope Cruz & Jennifer Lawrence

E Change partners. In pairs, st A talks about family A and st B talks about family B. Sts use family words from p. 21. Monitor closely for accuracy. At the end, ask a student to describe family A (the Dunphy family from the U.S. TV series *Modern Family*) and another student to describe family B (the Parr family of superheroes from *The Incredibles* movies). Names of some characters may be different in some countries.

F **Make it personal** Ask sts to complete the chart with frequency adverbs such as *always, often, usually, sometimes, occasionally, never*, according to their own habits. In pairs, sts take turns saying how they spend their weekends and find similarities and differences between them. Round off by asking sts to tell the whole class what they have in common.

G **Make it personal** Sts think of names of people and places for the blanks. Ask a student: *What name do you have for number 1?* Ask questions to encourage more discussion, e.g. *How do they make money? What do you know about [person's name]?*

H Allow sts some time to read about their roles. In pairs, sts prepare what they will say and role-play the situation.

> **Weaker classes** Ask sts to write the mini-dialogue before they role-play it so they have more time to plan their questions and answers. Monitor and help whenever necessary.

I **Make it personal** **Question time**. Sts look at the book map on p. 2–3 and take turns asking and answering the lesson titles from units 1 and 2. Monitor closely for accuracy and encourage sts to ask follow-up questions when suitable. At the end, ask them how they felt performing the task: *Do you feel comfortable with all of the questions? Which ones are easy? Which ones are difficult?*

> **Tip** As a form of evaluation, get sts to record themselves answering the questions in pairs, in or out of class, e.g. on their phones. When they listen to themselves, they will get much of the feedback they need. They can upload these recordings digitally to build a portfolio of themselves speaking English, which you can use as a proportion (e.g. 10–20%) of their overall marks. When you ask sts to record themselves as part of their assessment, they often re-record many times in order to get a satisfactory result, which is excellent practice for them.

3.1 What's the weather like?

1 Vocabulary Weather

A ▶3.1 Listen to a meteorologist and complete the weather chart.

Common mistakes

~~It's rain in this photo.~~ raining
It's usually rainy / It usually rains
~~It's usually rain in January.~~

	the sun	a cloud	wind	fog	rain	snow
noun						
adjective	sunny					
verb					to rain	to snow

B Study the chart and complete the rules.
1. To form adjectives from weather nouns, add _____.
2. For consonant-vowel-consonant words, double the final _____ and add _____.

C Match the temperature words to the correct thermometer position, a–d.
☐ cold ☐ cool ☐ hot [c] warm

D In pairs, use the photos and thermometer to remember the 10 adjectives.

E ▶3.2 Listen and identify the two photos the students are talking about.

F 🔴 Make it personal In pairs, do the same. Take turns describing the photos and guessing the place. Use *it's* + adjective.

In photo 1, it's really snowy. I think it's somewhere in the mountains in the U.S.

I disagree. The houses aren't American. Maybe it's Europe.

32

3

Unit overview: The main topics of unit 3 are the weather, months, present continuous, time expressions (*tomorrow morning*, *next week*, etc.), and making offers. The topics are introduced and practiced through the contexts of weather forecasts, phone conversations, and talking about what celebrities do. Sts also answer a questionnaire about their reasons for learning English and role-play a dialogue with informal language / chunks for making simple offers.

Unit 3 focuses on the use of present continuous for present use and is contrasted to the simple present. The present continuous for future use is introduced in unit 9 where it is contrasted with *going to*.

3.1 What's the weather like?

Lesson Aims: Sts continue to practice the verb *be* to ask and answer about the weather.

Function
Talking about the weather.
How's the weather in _____?

Language
What's the weather usually like in _____?
It's usually hot and windy.

Vocabulary: Weather words: hot, warm, cool, cold, sun, sunny, rain (verb / noun), rainy, fog, foggy, snow (verb / noun), snowy, cloud, cloudy, wind, windy.
Grammar: What's the weather like?
Skills: Analyzing your English.

Warm-up Books closed. Ask sts: *What's the weather like today?* to find out what vocabulary they already know. Write any correct vocabulary sts say on the board and tell them to teach meaning and pronunciation to the rest of the class.

Language tip In Portuguese and Spanish, the word for both *weather* and *time* is *tempo / tiempo*. As a result, speakers of these languages may use *time* when they mean *weather*. Pre-empt this by writing *weather* and *time* on the board and emphasizing that, although they both translate to the same word in the L1, they have different meanings in English.

1 Vocabulary Weather

A Point to the weather chart. Play ▶3.1 and sts complete the chart with the correct adjective under each noun. Paircheck. Drill pronunciation using opposing pairs of words so sts spot the differences: *sun—sunny*, *cloud—cloudy*, etc.

🔑 adjectives: cloudy, windy, foggy, rainy, snowy

▶3.1 Turn to p 312 for the complete audioscript.

B Write *sun* on the board and ask: *How do we make the adjective?* (add -*ny*). *What about wind?* (add -*y*). Check sts are clear on what CVC means and clarify the rule. Ask them to check they have spelled the other adjectives correctly.

🔑 1 -y   2 consonant, -y

Cultural note In some tropical regions, the concept of *cold* may vary according to the inhabitants' perspective. If you teach in a tropical climate region, your sts are likely to think (and argue) that 15 degrees means *cold* – but make sure they understand that in some English-speaking countries that would be considered *cool*. However, in the U.S., Fahrenheit is used rather than Celsius. So 15 degrees Fahrenheit is *very cold* (–9 degrees Celsius).

C Refer sts to the image of the thermometer and ask them to match the words to positions a–d. One answer is done.

🔑 a cold   b cool   c warm   d hot

D In pairs, sts cover **A** and **B** and refer to the thermometer and the photos. Have sts test each other and see how many weather words they can come up with. Monitor closely. Classcheck.

Stronger classes As you monitor, feed in synonyms and new weather words sts can use (e.g. *dry*, *wet*, *humid*, etc.).

E Play ▶3.2. Sts hear two people talking about two different photos. They have to listen and guess which two photos are being described. Paircheck. Classcheck. Tell sts to remember the words that made them guess the photos. There is more than one correct answer.

🔑 photos 1 and 2

F 🔴 **Make it personal** In pairs, sts perform the task about photos 1–8. Ask sts to refer to the AS on p. 161 if they need a model. Classcheck by playing a guessing game with the whole class: a pair of sts talk about a photo. The rest of the group listens and tries to guess which photo is being described. For small groups, repeat the procedure three times. For larger groups, repeat the procedure for five different photos in order to get more sts to participate.

Weaker classes Write some prompts on the board: *In this photo, the weather is … / It's (hot) and (dry). / Maybe it's (city). / Yes, I agree.*, etc.

🎵 *I want to know, Have you ever seen the rain, Comin' down on a sunny day?*

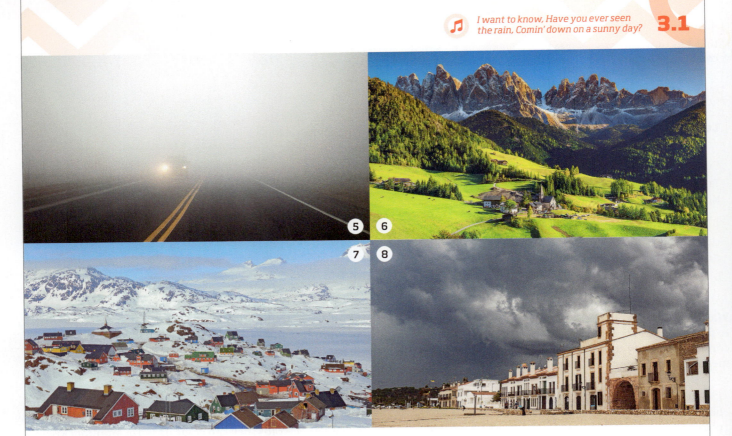

2 Listening

A ▶ 3.3 Listen to the TV show and number the places in the order you hear them, 1–5. Why do they say the weather is unusual?

	Usually	Now
☐ the Alps		
☐ the Amazon rainforest		
☐ the Atacama Desert		
☐ Cancún		
☐ Chicago		

Common mistakes

How's the weather ~~like~~?
~~It's~~
~~Is~~ really hot.
   windy
It's ~~winding~~.

B ▶ 3.3 Listen again and complete the chart in **A** with adjectives / words for each place.

C Complete the three questions from the show.
1. And _____'s the weather in Chicago?
2. _____'s the weather usually like there?
3. What's it _____ this year?

D 🔴 **Make it personal** In pairs, ask and answer about the weather in the photos, and in your city / country. Use the model and point to the photos as you ask.

What's the weather usually like in the Amazon rainforest?   *It's rainy.*

And how is it now?   *It's very dry.*

3.1

🎵 **Song line:** Turn to p. 326 for notes about this song and an accompanying task.

2 Listening

A Focus on the five places from the chart and elicit where they are (the Alps: Europe; the Amazon forest: South America; the Atacama Desert: Chile; Cancún: Mexico; Chicago: the U.S.) and what sts think the weather is usually like in each of them. Play ▶ 3.3 and ask sts to number the places in the order they hear them. Paircheck. Classcheck. Ask sts: *Why do they say the weather is crazy?* Check what sts thought of the listening. Ask: *Was it easy / difficult? How much did you understand? What words helped you to find the answers you needed?* Refer to the AS on p. 161 to discuss.

Extra activity If you have an IWB and / or cell phones with Internet in the classroom, ask sts to guess (and write on a piece of paper) the temperature and weather conditions in a distant city at a certain month of the year (e.g. Moscow, Chicago, etc.). Collect the slips of paper and redistribute them so sts can check their classmates' guesses about the current weather conditions in that place. The winner is the one who gets closest to the real weather conditions.

> 1 the Amazon rainforest 2 the Atacama Desert
> 3 Chicago 4 the Alps 5 Cancún
> The weather is unusual because it's very different to how it usually is in each place.

B Now sts listen to ▶ 3.3 again and fill in the chart in **A** with the adjectives used to describe the weather in the five different places. Complete the first line of the chart together as an example. Pause the recording and ask sts to check their answers quickly with a partner, then elicit the answer from the class. Play the rest of the recording. Paircheck. Classcheck with answers on the board. Ask sts: *Is the weather crazy in your / our country, too? Why? / Why not?*

> the Alps: Usually snowy; Now warm, no snow
> the Amazon rainforest: Usually very rainy; Now no rain
> the Atacama Desert: Usually hot and sunny; Now cool and cloudy
> Cancún: Usually hot; Now really cold
> Chicago: Usually windy; Now no wind, cool, and foggy

C Ask: *Do you remember the questions from the weather forecast?* Elicit the missing word in the first question (*how*). Individually, sts complete questions 1–3. Paircheck. Classcheck with answers on the board. Check sts are clear on the difference between the verbs *like* and *be like*.

Weaker classes Real beginners might need to read the AS on p. 161 and look for questions 1–3 in it.

Common mistakes Ask sts to read and elicit what the weather is like now / is usually like in (your city).

> 1 how 2 What 3 like

D **Make it personal** Ask sts to read the speech bubbles. Ask: *What's the opposite of dry?* to check meaning and teach *wet*. Drill the questions *What's the weather like? / How's the weather now in …?* before sts perform the activity. In pairs, sts take turns asking and answering about the weather in their city and / or the photos from pp. 32–33. Classcheck.

➡ **Workbook** p. 14

3.2 Are you busy at the moment?

1 Vocabulary Everyday actions

A ▶3.4 Match photos 1–6 to the actions. Then listen to Maddie make five phone calls. Which action don't you hear?
- ☐ buying groceries
- ☐ doing homework
- ☐ running in the park
- ☐ cooking dinner
- ☐ riding a bike
- ☐ talking on a landline

B ▶3.4 Listen again and match the person to the activity that they are doing.
Maddie _____   Susan _____   Rita _____
Eli _____   Michael _____

C 🔴 Make it personal In pairs, say which of the activities you do and which you don't do. When do you do them? Can you name other activities that you do?

> Riding a bike?   Yes, I do this on Saturdays when it's warm and when it's not raining.

2 Grammar Present continuous (1)

A ▶3.5 Listen to Maddie's last phone call. Answer the questions.
1. Why is she looking for company?
   - ☐ To have dinner.
   - ☐ To go to a sports event.
   - ☐ She's feeling lonely.
2. How does the story end?
   - ☐ She gets depressed and cries.
   - ☐ She finally finds a friend who is free.
   - ☐ She does her homework.

> **Common mistakes**
>   *are doing*
> What ~~you do~~ now?
> *Are you*
> ~~You are~~ studying English?
>   Yes, ~~I do~~.
>   *am*

B Complete the grammar box.

> **1** Complete the examples with the verb *be*.
> ⊕ She _____ talking on the phone. → Subject + *be* + verb *-ing*
> ⊖ I _____ _____ running. → Subject + *be* + not + verb *-ing*
> ❓ What _____ they doing? → Question word + *be* + subject + verb *-ing*
>
> **2** Delete the incorrect options.
> Use the present continuous for actions that happen **every day / at the moment / sometimes**.
> Don't pronounce the /g/ in the *-ing* ending. It's /ɪn/ or /ɪŋ/ (like *king* and *ring*).
>
> → Grammar 3A p.142

C ▶3.6 In pairs, listen to the sound effects. What are the people doing?
1. They're cooking.   3. _____   5. _____
2. She _____   4. _____   6. _____

D Look back at p. 20. Take turns testing a partner about Jake's morning routine.

> What's Jake doing in "e"?   He's taking a shower.

E 🔴 Make it personal Role-play a conversation like Maddie's. **A:** You're calling five friends to do something. **B:** You're A's friends. Make different excuses. Change roles.

> Hi, this is Marcia. Are you busy?   Yes, I'm cooking dinner!   OK, call you later!   Bye!

> **Common mistakes**
> I'm
> ~~I~~ working on a new project.

3.2 Are you busy at the moment?

Lesson Aims: Sts continue to practice verb *be* to talk about the seasons and months. Sts learn the present continuous through the context of routine activities.

Function
Talking about seasons and months.
Describing actions which are happening at the moment.

Language
What's your favorite season? What are you doing?
Are you busy?
I'm cooking dinner now.

Vocabulary: Months, seasons, actions (buying groceries, cooking dinner, doing homework, riding a bike, running in the park, talking on a landline). Key phrases: Are you busy? Call you later. No problem.
Grammar: Present continuous.

Warm-up Display some weather photos around the class or on the IWB and have sts ask and answer: *What's the weather like? / It's …* Monitor closely for accuracy.

1 Vocabulary Everyday actions

A Explore photos 1–6 and guide sts to the correct activity / actions. Use gestures, mime some of the actions (e.g. running, cooking, riding a bike, and doing homework). Drill the pronunciation of each phrase. Sts match photos 1–6 to the correct actions. Play ▶ 3.4 and ask: *Which action was not in the audio?*

> 1 talking on a landline   2 running in the park
> 3 riding a bike   4 doing homework   5 cooking dinner
> 6 buying groceries
> You don't hear doing homework.

▶ **3.4** Turn to p. 312 for the complete audioscript.
Note: Have fun with Spanish and Portuguese-speaking sts by comparing *groceries* with *groserías* (curse words) or *grosseria* (rudeness)!

B Listen again and sts complete the matching. Classcheck. Ask sts *Was this listening useful? Were some people easier to understand than others?*

> Maddie: talking on a landline
> Eli: cooking dinner
> Susan: running in the park
> Michael: riding a bike
> Rita: buying groceries

C 🔴 **Make it personal**   Sts follow the model given in the speech bubbles.

2 Grammar: Present continuous (1)

A Point to photo 1, say: *Look at Maddie. Is she happy?* (No) *Why not?*, and let sts speculate. Play ▶ 3.5. Sts listen and answer the questions. Peercheck, classcheck..

> 1 To go to a sports event
> 2 She finally finds a friend who is free.

B Sts complete 1 in the grammar box with the correct forms of *be*. Write the first sentence on the board: *She is talking on the telephone.* Ask a few concept-check questions, e.g. *Is it past / present or future?* (present) *Is it about an action that happens every day, now, or sometimes?* (now). Sts cross out the incorrect options in 2. Read the tip with them and drill the pronunciation of *doing, talking, cooking* in isolation and within sentences / context. Refer to the example of *king* and *ring* on the Sounds and Usual Spellings chart on SB p. 159. Ask sts if this grammar is the same in their language.

➡ **Grammar 3A** p. 142

> 1 is, am / 'm, not, are   2 Delete *every day* and *sometimes*

C **Books closed.** Say: *Listen to the sounds. What are they doing?* Play the first sound effect ▶ 3.6 and elicit the answer. Play the others and ask sts to remember the actions. Paircheck.
Books open. Sts write the answers. Sts listen again to check answers. Classcheck.

> 2 's singing.   3 He's driving.   4 She's drinking.
> 5 He's cleaning.   6 They're eating.

D Refer to the speech bubbles as a model. Sts look back to lesson 2.2 and test each other in pairs.

E 🟢 **Make it personal**   Demonstrate the conversation with a volunteer st. Direct sts to the speech bubbles. Have sts look at AS 3.4 on p. 161 and look at some of the phone phrases together: *Are you busy? Call you later. Don't worry. Sorry, wrong number. No, problem. I can't hear you. The line's busy. My battery's dying.* Sts role-play Maddie's conversation and give different excuses. Listen and make a note of good use of present continuous. Go over this afterwards to reinforce the form and meaning, praising good language from sts.

3 Reading

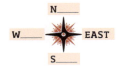

Winter, spring, summer or fall, All you've got to do is call and I'll be there, yeah, yeah, yeah, You've got a friend.

A ▶ 3.7 Study the months. Is the stressed syllable the same (S) or different (D) in your language? Listen to check. Then say your birthday month.

| January ☐ | February ☐ | March ☐ | April ☐ | May ☐ | June ☐ | July ☐ |
| August ☐ | September ☐ | October ☐ | November ☐ | December ☐ |

Common mistakes
My birthday's ~~on march~~. *in March*

B Read the extract from an encyclopedia and:
1 write the seven missing months.
2 circle the names of three more seasons in paragraph 1.
3 find two more seasons in paragraph 2.
4 find the names of one continent and two countries.
5 find the words to complete the compass.

N _____
W _____ ✦ EAST
S _____

Four seasons or two?

Countries with a temperate climate, like the ones in Europe and North America, have four defined seasons: hot summers in June, _____, and August; cold winters in December, January, and _____, with heavy snow in some countries; cool, windy falls in *September*, _____, and November, and warm springs in _____, April, and _____.

In contrast, tropical regions, especially around the equator, have only two seasons: the dry season and the rainy season. So, in places like India, West Africa, Central America, the north of South America, and the north coast of Australia, the rainy season is in their winter (_____, July, and _____), and it's accompanied by very high temperatures.

C ▶ 3.8 Listen to and read the encyclopedia extract. Any pronunciation surprises?

D In pairs, answer the questions.
1 Which months correspond to which seasons in your country?
2 What's your favorite season? What's the weather like in your favorite season?
3 Say three things you usually do in your favorite season, and three you don't.

I don't usually go out a lot in the rainy season. I watch a lot of TV!

E 🔴 **Make it personal** In groups. Think of a month and season. Mime an activity that you usually do in that season. Your group guesses what you are doing, the month, and the season.

Are you swimming? — Yes, I am. *Is it summer?* — Yes.
Is it December? — Yes, it is.

🎵 **Song line:** Turn to p. 326 for notes about this song and an accompanying task.

3 Reading Recognizing cognates

A **Books closed.** Ask: *When do we usually get lots of rain? What months? When is it usually sunny? What's your favorite month? Why?* Elicit some replies from different sts to assess their knowledge and pronunciation of the months. **Books open.** Sts read the months and, with the aid of the pink syllables, try to pronounce them in pairs. Ask them to write *S* if word stress is the same in their mother tongue and *D* when word stress is different. The words with no pink syllables have only one syllable. Play ▶ 3.7 so sts can check answers. Classcheck and have sts repeat their birthday month.

> **Cultural note** There are various definitions of *a continent*. In English-speaking countries, North and South America are considered to be separate continents. However, they are considered as one continent in Spanish and Portuguese-speaking countries.
>
> **Language tip** Remind speakers of Portuguese and Spanish that, although the months of the year are easy to identify because they are cognates, there is an important difference besides pronunciation and spelling. In English, they are always written with an initial capital letter. Ask what other words with initial capital letters are different in English and L1 (nationalities, days of the week).

B Focus on the encyclopedia text title and elicit / pre-teach the four seasons of the year. Go over 1–5 and make sure sts understand what they have to do. In small groups, sts read the text and help each other. Walk around the class and offer help when needed. Sts check their answers. Ask: *Was this information interesting / useful / easy / difficult? How much of the text did you understand? Any surprises?*

> 🗝
> 1 July, February, October, March, May, June, August
> 2 winter, fall, spring
> 3 dry, rainy
> 4 Continents: Europe, North America, South America, Africa
>   Countries: India, Australia
> 5 North, West, South

C Sts read the text in **B** and try to guess how to pronounce the words with pink syllables. Then, they listen to ▶ 3.8 to check. Classcheck and go over any words sts are not sure how to pronounce.

> **Tip** Encourage sts to make a note of new vocabulary and mark the stress as they do so by underlining the stressed syllable, drawing stress bubbles (winter Oo), or by using color. Sts could also list words together under the same stress pattern headings to help them remember the correct pronunciation and add to this as they learn new words.

D Ask: *What are the winter months here?* Elicit an answer. Sts discuss the questions in pairs. Monitor and help with pronunciation as needed. Have fun comparing the differences in seasons. Some sts may just have the "hot season" and the "very hot season"!

> **Weaker classes** Write some prompts on the board for 2: *My favorite season is … It's usually cool / warm / hot …*

E 👤 **Make it personal** Assign different groups. Tell sts to look at the speech bubbles. Demonstrate the task by miming an action. Drill short answers first. Have fun with this, adding more months and more activities. Let sts use dictionaries for lexis, e.g., local festival activities like picking grapes, wearing special clothes, etc. With adult groups, maybe get them to mime a few aspects of their job. In small groups, sts take turns miming and guessing. Round off the activity by asking a st from each group to report any interesting or unusual activities their classmates do and in which months.

➔ **Workbook** p. 15

3.3 What are you doing these days?

1 Listening

A ▶ 3.9 Listen and identify the people in the pictures.
1 Marisa   2 Jennifer   3 Kevin   4 Steve

B ▶ 3.9 Listen again. True (T) or False (F)? Correct the false statements.
1 Marisa is working at the moment. _____
2 She's studying art. _____
3 She's living with her parents. _____
4 She's dating Kevin. _____

2 Grammar   Present continuous (2)

A Complete the grammar box.

1 Put the questions in the correct column.
What are you doing these days?   Are you studying art?
Are you dating Kevin?   Where are you living?

Wh-?	Yes / No?

2 Which question type (*Wh-* or *Yes / No*) uses which structure?
 a verb *be* + subject + verb *-ing* _____
 b question word + verb *be* + subject + verb *-ing* _____

3 Delete the incorrect option.
We use the present continuous to talk about things happening:
 a right now.   b in the past.   c around now.

➡ Grammar 3B p.142

B Put the words in order to make questions. Ask and answer with a partner. Talk about other people, too.
1 you / are / doing / what / ?
2 working / where / you / are / ?
3 are / what / studying / you / ?
4 at home / living / you / are / ?
5 dating / are / you / ?

— What are you doing at the moment?
— Nothing special. I'm working a lot during the week.
— Oh, really! Where are you working?
— I have a new job now! At the aquarium. I feed the fish!

C 🟢 Make it personal   Invent a new personality! Ask and answer questions. Use the ideas below. Who has the most interesting life?

do a lot of exercise   go out a lot   listen to music   read   sleep well
speak more English   spend a lot of money   watch (a show on) TV

▶ Common mistakes

Are you coming
~~Do you come~~ for coffee?
           are you going
Hi! Where ~~do you go~~?
           I go home.
              'm going

3.3 What are you doing these days?

Lesson Aims: Sts ask and answer questions about different activities and work. Sts learn present continuous for talking about things happening around now. Sts discuss some problems related to technology.

Function
Giving opinions about technology.
Reading online comments about technology.
Listening to descriptions of people doing different activities.

Language
What are you doing these days?

Vocabulary: Technology (devices, social media, privacy, identity theft, addiction, isolation).
Grammar: Present continuous for actions happening around now.

Warm up Books closed. Sts think of friends and family and talk about what they are doing right now. Ask: *What do you think your parents are doing right now? What are your friends doing? What about other people you know?* Say: *My brother is working. My mother is probably working, too.* Sts talk about people they know.

1 Listening

A Books open. Sts look at the pictures and say what the people are doing. Play ▶3.9 and sts order the names. Paircheck. Classcheck.

Marisa, Jennifer Steve Kevin

▶3.9 Turn to p. 313 for the complete audioscript.

Language tip Portuguese and Spanish speakers tend to use *in the moment* instead of *at the moment* when they are learning English, because in both languages the preposition used in this expression (*no momento / en el momento*) is the equivalent to *in*. Remind sts that *at the moment* means right now, whereas *in the moment* has a focus on present time.

B Tell sts to focus on the picture of Marisa. Sts read the sentences before they listen and predict if true or false. Play ▶3.9 and sts write T or F and correct the false sentences. Paircheck. Classcheck.

1 F. She's at college.   2 F. She's studying Biology.
3 T.   4 F. She's dating Steve.

2 Grammar Present continuous (2)

A Sts look at the grammar box and write the questions in the correct column. Ask sts: *Do you remember any other Wh- or Yes / No questions from the listening? Can you invent more questions?* Write their examples on the board. Sts complete 2 to review the form. Sts complete 3 to confirm the meaning. Clarify that we use present continuous for different things: to talk about things happening right now **and** around now. Elicit more examples of both.

➔ **Grammar 3B** p. 142

1 Wh- ?: What are you doing these days? Where are you living?
Yes / No?: Are you studying art? Are you dating Kevin?
2 a Yes / No b Wh- 3 a, c

B Board presentation. Add the missing word to questions 1–4.

1 *What your sister doing these days?* 2 *Your brother studying in this moment?* 3 *Where your parents living?* 4 *The teacher watching us right now?*

Elicit corrections, and highlight correction of *in this moment* to *at the moment* in 2. Write more time phrases on the board, e.g. *at the moment, these days, on (Sundays/weekends), in the mornings, at (night), in your free time*.

Now refer to activity **2B** and complete 1 with the class. Tell sts to refer to the grammar box and complete 2–5. Teach the meaning of *Are you dating?* (You are in a romantic but not serious relationship.) Sts then ask and answer the questions. Monitor and correct errors with the present continuous as you hear them by prompting sts to self-correct.

1 What are you doing?   2 Where are you working?
3 What are you studying?   4 Are you living at home?
5 Are you dating?

C 🔵 **Make it personal** Check that sts understand the phrase *these days* in the title of the lesson. Refer sts to the speech bubbles and check they understand the task. Say: *Think of the most interesting job you can* and give sts a minute to think of a job and things they do in that job. Encourage them to use a dictionary. Sts work in small groups and take turns to ask questions and describe activities. After they have finished ask: *Who has the most interesting life in your group?*

3 Reading

🎵 *Don't stop me now, I'm having such a good time, I'm having a ball.*

A Match the technology problems 1–5 to photos a–e.
1. identity theft
2. addiction
3. consumerism
4. isolation
5. violence

B Read the online debate and match the person to the problem in **A** they write about.

Sammy
What do you think of technology?

Marsha
It's dangerous. Social media companies are changing the way we see privacy. Everyone is getting access to our personal information.

Lucinda
I don't like a lot of the new video games. They're getting more violent and it makes people act more violently.

KoolKat
People are going out less and spending more time alone with technology. We don't know our neighbors.

Dadofthree
People today are becoming obsessed with things! They want new clothes, new cars, new electronic devices, and they can buy it all online.

BBBaxter
My kids are spending more and more time on their devices and online, especially on social media. I don't know what to do. They panic when they don't have their phone with them. They just want to look at their phones.

C ▶ 3.10 Now listen and check your answers. Who do you most agree with? Practice saying what they say.

D 🎤 **Make it personal** What do you think the problems with technology are? List the problems in **A** in order of importance. Say why. Who agrees with you?

> What's your most important problem?

> Isolation. People are spending too much time on their phones.

> I agree. Communities are changing. I don't know my neighbors.

3.3

🎵 **Song line:** Turn to p. 326 for notes about this song and an accompanying task.

③ Reading

A **Books closed.** If you can, show the photos on the IWB. Sts look at the photos and describe what people are doing. Elicit examples and write relevant vocabulary on the board.

Sts look at items 1–5 and match them to photos a–e. Classcheck. Check pronunciation and ask questions to clarify that sts understand the vocabulary: *What other things can we be addicted to?* (alcohol, gambling) *When are people isolated?* (prison, live far away from other people) *What's the opposite of violence?* (peace)

> 1 e 2 c 3 b 4 a 5 d

B Ask: *Where do we read texts like this?* (online, in blogs and discussion forums). *Do you write texts like this in your own language?* Check understanding of *alone, privacy, devices.* Sts read and match the texts. Don't check answers yet.

> Marsha: identity theft
> Lucinda: violence
> KoolKat: isolation
> Dadofthree: consumerism
> BBBaxter: addiction

C Tell sts they can now check their answers. Play ▶3.10 and ask sts to correct their answers and think about who they agree with as they listen. Sts practice the phrases with a partner.

▶3.10 Turn to p. 313 for the complete audioscript.

> **Tip** Ask sts to turn to the AS on p. 162. Sts listen again and notice the pronunciation of /eɪ/ and /aɪ/.

D 🔴 **Make it personal** Ask a confident st: *Which problem is most serious, in your opinion? Why?* Use gestures to clarify the meaning of the superlative. Sts look at the photos and rank them from most serious / important problem to least serious / important in their opinion. Assign groups and have sts compare their ideas using the speech bubbles to manage their conversations.

> **Weaker students** If you have some lower level learners in your class, give all sts some time to prepare their ideas before they start the speaking task so they are more confident about sharing their opinions and giving reasons for their ideas.

➡ **Workbook** p. 16

3.4 What do you do after school / work?

1 Grammar Simple present vs. present continuous

A In pairs, can you recognize the celebrities in the photos? What do they do?

Who's this? *I think this is Naomi Watts.* *What does she do?* *I think she's a movie star.*

Spot the Celebrity

B Match photos 1–6 to these actions. What are the people doing? In pairs, take turns asking and answering.

- ☐ walk the dog
- ☐ watch a game
- ☐ shop
- ☐ listen to music
- ☐ watch a show
- ☐ drive a car

What's Steph Curry doing? *He's listening to music.*

C Complete the grammar box.

1. Read the paragraph and for sentences a–d write SP (simple present) or PC (present continuous).

    Jack Morley is a celebrity journalist. ᵃHe usually works from 8 a.m. to 5 p.m. in his office ☐, and ᵇhe talks to his editor every morning ☐. ᶜThis week, Jack's doing a lot of different things ☐. ᵈRight now he's interviewing a famous actor ☐.

2. Match the rules.

    a Use the present continuous to
    b Use the simple present to

    1 talk about routines.
    2 talk about something happening around now.
    3 describe actions in progress now.
    4 describe habits.

    ➔ Grammar 3C p.142

Common mistakes

I'm living
I'm live at home at the moment.
I like
I'm liking this movie.

3.4 What do you do after school / work?

Lesson Aims: Sts learn how to ask and answer questions about occupations. Sts learn simple present vs. present continuous through the context of routine activities.

Function
Asking and answering questions about occupations.
Talking about what people are doing.
Reading / Talking about a journalist's schedule.
Listening to / Talking about British Royal family members' daily life.

Language
What does she do?
What's he doing?

Vocabulary: Celebrities. Daily routine: walk the dog, ride a bike, carry shopping bags, etc. Time expressions: at the moment, right now, usually.

Grammar: Simple present vs. present continuous.

Warm-up Show some pictures of different people doing certain actions. You can mime some actions as well. Make sure you also clarify that the actions are happening at the moment you are miming them. You can reinforce the use of words such as *now* and expressions such as *at the moment* so that sts clearly understand that the actions are happening at that moment.

1 Grammar Simple present vs. present continuous

A Books closed. Have sts ask each other in small groups: *What do you do? I'm a / an ….* At the end, ask sts to tell the rest of the class what their partners do. Ask: *What does he / she do?*

Focus on one of the celebrities in the photos and ask: *Who's this?* (Sts: I think he / she is …), *What does he / she do?* (Sts: He / She is a …). Ask sts if they can remember Jay-Z and Beyoncé's daughter's name from unit 1 (Blue Ivy Carter). In pairs, sts do the same. Ask them to refer to the speech bubbles as a model and ask and answer about the celebrities in each photo. Classcheck.

1 Jay-Z 2 Steph Curry 3 Lionel Messi
4 J. K. Rowling 5 Naomi Watts 6 Salma Hayek

B Point to Naomi Watts (photo 5) and ask: *What is she doing?* (walking the dog). Sts match photos 1–6 to actions. Sts paircheck by asking each other *What's (J. K. Rowling) doing?* and answering *He / She is ….* Classcheck.

1 watch a game 2 listen to music 3 drive a car
4 watch a show 5 walk the dog 6 shop

C Draw a two-column chart on the board with headings SP (simple present) / PC (present continuous). Elicit time expressions and where they go in the chart, e.g. *now, at the moment, every day, sometimes, always, usually,* etc. Sts decide whether the sentences in 1 are in the SP or PC tense. Paircheck. Classcheck.

In pairs, sts reflect and decide about the rules in 2 for SP vs. PC use. Classcheck with answers on the board. *Ask Are uses 1–4 similar to or different from your language? Is the form similar too?* It can be easier for sts to make sense of rules when they translate or compare to L1.

➔ **Grammar 3C** p. 142

1 a SP b SP c PC d PC
2 a 2, 3 b 1, 4

Language tip In Portuguese and Spanish, main verbs do not need an auxiliary verb like *do* in the simple present for questions or negatives as they do in English. Before tackling the lesson title question (*What do you do?*) remind sts that, when the verb *do* is used in this way, it does not translate. Show sts by writing some examples of simple present questions with different verbs on the board. *What **do** you want? Where **do** you live?*

🎵 *I'm giving it my all, but I'm not the girl you're taking home, oh, I keep dancing on my own.*

D For each of the people in **A**, imagine what they usually do at these times and what they are probably doing right now or, more generally, around now.

	1	2	3	4	5	6
8:00 a.m.						
12:30 p.m.						
7:30 p.m.						

I think Steph Curry usually gets up before 8:00 a.m. Right now, I guess he's training. More generally, he's probably working on a new charity project.

E 🔵 **Make it personal** Make a timeline of what you usually do during a regular day. Are there any things that you are doing around now that you don't usually do?

I go to college on weekdays. But, I'm training for a marathon, so now I'm running every morning.

At the moment, I'm taking an English class at a language school.

🔵 **Common mistakes**

I'm running ~~all the mornings~~ *every morning* at the moment.

② Listening

A In pairs, share what you know about these celebrities.

That's George Clooney. He's married to a Lebanese-British lawyer.

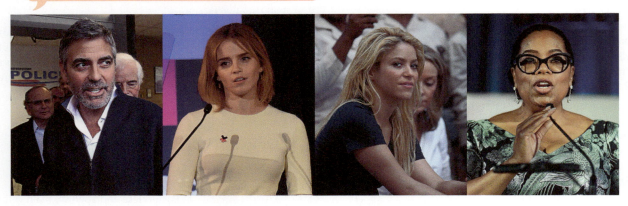

B ▶ 3.11 Listen to Jack Morley talk about celebrities. Does he think celebrity activists are a good thing or a bad thing?

C ▶ 3.11 Listen again and check (✓) which causes are mentioned.

☐ cyberbullying ☐ clean water ☐ corruption
☐ peace ☐ climate change ☐ animal rights
☐ education for girls ☐ women's rights ☐ racism

D ▶ 3.11 In pairs, complete these sentences. Then listen to check.
Celebrities _____ _____ a lot of publicity to these causes and people _____ _____ more money on the causes. But what do celebrities know about these _____?

E 🔵 **Make it personal** What do you think of celebrity activists? Give a reason.

I think Emma Watson is a good person and she helps people.

Yes, but she is an actor, not a politician.

But she's smart!

D Highlight new cognates *probably, more general(ly)*. Use the example in the speech bubble as a model for this activity. In pairs, sts do the same for the other times (noon, 7:30 p.m.) and take turns writing each time. Monitor closely for the correct use of simple present and present continuous. Classcheck by asking a pair of sts to act out the dialogue for two different times from the chart.

E 🟢 **Make it personal** Draw a timeline of your day on the board and mark some activities

E.g.

Get up at 8   go to English class   watch a new TV series
——— x ——————— x ———————————— x ———

Explain your activities to the sts. *I usually get up at 8:00 a.m. I always go to English class at 7:00 p.m. I am watching a new TV series.* Elicit questions. (*What series are you watching? Do you like it?*) Draw sts' attention to 🟠 **Common mistakes**. Ask sts to make a timeline with three activities from a regular day. Sts tell a partner about what they do, using simple present + *usually / always*, and present continuous. Monitor. Ask one or two sts to share information from their timeline with the class.

At this point, you could choose to briefly introduce the use of present continuous for future time (using Grammar Reference **3C**, p. 142) or leave this until unit 9.

🎵 **Song line:** Turn to p. 327 for notes about this song and an accompanying task.

2 Listening

A Sts look at the listening section. Ask: *Are you interested in celebrities? Yes? No? Sometimes?* Ask sts who say *Sometimes* to give reasons why. Sts name the celebrities (George Clooney, Emma Watson, Shakira, Oprah Winfrey). Ask sts to share what they know about these people. Ask for other examples of celebrities who are known for charity work, e.g. Rihanna, Angelina Jolie, or celebrities in sts' countries.

B Before sts listen to try to answer the question, ask them to predict what the journalist might say. Play ▶3.11 so they can check their ideas. Paircheck and classcheck.

🔑 He thinks they are a bad thing.

▶ **3.11** Turn to p. 313 for the complete audioscript.

C Explain the meaning of a *cause* (a principle, objective, or movement which people follow and sometimes take action to solve or support). For example, Emma Watson supports women's rights and spoke about it in a meeting of the United Nations. Read through the items and check understanding. Play ▶3.11 again and have sts check the causes mentioned. Paircheck. Classcheck. Ask: *Did you enjoy this activity? Did you learn anything new? Was the speaker easy / difficult to understand?*

🔑 cyberbullying, education for girls, clean water, climate change women's rights, animal rights, racism

Tip When sts are comparing answers, ask them to say why they checked the boxes and encourage them to make a note of relevant words or phrases they heard. They can then check this when they listen again. It might also help you see where there are issues with misunderstanding.

D Ask sts to read the sentence and try to remember or guess what words go in the gaps. Play ▶3.11 again so sts can complete the sentence. For pronunciation, drill *celebrities, publicity*. Highlight stress pattern on *-ity* and include more examples, e.g. *activity, ability*.

🔑 are bringing, are spending, problems

Weaker students Refer sts to the AS when you play the audio and ask them to listen and read. Encourage them to underline any sections they don't understand. A lack of understanding is usually because they don't know the words or because the words run together and don't sound the same as how they are written and how the sts expect to hear them. After listening, go over the sections they have underlined and focus on new vocabulary or chunks that sound different to how they are written. Encourage sts to think about how the words are connected so the next time they hear that chunk they recognize it.

E 🟢 **Make it personal** Sts use the sentences in **D** to help them discuss this question. Ask two sts to read the speech bubble dialogue. Ask the class: *What do you think?* Elicit some ideas. Ask: *Do you ever give to a charity? Do you do any work for a charity?* Sts discuss all the questions in pairs or small groups of three. Monitor and help with language and ideas. Go over any useful language that comes up.

Extra activity If sts have access to mobile devices and the Internet, ask them to search for other famous people who help people or have charities. Write some key words they can use to do an online search on the board (e.g. *celebrity charity causes*). Sts can do the search in pairs and then share the results in groups. (Pair stronger and weaker sts together if possible.)

Sts then talk about what celebrity causes they like the most. Write on the board: *Who do you think is doing a good job helping other people? What are the most important causes you read about?* Sts discuss in their groups and then share ideas with the class.

➡ **Workbook** p. 17

3.5 Why are you learning English?

ID Skills Analyzing your English

A Read the introduction to the questionnaire. Are questions 1–2 True (T) or False (F)?
1 We know exactly how many people speak English in the world.
2 The questionnaire is for the authors of this book.

Approximately 25% of the world speaks or is now learning to speak English, and this number is rapidly increasing. Please help the ID team to learn more about our users' motivation and experiences. Complete our questionnaire, checking (✓) all relevant answers, and let us know.

1 Why are you learning English?
   a ○ for my current or future job   ○ for school   ○ for college
   b ○ for pleasure   ○ I love learning languages
   c to communicate: ○ online   ○ in writing   ○ speaking
   d ○ to communicate with other people face-to-face
   e ○ to pass an exam
   f ○ to travel
   g ○ to emigrate
   h ○ other (what?) _____

2 Which are the three most important for you? Number them 1 to 3.
   a ○ grammar   d ○ listening   g ○ writing
   b ○ vocabulary   e ○ speaking   h ○ all equally
   c ○ pronunciation   f ○ reading   important

3 Which items in 2 do you find the most difficult?
   _____

4 How often do you do these things in English outside class? Mark them:
   E=Every day   V=Very often   S=Sometimes   O=Occasionally   N=Never
   a ○ read   e ○ watch TV / movies
   b ○ study   f ○ speak to people face-to-face
   c ○ write / send messages   g ○ communicate online
   d ○ listen to music / the radio   h ○ other (what?) _____

5 What do you like about your ID classes?
   a ○ the coursebook
   b ○ the workbook
   c ○ the ID student's learning platform
   d ○ my classmates
   e ○ other? _____

Common mistakes

~~to~~ *to*
I need ~~learn~~ English ~~for~~ pass my course.

~~to~~ *for*
I have ~~learn~~ English ~~to~~ my job.

job
I'm ~~needing~~ to get a new ~~work~~.

B Answer the questionnaire. In pairs, compare your answers.

C **Make it personal** In groups, explain your answers to the questionnaire.

I'm learning English for many reasons. I need it in school. I'm taking some exams in English.

I'm working at an international company at the moment. I need to talk to people from many different countries in English.

3.5 Why are you learning English?

Lesson Aims: Sts learn to talk about the reasons they are learning English. Sts learn to use *Do you want ...?* and *Would you like ...?* in the context of making offers.

Function
Reading the introduction of a questionnaire.
Answering a questionnaire.

Language
Why are you learning English?
I'm learning English for many reasons.
I'm going abroad next year.

Warm-up Books closed. Write *Why do people learn English?* on the board and elicit ideas. Write them on the board. Tell sts they are going to talk more specifically about why they are learning English in today's class.

ID Skills Analyzing your English

A Books open. Sts focus on the website photos and see if they can recognize what they are about (New York City, a woman / college student, London). Focus on the questionnaire. Sts read the introduction. In pairs, sts mark T (true) or F (false) for 1–2. Classcheck.

1 F   2 T

Tip Draw sts' attention to the stressed syllables in pink. Ask them to practice reading the introduction to each other in pairs to practice pronunciation.

B Refer to the **Common mistakes** to anticipate difficulties before sts discuss their answers to the questionnaire. Mention that certain verbs don't have a continuous form. Refer to the chart at the end of Grammar Reference 3C on p. 142 for more examples.

Individually, sts take the questionnaire in **A**. In pairs, they interview / read the questionnaire to each other and compare their answers.

Classcheck by asking some sts to report their partner's answers to the whole class.

Common mistakes Remind sts that although in their L1 the infinitive of a verb has no particle, the infinitive of verbs in English always come with the particle *to*. So, when you use *need* + verb, the verb must always come with the particle. *I need to work tomorrow.* (NOT *I need work tomorrow.*) *I need to get a new job.* (NOT *I need get a new job.*)

C Make it personal Assign groups and refer sts to the speech bubbles. Sts then share their results and ask for further information. Take this moment to get to know your sts' needs as much as possible by monitoring and asking for more details.

Tip Assign a secretary in each group and ask them to make a note of any relevant details from sts' answers that might be useful for you when planning future classes. Collect the notes at the end of the lesson.

3.5 Are you thirsty?

 So one last time, I need to be the one who takes you home. One more time, I promise after that, I'll let you go.

ID in Action Making offers

A ▶ 3.12 Listen to two friends and answer 1–5.
1 What time is it?
2 What's Linda working on?
3 When does she have to finish it?
4 How many more pages does she have to write?
5 Is she tired?

B ▶ 3.12 Listen again and write Mark's three questions. Guess what happens next.

Maybe Linda decides to go home. *Yeah. Perhaps. Or maybe she doesn't …*

C ▶ 3.13 Listen to the next part of the conversation to check. What does Linda want?

D ▶ 3.12 and 3.13 Listen again and match the formal and informal expressions.

Grammatical English		Informal English	
1	Are you tired?	a	Yep. / Yeah.
2	Do you want to go home?	b	Cookie?
3	Yes.	c	You tired?
4	Would you like a cookie?	d	Wanna go home?

E ▶ 3.12 and 3.13 Listen again. In pairs, role-play the dialogue using the picture clues.

Mark		Linda
☕	→	U/1?
✓	→	✓ ● no 🥄
🍔 too?	→	✗
🍪 ?	→	✗
☕ ⬆	→	U R GREAT !

Common mistakes
~~I don't have~~ I'm not hungry, but I'm ~~with thirst~~ thirsty.
~~Do~~ Would you like a drink?

F ▶ 3.14 Match the questions and offers. Listen, check, and practice the different responses.

Questions	Offers	Responses
Are you bored?	Do you want a sweater / to use my jacket?	Yes, please. Great!
Are you cold?	Do you want a sandwich? / Wanna cookie?	Sure. Why not?
Are you hot?	Would you like a coffee / to go home?	Yep / Yeah!
Are you hungry?	Would you like a drink?	Uh-huh, just …
Are you thirsty?	Do you want a cold drink / some ice cream?	No, thanks.
Are you tired?	Maybe you need a vacation / a new job?	No, really, I'm fine.
Are you stressed?	Wanna go out for a coffee / a walk?	That sounds great!

G 🔴 **Make it personal** In pairs. **A:** Mime an adjective from the chart in **F**. **B:** Ask a question and make an offer from the chart or one of your own. **A:** Respond.

Are you bored? Wanna read my newspaper?

3.5 Are you thirsty?

Lesson Aims: To practice making offers.

Function
Listening to two friends talking.
Making offers.
Responding to offers.

Language
What time is it?
What's Linda working on?
When does she have to finish it?
How many more pages does she have to write? Is she tired?

Vocabulary: Informal English: You tired? Wanna go home?

Grammar: Use of *have* to express obligation, use of *to* + verb and *for* + noun, questions (*Are you bored?*), offers (*Would you like to go home?*) and responses (*Yes, please. / No, thanks.*).

Song line: Turn to p. 327 for notes about this song and an accompanying task.

ID in Action Making offers

A Sts look at the photo. Ask: *What is happening?* Elicit ideas and encourage sts to use present continuous. Play ▶3.12 and have sts listen to Linda and Mark and answer questions 1–5. Paircheck. Classcheck with answers on the board.

> 1 1 a.m.   2 a report   3 tomorrow   4 three
> 5 Yes, kind of.

▶3.12 Turn to p. 313 for the complete audioscript.

B Sts listen again and write down Mark's questions. Paircheck. Classcheck with answers on the board. Elicit what sts think will happen next.

> 1 What are you doing?   2 Is it a big report?   3 You tired?

Tip Ask sts to turn to the AS on p. 162. Sts listen again and notice *have to* /f/ and *kind of* /v/.

C Play ▶3.13 for sts to check their guesses. Paircheck. Classcheck.

> Linda wants a black coffee.

D Sts read the chart and match the phrases. Play ▶3.12 and ▶3.13 so they can check. Classcheck and drill the pronunciation of all the phrases. Ask: *Did Mark and Linda use grammatical or informal phrases?* (Informal)

> 1 c   2 d   3 a   4 b

Common mistakes Draw attention to the mistakes here. Remind sts that we use the verb *be* with adjectives to describe how we are feeling.

E Play the audio again. Elicit the dialogue from the pictures in the chart and check how much sts can remember. In pairs, sts role-play the dialogue. Monitor for accuracy and intonation. Ask a pair of sts to act out the dialogue for the whole group.

F Sts match the first two columns in the chart. Paircheck. Play ▶3.14 to check their answers. Classcheck.

In pairs, sts role-play mini-dialogues using the questions, offers, and responses from the chart. Monitor closely for accuracy and appropriateness. At the end, ask three pairs of sts to act out different dialogues to the whole class.

> Are you cold?   Do you want a sweater / to use my jacket?
> Are you hot?   Do you want a cold drink / some ice cream?
> Are you hungry?   Do you want a sandwich? Wanna cookie?
> Are you thirsty?   Would you like a drink?
> Are you tired?   Would you like a coffee / to go home?
> Are you stressed?   Maybe you need a vacation / a new job?

Tip Encourage sts to use informal versions of the questions and offers, e.g. *You hungry? Wanna sandwich?*

G **Make it personal** In pairs, st A mimes an adjective. St B asks a question and makes an offer from the chart. St A replies with one of the responses from **F**. Sts change roles. Round off the lesson by asking volunteers to mime adjectives to the whole class and have the group as a whole ask questions and make offers.

➔ **Workbook** p. 18

➔ **Richmond Learning Platform**

➔ **Writing** p. 42

➔ **Café** p. 43

Writing 3 A language profile

 *Louder, louder, And we'll run for our lives, I can hardly speak I understand.*

A Read two student profiles and label the diagrams.

Personal details
My name's Marta and I'm 20.

Why are you learning English?
I often travel _____ other countries, so English is very important. I want _____ go _____ Los Angeles and India.

Which aspect of language is the most important for you?
_____ me, the most important thing is speaking. I need _____ communicate _____ people when I go on vacation.

What aspects of language are you good / bad at?
I'm not good _____ writing. I know how to say English words, but they are difficult _____ spell! I enjoy speaking _____ people and exchanging opinions. I'm good _____ talking – in fact, I never stop!

How do you practice English outside your classroom?
I use the Internet all the time, so I read the news _____ English and talk _____ my cousins in Canada online.

Personal details
My name's Mateo and I'm 24 years old.

Why are you learning English?
English is important for my career. I often have to read documents in English and I hope to get a promotion soon. Also, I'm going to New York next month!

Which aspect of language is the most important for you?
For me, the most important thing is pronunciation. It's often difficult to communicate with people because they don't understand me – and I don't understand them. It's very frustrating!

What aspects of language are you good / bad at?
I'm terrible at speaking! I want to speak to other people, but it isn't easy. When I'm reading, I go slowly and use a dictionary. I think I'm good at vocabulary, especially because many English words are similar to Italian words!

How do you practice English outside your classroom?
I don't have much time to practice at home because I work a lot. I occasionally watch American movies and read the subtitles. I need to practice more!

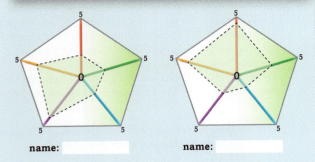

name: _____   name: _____

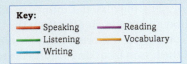

Key:
— Speaking   — Reading
— Listening   — Vocabulary
— Writing

D Complete the diagram in **A** for you. Rate each aspect of language 0–5.

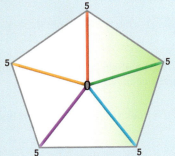

B Read **Write it right!** In Mateo's profile, circle five more words / phrases followed by *to* + infinitive.

> ✓ **Write it right!**
>
> *To* + infinitive and prepositions are often difficult to remember. When you read, try to notice phrases, and then use them when you write and speak.

C Notice the underlined preposition phrases in Mateo's profile. Complete Marta's profile with *to, for, with, at,* and *in*.

E ⬤ **Make it personal** Write your language profile in 80–120 words.

Before	Use the diagram in **D** and the questionnaire on p. 40.
While	Use prepositions carefully.
After	Read a partner's profile and draw their diagram.

42

Writing 3 A Language Profile

🎵 **Song line:** Turn to p. 327 for notes about this song and an accompanying task.

A Point to the two diagrams and ask sts to look at the key (below the diagrams) and discuss in pairs what the diagrams represent. Classcheck. Tell sts each diagram represents a student (point to the texts above), Marta or Mateo. Sts read both profiles and label the diagrams as being Marta's or Mateo's. Check any new vocabulary, and pay particular attention to the pronunciation of the pink-stressed words. Paircheck. Classcheck.

Note The blanks in Marta's profile will only be used / completed later on in **C**.

🔑 Diagram 1. Mateo   Diagram 2. Marta

B Read **Write it right!** with the whole class. Ask sts to look at Mateo's profile in **A** and notice the words in the circle, which are followed by *to* + infinitive. Ask them to find and circle five more words / phrases followed by *to* + infinitive. Paircheck. Classcheck with answers on the board or on the *Digital Book for Teachers*.

🔑
I hope to get a promotion.
It's often difficult to communicate.
I want to speak.
I don't have much time to practice.
I need to practice.

C Now refer sts to the underlined prepositions and preposition phrases in Mateo's profile. Sts fill in the blanks in Marta's profile in **A** with *to, for, with, at, in*. Tell sts to refer back to Mateo's profile in case they are uncertain about which preposition to use. Paircheck. Classcheck with answers on the board.

🔑 to, to, to, For, to, with, at, to, to, at, in, to

D Sts complete the diagram about themselves. Remind them / Elicit what each color stands for. (Key in **A**.) Sts assess their performance in each skill 0-5 and draw their own diagram. Sts can use this at any time to check progress.

Integrated speaking Ask sts to compare / talk about their diagrams in pairs. Write some prompts on the board to help them: *I'm (not) good at … / I know how to … / I like … / I need to …*, etc. Monitor closely for preposition use. At the end, ask sts to talk about their partners' diagrams to the whole class.

E 🔵 **Make it personal** Read the steps Before, While, and After with sts so as to guide them to write their own language profiles. Tell them to refer to Marta's and Mateo's profiles in **A** as a model and draw their attention to the length of the composition, that is, approximately 80–120 words. As a follow-up activity and before they hand in their texts, ask sts to exchange compositions and draw their partner's diagram.

3 Storm tracker

1 Before watching

A What are they doing? Look at the photo and check (✓).

August	Daniel	
		is looking in a bag.
		is sitting on a sofa.
		is standing behind the sofa.
		is using a computer.
		is checking a list.
		is holding a smartphone.

B Cover the chart. In pairs, take turns describing the scene.

The two guys are at home. August is …

C Put the words in the correct column. Watch and number them 1–10 in the order you hear them.

clouds   fast   heavy   lightning   storm
steady   filmmaker   video disc   shaky
zoom lens

Weather	Equipment	Adjectives	Job

2 While watching

A What's Daniel doing? Write Yes (Y) or No (N).

Daniel's …
1 carrying the equipment.   ☐
2 reading the list.   ☐
3 carrying the keys.   ☐
4 driving the car.   ☐
5 keeping the camera steady.   ☐
6 applying for an internship.   ☐
7 filming the storm.   ☐
8 introducing his storm tracker.   ☐

B In pairs, take turns asking and answering about 1–8 in A.

Is Daniel filming the storm?

No, he's not. August is filming the storm.

3 After watching

A Write True (T) or False (F). Correct what's false.
1 August uses the tripod.
2 Daniel's talking slowly into the microphone.
3 The storm's coming at 3:33.
4 The clouds behind Daniel aren't moving fast.
5 There's no lightning in the sky.
6 It's raining while August is filming.
7 They're making the video before the rain comes.
8 Daniel drops the microphone.
9 August keeps the camera steady.
10 Daniel is disappointed with the video footage.

B Order the story 1–9. In pairs, take turns saying a line of the story at a time.

☐ Daniel and August get wet and go home.
☐ Daniel and August are checking their list and Daniel asks about the tripod.
☐ Daniel invents a storm tracker app.
☐ Daniel checks if August can hear him.
☐ August doesn't bring the tripod.
☐ Daniel gets annoyed with August about the video footage quality.
☐ August and Daniel drive to the field.
☐ August films Daniel while the storm's passing over them.
☐ There's lightning just before they make the video.

C ◯ **Make it personal** In groups, talk about photography. Who uses their camera the most?
1 In an average week, how many photos and videos do you take?
2 What do you usually take photos and videos of?
3 Do you ever use a tripod or selfie stick?
4 What's your best recent photo or video?
5 How often do you share or upload photos?

It depends. I like to take photos of nature.   *I don't normally take videos, except when I'm out with friends.*

43

ID Café 3 Storm tracker

1 Before watching

A Point to the photo of August and Daniel, ask: *Who are they? What are they doing?* and point to the chart. Sts check who is doing what (August or Daniel) in the video. Paircheck. Classcheck.

August	Daniel	
✓		is looking in a bag.
	✓	is sitting on a sofa.
✓		is standing behind the sofa.
	✓	is using a computer.
✓	✓	is checking a list.
✓	✓	is holding a smartphone.

B Ask sts to cover the chart in **A** and, in pairs, take turns describing what August and Daniel are doing. Monitor closely for accuracy. Classcheck by asking several sts to say a sentence each to the whole class.

C Elicit / Drill pronunciation of all words in the box. Point to the table and ask: *Which words are related to the weather?* Get sts to work in pairs and write the words from the box under the correct category. Classcheck.

Weather	Equipment	Adjectives	Job
clouds	video disc	fast	filmmaker
lightning	zoom lens	heavy	
storm		steady	
		shaky	

2 While watching

A Explore the photo. Ask: *Where are Daniel and August? What are they doing?* and listen to sts' guesses. Point to sentences 1–8 and ask sts to pay attention to Daniel in the video. Read all sentences with the whole class and teach new vocabulary items, e.g. *keeping the camera steady* (pretend you are going to take a photo with your cell phone and mime you are trying to keep it still / not to shake it), *applying for an internship* (explain an internship is a period of time spent doing / learning a job to become qualified).

Tell sts to write Y (yes) or N (no) while they watch the video. Play **Video 3**. Paircheck. Replay the video if necessary. Classcheck.

1 N 2 Y 3 N 4 N 5 N 6 Y 7 N 8 Y

B Change partners. Tell sts to cover the answers in **A**, but to look at 1–8 in **A**. In pairs, sts talk about what Daniel is doing in the video. Have two sts read the model dialogue in the speech bubbles.

Elicit a few questions for sts to perform the activity, e.g. say: *What's the question to number 1 (in A)?* (Is Daniel carrying the equipment?) Drill pronunciation for the questions you elicit. Encourage sts to give short answers (No, he isn't.), and also correct the information (when suitable) as shown in the model dialogue.

Monitor closely for accuracy. Round off by getting sts to ask other classmates the same questions (open pairs).

3 After watching

A Read sentence 1 with sts and ask: *Is it true or false?* (False.) Sts continue deciding whether sentences 2-10 are true or false, and correcting the false ones. Paircheck. Classcheck.

1 F August doesn't use the tripod. He holds / is holding the video camera.
2 F Daniel's talking quickly.
3 F The storm's coming at 4:44.
4 F The clouds are moving very quickly.
5 F There's lightning in the sky.
6 F It's not raining while August is filming.
7 T
8 T
9 F Daniel doesn't keep the camera steady.
10 T

B Point to the sentences and tell sts they are in the wrong order. Individually, sts reorder the story according to what they remember from the video. Paircheck. If necessary, replay the video to check answers. Classcheck.

In pairs, sts take turns retelling the story. Round off with a collaborative storytelling activity: have nine sts retell the story to the whole class, pick one student at a time, or have the last student to read a line choose the next st to continue.

8 Daniel and August get wet and go home.
2 Daniel and August are checking their list and Daniel asks about the tripod.
1 Daniel invents a "storm tracker" app.
5 Daniel checks if August can hear him.
3 August doesn't bring the tripod.
9 Daniel gets annoyed with August about the video footage quality.
4 August and Daniel drive to the field.
7 August films Daniel while the storm's passing over them.
6 There's lightning just before they make the video.

C **Make it personal** Sts talk in groups about photography. Refer to the questions and the model dialogue. At the end, sts tell their partners' answers to the whole class.

Extra activity Have sts show each other their favorite photos on their phones and talk about when and where they took them.

99

4.1 Do you like tennis?

Unit overview: The main topics of unit 4 are sports, *can / can't*, possessive pronouns, clothes, and general abilities. Language points are introduced and practiced through the contexts of a sports TV program, a man's first day at the gym, questions about abilities such as using Google efficiently, cooking and dressing appropriately, and a job interview. Sts also listen to a speech by Malala, the human rights activist.

4.1 Do you like tennis?

Lesson Aims: Sts talk about sports.

Function
Listening to a sports program.
Listening to people talk about their favorite sports. Talking about sports.

Language
Today's exciting events at the Olympic Games include basketball, soccer, tennis, volleyball, cycling, running …
Skiing. I love to ski.
I like volleyball and cycling.
Our country is usually good at soccer.

Vocabulary: Sports.
Grammar: Definite article *the*.
Pronunciation: : /ə/ and /ɪ/ in *the*.

Warm-up In pairs, sts take turns asking and answering the questions from unit 3. Ask: *What's the weather like?*, *Are you busy at the moment?* and elicit some answers. Tell sts to work alone and choose four or five questions from unit 3 to ask a partner. They shouldn't write them down, just mark them in the book. Sts ask and answer the questions. Monitor closely for accuracy and afterwards ask each st to tell you one interesting answer they got from their partner.

No time for losers, 'cause we are the champions of the world.

1 Vocabulary Sports

A ▶4.1 Match the sports with photos 1–7. Try to pronounce them. Then listen to part of a sports show to check. Find two reasons why they are in two groups.

- [1] **ba**sketball ✓
- [ ] **vo**lleyball
- [ ] **te**nnis
- [ ] **so**ccer
- [ ] **cy**cling (bike riding)
- [ ] **swi**mming
- [ ] **ru**nning

Maybe it's because the first four we play …

B Listen to and repeat what your teacher says only if it's true for you. In groups, do the same.

Teacher: I like tennis.   *Some students: I like tennis.*

C ▶4.2 Listen to more of the sports show and check (✓) in **A** the five sports Mac mentions. Can you remember the six countries, too?

D ▶4.2 Listen again and match the times to the places.

1 9:00 [ ] the Igloo
2 9:30 [ ] North Park
3 10:00 [ ] the O**lym**pic A**re**na
4 10:30 [ ] the Olympic Sta**di**um
5 11:00 [ ] the Central Courts

E ▶4.2 Say the places in **D**. What's the difference in the pronunciation of *the*? Complete the rules with *th*/ə/ ("the") or *th*/iː/ ("thee"). Listen to check.
1 Before a vowel sound, pronounce *the* _____.
2 Before a consonant sound, pronounce *the* _____.

F ▶4.3 Listen and repeat the noun with th/ə/ or th/iː/ before you hear the beep.
Airport: *The airport.*

G ▶4.4 Listen to four interviews and order the sports you hear, 1–6. Which sports don't you hear?

- [ ] **base**ball
- [ ] **foot**ball
- [ ] golf
- [ ] **ho**ckey
- [ ] **rug**by
- [ ] **skate**boarding
- [ ] **ski**ing
- [ ] soccer
- [ ] **surf**ing
- [ ] **ta**ble tennis

H 🔴 **Make it personal** Answer in pairs. Which sports in this lesson …
1 need a ball?
2 need a net?
3 can you practice in the ocean?
4 are your favorite to watch / practice?
5 are your country usually good at in the Olympics?
6 are the most and the least dangerous?

Our country is usually good at …   *For me, the most dangerous is …*

In my opinion, the least dangerous sport is …

Common mistakes
I love ~~the~~ games.
I don't like ~~the~~ fruit.
I hate ~~the~~ soccer.
Don't use *the* with plural nouns or uncountable nouns or to talk about things in general.

4.1

🎵 **Song line:** Turn to p. 327 for notes about this song and an accompanying task.

1 Vocabulary Sports

Focus on the photos on p. 44 and ask: *Do you like sports? Do you watch sports on TV? Do you play sports? Do you like / watch the Olympic Games?*

A Sts match two groups of sports with photos 1–7. In pairs, they check their answers and try to pronounce the name of each sport. Play ▶ 4.1 so sts can notice if their pronunciation was correct. Classcheck.

> 🗝 2 soccer 3 tennis 4 volleyball 5 cycling (bike riding)
> 6 running 7 swimming

▶ **4.1** Turn to p. 313 for the complete audioscript.

⚠ **Common mistakes** Encourage sts to make comparisons between the use of the definite article in their mother tongue and in English. Highlight the fact that there is only one form of *the* in English (you could ask them how many forms of *the* exist in their L1 to compare). Read the rule in the box.

Note: Countable vs. Uncountable nouns is not taught until unit 6. You could explain briefly that some nouns cannot be counted, e.g. *water, homework*, and explain they will cover this in unit 6.

B A nice way of integrating cognitive thinking into behaviorist drills is by drilling any *I like* sentences inside sts' vocabulary range. Sts only repeat if the sentence is true for them. Suggestions: *I like swimming / basketball / cycling / volleyball / sandwiches / big cities / Mondays / English / my teacher*, etc.

> **Tip** As with any teacher-led drill, give a clear, strong signal, like a conductor's signal, or a sweep of the hands, after you have said a sentence so sts repeat it together.

C Sts listen to more of the same sports show ▶ 4.2 and check the sports they hear the TV presenter Mac say in **A**. Paircheck. Classcheck. Ask: *How does Mac feel? Can you remember the six countries?* and move on to **D**.

> 🗝 basketball, volleyball, tennis, soccer, cycling
> Cuba, Russia, Uruguay, Italy, the U.S., Australia

▶ **4.2** Turn to p. 313 for the complete audioscript.

D Sts listen again and write the correct number in the boxes as they listen. Paircheck and classcheck. If sts ask why *North Park* doesn't have *the*, you can explain the rule that we do not use *the* with streets, parks, cities, states, counties, most countries, continents, bays, single lakes, single mountains, and islands.

> 🗝 1 the Olympic Arena 2 the Central Courts
> 3 the Olympic Stadium 4 the Igloo 5 North Park

E Sts read the instructions. Help them with the phonemic symbols, perhaps referring to the Sounds and Usual Spellings chart on p. 158 to remind them of the picture words for /ə/ and /ɪ/. Drill the pronunciation of *the* in different phrases (*the Igloo / the Central Courts*, etc.). Sts listen again and match times and places. Paircheck. Classcheck with answers on the board.

> **Stronger classes** Instead of beginning with the box, focus on the AS on p. 162. Write *the* on the board and tell sts it can be pronounced in two different ways, /ə/ or /iː/. Drill both forms.

> 🗝 1 th/iː/ 2 th/ə/

F Play ▶ 4.3. Refer to the speech bubble example. Pause after each *the* phrase and elicit the pronunciation used in each case.

> **Tip** Write on the board some famous examples they will have seen many times but may have mispronounced, e.g. *the Americans, the end, the Incas, the iPhone, the Olympic Games, the subway*, etc., so they can enjoy saying them correctly now.

G Play ▶ 4.4 Sts listen to four short interviews for a street survey and number the sports in the order they hear them. Paircheck. Classcheck.

> 🗝 1 skiing 2 golf 3 soccer 4 skateboarding
> 5 baseball 6 surfing
> You don't hear: football, hockey, rugby, table tennis

▶ **4.4** Turn to p. 313 for the complete audioscript.

> **Tip** Notice the difference between UK English and U.S. English. Play ▶ 4.4 again and ask them to raise their hands when they hear a British person speak. Is there anything else they notice about British pronunciation, apart from the words *football / soccer*?

H ⬤ **Make it personal** In pairs, sts answer the questions about sports. Use photos to teach *net*. Direct them to the speech bubbles for help. Monitor and make a note of good language use and any pronunciation errors and go over this when sts have finished.

➔ **Workbook** p. 19

4.2 Can you drive a tractor?

1 Grammar Can: Yes / No

A ▶ 4.5 It's Mark's first day at the gym. Listen and complete the form.

Name: Mark
Age:

Activities
can
can, but not very well
can't (at all)

B ▶ 4.5 Listen again and complete the grammar box. Notice the weak pronunciation of *can* in the questions.

Yes / No ? with can	Short answers
1 _____ you run two kilometers?	No, I _____.
2 _____ you swim?	Yes, I _____.

➡ Grammar 4B p.144

> **Common mistakes**
> Can you play soccer well?
> ~~You can play well the soccer?~~

C Ask two friends the same questions and complete this form with ✗ or ✓. Now ask about four other sports. How many *Yes* answers can you get?

Name	Activities				

D ⬤ **Make it personal** Match the verbs to the noun groups. Ask your classmates about these abilities using *Can …?* Find someone who can do each one well.

play	drive	sing
speak	cook	

> Can you cook Chinese food?
>
> No, I can't. Not at all! Can you?
> Yes, I think so. But not very well.

the piano	English	in harmony	a tractor	Chinese food
the guitar	French	karaoke well	a truck	Mexican food
the saxophone	Chinese	a song in a		French food
the drums	German	third language		Japanese food
the violin				

4.2 Can you drive a tractor?

Lesson Aims: Asking and answering questions using *can*. Sts listen to a speech and discuss how to change the world.

Function
Listening / Reading / Talking about abilities.
Listening to a talk and giving opinions.

Language
Can you run two kilometers?
Can you swim?

Vocabulary: Various abilities (play a musical instrument, drive, cook well, sing, bargain, dress appropriately, understand directions, etc.).

Grammar: *Can* questions / short answers.

Warm-up Sts play a spelling guessing game in groups of three with the sports they learned in the previous lesson. St A spells out a sport, e.g. T-E-N-N-I-S, and the first to guess the sport before st A finishes spelling the complete word scores one point. St B now spells out a different sport from p. 45, and sts A and C compete to guess it. Sts change roles. Round off the activity by asking one group to challenge the others.

1 Grammar *Can: Yes / No*

A Focus on the lesson title and the photo of the tractor. Ask: *Can you drive a tractor?* and see how many people raise their hands. Tell sts that today's lesson is about abilities, what they can and can't do. Point to Mark's photo and ask: *What's his name?* (Mark) *How old is he?* (sts guess) Tell sts it is Mark's first day at the gym. Ask: *What's the name of the gym?* (Jimbo's) Elicit the activities / sports in the pictures. Ask: *Do you think Mark can run? Can he swim?* Highlight the three options. Sts listen to ▶ 4.5 and check the correct options. Paircheck. Classcheck.

> can: ride a bike
> can, but not very well: swim
> can't (at all): play tennis, run

▶ 4.5 Turn to p. 313 for the complete audioscript.

B Sts focus on the grammar box and complete with the correct words. Play ▶ 4.5 so sts can listen and check.

Common mistakes Draw sts' attention to the fact that the bare infinitive (without *to*) must be used after *can*. Drill some questions, e.g. *Can you dance / cook / swim / play volleyball / speak English / Chinese well?* Remind them that they usually make this kind of mistake when trying to translate directly from L1.

➡ **Grammar 4B** p.144

> 1 Can, can't   2 Can, can

Tip The formation of the infinitive with the particle *to* doesn't occur in Romance languages. Once sts learn this, they tend to overuse *to* in all situations where they would use the infinitive of a verb. Explain that, when the modal *can* comes with a verb in the infinitive, this verb <u>does not</u> take the particle *to*, as opposed to what happened with *need*. Write on the board *I **need to work** on Sundays / I **can work** on Sundays* and have sts practice with other examples.

C Write *Play* on the board and elicit sports which go with it, (e.g., basketball / volleyball / soccer, etc.). In pairs, sts ask each other *Can you +* sports questions. If you sense sts are tired of sports, replace with other activities.

Tip Try to avoid the *play / go / do* distinction at this stage, unless your class want to talk about activities they need *do* for (gymnastics, karate, yoga, etc.). Put the third column in the board and explain the difference:

play + ball sports / competitive games against another person / musical instruments

go + *-ing* adjectives (fishing, motor racing)

do + recreational activities / non-team sports without a ball (ballet, puzzles)

D **Make it personal** Refer to the box and elicit *Can you + activity?* question from sts for the first column. Encourage sts to add more examples as an extension to this activity e.g *Italian food, fly a plane*, etc. Sts read the speech bubbles. Focus on *not at all* and teach *I think so*. Sts then complete the rest of the chart and any additional examples. Classcheck. Highlight *the* before musical instruments and review other article rules from previous lesson. Demonstrate the task by asking different sts *Can you ..?* until one says *yes*. Tell sts to walk around and do the same.

> play, speak, sing, drive, cook

Tip This can become much more fun if sts start to mime activities which they can't yet express in English, like whistle, touch their nose with their tongue, stand on their head, bend their arms / fingers to funny angles, etc.

2 Listening

🎵 *Heal the world, Make it a better place, For you and for me, And the entire human race.*

A What do you know about Malala Yousafzai? In pairs, say what you know about her, or make guesses. Read the article to check.

Malala Yousafzai is probably the world's most famous Pakistani. Her 2009 blog about life under the Taliban for the BBC, and her activism made her many enemies. She was shot in the head when she was only 15 years old. But she survived, and in 2012 won the Nobel Peace Prize. She lives in the UK now and campaigns for education for girls across the world.

B ▶ 4.6 Watch / Listen and order the words as you hear them, 1–8. Which items are in the photos?

☐ book
☐ child
☐ education
☐ pen
☐ powerful
☐ solution
☐ teacher
☐ weapons

C ▶ 4.6 Watch / Listen again and write Malala's speech. In pairs, compare. Check your answer in AS 4.6 on p. 162.

D ▶ 4.7 58% of English comes from Latin, so you can guess many English words, like words with the suffixes -tion and -sion. Do you recognize the words below? Read the pronunciation rule. Then try to pronounce the words correctly. Listen to check.

> With suffixes -tion and -sion, always stress the syllable before the suffix.

action	corruption	motivation
combination	expression	opinion
conversation	information	organization
cooperation	isolation	question

E 🔴 **Make it personal** Which of the items in the photos in B can best change the world? In pairs, order them 1 to 4 from the most to the least powerful. Then compare with another pair. Do you agree?

Number 1?   *We think it's a teacher.*

We believe a book can be more powerful.   *For us, that's number 2.*

4.2

🎵 **Song line:** Turn to p. 327 for notes about this song and an accompanying task.

2 Listening

> **Cultural note** Malala Yousafzai is a Pakistani activist for female education. She's the youngest winner of the Nobel Peace Prize. She was born in 1997. According to *Time* magazine, she's one of the world's most influential people.

A Sts focus on the photo of Malala. Show phonetics or drill to help with pronunciation of her name (/məlalɑ/). Ask sts to say what they know about her. Sts read the text and check their ideas.

> **Tip** If sts have access to a mobile device and Internet connection, ask them to look up information about Malala and share their results in small groups. Ask the groups: *What are some of the most interesting things you know about Malala?*

Extra activity To continue article focus, prepare a gap fill or write the text about Malala on board, omitting *the*. Sts close books. Complete the first gap together as a model. Sts complete the text with *the*. Paircheck. Classcheck.

B Sts focus on the photos and think about how they might relate to Malala and helping the world. Ask sts to discuss their ideas in pairs before you ask the class for ideas. As they share ideas, write useful language on the board. Drill *education, powerful, solution, weapons*. Tell sts they're going to watch / listen to Malala speaking before the United Nations in July 2013. Play ▶ 4.6 and tell sts to order the items by writing numbers in the boxes. Ask: *Was this easy? Difficult? Were there any surprises?*

> 🔑
> 1 book 2 pen 3 powerful 4 weapons 5 child
> 6 teacher 7 education 8 solution

▶ 4.6 Turn to p. 314 for the complete audioscript.

C Play ▶ 4.6 again and have sts write the speech. Watch the whole thing and tell sts to write the words they hear as they watch. Watch again and pause every few words. Then, tell sts to compare their notes with a partner. Sts turn to AS on p. 162 to correct their speech texts. Sts could practice reading her speech out loud, and listen for connected words.

> **Tip** This is a good opportunity to discuss accents. You could explain that non-native English speakers outnumber native speakers 4 to 1, and that approximately 90% of English teachers are non-native speakers of English. Therefore, having an accent is inevitable, and almost all of our accents are different.

D Write *education* on the board and check pronunciation. Ask: *Is this word similar in your language?* Refer sts to the text in the box and ask them to read it. Sts work in pairs and try pronouncing the words. Play ▶ 4.7. Sts listen and check. Use the audio as a drill, getting sts to repeat the examples in pairs three times together for fun. Try to elicit a few more, e.g. *preposition, pronunciation, reservation, nation, description*.

> **Tip** Tell sts to underline the stressed syllables to help them pronounce the words correctly. Sts listen to ▶ 4.7 again to check their pronunciation.

E 🎤 **Make it personal** Ask: *Which objects are most important to change the world? Why?* Elicit some ideas. Tell sts to think about this for one minute individually. Tell them to put the photos from **B** in order, from most to least powerful. Direct sts to the speech bubbles. Then, sts work in small groups and share ideas and opinions. Monitor and help with ideas and language. Ask some sts to share what they spoke about with the class.

Extra writing Sts research Malala and write a short biography about her describing her causes and what she does to try and change the world.

➔ **Workbook** p. 20

4.3 What languages can you speak?

1 Grammar Can: ➕ ➖ and Wh- ❓

A ▶ 4.8 Listen to the interviews. Complete sentences 1–6 with *can* or *can't*. Listen again to check.
1 I _____ dance very well, but my wife _____. She's a very good dancer.
2 My father _____ cook really well. His food is delicious.
3 My best friend _____ play baseball or volleyball. He doesn't like team sports.
4 I _____ skate, but I _____ ski at all. Skiing is too difficult!
5 My friends _____ play soccer very well. They play every weekend.
6 _____ you do any martial arts? Yes, I _____. What _____ you do? Tae Kwondo.

B Complete the grammar box.

> 1 We use *can* to talk about ability. Study the examples in **A** and circle the correct option.
>   a *Can* goes **before / after** the main verb in a sentence.
>   b *Can* **changes / doesn't change** form in the 3rd person.
> 2 Complete rules c and d with the words.
>
> | can | Wh- question word | person | verb |
>
>   c To form a *Yes / No* question with *can* use: _____ + _____ + _____.
>   d To form a *Wh-* question with *can* use: _____ + _____ + _____ + _____.
>
>   ➡ Grammar 4B p.144

C ▶ 4.8 Listen again and notice the pronunciation of *can* and *can't*. In pairs, practice pronouncing the sentences in **A** correctly.

D 🟢 Make it personal Write three true and three false sentences about you and people you know and their abilities. In pairs, decide which are true and which are false.

> *Anna can play the guitar well.*   *I think that's false. Anna can't play the guitar at all!*

E 🟢 Make it personal *Can* is also used for requests. Read and choose the three most useful phrases for 1) everyday life and 2) English classes. Compare with a partner. Any similarities?

Can you help me?   Can I say it in (my language)?
Can you **trans**late this?   Can I open the window?
Can you **loud**er?   Can I park here?
Can you spell it, please?   Can I have a little more (coffee)?
Can you close the door?   Can I go home now?
Can I go to the bathroom?

48

4.3 What languages can you speak?

Lesson Aims: Sts talk about general abilities and key abilities for being successful at work and listen to a job interview. Sts interview each other about their abilities to practice *can* in + – and questions.

Function
Describe people's general abilities.
Ask and answer questions about abilities related to work.

Language
I can dance but my wife can't.
Can you speak Portuguese?
No, I can't.
Can you use simple tools?
What can you play?

Skills: Read about keys to success. Listen to a job interview.
Vocabulary: Abilities for work (use simple tools, dress appropriately).
Grammar: *Can*: + – and *Wh-* questions.

1 Grammar *Can*: ➕ ➖ and *Wh-* ❓

Warm-up Books closed. Ask sts to write two sentences with *can / can't* about two classmates, based on what they remember, e.g. *Julia can't drive a tractor. / Victor can play the piano.* Sts take turns reading their sentences aloud, and the st mentioned comments as to whether the information about him / her is true or false.

A Books open. Sts fill in the blanks in 1–6 with *can* or *can't*. Elicit the possible answers for 1. Sts do 2–6 on their own. Paircheck. Play ▶ 4.8 so sts can check their answers. Highlight that *can / can't* is the same for all persons. Have sts guess context for each exchange before teaching the grammar. Ask: *Have you had any similar exchanges recently?*

> 1 can't, can   2 can   3 can't   4 can, can't   5 can
> 6 Can, can, can

▶ 4.8 Turn to p. 314 for the complete audioscript.

B Sts complete the grammar box. Ask them to do this individually, then pair check and classcheck. Ask: *How similar / different is **can** in your language?*

> 1a before   b doesn't change
> 2c can, person, verb   d Wh- question word, can, person, verb

➡ **Grammar 4B** p. 144

C Play ▶ 4.8 again and ask sts to notice the pronunciation of *can* and *can't*. Give examples of full form and weak forms of *can*. Explain we use the full form *can* /kæn/ for short answers and for emphasis, but we pronounce *can* /kən/ (weak form) when it's unstressed (before a verb or as a question). Always pronounce the negative form *can't* /kænt/. Sts listen and repeat the sentences in **A** then circle the weak forms of *can*. Listen again to check.

D 🔵 **Make it personal** Tell sts the goal of this task is to guess when their partner is lying. Sts write their sentences. Monitor and check for accuracy. Then, look at the speech bubbles and do the same. Tell sts to focus on their pronunciation as they speak. After they finish, ask some pairs if they guessed the lies correctly.

> **Tip** Listen for sts using *to* after *can* and before the main verb. This is a typical error when using modal verbs.

E 🔵 **Make it personal** Ask sts to read the sentences and label the three most useful for 1 and 2. Elicit / add in any other useful ones for classroom use: *Can you say that again, please? Can I help you? Can I use your Internet connection? I can't find my pen. I can't see the board.* etc. Tell sts to practice saying the phrases to each other to sound polite. Give feedback on their pronunciation of the weak and full forms of can and how polite they sound.

🎵 *Filled with all the strength I found, There's nothing I can't do! I need to know now, Can you love me again?*

② Reading

A ▶ 4.9 Listen, read, and match photos a–f to six of the abilities.

Ten Keys to 21st Century Success

To fly high in the modern world, certain abilities are essential. Here are our top 10 in no particular order:

1 to Google efficiently
2 to understand directions quickly
3 to cook the basics
4 to remember names
5 to use simple tools
6 to speak two common languages
7 to dress appropriately
8 to bargain well
9 to make friends easily
10 to make a good first impression

B Many adverbs are formed adjective + -ly, e.g., *probably, finally, especially, certainly, exactly*. Underline four examples in **A**. Can you find an irregular one, too?

C Use these symbols to mark the list in **A** according to your ability. Then interview a partner about their abilities. What can they do well?

XX = I can't at all.   **X** = I can't very well.   ✓ = I can.   ✓✓ = I can very well.

Can you use simple tools?   *No, I can't! I always ask my mom to help me.*

⚠ **Common mistakes**

I can type ~~quick~~. *quickly*
I can't cook ~~good~~. *well*

D 🔴 **Make it personal**   Choose the five most important abilities for you.

I'm at school and I don't have a job, so my most important are …

③ Listening

A ▶ 4.10 Listen to a job interview. Circle the job that Maddie wants.
a babysitter   a journalist   a secretary   a teacher

B ▶ 4.10 Listen again and complete with *can* or *can't*.
1 Maddie _____ speak Spanish very well.
2 She _____ play volleyball and tennis but not very well.
3 She _____ text fast.

C 🔴 **Make it personal**   In pairs, think of a job. Write a list of questions to ask about abilities for that job. You can use AS 4.10 on p. 163 to help you. Now interview another pair. Do you give them the job?

Can you speak Portuguese fluently?   *No, I can't.*   *Sorry. We're looking for a Portuguese teacher!*

4.3

🎵 **Song line:** Turn to p. 328 for notes about this song and an accompanying task.

2 Reading

A Ask: *Is it important to speak English these days? What about Spanish? If you're looking for a job, is it important to know how to use different technology?* Play ▶ 4.9. Sts match the photos and the abilities. Paircheck. Classcheck. Drill pronunciation as necessary, either modeling it yourself or having sts repeat after the audio. Ask: *Do you agree that these abilities are important? Was there any information that surprised you? Did you learn anything new?*

> **Language tip** Comparing and contrasting common suffixes in English to those in sts' L1 can help them understand the meaning of cognates. They may even experiment by using translanguaging techniques and creating words. Use the text in **A** to give sts examples of two common suffixes: *efficiently* (-ly = *mente*, transforming adjective to adverb); *direction* (-ion = -ión / -ão, transforming verb to noun). Ask sts to come up with more examples. *Note:* not all cognates ending with the suffix *ión* / *-ão* will have an *-ion* equivalent in English.

> **Tip** There are ten abilities, but only six photos to illustrate them because the others are either known or easily recognizable as cognates.

🔑 a 10   b 5   c 7   d 3   e 2   f 1

B Write *easy* on the board and elicit the part of speech (adjective). Ask sts to change it to an adverb (*easily*) and to make a sentence (e.g. *I learn new things easily.*). Sts read the instructions and find adverbs in the text. Classcheck. For position of adverbs, the rule is: *Adverbs of manner cannot be put between a verb and its direct object. They must be placed either before the verb or at the end of the clause.*

Note: The adverbs in this activity are very similar in Spanish and Portuguese.

🔑 efficiently, quickly, appropriately, easily
irregular: well

C Focus on the symbols and drill the four answers. Sts focus on abilities in **A** and use the four symbols to express what they can do, what they can do very well, not very well or can't at all.

In pairs, sts interview each other with *Can you* + ability? questions from the article. Drill some example questions with the abilities in **A** and other examples before sts perform the activity, e.g. *Can you understand directions quickly? Not very well, no. I'm useless with maps.* Their aim is to find out their partner's top five from the list (that he or she can do). Classcheck with reported answers.

D 👤 **Make it personal** Ask sts to circle the five most important abilities in **A** according to their opinion or profession and try to explain why. Use the example to set this up. Ask sts to report their top five abilities to the whole class. Encourage them to justify their choices.

> **Tip** Write all ten answers on the board and check them off each time they get a vote to work out easily and visually which are the class top five.

> **Stronger classes** Ask learners if there's anything else they consider important.

3 Listening

A Elicit some *Can you* + ability? questions from the text, that are likely to be asked in a job interview. Tell sts to write down these questions to use in **C**. Say: *Listen to a job interview and circle the job Maddie wants.* Play ▶ 4.10. Paircheck. Classcheck and ask: *What questions do you remember from the listening? What does he think of Maddie?*

🔑 a babysitter

▶ 4.10 Turn to p. 314 for the complete audioscript.

> **Tip** Ask sts to rate their listening comprehension from 0 to 4. Ask: *How much of the audio could you understand? 50%? 80%?* This is a useful activity to get quick feedback after listening. It also helps train sts to judge their own individual performance.

B Sts listen to ▶ 4.10 again for *can* or *can't*. Paircheck. Classcheck. Ask sts to rate their listening comprehension again. Ask: *Can you understand more when you listen again / for the 2nd time?* Ask: *Do you think Maddie gets the job? Do you think she wants it after that interview?*

🔑 1 can't   2 can   3 can

C 👤 **Make it personal** Write a job on the board, e.g. *teacher*, and ask sts for abilities you need for this job. Elicit questions to ask in a job interview using *can* for this job.

> **Weaker students** Write the questions on the board.

Refer sts to the AS on p. 163 for ideas. Sts then think of a different job and write questions to ask about abilities for that job. Direct sts to the speech bubbles and tell them to use their notes to role-play a job interview. Ask: *Who got the job?*

Extra writing Sts can write their answers to **C** in the form of sentences, or even a short paragraph, about their own abilities.

➡ **Workbook** p. 21

4.4 Are you an organized person?

1 Vocabulary Clothes

A ▶4.11 Listen to the fashion show. Who's JKK? Do you like the designs?

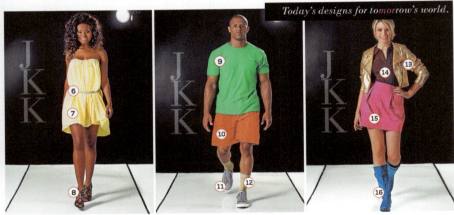

Today's designs for tomorrow's world.

B ▶4.11 Match 1–16 to the clothes items.

- ☐ a silver belt
- ☐ a brown blouse
- ☐ blue boots
- ☐ a gold jacket
- ☐ a yellow dress
- ☐ black sandals
- ☐ a purple shirt
- ☐ orange shorts
- ☐ a pink skirt
- ☐ beige socks
- ☐ a blue suit jacket
- ☐ blue shoes
- ☐ a green T-shirt
- ☐ a white tie
- ☐ gray sneakers
- ☐ blue suit pants

C Cover the words in B. In pairs, describe the four models.

D 🔴 **Make it personal** Look at what your classmates are wearing for a minute. In pairs, take turns describing without looking and guessing. Now do the same with photos of people on your phone.

> She's wearing a red sweater.   Is it Carmen?

⏰ Common mistakes

She always wears a green shirt and ~~a~~ gray pants to school.
~~wearing~~
He's ~~using~~ a suit.
~~pairs of~~
She has two ~~jeans~~.

> I have about twenty pairs of jeans.

> Twenty? I only have three pairs.

2 Reading

A Do you have a lot of clothes? Describe your closet to your partner.

B Answer the title question from the forum. Then read the three posts and match them to pictures 1–3.

Victoria: _____   Kyle: _____   Tanya: _____

Can organized and messy people live together?

It's not impossible, but it's difficult. At home, it's only me and my husband. My clothes and shoes are always organized, but his are not! Sometimes I get angry because he is messy and I'm neat, but usually it's OK. **Posted by Victoria**

I confess: I don't like to share – it's too difficult! So my wife and I have separate closets. I have more things than she does, so my closet is enormous and hers is not. We are both clean and organized, but the problem is our kids! We clean our room, but we never look in theirs! Their rooms are messy and full of dirty sports equipment – balls, rackets, skis, etc. Horrible! It's hard for people who are very different to live together, but if you're family you can do it! **Posted by Kyle**

In my house, we don't say "mine" or "yours". Everything is ours. Our house is small, and a little disorganized, but we like it like that. We share space and clothes. We occasionally have a conversation like this: "Whose sweater is this?" "It's yours!" "No, it's yours!" That's a big advantage of living with your twin sister! We are very similar. I can't live with people who are different from me. **Posted by Tanya**

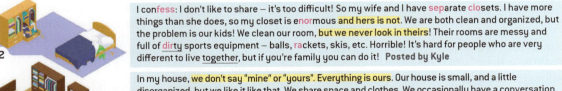

50

4.4 Are you an organized person?

Lesson Aims: Sts describe what people are wearing. Sts use possessive pronouns to talk about living with messy and tidy people.

Function
Listening to a fashion show.
Describing what people are wearing.
Read a forum.

Language
She's wearing black boots.
He's wearing a purple shirt.
This is my / your / her T-shirt.

Vocabulary: Clothes (What's *he/she* wearing)
Grammar: Use simple present and continuous. Learn possessive pronouns (my, her, his, etc.)

1 Vocabulary Clothes

A Focus on the four models and elicit the meaning of *fashion show*. Ask: *Are you interested in fashion?* Play ▶ 4.11 for sts to listen and answer the questions. Classcheck.

> Jacobelli   Klein   Karan

▶ 4.11 Turn to p. 314 for the complete audioscript.

B Point to the options and ask sts to match one item to a photo. The colors should guide them. In pairs, sts match numbers 1–16 from **A** to the items. Classcheck with answers on the board.

Drill the pronunciation of some phrases and encourage sts to notice that some pairs of *color + clothing item* have the same (S) vowel sound, e.g. a white tie (/aɪ/), blue boots (/uː/); and in some pairs the vowel sounds are not the same (NS), as in a silver belt (/ə/ and /e/).

Play ▶ 4.11 again so sts can pay attention to the pronunciation. In pairs, sts decide if the vowel sounds have the same (S) sound or not the same (NS) sound. Classcheck.

> 1 a purple shirt   2 a blue suit jacket   3 a white tie
> 4 blue suit pants   5 blue shoes   6 a silver belt
> 7 a yellow dress   8 black sandals   9 a green T-shirt
> 10 orange shorts   11 gray sneakers   12 beige socks
> 13 a gold jacket   14 a brown blouse   15 a pink skirt
> 16 blue boots

Tip Highlight the examples of alliteration, remembering words with the same (vowel) sound. Both are great ways to help sts learn two things for the price of one. To work on any individual sounds they found hard, and want more examples of, turn to the Sounds and Usual Spellings chart on p. 158.

C Ask: *What's Justin wearing?* on the board and point to Justin in **A**. Prompt *He's wearing ...* . In pairs sts describe the other models. Classcheck.

Common mistakes Read and elicit the explanation of mistakes from sts. Also highlight that we use the verb *wear* for all clothes and accessories (e.g. *we wear shorts*, and that we say *a pair of glasses*, etc.)

D Make it personal Ask: *What's (student's name) wearing?* (He's wearing ... .) Give sts 60 seconds to observe each other and memorize what their classmates are wearing. Sts take turns describing a classmate for other sts to guess who he / she is talking about.

Tip Ask one st to leave the classroom. Describe his / her clothes making errors in the colors. Sts correct you.

Extra activity Ask sts if they have photos on their cell phones. Sts select one or two photos and describe what the people in them are wearing. Classcheck by asking some sts to present and describe their photos to the whole class. Alternatively, if sts don't have any photos available, ask them to open the book to a random page and describe the clothes worn by someone on the page. Their partner then has to figure out who they are describing.

2 Reading

A Ask sts the question. Sts describe their closet in pairs.

B Focus on the title and ask: *Can organized and messy people live together?* Clarify the meaning and set a time limit for sts to read the forum and answer the question. Classcheck. Ask sts to read the text and notice the pronunciation of the words with pink letters. In pairs, sts try to repeat the pronunciation correctly. Sts match the posts to pictures 1–3.

> Victoria: 2   Kyle: 3   Tanya: 1

🎵 *Oh, oh, oh, Sweet child o' mine,*
Sweet love o' mine.

C **Complete the sentences with the names from the forum and *her* or *his*.**
1 _____ lives with _____ sister.
2 _____ lives with _____ husband.
3 _____ lives with _____ wife and children.
4 _____ is different from _____ children.
5 _____ can share easily.
6 _____ can't share at all.

D ▶ 4.12 **Match the four underlined words in B with their opposites below. In pairs, try to pronounce all the words in B with pink syllables. Listen to check. Any surprises?**

calm   clean   disad**van**tage   **sep**arately

E 🔵 **Make it personal** Who are you more similar to: Victoria, Kyle, or Tanya? Find one person in the class who is like you and one person who is different.

> *I share a room with my sister, but I'm organized and she isn't. I think I'm similar to Victoria.*

③ Grammar   Possessive pronouns

A ▶ 4.13 **Look at the highlighted phrases in 2B. Complete the grammar chart. Listen to check. Then answer questions 1–3.**

	Possessive adjectives	Possessive pronouns
This is	my closet	mine
	your closet	
	her	
	his	
	our	
	their	

1 How many possessive pronouns end in *s*?
2 Is the final *s* pronounced /s/ or /z/?
3 Read the rules and complete the dialogue with *hers*, *mine*, or *whose*.
   Use *Whose?* to ask about possession.
   Use a possessive pronoun to replace a possessive adjective + noun.
   A: _____ phone is that?
   B: I think it's _____. (not "her phone")
   C: No, it isn't. It's _____. (not "my phone")
4 Rewrite the dialogue above using *phones* instead of *phone*.

→ Grammar 4C p.144

🔴 **Common mistakes**
These glasses are ~~the~~ mines.
Whose pen is this?
~~Of who is~~ this pen?

It's ~~of~~ Maria. ('s)

B **In groups, take turns describing one item of clothing in the classroom to the rest of the group. Then point and say whose it is.**

> *It's a green and white T-shirt. Whose is it?*   *It's hers!*   *No!*   *It's his!*   *Yes.*

C 🔵 **Make it personal** Write your own post for the forum. Use the prompts to help you. Compare in pairs. How are you similar and how are you different?
I live with …
My room is …
I (don't) share my room …
I am (an organized / a messy …) person.
I (can / can't share) things (easily).
I think people who are different (can / can't) live together.

> *I share a room with my brother. We have a lot of things, and our room is very messy!*

C Do 1 with the class. Sts complete the sentences. Classcheck.

> 1 Tanya, her   2 Victoria, her   3 Kyle, his   4 Kyle, his
> 5 Tanya   6 Kyle

D Direct sts to the text in **B** and the underlined words. Ask sts to match one of the words with a word from the box. Sts complete the other four examples. Classcheck. Play ▶ 4.12 to check answers.

> angry: calm   dirty: clean   together: separately
> advantage: disadvantage

E **Make it personal** Ask a more confident st the question and encourage them to expand on their answer. Refer sts to the speech bubbles and tell them to ask and answer in pairs. If there is time, ask questions to encourage further discussion of the reading text and reflection. E.g. *Do you post in any forums online? Did you find this helpful? Did you learn any new vocabulary? Do you have any questions about the reading?*

🎵 **Song line**: Turn to p. 328 for notes about this song and an accompanying task.

3 Grammar Possessive pronouns

A Focus on the yellow highlighted sentences in **2B** and encourage sts to guess what they refer to, e.g. *his are not* = his clothes are not organized, *hers is not* = her closet is not enormous, etc. In pairs, sts complete the grammar box. Play ▶ 4.13 to check answers. Ask 1 and 2 to the whole class.

> Chart: yours, hers, his, ours, theirs
> 1 five
> 2 /z/
> 3 A Whose   B hers   C mine
> 4 A: Whose phones are those?
>   B: I think they're hers.
>   C: No, they aren't. They're mine.

➡ **Grammar 4C** p. 144

⚠ **Common mistakes** Read and elicit the correction of mistakes from sts. Highlight the use of 's for possession and follow up with more examples.

B Demonstrate the task. Refer sts to the speech bubbles. Do a similar example by describing an item of clothing one of the sts is wearing. Sts then work in groups of four and do the same. Monitor and correct errors in grammar and pronunciation. Ask: *Is this grammar similar in your language? How is it similar / different?*

C **Make it personal** Sts make true sentences about themselves and write a short forum post. Then compare in pairs. Ask some sts to report back anything interesting they learned about each other. Use their examples to write a few example sentences on the board, to help remaining sts with reporting back on what they learned about their partner, e.g. *We're both a bit messy, especially with our dirty clothes.*

➡ **Workbook** p. 22

4.5 Do you like spas?

Skills Reading for details

A Quickly look at the text and answer the questions.
1 Where do you think it's from? ☐ the Internet ☐ a book ☐ a magazine
2 What is it? ☐ a poster ☐ an ad ☐ a blog

{ALL YOURS}

Do you like healthy food and healthy living?

All Yours is the perfect place for you. There, in the same ultra-modern center, you can find:

† **Super Salon** with unisex hair stylists, manicurists, and pedicurists available from 8 a.m. to 10 p.m., seven days a week.

† **Natural Foods** restaurant that serves high-quality, healthy foods, specially prepared by our expert chefs and nutritionists. Open from 7 a.m. to midnight daily.

† **World Boutique** with unique fashion designs from around the world for everybody, young or old.

† **Marvelous Me** massage suite. Our fantastic therapists can eliminate all your stress.

† **Giant Gym**. A great place to stay in shape and keep your heart and muscles healthy.

B Read the text. True (T) or False (F)?
1 All Yours is a shopping mall.
2 The hair stylists work on Sundays.
3 It's possible to eat, buy clothes, de-stress, and exercise there.
4 It's for women and men.
5 Five different professions are mentioned.

C Find the words in the text that mean:
1 the opposite of different =   3 take away =
2 in good health =   4 continue to be =

Yes, the suffix -ist isn't stressed in English.

D ▶ 4.14 In pairs, pronounce the words with pink syllables. Listen to check. Any surprises?

E 🔴 **Make it personal** In pairs, plan the perfect day at All Yours. Tell another pair about your day. Who has the best day?

We arrive at 7 a.m. and go for breakfast at Natural Foods.   *We go to the gym first at 7 a.m.*

4.5 Do you like spas?

Lesson Aims: Sts practice reading an ad for details. They plan a perfect day at a spa to review talking about daily activities and the time.

Function
Reading a magazine ad.
Guessing the meaning and pronunciation of new words.
Talking about your favorite area in a spa.
Plan a perfect day at the spa.

Language
All yours! ... is the perfect place for you. ... serves low-calorie food.
I love to go to salons.
We arrive at 7 a.m.
Yours in the best day.

Pronunciation: Word stress in stylist, manicurist, restaurant, etc.
Grammar: Use simple present.
Skills: Reading for details.

Warm-up Go around the class picking up different items (pens, books, etc.), singular and plural. Ask: *Whose is this? Whose are these? Is this mine? Are these yours / hers / etc.?*, pointing to different sts to elicit positive and negative responses. If time allows, sts can do the same in groups, putting their possessions on a table and asking / answering together.

ID Skills Reading for details

A Begin by asking the lesson title question to gauge sts' interest in spas. Encourage them to say / express as much as they can. Don't correct much at this stage.

Tip This initial fluency practice based around answering the title question can always be repeated at the end of a lesson. At this point, sts should improve with more vocabulary and greater accuracy. This loop input (try – feel the need to learn some language – learn it – try again – feel progress) method can help sts feel short-term success and find real relevance / personalization in your classes.

Sts quickly read the text and answer the questions. Paircheck. Classcheck.

1 a magazine 2 an ad

Tip See if they notice / like alliteration and if it reminds them of anything they've seen earlier in the course. For fun, sts can easily alliterate each other's names with an adjective: Big Bernard, Cool Claudia, Easy Enrique, etc.

B Sts reread the text. In pairs, they decide whether sentences 1–5 are T (true) or F (false). Classcheck. Encourage sts to justify / explain false sentences with evidence from the text.

1 F 2 T 3 T 4 T 5 F

C In small groups, sts look for words in the text which match meanings 1–4. Do number 1 as an example. Classcheck with answers on the board.

1 same 2 healthy 3 eliminate 4 stay

D In pairs, sts try to pronounce the words in the text which have pink letters. Play 4.14 and pause after each comma or period, asking sts to repeat and confirm their guesses. Ask if there were any pronunciation surprises? Did they find the ad more convincing as a listening or as a reading? Why?

Tip We can organize words according to their affixes. Ask sts to underline all the words ending in *-ist* and *-ique* in the All Yours text. Elicit the pronunciation of each word sts underlined and drill their correct pronunciation.

Extra activity Write a prompt to a conversation on the board: *How often do you see a ...?* In pairs, sts interview each other using the professionals from the text (hair stylist, manicurist, therapist, etc.).

E **Make it personal** Change partners. In pairs, sts plan a day at the spa. Then, put pairs together to make groups of four or six and tell them to explain their days and decide on the most relaxing, fun, and unusual day.

4.5 What shoe size are you?

 You can't always get what you want. But if you try sometimes, yeah, you might find you get what you need.

ID in Action — Shopping for clothes

A ▶ 4.15 Listen to the dialogue and complete 1–4. Predict how it ends.
1. The man's at a …
2. He wants …
3. The color he wants is …
4. The size he wants is …

B ▶ 4.16 Listen to part two of the dialogue and answer the questions.
1. Who's the sweater for?
2. Why does he want it in blue?
3. Do you think the salesclerk is good at his job?

C Listen to ▶ 4.15 and ▶ 4.16 again and find:
1. the preposition we use before colors.
2. the verb that means "to test clothes on your body".
3. the name of the room where we go to do this.

D ▶ 4.17 Listen to and complete a short version of the dialogue. What three changes do you need to make if he asks for jeans?

Salesclerk:	Can I _____ you?
Jason:	Yes, please. Can I _____ the _____ in the window?
Salesclerk:	Sure! What _____? We have it in _____, blue or _____.
Jason:	_____, please.
Salesclerk:	All right. What _____?
Jason:	Extra _____.
Salesclerk:	_____ small in blue? OK, just a _____, please. Here you _____.
Jason:	Thanks. Can I _____ it on?
Salesclerk:	Sure. The fitting _____ are over _____.

Common mistakes

~~Do you like this pants?~~ → *these pants / them*
~~Yes, I like.~~ → *do / like them*

E In pairs, practice the dialogue in D. Use other clothes items from this unit. Be careful with singular and plural forms.

F ▶ 4.18 Punctuate the rest of the dialogue. Listen to check. Then cover and practice from the photos.

Jason:	nothanksjustthesweaterhowmuchisit
Salesclerk:	fortynineninetynine
Jason:	greatheresmycreditcard
Salesclerk:	thankyoupleaseenteryourpinnumber
Jason:	hereyougo
Salesclerk:	heresyourreceipthaveanicedaybyejackson

G 😀 **Make it personal** Go shopping!
1. In groups, discuss the questions.
   What do you wear …
   a to school / work?
   b to go to a party?
   c on the weekend?
   d to a job interview?
2. In pairs, go shopping for clothes for one of the situations in 1.
   A: You're the customer. **B:** You're the salesclerk.

   Hi! I like these black shorts. How much are they?

4.5 What shoe size are you?

Lesson Aims: To talk about what clothes you wear and to role-play shopping for clothes.

Function	Language
Shopping for clothes.	Can I help you?
Describing clothes.	What size?
	Extra small.

Vocabulary: Review clothes vocabulary and phrases for shopping.
Grammar: Use *can* in ? + −
Skills: Listen to a dialogue for details.

♪ **Song line:** Turn to p. 328 for notes about this song and an accompanying task.

ID in Action Shopping for clothes

A Explore the picture of the man and his dog. Ask: *How old is he? Is he small? Do you know people with small dogs like this?* Focus on sentences 1–4 and elicit possible endings for the sentences. Play ▶ 4.15. Sts complete the sentences and paircheck. Classcheck. Ask: *Can you predict how the dialogue ends?* Elicit ideas.

> 1 clothing store   2 a sweater   3 blue   4 extra small

▶ 4.15 Turn to p. 314 for the complete audioscript.

B Play part two of ▶ 4.16. In pairs, sts answer 1–3. Classcheck. Ask sts some follow-up questions, such as: *Do you have a dog? What's its name? Do you buy clothes for it?*

> 1 Jackson, the man's dog   2 It's Jackson's favorite color.
> 3 Suggested answer: Yes, because he's surprised that the man wants an extra small sweater, but he's polite and doesn't question him. He tries to sell the man some clothes for himself.

C Sts go to the AS on p. 163 and find answers. Classcheck. Tell sts to make a note of any new vocabulary.

> 1 in   2 try on   3 fitting room

D Play ▶ 4.17. Sts complete a short version of the same dialogue with the missing words. Paircheck. Classcheck. Ask sts: *What three changes do you need to make if he asks for jeans?* Guide them to singular vs. plural differences and write sentences on the board, e.g. *We have them in blue*, etc.

> help, see, sweater, color, black, green, Blue, size, small, Extra, moment, are, try, rooms, there
> Changes: Can I see the **jeans** in the window? … We have **them** in black, … Can I try **them** on?

E Sts practice the dialogue in **D**, paying attention to singular / plural changes. Ask them to choose clothes items from p. 50. Monitor closely for accuracy and prompt self-correction when you hear errors.

F Draw the following punctuation marks on the board: period, comma, apostrophe, hyphen, question mark. Ask: *What are these?* Elicit the name for each punctuation mark and write it on the board, marking the stress. Drill pronunciation. Divide the class into pairs. Sts read and punctuate part three of the dialogue. Ask one pair to write their punctuated dialogue on the board. Play ▶ 4.18. Then, in pairs, sts cover the words, and practice from the photos.

> Jason: No, thanks. Just the sweater. How much is it?
> Salesclerk: Forty-nine ninety-nine.
> Jason: Great! Here's my credit card.
> Salesclerk: Thank you! Please, enter your PIN number.
> Jason: Here you go.
> Salesclerk: Here's your receipt. Have a nice day! Bye, Jackson!

G 🎧 **Make it personal** Sts work in groups. They discuss the questions in 1. For 2, put sts into pairs and ask them to choose a situation and prepare and act out the role-play.

Weaker students Sts can refer to the dialogue in **D**.

Stronger students tell them to close their books and try to role-play without looking at the language from this lesson.

➔ **Workbook** p. 23

➔ **Richmond Learning Platform**

➔ **Writing** p. 54

➔ **Café** p. 55

Writing 4 A job application

*Sweet home Alabama,
Where the skies are so blue
Sweet home Alabama,
Lord, I'm coming home to you.*

A Read the job ad and find the names of
1 the company advertising the job.   2 the job the ad is for.   3 the person you have to write to.

Make this your best ever summer – at 50 States Summer Camp!

Would you like to: ◦ have the chance to visit the U.S.? ◦ spend the summer working with young people? ◦ teach a sport or a skill that you are passionate about? ◦ make amazing new friends and have a fantastic time?

If so, send an email to: rebecca@50states.com. Tell us about you, your skills, your likes and dislikes, and why you want to be a counselor at 50 States Summer Camp. Include any questions you'd like us to answer. One of our team will contact you for a phone interview.

To: Rebecca
Subject: 50 States Summer Camp Counselor
Today at 16:03
All Mail

Dear Rebecca,

I am an 18-year-old high school graduate from Granada in the south of Spain. Right now, I'm working in a local restaurant. I really enjoy it, but I'm planning to go to college in the fall to study sports science.

I can play most sports. I play soccer very well, and I'm a good swimmer, so I'm sure I can teach those. I'm teaching my younger brother to play guitar at the moment – I play the guitar quite well, but I can't sing at all, unfortunately. I'm good at languages – in addition to Spanish, I speak English and French.

As a person, I'm quite organized and tidy, and I'm not good at living with other people if they are messy. I like music and reading, but I really love being outside and spending time with my friends. I also love food. I can cook, but not very well. I hate shopping.

This summer, I want to do something that is connected to my future studies and also uses my skills. I like helping other people, and I love to see them enjoying the same things I do. And, of course, I'd love to visit the U.S.!

I look forward to hearing from you.

Sincerely,
Ana Sofía Reynoso

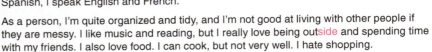

B Read Ana's email and underline.
1 her job and current plans.
2 five things she's good at and one she's not.
3 the languages she speaks.
4 two positive adjectives to describe her.
5 five things she does well and one she doesn't.
6 five reasons she wants the job.

C Imagine you want to apply for the job in **A**. Note your answers to 1–6 in **B**.

D **Make it personal** Write a similar email applying to 50 States Summer Camp (about 180–200 words).

Before	Use your notes in **C**. Add any information you think is important.
While	Use intensifying adverbs to describe your skills and likes.
After	Exchange emails with a partner. Decide who is the best candidate.

⊙ **Write it right!**
Use a variety of intensifying adverbs with adjectives, adverbs, or verbs – *not ... at all, not very, quite, really, very*.

54

Writing 4 A job application

♪ **Song line:** Turn to p. 328 for notes about this song and an accompanying task.

> **Tip** Adapt this lesson to your students' ages. For example, for 16 to 18-year-olds there are real summer camp job sites such as https://www.campleaders.com/gb/ or https://www.usasummercamp.com/, which have interesting videos and information. If your sts are slightly older, direct them to local or international job sites. Before the lesson, search for job ads your sts might be interested in, ideally with simple language and visuals.

A Sts skim read the ad and find the names of the three items. If you think it is appropriate, you could make this a race to see who can find the answers first. Sts can do this individually or in pairs.

> 1 50 States Summer Camp   2 counselor   3 Rebecca

B Ask: *Have you ever applied for a job? What information do you include in the cover email?* List sts' ideas on the board. Refer sts to the ad and clarify the meaning of *skills* and *counselor*. Ask: *What skills do you need for this job?* and elicit ideas on the board. Sts read Ana's email and find and underline 1–6. Classcheck.

> 1 restaurant worker, planning to go to college to study sports science
> 2 good at: sports, soccer, swimming, playing the guitar, languages
>   not good at: singing
> 3 Spanish, English and French
> 4 organized, tidy
> 5 does well: music, reading, being outside, spending time with friends, doesn't do well: cooking
> 6 wants to do something connected to her future studies, uses her skills, likes helping other people, loves to see people enjoying the same things as her, would love to visit the U.S.

C Read **Write it right!** with the class and check understanding of the intensifying adverbs. Sts can then find examples in the email. Tell sts they are going to apply for the job in the ad. Have them note down their own personal answers to 1–6 in **B**.

D 🔵 **Make it personal** If you researched other job sites, refer your sts to them now. Read the steps Before, While, and After with sts so as to guide them to write their own job application emails. Tell them to refer to Ana Sofia's email in **A** as a model, and draw their attention to the length of the composition – that is, approximately 180–200 words. As a follow-up activity and before they hand in their texts, ask sts to exchange compositions. Encourage them to suggest how to improve the application. Ask: *What did you like about your partner's email?* Discuss what makes a good job application email.

4 Whose action hero?  Café

1 Before watching

A Look at the photo. Where are Andrea and Lucy?
☐ at a tennis court ☐ at a gym ☐ at a stadium

B 🔘 Make it personal Check (✓) which are true for you and correct the others.
1. I can sing.
2. I can do acrobatics.
3. I can do martial arts.
4. I can box, but I can't do kickboxing.
5. I can dance, but I can't sing.

C 🔘 Make it personal In pairs, take turns asking and answering can / can't questions about the activities in B.

Can you sing? *No, I can't. What about you?*

2 While watching

A Check (✓) the correct columns according to what Lucy, Andrea, and Paolo say.

	Andrea		Lucy		Paolo	
	can	can't	can	can't	can	can't
talk to Paolo						
still join the class						
dance						
do gymnastics						
be in Lucy's film						
text their number						
help someone catch up						

B Write True (T) or False (F). Correct the false sentences.
1. Lucy and Andrea can't take Paolo's kickboxing class.
2. Andrea's film project is due next week.
3. Andrea can't do gymnastics.
4. Martial arts is Andrea's taste.
5. Andrea is flexible but not so strong.
6. Lucy says that Andrea can't be in her film.
7. Paolo offers to help Lucy catch up before the class starts.

3 After watching

A Complete this extract.
Lucy: Hey, what's up?
Andrea: I want to take an exercise class. Summer _____ coming.
Lucy: Summer? I _____ only think about _____ action film. It's due next week.
Andrea: _____ class should I take? Jim _____? Marie _____? Whose class _____ best?
Lucy: You see that guy over there? Whatever _____ taking.
Andrea: Martial arts? That's _____ taste, not mine.
Lucy: I think I just found _____ new action hero. Let's go.

B Complete with *his / her / their* or noun + possessive *'s*.
1. Lucy's going home to work on _____ script.
2. Paolo's taking Andrea to _____ class.
3. Lucy can text Paolo _____ number.
4. Andrea can also be in _____ film.
5. Lucy and Paolo are sharing _____ cell phone numbers.

C 🔘 Make it personal In groups of three, design your ideal superhero. What can she / he do? Present her / him to the class.

This is our superbot, Queen Fantastic! She can do many things ...

55

ID Café 4 Whose action hero?

1 Before watching

A Have sts look at the photo and answer the question. Classcheck. Ask: *Where are Andrea and Lucy?* (at a gym).

B 🔘 **Make it personal** Model the activity. Write *I can sing.* on the board and ask: *Can you sing?* Tell sts who say yes to check sentence 1 in their books. Elicit the negative form from sts who said no and correct the sentence on the board, *I can't sing.* Tell sts to do the same in their books.

Sts check sentences which are true for them and change the wrong ones to make true statements about themselves. If possible, walk around the classroom to monitor their writing. Sts paircheck below in **C**.

C 🔘 **Make it personal** Elicit / Drill *Can you ...?* questions about sentences 1–5 in **B**. In pairs, sts ask and answer questions about the activities in **B** as in the model dialogue in the speech bubbles. Ask sts to find three things in common. Monitor closely for accuracy. Ask sts to tell you and the whole class what they have in common, e.g. *We can't do acrobatics or kickboxing, but we can dance.*

2 While watching

A Tell sts they are going to watch a video showing Andrea, Lucy, and Paolo at the gym. Allow sts some time to briefly read the skills in the table and tell them to check what Andrea, Lucy, and Paolo *can* or *can't* do. Make sure sts know the meaning of all the skills listed.

Play **Video 4**. Paircheck. Replay the video. Classcheck with answers on the board. Check answers on the same page in the *Digital Book for Teachers*, if technology is available.

Skills	Andrea		Lucy		Paolo	
	can	can't	can	can't	can	can't
talk to Paolo		✓	✓			
still join the class	✓		✓			
do acrobatics				✓		
dance	✓		✓			
do gymnastics	✓			✓		
be in Lucy's film	✓				✓	
text their number			✓			
help someone catch up					✓	

B Point to sentences 1–6 and tell sts to write T or F according to what they remember from **Video 4**. Paircheck. If necessary, replay the video to check answers. Classcheck with answers on the board.

1 F Lucy and Andrea can take Paolo's kickboxing class.
2 F Lucy's film project is due next week.
3 F Andrea can do gymnastics.
4 F Martial arts is not Andrea's taste.
5 F Andrea is strong but not so flexible.
6 F Lucy says that Andrea can be in her film.
7 F Paolo offers to help Andrea catch up before the class starts.

3 After watching

A Point to the dialogue between Lucy and Andrea and tell sts that the conversation is a part of the video. Sts fill in the blanks with a suitable word each. Paircheck. Classcheck

Weaker classes Have sts work in pairs to complete the dialogue.

is can my Whose 's 's is he's your my

B Individually, sts complete sentences 1–5 with *his / her / their /* or noun + possessive *'s*. Paircheck. Classcheck with answers on the board.

1 her 2 his 3 her 4 Lucy's 5 their

C 🔘 **Make it personal** Ask: *What superheroes do you know? What powers do they have?* Put sts into groups and tell them to design a superhero. They should prepare a short presentation with images / drawings and a description. Put groups together so they can present their superheroes to each other. Ask sts what they liked about the other group's superheroes after their presentations.

R2 Grammar and vocabulary

A **Picture dictionary.** Cover the words on these pages and use the pictures to remember:

page	
32–33	10 weather adjectives
34	6 everyday actions
35	4 seasons
37	5 technology problems
38	6 activities
45	7 sports
46	5 abilities
48	6 talents
50	16 clothes items
53	the clothes store dialogue
158	10 picture words for diphthongs

B Complete with weather adjectives and the month (January = 1, December = 12).
1 In <u>December</u> (12), New York is usually very c o l d.
2 Lima is a very c_ _ _ _y city in _____ (7).
3 London is a r_ _ _ _y place in _____ (10).
4 The coast of Canada is very f_ _ _y, especially in _____ (1).
5 It is s_ _ _y in Bariloche. Winter there starts in _____ (5).
6 Sydney's very s_ _ _y, especially in _____ (2).
7 La Mancha's very w_ _ _y in _____ (8).

C 🎤 **Make it personal** Match questions 1–3 to answers a–c. Complete a–c so they're true for you.
1 What's the weather usually like in your city in July?
2 Is it raining at the moment?
3 Does it usually rain a lot in your city?
  a _____, _____ does / doesn't.
  b It _____ and _____.
  c _____, _____ is / isn't.

D 🔊 R2.1 Circle the correct alternatives. Listen to check. In pairs, role-play the dialogue.
Tyler: Hello?
Shannon: Hi, Tyler. This is Shannon. What **are you doing / do you do**?
Tyler: Oh, hi, Shannon. I **'m watching / watch** the football game.
Shannon: Oh? Who **'s playing / plays**?
Tyler: You **'re kidding / kid**, right?
Shannon: Tyler, you **'re knowing / know** that I **'m not liking / don't like** sports.
Tyler: OK, OK ... the Cowboys and the Giants **'re playing / play** right now.
Shannon: And who **'s winning / wins**?
Tyler: The Giants, 31–14. They **'re always winning / always win**.
Shannon: Sorry to hear that! Um ... **do you want / are you wanting** to go out later?

E Cross out the incorrect response.
1 When are you leaving?
  a Every day at 6:30 a.m.
  b Tomorrow morning.
  c In two weeks.
2 Can I see the sweater in the window?
  a Sure. What size are you?
  b Sure. How much is it?
  c Sure. What color do you prefer?
3 Here are the boots.
  a I like them very much.
  b How much are they?
  c Can I try it on?
4 Are you busy on the weekend?
  a No problem.
  b Yes, I'm working both days.
  c Not really. What are you doing?
5 Can you sing?
  a I can, but not very well.
  b Not at all.
  c Yes, I am.
6 What sports can you play?
  a No, I can't.
  b I can play volleyball and tennis.
  c I can't play any sports.

F 🎤 **Make it personal** In pairs, ask and answer 4–6 in E. Make more questions by changing the verbs.

G 🎤 **Make it personal** Play *Last-to-first Race!* In pairs, take turns saying these in reverse order.
1 The months: December, ...
2 The days of the week: Sunday, ...
3 Numbers 1 to 20: Twenty, ...
4 Your daily routine: I go to bed, ...
5 Your phone number: ...

H Correct the mistakes. Check your answers in units 3 and 4.
1 How's the weather like in June? (1 mistake)
2 Is raining in Patagonia at the moment. (1 mistake)
3 Do you hungry? You would like a sandwich? (2 mistakes)
4 Is usually cold in december in Canada. (2 mistakes)
5 My daughter studying at the moment. (1 mistake)
6 What your best friend is doing now? (2 mistakes)
7 He go to Europe the next month. (2 mistakes)
8 Patty can to play very well the tennis. (3 mistakes)
9 Gloria is using a blue jeans. (2 mistakes)
10 Of who are these shoes? They're of Jane. (3 mistakes)

56

Review 2 Units 3-4

Grammar and vocabulary

A Picture dictionary. Pairwork. Sts test each other and review the main vocabulary items learned in units 3 and 4. There are some possible techniques mentioned on p. 9 of the introduction section on how to work with the picture dictionary in order to review vocabulary. You can select whichever of these best suit the needs of your class.

B Individually, sts complete sentences 1–7 with weather words and months. Sts can refer to p. 32 and p. 33 if they are not sure. Paircheck. Classcheck with answers on the board. At the end, elicit / drill pronunciation of all answers on the board. Note that the numbers in parentheses refer to the months of the year. For example, 12 refers to December.

> 2 cloudy, July 3 rainy, October 4 foggy, January
> 5 snowy, May 6 sunny, February 7 windy, August

C **Make it personal** In pairs, sts match questions 1–3 to answers a–c. Tell them not to fill in the blanks yet. Classcheck Individually, sts complete answers a–c. Paircheck. Classcheck with answers on the board.

> 1 b It's (adjectives). 2 c Yes, it is. / No, it isn't.
> 3 a Yes, it does. / No, it doesn't.

D Sts read the dialogue and circle the correct options. Play ▶R2.1 so sts can check their answers. Classcheck. At the end, replay the track and ask sts to repeat after each sentence. In pairs, sts role-play the dialogue. Sts change roles and act out the dialogue once more. Ask two sts to act it out for the whole class.

> What **are you doing**?
> Oh, hi, Shannon. I**'m watching** the football game.
> Oh? Who**'s playing**?
> You**'re kidding**, right?
> Tyler, you **know** that I **don't like** sports.
> Fine. The Cowboys and the Giants **are playing** right now.
> And who**'s winning**?
> The Giants, 31–14. They **always win**.
> Sorry to hear that! Um… **do you want** to go out later?

E Do number 1 with the whole class. Read the question and elicit which answer is incorrect (a Every day at 6:30 a.m.) Individually, sts continue choosing the incorrect answers to questions 2–6. Paircheck. Classcheck.

> 1 a 2 b 3 c 4 a 5 c 6 a

F **Make it personal** In pairs, sts ask each other questions 4–6 from **E**. Monitor closely for accuracy. Ask sts to report their partners' answers to the whole class.

G **Make it personal** Read the instructions with the class and challenge a st to say item 1 (the months of the year) in reverse order as fast as they can, starting with December. Other sts listen and check if the order is correct. To add a further element of competition, have sts time their partner using a watch or phone. Have the two quickest sts compete against each other to be the class winner of the Last-to-first Race!

H Draw sts' attention to the number of mistakes between parentheses. Elicit corrections to sentence 1 and mark the phrase on the board.

In pairs, sts correct sentences 2–10. Whenever sts are uncertain, encourage them to flip back and check their answers in units 3 and 4. Classcheck with answers on the board.

> 1 What's the weather like in June? OR How's the weather in June?
> 2 It's raining in Patagonia at the moment.
> 3 Are you hungry? Would you like a sandwich?
> 4 It's usually cold in December in Canada.
> 5 My daughter's studying at the moment.
> 6 What is your best friend doing now?
> 7 He is going to Europe next month.
> 8 Patty can play tennis very well.
> 9 Gloria is wearing blue jeans.
> 10 Whose shoes are these? They're Jane's.

Skills practice

R2

♪ *California girls, we're undeniable, Fine, fresh, fierce, we got it on lock, West Coast represent, now put your hands up.*

A ▶R2.2 Listen to an interview with Paralympic swimmer Ricky Pietersen and number the questions in the order you hear them, 1–4.
- ☐ What else do you like doing when you're not swimming or watching your team?
- ☐ Do you like soccer?
- ☐ What is your next big challenge?
- ☐ So, Ricky, what's your favorite sport?

B ▶R2.2 Listen again and correct 1–5.
1. Well, I love singing, of course.
2. Yes, I love to watch my team win.
3. I like to read to young kids with disabilities.
4. I'm working hard to prepare for the next Panamerican Games.
5. I have to beat my own result.

C Match words 1–3 from the interview to their meanings a–c.
1. Paralympics
2. disability
3. beat the record

a. a physical or mental condition that limits a person's activities
b. to do better than the last person to hold the record
c. the Olympic Games for athletes with disabilities

D In pairs, use the information in **A** and **B** to role-play the interview. Then change roles.

> So, here I am with today's guest, Paralympic swimmer, Ricky Pietersen. Hi, Ricky!

E ▶R2.3 Read the blog page. Can you guess the missing words? Listen to check your answers.

My name is Cristina Valenzuela and I ¹_____ twenty-three years ²_____. I live in Santa Monica, California. My parents are originally ³_____ Chile, so I ⁴_____ speak Spanish very well. I love sports. I go to the beach every day, and I surf and swim when the ⁵_____ is good. It's usually very ⁶_____ and sunny here! I love it!

I'm ⁷_____ very casual person. I usually ⁸_____ shorts and a T-shirt during the day and jeans at night. When it's cold, I sometimes wear ⁹_____ sweater, but I don't like it very ¹⁰_____. I prefer to wear summer ¹¹_____. Write me an email! Maybe we ¹²_____ go to the beach together next summer.

F Answer questions 1–4 about her blog page.
1. Why can Cristina speak Spanish well?
2. What sports does Cristina usually practice?
3. What's the weather usually like in Santa Monica?
4. What does she like to wear?

G 🎤 **Make it personal** Question time.
In pairs, practice asking and answering the 12 lesson titles in units 3 and 4. Use the book map on p. 2–3. Where possible, ask follow-up questions, too. Can you comfortably ask and answer all the questions?

> What's the weather like? It's very hot again!
> Is it windy, too? No, it's not. No wind, no rain, only sun!

Skills practice

A Explore the photo. Ask: *What's he doing? Where is he? Anything special about him?*, etc. Sts will hear an interview with Paralympic swimmer Ricky Pietersen. Allow sts a few seconds to read the questions. Tell sts to number the questions in the order they hear them, 1–4. Play ▶R2.2. Paircheck. Classcheck with answers on the board.

> 1 So, Ricky, what's your favorite sport?
> 2 Do you like soccer?
> 3 What else do you like doing when you're not swimming or watching your team?
> 4 What is your next big challenge?

B Sts listen to the interview again. Point to answers 1–4 and tell sts they are all incorrect. Sts listen to ▶R2.2 and correct the sentences according to what they hear. Paircheck. Classcheck.

> 1 Well, I love ~~singing~~ swimming, of course.
> 2 Yes, I love to watch my team ~~win~~ play.
> 3 I like to ~~read to~~ help other kids with disabilities.
> 4 I'm working hard to prepare for the next ~~Panamerican~~ Paralympic Games.

C In pairs, sts match words 1–3 to definitions a–c. Classcheck.

> 1 c   2 a   3 b

D Change partners. Assign roles A and B: Ricky Pietersen and the reporter. Tell sts to use the questions from **A** and answers in **B** to role-play the interview. Sts change roles and act out the interview again. At the end, ask two sts to role-play the dialogue for the whole class.

E Point to the photo and blog post. Ask sts: *What's her name? Where does she live? Can she speak Spanish?* and have sts scan the text to find the answers. Tell sts to read the text and, in pairs, try to guess the missing words. Play ▶R2.3 to check answers. Classcheck.

> 1 am   2 old   3 from   4 can   5 weather   6 hot   7 a
> 8 wear   9 a   10 much   11 clothes   12 can

F In pairs, sts take turns asking and answering questions 1–4. Classcheck.

> 1 Because her parents are originally from Chile.
> 2 Swimming and surfing.
> 3 Hot and sunny.
> 4 Summer clothes, shorts, T-shirts, and jeans.

G **Make it personal** **Question time.** Sts look at the book map on p. 2–3 and take turns asking and answering the lesson titles from units 3 and 4. Monitor closely for accuracy and encourage sts to ask follow-up questions when suitable. At the end, ask them how they felt performing the task: *Do you feel comfortable with all of the questions? Which ones are easy? Which ones are difficult?*

Tip Print out and cut up all the question titles from units 1–4 and put them in envelopes, for sts in pairs to pull out random questions and ask each other.

5.1 Is there a mall in your area?

1 Vocabulary Public places

A ▶5.1 How do you pronounce places 1–8? Listen to check. Name one real example you like of each.

1 a bar
2 a club
3 a hotel
4 a museum
5 a park
6 a restaurant
7 a stadium
8 a theater

☐ 9 a bookstore
☐ 10 a bridge
☐ 11 a library
☐ 12 a mall
☐ 13 a movie theater
☐ 14 a racetrack
☐ 15 a river
☐ 16 a swimming pool

I really like the Japanese restaurant on my street. It's excellent.

B ▶5.2 Match places 9–16 to photos a–g. Listen to check.

C ▶5.3 Listen to the tourist information about Louisville and number the places in the order you hear them. Which two places are not mentioned?

D Make it personal Read the rule. In your opinion, which place in Louisville is a) the most interesting b) the most boring?
Use *the most* + adjective to form the superlative:
Tokyo is the most populated city on Earth.

I think the most interesting place is probably the racetrack.

Common mistakes
bookstore
We go to the ~~library~~ to buy books.

5

Unit overview: The main topics of unit 5 are describing places around a city and your own neighborhood, verbs of emotion, everyday activities, different types of vacation and vacation activities, as well as following directions. We go from Kentucky to a talent show in Britain, then from snorkeling and sunbathing on a cruise in Mexico to yoga in Costa Rica, then feeding a friend's pet and back to San Francisco!

5.1 Is there a mall in your area?

Lesson Aims: Sts use *there + be* to talk about public places. They learn vocabulary to compare towns and describe a neighborhood they know.

Function
Listening to a description of a city.
Talking about interesting places in a city.
Talking about what you can do in a place.
Describing (comparing) your hometown and Louisville.

Language
A bar, a club, a hotel, etc.
Welcome to Louisville …
I think the most interesting place is probably the racetrack.
You can eat out.
In Louisville there's a baseball stadium, but there's no baseball stadium in my hometown.

Vocabulary: Public places. Use of *the most + adjective*.
Grammar: *There is / are, There's no / There aren't any*. Review *can*.

Warm-up Play *Messenger Race*. Stick a previously printed dialogue on a wall outside the classroom. Number the dialogue lines from 1 to 10. Split the class into groups of four or five sts. Each st goes outside, one at a time, reads and memorizes one sentence from the dialogue, and comes back to dictate the sentence to his / her group. All sts should copy the sentence. A second st goes outside and does the same. The group who completes the dialogue first is the winner. Classcheck.

1 Vocabulary Public places

A Focus on the photos and ask: *Are these things in your town?* Focus on the list of places 1–8. In pairs, sts try to say places 1–8. Play ▶5.1 to check. Read the example in the speech bubble with sts. They then name one real example they like of each place.

Ask: *Are these words (1–8) similar in your language? Which ones do you find difficult to pronounce?*

Tip Encourage sts to make a note of cognates as they are easy to remember. They could start a cognates page in their notebooks.

▶5.1 Turn to p. 315 for the complete audioscript.

B Sts match the photos to words 9–16. Paircheck. Play ▶5.2 to check.

9 f 10 g 11 b 12 a 13 c 14 d 15 g 16 e

C Sts listen to an ad for Louisville and check the places in **A** (1–16) in the order that they are mentioned in the audio. Play ▶5.3. Paircheck. Classcheck. Listen again to confirm.

Historical and geographical note Originally a part of Virginia, in 1792 Kentucky was the 15th state to join the Union. Kentucky is the 37th most extensive and the 26th most populous of the 50 states in the United States. Its capital is Frankfort, but its largest city is Louisville.

1 river 2 park 3 museum 4 theater 5 racetrack
6 stadium 7 mall 8 library 9 restaurant
10 swimming pool 11 bar 12 club 13 movie theater
14 hotel
Not mentioned: bookstore, bridge

▶5.3 Turn to p. 315 for the complete audioscript.

Common mistakes Point out the difference between *library* and *bookstore*.

D **Make it personal** Sts read the rule about superlatives. Refer to the speech bubble and tell sts to share opinions. Remind them to ask *Why?* to get more information.

Tip Explain that basic comparatives and superlatives are easy for sts to understand and use immediately. The basic rule is *more + adjective* and *the most + adjective*. They will learn more rules in unit 10.

2 Grammar There is / are ➕➖❓

A ▶5.4 Complete 1–4 in the grammar box with *a*, *any*, *are*, or *no*. Listen to check.

	➕	➖	❓
Singular	There is a …	There is no …	Is there a …?
Plural	There are …	There are no … / There aren't any …	Are there any …?

1 There _____ seven museums downtown.
2 There's _____ famous racetrack at Churchill Downs.
3 There aren't _____ swimming pools in downtown Louisville.
4 There are _____ unfriendly people.

➡ Grammar 5A p.146

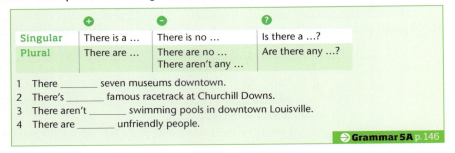

> 🎵 There's nothing you can't do,
> Now you're in New York.
> These streets will make you feel brand new
> Big lights will inspire you.

Common mistakes

There's a
~~Have one~~ famous baseball stadium in Louisville.

There are no
~~No have~~ swimming pools in downtown Louisville.

B In pairs, each ask four *Can you …?* questions about Louisville using these verb phrases.

eat out   go to the beach / the movies / the theater
go shopping / skiing / swimming   stay in a nice hotel   watch horse racing

> Can you go skiing?
>
> No, you can't. There aren't any mountains.

C 🟢 **Make it personal** Compare your hometown to Louisville. Find at least five differences.

> In Louisville there's a baseball stadium, but there's no baseball stadium in my hometown.

3 Reading

A ▶5.5 Read and complete the brochure with *a*, *an*, *is*, *are*, or *no*. Listen to check.

Come to Markville!

It's __a__ great place to live. There ____ two museums and ____ great public library. There ____ also a movie theater, so you can see ____ movie if you want. There's ____ mall, but there ____ lots of cool shops and ____ historical bank. Markville has two hotels: there's ____ old traditional hotel and there ____ a new modern one, so you can choose where you stay. There are ____ clubs, but there ____ a bar inside one of the hotels. For food lovers, there ____ two delicious restaurants, one French, the other Mexican, and ____ interesting café, too. Downtown is for pedestrians, so there are ____ cars to ruin the peace. People are warm, the weather is, too. The food is great, so see you soon!

B Which picture is Markville, 1 or 2? Explain.

C Work in pairs. **A:** Look at the pictures and answer.
B: Don't look! Ask **A** questions to find four differences between the two pictures.

> Is there a …?   Are there any …?

D 🟠 **Make it personal** In groups, describe a town or neighborhood you know. Is it a great place to live?

> is a nice place to live. There is a big mall downtown and so many things to do.

5.1

🎵 **Song line:** Turn to p. 329 for notes about this song and an accompanying task.

2 Grammar *There is / are* ➕ ➖ ❓

A Ask the lesson title question and get sts to raise their hands if there is a mall on their street. Elicit from the sts who raised hands the answer *Yes, there is*, and the others *No, there isn't*.

🔑 **Common mistakes** This is particularly difficult for Portuguese speakers, which is why there are so many errors here.

Focus on the grammar box. Sts complete sentences 1–4 with the words *a*, *any*, *are*, or *no*. Paircheck. Listen to the extracts in ▶ 5.4 to classcheck. In pairs, sts study sentences 1–4. Elicit some examples of *there is / are* sentences, using places from the lesson and talking about sts' own neighborhood.

➡️ **Grammar 5A** p. 146

> 🔑 A 1 are 2 a 3 any 4 no

B Continuing the theme of what you can / can't do in cities, sts ask and answer *Can you …?* questions with the verb phrases. Use the example in the speech bubble to model it.

> **Tip** Ask a few individual sts questions about New York or another city first to set this up, so the questions they ask and answer in pairs about Louisville are fresher.

St A asks st B four of the questions, then they change roles. Monitor and praise / correct use of *there is / are*. When they finish, extend the speaking activity by having them ask the same questions about their own town. Classcheck. Highlight any pronunciation difficulties, e.g. /skiː/ not /skaɪ/.

> 🔑 Can you eat out?   Yes, you can.
> Can you go to the beach?   No, you can't.
> Can you go to the movies?   Yes, you can.
> Can you go to the theater?   Yes, you can.
> Can you go shopping?   Yes, you can.
> Can you go skiing?   No, you can't.
> Can you go swimming?   Yes, you can.
> Can you stay in a nice hotel?   Yes, you can.
> Can you watch horse racing?   Yes, you can.

Stronger classes Encourage them to experiment with locally important places and activities, and write more examples on the board, e.g. *swim in a lake, climb a mountain, watch soccer, skate, eat ceviche*, etc.

C 👤 **Make it personal** In small groups, sts compare Louisville to their hometown with *There is / are* sentences. Use the example to set this up. Ask sts to find four differences between the two cities. Round off the activity by asking some sts to report and compare their answers.

Extra writing Sts can describe the differences between Louisville and their city in a written paragraph.

3 Reading

A Sts read about a different town, Markville. Say: *Don't look at the pictures now, just at the text. Quickly read and answer this question: How many different places are mentioned in the text?* Sts read and find the number of places and name them (two museums, a library, etc.). Sts reread and complete the text with *a*, *an*, *is*, *are*, or *no*. Paircheck. Play ▶ 5.5 for sts to check answers and try to remember the pronunciation of the words with pink letters. Write problematical answers on the board and drill pronunciation as necessary. Ask: *What is the purpose of the advertisement?* (to invite people to live here). *Where do you think people would see or hear an advert like this?* (On the radio, at the tourist office, in a magazine …)

> 🔑 are, a, is, a, no, are, an, an, is, no, is, are, an, no

> **Tip** Visually beat the stress when you drill words like pe-des-tri-an oOoo, to help sts "see" and "feel" the stress. Clearly show there are four beats (syllables), raising your hand high on the stressed syllable.

B Focus on the two pictures. Elicit what places sts can see. In pairs, sts reread the text in **A** and decide which picture, 1 or 2, shows Markville. (Picture 1) Classcheck. Ask: *Would you like to visit Markville? Why (not)? What are two good / bad things about Markville?* to get some feedback and help them prepare for the next activity.

C To review *Is / Are there*, in pairs, sts find four differences between pictures 1 and 2 in **A**. Have st A turn her / his back to st B so she / he can't see the picture. Sts then find the differences by asking questions with *Is there a … / Are there any … .*

D 👤 **Make it personal** In pairs, sts talk about their own neighborhood. Model this with a town / neighborhood you know well and they don't, and tell them about it / let them ask questions. With a weaker class, prompt the sentences on the board. Write *There's a / an … / There are … / There are no …* In small groups, sts describe a place they know well.

> **Tip** Either split the sts from the same place into groups so they enjoy talking about local places together, or split them into different groups so the communication between people from different places is more genuine / informative.

In class or for homework, sts can write a brochure about their town / neighborhood. If you set it for homework, give them a word count of 100–120 words, and some guidance criteria: who their audience is, how many paragraphs, etc. Alternatively, sts could prepare a presentation to give to the class.

> **Tip** The website www.glogster.com is great for making a brochure.

➡️ **Workbook** p. 24

5.2 What are your likes and dislikes?

1 Vocabulary Free-time activities

A ▶5.6 Listen to Sandy and complete her blog post with the words.

cleaning   cooking   eating   going   playing   shopping   watching

Sandy's blog

Home | About me | Archive | Contact me

Here are the 10 things I do most every week in order of how much I like them. ☺

1. _____ video games ☐
2. going out with friends ☐
3. _____ ☐
4. _____ out ☐
5. blogging ☐
6. _____ to work ☐
7. _____ with a friend ☐
8. working out / exercising ☐
9. _____ TV ☐
10. _____ the house ☐

What about you? Are you like me? ☺

B ▶5.7 Match her blog activities to photos a–j. Listen and write the number of the activity in the chart.

😍 love	😀 like	😐 don't mind	😟 don't like	🤢 hate
1				

C 🎤 Make it personal   Make a chart like the one in **B** and write 10 activities. Compare in pairs. Find two things you have in common.

I hate going to the dentist, and I don't like exercising.   *We both love dancing salsa.*

2 Grammar *like / love / hate / not mind* + verb *-ing*

A Match the statements that have similar meanings.

1 I like to clean the house.
2 She hates swimming.
3 He doesn't like to clean the house.
4 I don't mind swimming.

a Swimming is OK with me.
b He hates cleaning the house.
c She doesn't like swimming.
d I like cleaning the house.

5.2 What are your likes and dislikes?

Lesson Aims: To talk about likes and dislikes.

Function
Reading / Listening about free-time activities.
Talking about free-time activities you like / dislike.
Understanding stress / intonation in short sentences.

Language
Sandy loves playing video games and going out with her friends.
I don't mind cooking but I love eating out.
I hate doing the laundry.

Vocabulary: Free-time activities (clean, cook, eat out, etc.), weird, mind (v), fun, I'm joking, sad, surprised. House chores (cleaning, tidying, etc.)

Grammar: like / love / hate / not mind + verb -ing

Warm-up Recycle giving opinions and object pronouns. Draw a chart on the board, as shown below. Ask sts to write one example under each category. In small groups, sts ask each other *What do you think of (Shakira)?* and answer with *I like (her). I think (she's) a great singer.* Get class feedback on any interesting disagreements.

| An artist / type of music | A soccer player / an athlete / a team | A TV program / film | A country / city | A famous local person |

Language note If they ask / talk about soccer teams the pronoun is *them*: *What do you think of (Chelsea)? I hate them.*

1 Vocabulary Free-time activities

A Focus on Sandy's blog. Ask: *What is Sandy's blog about? Do you follow blogs like this?* Ask sts to read the blog and predict where the words go. Play ▶5.6 for sts to listen / read and complete the gaps. Classcheck.

1 playing 3 cooking 4 eating 6 going 7 shopping
9 watching 10 cleaning

B Play ▶5.7 and have sts match a–j to sentences 1–10. Listen again, pausing and repeating the phrase she uses about each activity.

Focus on the emoticons and tell sts to listen again and write the numbers under the correct emotion. Tell them to listen to the pronunciation and what emotion it shows. Play the track again and tell sts to try and mimic the intonation.

Tip Help shyer sts with simple gestures to convey and consolidate meaning. Again, the idea of miming as they repeat is to add meaning, their own feelings / identity and memorability to what is otherwise just mechanical repetition. For further practice, you can lead the class in "repeat if it's true" mode. One st says a phrase (I hate cooking) and the class repeats it if they share that feeling.

1 e 2 a 3 b 4 d 5 g 6 h 7 c 8 i 9 j 10 f
love: 2
like: 4, 5, 7
don't mind: 3, 6
don't like: 8, 9
hate: 10

▶5.7 Turn to p. 315 for the complete audioscript.

C 🔵 **Make it personal** Now focus on Sandy's final questions, *What about you? Are you like me?* and elicit answers. Following the chart in **B**, sts make their own lists. Then, in pairs, sts tell each other about what they like or don't like doing and find one thing in common. Classcheck two things they have in common from each pair. Ask: *Is anyone like Sandy?*

2 Grammar like / love / hate / not mind + verb -ing

A Tell sts to read the sentences and complete the exercise. Emphasize how common verb + -ing is in English (as subject, after verbs of emotion, in continuous verb forms), compared with Latin languages.

Language note American English uses both verb forms with no difference. British English tends to use the gerund when *like* means *enjoy*. It is possible to use *to* + infinitive in a subject position; however, this is not very common and is usually used in dictionaries, instructional material, and quotes. A subject infinitive is usually followed by the verb *be* or a stative verb.

1 d 2 c 3 b 4 a

Language tip The structure that Spanish speakers use to say that they like doing something can lead to confusion when learning how to express likes and dislikes. Spanish speakers say *(A mi) Me gusta trabajar aqui*, which, as a result of mental translation, they tend to translate as *I'm like work here*. Pre-empt this by highlighting this difference between L1 and English.

♫ *I don't mind spending every day,*
Out on your corner in the pouring rain,
Look for the girl with the broken smile.

B Use the statements in **A** to help you complete the grammar box.

> **Choose the correct answer.**
> a With *love, like, hate*, use:
>   1 *to* + verb   2 verb *-ing*   3 both are possible
> b With *not mind*, use:
>   1 *to* + verb   2 verb *-ing*   3 both are possible

➡ **Grammar 5B** p.146

⚠ **Common mistakes**
~~drive~~ *driving*
I hate ~~drive~~ in traffic.
~~to drive~~ *driving*
I don't mind ~~to drive~~ at night.

C Order the words to make sentences.
1 like / soccer / on / don't / I / watching / games / TV / .
2 friend / loves / go / to / movies / my / best / the / to / .
3 mind / in / don't / shopping / I / malls / .
4 my / hate / out / work / sisters / to / .

D 🟢 **Make it personal** Change the sentences in **C** so they are true for you. Find someone who has the same sentences as you.

> *I don't mind watching soccer on TV.*   *I don't mind either!*

③ Pronunciation

A ▶ 5.8 Listen to the people talking about household chores. Match sentences 1–4 to photos a–d.
1 I don't <u>mind</u> cleaning the <u>bath</u>room.
2 I love <u>ti</u>dying my room.
3 I hate doing the <u>laun</u>dry.
4 I like <u>wash</u>ing the dishes.

B ▶ 5.8 Listen again. <u>Underline</u> the stressed words in sentences 2–4. Are pronouns, articles, and possessive adjectives normally stressed or unstressed?

> *I don't mind washing the dishes, but I hate doing the laundry.*

C 🟠 **Make it personal** Change the sentences in **A**, 1–4, so they are true for you. Compare with a partner. Do you agree?

④ Listening

A Read the ad for the show. Guess the answers to questions 1–3.
1 How old is she?
2 What does she love to do?
3 Who does she want to be like?

B ▶ 5.9 ▶ Watch the video and check your guesses. Do you think she has talent?

C 🟠 **Make it personal** Imagine you're on a talent show. Introduce yourself and say what you love doing and who you want to be like.

> *Good evening, everybody, I'm Sam, and I love to rap. I want to be like Jay-Z.*

The *Got Talent* <u>fran</u>chise is a very popular TV <u>tal</u>ent show. There are <u>ver</u>sions of this show in more than 50 countries. Before the con<u>tes</u>tant shows his or her talent, there is an intro<u>duc</u>tion to the person.

5.2

♪ **Song line:** Turn to p. 329 for notes about this song and an accompanying task.

B Direct sts to the grammar box. Sts complete the rules with *to + infinitive* and / or *verb -ing*. Paircheck. Classcheck with answers on the board. Refer to 🔑 **Common mistakes**. Then write *To drive on Sundays is fun.* on the board and elicit the mistake. Give / Elicit other wrong examples yourself for sts to correct you.

🔑 a 3 b 2

➡ **Grammar 5B** p. 146

C Do number 1 together. Sts do 2–4. Classcheck.

🔑
1 I don't like watching soccer games on TV.
2 My best friend loves to go to the movies.
3 I don't mind shopping in malls.
4 My sisters hate to work out.

D 🔘 **Make it personal** In pairs, sts say the sentences, changing them to make true statements about themselves and their family / friends. Highlight the speech bubble example. Classcheck by asking sts to report their partner's answers. Put some more locally relevant jumbled sentences on the board to personalize this further, e.g. *5 hate / watching / I / (local soccer team) / lose 6 to love / eat / (bad local restaurant)*.

Tip As with any exercise like this, fast finishers can make another jumbled sentence for a partner to order, or you can set this as written homework.

3 Pronunciation

A Point to photos a–d and ask: *What are they doing?* (but don't teach the new phrases yet). Play ▶ 5.8 and ask sts to complete the matching exercise. Paircheck. Classcheck with answers on the board. Drill pronunciation. Sts practice saying the phrases noticing the pink syllables for the correct word stress. To personalize, sts could order the activities from best to worst for them and then compare with a partner. Ask: *Do you agree?*

🔑 1 a 2 d 3 b 4 c

Tip Have sts in pairs quickly cover sentences 1–4 and remember what each person said for the four photos. Don't give feedback.

B Refer sts to sentence 1 in **A** so they notice the underlined words. Play the audio for that sentence so they can notice the sentence stress. Sts listen and mark the stress in 2–4. Sts listen again and notice the grammar words (*the, my*, etc.) are not stressed.

Tip Explain that English usually stresses the content words and the grammar words are usually not stressed. This means they are often hard to hear. This leads sts to think that in English we "eat" words sometimes.

🔑 Underline: 2 love, tidying 3 hate, laundry 4 like, washing Pronouns, articles and possessive adjectives are normally unstressed.

C 🔘 **Make it personal** Ask sts about the household chores in **A**: *Do you like cleaning the bathroom / tidying your room?* Sts rewrite sentences 1–4 from **A**, making true sentences, e.g. *I hate cleaning the bathroom. I don't mind washing the dishes.* Have sts compare their answers in pairs.

Ask the whole class: *Which household chore do you hate the most? Which do you think is the most unpopular?* Use a show of hands to vote.

4 Listening

A Ask: *Do you like watching talent shows on TV? What shows do you watch?* (Use America's / Britain's Got Talent as examples). Sts read the ad for the show and, in pairs, guess some information about the girl in the photo by answering questions 1–3.

B Play ▶ 5.9 for sts to watch / listen and check their answers. Classcheck. Ask: *Do you know any girls like her? / Do you know / like Beyoncé / the Alicia Keys song she's going to sing?*

Tip To best answer the last question about her talent, you could have sts search on the Internet for the original video.

🔑 1 10 years old 2 She loves to sing 3 Beyoncé

▶ 5.9 Turn to p. 315 for the complete audioscript.

Tip Ask sts to turn to the AS on p. 163. Sts listen / watch again and notice main sentence stress on content words and at the end of phrases.

C 🔘 **Make it personal** Ask *Do you have any hobbies / talents? Do you like singing / dancing / playing a musical instrument? What would you do on a talent show?* Sts read the instructions and the speech bubble example. Sts pretend they are taking part in a talent show and introduce themselves in small groups or to the class.

➡ **Workbook** p. 25

5.3 What do you like doing on vacation?

1 Vocabulary Vacation

A ▶5.10 Listen to and repeat 1–7, but say *I like* or *I don't like* before the activities.

Subject		Emily	Josh	You
1	camping			
2	cooking			
3	dancing			
4	hiking			
5	eating out			
6	buying souvenirs			
7	swimming			
8	visiting museums			
9	kayaking			
10	reading novels			
11	sightseeing			
12	snorkeling			
13	sunbathing			
14	taking a class			

B ▶5.11 Match activities 8–14 to the photos. Listen to check.

Common mistakes

~~with~~ *to*
He's similar ~~with~~ you.

C ▶5.12 In pairs. Listen to Emily and Josh. **A:** Check (✓) Emily's likes in the chart. **B:** Check (✓) Josh's likes. Check together, and listen again to confirm. Do you think they can go on vacation together?

> I think they really can't go on vacation together, because …

D 🔵 **Make it personal** Check (✓) the activities you like doing on vacation. Are you more similar to Emily or Josh? Why? Tell a partner.

> I love to swim, and I don't like camping, so I'm more similar to Emily.

5.3 What do you like doing on vacation?

Lesson Aims: Sts read about different vacations and then design their own perfect vacation.

Function
Reading two ads for vacations.
Talking about vacation preferences.

Language
Don't miss …
I prefer the retreat because I enjoy relaxing on vacation.

Vocabulary: Review vacation activities. Vacation words (sunset, massage, hammock.) Enjoy + -ing.

Warm-up Books closed. Write *vacation* on the board and elicit words and phrases related to types of vacation, vacation activities, adjectives to describe different vacations. Draw a mind map on the board with those headings as satellites. When you have some examples on the board, ask: *Do you like (+ activity)?* Sts answer using the adjectives on the board. *Yes, it's fun. No, it's boring.*

1 Vocabulary Vacation

A Focus on the list of vacation activities. Conduct this exercise as a meaningful drill. Play ⏵5.10 and have sts repeat each activity (1–7), but say them in *I like / I don't like …* sentences.

B Use photos a–g to present new vocabulary / activities. Sts match activities 8–14 to the photos. Paircheck. Play ⏵5.11 to check answers. Play the track again and have sts repeat the activities after the model. Add or elicit more vacation activities using examples or images, e.g. *wearing different clothes, relaxing taking selfies, doing something different …*

> 8 d 9 g 10 e 11 a 12 f 13 c 14 b

Language tip As sts have already learned about the present continuous, they have probably started to associate the suffix *-ing* to continuous forms of verbs, which in Portuguese and Spanish are formed with *-ndo*. In English, *-ing* forms of verbs can also be used as nouns, which is the case for all vacation activities in **A**. Tell sts that, to identify when *-ing* means the same as *-ndo* in the L1, they should look for the verb *to be* in the sentence which would indicate a continuous action.

C Point to the names *Emily* and *Josh* in the chart in **A** and tell sts they will listen to Emily and Josh talk about activities they like. Divide the class in two groups. Group A checks off Emily's activities while they listen. Group B checks off Josh's activities. Play ⏵5.12. Sts paircheck their answers within their groups, A or B. Listen again to confirm / catch anything they missed.

For extra practice, pair-up sts A and B (one st from each group). In pairs, sts exchange information about Emily and Josh to complete the chart. St A asks: *Does Josh like camping / cooking / dancing?* and st B asks about Emily. Play the track again so sts can check their answers. After, ask what sts thought about the listening. *Was it easy / difficult? Was one person easier to understand than the other?*

> Emily: 13, 7, 10, 5, 3, 11
> Josh: 12, 9, 14, 8, 1, 6, 2, 4

⏵5.12 Turn to p. 315 for the complete audioscript.

D **Make it personal** Sts check activities they like in the *You* column. Read the speech bubbles together, then draw sts' attention to the **Common mistakes**. In small groups, sts compare preferences and decide whether they would prefer to go on vacation with Josh or Emily, or with a classmate. Classcheck to see their preferences by raising their hands and encourage open-class feedback as they attempt to explain why.

Stronger classes Stronger classes Ask sts to read the question in the rubric *Check (✓) the activities you like doing on vacation.* and rephrase it, using "like to" (Check the activities you like to do on vacation.). Write more examples on the board for sts to rephrase in the same way e.g. *What do you like eating on vacation?* (like to eat) *What music do you like listening to?* (like to listen to).

Tip For additional practice, sts can each imitate ⏵5.11, but racing to say their favorite vacation activities in a maximum of ten seconds. This could be done for homework, where they record themselves on a site like www.vocaroo.com, then send the recordings to you to be played in the following class.

2 Reading

A ▶5.13 Read the two vacation ads quickly and answer questions 1–3 for each. Listen to check.
1 What country is the ad for?   2 What kind of vacation is it?   3 When can you go?

Tropical Trek

Our backpacker bus tours offer something for everyone who enjoys adventure.

What to do: Swim, snorkel, scuba dive, kayak, visit ancient Mayan pyramids, hike through a fantastic rainforest, search for crocodiles, camp in the jungle.

Don't miss the spectacular sunrises, the howler monkeys, and the flamingos!

Don't forget to lie in a relaxing hammock under a tree and spend some time doing nothing.

When to go: Mexico is a year-round destination and the fun never stops.

YOGA RICA

Discover our yoga retreats offered by local and international yoga professionals.

What to do: take a yoga class, meditate, have a massage, relax and read, walk in the forest, drink herbal tea.

Don't miss our guided tours to an active volcano, wonderful waterfalls, rivers, mountains, and beautiful beaches.

Don't forget to finish your day with a gourmet vegetarian meal in our restaurant.

When to go: we offer retreats all year round in Costa Rica.

B Read the rule, then answer the questions.
Use *more* + adjective to form the comparative.

Which vacation in **A**:
1 is more active?   3 has more variety?   5 is more dangerous?
2 is more relaxing?   4 is more healthy?   6 is more adventurous?

C ▶5.14 Match the highlighted words and phrases in the ads to photos 1–9. Listen, check, and repeat them. Which of the words with pink syllables are similar to your language?

D Which vacation do you prefer? Why?

I prefer the yoga retreat because I love relaxing on vacation, and I don't like hiking!

Common mistakes

taking
I enjoy ~~to take~~ selfies.

E 🎤 **Make it personal**   In groups, design the perfect vacation. Decide:
a what type of vacation?   d how long?
b when?   e what activities?
c where?

5.3

🎵 **Song line:** Turn to p. 329 for notes about this song and an accompanying task.

② Reading

A Say: *Look at the ads for 20 seconds and try to remember as much information as you can.* After 20 seconds, say: *Close your books. Tell your partner what you remember from the ads.* Ask sts to tell you some examples of what they remember. **Books open.** In pairs, sts look at the words with pink letters and agree on the best pronunciation for those words. Classcheck. Focus on the two ads and their titles. Sts quickly read (scan) them and answer questions 1–3. Play ▶ 5.13. Sts listen to check answers. Listen again to check pronunciation of the words in pink in the text.

> **Tip** These texts are quite long, with several new words, so you might want to use the listen and read option provided by ▶ 5.13 either here, or at stages **B** or **C**, or as a final listen and enjoy activity.

> Tropical Trek: 1 Mexico 2 backpacker bus tour 3 all year round
> Yoga Rica: 1 Costa Rica 2 yoga retreat 3 all year round

B Sts discuss these questions in pairs checking information in the texts as they work through the questions. After, ask sts to give some answers referring to the texts. Note: This activity is a more gradual way of teaching comparatives. You may choose to explain this to your sts.

> 1 Tropical Trek 2 Yoga Rica 3 Tropical Trek
> 4 Yoga Rica 5 Tropical Trek 6 Tropical Trek

C Elicit what sts can see in photos 1–9. Draw sts' attention to some cognates, such as *pyramids, vegetarian, herbal, professionals, options, spectacular, massage, relax, meditate, volcano, mountains*. Drill pronunciation. In pairs, sts match the highlighted words from the ads to photos 1–9.

Play ▶ 5.14 to check answers. Play it again and sts repeat the phrases.

> **Tip** Instead of just repeating after the audio, drill by asking a variety of questions to make sts say different phrases each time: *Which of the items / phrases do you like best / sound the nicest in English / is the quietest / is best for your health / is the smallest / would you like to enjoy right now / do you have in your country?*

> 1 backpacker bus tours 2 camp in the jungle
> 3 fantastic rainforest 4 relaxing hammock
> 5 spectacular sunrises 6 yoga retreats 7 herbal tea
> 8 wonderful waterfalls 9 beautiful beaches

D Do a quick review of last lesson's grammar if necessary and check rules on which verbs are followed by + verb, + verb -*ing*, both. Look at the **Common mistakes** as an example of *enjoy* + verb -*ing*. Sts look at the speech bubble as an example and compare their opinions of the two vacations. Monitor and check accuracy of grammar and vocabulary.

E 🗨 **Make it personal** Ask sts to put their hands up if they preferred the yoga vacation. Use this information to group sts into those who like more relaxing vacations and those who like active vacations. Check sts are clear on the task. Sts plan a vacation in pairs. Put pairs together to make groups of four or six and tell them to compare vacations.

Extra speaking Open up as a class discussion with more questions. Ask: *Have any of you been to Costa Rica / Mexico / to a yoga retreat / on a cruise? What do you know about these countries / activities?*

Extra writing You could ask sts to create a poster or brochure after the speaking task. They create a brochure to advertise the vacation they created. Tell them to use the texts as a model.

➔ **Workbook** p. 26

5.4 How often do you leave voice messages?

1 Listening

House sitters
Young, active, professional couple looking to house sit in downtown area before buying. No kids, no pets. We totally understand the importance of loving your home. References provided.

A ▶5.15 Read the ad and guess True (T) or False (F). Listen to / Watch the video to check.

A house sitter is someone who:
1 usually pays to stay in a house.
2 lives in a house all the time.
3 cleans and cooks for the owner.
4 often takes care of pets.
5 leaves when the owner comes back.

B 🗣 **Make it personal** In pairs, think of two advantages and disadvantages of being a house sitter. Would you like 1) to be or 2) to have a house sitter? Why (not)?

> One advantage is that you can see if you like the area.

> A disadvantage is that you have to leave when the owners return.

2 Vocabulary House sitting

A ▶5.16 Match the phrases to a–h in the picture. Listen, check, and repeat. Mime a phrase for a partner to say.

- [d] feed the cats / dog ___
- [ ] give the cats / dog some water ___
- [ ] turn on / off the lights ___
- [ ] walk the dog ___
- [ ] open / close the windows ___
- [ ] pick up / put the mail on the table ___
- [ ] water the plants ___
- [ ] don't let the cats out ___

64

5.4 How often do you leave voice messages?

Lesson Aims: Sts talk about house sitting and practice giving instructions in a phone message for someone coming to look after their house.

Function
Talk about advantages and disadvantages.
Understand a phone message.
Leave a phone message.

Language
One advantage is you can ...
I want to be a house sitter
Take the dog for a walk
I think it's important to ...

Vocabulary: House sitting (feed the cat, open the windows ...).
Grammar: Imperatives (Feed the cat, don't open the windows).

Warm-up Books closed. Ask: *Do you have a cat? A dog? A hamster? A snake?* to find out what pets they have. Ask: *What happens to your pets when you go on vacation?* or, if they don't have pets, ask: *Does anyone stay in your house when you go on vacation? Have you stayed in someone's house while they were on vacation?* Sts discuss in pairs or small groups. Monitor and promote conversation, asking more questions as necessary.

1 Listening

A Point to the woman in the photo and ask: *What's her job? What's she doing?* (Don't give the answer yet.) Sts read the ad and guess true or false for the five sentences. Don't give answers yet. Play ▶5.15 for sts to listen / watch and check their answers. Write some more examples on the board, after listening, for sts to mark true or false, e.g. *takes care of plants* (T), *looks after children* (F), *provides security* (T), *never goes out* (F). Classcheck.

1 F 2 F 3 F 4 T 5 T

B 🔘 **Make it personal** Refer sts to the speech bubbles. Give your own opinion as a further model. Sts then discuss the question in pairs or small groups. Listen for good examples of vocabulary and go over this afterwards, praising learners for their language use.

Extra activity In pairs, sts could role-play a phonecall between the homeowner and the person who wrote the house sitter ad. Ask pairs to volunteer to perform their dialogue for the class.

2 Vocabulary House sitting

A Sts read the eight verb phrases and match them to objects a–h in the picture. Play ▶5.16 to check answers. Classcheck. Play the track again and have sts repeat the phrases. In pairs, sts test each other and take turns miming and guessing the phrases.

Tip Do not go into the grammar of phrasal verbs at this stage, just stick to teaching them as chunks. These are introduced in levels 2 and 3.

a turn on / off the lights   b open / close the windows
c don't let the cats out   e give the cats / dog some water
f pick up / put the mail on the table   g walk the dog
h water the plants

B ▶5.17 Listen to a phone message for a house sitter. Number the activities in A in the order you hear them, 1–8.

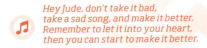
Hey Jude, don't take it bad, take a sad song, and make it better. Remember to let it into your heart, then you can start to make it better.

C ▶5.17 Listen again and complete Lori's notes with these pronouns. What does each pronoun refer to?

him   it   me   them (x 4)   us

1- Open the windows and close _____ again every day.
2- Pick up the mail, and put _____ on the table.
3- Feed the animals in the morning and evening (don't give _____ too much food).
4- The lights and air-conditioning - turn _____ off when you go out.
5- Don't forget to give _____ some water.
6- Walk Chips in the morning and afternoon (don't take _____ near the road).
7- Call _____ if you have any questions.
8- Please tell _____ if Salt, Pepper, or Chips escape.

➡ **Grammar 5C** p. 146

D 🔴 **Make it personal** Which is the most important thing to do when you house sit? Which is the least important? Compare in groups.

I think it's most important to feed the animals.

I think it's more important to give them water.

⚠ **Common mistakes**
                          most important thing
Which is the ~~thing most important~~?
               least
The ~~less~~ important thing is to put it on the table.

3 Grammar Imperatives

A Listen and read Lori's instructions in 2C again and circle the correct options in the grammar box.

> Imperative verb forms:
> 1 **have / don't have** a subject.
> 2 use **don't / doesn't** for negative forms.
> 3 are statements of fact / tell you to do something.
> 4 go **up ↗ / down ↘** at the end.

➡ **Grammar 5D** p. 146

B In pairs, make ten instructions combining the words. Try them out with another pair. Use *please* to sound more polite.

open / close   your book / eyes
pick up / put down   your phone / pen
turn on / off   the lights / the air conditioning
point to   the teacher / the door

Please close the door. Don't open it again!

C 🟢 **Make it personal** Imagine you're going on vacation.
1 Complete this list of instructions for a house sitter. Compare in groups. Who has the most useful instructions?
   1 Don't forget to _____.
   2 Please _____.
   3 Please don't _____.
   4 Remember to _____
   5 _____

Please don't have a party!

2 Leave a phone message for the house sitter. Use AS 5.17 on p. 163 to help you.

B Tell sts they will hear a phone message for a house sitter. Play ▶5.17. They number the tasks in **A** (1–8) in the order they hear them. Paircheck. Classcheck with answers on the board.

> 1 f   2 b   3 h   4 a   5 d   6 e   7 g   8 c

▶5.17 Turn to p. 315 for the complete audioscript.

Tip Ask sts to turn to the AS on p. 163. Sts listen again and notice the pronunciation of object pronouns in speech.

C Sts listen again and complete Lori's notes with the pronouns. Paircheck. Classcheck with answers on the board. Ask *What does it / them / her / him refer to?* for each sentence as you check sts' answers. Explain that animals are referred to as *it* in English, but domesticated animals (pets) are usually referred to as *he / she / him / her*.

> 1 them (windows)   2 it (mail)   3 them (animals)
> 4 them (lights and air-conditioning)   5 them (animals)
> 6 him (Chips)   7 me (home owner)
> 8 us (home owner + partner)

➔ **Grammar 5C** p. 146

D **Make it personal** Refer to the speech bubbles and tell sts they need to practice all the phrases to talk about house-sitting jobs. Draw sts' attention to the **Common mistakes** and remind them that these mistakes are most often made when they try to translate directly from L1. Tell sts to think of some ideas before they speak and then assign groups for sts to share ideas.

♪ **Song line:** Turn to p. 329 for notes about this song and an accompanying task.

3 Grammar Imperatives

A Write *Open the windows* on the board. Ask: *How do you say this in the negative?* (Don't open the windows.) Explain this kind of structure is an imperative. It's an instruction. Sts read the grammar box and complete the exercise. Classcheck.

> 1 don't have   2 don't   3 tell you to do something
> 4 down

➔ **Grammar 5D** p. 146

Language tip In Portuguese and Spanish, negative imperatives are formed by adding *no* (*não / no*) in front of the affirmative forms. This leads sts to do the same in English. **No** *swim in the ocean.* **No** *drink and drive.* Pre-empt by explaining that, in English, you always use the auxiliary *don't* for negative imperatives. **Don't** *swim in the ocean.* **Don't** *drink and drive.*

B Write one example on the board using the words. Refer sts to the speech bubble example and set a time limit of five minutes for sts to complete nine more instructions. Tell sts that *please* can go at the start or the end of the imperative. Ask some sts to say their instructions to the class.

Tip Make this activity physical. Sts take turns to read their instructions to a partner who has to do the action, e.g. *Point to the teacher. Close the door. Open your book.*

C **Make it personal** Say: *Now think about your home. Imagine you're going on vacation and your classmate will house sit for you. Write him / her a list of instructions.* They complete the sentences and then discuss question 1. Ask sts to refer to AS on p. 163 for help with number 2. Ask sts to sit back to back and leave their messages to each other. For stronger sts or faster finishers, you could add *Be careful (not) to ...* to this list.

Tip Sts can record their message for homework, e.g. sts might record their messages online via www.vocaroo.com or directly on a mobile device, and send the link via email or SMS to a classmate(s). These sites are free. Say: *Please don't forget to do your homework!* to finish the lesson.

➔ **Workbook** p. 27

5.5 What's a staycation?

ID Skills Understanding instructions

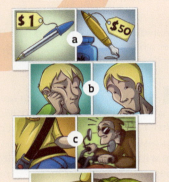

A ▶5.18 Listen to the pairs of opposite adjectives and match them to pictures a–d. In pairs, can you think of others?
1. boring – fun / interesting
2. expensive – cheap
3. safe – dangerous
4. neat – messy

How about rude and polite?

B ▶5.19 Listen, and read about two alternative types of vacations, 1 and 2. Match them to their best definition. There's one extra.
- ☐ You take a vacation at home.
- ☐ You go and stay in another person's home.
- ☐ You pay to stay in someone's home.

Vacations for less!

1 Couchsurfing helps you stay free in about 200,000 cities around the world. Couchsurfing.org is an international network and there are more than 12 million members. Members offer people a place to stay in their homes. In return, they can stay free at another member's home. Members are students and professionals. You can be a surfer or a host or both!

If you want to couchsurf, here's what to do:
- Find a host who has positive references and a complete profile.
- Look for a host who has similar interests.
- Write a request to your potential host.
- Be a good guest.
- Don't be rude or messy! Help with the household chores.
- Write a reference as soon as possible to help other couchsurfers.

2 A **stay**cation is a vacation that you spend at home! It's a way to have a rest from work and your routine without spending much money. Maybe it sounds boring, but it doesn't have to be.

Here are some tips to make your staycation fun:
- Spend time at home. Invite friends to use your pool or have dinner.
- Visit local parks and museums. There are often really cool things in your hometown.
- Find out about local festivals in your area.
- Change your routine – don't do what you usually do every day. Do something different. Get up late. Change stores. Eat different foods. Take a bus, ride a bike, or walk for a change.
- Relax and don't think about work until your staycation is over.

C Read again and write True (T) or False (F).
1. Couchsurfing only happens in Europe.
2. You don't pay to couchsurf.
3. Couchsurfers write references and requests.
4. Staycations are for boring people.
5. People on staycation don't go out.
6. On a staycation, the idea is to do different things.

D ▶5.20 Listen to six sentences from the text and say *staycation* or *couchsurfing* after each.

E 🔴 Make it personal In pairs. Write five instructions for:
a) a couchsurfer visiting your town OR
b) a person who wants to staycation in your hometown.

Compare instructions with another pair. Do you agree with theirs?

Our first instruction for a couchsurfer is: Don't make noise. *That's a good one. That's very important.*
For a staycation in our hometown: Visit the market.

66

5.5 What's a staycation?

Lesson Aims: Sts get further practice in understanding instructions and compare two more types of vacations.

Function
Asking about opposites.
Reading about two more types of vacations. Talking about / Comparing vacations.

Language
What's the opposite of ...?
A staycation is a vacation that you spend at home! In my opinion, it can be boring.

Vocabulary: Newly invented words (staycation, couchsurfing.) Adjectives (boring, relaxing, exciting, interesting, rude, polite, safe, dangerous, tidy, messy.)
Grammar: -ing adjectives.

Warm-up Review the alphabet and adjectives of opinion. Either play *Hangman* or a *How do you spell ...?* with the words *boring, fun, expensive, interesting, cheap, relaxing, safe,* and *dangerous*.

ID Skills Understanding instructions

A Sts match pairs of opposites 1–4 to pictures a–d. Paircheck. Play ▶5.18 to check answers. In pairs, sts think of any other opposite adjectives they know. Classcheck.

> **Tip** If time allows, with a stronger class, compare adjectives ending in *-ing* with *-ed* adjectives as in *I'm excited / tired / bored*, as opposed to *It's exciting / tiring / boring*.

1 b 2 a 3 c 4 d

B Ask: *Where are you going for your next vacation?* to see what their plans are. Ask the lesson title question: *What's a staycation?* to see what they can come up with. Do the same with *What's couchsurfing?* but don't give them the answers yet if they don't know. Focus on the definitions and tell them to read the two texts to find which is which. Play ▶5.19 so sts can listen and read the texts. Sts match texts 1 and 2 to the best description. Ask: *Have any of you tried either of these vacations?*

> **Tip** After any (listening and) reading activity like this, it can be useful to get sts to cover the text and in pairs tell each other what they can remember from it. This gives you instant feedback on what they've understood, where pronunciation problems lie, etc.

Elicit or tell sts that *couchsurfing* also includes the possibility of a couchsurfer asking for local advice and going out with another couchsurfer for a meal or a tour in a town without necessarily staying at his / her house. For further information, sts can go to www.couchsurfing.org

1 You go and stay in another person's home.
2 You take a vacation at home.

Tip Look at the words *couchsurfing* and *staycation* in the text and ask which two words formed each (couch + surfing, stay + vacation). Encourage sts to think of other examples. Possible answers: *emoticon* (emotion + icon), *guesstimate* (guess + estimate), *chillax* (chill + relax). Ask: *Does this happen in your language?* Explain that languages adapt very fast to changes in our world and new words like this are invented every day.

C Ask sts to cover the texts in **B** and decide whether sentences 1–6 are true or false based on what they remember. Sts reread and check if their guesses were right. Classcheck.

1 F 2 T 3 T 4 F 5 F 6 T

D Play ▶5.20 and pause after each sentence. Sts say *staycation* or *couchsurfing* for each sentence they hear. Check answers one by one as sts say their guesses.

1 couchsurfing 2 staycation 3 staycation
4 couchsurfing 5 staycation 6 couchsurfing

▶5.20 Turn to p. 315 for the complete audioscript.

E **Make it personal** Ask: *Would you / Do you prefer to be a host for a couchsurfer or a staycation friend / colleague / guest? Why?* Tell sts they have to choose one of these options and write some instructions for a guest. Pairs read the speech bubbles to get some ideas. Check meaning of *noise* and teach / elicit *noisy*. Sts write their instructions and change with another pair. Sts read the instructions and say if they agree with them.

> **Tip** Encourage peer feedback by telling pairs to check each other's texts for grammar and vocabulary and give positive feedback as well as pointing out any errors.

5.5 Do you live near here?

 In my place, in my place. Were lines that I couldn't change, And I was lost, oh yeah, I was lost.

ID in Action Giving directions

A ▶5.21 Match the phrases to photos 1–6. Listen, repeat, and mime them.

☐ a corner
☐ cross at the stoplight
☒ 1 go straight
☐ a stop sign
☐ turn left
☐ turn right

B In pairs, share what you know about San Francisco in one minute.

I know it's a large city on the west coast of the U.S.

Common mistakes

Do you know where ~~is~~ the *is* stadium?

Turn ~~to~~ left.

C ▶5.22 Listen to and order the tourist's questions, 1–4. How many people does he speak to?

☐ Is there a movie theater around here?
☐ Are there any bookstores near here?
☐ Where's the mall?
☐ Do you know where the library is?

D ▶5.22 Listen again and complete 1–4. Do you think he understands the last man?

1 It's _____ front of you _____ Market Street. Cross _____ at the stoplight.
2 Go _____ on Market Street and turn _____ on Fourth Street. Go _____ for one block, and the movie theater's on the _____ of Fourth and Mission Street.
3 Turn _____ on Grove Street.
4 Go straight for about _____ blocks. The bookstore's on your _____.

E In pairs, use the language above to ask for and give directions to places 1–4. Start at Powell Street Station.

1 City Hall
2 the Museum of Modern Art
3 Union Square Park
4 a parking garage

F **Make it personal** In pairs. **A:** Give directions to your home from school. **B:** Follow the directions on a map until you find where **A** lives.

Leave the school and turn left. Go straight for two blocks. My house is on the left.

5.5 Do you live near here?

Lesson Aims: Sts understand and give simple directions.

Function
Listening to and asking for directions.

Language
Cross at the stoplight.
Leave the school and turn left.
How do I get to …?

Vocabulary: Directions: turn left / right, cross at the stoplight, go straight, a corner, a stop sign. Review vacation activities, places around town, prepositions of place and movement.
Grammar: Imperatives review.

 Song line: Turn to p. 329 for notes about this song and an accompanying task.

Before the lesson Gather some photos of San Francisco, either digital or printed. Pick up some maps of the local area from the Tourist Information office, or print some from the Internet.

ID in Action Giving directions

A Ask the title question: *Do you live near here? Where exactly? How do I get there?* to see what the class can come up with. Leave the question on the board until the end of the lesson when they will have learned to answer it more effectively.

In pairs, sts match phrases to the photos 1–6. Play ▶ 5.21 to check answers. Play the audio again and have sts repeat and mime all the phrases. In pairs, sts mime signs and phrases for their partners to guess and say.

Elicit more signs / instructions which can be easily mimed when giving or asking for directions. Focus on the ⊙ **Common mistakes** . Write *Cross in the stoplight*. on the board and elicit the correction that is needed (at the stoplight).

2 turn left   3 turn right   4 a stop sign
5 cross at the stoplight   6 a corner

B Bring in photos of San Francisco or look some up, e.g. of the Golden Gate Bridge or Alamo Park. Refer to details in the cultural note below. Sts share information in pairs.

Cultural note San Francisco: about 8 million people live in S.F. Bay area, which includes San Jose and Oakland, and it's the 14th most populous city in the U.S. Famous events: 1849 California Gold Rush; 1906 earthquake and fire; 1970s hippies and summer of love, gay rights movement. It's the 35th most visited city worldwide, famous for cool summers, fog, steep hills, eclectic architecture. Landmarks include the Golden Gate Bridge, cable cars, and Chinatown.

C **Books closed.** Sts will hear a tourist in San Francisco asking for information in the street. Ask: *How many people does he speak to?* Play ▶ 5.22. Classcheck. **Books open.** Sts read the four questions. Listen again and sts number the questions in the order they hear them. Classcheck.

1 Where's the mall?
2 Is there a movie theater around here?
3 Do you know where the library is?
4 Are there any bookstores near here?
He speaks to six people.

▶ 5.22 Turn to p. 316 for the complete audioscript.

D Sts listen again and complete 1–4. Classcheck. Ask: *Do you think he understood the last man?*

1 in, on, here   2 straight, right, straight, corner   3 right
4 four, left
He probably doesn't understand the last man.

E Focus on the map and give some instructions to one of the points. Tell sts to follow you and say where you go. Sts look at the map and take turns asking and giving directions for places 1–4.

Weaker students Tell them to refer to the sentences in **D** for help. Or give them time to write out some directions for this activity before they speak.

F ⊙ **Make it personal**   Go back to the initial question *Do you live near here?* Give a model yourself, e.g. how to get to your own home, and see if they can follow your directions. In pairs, sts do the same. If possible, have some local maps available or sts can use their cell phones. You can even get sts to try to draw the instructions they hear from their partner. Monitor and correct as necessary.

Round off by returning to the question you wrote on the board at the start of the lesson and ask sts if they feel they can answer it better.

➔ **Workbook** p. 28
➔ ⓘⒹ **Richmond Learning Platform**
➔ **Writing** p. 68
➔ ⓘⒹ **Café** p. 69

Writing 5 A city brochure

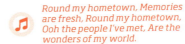
Round my hometown, Memories are fresh, Round my hometown, Ooh the people I've met, Are the wonders of my world.

A What do you know about Vancouver? Say what you see in the photos.

B Read the brochure entry and answer questions 1–8.
1. Where's a good place to start the day?
2. Where's a beautiful place for photos?
3. What's a good place to go when it's rainy?
4. What's a good place to go to buy souvenirs?
5. What are three examples of places to eat lunch?
6. Is there a romantic place in this city?
7. What can tourists do at night?
8. Is this city famous for anything?

C Study the underlined words in **B** and answer 1–3.
1. Do adjectives come before or after a noun?
2. Do adjectives come before or after the verb *be*?
3. Can you make adjectives plural?

D Order the words to make sentences.
1. is / wine / for / France / famous / .
2. the / try / cheese / local / .
3. spectacular / a / there / view / is / .
4. mountains / can / in / beautiful / the / walk / you / .
5. visit / amazing / can / you / museum / the / .

E Read **Write it right!** and find eight sequencing words in **B**.

> **Write it right!**
>
> Use sequencing words to order actions: *before, after, when, first, then, finally,* etc.
> You can take photos in the park. **After that**, go to the museum.
> **After** taking (or **After** you take) photos, go to the museum.
> **Before** going (or **Before** you go) to the museum, take some photos in the park.

A DAY IN VANCOUVER

- Welcome to Canada's third – but most beautiful – city! First, have breakfast at Purebread Bakery in Gastown. The coffee and chocolate brownies <u>are delicious</u>!
- After eating, rent a bike and ride to Stanley Park. This is an <u>enormous park</u> downtown with lots of monuments, live concerts, street artists, and wildlife. There are <u>beautiful views</u> of the mountains. Before leaving, visit Prospect Point and take some photos of the ocean.
- After that, take the subway to the Museum of Vancouver. Vancouver is famous for its First Nations art, and you can see some amazing <u>old and modern art,</u> and <u>cultural objects</u>.
- When you leave the museum, go back downtown. There are hundreds of restaurants for lunch: Asian noodle restaurants, Canadian seafood cafés with <u>fresh fish</u>, and lots of great American burger bars. Go to Main Street after lunch and shop in the local <u>independent stores</u>, then take a water taxi to the public market at Granville Island.
- Finally, Vancouver has great nightlife, with many clubs and music venues. And you have to visit the Top of Vancouver revolving restaurant for a night-time view of this incredible city – <u>it's very romantic</u>.

F Note your answers to 1–8 in **B** for your town or city.

G **Make it personal** Imagine a tourist is coming to your town / city. Plan a day for her / him.

Before	Use your notes for **F**. Give extra information, too, e.g., your opinion.
While	Use adjectives and a variety of sequencing words.
After	Check your writing carefully and / or email it to a partner before giving it to your teacher.

68

Writing 5 A City Brochure

🎵 **Song line:** Turn to p. 330 for notes about this song and an accompanying task.

A Point to the photos and ask sts what they know about the Canadian city of Vancouver. Ask: *Where is Vancouver? What can you see in the photos?* Elicit *(tall) buildings, water, parks, mountains, clouds, trees, boats, harbor, houses*, etc.

B Point to questions 1–8 and tell sts to read them and find the answers in the text. Paircheck. Classcheck.

> 1 Purebread Bakery, Gastown.
> 2 Prospect Point.
> 3 The Museum of Vancouver.
> 4 Main Street, downtown.
> 5 Asian noodle restaurants, Canadian seafood cafés, and American burger bars.
> 6 Yes, the Top of Vancouver revolving restaurant.
> 7 Visit a club or music venue, or the Top of Vancouver revolving restaurant.
> 8 Yes, its First Nations art, which you can see at the Museum of Vancouver.

C Sts look at the underlined words in **B**. Remind them that all the underlined phrases contain adjectives. In pairs, sts study the phrases in **B** and answer questions 1–3 about the rules for adjective use. Classcheck.

> 1 Adjectives come before a noun.
> 2 Adjectives come after the verb *be*.
> 3 No, you can't make adjectives plural.

D Elicit the correct order for sentence 1. Individually, sts order sentences 2–5. Paircheck. Classcheck with answers on the board.

> 1 France is famous for wine.
> 2 Try the local cheese.
> 3 There is a spectacular view.
> 4 You can walk in the beautiful mountains.
> 5 You can visit the amazing museum.

E Read **Write it right!** with sts and ask them to find eight sequencing words / phrases in **B**. Paircheck. Classcheck with answers on the board or use the *Digital Book for Teachers*.

> First, After eating, Before leaving, After that, When, after lunch, and then, finally.

F In pairs, sts take turns asking and answering the questions in **B** about their town or city. Classcheck by having a different st answer each of the questions. Encourage other sts to suggest different answers.

G 🎧 **Make it personal** Tell sts to imagine a tourist is coming to their town or city. Read the steps Before, While, and After with sts so as to better guide their writing. Tell them to refer to text **B** as a model to write a one-day plan for the tourist. Remind them to use adjectives and sequencing words.

> **Tip** To encourage creativity, ask sts to write an alternative guide, suggesting and describing places visitors wouldn't normally visit.

5 Miss GPS

ID Café

1 Before watching

A Match the nouns with the verb phrases to make sentences.

1. A map — gets you from one place to another.
2. A car — picks up a signal so you can make a call.
3. GPS / sat nav — always shows you where north is.
4. A compass — shows roads and highways.
5. A cell phone — can give you directions by voice.

B Number the items 1–8 in your order of importance for a road trip to a new place.

- a car / motorbike ☐
- a cell phone ☐
- a map ☐
- extra batteries ☐
- a phone charger ☐
- food and drink ☐
- good company ☐
- music you enjoy ☐

C 🔘 **Make it personal** Compare and explain in pairs. Many differences?

> I hate maps, so for me that's number 8. My number 1 is good company!

> I'm different. I like to travel alone, so my number 1 is music I enjoy.

D In pairs, choose four items from A and B you think the actors use on their trip. Watch to check. Were you right?

2 While watching

A Complete 1–12 with the correct form of the verbs. Who says them?

| avoid | hate | have | go | like | love (x 2) |
| save | take | tell | use | waste | |

1. Does anyone _____ a map?
2. Maps? Who _____ maps anymore?
3. I _____ using maps. Especially old maps.
4. Here she is. Miss GPS. You _____?
5. We don't _____ anywhere without GPS, right Auggie?
6. Technology _____ all the fun out of traveling.
7. I disagree. Technology _____ time.
8. And it _____ us where we're going, while we're driving.
9. Come on. Let's not _____ time arguing.
10. And a GPS helps us _____ traffic. A map can't do that.
11. And I _____ hearing the sound of my GPS girl's voice.
12. I _____ hearing that voice. It's so annoying!

B 🔘 **Make it personal** In pairs, talk about technology. Which items do you love? Any you find annoying?

> I love electricity. Without it, I can't do anything!

> I love cell phones, but sometimes ring tones are annoying.

3 After watching

A What happens on the trip? Write True (T) or False (F). Correct the false sentences.

1. They get lost.
2. Daniel forgets to plug in the GPS.
3. The GPS battery's dead.
4. August has a strong signal on his cell phone.
5. They stop the car and ask for directions.
6. Andrea uses a map and gives directions.
7. August gets a signal on his cell phone.

B Who says it? Match 1–8 to Andrea (An), August (A), Daniel (D), Lucy (L). Watch again and imitate the actors.

	An	A	D	L
1 GPS! Not always reliable.				
2 Are you kidding me?				
3 Not a car in sight and no signal. We are so lost.				
4 Especially when you forget to plug it in.				
5 I'm gonna get a signal, don't worry.				
6 What are we gonna do? Turn back?				
7 Lucy and I will give directions from now on.				
8 After that, we're back on the main road.				

C 🔘 **Make it personal** Which do you prefer? Compare in pairs. Why?

1. giving the driver directions or driving the car
2. driving or taking a taxi
3. driving in the city or in the country
4. walking or cycling
5. using a GPS with the voice on or off

> I like driving and I'm not good with maps. So, I prefer driving.

ID Café 5 Miss GPS

1 Before watching

A Write the questions below on the board and have sts ask and answer them in pairs. Classcheck.

Can you drive?

Do you like traveling by car?

Do you enjoy driving long distances?

Ask: *What do you need for a road trip?* Point to words / phrases 1–5 and ask sts to complete the matching activity

Sts match items 1–5 to the definitions. Paircheck. Classcheck with answers on the board.

> 1 A map shows roads and highways.
> 2 A car gets you from one place to another.
> 3 GPS / sat nav can give you directions by voice.
> 4 A compass always shows you where north is.
> 5 A cell phone picks up a signal so you can make a call.

B Ask sts to read through the items and check understanding of vocabulary. Ask: *Which items are most important for a road trip to a new place?* Tell sts to order the items individually.

C **Make it personal** Have sts compare their answers in **B**. Ask some sts to share their answers with the class and give reasons for their answers.

D Tell sts they are going to watch a video showing Andrea, August, Daniel and Lucy going on a road trip. Sts choose four items from **A** and **B** that they think the people in the video will use on their trip. Come back to this question when sts have watched the video and see if their guesses were correct.

2 While watching

A Point to the verbs in the box and pre-teach *avoid* and *waste* – provide sts with some simple example sentences, e.g., *I avoid going to the supermarket on Fridays. There are always too many people! Don't waste your time phoning her. She's not home.*

Give sts time to read the phrases from the video and predict answers.

Play **Video 5**. Sts complete the phrases with the verbs from the box, then identify who says each sentence. Paircheck. Classcheck.

> 1 have   2 uses (August)   3 love (Andrea)   4 like
> 5 go (Daniel)   6 takes (Lucy)   7 saves (Daniel)   8 tells
> 9 waste   10 avoid (August)   11 love   12 hate

B **Make it personal** Point to the dialogue in the speech bubbles and have two volunteers read the conversation. Ask the whole class: *What do you think about using technology? Do you like it? Hate it?* Sts discuss their answers in pairs. Tell them to use at least three verbs from **A**. Monitor closely for the use of verbs of emotions + verb *-ing*. At the end, ask sts to tell the class their partners' opinion.

3 After watching

A Point to statements 1–7 and ask sts to check the true sentences and correct the false ones. Paircheck. Classcheck.

> 1 True   2 True   3 True   4 False – August does not have a strong signal on his cell phone.   5 False – They stop the car and Andrea looks at the map.   6 True   7 False – August gets no signal on his cell phone.

B Focus on the table and have sts check which character says each sentence in the video. Paircheck. Replay **Video 5** for sts to check answers. Pause the video for sts to repeat the phrases, copying the actors' intonation. Classcheck.

Skills	An	Aug	Dan	Lu
1 GPS! Not always reliable.	✓			
2 Are you kidding me?				✓
3 Not a car in sight and no signal. We are so lost.		✓		
4 Especially when you forget to plug it in.			✓	
5 I'm gonna get a signal, don't worry.				✓
6 What are we gonna do? Turn back?			✓	
7 Lucy and I will give directions from now on.	✓			
8 After that, we're back on the main road.			✓	

C **Make it personal** Read the first question with sts and have a volunteer read the answer in the speech bubble. Sts work in pairs to discuss questions 2–5. Encourage sts to give reasons for their answers. Classcheck by asking individual sts to report their partner's answer for each question.

Mid-term review Play *Thirty Seconds*.

- 4 to 8 players. Divide into 2 teams.
- From the start, teams go in opposite directions.
- Toss a coin.
     Heads move 1 square.
     Tails move 2 squares.
- Talk about the topic, answer the question, or do the activity on the square. Maximum 30 seconds per person.
- The winning team is the first to complete the full circuit.

Mid-term review Play *Thirty Seconds*.

Sts work in groups of four or eight. Within their groups, sts form two teams to play against each other. There are two starting points, one for each team (teams go in opposite directions.) Point to the coins in the instructions box on top of p. 70, and explain to sts that they will toss the coin each time to determine whether they move one square or two. If they get heads, they move one square; if they get tails, they move two squares.

 heads   tails

At each square they stop at, sts from the same team take turns talking about the suggested topic. (For more info, refer to the chart on p. 155). The winning team is the first to complete the full circuit. Draw sts' attention to the language prompts in both inner curves of the circuit, and to the winner's "prize" (talk about himself / herself for 30 seconds) at the finishing point. Monitor closely for accuracy and offer help whenever necessary.

When sts are uncertain about what to say at a specific square, offer help by either prompting language or telling them the pages where they can find the items / topics, as listed in the chart on p. 155.

St A is the one who tosses the coin and is expected to either speak on his / her own, or answer a question. The questions should be asked by a member of the same team, referred to as st B in the chart. Do not allow strong sts to monopolize the activity – vary participants as much as possible so that no learner is left out.

Topics	Reference	Expected language production
Your family	p. 22	St A: I have a (small) family. My mother's name is (Sarah) and my father's name's (Anthony) I have (two) brothers, (Juan) and (Carlos).
Favorite season	p. 35	St B: What's your favorite season? St A: My favorite season is summer because … .
Describe a friend's routine.	p. 20–21	St A: (Nathan) usually gets up at 6 a.m., has breakfast at 6:30 and leaves home at … . He/She starts work at … .
Sports	p. 45	St A names five sports.
Why are you learning English?	p. 40	St B: Why are you learning English? St A: I have to learn English for my job.
What are they wearing? Describe a classmate.	p. 50	St A describes a classmate: (Luis) is wearing a brown jacket, blue jeans and a white T-shirt.
Vacation activities	p. 62	St A: On vacation I enjoy sunbathing and sightseeing. I don't like camping.
Chores + / −	p. 61	St A: I hate washing the dishes. I don't mind doing the laundry.
Spell your full name.	p. 8–9	St B: How do you spell your first name? St A: M-A-R-I-A.
Introduce yourself. (Name /Age / Nationality)	p. 6–7	Hi! I'm Rebecca. / My name's … and I'm (18) years old. I'm (Canadian).
What am I doing? (Mime an action.)	p. 34	St A mimes an action for his / her team to guess (using the Present continuous).
Next weekend	p. 36, 142	St B: What are you doing next weekend? St A: I'm watching a DVD and studying for a test.
How often do you go to the grocery store?	p. 18, 25	St B: How often do you go to the grocery store? St A: I (usually /always / etc.) go to the grocery store on (Saturday) (afternoon).
A celebrity you like / don't like	p. 38	I think Taron Egerton is a fantastic actor. He's British. I think he's about (30) years old. I love his movies.
Your town	p. 58	St A: In my town, there are seven museums, a lot of shopping malls, and theaters. There's a … . There aren't any … .
What's this? (Describe a picture from these pages)	photos on game page	St B: (pointing to an object) What's this? St A: It's a …
Abilities + / −	p. 46	St A talks about two things he / she can do well, and two things he /she can't do.
Morning routine	p. 20–21	St A: I get up at … . I brush my teeth … . I have breakfast at … .
The weather	p. 32	St B: What's the weather like today? St A: It's cloudy and cool.
Free-time activities	p. 60	St B: What do you usually do in your free time? St A: I usually go out with friends. / I like going out with friends.
Winner's Prize! Talk about yourself for 30 seconds.	Units 1–5	Introduce yourself / Talk about abilities / likes and dislikes / family / routine.

6.1 What's in your refrigerator?

1 Vocabulary Food and drink

A ◯ 6.1 Match the food on the counter 1–8 to these words. Try to pronounce them. The highlighted letters are all pronounced /ə/. Then listen to Jeff making a shopping list to check.

- ☐ bananas
- ☐ oil
- ☐ spaghetti
- ☐ tomatoes
- ☐ chocolate
- ☐ salt
- ☐ tea
- ☐ vinegar

72

Unit overview: The main topics of unit 6 are countable vs. uncountable food items and nouns, quantifiers and *How much* vs. *How many*, which are presented by different people talking about their eating habits and preferences. In this unit, sts also read / scan a menu for specific information and learn / practice how to order a meal at a restaurant.

If you're doing this as the first unit of English ID split edition, use the Question syllabus from the ID Language map at the start of this book to revise units 1–5. Sts can ask and answer in pairs, to diagnose what, if anything, needs to be reviewed.

6.1 What's in your refrigerator?

Lesson Aims: Sts learn to talk about food and drink items.

Function
Naming food and drink items.
Talking about food and drinks you like / dislike.
Listening to a couple talk about what they have in their fridge.

Language
I really like bananas, but I hate vinegar.
Why's there all this food on the counter?
There's also some salt, some tea …

Vocabulary: Food and drink items, bananas, chocolate, oil, salt.
Grammar: Countable vs. uncountable, *some*, *any*.

Warm-up Books open. Point to the photo in the book or display it on the IWB. Say: *Do you usually have these things in your kitchen? Tell a partner. Point to the images if you don't know the names of the food. We will learn that in a minute!* Sts tell each other using the photo.

1 Vocabulary Food and drink

A Point to the photo again and elicit the word *kitchen*. Draw sts' attention to the fridge and counter and for each of them ask: *What do you call it?* Focus on the food on the counter and elicit food and drink vocabulary. Point to the list of words and have sts match them to the items on the counter in the photo. These are familiar food words and / or cognates. The rest are introduced in **B**. Help sts notice stress on the words and try to guess how to pronounce them, then highlight spelling and pronunciation differences. Celebrate the fact that these are easy for them as they are similar in L1 (except *oil*). Elicit more words with sound /ɔɪ/ as in *oil*, e.g. *toy*, *boy*, and refer to the Sounds and Usual Spellings chart on page 158 to show them the symbol.

Extra activity Point to a shelf in the refrigerator and elicit or teach *shelf*. In pairs, sts can play a game, taking turns to close their eyes and test each other's memory about what items are in the refrigerator, on the top shelf, on the counter etc. Write questions on the board for them to ask their partner, e.g. *What is on the top shelf? Is X on the counter or in the refrigerator?*

Cultural note fridge = refrigerator

Write *banana* on the board and highlight the first and last *a*. Drill the pronunciation of the word and draw sts' attention to the schwa sound /ə/. Do the same with *pajamas* and remind sts they have the picture words in the Sounds and Usual Spellings chart on p. 158.

Drill the sound (e.g. mime hitting yourself in the stomach so they make the right unstressed "uh" noise!) using the two picture words from the Sound and Usual Spellings chart. If time allows, elicit other examples they know with schwas. Tell them all highlighted letters have schwa /ə/ sounds.

In pairs, sts try to pronounce all the words on the list. Monitor closely for accuracy and offer help / model pronunciation if necessary. Play ▶6.1 for sts to notice how words are pronounced. Conduct a repetition drill. Ask: *Who is Jeff talking to?* (himself)

> 1 spaghetti 2 oil 3 vinegar 4 tomatoes 5 bananas
> 6 chocolate 7 salt 8 tea

▶6.1 Turn to p. 316 for the complete audioscript.

> **Tip** For extra practice on pronunciation, go to the AS on p. 164 and ask sts to notice the schwa sounds.

B ▶ **6.2** Match the food in the refrigerator to these words. Try to pronounce them. Then listen to Jeff completing his list to check.

♪ *Your sugar, Yes, please, Won't you come and put it down on me?*

- [ ] apples /ˈæpəlz/
- [ ] bread /brɛd/
- [ ] butter /ˈbʌtər/
- [ ] carrots /ˈkærəts/
- [ ] cheese /tʃiːz/
- [ ] chicken /ˈtʃɪkən/
- [ ] eggs /ɛgz/
- [ ] fish /fɪʃ/
- [ ] lettuce /ˈlɛtəs/
- [ ] milk /mɪlk/
- [ ] onions /ˈʌnjənz/
- [ ] oranges /ˈɔrəndʒəz/
- [ ] potatoes /pəˈteɪtoʊz/
- [ ] sugar /ˈʃʊgər/

C In pairs, cover the words in **A** and **B**, and name all the items in the photo.

> *Five oranges ...*

D ▶ **6.3** In pairs, listen to Sandra and Jeff. What's their problem?

E ▶ **6.3** Listen again and number the items in **B** in the order you hear them. Then ...
1. What three items can they put in the freezer?
2. What fruit doesn't Sandra like? What food doesn't she eat?
3. What three items can they can use for dinner?

F 🔵 **Make it personal** In pairs, ask and answer. Which items on p. 72–73 do you eat / drink
- (almost) every day?
- more or less every week?
- occasionally?
- never?

> *I eat bananas almost every day. I love them!*
> *Really? I like bananas, too, but I only eat them occasionally.*

2 Grammar Countable vs. uncountable nouns

A Look at the words in exercises **1A** and **1B**. In pairs, answer 1 and 2.
1. Circle the eight plural words. Are the other words usually singular or plural in your language?
2. Which of these foods can you have more than one of?
   a coffee   b egg   c orange   d rice   e spaghetti   f sugar   g juice

B Read the grammar box. Then complete the sentences.

Countable nouns		Uncountable nouns
a carrot	carrots	butter
an egg	eggs	cheese
a mango	mangoes	fish
a melon	melons	ice
a potato	potatoes	juice
		milk
		water

Countable nouns have plural forms that end in _____, and the word *a* or _____ before them in the singular. We use _____ when the word begins with a vowel. Uncountable nouns have only _____ form and do _____ have *a* or *an*.

▶ **Grammar 6A** p. 148

▶ **Common mistakes**
We have ~~a~~ bread for breakfast.
I don't eat fish~~es~~.

C In pairs, take turns asking and answering about the items in the photo.

> *What's this?*   *It's chocolate.*   *What are these?*   *They're fish.*

D 🔵 **Make it personal** Play *Refrigerator Secrets*!
1. Make a list of 10 items you usually have in your refrigerator.
2. In pairs, take turns asking and answering. Who can guess all 10 items first?

> *Do you usually have milk?*   *Yes, I do. And you?*
> *Do you usually have soft drinks?*
> *Yes. I usually have two or three soft drinks in my refrigerator.*

6.1

B Now focus on the food and drink items in the fridge. These are in a second group because most are non-cognates for Latin language speakers. Point to some of the items and elicit how to say them in English. Name what sts do not know and ask: *Do you like it / them? How often do you eat / drink ...?* about a few of them. Individually, sts match the words to the items in the fridge. Sts listen to ▶6.2 to check. Paircheck. Classcheck with answers on the board. In pairs, sts try to pronounce the words.

> 9 sugar   10 apples   11 oranges   12 lettuce   13 butter
> 14 cheese   15 eggs   16 chicken   17 bread   18 milk
> 19 fish   20 onions   21 carrots   22 potatoes

Tip Ask sts to list the food items that are recognizable from their language. This kind of activity helps sts remember, practice, and feel good about English vs. their language.

Extra activity Ask sts to think about their own fridges and think about what they need to buy. Ask sts to write a shopping list. In pairs, sts compare their lists, e.g. *I need to buy (some) milk, eggs, etc.* The *some / any* distinction is taught in lesson 6.2 so don't correct it here.

C Sts test each other by looking at the photo covering the words and naming as many items as they can.

D Focus on the photo and tell sts that they are Jeff and Sandra. Sts listen to ▶6.3 and answer the question. Paircheck. Classcheck.

> They are leaving tomorrow (so don't need all this food).

▶6.3 Turn to p. 316 for the complete audioscript.

E Sts listen again and number the items in **B** as they hear them, then answer 1–3. Paircheck. Classcheck. Ask: *Do you keep all these items in your fridge / freezer?* Use the AS on p. 164 to help sts process the language through reading, and for extra pronunciation practice.

> 1 apples   2 oranges   3 onions   4 potatoes   5 chicken
> 6 fish   7 milk   8 cheese   9 butter   10 lettuce   11 carrots
> 12 eggs   13 bread   14 sugar
> 1 bananas, chicken, fish
> 2 She doesn't like apples. She doesn't eat potatoes.
> 3 lettuce, carrots, eggs

F 🎤 **Make it personal**   Direct sts to the speech bubbles and give your own examples pointing to the list of foods in **B**. Ask: *Do you like apples?* Sts work in pairs and ask and answer questions. Monitor and listen for good examples and errors in pronunciation and go over these when they are finished. Ask: *What do you both like?*

🎵 **Song line:** Turn to p. 330 for notes about this song and an accompanying task.

2 Grammar Countable vs. uncountable nouns

A Sts should have encountered this grammar point before so approach it as a review, checking understanding rather than explaining. Refer to the list of words in **1A** and **1B** above and ask: *Can you give me an example of a plural noun?* Sts complete 1 and 2 and paircheck. Ask: *Why aren't the other words (oil, vinegar, tea, etc.) plural?* (Because they are uncountable.)

> 1 bananas, tomatoes, apples, carrots, eggs, onions, oranges, potatoes
> 2 b, c

Tip To help with the concept, mime the futility of trying to count sugar, rice, or water.

Language tip Sts who speak Portuguese or Spanish as their L1, tend to use *coffee, water, beer*, etc. as countable nouns, e.g. *three coffees, four beers, two waters*. In English, this is accepted when ordering drinks in a restaurant but point out that you would say *I drank **five cups of coffee** yesterday*.

B Have sts read the grammar box and, in pairs, fill the blanks. Tell sts that uncountable nouns are usually liquids, items that come in (small) parts, or items you eat only a part of. In pairs, sts add two more items to each category. Paircheck. Classcheck with answers on the board. Elicit more words for each column, e.g. *ketchup*. Use the photo on p. 72.

➔ **Grammar 6A** p. 148

🔶 **Common mistakes**   Ask sts to read the box and remind them that *bread* is uncountable. Explain *fish* when we are talking about it as food is uncountable (as with *chicken* and *meat*), and elicit or write some more examples, e.g. *We eat a lot of fish at home. / I eat fish but I don't eat meat.*

> -s, an, an, one, not

C Direct sts to the speech bubbles. Sts work in pairs to ask and answer questions.

D 🎤 **Make it personal**   Sts should work in new pairs if possible. Demonstrate the task by having sts guess what 10 items are in your refrigerator. Give them time to write their lists. Encourage them to use uncountable nouns and say countable nouns in the plural as in the examples. Classcheck by asking individual sts to report what their partner has in their refrigerator. Ask: *Any surprises?*

➔ **Workbook** p. 29

6.2 What do you eat for lunch and dinner?

1 Vocabulary Food portions and containers

A ▶ 6.4 Match photos 1–13 to the food items. Listen to check. Which item isn't very healthy?

- ☐ a bottle of water
- ☐ a bowl of rice
- ☐ a cup of tea
- ☐ a glass of juice
- ☐ a piece of cake
- ☐ a piece of fruit
- ☐ a slice of bread
- ☐ some carrots or nuts
- ☐ some eggs
- ☐ some meat
- ☐ some fish
- ☐ some salad
- ☐ some vegetables

B ▶ 6.5 Listen to Tony recording Day One of his healthy eating plan. Write Breakfast (B), Lunch (L), Dinner (D), or Snack (S) next to the items in **A** that he eats.

C ▶ 6.6 Listen to Tony and his friend María. True (T) or False (F)? Correct the false sentences.
1. Tony doesn't like cake.
2. His juice is natural.
3. He thinks potato chips are healthy.
4. He eats a slice of bread only in restaurants.
5. María wants to eat healthy food, too.

D 🔵 Make it personal Each day you can eat only five of the items in the photos, and each week you can eat a particular food no more than three times. In pairs, plan your weekly menu.

> How about some salad for lunch on Monday?   OK. And let's have fish on Tuesday.

⚠️ **Common mistakes**
for
I don't like ~~the~~ tea ~~in the~~ breakfast, I prefer ~~the~~ coffee.

2 Grammar Quantifiers: *some* and *any*

A ▶ 6.7 Complete the extracts using *some* or *any*. Listen to check. In pairs, change 1–4 to make them true for you.
1. I usually have _____ brown rice.
2. I don't eat _____ red meat. I'm a vegetarian.
3. I never eat _____ sugar.
4. I have _____ bread every day with meals.
5. Do you want _____ water?
6. No, I don't want _____ , thanks.

74

6.2 What do you eat for lunch and dinner?

Lesson Aims: Sts listen to people talking about their diets and eating habits. They learn to use *some* and *any* in the contexts of planning a menu and talking about what they eat.

Function
Talking about portions of food.
Listening to a woman talk about her diet. Talking about your own diet.

Language
I usually have a slice of bread and a piece of fruit for breakfast. For lunch, it's a bowl of rice, two spoons of beans …
For dinner, I often have a bowl of rice and some fish or chicken.

Vocabulary: Portions of food (a bowl of rice, 2 spoons of beans, 1/2 pound of meat, a can of diet soda, etc.) Healthy / junk food, liquids.

Grammar: Quantifiers, *some* and *any*.

Warm-up Play the *Memory Race* game with food and drink items. Sts have one minute to write down all the items they can remember. Classcheck with answers on the board. Include *(s)* after each countable noun to help with the next activity: *apple(s), banana(s).* etc.

1 Vocabulary Food portions and containers

A Direct sts to the photos of food and tell them to cover the list. Test their vocabulary of each item. Ask: *Is this food all healthy?* Point to the list and ask: *What number is a bowl of rice?* (6). Tell sts to write the number in the box. Play ▶6.4. Sts match the items, writing the numbers in the boxes. Check answers. Drill *vegetables* and highlight that the only other word which sounds like this is *comfortable*! Elicit more food vocabulary items from the class, particularly foods that they eat regularly at home.

Use photos to teach more cognates, e.g. *(some) broccoli, pineapple, papaya,* etc. (items which you eat a portion of, not a whole one).

> 1 a glass of juice 2 a cup of tea 3 some salad
> 4 a slice of bread 5 a piece of fruit 6 a bowl of rice
> 7 some meat 8 some fish 9 some eggs
> 10 some vegetables 11 a bottle of water
> 12 a piece of cake 13 some carrots or nuts

Tip Help sts to remember and process the vocabulary by having them categorize the food items, e.g. *Which do you eat most / least? Which are the most / least expensive?*

B Sts will hear Tony recording Day One of his healthy eating plan. Elicit what he has for each meal, but don't give the correct answers. Play ▶6.5 and tell sts to listen and write the correct letter next to the food items they hear. Paircheck. Classcheck.

▶6.5 Turn to p. 316 for the complete audioscript.

> a cup of tea (B), a slice of bread (B), a piece of fruit (B)
> a bowl of rice (L), some meat (L), some vegetables (L), a bottle of water (L)
> some carrots or nuts (S)
> some salad (D), some fish (D), some eggs (D), a glass of juice (D)

Cultural note
1 lb = 1 pound = 453,6 grams
1/2 lb = half a pound = 226,8 grams

C In pairs, sts try to predict possible answers to questions 1–5. Play ▶6.6 for them to check their answers. Classcheck. Ask: *Do you always eat meat for lunch? Do you like the same food as Tony?*

> 1 F. He sometimes has a piece of cake in restaurants.
> 2 T
> 3 F. He refers to them as junk food.
> 4 F. He has a slice of bread with his lunch.
> 5 T

▶6.6 Turn to p. 316 for the complete audioscript.

Tip Ask sts to turn to the AS on p. 164. Sts listen again and notice /ʌ/, /ʊ/ and /uː/.

D 🔴 **Make it personal** Direct sts to the speech bubbles and explain the task. Sts then discuss and create their menus. They can then work in groups of four or six and read each other's menus and decide on who has the healthiest menu.

2 Grammar Quantifiers: *some* and *any*

A Sts complete the sentences. Paircheck. Play ▶6.7 for sts to check their answers. Classcheck. Sts then work in pairs to make new sentences for 1–4.

> 1 some 2 any 3 any 4 some 5 some 6 any

B Complete the grammar box examples and rules 1–4 with *some* or *any*.

 You want a piece of me, I'm Mrs. Lifestyles of the rich and famous, You want a piece of me.

There's **some** coffee and _____ tea here. And there's also **some** sugar.
Do you have **any** vinegar? Yes, but I don't have **any** salt or _____ pepper.
Do you want **some** cold juice? It's really hot!
Do we have **any** pasta? I want to make dinner.

1 Use _____ in affirmative sentences ➕.
2 Use _____ in negative sentences ➖.
3 Use _____ in questions when you think the answer is "yes."
4 Use _____ in questions when you think the answer is "no" or aren't sure.

➡ **Grammar 6B** p.148

Common mistakes

Do you have any ~~informations~~? *information*
That was ~~a~~ bad news!
NB: The word *news* is an uncountable noun, not a plural.

C ▶6.8 Circle the correct form. Then listen to check. Are you similar to or different from Lucas?

Judy: So, Lucas, what do you usually have when you get up?
Lucas: I only have **some / any** water.
Judy: Wow! You don't eat **some / any** food?
Lucas: Well, I have **some / any** bread and **some / any** fruit two hours later.
Judy: Two hours later? And do you have **some / any** coffee? You know, to stay awake?
Lucas: I don't need **some / any** coffee. I don't get up until noon!

D 🎤 **Make it personal** In groups. What do you usually eat / drink in the morning? Whose morning diet is the healthiest?

I always drink some water when I get up.

3 Listening

A ▶6.9 Use the photos to guess what Amy is going to have for breakfast during her trip to Japan. Listen to Amy and her friend Bill to check.

B ▶6.9 Listen again. Choose the correct answers.
1 Amy's trip to Japan is for **vacation / work**.
2 Tourists usually like the **Western / Japanese** breakfast.
3 Bill **often / never** goes to Japan.
4 Miso soup **has / doesn't have** a lot of salt.
5 Green tea **has / doesn't have any** caffeine.
6 In Japan, you can buy coffee in a **bottle / can**.
7 A good way to go to your hotel in Tokyo is by **taxi / train**.
8 Amy **is / isn't** nervous about her trip.

C 🎤 **Make it personal** In pairs, compare your answers to these questions. Any surprises?
1 Would you like to try a Japanese breakfast? Why (not)? Any other unusual meals you like or would like to try?
2 What's your ideal breakfast, lunch, and dinner? Where, when, who with, what food?

My ideal lunch is me and Justin Bieber on a beautiful beach, eating fish and drinking coconut water.

My ideal lunch is me and my family eating my mom's home-cooked food!

B Have sts decide in pairs how to best complete the grammar box about the use of *some* and *any*.

🕑 **Common mistakes** Draw sts' attention to the rules. Ask: *Which of these mistakes have you made?*

For a quick practice activity, get sts to practice offering and accepting / refusing the food in the photos here and in the previous lesson. *Do you want some bread / rice, etc.? Yes, please / No, thanks.*

➡ **Grammar 6B** p. 148

> some, any
> 1 some 2 any 3 some 4 any

C Individually, sts circle the best options in the dialogue. Paircheck. Play ▶6.8 so sts can check their answers. Ask for sts' opinion about Lucas' diet e.g. *Is his diet healthy?*

> some, any, some, some, some, any

▶6.8 Turn to p. 316 for the complete audioscript.

D 👤 **Make it personal** In groups, sts tell each other what they usually have for breakfast. Tell them they need to use at least two quantifiers from **1A** (*a slice of, a cup of*, etc.). Encourage them to say which morning diets are healthy or unhealthy.

> **Weaker classes** Write prompts on the board *For breakfast, I usually have a cup of ..., For lunch, I usually ...* so sts know where to start from.

🎵 **Song line:** Turn to p. 330 for notes about this song and an accompanying task.

3 Listening

A Tell sts to look at the photos of Amy and the city. Ask: *What country is this?* (Japan) Ask: *What do they eat for breakfast?* Direct sts to the three photos and ask them to predict what her breakfast will be. Play ▶6.9 and tell sts to check their prediction.

> the Japanese breakfast (rice, fish and soup)

▶6.9 Turn to p. 316 for the complete audioscript.

B Tell sts to read through the sentences and try to remember which are the correct options. Play ▶6.9 again and ask them to check their ideas and circle the correct answers. Paircheck and classcheck. Ask: *Have you eaten Japanese food? Do you like it?* Ask more questions to check comprehension of the listening task and discuss any challenges, e.g. *Was this useful? Did you find it easy or difficult? Did you find it interesting? Why? What did you learn about listening? How will you try to listen differently next time?*

> 1 work 2 Western 3 often 4 has 5 has 6 can
> 7 train 8 is

C 👤 **Make it personal** Draw from your own experience and opinions as an example of the task for sts. Refer to the speech bubbles. Drill *ideal*. Sts ask and answer the questions. Encourage them to use quantifiers from this lesson, e.g. *I don't like Mexican food. It has a lot of salt and spices in it.*

➡ **Workbook** p. 30

6.3 How often do you eat chocolate?

1 Reading

A ▶6.10 Read the title of Nelly's blog. Do you think the answer is *yes* or *no*? Then read and listen to the blog and the article and see if the writer agrees with you.

Food & Life

HOME ABOUT RECIPES MISC

Is Chocolate Really Good For You?
September 3rd by Nelly

I have a confession to make: I love sugar ♥. But I don't really eat a lot of candy. The secret to a "sweet" life 🙂 is quality, not quantity. When I really want some candy or a dessert, I always go for the most delicious and the most attractive that I can find. And they even say chocolate is good for you!

Maybe you're smiling because Nelly's blog sounds familiar. That's not surprising. Chocolate tastes good! And some claim it has health benefits, too.

- If you have a lot of pressure and stress in your life, chocolate can make you feel better mentally and physically. Chocolate gives you energy!
- Chocolate will reduce your appetite. If you eat a small quantity of dark chocolate before a big lunch, your appetite might be 15% less!
- Chocolate can improve your heart! Some even say your cholesterol may improve, too.
- Chocolate keeps your skin hydrated, and it also has anti-aging properties that help you stay young.
- Chocolate has a little caffeine, but much less than coffee. And it has some sugar. Be sure to check the ingredients before you buy. And make sure your chocolate is at least 85% chocolate.

So, is chocolate really good for you? No, not really! We usually eat it with a lot of fat and sugar, which aren't so good for you. But, the good news? A little chocolate now and again won't hurt you – and, of course, it tastes delicious!

B ▶6.10 How much can you remember? Complete the notes about chocolate. Listen to and read both texts again to check. Repeat the pink-stressed words.

People say:
1. It's good for pressure and _____.
2. It gives you _____.
3. Eat a little piece before a big _____, and you eat less.
4. It's good for your _____.
5. It makes you look _____.
6. But chocolate usually contains _____ and _____, so it's good to only eat a _____!

C 🗨 Make it personal Discuss the questions in groups.
1. Are you similar to or different from Nelly?
2. Does any information in the article surprise you? Anything missing?
3. Do you keep a blog or regularly read any blogs?

> It doesn't mention the origin of chocolate. It comes from …

6.3 How often do you eat chocolate?

Lesson Aims: Sts learn to use quantifiers with countable and uncountable nouns. Sts also learn to say large numbers.

Function
Reading and talking about sugar / sweet items.
Listening to a couple decide what to have for lunch.
Listening to information about a Nutrition Facts chart.
Saying quantities and numbers.
Talk about how much you do different things.

Language
When I eat a lot of chocolate, I compensate the next day.
Are you ready for lunch?
How much cholesterol does the vegetarian burrito have?
I eat everything and never worry about calories.
I don't spend a lot of money.

Vocabulary: Words related to sugar (sugar, sweet, candy, dessert, chocolate, mousse, fruit, Nutella). Nutrition Facts (calories, cholesterol, total fat, fiber, protein, sodium). Large numbers.
Grammar: Quantifiers *a lot of*, *a few*, and *a little*.

Warm-up Ask: *Do you eat a lot of sugar? What's your favorite sweet item?* Ask sts to tell a partner what sweet things they eat in a typical week, e.g. *I eat some chocolate but not every day. I don't eat any sweets*. Teach the meaning of *having a sweet tooth* (someone who likes sweet food). Ask: *Who has a sweet tooth?*

1 Reading Recognizing cognates

A Focus on the photo of Nelly. Say: *She's Sandra's friend. She writes a blog about food*. Sts read the title of the text and predict if the answer will be *yes* or *no*. Highlight pronunciation of *chocolate* and the silent letters in it. Ask if they have words with syllables that disappear in their language. Sts read quickly for gist to check their ideas. Paircheck. In pairs, sts can guess pronunciation of words with stress marked in pink (before listening). Play ▶6.10. Pause after listening to the introduction to to check comprehension and pronunciation of any words. Sts reread and listen to the text in pairs and discuss what else they understood. Tell them to give evidence from the text to justify their answers. Classcheck. Then check their pronunciation predictions for words with stress marked. Ask: *How many did you get right?* Note: You can mention here that *will / won't* is the future of *be*, which sts will see later in English ID 1 and in English ID 2.

> no

Tip Keep a glossary on the board of pink-stressed, non-cognate vocabulary from the text, to help sts as they complete the activities, e.g. *smile*.

B Tell sts to read through the sentences and then discuss in pairs what goes in the blanks. Then they read and listen to the text again to check answers. Classcheck.

> 1 stress 2 energy 3 lunch 4 heart 5 young
> 6 fat, sugar, little

Find out more about sts' experience of this reading activity and encourage them to reflect on it. Ask: *Did you enjoy reading this text? Did you learn anything new? Do you find the subject interesting? How much of the text did you understand the first time you read it? Did the pronunciation of any words surprise you?* etc.

C **Make it personal** This task asks sts to respond briefly to the text. Ask them to discuss the questions in groups.

2 Grammar Quantifiers: *a little, a few, a lot of*

🎵 *All I'm askin', (ooh) Is for a little respect when you come home (just a little bit).*

A Circle the correct words in a–d and complete rules 1–3 with *a few*, *a little*, or *a lot of*.

a Nelly doesn't eat **a lot of / a little** candy.
b **A little / a few** chocolate satisfies her.
c If you have **a lot of / a few** stress, chocolate can make you feel better.
d We all have **a few / a little** bad habits.

1 Use _____ with countable nouns. It means a small number.
2 Use _____ with uncountable nouns. It means a small quantity.
3 Use _____ with countable and uncountable nouns. It means a large quantity or number.

➔ **Grammar 6C** p.148

Common mistakes
I have a little ~~of~~ money in my purse.

3 Listening

A ▶ 6.11 Listen to Sandra and Joe talk about lunch at a Mexican restaurant. What do they decide to eat?

B ▶ 6.11 Listen again and complete the chart. Which meal would you choose? Why?

Common mistakes
six ~~hundreds~~ fifty grams

NUTRITION FACTS
Serving Size: 1 burrito (198 g)

Quantity Per Serving	Chicken burrito	Meat burrito	Vegetarian burrito
Total Fat	___ g	5 g	4 g
Cholesterol	30 mg	___ mg	___ mg
Sodium	880 mg	890 mg	730 mg
Fiber	6 g	5 g	___ g
Protein	___ g	___ g	14 g

C 🔶 **Make it personal** In pairs. Use the words in 1–6 and *a lot / a little / a few* to have short conversations about you and your friends. Any surprises?

1 eat / Mexican food
2 have / English-speaking friends
3 spend / money
4 do / exercise
5 download / songs
6 take / selfies

Do you take a lot of selfies?   *No, only a few. I don't really like selfies.*

6.3

🎵 **Song line:** Turn to p. 330 for notes about this song and an accompanying task.

2 Grammar Quantifiers: *a little, a few, a lot of*

A Tell sts to decide in pairs how to complete the grammar box. Monitor and check progress.

➔ **Grammar 6C** p. 148

a lot of, A little, a lot of, a few
1 a few   2 a little   3 a lot of

Language tip In this activity, the meaning of *a little* relates to quantity, not size, translating to (*pouco(a)/poco(a)*) in Portuguese and Spanish, respectively. In this case, sts must always use the article *a* before (*a little*).

Tip Ask sts to write 3–5 sentences using the quantifiers about their diet. Sts share sentences with a partner to see if they have anything in common. Monitor to check grammar and prompt sts to self-correct errors.

Draw sts attention to the **Common mistakes**. Add more examples, e.g. *I have few money.* and correct as a class.

3 Listening

A Write the following numbers on the board and elicit how we say and write them: *880, 890, 730*. Sts prepare their answers in pairs. Classcheck. Write a few more examples of high numbers if sts need more practice with this. Tell them Sandra and Joe are going to have lunch together. Sts listen to ▶ 6.11 and take notes of the food they hear. Paircheck. Classcheck with answers on the board. Ask: *Do they like / eat a lot of Mexican food?*

Sandra: chicken burrito
Joe: meat burrito

▶ **6.11** Turn to p. 317 for the complete audioscript.

B Point to the Nutrition Facts chart and check if sts are familiar with the vocabulary in the first column. Ask: *Which burrito is the healthiest / best for Sandra's diet?* and listen to sts' first opinions. Ask: *Which would you eat?* Play ▶ 6.11 again for sts to complete the chart. Paircheck. Classcheck with answers on the board. Ask: *Do you find it easy or difficult to understand numbers when listening? Is this kind of listening activity interesting or useful? Why / why not?*

Chicken: 5 g, 18 g
Meat: 35 mg, 19 g
Vegetarian: 5 mg, 14 g

Tip Ask sts to turn to the AS on p. 164. Sts listen again and notice the dark *l* vs. normal *l*.

▶ **6.11** Turn to page 317 for the complete audioscript.

C **Make it personal** Elicit the *Do you …?* questions. Get them to interview you first to set this up and practice pronunciation. Refer sts to the speech bubbles to help clarify the task. Tell sts to take turns asking and answering the questions. Ask sts to report their partners' answers to the whole class.

➔ **Workbook** p. 31

6.4 How many meals do you cook a week?

1 Grammar *How much* vs. *how many*

A ▶ 6.12 Listen to and complete the conversation with *how much*, *how many*, *a lot*, *a few*, or *a little*.

Richie: OK, the chili's almost ready.
Grandpa: You can add some mushrooms, if you want.
Richie: _____ mushrooms?
Grandpa: I don't know! _____ if you like them or _____ if you don't.
Richie: OK – I get it. And how do I serve it?
Grandpa: With some rice.
Richie: _____ rice?
Grandpa: _____ if you're hungry, _____ if you're not.

B Circle the correct answers and complete the examples in the grammar box.

> 1 Use **how much** / **how many** with uncountable nouns: "_____ money do you have?"
> 2 There's always a plural noun after **how much** / **how many**: "_____ carrots are there?"
> 3 *A few* is an answer to **how much** / **how many**: "_____ eggs are there?" "A few."
> 4 *A little* is an answer to **how much** / **how many**: "_____ cheese is there?" "A little."
>
> ▶ Grammar 6D p.148

> **Common mistakes**
> ~~movies~~
> How many ~~movie~~ do you see a month?
> ~~much~~
> How ~~many~~ time do you spend in the shower?

C Complete the examples with *how much* or *how many*. In pairs, research these foods and role-play choosing something to eat.

a chicken burrito   a hamburger   a salmon burger
a veggie burger   a tofu burger

fat   fiber   salt   cholesterol   protein

> Do you want a chicken burrito?
> I'm not sure. _____ fat does it have?
> Five grams.
> And _____ grams of fiber does it have?
> Only six.

D Complete 1–10 with *How much* or *How many*. Ask and answer in pairs.

1 _____ restaurants do you go to every month?
2 _____ coffee / tea / water / milk do you drink every day?
3 _____ people do you live / work / study with?
4 _____ hours do you work / study / exercise on the weekends?
5 _____ time do you spend studying English / listening to music / on social media a week?
6 _____ money do you spend on clothes / going out / traveling / food a month?
7 _____ meat / rice / fruit do you eat a week, on average?
8 _____ phones / computers / TVs / cars does your family have?
9 _____ texts / emails / Tweets, on average, do you send a day?
10 _____ times do you go out / go to the beach / play sports each month?

E **Make it personal** Choose a topic 1–10 in D, and take a class survey. Share your answers with the class.

> Most of us are on social media all the time, except Victor.
> On average, we spend about X a month on clothes.

78

6.4 How many meals do you cook a week?

Lesson Aims: Sts learn to use *how much* and *how many* to talk about food.

Function
Asking and answering questions about quantities.
Choosing food at a restaurant.
Reading / Taking a pop culture quiz.
Asking and answering questions about eating habits and lifestyle.

Language
How many calories do you eat a day?
How much coffee do you drink in a day?
Do you want a tofu burger?

Vocabulary: Recycling nutrition facts (calories, cholesterol, total fat, grams of fiber, protein, sodium).
Grammar: *How much* vs. *How many*. Recycling quantifiers (*a lot of, a few* and *a little*).

Warm-up Write question prompts on the board:
What / you have for breakfast this morning?
What / you eat for dinner last night?
What / you have for lunch earlier / yesterday? / you have any snacks?
How much water / you drink yesterday?
How many calories / you think you had yesterday?

Focus on the weak pronunciation of *did you* /dɪdʒə/. Elicit the complete questions and have sts ask and answer them in pairs. Ask sts to report their partner's answers to the whole class. Establish that *have* and *eat* are synonyms in this context.

1 Grammar *How much vs. how many*

A Explore the photo. Ask: *Who can you see? Where are they? What are they doing?*, etc. Individually, sts complete the dialogue between Richie and his grandpa with *how much, how many, a lot of, a little,* or *a few*. Paircheck. Play ▶6.12 for sts to check their answers. Classcheck.

> How many, A lot, a few, How much, A lot, a little

> **Stronger classes** Do this activity as a *dictagloss*. Have sts close their books, listen and write down as much of the dialogue as they can. Paircheck. Repeat two or three times. Then have sts open their books, check spelling and see how much they got right.

B Sts read and complete the grammar box. Check answers. Elicit more questions with *How much / many...?* and write them on the board.

> 1 how much, How much
> 2 how many, How many
> 3 how many, How many
> 4 how much, How much

➡ **Grammar 6D** p. 148

C Point to the speech bubbles, elicit the missing words and have two sts act out the conversation. Help with pronunciation when necessary, reviewing the grammar box in **B**. Check understanding of *fiber, cholesterol,* and *protein*. In pairs, sts role-play choosing food. Make sure they include *How much / many* questions in their dialogue. Monitor closely for accuracy.

> How much, how many

D Change partners. In pairs, sts complete 1–10 and then ask and answer questions. Make sure they ask all the relevant options. Classcheck. Ask: *How many answers did you get right?* Make sure they are applauded at the end.

> 1 How many 2 How much 3 How many
> 4 How many 5 How much 6 How much
> 7 How much 8 How many 9 How many
> 10 How many

E 🔵 **Make it personal** Sts choose one of the question options, 1–10, and then mingle to ask the whole class and produce a class survey. Focus on the speech bubbles to show them what they should be able to say by the end of the activity. Ask volunteers to share their answers with the class.

2 Reading

But she said where d'you wanna go?, How much you wanna risk?, I'm not looking for somebody, With some superhuman gifts.

A In pairs, take the quiz, but don't read the article! Try to guess the correct answers.

HOW MUCH DO YOU KNOW ABOUT WHAT YOU EAT?
by Sally Larouche

1 Which of these foods doesn't have a lot of pot**a**ssium?
   a potatoes   b beans   c bananas   d apples

2 Which of these drinks is the best way to reh**y**drate the body?
   a water   b tea   c sports drinks   d orange juice

3 Which of these drinks is really a food item?
   a tea   b coffee   c milk   d c**o**conut water

4 Which of these vegetables has a lot of protein?
   a beans   b carrots   c sp**i**nach   d onions

5 Which of these foods is NOT rich in v**i**tamin C?
   a str**a**wberries
   b pears
   c k**i**wis
   d tomatoes

B ▶6.13 Skim the article and, in pairs, answer 1 and 2. Think of ten more cognates you know.
1 Words that are similar in two languages are called *cognates*. How many of the highlighted words in paragraph 1 do you recognize? Is the pronunciation similar or different in your language? Listen to check.
2 Examples can help you know the meaning of words, too. Can you guess the meaning of the highlighted words in paragraph 3?

How do we decide what to eat?
It's not easy because modern grocery stores offer many, many choices. The first step to a healthy diet is learning as much as we p**o**ssibly can about the foods we eat. Let's look at the answers to the quiz.

1 Apples are good for you in many ways, but they're not rich in **potassium** like the other foods are. Potassium keeps our **muscles** strong and helps **eliminate** salt from the body. Apples are very **nutritious**, though, and have a lot of vitamin C and fiber.

2 As you've probably guessed, water is absolutely the best way to rehydrate the body. When it's hot out, drink, drink, drink, and always carry a bottle of water with you. Water also inc**rea**ses our energy, helps us con**centrate**, and pre**vents head**aches.

3 Because it con**ta**ins a lot of **nutrients**, including cal**cium**, protein, and potassium, milk is a food. It's a food you can drink! But if you don't like the taste of milk, be sure to con**si**der other **dairy products**, such as cheese and yo**gurt**.

4 Do you remember Popeye? He loved spinach. Well, all of the foods in question 4 are good for you, but beans have a lot of protein, more than spinach, carrots, or onions. Maybe you eat beans often, but, if not, now is a good time to start. They taste good, too!

5 And finally, everyone knows that vitamin C is good for you, but which of these fruits is NOT rich in vitamin C? It's not the **tiny** strawberry. The answer is pears. The good news is that pears contain no fat and are a good source of fiber.

So ... happy, healthy eating! Please share my article with all of your friends. Thank you!

C ▶6.13 Listen to and read the article again. In pairs, take turns asking and answering the quiz in **A**. Check your answers in the article. Do you remember any interesting facts?

Here's one. Apples have a lot of vitamin C.

D 🎤 Make it personal   In pairs. Ask and answer 1–4. Are your answers similar?
1 Do you Google information you don't know?
2 How many times a week do you check Wikipedia?
3 Did any answers to the quiz surprise you? Which ones?
4 Does it make you want to change anything about the way you eat?

I use Google a lot!

Me, too. I check Wikipedia every day.

6.4

🎵 **Song line:** Turn to p. 330 for notes about this song and an accompanying task.

② Reading

A In pairs, sts scan text looking for words with pink highlighting. They can categorize them into familiar or unfamiliar, and guess pronunciation. Sts do a quiz to check how much they know about what they eat. Tell them they will find out the answers later.

> 1 d 2 a 3 c 4 a 5 b

B Set a time limit of one or two minutes so sts read quickly. Tell them to read and focus on the highlighted words. Sts then discuss the questions with a partner. Play ▶6.13 then classcheck.

> 2 nutrients: chemicals that give us what we need to live and grow
> dairy products: things made from milk

Tip Sts can start using cognates quickly if they are confident they have the same meaning in English as their L1. Encourage them to make a note of sentences to remember how they are used in a phrase and confirm the meaning.

C Sts listen again and read to understand more details. Tell sts to return the quiz and check their answers with their partner. Tell them to take turns reading the questions. Check answers and then ask the final question to the class.

Language tip Use the article to emphasize how sts who speak Romance languages can benefit from the amount of real cognates between their L1 and English. Encourage sts to find and underline as many similar words to their L1 as they can. Have them share their lists.

D **Make it personal** Ask sts how they would usually find the answers to the quiz questions. Ask: *Would you use Google?* Sts then discuss the questions in pairs. Ask some sts to share any interesting things they discussed with the class.

➔ **Workbook** p. 32

6.5 Are you hungry?

🆔 Skills Scanning a menu

A Scan the menu. In pairs, answer 1–5.
1 What do the symbols (V), (vegan), (&) mean?
2 How many meat-free dishes are there?
3 What are the two types of starters?
4 How many main courses and desserts are there?
5 Write the price of each dish on the photos.

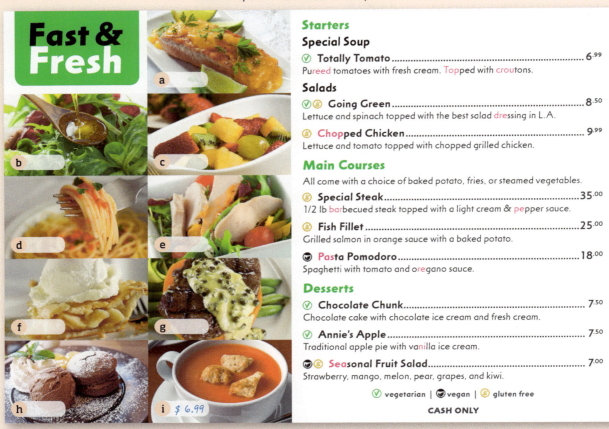

Starters
Special Soup
(V) Totally Tomato 6.99
Pureed tomatoes with fresh cream. Topped with croutons.
Salads
(V)(&) Going Green 8.50
Lettuce and spinach topped with the best salad dressing in L.A.
(&) Chopped Chicken 9.99
Lettuce and tomato topped with chopped grilled chicken.

Main Courses
All come with a choice of baked potato, fries, or steamed vegetables.
(&) Special Steak 35.00
1/2 lb barbecued steak topped with a light cream & pepper sauce.
(&) Fish Fillet 25.00
Grilled salmon in orange sauce with a baked potato.
(vegan) Pasta Pomodoro 18.00
Spaghetti with tomato and oregano sauce.

Desserts
(V) Chocolate Chunk 7.50
Chocolate cake with chocolate ice cream and fresh cream.
(V) Annie's Apple 7.50
Traditional apple pie with vanilla ice cream.
(vegan)(&) Seasonal Fruit Salad 7.00
Strawberry, mango, melon, pear, grapes, and kiwi.

(V) vegetarian | (vegan) vegan | (&) gluten free
CASH ONLY

B ▶ 6.14 Listen to the ad for Fast & Fresh and check (✓) the dishes you hear on the menu.

C Read the menu again. True (T) or False (F)?
1 Croutons are bread and are only served in salads.
2 The fish and the steak are grilled.
3 There are three different kinds of potatoes.
4 The vegetables are fried.
5 The fruit salad has strawberries.
6 You can pay by cash or credit card.

D 🗣 **Make it personal** In pairs. Imagine you're at Fast & Fresh. Order a three-course meal.

For my starter, I'm having …   *And I'd like …*

6.5 Are you hungry?

Lesson Aims: Sts read a menu and discuss what they will have.

Function
Reading a menu.
Choosing dishes from a menu.

Language
Salads. Going Green: lettuce and spinach topped with the best salad dressing in L.A.
Chocolate Chunk: Chocolate cake with chocolate ice cream and fresh cream.
For my starter, I'm having the soup.

Vocabulary: Dishes and drinks in a restaurant. Fruit and vegetables. Meals, starters, salads, the main course, desserts, beverages, the check / bill, decaf coffee, chamomile tea.

Warm-up *Find someone who …* Write the prompts below on the board or print them out before class and hand out copies to sts. Elicit the questions sts will need to ask for the activity and have them stand up and talk to as many classmates as possible.

Find someone who …
1) … eats out every day.
2) … loves Japanese food.
3) … is vegetarian.
4) … never has salads.
5) … had dinner at a special restaurant last weekend.
6) … cooked dinner last night.
7) … prefers fruit juice to soda.

Language tip Focus on the lesson title. Remind sts that *I am hungry* (subject + verb *be* + adjective) is the correct structure in English. In their L1, Spanish and Portuguese speakers say *Yo tengo hambre / Eu tenho fome* (subject + verb *have* + noun), so, tend to say, "I have hungry." Remind sts that *Yo estoy hambriento / Eu estou faminto* uses the same structure as English, to help them remember.

ID Skills Scanning a menu

A Ask the lesson title question and see what they say. Focus on the photos. Elicit all the food items they can see. Ask: *What's the name of the restaurant?* (Fast & Fresh) *Does it look good?* Now ask: *Are you hungry now?* to see if anybody has changed their mind. Sts work in groups of three or four. Within their groups, sts help each other find the answers to questions 1-5. Walk around the classroom and offer help when necessary. Classcheck. Drill pronunciation as necessary.

1 vegetarian, vegan, gluten free
2 seven
3 soup, salad
4 main courses: three; desserts: three
5 a $25.00 b $8.50 c $7.00 d $18.00 e $9.99
  f $7.50 g $35.00 h $7.50 i $6.99

Tip Elicit examples of alliteration from the menu (**S**easonal **S**alad, **F**ish **F**illet, **Ch**opped **Ch**icken). Explain that this is a repetition of sounds, usually in the first syllables of words. Alliteration is used in literature, poetry, and brands (**D**unkin' **D**onuts, **P**ay**P**al, **Co**ca-**Co**la).

B Sts listen to an ad for Fast & Fresh. Play ▶6.14 and sts check which dishes on the menu are mentioned. Paircheck. Classcheck. Use the AS on p. 165 to clear up any doubts. Ask: *Did you like the ad / find it convincing? Would you like to go to Fast & Fresh this weekend?* Point out the silent letters in -ed endings, e.g. *grilled, topped*, etc. Drill.

Chopped Chicken, Fish Fillet, Special Steak, Seasonal Fruit Salad

C Sts reread the menu in **A** for specific information. In pairs, they decide whether sentences 1-6 are true (T), or false (F). Ask them to justify the false ones with evidence from the text. Classcheck with answers on the board.

1 F 2 F 3 T 4 F 5 T 6 F

D To help sts prepare for this task, turn to p. 81 and look at the **Common mistakes** together, and highlight forms and options. Say: *We use* **I'll have, I'm having,** *or* **I'd like to order** *in a restaurant.*

Make it personal Say: *Imagine you're at Fast & Fresh. What are you ordering?* Ask sts to choose one option under each heading (starters, main courses, desserts) following the example. Model their dialogues with present continuous sentences, e.g. *For my main course, I'm having the Fish Fillet.* In pairs, sts tell each other their choices. Ask: *Did any of you order the same meal?*

6.5 What would you like for lunch?

I am sitting in the morning, At the diner on the corner, I am waiting at the counter, For the man to pour the coffee.

in Action   Ordering food

A ▶6.15 Listen and check (✓) the items Marie and Phil order.

B ▶6.16 Listen and order the second part of the dialogue 1–10. Complete the dialogue with the food Phil and Marie order.

	Server:	OK. And you, sir?
	Marie:	Great, thanks.
	Marie:	Yes, please. I'd like the _____, please.
	Server:	OK. How are your starters?
	Phil:	Can I have _____, please?
	Server:	Would you like to order the main course now?
	Phil:	I'll have the _____, please.
	Server:	Any drinks with your meal?
	Server:	Sure. I'll be right back with those.
	Marie:	And I'll have _____, please.

Common mistakes

~~I~~ *I'd* like pizza, please.
"I like pizza" = generally.
"I'd like pizza" = now.
~~I~~ *I'll* have a mint tea, please.

C Read the dialogue in **B** again and find three different ways to order food in a restaurant.

D ▶6.17 Listen and check (✓) the desserts and hot drinks Phil and Marie order. What's the last thing Phil asks for?

E 🔴 **Make it personal** Restaurant role-play in groups of four. **A**, **B**, and **C**: you're at Fast & Fresh for a three-course lunch. **D**: you're the server.

Hi! I'm Gaby, and I'm your server today. What would you like to start?

I'd like the soup, please.

Excellent choice! And for your main course?

81

6.5 What would you like for lunch?

Lesson Aims: Sts role-play ordering and serving food at a restaurant.

Function
Ordering and serving a meal.

Language
Can I have the Chopped Chicken, please?
I'd like a can of soda, please.
Would you like to order the main course now?

Vocabulary: Food and drink items: lettuce, green peppers.
Grammar: Polite requests with *Can I have, I'd like, I'll have*.

♫ **Song line:** Turn to p. 331 for notes about this song and an accompanying task.

Warm-up Ask sts what they remember about the Fast & Fresh restaurant from the last lesson. Elicit the type of restaurant it is and examples of the food they serve.

ID in Action Ordering food

A Direct sts to the photo and ask: *Where are they?* (At Fast & Fresh.) Point to the screen on the right and briefly read what customers might order for starters and salads. Say: *Now imagine you're the server. Listen to the customers and check what they order.* Play ▶6.15. Paircheck. Classcheck.

> Totally Tomato: croutons
> Chopped chicken: lettuce, spinach, green peppers, red peppers, tomato

▶6.15 Turn to p. 317 for the complete audioscript.

B Tell sts to read part two of the dialogue and order it 1–10. Play ▶6.16 so they can check answers. Paircheck. Play the audio again and tell them to complete it with food items. Classcheck with answers on the board.

> 1 Server: OK. How are your starters?
> 2 Marie: Great, thanks.
> 3 Server: Would you like to order the main course now?
> 4 Marie: Yes, please. I'd like the **Pasta Pomodoro**, please.
> 5 Server: OK. And you, sir?
> 6 Phil: I'll have the **Special Steak**, please.
> 7 Server: Any drinks with your meal?
> 8 Phil: Can I have **mineral water**, please?
> 9 Marie: And I'll have lemonade, please.
> 10 Server: Sure. I'll be right back with those.

C Highlight the three ways to order. Ask: *Do you say **please** and **thank you** a lot in your language, too?*

> I'd like …, I'll have …, Can I have …

D Focus on the Hot drinks and Desserts list on the second screen. Play ▶6.17. Sts listen to part three of the dialogue and check the drinks and desserts they order. Paircheck. Classcheck. Ask: *What is the last thing they order?* (the check.)

> Coffee: decaffeinated
> Tea: chamomile
> Dessert: Chocolate Chunk
> Phil asks for the check.

Tip Ask sts to turn to the AS on p. 165. Sts listen again and notice /tʃ/ and the connecting sounds.

E **Make it personal** Sts work in groups of four and decide who is the server. The others order a meal (friends at the same table). Sts role-play the full meal in four stages: 1) order starters and drinks; 2) the main course; 3) the dessert; 4) the check. Monitor closely for accuracy. Have one or two groups act out their conversations for the whole class.

Tip To add fun, it is probably best to be the server yourself first to briskly / humorously show sts what to do and then to move quickly through the different stages.

Extra writing Sts could write up their own version of the complete restaurant role-play at a restaurant of their choice. See if they can get an English menu so they learn a few more words as they do so. They could find one online.

➔ **Workbook** p. 33

➔ **Richmond Learning Platform**

➔ **Writing** p. 82

➔ **Café** p. 83

Writing 6   A food diary

Have some more chicken, have some more pie, It doesn't matter if it's broiled or fried, Just eat it.

My Life in Food

The healthy eater
Monica, age 22, personal trainer

I try to eat well, as I have a very active job. I believe there's a connection between what we eat and our physical health, so I like to eat food that's fresh and nutritious.

For breakfast, I usually have fruit juice, cereal with honey, and a cup of hot water. I drink a lot of water every day, because it's important to stay hydrated. I never drink sugary drinks. However, I love coffee, and I often have an espresso after lunch.

Mid-morning, I often have a snack, like a piece of fruit. I never eat chocolate or candy. I eat a lot of fruit and vegetables. I don't eat a lot of meat, but I do eat fish because it has protein without much fat.

I always eat lunch, as I need to maintain my energy level through the day. A typical lunch for me is a big salad, with tuna, bread, and more fruit. In the evening, I'm usually tired, so I eat something easy to prepare – for example, spaghetti with vegetables.

The junk food addict
Jude, 19, college student

I eat a lot of junk food, _____ I know it's bad for me and makes me put on weight.

I never eat breakfast _____ I always get up late, but when I get to college, I usually have a donut and a cup of coffee. I drink a lot of soda, _____ it's cheap and it tastes good, and the sugar helps me to stay awake in class.

I eat a lot of snacks through the day – _____, candy bars, chocolate, and potato chips. For lunch, I usually have a burger with some fries and a bottle of soda. I hate fish, and I don't eat fruit or vegetables; _____, I like banana ice cream!

I eat dinner alone _____ my mom works in the evenings. I usually get a take-out, _____ pizza, or sometimes Chinese food. I stay up late playing video games, _____ I often eat another slice of pizza or some chocolate at night. I'm surprised how unhealthy my diet is – I know I need to change it.

A Read what two people with very different diets eat in a typical day. Check (✓) the things they eat and drink.

	Monica	Jude	You
breakfast	☐	☐	☐
water	☐	☐	☐
coffee	☐	☐	☐
fruit	☐	☐	☐
vegetables	☐	☐	☐
fish	☐	☐	☐
meat	☐	☐	☐
soda	☐	☐	☐
chocolate	☐	☐	☐

B Read **Write it right!** In Monica's diary, circle the six connectors.

Write it right!

To improve your writing, use a variety of connectors.
- to give reasons: *because, as,* and *so*
- to give examples: *for example* (or *e.g.*), *like*
- to introduce a different idea: *however, but*

C Complete Jude's diary with *because, as, so, for example / e.g., like* and *however*.

D Complete the chart in **A** for you. Think about why you eat what you eat. Anything you need to change?

E **Make it personal** Write your own food diary in 150–180 words.

Before	Use your notes in D and the vocabulary in Unit 6.
While	Use connectors carefully.
After	Read a partner's diary and comment on her / his diet.

Writing 6 A food diary

♪ **Song line:** Turn to p. 331 for notes about this song and an accompanying task.

A Refer sts to the photos of Monica and Jude. Ask: *What foods do you think they eat?* Put sts into pairs and tell them to make two shopping lists of food, one for Monica and one for Jude. Set a time limit of two minutes. Ask the pair with the most items to read out their lists. Write the more difficult words they say on the board to check understanding and pronunciation.

Refer sts to the chart and do the first example of breakfast with the class. Sts read the texts and complete the chart. Tell them to look up unknown words in a dictionary. Monitor and write words they don't know on the board. Classcheck. Call sts' attention particularly to the pronunciation of pink-stressed words.

	Monica	Jude	You
breakfast	✓		
water	✓		
coffee	✓	✓	
fruit	✓		
vegetables	✓		
fish	✓		
meat		✓	
soda		✓	
chocolate		✓	

B Read **Write it right!** with the class. Sts then find six connectors in Monica's diary.

Tip If you have an IWB, display Monica's diary and ask sts to come up to the board and circle examples.

I try to eat well, (as) I have a very active job. I believe there's a connection between what we eat and our physical health, (so) I like to eat food that's fresh and nutritious.

For breakfast, I usually have fruit juice, cereal with honey, and a cup of hot water. I drink a lot of water every day, (because) it's important to stay hydrated. I never drink sugary drinks. (However,) I love coffee, and I often have an espresso after lunch.

Mid-morning, I often have a snack, (like) a piece of fruit. I never eat chocolate or candy. I eat a lot of fruit and vegetables.

I don't eat a lot of meat, (but) I do eat fish (because) it has protein without much fat.

I always eat lunch, (as) I need to maintain my energy level through the day. A typical lunch for me is a big salad, with tuna, bread, and more fruit. In the evening, I'm usually tired, (so) I eat something easy to prepare – (for example,) spaghetti with vegetables

C Refer sts to Jude's diary. Have them complete it with the connectors given.

but, because / as, as / because, for example / e.g., however, as / because, like, so

D Refer sts back to the table in **A** and ask them to check the items they eat and drink. Sts then work in small groups and talk about their diets and what, if anything, they think they could change.

Tip Help weaker sts by writing some phrases on the board and giving your own examples, before sts start **D**.
I should eat/drink more/less… + FOOD
I could stop eating/drinking.. + FOOD

E 🔵 **Make it personal** Read the steps Before, While, and After with sts to guide them to write their own food diaries. Tell them to refer to the texts in **A** as models and draw their attention to the length of the composition – that is, approximately 150–180 words. As a follow-up activity and before they hand in their texts, ask sts to exchange compositions and talk about things they found interesting in each other's diets.

Tip If appropriate, you could ask sts to keep a note of all the food they eat between now and the next class. Sts can compare their lists at the start of the next lesson.

6 Party planners

Café

1 Before watching

A Match 1–5 to their definitions.
1 split — be certain
2 tasting — small, red, sweet fruit
3 make sure — share
4 have no idea — not know at all
5 cherries — trying

B In pairs, guess where August and Andrea are, and what they're doing. Then watch to check.

> I think they're sitting in …

2 While watching

A Listen and complete the extracts with *like, love, would like / 'd like,* or *will have.*

August: OK. I _____ to try the beef, for sure. But I do _____ chicken.

Andrea: That's OK. You get those. And I _____ to try the fish and vegetarian dishes. I'd also _____ a bowl of rice and a salad plate. So you could get the pasta and potatoes, OK?

Server: _____ you _____ to order dessert?

Andrea: Yes, please. I _____ the white chocolate cake. And also a cup of tea, please. Thank you.

August: And I _____ a slice of Black Forest cake and a coffee. Thanks.

B Complete 1–5 with *how much* or *how many*. In pairs, take turns asking and answering.
1 _____ food do they order?
2 _____ main and side dishes are there?
3 _____ slices of cake do they order?
4 _____ cups are there on the table?
5 _____ dishes does Andrea order?
6 _____ cake do they eat?

> They both order a lot of food!

C Match food portions 1–4 to the correct group. Then add the food items to the groups.

| bread | cereal | coffee | pie |

1 A bowl of — paper, gum, _____
2 A cup of — pizza, cake, _____
3 A slice of — tea, hot chocolate, _____
4 A piece of — rice, pasta, _____

3 After watching

A True (T), False (F), or Not Given (NG)?
1 August and Andrea are at their favorite restaurant.
2 They're planning a surprise for their parents.
3 Andrea loves all red fruit.
4 August doesn't enjoy the Black Forest cake.
5 They thought they were trying the regular menu.
6 They don't have enough money to pay.

B Match questions 1–6 to the responses.
1 Are you ready to order?
2 What are you having?
3 Can I take your order?
4 What can I get you?
5 Can I get you anything else?
6 Would you like to see the menu?

- I'll have the chicken, please.
- Spaghetti and meatballs, please.
- Sure. Could I get the beef, please?
- Yes, thanks.
- Yes, I am. I'd like the fish.
- No, thanks. Just the bill, please.

C Complete 1–5 with expressions from the video.
1 _____ they don't know about the surprise party?
2 I think we have to try all of those things to _____ they're good.
3 Here comes the server … _____.
4 Dessert? _____ We have to try those, too.
5 _____ we just ate two main courses?

D ● **Make it personal** In groups of three, role-play the situation. Eat a lot and pay too much!

> Good evening sir, madam. A table for two?

83

ID Café 6 Party planners

1 Before watching

A Tell sts to look at words / phrases 1–5. Ask: *Do you recognize any of these words / phrases?* Have sts match 1–5 to their meanings. Paircheck. Classcheck.

> 1 share 2 trying 3 be certain 4 not know at all
> 5 small, red, sweet fruit

B Explore the photo. Sts predict what August and Andrea are doing. Classcheck by listening to their guesses and telling them what **Video 6** will be about.

> They're at a restaurant. They are planning a surprise party for their parents and are at the restaurant to taste and choose which food will be served at the party.

2 While watching

A Play **Video 6** for sts to get an overall idea of what August and Andrea are doing. Ask: *How much food do they eat, a lot or a little?* (A lot.)

Point to the dialogue and ask sts to fill in the blanks with *like*, *would like*, *will have*, or *love*. Paircheck. Replay **Video 6** for sts to check their answers. Classcheck.

> would like, love, would like, like
> Would, like, will have, will have

B Sts complete questions 1–5 with *how much* or *how many*. Paircheck. Classcheck.

In pairs, sts ask and answer questions 1–5 according to what they remember from **Video 6**, as in the model dialogue in the speech bubbles. Monitor closely for accuracy. Classcheck.

> 1 How much food do they order?
>   They order a lot of food.
> 2 How many main and side dishes are there?
>   There are eight different dishes.
> 3 How many slices of cake do they order?
>   They order two slices of cake.
> 4 How many cups are there on the table?
>   There are two cups on the table.
> 5 How many dishes does Andrea order?
>   She orders four dishes and one slice of cake.
> 6 How much cake do they eat?
>   They eat two slices of cake.

C Sts match food portions 1–4 to the correct group. Then they add the food items in the box to the correct group. Paircheck. Replay **Video 6** to check answers. Classcheck.

> 1 a bowl of rice, pasta, cereal
> 2 a cup of tea, hot chocolate, coffee
> 3 a slice of pizza, cake, pie
> 4 a piece of paper, gum, bread

3 After watching

A Change partners. In pairs, sts decide whether sentences 1–6 are T (true) or F (false) or if the answer is not given (NG). Classcheck with answers on the board.

> 1 NG 2 T 3 NG 4 T 5 F 6 NG

B Elicit the best response to question 1. Sts write 1 in the correct box (Yes, I am. I'd like the fish.). Sts continue the activity and match questions 2–6 to the correct responses. Paircheck. Classcheck with answers on the board.

> 1 Are you ready to order? Yes, I am. I'd like the fish.
> 2 What are you having? I'll have the chicken, please.
> 3 Can I take your order? Sure. Could I get the beef, please?
> 4 What can I get you? Spaghetti and meatballs, please.
> 5 Can I get you anything else? No, thanks. Just the bill, please.
> 6 Would you like to see the menu? Yes, thanks.

C Individually, sts try to remember the expressions from the video and fill in the blanks 1–5. Play the video so that sts can fill in the blanks with the expressions they could not remember. Paircheck. Replay the video once so sts can check their answers. Classcheck with answers on the board.

> 1 Are you sure 2 make sure 3 Just in time
> 4 I guess you're right 5 Can you believe

D ● **Make it personal** Ask the whole class: *What was the problem? Why did they eat a lot and pay too much?*

> They thought the menu they used was a tasting menu. They just wanted to taste items and choose the food for the surprise party. But they ordered from the regular menu.

Refer sts to the speech bubble and ask: *What is the next line in the dialogue?* Tell sts to build up a dialogue to role-play the situation. Monitor and make a note of good language. Go over this after they have finished speaking.

R3 Grammar and vocabulary

A **Picture dictionary.** Cover the words on these pages and use the pictures to remember:

page	
58	8 places around town
60	10 free time activities
61	4 household chores
62	14 vacation activities
64	8 house sitting jobs
67	4 traffic signs
72–73	22 food and drink words
159	16 picture words for lines 1 and 2 of consonants

B **Make it personal** Play *Mime it!* Think of examples for 1–8. Mime them for a partner to guess. Were any of your choices the same?
1. Two spectacular animals.
2. Two useful *Can I ...?* questions.
3. Three boring activities.
4. Three relaxing places.
5. Three items in your fridge.
6. Two household chores.
7. Your favorite dessert.
8. One vegetable and one fruit.

No idea! Maybe a lion?

C Circle the correct alternative to complete 1–10.
1. _____ a good café with WiFi near here?
   a There is   b Is there   c Have
2. Today, _____ over 5 billion cell phones in the world.
   a there is   b there are   c there are some
3. Are there _____ cookies in the kitchen?
   a the   b a   c any
4. How _____ people are there at the party?
   a much   b a lot of   c many
5. _____ a great new store on the corner.
   a There is   b Is   c Is there
6. Can I have _____ water, please?
   a some   b any   c glass of
7. This vegetable soup has _____ salt.
   a much   b any   c a lot of
8. We _____ like watching TV.
   a same   b the two   c both
9. I love _____ to the gym and shopping.
   a go   b going   c goes
10. I hate cooking, but I don't mind _____ the dishes.
    a wash   b to wash   c washing

D ▶R3.1 Complete with *some* or *any*. Listen and check. Then in pairs, role-play using different food items.
Tina: I'm thirsty. Is there _____ juice in the fridge?
Carl: No, we didn't buy _____ juice this week. But, look, there are oranges. Do you want me to make you _____ juice?
Tina: Yes, thanks. Uh, and did we buy _____ cookies?
Carl: No, but there are still _____ cookies in the cabinet.
Tina: Great, thanks!

E Circle the correct words.
Dan: Do we have **a lot of / many** homework for next class?
Lee: No, just **a few / a little**. Maybe half an hour.
Dan: How **many / much** exercises?
Lee: I'm not sure, Dan. Only **a little / a few**. Why do you ask?
Dan: I have a party tonight and **much of / a lot of** my friends are going, so I don't have **many / much** time for homework! Hey, do you want to come, too?
Lee: Sure, why not? It sounds fun.

F Match the two parts to make activities.

cleaning	in rivers / in the ocean / in a pool
going	video games / soccer / cards
watching	museums / relatives / a friend
playing	the house / the bathroom / the car
taking	the sunrise / old movies / TV
doing	a class / a shower / a course
visiting	the dishes / the laundry / homework
swimming	online / out with friends / to the gym

G ▶R3.2 Complete with a pronoun. Listen to check.
1. Hi Mike, how are *you*?
2. This is Nick and this is Steve, I work with _____.
3. Your coat is on the floor. Please put _____ on your chair.
4. That's Jessica. I go to school with _____.
5. This is David's phone. Can you give it to _____?

H Correct the mistakes. Check your answers in units 5 and 6.
1. A house sitter take care your house when you're away. (2 mistakes)
2. I love to walking in the beach. (2 mistakes)
3. To swim is good for you. (1 mistake)
4. I no really enjoy to do the dishes. (2 mistakes)
5. Do you know where is the soccer stadium? (1 mistake)
6. For dinner we ate a bread and a few yogurt. (2 mistakes)
7. You look hungry. Would like any biscuit? (2 mistakes)
8. It's my sister's book. Please give him to it. (2 mistakes)
9. I hate use maps, especially old maps. (1 mistake)
10. Stop! No do that! Please to sit down. (2 mistakes)

Review 3 Units 5-6

Grammar and vocabulary

A Picture Dictionary. Pairwork. Sts test each other and review the main vocabulary items learned in units 5 and 6. There are some possible techniques mentioned on p. 9 of the introduction section on how to work with the Picture Dictionary in order to review vocabulary. You can select whichever of these best suit the needs of your class.

B **Make it personal** Ask each student to write an example for 1–8. In pairs, sts compare their answers. Classcheck.

> **Tip** Encourage sts to use words they think they know and then sts use their cell phones or a bilingual dictionary to check spelling if necessary.
> Help them with pronunciation, focusing on aspects of the words which make them difficult to understand such as incorrect word stress and pronunciation of consonant sounds.
> And, at this low level, where possible, encourage use of cognates, e.g. to choose *crocodile* over *alligator*, *Can you repeat that?* rather than *Can you say that again, please?*

C Individually, sts choose the best alternatives to complete sentences 1–10. Paircheck. Classcheck.

> 1 b 2 b 3 c 4 c 5 a 6 a 7 c 8 c 9 b 10 c

D Do the first line with the class and then have sts complete the dialogue. Play ▶R3.1 to check answers.

> any, any, some, any, some

E Sts select the correct words. Paircheck. Classcheck.

> **Tip** If time is available, have sts work in pairs and read out the dialogues in **D** and **E** until they can repeat them without looking at the book.

> a lot of, a little, many, a few, a lot, much

F Individually, match the verbs and nouns to make activities. If you have time, ask sts to ask and answer questions with *Do you like …?* with some of the activities.

> cleaning the house / the bathroom / the car;
> going online / out with friends / to the gym;
> watching the sunrise / old movies / TV;
> playing video games / soccer / cards;
> taking a class / a shower / a course;
> doing the dishes / the laundry / homework;
> visiting museums / relatives / a friend;
> swimming in rivers / in the ocean / in a pool

G Sts complete the dialogue with the correct pronouns. Play ▶R3.2 to check answers.

> 2 them 3 it 4 her 5 him

H Tell sts to correct the sentences. Call sts' attention to the number of mistakes between parentheses. Read sentence 1 and elicit corrections from the whole class.

In pairs, sts correct sentences 2–10. Whenever sts are uncertain, encourage them to flip back through units 5 and 6 and check their answers. Classcheck with answers on the board.

> 1 A house sitter takes care of your house when you're away.
> 2 I love walking on the beach.
> 3 Swimming is good for you.
> 4 I don't really enjoy doing the dishes.
> 5 Do you know where the soccer stadium is?
> 6 For dinner we ate bread and some yogurt.
> 7 You look hungry. Would you like some biscuits?
> 8 It's my sister's book. Please give it to her.
> 9 I hate using maps, especially old maps.
> 10 Stop! Don't do that! Please sit down.

> **Tip** Write these sentences with errors on strips of paper and stick them on the walls of the classroom. Sts work in pairs and walk around the room, trying to correct the errors. Tell them to take a notebook so they can write the correct sentences. Classcheck after they have finished.

Skills practice

🎵 *There's a mountain top that I'm dreaming of, If you need me you know where I'll be, I'll be riding shotgun underneath the hot sun.*

R3

A 🔴 **Make it personal** Do you like doing these activities? In pairs, compare. Anything in common?

| hate | don't mind | like | love |

- clean the bathroom   cook   do the dishes
- do the laundry   exercise   go online
- play video games   read novels
- shop in malls / online   spend money   sunbathe
- take selfies   tidy my room   water plants

I don't mind doing the laundry, what about you?

Oh, no! I hate doing the laundry.

B Try to match breakfasts a–f to the country they are typical of. Then read the blog to check your guesses.

1 Brazil   3 Japan   5 Norway
2 China   4 Mexico   6 The UK

What's your perfect breakfast?

"On the weekend I love to eat eggs, bacon, sausage, tomatoes, mushrooms, and toast. And lots of tea! I don't have time to make such a big, cooked breakfast from Monday to Friday."
Julia, London, UK

"My favorite breakfast is eggs in hot sauce with refried beans, tortillas, and some coffee."
Juan, Guadalajara, Mexico

"I eat the same thing every day – fruit, bread, pastries, some juice, and some coffee."
Milton, Salvador, Brazil

"On weekends or special occasions, I usually eat smoked salmon and scrambled eggs with some rye bread. Other days I just have some bread and cheese – and black coffee, of course! I don't usually eat much in the mornings."
Alexander, Oslo, Norway

"I always eat rice with some fish and soup for breakfast. I don't have time to eat again until the evening so a good breakfast is important to maintain my energy level through the day."
Kimiko, Tokyo, Japan

"Rice porridge with chicken is my best breakfast. I have this about three times a week."
Lin, Beijing, China

C Read again and name the person / people who …
1 eats the same thing every day? _____
2 has a different breakfast on weekends? _____
3 enjoys eggs with hot sauce? _____
4 eats meat for breakfast? _____
5 doesn't eat any meat or fish for breakfast? _____
6 eats rice for breakfast? _____

D 🔊 **R3.3** Listen and follow the directions. Write the letter in the correct place on the map.
a the bookstore   c the mall
b the movie theater   d the gym

E 🔴 **Make it personal** In pairs, are 1–5 True (T) or False (F) for your area? Any interesting differences?
1 There's a very good restaurant near my house.
2 There is a nice park at the end of this street.
3 There's no good shopping mall near here.
4 There are no interesting museums around here.
5 There aren't any cheap hotels in this area.

There are a lot of excellent restaurants near my house.

Really?! Lucky you! There aren't any near mine.

F 🔴 **Make it personal** **Question time.**
In pairs, practice asking and answering the 12 lesson titles in units 5 and 6. Use the book map on p. 2–3. Where possible, ask follow-up questions, too. Can you comfortably ask and answer all the questions?

Is there a mall in your hometown?   *Yes, but it's only small.*

Do you go there often?   *Not really.*

Skills Practice

🎵 **Song line:** Turn to p. 331 for notes about this song and an accompanying task.

A 🔑 **Make it personal** Refer to the model dialogue in the speech bubbles. In pairs, sts talk about the activities in the box and say if they *hate / don't mind / like / love* doing each of them. Monitor for *-ing* use of the verbs after *hate / don't mind / like / love*.

At the end, ask sts to report some of their partners' phrases to the whole class, e.g. *He hates cleaning the bathroom. He doesn't mind cooking.* Monitor closely for present simple third person *-s / doesn't*.

B Ask sts what food they see in the photos and correct any issues with pronunciation. Sts match the photos to the countries. Ask sts to discuss in small groups or pairs whether they like these foods.

🔑 1 c 2 e 3 d 4 a 5 f 6 b

C Ask sts to read the text again and complete the exercise. Ask: *Who has the most similar diet to you? Who has the healthiest / unhealthiest diet?*

🔑 1 Milton 2 Julia 3 Juan 4 Julia and Lin
5 Juan and Milton 6 Kimiko and Lin

D Sts will hear four people asking for directions to places a–d. If an IWB is available, use the *Digital Book for Teachers* to better explore the map. Point to the four white squares on the map and tell sts they need to discover which places are a, b, c, and d. Draw sts' attention to the street names and the notes next to the green squares.

Play ▶ **R3.3** and pause after dialogue A. Allow sts some time to find where the bookstore is. Paircheck. Classcheck.

Play the rest of the audio for dialogues B–D. Paircheck. Replay the track if necessary. Classcheck.

▶ **R3.3** Turn to p. 317 for the complete audioscript.

E 🔑 **Make it personal** Sts read sentences 1–5 and talk about their own neighborhood or town. Refer to the model dialogue in the speech bubbles before sts compare answers in pairs. Tell them not to use the words *true* or *false* (~~For me number 4 is false~~) when comparing, but to say sentences using *there's / isn't / there are /aren't*. At the end, ask each pair to tell you one similarity and one difference between their neighborhood or street.

F 🔑 **Make it personal** **Question time.** Sts look at the book map on p. 2–3 and take turns asking and answering the lesson title questions from units 5 and 6. Monitor closely for accuracy and encourage sts to ask follow-up questions when suitable. At the end, ask them how they felt performing the task: *Do you feel comfortable with all of the questions? Which ones are easy? Which ones are difficult?*

7.1 Do you live in a house?

1. Take a shower in …
2. You can cook in …
3. You wash and dry clothes in …
4. Store things you don't need in …
5. You sleep in …
6. People usually eat in …
7. People work in …
8. We watch TV in …
9. We keep our car in …

1 Vocabulary Rooms and furniture

A ▶ 7.1 Match clues 1–9 to the rooms. Listen to a guessing game to check.

- [ ] the basement __
- [ ] the dining room __
- [ ] the living room __
- [1] the bathroom __
- [ ] the garage __
- [ ] the office __
- [ ] the bedroom __
- [ ] the kitchen __
- [ ] the laundry room __

B ▶ 7.2 Listen to Tom showing his house to Anna, a potential roommate. Number the rooms in **A** in the order you hear them, 1–6. Which three rooms in **A** are not mentioned?

C Match the words below to furniture a–s in the picture. First match the words on the left, then those on the right. How many of the words do you already use?

- [✓] a bed
- [ ] a sofa
- [ ] an armchair
- [ ] shelves
- [ ] a chair
- [ ] a table
- [ ] a bathtub
- [ ] a sink
- [ ] a closet
- [ ] a TV
- [ ] a fan
- [ ] storage space
- [ ] a refrigerator
- [ ] a toilet
- [ ] a fireplace
- [ ] a stove
- [ ] a shower
- [ ] a microwave
- [ ] the stairs

D **Make it personal** In pairs, decide which items of furniture are essential at home and which are optional. Make two lists.

In my opinion, a bed is absolutely essential.

7

Unit overview: The main topics of unit 7 are rooms and furniture, *there was / there were*, party items, talking about the past and saying years (1998, 2009, etc.), describing where objects are, and making invitations. Sts learn and practice through the contexts of describing homes, describing cities, listening to a party planner's tips, talking about events, and role-playing short dialogues inviting, accepting, and refusing invitations to different events.

7.1 Do you live in a house?

Lesson Aims: Sts learn to describe rooms and contents in a house and talk about houses in the past.

Function
Naming and identifying rooms and furniture.
Talking about essential and optional items in a house.
Reading and watching a video about tiny homes.
Listening about and describing homes in the past.

Language
You sleep in a bedroom.
In my opinion, a bed is essential. There are two chairs.
There was a living room.
There wasn't a bathtub.
There weren't any windows.

Vocabulary: Rooms (a bedroom, a bathroom, the basement, the kitchen, the office, the utility room, the garage, etc.) and furniture (a closet, a bed, a sink, storage place, etc.).
Grammar: *There was / There were*. Review: *There is / There are*.

♪ **Song line:** Turn to p. 331 for notes about this song and an accompanying task.

Warm-up Before sts arrive, have these prompts written on the board: *How many hours / you sleep a day? Where / you usually eat? How often / you cook? What time / you usually take a shower? How often / you wash your clothes? Where / you keep your car?*

Elicit and drill the questions. In pairs, sts ask and answer the questions from the board. Monitor and prompt self-correction of the questions forms. If time allows, they can change partners and report what they remember.

1 Vocabulary Rooms and furniture

A Ask the title question to see what vocabulary sts know to describe rooms and their contents. Explore the picture, pointing to it and asking: *Is this a house or an apartment?* (a house). Use the picture to elicit or teach *garden*, too. Help sts find numbers 1–9 in the picture. Ask: *Where's number 1? / Can you see number 1?* and point to it in the bedroom, but do not name rooms yet. Play a quick game. You say the number, sts find it in the picture. Say: *Where's number 2? 3?* and so on. That will help sts focus on numbers only—letters a–s are only dealt with in **C**.

Model the activity. Point to number 1 in the picture, ask: *What do people usually do in number 1?* and say: *You take a shower in ...*, letting sts complete your sentence (a bathroom). Do the same for number 2 (the kitchen). Ask *What do people do in number 2?* (cook). In pairs, sts match the clues 2–9 to the correct room. Play ▶7.1 for sts to listen and check their answers.

> 2 the kitchen 3 the laundry room 4 the basement
> 5 the bedroom 6 the dining room 7 the office
> 8 the living room 9 the garage

▶7.1 Turn to p. 317 for the complete audioscript.

B Write the word *roommate* on the board and elicit its meaning. Play ▶7.2. Sts listen to Tom showing his house to Anna, a potential housemate, and number the rooms in the order they hear them. Paircheck. Classcheck. Ask: *Which three rooms in A are not mentioned?*

> 1 the living room 2 the kitchen 3 the dining room
> 4 the bathroom 5 the bedroom 6 the laundry room
> Rooms not mentioned: the basement, the garage, the office

▶7.2 Turn to p. 317 for the complete audioscript.

C Point to the picture of the house again and ask: *What's letter a?* Focus on the words on the left and ask sts to match them to letters in the picture. Sts then match the words on the right. Paircheck. Classcheck and drill pronunciation.

> a a bathtub   b a shower   c a refrigerator   d a microwave
> e a sink   f a stove   g the stairs   h a closet   i a table
> j storage space   k a toilet   l a bed   m a TV   n a fireplace
> o an armchair   p a chair   q shelves   r a fan   s a sofa

Note: Words are grouped by familiar and cognates first, and new or more difficult words after. By familiar, we mean either that they have already seen the words in previous lessons, or that they are recognizable cognates. Recognizing cognates is a special feature of English ID. See TB Introduction, p. 8–23, "Advantaging monolingual classes."

D 🔴 **Make it personal** In pairs, sts write two lists with items they think are essential or optional at home. Encourage sts to share their conclusions (*We think a bed and a refrigerator are essential*, etc.). For fun, you could limit them to the eight most essential items. Ask some sts to read out their essential lists and give reasons for their choices.

185

E ▶ 7.2 Listen again and list the furniture Tom mentions in each room. Do you think Anna likes the house? Why or why not?

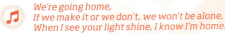
We're going home,
If we make it or we don't, we won't be alone,
When I see your light shine, I know I'm home.

F 🔴 **Make it personal** Give a tour of your home. Draw a floor plan and describe it to your partner. Are your homes similar?

This is the living room with a big sofa. And this is my bedroom.

2 Reading

A Look at the photo and guess what Jay says about his house. Then, read his blog post and answer the questions.

Hi! I'm **Jay Shafer** and I live in a small house because it doesn't cause problems for the environment. Also, this way, I don't buy more things than I really need. My house is only 89 square feet (that's 8.3 m²). It has a very small living room, a tiny kitchen, a small bedroom, and bathroom. During the day, my bed is in the wall. You can have a small house, too! Dream big. Live small.

1 What rooms does Jay's house have?
2 What are some good things about a tiny house? Can you think of any others?

B ▶ 7.3 Watch the video with the sound off. In pairs, name everything you saw in one minute. Who remembered the most?

two chairs   a toilet

C ▶ 7.3 Watch again and circle the correct answers. Is his house comfortable?
1 Jay's living room has two chairs and a tiny **fireplace / sofa**.
2 The kitchen has a sink, stove, refrigerator, and a **dishwasher / toaster oven**.
3 The shower is **the bathroom / in the bathtub**.
4 Jay sleeps in **a bedroom / the loft**.
5 When it's hot, he uses **air conditioning / a fan**.

3 Grammar Past of *be*: *there was / there were*

A ▶ 7.4 Listen to Katie and Lenny talking about a tiny house. Complete the grammar box with *was, were, wasn't,* or *weren't*. How many syllables in *wasn't* and *weren't*?

	+	–	?	Short answers
Singular	There _____ a window.	There was no stove. There wasn't a stove.	_____ there a bathtub?	Yes, there _____. / No, there wasn't.
Plural	There were two closets.	There _____ any closets.	_____ there any bedrooms?	Yes, there _____. / No, there weren't.
When something is negative, we use *there* _____ if it's singular, and *there* _____ if it's plural.				

→ **Grammar 7A** p. 150

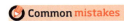 **Common mistakes**

there
~~Was~~ a bathtub?
There wasn't a
~~No had~~ garden in my old home.

B 🔴 **Make it personal** Imagine you're now living in a tiny house. In pairs, compare it to your "old home."

In my old home, there was a … but now there's no …!   *Were there any … in your old home?*

7.1

E Sts listen again for items of furniture. This will help them hear the pronunciation of the new lexis. Play ▶ 7.2 and tell sts to list the items in **C** they hear. Paircheck. Play again if necessary. Ask sts if they think Anna likes the house. Tell them to check the AS on p. 165 if they are not sure about the answer.

> the living room: a fireplace, a TV, armchairs, a sofa
> the kitchen: a stove, a microwave, a sink, a refrigerator, a table, chairs
> the dining room: a table, chairs
> the bathroom: a toilet, a shower, a bathtub
> the bedroom: a bed, a table, a closet, storage space, a fan
> the laundry room: storage space, shelves
> No, Anna doesn't like the house. She makes negative comments in almost every room.

F **Make it personal** Demonstrate this with a drawing of the floorplan of your house on the board. Sts then do the same. Monitor and check pronunciation of the vocabulary. Ask: *Are your houses similar or different? What's different?*

2 Reading

A Focus on the photo and ask: *Is it a big house? Why do you think Jay lives in this house?* Read questions 1 and 2 with sts and give them one minute to find the answers in the text. Classcheck.

> 1 a living room, a kitchen, a bedroom, a bathroom

B Play ▶ 7.3 or the video and tell sts to try and remember / list all the things they see. When it finishes, tell sts to try and write all the things they saw / heard mentioned. Set a time limit of one minute. Then, sts compare their lists. Ask: *Who remembered the most things? Would you like to live in this house?*

Cultural note Jay mentions a *faux fireplace*. In case sts ask for clarification, explain *faux* is pronounced /fo/ as it comes from French, meaning *fake*.

Note The authentic video here has quite a few tricky words, so for weaker classes, or if you just wish to keep it really simple, we have recorded an easier version for you to use without the video. This is available on the Richmond Learning Platform. You might like to play one then the other. Choose what's best for your classes. The main point is to practice listening in a useful way, and build confidence, so if you do use the harder version, ensure sts realize that comprehending even 50% is a great success, and that they really shouldn't either worry about nor expect to fully understand every word.

▶ 7.3 Turn to p. 318 for the complete audioscript.

C Elicit / Drill the pronunciation of the words in bold. Sts listen to ▶ 7.3 again or watch the video to choose the correct options. Paircheck. Classcheck. Ask sts if they think Jay's house is comfortable.

> 1 fireplace 2 toaster oven 3 the bathroom
> 4 the loft   5 a fan

3 Grammar Past of *be*: *there was / there were*

A Sts hear Katie and Lenny talk about a small house after visiting it. Play ▶ 7.4. Ask: *Did they like the house?* Classcheck. Tell sts to complete the grammar box and listen again to check answers. Ask: *Are they talking about the past or the present?* (the past).

Common mistakes Have sts focus on *There was / There were* examples to check answers.

> **Tip** For immediate practice, sts close their books and, in pairs, write down as much as possible about the house on p. 86 and its contents using *There was / there were*.

Help sts to notice that the positive form is unstressed but the negative (including *no*) is stressed.

➡ **Grammar 7A** p. 150

> + was
> – weren't
> ? Was, Were
> Short answers: was, were
> wasn't, weren't

Language tip Remind Portuguese speakers that, in English, we never use the verb *have* to indicate existence. Instead, we use *there + to be*, conjugating the verb *to be* according to the tense used. So, **There was** *a car in front of your house.* NOT **Had** *a car in front of your house.*

B **Make it personal** To model the activity, tell sts that you now live in a tiny house and that you will compare it to your old home. Refer to the speech bubbles on the page and make sure sts understand they are supposed to talk as if they now live in a tiny house like Jay's. Monitor closely for singular and plural uses of the past form of *There + be*. Ask two or three sts to share their comparisons with the whole class.

➡ **Workbook** p. 34

7.2 Where were you last night?

1 Vocabulary Party items

A In pairs, name each item and its color.

a red teapot, colored invitations, ...

- [ ] coffee
- [ ] glasses
- [ ] plates
- [ ] presents
- [ ] juice
- [ ] a cake
- [ ] tea
- [ ] water
- [ ] balloons
- [ ] birthday cards
- [ ] candles
- [ ] invitations
- [ ] napkins
- [ ] snacks
- [ ] soft drinks

B ▶7.5 Listen to Liz, a party planner, talking about how to have a good party. Number the items in **A** 1–15 in the order she mentions them.

C ▶7.5 Listen again. What does Liz consider essential for a party that is not shown in **A**?

D 🔴 Make it personal In pairs, compare your last party. Which items in **A** and **C** were(n't) there?

My last party was fantastic!   *There were a lot of ...*

2 Grammar Past of *be*: statements and questions

A ▶7.6 Listen to Martha and Rob, and find Martha (1), Rob (2), Jane (3), and Rick (4) in the photos.

7.2 Where were you last night?

Lesson Aims: Sts learn to use the simple past and past time expressions by talking about a party and finding out about each other's past.

Function
Naming and identifying party items.
Listening to a description of how to give a good party.
Talking about the last party you went to.
Reading an informal email.
Asking and answering questions about past events.

Language
There was a lot of wine.
We need snacks, beer, a cake.
I was at a fantastic party last week.
There was great music and dancing.
Where were you last night?
Were you at home last Sunday?

Vocabulary: : Party-related vocabulary (balloons, beer, invitations, snacks, plates, etc., space to dance, music). Past time expressions (yesterday + morning, night, afternoon; at + time; last + night, Sunday, weekend, etc.).
Grammar: Recycle: *There was / There were*. Verb *be* (simple past).

Warm-up Books closed. Elicit what sts can remember about Jay's tiny house from lesson 7.1. Ask sts to make true sentences about Jay's home using *There was / There were*. In large groups, sts collaboratively try to describe the tiny house.

1 Vocabulary Party items

A Books closed. You could use some realia to present party-related vocabulary. Tell sts you're having a party and show what you have brought. Ask *What else do we need for a party?* Encourage contributions and see what sts suggest.

Note: The use of realia is widely employed by language teachers to convey meaning and strengthen sts' associations. Although technology offers quick and practical tools to present vocabulary, bringing in real items is still a great technique to make words tangible, real, and memorable in the classroom.

Books open. Explore the photo and ask sts to point to items in it. In pairs, sts name each item and its color. Classcheck. Elicit that of the two columns, column 1 contains words they know already. Ask: *Which are countable? Which are uncountable?*

black coffee; red cups; white plates; blue, red, and gold presents; orange juice; a yellow cake; red teapot; yellow, orange, blue, and pink balloons; colored birthday cards; blue, green, and red candles; colored invitations; green napkins; green and orange snacks

B Ask: *What's important for a good party?* Get some ideas from sts. Sts listen to Liz, an events planner, talk about how to give a good party. Sts listen to ▶7.5 and order items 1–15 in the boxes in **A**. Paircheck. Classcheck with answers on the board.

1 invitations   2 soft drinks   3 water   4 tea   5 coffee
6 juice   7 snacks   8 plates   9 glasses   10 napkins
11 a cake   12 birthday cards   13 balloons   14 candles
15 presents

▶7.5 Turn to p. 318 for the complete audioscript.

C Play ▶7.5 again. Elicit what Liz talked about that wasn't shown in **A**. Paircheck. Classcheck.

music and space for people to dance

D Make it personal   Ask sts to remember the last party they went to. In pairs, sts talk about their last party, saying which items in **A** and **C** there was(n't) / there were(n't). Refer to the speech bubbles in **D** as a model. Add extra questions that they can ask each other, e.g. *Was there a theme?*

Extra activity Sts think of an idea for a class party. They think of ingredients, location, a theme, etc. Sts do this in small groups and then present their ideas to the class to decide on the best idea.

2 Grammar Past of *be*: statements and questions

A Ask sts to describe the photos using *There is / There are*, e.g. *There's a cake, There's a man,* etc. plus their ages, clothes, what they are doing, etc. Tell sts Martha went to a party yesterday, and she is now talking to Rob about it. Tell sts they will listen to the conversation and identify the people in the photos. Play ▶7.6. Paircheck. Classcheck.

1 a   2 d   3 b   4 c

Ask: *Why does Rob know Jane's parents? How does Rob feel? Why does Martha change the topic of conversation at the end?*

▶7.7 Turn to p. 318 for the complete audioscript.

Tip Ask sts to turn to the AS on p. 165. Sts listen again and notice the ↗ and ↘ intonation.

7.2

B ▶ 7.6 Order these words to make sentences. Who said them? Martha or Rob? Listen again to check.

1 was / I / party / great / at / yesterday / a / .
2 it / was / where / ?
3 was / it / Jane Foster's / at / home / .
4 birthday / was / it / her / .
5 there / Jane's / was / boyfriend / ?
6 he / yes, / was / .
7 parents / Jane's / there / were / ?
8 they / no, / weren't / .
9 boyfriend / I / before / Jane's / Rick / was / .
10 party / great / that / the / wasn't / .

 'Cause we were just kids when we fell in love, Not knowing what it was, I will not give you up this time.

Common mistakes

~~Was your brother~~
~~Your brother~~ was at the party last weekend?

                          was
Were you alone? Yes, I ~~were~~.

C Read the grammar box and complete with *was, were, wasn't,* or *weren't.*

	+	**−**	**?**	**Short answers**
Singular	I was at home. You were … She / He / It was …	I wasn't there. You _____ … She / He / It wasn't …	Were you at home? _____ she / he / it good?	Yes, I was. / No, I _____. Yes, he / she / it was. No, he / she / it _____.
Plural	We were there. You _____ … They were …	We _____ there. You weren't … They _____ …	_____ you there? Were they …?	Yes, we _____. / No, they weren't.

Don't forget the pronoun with *Wh-* questions:
Where were you? I was at school.
When was Julia at school? She was there all day.

➔ **Grammar 7B** p. 150

D Complete the email with the verb *be*. Where was Stacey yesterday?

> To: **Martin**   Today at 10:58
> Subject: R U OK?   All Mail
>
> Hi Martin!
> Where _____ you yesterday evening? Sleeping again? Well, I _____ at Lina's party, and it _____ amazing! There _____ some great music from the DJ, lots of dancing and the food _____ absolutely delicious! _____ you at home? Your cell phone _____ on all night, and I couldn't talk to you. That's why I _____ emailing you now. Are you OK? You _____ at school last week, and you _____ at the party. Where _____ you now??? 😐
>
> I hope everything _____ OK.
>
> Write back, text, or call me, please!
>
> Stacey xx

E Complete the chart of past time expressions.

afternoon	evening	Monday	month
morning	night	summer	weekend	year

yesterday	last
evening	

Common mistakes

last Monday morning
I was at work ~~the last Monday in the morning~~.

                  all evening
We weren't at home ~~all the night~~.

F 🟢 **Make it personal** In five minutes, find out all you can about your partner's week. Use *Were you …?* or *When / Where were you …?* + past time expressions. Mime what you can't express in English. Change partners and report what you remember. Who had the most boring / interesting week?

> Were you at home last night?

> Yes, I was, all evening. Where were you yesterday morning?

B **Common mistakes** Remind sts of word order for Yes / No questions. Ask them to look for sentences which are questions in lines 1–10. In pairs, sts write questions 2–5–7 in the correct order. Classcheck with answers on the board. Now elicit the correct order for 1. In pairs, sts order the rest of the sentences. Classcheck with answers on the board.

1 I was at a great party yesterday. (Martha)
2 Where was it? (Rob)
3 It was at Jane Foster's home. (Martha)
4 It was her birthday. (Martha)
5 Was Jane's boyfriend there? (Rob)
6 Yes, he was. (Martha)
7 Were Jane's parents there? (Rob)
8 No, they weren't. (Martha)
9 I was Jane's boyfriend before Rick. (Rob)
10 The party wasn't that great. (Martha)

Ask: *Do you remember who said each line? Was it Martha or Rob?* Give sts a minute to guess who said each line and write Martha or Rob. Play ▶ 7.6 again so sts can check if their guesses were right. Classcheck.

C Sts study 1–10 in **B** and complete the grammar box with the correct past forms of *be*. Paircheck. Classcheck with answers on the board.

+ were
- weren't, weren't, weren't
? Was, Were
Short answers: wasn't, wasn't, were

Tip Explore the grammar box. Ask: *How many different forms are there for the verb **be** in the past?* (two forms: was / were). *When do we use **was**?* (with I / he / she / it). *And **were**?* (with we / you / they). Remind sts that English has one form of *you* so they should be careful with *Were you ...? Yes, I was.* In pairs, sts can cover the grammar table and try to reproduce it with examples of their own.

➔ **Grammar 7B** p. 150

D Point to the email. Tell sts to skim through it and ask them *What type of text is this?* (an email); *How do you know it's an email?* (boxes *to, cc, subject*; text format); *Who is it from?* (Stacey); *Who is it to?* (Martin); *What is it about?* (a party yesterday). Sts fill in the blanks with the correct form of *be*. Paircheck. Classcheck with answers on the board.

were, was, was, was, was, Were, wasn't, am, weren't, weren't, are, is
Stacey was at Lina's party; Martin was possibly at home.

E Refer to the example in the chart and sts complete the columns with the correct words. Pair and classcheck.

yesterday: afternoon, morning
last: Monday, month, night, summer, weekend, year

Tip Highlight any common mistakes sts are likely to make by transferring from their L1 (e.g. *yesterday in the evening* and *all the day*. Drill *Were you / Where were you ...* + past time expression questions, e.g.:
T *Where were you yesterday morning?*
Sts (Repeat)
T *Yesterday evening.*
Sts *Where were you yesterday evening?*
etc.

F **Make it personal** Encourage sts to mime as much as possible what they can't say yet, e.g. *born, flying, driving,* etc. They should be able to express a lot even though they will almost certainly make mistakes with verb forms and prepositions but this will obviously get better with practice. Focus your corrective feedback on helping them to get *was / were* and the time phrases right for now. Refer to the speech bubbles as a model.

In pairs, sts have five minutes to discover as much as possible about their partner's past activities. Classcheck by asking sts to report on what their partner said. Ask: *Who had the most boring / interesting week?*

 **Song line:** Turn to p. 331 for notes about this song and an accompanying task.

➔ **Workbook** p. 35

7.3 Where were you last New Year's Eve?

1 Reading

A Which cities do the photos illustrate? What can you see in them?

> The Opera House. That's in Sydney.

B ▶ 7.7 Who has good memories of New Year's Eve last year? Who doesn't? Read and write + or – next to what each person says. Listen to check.

New Year's Eve around the world

Billions of people glo**b**ally welcome New Year's Eve with spectacular celebrations. How was your last New Year's Eve?

It was awesome! Our city was the first place in the world to really celebrate the New Year. And, of course, the first babies of the year were born here!
Kerry, Gisbourne, New Zealand.

Amazing! I'll never forget it. This was my first year in Sydney. There were fantastic fi**re**works, and there were hundreds of boats on the water!
Dave, Sydney, Australia.

It was cold! The music was good, but there were so many people a**lo**ng the River Thames! And there were no rest**rooms** near us, so we didn't stay long!
Kirsty, London, England.

I was at the concert at the pyramids of Giza. It was ma**g**ical! Incredible to think they're nea**r**ly 5,000 years old!
Habibah, Cairo, Egypt.

There were thou**s**ands of lights on the Eiffel Tower. It was abso**lu**tely beautiful!
Sabine, Paris, France.

It wasn't too good. I don't really like fireworks. But I was with a big group of friends. We were all a**s**leep by 12:30!
Lindsey, Los Angeles, the U.S.

It was just like every other day. It wasn't really very special. The family was all together, and dinner was delicious, but it always is. My brother is a chef.
Larry, Santiago, Chile.

There were tons of confetti falling on Times Square. It was a fa**b**ulous sight. The snow was beautiful, too, but too many people, and all the trash on the streets wasn't very nice.
Kevin, New York, the U.S.

It was my birthday. It was New Year's Eve and then su**d**denly I was 12, too! Wonderful!
Jodie, Berlin, Germany.

Fantastic! I was on the beach all night. There was dancing, and then there was a terrific sunrise. Beautiful colors!
Luís, Guadalajara, Mexico.

C Answer the questions.

Who ...
1 was cold?
2 was on the beach?
3 was a child?
4 doesn't like fireworks?

Where ...
1 were the first babies born?
2 was there music along the river?
3 were there a lot of boats?
4 was there confetti?

D **Make it personal** What happens in your town or city on New Year's Eve? In pairs, imagine you were together last year. Write a post to the website.

> Traditionally here, people eat 12 grapes at midnight.

7.3 Where were you last New Year's Eve?

Lesson Aims: Sts read about five different New Year's Eve celebrations and talk about a party they remember. Sts also learn prepositions of place.

Function
Reading and writing about a past New Year's Eve celebration.
Saying years.
Talking about a party you remember.
Listening to and describing positions.
Reading and writing text messages.

Language
It was cold.
There were fantastic fireworks.
We were all asleep by 12:30!
There were a lot of drinks and food.
The mouse is under the bed.
Wan 2 come 2 a party?

Vocabulary: Recycle: Party vocabulary. Adjectives (amazing, dangerous, anxious, worried, cold, awesome, magical, fabulous). Numbers for saying years.

Grammar: Recycle: Past forms of *be*. Prepositions of place.

Warm-up Recycle furniture and party items with a one-minute race game. Give each pair of sts a sheet of paper and tell them they will have one minute to write as many words as possible about a topic given by you. Start with furniture items and give sts one minute to list all the items they can remember from lesson 7.1. When time is up, ask them to count how many words they have. The pair with the highest number reads their list aloud. Check spelling and pronunciation on the spot. Repeat the procedures for party vocabulary.

1 Reading

A To prepare for this reading text, write the cognates on the board before sts enter the classroom. In pairs, sts can try to pronounce them. Ask them to guess what they think this lesson will be about.

Books open. Tell sts (if they haven't guessed) that today's lesson is about a special celebration in December. Point to the photos and ask: *What's this celebration? Do you recognize the places / cities in the photos? Have you been to any of them?*

> New York   Paris   Sydney   London

B Focus on the web forum and ask: *What are people writing about?* (New Year's Eve in different places). Ask: *What date is New Year's Eve?* and lead into a revision of dates and prepositions of time from p. 27, adding December 31. You may want to write other dates on the board with errors, for sts to correct. Paircheck. Classcheck.

Ask: *Are your memories positive or negative of last year's celebrations?* Tell sts to read the text and write + or - next to each post. Play ▶ 7.7. Sts read the text and listen to check their answers. Paircheck. Classcheck. Draw sts attention to the words with pink syllables and practice pronouncing the words with the correct word stress.

> Kerry +, Dave +, Kirsty -, Habibah +, Sabine +, Lindsey -, Larry -, Kevin -, Jodie +, Luis +

C Elicit what sts can remember from the texts in **B** and ask: *Who was cold?* (Kirsty) *Who was in a big city?* (Dave, Kirsty, Habibah, Sabine, Lindsey, Larry, Kevin, Jodie and Luis). Sts answer the questions. Classcheck.

> Who: 1 Kirsty   2 Luis   3 Jodie   4 Lindsey
> Where: 1 Gisbourne   2 London   3 Sydney   4 New York

D 🔵 **Make it personal**   Ask: *Are any of the posts similar to your experiences? What's New Year's Eve like where you live?* Tell sts to write a similar post in pairs. Monitor closely for the use of past forms of *be*. Round off with sts reading each other's posts and asking follow up questions in small groups of three or four.

At the end of the lesson, go back to this list and see how much of the lesson sts can remember around the cognates that you looked at at the start of the class. Celebrate the advantage of being able to use L1 to help with learning English.

7.3

2 Listening

A ▶ 7.8 Where's the mouse? Listen. Match mice 1–10 to the prepositions.
- ☐ above the TV
- ☐ across from the people
- ☐ behind the TV
- ☐ between the sofa and the table
- ☐ in front of the TV
- ☐ in the bed
- ☐ in the box
- ☐ next to the sofa
- ☐ on the bed
- ☐ under the table

But here I am, Next to you, The sky's more blue, in Malibu.

B ▶ 7.9 Listen to the couple and circle the seven mice they mention in the picture in **A**.

C ▶ 7.9 Listen again. Draw the mouse's new route on the picture. Describe the route to your partner using the phrases in **A**.

First, the mouse was under the table. Then it was …

D ◯ **Make it personal** In pairs, follow these steps.
1 A: Say where the mouse is. B: Point to the correct picture.
2 A: Point to a picture. B: Describe where the mouse is.
3 Close books and remember!

It's on the …

Common mistakes
mice
I don't like ~~the mouses~~.
mice = irregular plural, like *women*, *men* and *people*

3 Grammar Prepositions of place

A Read and complete the grammar box. Which are opposites? Mime one to test a partner.

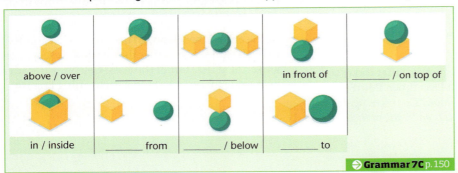

| above / over | _____ | _____ | in front of | _____ / on top of |
| in / inside | _____ from | _____ / below | _____ to | |

→ Grammar 7C p.150

B In pairs, say where these items are in **2A**. Test each other with more items, too.
1 the pillow / sofa   3 the fruit / table   5 the CDs / TV
2 the plant / TV   4 the picture / TV   6 the bed / chairs

The pillow is on the sofa.

C ◯ **Make it personal** Play a memory game in pairs. You each need five personal objects.
A: Close your eyes. B: Move an object.
A: Look and say where the object was and where it is now.

The … was next to the … but now it's under the …
Hmm … Where was the …? Now it's between …
There was a … in front of … It wasn't behind …

7.3

🎵 **Song line:** Turn to p. 332 for notes about this song and an accompanying task.

2 Listening

A Tell sts to look at the picture and ask where the mice are. Sts listen to ▶7.8 and match them to prepositions. Paircheck. Classcheck. Remind them that they have seen lots of songs with prepositions in them. Sts could look through the book to find them, underlining the prepositions.

> 1 in the box
> 2 under the table
> 3 between the sofa and the table
> 4 next to the sofa
> 5 in the bed
> 6 on the bed
> 7 across from the people
> 8 in front of the TV
> 9 behind the TV
> 10 above the TV

▶7.8 Turn to p. 318 for the complete audioscript.

Language tip Some prepositions of place, e.g. *above*, *behind* and *under* are formed by two prepositions in Portuguese and Spanish and combined with the equivalent to *of*. So, sts might say, *The mouse is **behind of** the TV*. Make sure sts understand that this is incorrect in English.

B Sts listen to a conversation between the couple about mice in their house. Play ▶7.9 and tell sts to circle the seven mice they mention. Paircheck. Play it again if necessary. Classcheck.

> 2, 4, 8, 9, 6, 5, 1

▶7.9 Turn to p. 318 for the complete audioscript.

C Ask: *Where was position 1? What about position 2?* and see what they can remember from the mouse's route. Tell them to draw the mouse's route on the picture as they listen to the couple again. Play ▶7.9 again. Write on the board a few simple narrative markers such as *first, then, after that, finally*. Focus on the speech bubble to model the speaking task and focus on the past form of *be* (*First, the mouse was under the table ...*). In pairs, sts retell the mouse's route in the picture. Invite one st at a time to say where the mouse was until the full route is told.

D 🅾 **Make it personal** Demonstrate the task with a st. Sts then decide who is A and B and do the activity. Monitor and check they are using the correct prepositions.

3 Grammar Prepositions of place

A Review prepositions sts know by writing song lines from previous lessons on the board and blanking out prepositions for sts to complete.

1 You can stand ____ my umbrella. (under)
2 We all live ____ a yellow submarine. (in)
3 Our house ____ of our street. (in the middle)
4 I don't mind spending every day out ____ the corner in the pouring rain. (on)

Focus on the pictures in the grammar box and elicit prepositions. Sts complete the box. Classcheck. Ask: *Do these words exist in your language? Are they used in a similar way?*

> behind, between, above, across, under, next

➡ **Grammar 7C** p. 150

B Refer to the picture in **2A**. Do number 1 with the class to make a full sentence with the correct preposition.

Weaker classes Write the sentence on the board as an example.

> 1 The pillow is on the sofa.
> 2 The plant is next to the TV.
> 3 The fruit is on the table.
> 4 The picture is above the TV.
> 5 The CDs are under the TV.
> 6 The bed is across from the chairs.

C **Make it personal** In pairs, sts test each other. Refer to the speech bubbles. Place five objects on your desk and give sts 30 seconds to memorize their positions. Tell them to close their eyes while you move one object. Sts open their eyes and say what has changed, e.g. *The pen was next to the book, now it's under the book*. Sts play this memory game with their own objects in pairs. If you have a suitable classroom, you could ask them to place objects around the room to make it more challenging.

For more practice of *on / at / in*, write more common mistakes on the board for sts to correct, e.g. *in the beach, in the bus, in the bus stop, in the check in, in/at the movie theater* etc.

Extra activity Refer sts back to p. 86. In pairs, sts take turns describing a room in the house for a partner to guess it. Model the language, writing an example on the board to help sts get started, e.g. *There's a sink in the corner and next to it, there's ...*

Fast finishers / Stronger classes could match together prepositions of place and time. Refer to the expressions from **E** on p. 89 and write sentences on the board for sts to complete, e.g. *We were in Sydney ___ December. / I can meet you ___ 2 p.m ___ Michael's house ___ the morning.*

➡ **Workbook** p. 36

7.4 Was your hometown different 10 years ago?

1 Vocabulary Dates

A ▶ 7.10 Listen to and number the dates in the order you hear them. Then circle the correct options.

YEAR 1980 YEAR 2000 YEAR 2013 YEAR 1985 YEAR 2005 YEAR 2017 YEAR 1997 YEAR 2010 YEAR 2023

We say years like 1980 and 2017 as **two / three** numbers. For 2019, you can also say two **thousand / thousands** nineteen.

B ▶ 7.11 Listen to Núria describe her hometown. Write the dates.

I was born in Barcelona in _____. The city was very different then. In my neighborhood, there were a lot of old buildings and factories. Until _____, there were only two coffee shops (we call them "bars"), and there were no other restaurants on my street. By _____, the neighborhood was a little different, and by _____, there were many new businesses. Now it's _____, and there are families from all over the world. You can enjoy food from many countries, too!

C  In pairs, describe a real or imaginary city on three different dates.

> It was very different. In ..., there was ...

2 Reading

A Is this photo of San Diego, California, from 1990 or 2018? In pairs, give three reasons. Which is the most convincing?

> I think it's 2018. There are a lot of tall buildings.

B Read the article about Bill Watson's trip to the future. It's now 2030! Is San Diego a little different or a lot different from his last visit? Does he like the city now?

San Diego, a changing city
by Bill Watson

As I arrive at my hotel in downtown San Diego in 2030, I am shocked. I was last here in 2018, and the city is very different. I almost think I'm in the wrong place!

Like many American cities, there has been urban renewal, and the downtown area has been renovated. It wasn't very nice when I was here in 1990, but, by 2018, visitors were able to enjoy good food, music and theater, or even a baseball game at Petco Park. Now, in 2030, the neighborhood near my favorite hotel is completely transformed!

There are new roads, a park, and new traffic lights. There wasn't so much traffic in 2018, but now traffic lights on every corner are essential. There were some good grocery stores downtown before, but now there are three new ones on my block where you can send your robot to do the shopping. And there's more! When I was here in 2018, there was a movie theater next to the bank. I went there often. But now, there's an enormous movie complex with six large theaters! And there are security cameras everywhere, but there weren't any in 2018. Maybe that's because there's a new school across from the movie complex. In 2018, there weren't any schools in this area.

My recommendation: This is a great city! Beautiful weather, clean, too, and there are a lot more cars in Los Angeles!

7.4 Was your hometown different 10 years ago?

Lesson Aims: Sts review prepositions and learn to use *there was / there were* to talk about the changes in their town.

Function
Reading about changes in a city.
Talking about your town back then and now.

Language
There wasn't a lot of traffic.
Twenty years ago, there was a park near my house … Now, there's a swimming pool complex in the same place.

Vocabulary: Recycle places in town. Past time expressions with *ago*.
Grammar: *There was / There were*. Review: Past forms of *be* and prepositions of place.

🎵 **Song line:** Turn to p. 332 for notes about this song and an accompanying task.

Warm-up Review comparatives. Write a list of sentences on the board before sts arrive, e.g. *The U.S. is a beautiful country. English is an easy language. Chicago is a very cold city*. In small groups, sts discuss and write a response for each sentence, to contest it, using comparatives, e.g. *We think Brazil is more beautiful than the U.S. / I think Spanish is easier than English. / La Paz is colder than Chicago*. Monitor closely and correct on the spot.

1 Vocabulary Dates

A Ask: *What's the date today?* Correct sts and write the date on the board. Refer sts to the dates and ask sts to say them to a partner as they think they are said. Play ▶ 7.10. Sts listen and number the dates in the order they hear them. Paircheck. Sts circle the correct options in the rules. Classcheck. Clarify how we say the dates using the sentence with 1980 and 2017 as examples. Write other dates on the board for sts to say.

🔑 1 2017 2 1997 3 2000 4 2010 5 1985
6 2023 7 1980 8 2005 9 2013
two, thousand

Language tip The interesting dates come after 2000. These are the rules to help sts generalize:
1900 – nineteen hundred (only if last two digits are zero)
1983 – nineteen eighty-three (no "hundred"!)
2000 – two thousand
2001 – two thousand one
2019 – twenty nineteen OR two thousand nineteen

Extra activity Elicit the months for a quick revision, and have sts jump up and make a line, as fast as possible, placing themselves in order of when their birthdays are, from January to December.

B Refer to the photo of Las Ramblas in Barcelona and ask: *Where is this?* Tell sts they are going to listen to Núria talk about her hometown, Barcelona. Check sts understand *buildings*, *factories*, and *neighborhood*. Play ▶ 7.11. Sts listen and write the dates. Paircheck. Classcheck.

🔑 1985, 1997, 2005, 2013, 2018

C 👤 **Make it personal** Sts could research this if they are too young to remember changes in their city. Or, they can invent changes. It will help to suggest some types of changes if they want to invent. Sts then take turns to describe the changes. Encourage sts to peer correct any errors they hear with dates.

Extra activity Sts think of three important events from their past (either personal or famous). They write them down and their partner asks *Yes / No* questions to find out what happened in that year.

A: *Did you start school in 2003?*
B: *Yes*.

Don't worry if they get the grammar wrong. Focus on how they say the dates. Encourage them to ask follow-up questions about the events.

2 Reading

A Refer sts to the photo and ask: *Where is San Diego?* (In the U.S). *Is this photo from 1990 or 2018? Why?* Elicit reasons. Find out if any of your students have ever been to San Diego.

B Read the instructions with the sts and tell them to read the article quickly to find answers to the two questions. Paircheck. Classcheck.

🔑 It's a lot different.
Yes, he does.

After reading, ask: *Did you enjoy reading this text? Is it the sort of text you'd choose to read in Spanish / Portuguese? Did you lose concentration or skip any bits?*

7.4

C ▶7.12 Read the article again and complete the chart about the neighborhood near Bill's hotel. Listen to check.

*Was it all in my fantasy?
Where are you now?
Were you only imaginary?
Where are you now?*

Back then, 2018	Today, 2030
1 There _____ so much traffic.	There _____ a lot of _____ lights.
2 There _____ some good grocery stores.	There are _____ new ones on the block.
3 There _____ a movie theater _____ _____ the bank.	There _____ a movie complex with _____ theaters.
4 There _____ no _____ cameras.	There are a lot of _____ cameras.
5 There _____ any _____ in the area.	There _____ a _____ across from the _____ _____.

D 🗣 **Make it personal** Imagine that you live in San Diego in 2030. In pairs, say which city you prefer, San Diego in 2018 or San Diego in 2030.

San Diego was great in 2018. It was so quiet!   *Yes, but there were no …*

③ Listening

Shanghai Then and Now

A In pairs, use the photos of Shanghai, China, in 1992 and 2018 to find two things that are the same and two that are different.

There is a big lake in both photos.

B ▶7.13 Listen to a conversation about Shanghai then and now. Which changes are mentioned that you can see in the photos in **A**?

C ▶7.13 Listen again. Complete the chart on Shanghai. Write + (*a lot*), - (*not much / many*), or a number.

	1990	Today
Traffic		
Population		
Pollution		
Tall buildings		
Famous sights		

⚠️ **Common mistakes**

There were ~~much~~ *many* more low buildings.

I ˇ*was* born in Quito.

D 🗣 **Make it personal** Find out about your own city or town.
1. Google your hometown or another place you're interested in. Find five ways it was different 20 years ago. (Try to read online texts in English!)
2. In pairs, describe the changes. Mime what you can't express in English.
3. Share your information with the class. Who found the most interesting changes?

Twenty years ago, Curitiba was / wasn't very clean / big / busy.

There was / were / wasn't / weren't a lot of malls / traffic / people.

C Sts read the text to find answers to the sentences. Don't check answers. Play ▶ 7.12 and tell sts to read and listen and check their answers.

1 wasn't, are, traffic
2 were, three
3 was, next to, 's, six
4 were, security, security
5 weren't, schools, 's, school, movie complex

Tip Focus on the stress of the auxiliary verb in negative sentences *There **wasn't** as much **tra**ffic* and the weak form in positive sentences *There were some **good gro**cery **stores**.* Sts practice saying the sentences with correct sentence stress.

D **Make it personal** Ask: *Do you think San Diego is better now or was it better before all the changes?* Refer sts to the speech bubbles. Sts then discuss their preferences.

Stronger students Tell them to take opposite positions and defend their ideas. St A thinks it was better before and st B thinks it is better now.

3 Listening

A **Books closed.** Use clues to help sts guess the name of the city, Shanghai. Sts get more points the fewer clues they need to guess it, e.g. most populated city in the world; world financial center; in Asia; on the east coast of China; starts with "S"… . Ask them to write it down if they know it, but not to shout it out. **Books open.** Ask sts to look at the photos. Ask: *Can you tell me one thing that is different?* Refer sts to the speech bubbles. In pairs they think of two more similarities and differences.

B Tell sts to listen and see if their ideas are mentioned. Play ▶ 7.13. Paircheck. Classcheck.

clean air / smog, few tall buildings / lots of tall buildings, no landmarks / landmarks (Oriental Pearl Tower, Shanghai Tower)

▶ 7.13 Turn to p. 318 for the complete audioscript.

C Refer sts to the chart. Sts listen to ▶ 7.13 again and complete the chart. Paircheck. Play again and ask them to check their answers.

Traffic:	–	+
Population:	11 million	24 million
Pollution:	–	+
Tall buildings:	–	+
Famous sights:	–	+

After listening the second time, ask: *Did you find this interesting? How much did you understand the first time you listened? Which parts did you only understand the second time you listened? How will you try to listen differently next time?*

Language tip A common mistake for Romance language speakers is the incorrect use ***a lot of*** or ***many** time ago* (L1 *muito tempo atrás / mucho tiempo atrás*). Make sure they understand the correct expression in English is ***a long** time ago*.

D **Make it personal** To set up this task, you could display photos of your hometown from 20 years ago and now and talk about changes.

Refer sts to the speech bubbles. Ask them to search for photos and find information (in English if possible) about how things have changed in their city or town and make some notes. Tell them not to write full sentences. Sts then work in pairs and talk about the changes they found before they share information with the class. If sts are from same town, they could choose another city where they may have family, or a city / place abroad they want to visit. Sts share their information with the class. Ask: *Who found interesting changes?*

Stronger students To add challenge, tell them to look for two good changes and two negative changes.

Extra writing Sts write a summary of the changes in their town / city for homework. They could also interview an older person in their family about changes and include that in their writing.

➔ **Workbook** p. 37

7.5 Do you enjoy weddings?

Skills Predicting from context

A Match the events to photos 1–5. What do you know about the five events?
- ☐ The 1985 Live Aid Concert
- ☐ Prince Harry and Meghan Markle's wedding in 2018
- ☐ The 1970 World Cup
- ☐ The 2016 Olympic Games in Rio
- ☐ The first Oscars in 1929

B ▶ 7.14 Read and listen to check your answers to **A**.

Dream tickets

It was at the Hollywood Roosevelt Hotel in Los Angeles, California, on May 16, 1929, and was a private dinner with 36 tables, and only 270 people. Believe it or not, tickets were only $5. Actors and actresses arrived at the hotel in luxury cars, and there were many fans waiting to greet them. It was not on radio or television. Douglas Fairbanks, president of the Academy of Motion Picture Arts and Sciences, was the host, and the ceremony was just 15 minutes long.

There were 600 people at the "small" ceremony and reception, but 1,200 guests came to greet the happy couple at Windsor Castle. An incredible 18 million people watched the event live on TV in the UK and 29 million in the U.S. The location of the honeymoon was secret!

It was the first World Cup in North America and the first outside South America or Europe. The Brazilian team were fantastic. Brazil beat Italy 4–1 in the final. It really was a great competition – the third World Cup victory for Brazil. It was Pelé's fourth and final World Cup. Pelé is about 80 years old now, but he's still considered the best player of all time.

This spectacular charity event was organized to raise money for the terrible famine in Ethiopia. There were two simultaneous concerts, one at Wembley Stadium in London, the other at JFK Stadium in Philadelphia. There were 72,000 people at the concert in London, and 100,000 in Philadelphia. On the same day, the event also inspired concerts in Australia and Germany. About 1.9 billion people, in 150 countries, watched it all live on TV. Artists included Queen, U2, David Bowie, and Paul McCartney.

C Cover the text. Uncover only line 1 and guess the word that comes next. Uncover line 2 to check, then guess the first word in line 3. Continue like this until the end. How many of your guesses were right?

D ▶ 7.15 *Race the Beep!* Listen to 12 numbers from the text in **B**. You have only 10 seconds to find the number and say what event it refers to.

E 🗣 **Make it personal** In pairs, follow these steps. Then change roles.
- **A:** Imagine you were at one of the events. How was it? Tell your partner. You can add any information you want!
- **B:** Ask your partner questions. What do you want to know?

I was at the … It was amazing! There was a lot of great music and dancing.

Were there a lot of people?

⚠ Common mistakes
million
two ~~millions~~ of people

94

7.5 Do you enjoy weddings?

Lesson Aims: Sts describe experiences of past events.

Function
Reading about events.
Listening to numbers and quickly relating them to facts in the texts.
Talking about your favorite event.

Language
There were about 200 guests.
My favorite event is the World Cup because …

Vocabulary: Events and celebrations.
Grammar: Past forms review: *there was / were …*

Warm-up Books open. Sts look at the photos and describe what they see. Make a note of relevant vocabulary.

ID Skills Predicting from context

A Sts match photos 1–5 to the events. Paircheck. Classcheck.

Extra activity Sts work in small groups. Tell them you are going to dictate some information twice, and that they should listen and note down only key words and numbers, but not every word. They will then rewrite the information in their groups. Focus on photo 2. Read the following information twice: *At the 2016 Rio Olympics, Usain Bolt won the 100 meters with a time of 9.81 seconds, the 200 meters, and the 4 x 100 meter relay, to secure his third consecutive triple gold at the Olympics, the only man in history to do so.* Monitor to support sts in preparing their texts. Each group can read their text for the class. Go over any common errors after they finish. Ask: *Who watched Usain Bolt in the Olympics? What was his gesture for winning?* (the bolt).

1 The first Oscars in 1929
2 The 2016 Olympic games in Rio
3 Prince Harry and Meghan Markle's wedding in 2018
4 The 1970 World Cup
5 The 1985 Live Aid Concert

B Point to the text. Sts listen to and read the reports and discover which event they describe. Play ▶ 7.14. Paircheck. Classcheck. Refer sts to **Common mistakes** at this point.

C Ask sts to cover their texts with a sheet of paper. In pairs, sts uncover and read the first line and try to guess the upcoming word on the following line. Each correct guess equals one point. Sts continue uncovering one line at a time trying to guess the following word(s) in the line below. Do this for the first column. Ask sts how many points they scored. As they may have either come up with different alternatives for some of the lines or not understood certain links in the text, ask sts if they have any questions.

D Sts hear twelve numbers which appear in the texts in **B**. Play ▶ 7.15 and pause after *36*. Ask them to find the numbers in the text and say what each number refers to. On the audio they only have four or five seconds to beat the beep. You may want to extend this to ten or more seconds by pausing the audio yourself, especially if you are asking them to write down their answers. Give them ten seconds to say what the numbers refer to.

36 tables (Oscars)
final score 4–1 (World Cup)
1,200 guests at Windsor Castle (royal wedding)
150 countries showed it on TV (Live Aid)
270 guests (Oscars)
600 guests at the ceremony and reception (royal wedding)
1.9 billion watched it (Live Aid)
the first ceremony was in 1929 (Oscars)
29 million watched it in the U.S. (royal wedding)
100,000 went in Philadelphia (Live Aid)
first one in North America (World Cup)
it lasted 15 minutes (Oscars)

Tip This can be a fun, competitive game where sts have to write down what each number referred to, and made harder if you don't let them look back at the text. Add up the correct guesses at the end!

E **Make it personal** Point to photos 1–5 in **B** again and ask the whole class: *What's your favorite type of event?* Sts imagine they were at that event. Give them time to think about how they will describe it. Remind them to use the past of *be*. Refer them to the speech bubbles for support. Sts then describe their events in pairs and ask questions to find out more information. After they have finished, ask some sts to share what events their partners described.

Extra writing Ask sts to write a description of their Dream Ticket event.

7.5 How about a barbecue on Sunday?

This is an invitation across the nation, A chance for folks to meet, There'll be Dancing in the streets.

ID in Action Making invitations

A Read the invitations. What kind of event is each one for?

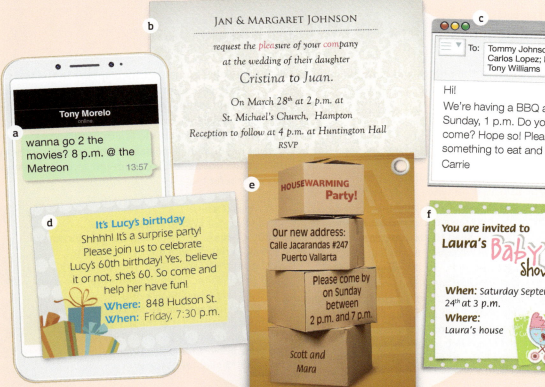

B ▶ 7.16 Listen and match conversations 1–6 to invitations a–f.
1 ____ 2 ____ 3 ____ 4 ____ 5 ____ 6 ____

C ▶ 7.16 Listen again and choose the expression you hear. Is the person making an invitation (M), accepting an invitation (A), or refusing an invitation (R)?
1 Can you and Sandy come? / Do you and Sandy want to come?
2 Sure. Sounds good. / Sure. Sounds great.
3 I'm sorry. We already have plans. / I'm sorry. We can't.
4 Great. I'd love to. / Sounds great.
5 Are you free on Friday? / Can you come on Friday?
6 Of course we can! What time? / Yes, we can! What time?

D 🗣 **Make it personal** In pairs, imagine an event and write the invitation. Go around the class and invite others. Note if they accept or refuse. Who has the most people going to their event?

We're having a Halloween party next weekend. Can you and your partner come?

We'd love to! What time?

⚠ Common mistakes

I'm going
~~I go~~ to a wedding this weekend.

I'm taking
Sorry, I can't go. ~~I go take~~ my mom to the hospital.

Use the present continuous, NOT the simple present for future plans.

7.5 How about a barbecue on Sunday?

Lesson Aims: To practice making invitations to different events.

Function
Reading and writing invitations to parties.
Listening to people invite, accept, and refuse invitations.
Inviting, accepting, and refusing invitations.

Language
Do you want to come to a barbecue on Sunday?
How about going _____?
Sure. That sounds great!
I'm sorry. We already have other plans.

Vocabulary: Invitations and events, celebrate, wedding, reception, barbecue.

♪ **Song line:** Turn to p. 332 for notes about this song and an accompanying task.

Warm-up Review party items. Ask sts to work in pairs and try to remember what items they looked at in lesson 7.2. Then sts go to that lesson and check their ideas.

ID in Action Making invitations

A Books closed. Write the lesson title on the board and elicit the meaning of *barbecue*. Point to a–f and ask: *What are these?* (invitations). Encourage sts to say what type of invitation each one is, e.g. a text message, a formal invitation, an email, etc. Ask: *What kind of event is each one for?*

🗝
a trip to the movies   b wedding   c barbecue lunch
d birthday party   e housewarming party   f baby shower

B Sts will hear people talking about the events in **A**. Play ▶7.16 conversation 1 then pause. Point to the invitations and ask: *Which event are they talking about?* (invitation e). Sts write e in 1. Play the rest of the audio. Paircheck. Classcheck with answers on the board.

🗝
1 e   2 a   3 c   4 b   5 d   6 f

▶7.16 Turn to p. 319 for the complete audioscript.

C Ask: *Do you remember if people accepted or refused the invitations?* Elicit what phrases were used to accept and refuse invitations. Sts listen to ▶7.16 again and put a check (accept) or a cross (refuse) in the boxes. Paircheck. Classcheck with answers on the board.

🗝
1 Can you and Sandy come? (M)
2 Sure. Sounds good. (A)
3 I'm sorry. We can't. (R)
4 Great. I'd love to. (A)
5 Are you free on Friday? (M)
6 Of course we can! What time? (A)

Tip Ask sts to turn to the AS on p. 166. Sts listen again and notice weak forms of *to*, *at*, *for*, and *of*.

Common mistakes Remind sts that we don't use simple present for future plans, we always use present continuous. Point out invitation C: *We're having a BBQ at ours on Sunday, 1 p.m.* Give other examples: *I'm having a party, I'm going for a coffee.*

Extra activity Tell them to use the phrases from **C** to take turns inviting and accepting or refusing invitations. Monitor closely for accuracy.

D Make it personal Ask sts to pretend they are throwing a party or any kind of event shown in **A** and write an invitation for it. Sts stand up and invite as many people as possible to their event. Remind them they need to use phrases from **C** to invite, accept, or refuse. Teach or elicit some more phrases with present continuous, e.g. *I can't, I'm meeting a friend / studying ... What are you doing [on Monday]?* Look at the speech bubbles. Highlight *next weekend* and write *the next weekend* on the board to show sts a common mistake when translating from L1. Draw attention to new language *We'd love to* and teach *I'd like / love to (but) ...* . When they finish, give them feedback on the language used and ask: *Who has the most people going to their event?*

➔ **Workbook** p. 38

➔ **Richmond Learning Platform**

➔ **Writing** p. 96

➔ **Café** p. 97

Writing 7 An online review

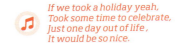
*If we took a holiday yeah,
Took some time to celebrate,
Just one day out of life,
It would be so nice.*

A Read the ad and underline the positive features of this city-center apartment.

Beautiful luxury apartment, with garage.

👤 2 guests 📶 Wi-Fi 🚗 Parking

Ideal for a weekend city break. In quiet location, only 10 minutes from city center and close to transportation. All modern conveniences, including superfast Wi-Fi, well-equipped kitchen, terrace with great views. Sheets and towels provided. $300 per night for two people.

B Read the review and circle the features in the ad that weren't good or weren't true.

Review by Alisha2001
●○○○○

Apartment sounds great, but was terrible – don't stay there!

My mom and I wanted a relaxing city break, but we were very disappointed. Yes, it's beautiful inside, but ...

The first problem was car parking – the garage is over 100 meters away across a busy street!

Secondly, the ad says "close to transportation." That's true – kind of! There was a huge highway in front of the building, and a busy subway station at the back, too! Also, the apartment was not 10 minutes from the city center. Walking fast, it was over 30 minutes.

Then there were the "modern conveniences." There was a refrigerator and a microwave but no dishwasher or washing machine ... not even a toaster! Plus, the sheets weren't clean, and the Wi-Fi was really slow.

Finally, there was the noise. Unbelievable! Thousands of cars, and trains passing all night so we never opened the terrace doors!

C Read **Write it right!** and underline the connectors in the text in **B**.

✓ Write it right!

In a review, start with a statement summarizing your feelings / opinion. Use connectors to:
- sequence – *the first problem was, secondly, another thing was, then there was / were, finally.*
- add information – *also, too, plus.*

D Use connectors from **Write it right!** to complete the review. Circle the eight problems.

My friends and I rented a camper van from ZZ Rentals last weekend – it was a disaster!

(1) _____ there was no record of our reservation.
(2) _____, there was only one very small camper available, so we had to take that.
(3) _____, because it was so small, there was no bathroom, and there wasn't a kitchen. It was (4) _____ dirty, and we had to ask for clean towels and sheets (5) _____, when these were supposed to be included.
(6) _____ the insurance. There was an extra $100 per person to pay because we were all under 24. (7) _____, there was a deposit of $1,000 in case of damage!
(8) _____, when we were on the road, we realized there was no gas in the tank! I will never rent a camper van from this company again.

E 🔵 **Make it personal** Write a review of a bad experience at a hotel, in a restaurant, or on vacation.

Before	Use ideas from **B** and **D**, or your own experience.
While	Use a variety of connectors.
After	Check your review carefully and exchange it with a partner. Think of two questions to ask your partner about their experience.

96

Writing 7 An online review

♪ **Song line:** Turn to p. 332 for notes about this song and an accompanying task.

Integrated speaking skills. Ask sts to work in small groups and talk about bad experiences they have had at a hotel, restaurant or on vacation. Monitor and make a note of useful vocabulary and go over this after they finish. If your sts are younger and don't have these types of experiences, you could tell them about a bad experience and encourage them to ask questions to find out what happened.

A Refer sts to the ad and ask sts to underline the positive features of the apartment. Classcheck. Ask: *Would you like to stay in this apartment? Why (not)?*

> **Tip** Explain *conveniences* using the word *convenient*, which is a cognate with Latin languages. Things which make living in a flat convenient, e.g. Wi-Fi, heating, air-conditioning, etc.

> Ideal for a weekend city break. In quiet location, only 10 minutes from city center and close to transportation. All modern conveniences, including superfast Wi-Fi, well-equipped kitchen, terrace with great views. Sheets and towels provided. $300 per night for two people.

B Refer sts to the review and the circle ratings. Ask: *What do the circles show?* Sts read the review. Check any vocabulary that sts may not know, focus especially on the pronunciation of the pink-stressed words. Refer sts back to the ad in **A** and have them circle features that weren't good or true according to the review. Paircheck. Classcheck.

> the garage is over 100 meters away across a busy street
> huge highway in front of the building
> busy subway station
> city center ... was over 30 minutes
> no dishwasher or washing machine ... not even a toaster
> sheets weren't clean
> Wi-Fi was really slow
> noise ... Thousands of cars, and trains passing all night

C Read **Write it right!** with the class. Sts underline the connectors in the review in **B**. Paircheck and classcheck. Point out that we use commas after *firstly, secondly, also, plus,* and *finally*.

> The first problem was
> Secondly,
> too
> Also,
> Then there was
> Plus,
> Finally,

D Tell sts to read the review quickly and summarize what the problems were. Sts then use the connectors in **Write it right!** to complete the review. Classcheck.

> 1 The first problem was
> 2 Secondly
> 3 Another thing was
> 4 also
> 5 too
> 6 Then there was
> 7 Plus
> 8 Finally

E 🔵 **Make it personal** Ask one or two sts if they have had bad experiences in a restaurant, in a hotel, or on vacation. Elicit some ideas about what happened, and write useful vocabulary on the board. Read the steps Before, While, and After with sts so as to guide them to write their own reviews. Tell them to refer to the reviews in **B** and **D** as models. As a follow-up activity and before they hand in their texts, ask sts to exchange compositions and ask each other questions to find out more details.

7 House rules

 Café

1 Before watching

A 🎤 **Make it personal** In pairs, describe your home. Find six differences.

> Bea lives in a new apartment block, but I live in an old house.

B Match photos 1–5 to these words.

- [ ] antique furniture
- [ ] an indoor pool
- [ ] an attic
- [ ] a lake house
- [ ] a cellar

C Complete 1–6 with the prepositions.

| at | behind | in | in front of | next to | on |

1 August has a computer _____ his lap.
2 Andrea has a cell phone _____ her hand.
3 August's sitting _____ Andrea on the sofa.
4 The window's _____ the sofa.
5 Andrea and August are _____ home.
6 The sofa's _____ the window.

2 While watching

A Check (✓) the correct answer.
1 Andrea says they'll be the best ever …
   - [ ] students
   - [ ] owners
   - [ ] renters.
2 Andrea and August are going to a lake house …
   - [ ] on the ocean
   - [ ] in the mountains
   - [ ] on the beach.

B Check (✓) or correct all the rules they mention.
1 Don't sit on the furniture in the huge sitting room.
2 Don't go in the cellar.
3 You cannot go in the attic.
4 You can sleep in the master bedroom.
5 Don't swim in the lake.
6 Absolutely no parties.

C True (T) or False (F)? Correct the false sentences.
1 There are ten rules on the list.
2 August's status update doesn't mention the party.
3 Daniel says "My holiday is over."
4 Lucy says she'll clean the downstairs bedroom.
5 Andrea is sad because now they can't go to the beach.
6 Daniel says he'll put the dining room furniture back and vacuum.

3 After watching

A In pairs, describe the photo. Then complete 1–6 with was(n't) / were(n't).

> Three of them are sleeping. Andrea is …

1 It obviously _____ a small, quiet party.
2 There _____ probably a lot of people there.
3 There _____ probably a lot of food and drink.
4 Lucy _____ at the party, but Genevieve _____ .
5 After the party, everyone except Andrea _____ sleeping.
6 All the rooms _____ very messy.

B Order the events, 1–6.
- [ ] The cleaning crew arrives.
- [ ] The crew goes upstairs.
- [ ] August sends an email to someone.
- [ ] August says he is selling his car.
- [ ] Everyone goes to the beach.
- [ ] They all start cleaning except August.

C 🎤 **Make it personal** In pairs, describe the last party you went to. Were your parties similar?

> My last party was at a hotel. It was my cousin's 15th birthday.

ID Café 7 House rules

1 Before watching

A **Make it personal** Give a short description of your house as shown in the speech bubbles. Introduce the question: *What's your house like?* In pairs, sts ask and answer about their houses. Monitor and make a note of useful language sts use. Go over this with the class afterwards.

B Briefly elicit some parts of the house (living room, bedroom, etc.) Point to photo 4 and ask: *What's this?* (Sts may say *a swimming pool*.) Tell them it's *an indoor pool* and have sts write 4 in the correct box. Go on exploring the photos and use them to present new vocabulary. Drill pronunciation of all words, especially *cellar* /ˈsɛlər/, *attic* /ˈætɪk/, and *antique* /ænˈtiːk/. Sts match photos 2–5 to the correct words / phrases. Classcheck.

> 3 antique furniture 2 an attic 1 a cellar
> 4 an indoor pool 5 a lake house

C Refer sts to the photo showing Andrea and August and ask them to complete sentences 1–6 with the correct preposition. Paircheck. Classcheck.

> 1 on 2 in 3 next to 4 behind 5 at 6 in front of

2 While watching

A Elicit what sts can remember about the characters they have met in **ID Café** so far. Can they remember their names and what they do? Play the first part of **Video 7** (August and Andrea on the sofa). Sts choose the correct option for 1 and 2. Paircheck. Classcheck.

> 1 renters
> 2 on the beach

B Tell sts there's a list of rules in the house. Play **Video 7**.

Point to rules 1–6 and get sts to check the rules they remember from the video. Paircheck. Classcheck.

> The rules mentioned are: 2 3 6

C Ask: *Why does August say, "Uh-oh"? Are they giving a party at the house? Let's see!* Play the rest of the video. Point to sentences 1–6 and have sts decide in pairs whether they are true or false. Classcheck.

> 1 T 2 F 3 F 4 F 5 T 6 T

3 After watching

A Point to the photo showing Andrea, Lucy, August and Daniel, all asleep at the table and on the sofa. Ask sts: *Is it before or after the party?* (after). *What kind of party was it?* Sts describe the party with their partner. After they finish ask some pairs to describe the photo. Correct any errors with *was / were*.

Ask sts to fill in the blanks with *was / were*, affirmative forms only. Paircheck. Classcheck.

> 1 wasn't 2 were 3 was 4 was / wasn't 5 was 6 were

B Change partners. In pairs, sts reorder events, 1-6, according to what they remember from the video. Replay **Video 7** if necessary. Classcheck.

> 4 The cleaning crew arrives.
> 5 The crew goes upstairs.
> 1 August sends an email to someone.
> 3 August says he is selling his car.
> 6 Everyone goes to the beach.
> 2 They all start cleaning except August.

C **Make it personal** Refer sts to the speech bubble and also give your own example. Give clear examples using *was / were*. Then, sts describe parties they have been to. Monitor and make a note of good examples of *was / were* and errors, and go over this after they finish. Ask the class to share any fun stories they heard to end the lesson.

8.1 When did you start school?

1 Reading

A Name someone famous from the past. Your partner says something they know about that person. If they are correct, they get a point. Take turns.

Pablo Picasso. — *He was an artist. I think he was Spanish.* — *That's right!*

B ▶8.1 Match pictures 1–10 to a–j. Complete with *in*, *to*, or ө. Listen to check.

a marry _____ him
b learn how _____ tat**too**
c want _____ go out with her
d stop _____ work (n.)
e be born _____ 1877
f die _____ 1961
g work _____ the circus
h agree _____ see him
i start _____ tattoo lessons at nine
j study _____ hard

C ▶8.2 Read and listen to Maud's biography. What were her two professions?

MAUD STEVENS WAGNER Famous … as a tat**too** artist!

Maud Stevens was born in 1877 in Kansas in the United States. She was a circus performer who **worked** in the circus for many years, but that's not all. She was also a tattoo artist, the very first female tattoo artist in the U.S.

In 1909, Maud **married** Gus Wagner, who was a tattoo artist, too. His body was completely covered – there were tattoos all over it! When Gus first **wanted** to go out with Maud, she **didn't want** to go out with him. She only a**greed** to see him in ex**change** for a tattoo lesson. Maud **studied** hard, and soon she **learned** how to tattoo.

Maud **didn't stop** working in the circus, but she **covered** her body with tattoos. Soon, everyone wanted a tattoo from Maud. Maud and Gus's daughter Lotteva **started** tattoo lessons when she was only nine years old. They **toured** the U.S., giving tattoos to people everywhere. Finally, they **moved** to Lawton, Oklahoma, where Maud **died** in 1961 at the age of 84.

D ▶8.2 Write the verbs in the correct group, according to the pronunciation of their *-ed* endings. Read and listen again to check. Any surprises?

agreed covered died learned married moved
started studied toured wanted worked

/t/	/d/	/ɪd/
stopped	lived	needed

Common mistakes

/askt/
I asked /askɪd/ my teacher a question.

98

Unit overview: The main topic of unit 8 is the simple past with both regular and then irregular verbs. The contexts are the story of a famous tattoo artist from the 1870s, Frida Kahlo's biography, talking about your last vacation, and an interview with a songwriter. Questions with and without auxiliaries (subject questions) are introduced and practiced through a quiz on pop culture. The unit ends practicing more phone language and polite requests and responses.

8.1 When did you start school?

Lesson Aims: Sts start using the simple past in the affirmative form. The rules are taught in the next lesson.

Function	Language
Talking about past events. Listening and reading a famous tattoo artist.	She was born in 1877. She studied hard. She married Diego Rivera. I started school in …

Vocabulary: Recycle saying years (1983, 2009). Biography vocabulary (be born, start school, get divorced, get married to). Vocabulary related to text (get piercings / tattoos, trouble, musicians, receive an award, record an album, play the guitar).
Grammar: Simple past regular verbs + and –

Warm-up Books closed. Write *tattoo* on the board. Ask: *What's a tattoo? Do you like tattoos? Do you know any famous people with tattoos? Do you have any tattoos?* Sts can discuss these questions in pairs or as a whole class.

1 Reading

A Books open. Name a famous person from the past you think your sts will know. Ask: *What do you know about _____?* Sts offer ideas. Every time someone says something correct, write a point on the board. Sts then do the same in pairs.

B Refer sts to the photo of Maud Stevens Wagner and ask: *Have you heard of her? What tattoos can you see on Maud?* Tell sts they are going to learn about Maud's life. Tell sts to look at the pictures and complete the matching activity. Play ▶8.1 so they can check their answers. Sts complete the gaps with the correct preposition. Play the audio again so they can check their answers. Note: Tell sts that Maud and her husband gave traditional "hand-poked" tattoos to people all their lives despite the invention of the tattoo machine. Interesting—and painful!

> 1 e, in 2 g, in 3 c, to 4 h, to 5 a, – 6 j, – 7 b, to
> 8 d, – 9 i, – 10 f, in

▶8.1 Turn to p. 319 for the complete audioscript.

Tip Sts often say *stop **to** work* and *marry **with** a person*. Tell them that, in English, these phrases don't have prepositions. To help consolidate all phrases, tell sts to test each other by pointing to the pictures and asking their partner to say the correct phrase.

C Check sts are clear that *profession* means *job*. Play ▶8.2 so sts can listen and read then answer the questions. Paircheck and classcheck.

> circus performer, tattoo artist

D Say: *agreed, studied, worked* and ask sts what column they go in and ask why.

Common mistakes Show sts that /ɪd/ is in fact adding another syllable onto the word and we only do this with words that end in the sounds /d/ or /t/.

> /t/   worked
> /d/   agreed, died, married, moved, toured, studied, covered, learned
> /ɪd/ started, wanted

Tip Show sts /t/ is unvoiced and /d/ is voiced. Ask them to put their hand on their throat and say the sounds. With /d/ they should feel some vibration and with /t/ none. Tell sts we add /t/ to verbs that end in unvoiced consonants, e.g. *ask*, and we add /d/ to verbs that end in voiced consonants or vowels, e.g. *travel*.

Sts look at the examples and complete the columns. Play ▶8.2 for sts to check. Paircheck and classcheck.

209

E In pairs, decide if 1–5 are True (T) or False (F). Then cover each paragraph in turn, and remember all you can from it.
1. Gus was a tattoo artist, but he didn't have any tattoos.
2. Maud wanted to go out with Gus, but Gus didn't want to go out with Maud.
3. She didn't learn how to tattoo before she married him.
4. Maud and Gus's daughter Lotteva didn't learn how to tattoo.
5. There were no female tattoo artists in the U.S. in 1877.

So wake me up when it's all over, when I'm wiser and I'm older. All this time I was finding myself, And I didn't know I was lost.

Common mistakes

Maud ~~work~~ *worked* in many places.
She ~~no lived~~ *didn't live* in Mexico.

F 🟠 **Make it personal** Choose a famous person from the past. Research their life and write five sentences about them. Share your information with a partner.

Avicii was a Swedish musician, DJ, and record producer. He died in Oman in 2018 when he was only 28. He didn't have any children. I loved his music, especially "Wake Me Up" and "Hey Brother".

2 Grammar Simple past regular verbs ➕ and ➖

A Complete the grammar box. Does the simple past in your language have more or fewer forms?

> Study the bold verbs in Maud's biography (and the negative verbs in **1E**). Complete the rules.
> 1. Positive and negative forms have **more than one / only one** form for all persons.
> 2. For negatives, use **doesn't / don't / didn't** + the infinitive.
> 3. To form the simple past tense:
>   the usual ending is _____.
>   when a verb ends in *-e* (*agree, live, like*), add only _____.
>   when a verb ends in *-y* (*study, marry*), change the *y* to _____ and add _____.
> 4. For positive *-ed* endings, there are three possible pronunciations: /t/, /d/, or /_____/. The most common is _____.
>   Only add an extra syllable for *-ed* endings with verbs ending in the letters *d* and *t*.
>
> ➡ **Grammar 8A** p. 152

B ▶ 8.3 Write the simple past verbs. Then listen to information about the Mexican painter Frida Kahlo, and match the information to the dates.

1928	was born	in Coyoacán, Mexico City (**be born**)
1907	_____	in Casa Azul with her family (**live**)
1920s and 1930s	_____	to be a doctor (**want**)
1954	_____	to be a painter after a bus accident (**decide**)
1907 to 1928	_____	Diego Rivera, the world famous muralist (**marry**)
before 1925	_____	to the U.S. (**travel**), and _____ a unique style (**develop**)
childhood to 1954	_____	her entire life, and was famous for her self-portraits (**paint**)
1925	_____	in bed at the Casa Azul in Mexico City (**die**)

C ▶ 8.3 Listen again. Choose the correct answer.
Frida **enjoyed / didn't enjoy** her time in the U.S., but she **liked / didn't like** some aspects of American society. She **didn't travel / traveled** outside North America.

D In pairs, take turns telling Frida's story. Try to help each other with pronunciation.

E 🟢 **Make it personal** Write your own short biography using six of these verbs. Tell your story to the class.

> be born   decide   learn   live   marry   move   start   study   travel   work

I was born in Bogotá, Colombia. I lived there for five years before we moved to Baranquilla. I started school in 2009.

E Ask the class to say if they think the sentences are true or false. Then they read and check their answers in pairs. Then, tell them to take turns covering each paragraph and trying to remember what they can. Their partner reads and tells them what information they remembered correctly. Ask: *What do you think of Maud?*

> 1 F   2 F   3 F   4 F   5 T

F 🔵 **Make it personal**   This is an ideal homework task. However, if sts have access to the Internet they can research someone online and do the activity in class. To help direct the task, tell sts to find out when their chosen person was born, what they did that made them famous, any relationships and children they had, one or two interesting facts about them, and when they died. Monitor and check their sentences but don't correct the simple past grammar yet. Focus on prepositions. Sts then use their sentences to tell a partner about the person. Encourage them to summarize the information, not just read what they wrote. Ask sts to share any interesting information they learned from their partners with the class.

🟠 **Common mistakes**   Remind sts to use the simple past when referring to finished past events.

2 **Grammar** Simple past regular verbs ➕ and ➖

🎵 **Song line:** Turn to p. 332 for notes about this song and an accompanying task.

A Do the first example in the grammar box with the class. Ask: *What do we add to the end of regular verbs to make into simple past?* (*-ed* or *-d*). Then sts complete the rest of the box. Paircheck. Classcheck.

> 1 only one   2 didn't   3 -ed, -d, -i, -ed   4 /id/, /d/

➡️ **Grammar 8A** p. 152

B Tell sts to look at the photo of Frida Kahlo. Ask: *What do you know about Frida?* Ask sts to read out the dates to review how we say dates. Then sts fill in the information with the correct form of the verbs. Play ▶️8.3 so they can check answers. Classcheck.

> lived: 1907 to 1928
> wanted: before 1925
> decided: 1925
> married: 1928
> traveled, developed: 1920s and 1930s
> painted: childhood to 1954
> died: 1954

▶️**8.3** Turn to p. 333 for the complete audioscript.

C Ask sts to predict the answers. Play ▶️8.3 again so they can check. Classcheck.

> enjoyed, didn't like, traveled

Tip Ask sts to turn to the AS on p. 166. Sts listen again and notice *-ed* endings.

D Give sts two minutes to make notes individually about what they can remember. Tell them to write down key verbs, e.g. *was born* + date, *married* + person, etc. Then, sts work with a partner to describe Frida's life with as many facts as possible. Monitor and correct errors in grammar or pronunciation as you listen. Go over any common errors after they finish.

E 🔵 **Make it personal**   Refer sts to the example in blue. Then, tell them to write their own biography. With younger classes, try writing the biography of another person (sts can choose). Or, in pairs or small groups, sts could write the biography for a famous person. Monitor and prompt self-correction of simple past and preposition errors.

Extra activity   Take in all the texts and give them out to different sts. Put sts into groups of four and tell them to take turns reading out the biographies without saying the name of the person. The listeners guess whose biography it is.

➡️ **Workbook** p. 39

8.2 Did you go out last weekend?

1 Listening

A In pairs, guess which question goes with each picture.
How was your ...?

| day off | day yesterday | summer | Sunday | Thanksgiving | weekend |

I think "How was your day off?" is "b."   *Really? I think it's "e."*

B ▶8.4 Listen and complete 1–6 with the words in **A**. Match them to the correct picture.

1 **A:** How was your _____ _____?
   B: Oh, perfect! I didn't do much. I **took** it easy and I **read** my book.
2 **A:** How was your _____ _____?
   B: I **slept** late. Then I **made** brunch and **had** a good time with my friends.
3 **A:** How was your _____?
   B: Great! My sister and her family **came** over, and we **ate** a lot!
4 **A:** How was your _____?
   B: Slow! I **didn't get up** until midday. Then I **met** some friends, and we **saw** a movie.
5 **A:** How was your _____?
   B: Fantastic! We **got up** late every day and then we **went** to the beach.
6 **A:** How was your _____?
   B: Saturday, I **went** shopping and **bought** some new jeans. I **did** chores all day Sunday.

C ▶8.5 Listen to the pronunciation of 14 common past tense irregular verbs and repeat.

buy – bought /ɔ/	go – went /ɛ/	say – said /ɛ/
come – came /eɪ/	have – had /æ/	see – saw /ɔ/
do – did /ɪ/	know – knew /u:/	take – took /ʊ/
get – got /ɑ/	make – made /eɪ/	think – thought /ɔ/
give – gave /eɪ/	meet – met /ɛ/	

D 🔴 **Make it personal** Tell the class at least two things you did last weekend.
I met some friends and we decided to go to a nightclub. We had a great night.

2 Grammar Simple past irregular verbs ⊕ and ⊖

A Complete the grammar box.

1 Complete the sentences with the simple past ⊕ form of the verbs in parentheses.

	Subject	Verb	
1	I		my homework last night. (**do**)
2	You		me a really nice gift. (**give**)
3	He		really late after his final exam. (**sleep**)
4	She		good-bye at the airport. (**say**)
5	We		your parents at the mall. (**meet**)
6	They		some expensive clothes last weekend. (**buy**)

In the simple past, ⊕ irregular verbs only have one form for all persons.

2 Complete the rule for ⊖ sentences.
We saw Vero but she **didn't see** us.   Leo **didn't play** soccer because he **didn't feel** well.
Use the auxiliary _____ + infinitive for ⊖ regular and irregular simple past verbs.

➡ **Grammar 8B** p. 152

🔴 **Common mistakes**
We didn't ~~had~~ *have* a class yesterday.

8.2 Did you go out last weekend?

Lesson Aims: Sts learn the form and uses of both regular and irregular verbs in the simple past + and -

Function
Listen to short conversations.
Practice pronunciation of past verbs.
Talking about last weekend.
Talk about family members and bithdays.

Language
How was your day off?
I slept late.
I went shopping.
She was born on March 14th, 1861.

Vocabulary: Recycle saying years (1971, 1943). Recycle: be born, start school, get divorced, get married to, record a song and finish school. Two different uses of *so* (to intensify and conclude.) Irregular verbs – simple past forms: had, did, said, went, made, knew, thought, took, saw, came. Dates and ordinal numbers.
Grammar: Simple past. Irregular simple past forms.

♪ **Song line:** Turn to p. 333 for notes about this song and an accompanying task.

Warm-up Recycle weather. Ask: *What's the weather like today?* or *How's the weather today?* (It's sunny, cold, etc.) Elicit the same question *What was the weather like?* in the past, e.g. *yesterday*. Write some past time expressions on the board, e.g. *yesterday, last Sunday, last Saturday, last vacation, last winter*, and in pairs have sts ask each other: *What was the weather like* (+ past time expression)?

1 Listening

A Look at the pictures and ask: *Who can you see in the pictures? Where are the people? Do you do these things on your days off?* Then, direct them to the task and ask them to discuss it in pairs. Classcheck. Ask: *Why?* so sts give reasons for their answers.

B Sts listen to ▶8.4 and match to the pictures to check their ideas in **A**. Check understanding and pronunciation of *noon* and *chores*. Tell sts to look at the verbs in bold and elicit their form in the present but don't say if they are correct.

> 1 b day off   2 f day yesterday   3 d Thanksgiving
> 4 a Sunday   5 c summer   6 e weekend

C Tell sts to check their ideas about the present forms of the verbs. Ask: *Were you correct about the verbs?* Tell sts to look at the verbs and the symbols and have a go at pronouncing them. Play ▶8.5 and ask sts to listen only. Ask: *Was your pronunciation correct?* Play it again and sts listen and repeat. Ask: *Which verbs have the same vowel sound in the past?* e.g. came / gave / made, went / said / met, saw / thought / bought, Highlight spelling differences. Elicit other words they know with same patterns.

> **Tip** Get sts to test each other's pronunciation by asking them to take turns pointing to the verbs so their partner can say them. Or one st says the verb in present and the other says it in past. Encourage them to correct each other's pronunciation.

D 🔵 **Make it personal** Refer sts to the lesson title. Ask: *What did you do last weekend?* Elicit answers from sts. Sts could ask and answer the question in small groups or in a milling activity where they walk around and ask different sts.

2 Grammar Simple past irregular verbs ➕ and ➖

A Use some examples from the last activity and write sentences on the board with the verb missing, *(Name of st) _____ last weekend*. Ask sts to give more examples. Refer them to the grammar box and ask them to complete the rules. Paircheck and classcheck.

> 1 1 did   2 gave   3 slept   4 said   5 met   6 bought
> 2 didn't

➡ **Grammar 8B** p. 152

B Complete Laura's email to her friend Barbara with the simple past form of these verbs. Use each verb only once.

buy	come	get up	give	go 🟢	go 🔴
know	make	meet	relax	see	sleep

♫ *I knew it when I met him,*
I loved him when I left him.
Got me feelin' like, ooh, and then I
had to tell him, I had to go, Havana.

8.2

To: **Barbara** Monday at 09:23
Subject: Hello!

Hi Barbara,

How was your weekend? Mine was pretty good! Saturday I _____ _____ early and _____ shopping downtown with my brother. You _____ him at my party, remember? I _____ some new sandals, and I'm wearing them now! Then we _____ a really good movie. In the evening, my old school friend, Bill, _____ over, and I _____ dinner. And guess what? He _____ me a gift! I _____ he liked me! I _____ to the beach Sunday because I _____ until noon, and then it started raining 🙁. So, I just _____ at home. Perfect!

Call me! Let's get together soon.

Laura xx

⚠️ **Common mistakes**

Did you know my father?
                    met
Not really. I only ~~knew~~ him once.

C 🟢 **Make it personal** List three things you did yesterday. Go around the class. Find at least two people who did the same things.

🗨️ *I ate pizza yesterday.* 🗨️ *Me, too!* 🗨️ *Oh, I ate fish.*

3 Vocabulary Ordinal numbers

A ▶ 8.6 In pairs, read the rules and practice saying the dates. Listen to check.

June 1st, 1996   March 2nd, 2001   December 3rd, 2018
February 4th, 1988   May 5th, 2016   August 6th, 2005
September 7th, 1803   January 8th, 1943   July 9th, 1994

> 1–3 are irregular: *first*, *se*cond, *third*. Other numbers add -*th*: *fourth*, *fifth*, *six*teenth.
> Over 20: *twenty-first*, *thirty-seventh*.

B Add three family members to the chart. In pairs, share your information.

	Born on	Died on
My great grandmother	October 14th, 1861	April 3rd, 1961

🗨️ *My great grandmother was born on October 14th, 1861, and died on April 3rd, 1961.*

🗨️ *Wow! She was nearly 100 years old!*

C 🟢 **Make it personal** Make a class birthday line. Which month and date have the most birthdays?

1. Stand up and ask "When's your birthday?" to form a class birthday line, from January 1st to December 31st.
2. Tell five classmates what you did on your last birthday. Any unusual celebrations?

🗨️ *What did you do on your last birthday?* 🗨️ *I had a big party.* 🗨️ *Lucky you! I didn't do anything special.*

⚠️ **Common mistakes**

Miley Cyrus was born in 1992,
~~in~~ November 23rd.
 on

B Explain that Laura and Barbara are friends. Ask sts to read the email quickly and ask: *What's it about?* (last weekend). Sts complete the email with the correct verb forms. Classcheck. Ask sts to find the regular verbs in the text (*like, start*).

Extra activity Prepare different versions of the text with sections missing for sts to complete, to check understanding and see what they remember. You could prepare various versions of increasing difficulty, with gaps getting longer each time.

> got up, went, met, bought, saw, came, made, gave, knew, didn't go, slept. relaxed

C 🔘 **Make it personal** Demonstrate the task of finding something in common. Write *Me too!* and *Sorry, I didn't do that* on the board. Say your sentence to different sts and ask them to reply using the phrases on the board. Sts then do the same speaking to different people in the class. After they finish, ask *Who did the same as you?* You could repeat the game, this time with different verbs and playing it in the negative, i.e. *List three things you didn't do yesterday*.

3 Vocabulary Ordinal numbers

A Ask: *What date was it last Saturday?* Write it on the board and check that sts remember how to say the year. Remind them we say 1990 *nineteen ninety* and 2018 *twenty eighteen* or *two thousand eighteen*. Write *1* and *1st* on board and ask: *How are these numbers different?* (The first is used to count quantities / amounts and the second is used to put things in order.) Refer sts to the rule box. Tell sts to try saying the dates. Play ▶ 8.6 and ask sts to listen. Ask: *Were you correct?* Play again for sts to listen and repeat. To help with pronunciation of *th*, elicit *teeth + thief* and our /th/ pictures from the Sounds and Usual Spellings chart on p. 158.

> **Stronger students** Use the first three or four to do a dictation activity. Sts listen and write the dates they hear.

> **Language tip** In Portuguese and Spanish, dates are written DD/MM/YYYY, not MM/DD/YYYY as in American English. So, 08/10/2018 in their L1 is 8th October 2018, whereas in the U.S., for example, it means August 10, 2018. Write a few dates on the board in the American English format and have sts practice saying them.

B Do your own example on the board. Ask sts to say the dates and correct when necessary. Sts complete their own chart and tell each other about their family members. Refer them to the speech bubbles for help. Ask: *Who has the oldest family member? When were they born?* Refer to ✓ **Common mistakes** here.

C 🔘 **Make it personal** Drill the question: *When's your birthday?* and have sts discover each other's birthdays to form the line in the correct order. At the end, check if they got it right: do a chain drill (A asks B, B asks C, C asks D, etc.) and have sts ask the next person in line: *When were you born?* Drill pronunciation first and say it is another way to ask about birthdays. Make sure they reply using: *I was born on …* before the dates. Still in line, get the first five sts to form a group, the following five form another, and so on. In groups of five, sts interview each other. Use the speech bubbles to model their conversation.

➔ **Workbook** p. 40

8.3 Where did you go on your last vacation?

1 Grammar Simple past questions and short answers

A ▶8.7 In pairs, make sure you know the simple past of these verbs. Listen to the conversation, then complete David's blog about his vacation.

| be | drink | eat | go | have | meet | see | stay | take | travel | visit | walk |

On my last vacation, my girlfriend and I _traveled_ to Ilha Grande – that's Big Island in English! We _____ by car and then _____ the ferry. There are no cars there, so we _____ a lot! The island's incredible, the forest is really beautiful, and the smell of nature is absolutely fantastic. We _____ lots of beautiful beaches, too, and I _____ three dolphins! We _____ fresh fish every day. It _____ very hot, so I _____ a lot of cold soda, too! We _____ in a tiny hotel right across from the beach, and _____ some cool tourists from Argentina. We _____ a wonderful time, and I can't wait to go back.

B ▶8.7 Listen again. Which word is missing in these questions? How is it pronounced? Now complete the grammar box.

How _____ you get there?   What _____ you do?
What _____ you eat?   _____ you stay in a hotel?

Yes / No questions (ASI)			**Short answers**	
Auxiliary	**Subject**	**Infinitive**	**Subject**	**Auxiliary**
Did	you	enjoy your vacation?	Yes, I	did.
	she	go to Brazil?	she
	we	buy water?	No, we	didn't.
	they	have a car there?	they

Wh- questions (QASI)

Question word	Auxiliary	Subject	Infinitive
When	_____	you	go?
What	did	he	see?
Where	_____	she	stay?
	did	we	eat dinner?

To form simple past questions, use the auxiliary _____ . To answer Yes / No questions, use _____ ➕ or _____ ➖.

➡ Grammar 8C p. 152

Common mistakes
~~Where she went?~~ → did go
She went to Miami.

C ▶8.8 Listen and point to the four questions you hear. Which has more emphasis – *did you* or the verb after it?

What did you do on your last vacation?
├── I went out of town.
└── I stayed here.

Where / go?
Who / go with?
How / get there?
Where / stay?
/ meet anyone interesting?
/ do a lot of shopping?
/ take many pictures?
/ have any problems?

/ eat well?
/ drink a lot of soda?
/ have a good time?

Why / stay here?
/ relax?
What time / wake up?
What / do every day?
/ visit anybody?
/ watch a lot of TV?
/ go out a lot?
/ do anything unusual?

What did you do on your last vacation?
I traveled. / I stayed at home.

D 🔘 **Make it personal** In pairs, ask and answer about your last vacation.

8.3 Where did you go on your last vacation?

Lesson Aims: Sts learn to form simple past questions to talk with some fluency about their last vacation, then move on to dates of birth and birthdays.

Function
Asking and answering about your last vacation.

Language
What did you do last vacation? Where did you go?
How did you get there?
I traveled to Europe.

Vocabulary: Verbs and noun collocations for vacation (stay in a hotel, take a ferry, visit beaches).
Grammar: Simple past. Prepositions.

Warm-up Write the sentences below on the board. Sts work in small groups and have to complete each sentence with a verb.
1 I _____ cereal for breakfast this morning.
2 I _____ to the theater last night.
3 I _____ to class by bus today.
4 I _____ an interesting movie yesterday.

In pairs, sts make true sentences about themselves, saying sentences 1–4 in affirmative or negative forms, e.g. *I didn't have cereal for breakfast this morning. I had bread and coffee.* Monitor closely for accuracy. Ask some sts to report their sentences to the whole class.

1 Grammar Simple past questions and short answers

A Ask: *Do you know Ilha Grande?* Explain it is a big island located off the south coast of Rio de Janeiro in Brazil, hence the name Ilha Grande! Elicit the past forms of all the given verbs. Play ▶8.7. Sts listen to the conversation then complete the blog post with the appropriate verb. Paircheck. Classcheck. Ask: *Would you like to visit Ilha Grande?*

> went, took, walked, visited, saw, ate, was, drank, stayed, met, had

▶8.7 Turn to p. 319 for the complete audioscript.

B Say: *These were the questions in the conversation* and point to the questions. In pairs, sts fill in the blanks. Play ▶8.7 again for sts to check their answers. Classcheck with answers on the board. Sts then complete the grammar box. Paircheck and classcheck. Highlight pronunciation of *did you* /didja/. Ask: *Who did he go with?* and write the question on the board with a checkmark next to it. Write *With who did he go?* and cross it out to show that it's incorrect.

> did you, did, did, Did
> Wh- questions: did, did
> did, did, didn't

▶ **Grammar 8C** p. 152

C Highlight the two routes – left or right – depending on the first answer. The questions in the middle work for either response. Point to the questions in the flowchart. Play ▶8.8. Sts have to find and point to the questions they hear. Pause after each question so you can monitor more efficiently.

⚠ **Common mistakes** Draw sts' attention to the tips.

Stronger classes Strong groups can have an extra challenge. In pairs, sts decide if the questions in the flowchart have rising or falling intonation.

Weaker classes Elicit all the questions. Make sure they understand that each "/" stands for *did you*. Drill the rising intonation for *Yes / No* questions and falling intonation for *Wh-* questions. Have sts take turns asking you all the questions in the flowchart.

> The verb after *did you* has more emphasis.

Tip Write *did you* on the board. Point and ask: *How do you pronounce this?* Draw sts attention to the connection of sounds when *did you* is pronounced. To help them produce it, drill some of the questions in the chart, and beat the stress on the question and main verb and encourage them to accelerate on the unstressed parts.

D 🗣 **Make it personal** Model the activity with the whole group and have sts interview you about your last vacation before they get to work in pairs. Then, in pairs, sts ask and answer questions about their last vacation. Monitor closely for accuracy. Make sure the st who is answering doesn't look at the flowchart, but instead makes eye contact with his / her partner.

Discuss any interesting answers they want to share with the class. Pay special attention to accurate use and pronunciation of *did you* when sts ask the questions.

Extra writing For extra writing practice, sts can write up their own (or their partner's) last vacation as a blog. If they email them to you, you can post them on the Learning Platform so they can all read and enjoy each other's stories about their last vacation.

2 Reading

A Quickly read a radio show interview and put the pictures a–e in order 1–5.

Oops, I did it again. I played with your heart, got lost in the game. Oh baby, baby.

A BAD TRAVEL EXPERIENCE? Not really!

Travel the World: Next call, please.
Ms. Riggs: Hi! My name's Pamela Riggs.
TtW: Hi, Ms. Riggs. So, can you tell us about a bad experience you had on a trip?
Ms. R: Well, I don't usually have big problems on my trips, but here's an interesting story for you. Two years ago, I went to Turkey. It's a fantastic country – half European, half Asian!
TtW: Yes, it's amazing. Who did you go with?
Ms. R: Nobody. It was a business trip. Anyway, I got to Istanbul airport early in the morning, and I had a connection to Cappadocia, but the airline canceled the flight because of bad weather.
TtW: Really?
Ms. R: Yes, there was no flight until the next day!
TtW: Oh no! And what did you do?
Ms. R: Well ... at first, I just cried! But then I saw a familiar face. It was Semir, my lovely neighbor from New York!
TtW: That's an incredible coincidence! What did he say?
Ms. R: He said, "I also had a ticket on that flight. But I need to get to Cappadocia tonight, so I rented a car. Do you want to come with me?"
TtW: So did you accept his offer?
Ms. R: Of course! But the trip took us around 13 hours.
TtW: But why did it take so long?
Ms. R: Well, Cappadocia is about 740 kilometers from Istanbul by car. And Semir knew the way very well, so we stopped a few times, and I saw some really interesting places. We also had a delicious Turkish meal at a fantastic restaurant in Ankara. We ate and talked for hours. It was great!
TtW: Wow ... So the airline canceled the flight, but your trip to Cappadocia wasn't bad after all.
Ms. R: Not at all. On the contrary, I thought it was fantastic! It was one of the best trips of my life. And, um ... I don't think I told you, I'm now married to Semir. Thanks to that bad weather!

B ▶8.9 Read and listen to the interview, and then complete 1–5 with two words. Do you know of any similar travel stories with a happy ending?

1. She arrived in Istanbul to _get a_ flight.
2. She cried because the airline _____ the _____ to Cappadocia.
3. Semir _____ a ticket for the same _____.
4. The trip to Cappadocia took around _____ _____.
5. She _____ a delicious Turkish _____ with Semir in Ankara.

C Circle the past tense verbs in the interview. In pairs, think of five past tense questions to ask Pamela Riggs in an interview.

D 🔒 **Make it personal** In pairs, role-play the interview with Pamela Riggs.

So, Ms. Riggs, where did you go for this trip? | *I went to Turkey.* | *I see. Did you fly to the capital, Ankara?*

> **Common mistakes**
>
> *at*
> She arrived ~~to~~ the hotel late.

3 Pronunciation *Did you*

A ▶8.10 Read the explanation. Then listen to six questions. Are they present or past? Compare in pairs. Then listen again to check.

> In rapid, informal speech, *did you* is often pronounced /dʒə/, but *do you* is pronounced /dəjə/. Can you hear the difference?

1. Where did you go?
2. Do you watch a lot of TV?
3. Did you relax?
4. Where did you stay?
5. Do you eat well?
6. When did you go on vacation?

B 🔒 **Make it personal** In pairs. A: tell B about a trip. B: ask questions about it using *do / did you*. Then change roles.

Last year I went to see my grandmother. | *Oh, when did you go?*

8.3

♫ **Song line:** Turn to p. 333 for notes about this song and an accompanying task.

② Reading

A Focus on the five pictures and ask: *Where do you think Ms. Riggs traveled to?* Elicit some guesses. (She went on a trip to Turkey). Explore what is happening in all the pictures. Ask: *What is she doing in c? What about d?*

> **Tip** Before sts read, ask them to cover the text with a piece of paper. Focus on the title and the pictures. Get them to speculate on what they can see. Elicit some guesses then uncover the text.

Sts quickly read the interview (set a timer for three minutes to encourage them to read quickly) and number the pictures a–e in the order the events happen in the text.

> 1 b   2 e   3 d   4 c   5 a

B Sts listen to ▶ 8.9 and read the interview with Ms. Riggs. Pause the track from time to time and ask sts to echo the last word and tell you the next, then listen and check. This will help to sure they're listening, not just reading. then complete the blanks. Paircheck. Classcheck. Ask: *Do you know any travel stories with a happy ending?* Sts tell the class examples, or they can discuss this in groups.

> 2 canceled, flight   3 had, flight   4 13 hours   5 had, meal

C As sts circle the verbs, ask them to notice which are regular and irregular. Elicit one verb and write it on the board. Ask: *What's the question?* and get sts to help you form it on the board. Sts then write five questions individually. Monitor and help with grammar, prompting self-correction.

> had, went, did / go, was, got, had, canceled, was, did / do, cried, saw, was, did / say, said, had, rented, did / accept, took, did / take, knew, stopped, saw, had, ate, talked, was, canceled, wasn't, thought, was, was, told

D 🅜 **Make it personal** Look at the 🧹 **Common mistakes** and add: *I don't think I told to you.* Write the incorrect sentence on the board and elicit the correction. (*I don't think I told you*). Sts role-play the interview. They take turns to ask and answer questions.

③ Pronunciation *Did you*

A Write *Did you go?* on the board and check that sts remember how it's pronounced. Refer them to the explanation in the box to clarify the difference between *did you* and *do you*. Play ▶ 8.10 and ask: *Are these in the past or present?* Play the audio again and ask sts to listen and repeat.

> 1 past   2 present   3 past   4 past   5 present   6 past

B 🅜 **Make it personal** Draw sts' attention to the title question: *Where did you go on your last vacation?* Refer them to the speech bubbles. Use *Oh, when did you go?* to drill pronunciation of *did you* again quickly. In pairs, sts ask and answer the lesson title question. Ask sts to share any interesting things they heard with the class after they have finished speaking.

→ **Workbook** p. 41

8.4 When do you listen to music?

1 Listening

A ▶8.11 Listen to an interview with Jay De La Fuente, a young songwriter. Order his actions yesterday 1–13.

- [1] He got up at about 6 o'clock.
- [ ] He took a shower.
- [ ] He played the keyboard and wrote a song.
- [ ] He ate breakfast.
- [ ] He answered 30 emails.
- [ ] He brushed his teeth.
- [ ] He had lunch.
- [ ] He turned on the computer.
- [ ] He ran a mile.
- [ ] He answered the rest of the emails.
- [ ] He went to sleep.
- [ ] He went to visit friends.
- [ ] He made coffee.

B ▶8.11 Listen again. In pairs, try to remember Jay's day.

> What was the first thing he did? — He got up at about 6 o'clock. — What did he do next?

C ▶8.12 Listen to excerpts and number the "How to sound impressed" phrases in the order you hear them, 1–4.

D 🎤 **Make it personal** Interview role-play. **A**: interview **B**, a famous person, about yesterday. Sound very impressed! Then change roles. Who has the funniest interview?

> What did you do first yesterday? — I got up at about 5 o'clock. — Wow! So early. That's amazing!

How to sound impressed
- [ ] You're kidding! That's incredible.
- [ ] Wow! That's amazing.
- [ ] That's fantastic!
- [ ] That's great!

2 Grammar — Subject questions vs. object questions

A ▶8.13 How much do you know about music? Take the ID Pop Quiz and find out!

B ▶8.14 Listen to check. How many did you get right?

C Complete the grammar box. Choose the correct options. Is your language similar?

Object questions (QASI)

Who	does	Jay	live with?	He lives alone.
What	did	he	say?	He said he loves his job.
Where	did	he	go?	To a friend's house.

Subject questions (QV)

Who	sings	that song?	Michael Jackson.
Who	wrote	it?	Michael Jackson.
What	happened to	him?	He died in 2009.

1. In **subject** / **object** questions, you know the subject and want information about the action.
2. In **subject** / **object** questions, you know the action and want to discover who or what is responsible.
3. **Subject** / **Object** questions need an auxiliary.
4. Quiz questions 1-8 are **subject** / **object** questions.

➡ **Grammar 8D** p.152

⚠ Common mistakes

What ~~did~~ happen**ed** on Sunday?
What ~~said~~ **did** our teacher ~~say~~?

8.4

8.4 When do you listen to music?

Lesson Aims: Sts learn to ask subject questions to interview someone. Sts also learn to use ordinal numbers.

Function
Talking and listening / watching a video about past routine.
Asking and answering about yesterday.
Reading / Taking a pop culture quiz.
Asking and answering about cultural facts.
Writing your own quiz.

Language
Jay got up at about 6 o'clock. Then, he had breakfast.
What did you do yesterday? I read a book.
Who recorded more songs?
Which singer won six Grammys in 2012? Which band composed?
Who composed the song "Imagine"?

Vocabulary: Recycle routine verbs. Expression to show you're impressed (Wow, so early! / No! I can't believe it!, etc.)
Grammar: Subject questions vs. object questions.

Warm-up Recycle dates by writing these prompts on the board: *Christmas, Halloween* (local holidays, e.g. Mother's Day), *your best friend's / teacher's birthday*. Sts take turns asking *When is _____?* questions and practice saying dates in English.

1 Listening

A Ask: *What's his job?* Sts read the instructions. Point to the example phrase and ask: *What did he do first?* (He got up at about 6 o'clock.) Sts listen to ▶8.11 and order the events. Paircheck. Write the following on the board and elicit the links, marking them with red lines: *got up, took a, brushed his, turned on, ran a*. Drill the linked pronunciation.

> 2 He brushed his teeth.
> 3 He made coffee.
> 4 He ate breakfast.
> 5 He turned on the computer.
> 6 He answered 30 emails.
> 7 He ran a mile.
> 8 He took a shower.
> 9 He had lunch.
> 10 He answered the rest of the emails.
> 11 He played the keyboard and wrote a song.
> 12 He went to visit friends.
> 13 He went to sleep.

▶8.11 Turn to p. 319 for the complete audioscript.

Tip Ask sts to turn to the AS on p. 166. Sts listen again and notice / imitate the connections.

B In pairs, sts tell each other what they remember from the audio. Encourage them to use ordinal numbers to ask: *What was the first thing he did? And the second? The third?* Classcheck the correct order. Ask: *How many did you get right? Did anybody guess the whole order correctly? What else did you learn about Jay?*

C Now sts listen to ▶8.12 and number phrases, 1–4, as they hear them. Paircheck. Classcheck. Elicit more "How to sound impressed" phrases e.g. *awesome, no way ...*

> 1 Wow! That's amazing.   2 That's great!
> 3 You're kidding! That's incredible.   4 That's fantastic!

D 🔴 Make it personal Change partners. In pairs, sts interview each other. Tell sts the interviewer has to look / sound impressed, and use some of the phrases in **C** with the appropriate intonation. Model this yourself, with sts asking you the questions. Then ask one pair to act out their dialogue for the class.

2 Grammar Subject questions vs. object questions

A Before starting, clarify subject vs. object. Say: *Remember, the subject does the action, the object receives it*. Ask: *Do you know a lot about art, songs, books, and films? Where do you learn about these things?* Point to the Pop Quiz photos and elicit who some of the people are. Play ▶8.13. Sts read and listen to take the quiz. Highlight difference in stress between *records* and *recorded* in question 1. Drill. Ask: *Does anyone have any records at home?*

B Play ▶8.14 for sts to check their guesses. Check who got the most answers right.

> 1 b 2 a 3 b 4 a 5 a 6 c 7 a June 26th, Florida
> b March 1st, London   c February 20th, Barbados
> d August 8th, Toronto 8 c 9 c 10 c

▶8.14 Turn to p. 320 for the complete audioscript.

C Sts read the examples and complete the rules in the grammar box.

➡ **Grammar 8D** p. 152

> **Weaker classes** Sts may need more guidance to understand the difference between object and subject questions. Write two questions on the board: *1) What did Alexander Graham Bell invent?* vs. *2) Who invented the telephone?* Help them see the differences in grammar and meaning.

> 1 object 2 subject 3 Object 4 subject

8.4

🎵 *Right now, I'm in a state of mind
I wanna be in like all the time,
Ain't got no tears left to cry.*

🆔 Pop Quiz

1. **Who sold more than 100 million records and re**cor**ded the most songs?**
   a Elvis Presley
   b The Beatles
   c Michael Jackson

2. **Who became the first artist to sur**pass **50 billion streams worldwide in 2018?**
   a Drake
   b Coldplay
   c Justin Bieber

3. **Who sang "Let it Go" in Disney's movie *Frozen*?**
   a Celine Dion
   b Idina Menzel
   c Demi Lovato

4. **Who wrote the first rap song to win an Oscar?**
   a Eminem with "Lose Yourself"
   b Kanye West with "Stronger"
   c Jay-Z with "Run this Town"

5. **Who made a** ma**ssively popular music video in which the singer(s) walk and sing in the street, wearing** co**lored suits?**
   a Mark Ronson and Bruno Mars
   b Ed Sheeran
   c Maroon 5

6. **Who had the first song in Spanish to surpass a billion views on YouTube?**
   a Ricky Martin ("Livin' la Vida Loca")
   b Enrique Iglesias ("Bailando")
   c Luis Fonsi featuring Daddy Yankee and Justin Bieber ("Despacito")

7. **Who was born when and where? Match the singer to their birthday and birth place.**
   a Ariana Grande
   b Justin Bieber
   c Rihanna
   d Shawn Mendes

   • March 1st 1994; London, Canada
   • February 20th, 1988; St. Michael, Barbados
   • August 8th 1998; Toronto, Canada
   • June 26th 1993; Florida, the U.S.

8. **Who didn't sing at President Barack Obama's inau**gu**rations?**
   a Beyoncé
   b Kelly Clarkson
   c Lady Gaga

9. **Where did Reggaeton begin in the late 1990s?**
   a Brazil
   b Colombia
   c Puerto Rico

10. **What did Bob Marley say to his son, Ziggy, just before he died?**
    a "Love one another"
    b "No woman, no cry"
    c "Money can't buy life"

D In pairs, take turns asking and answering subject and object questions about facts 1–5.

INTERESTING FACTS!

1. _____ landed on the moon in _____.
2. _____ di**re**cted *The Shape of Water* in _____.
3. _____ won their second soccer World Cup in Russia in _____.
4. _____ be**ca**me U.S. President again in 2012.
5. _____ won five gold **me**dals and one silver medal at the Rio Olympic Games in _____.

Answers: 1 Neil Armstrong / 1969 2 Guillermo del Toro / 2018 3 France / 2018 4 Barack Obama 5 Michael Phelps / 2016

> Who landed on the moon in … I think … 1968?

> No, it was 1969, and I think it was Buzz Aldrin and ….

E 🟢 **Make it personal** In groups, write five questions for a class quiz. Include at least three subject questions. Exchange with another group and take their quiz. Which group got more answers right?

> Which driver won the 2018 Formula One Championship?

105

D 🕐 **Common mistakes** Clarify the rules on p. 104. In pairs, sts take turns asking subject and object questions. Monitor closely for accuracy. Get sts to cover answers or close books. Have some more locally relevant questions prepared, and write them on the board to extend this activity. Sts check their answers and facts they do not know (see right of facts). Classcheck.

> **Tip** Refer throughout the lesson to **Common mistakes** whenever you need to correct sts' mistakes on the spot or for delayed correction afterwards.

🔑 Suggested questions:
1. Who landed on the moon in 1968?
   When did Neil Armstrong land on the moon?
   What did Neil Armstrong do in 1968?
2. Who directed *The Shape of Water* (in 2018)?
   When did Guillermo del Toro direct *The Shape of Water*?
   What film did Guillermo del Toro direct in 2018?
3. Who won their second soccer World Cup in Russia in 2018?
   When did France win their second soccer World Cup?
   What did France win in Russia in 2018?
4. Who became U.S. President again in 2012?
   When did Barack Obama become U.S. President again?
5. Who won five gold medals and one silver medal at the Rio Olympic Games (in 2016)?
   What did Michael Phelps win at the Rio Olympic Games (in 2016)?
   When / Where did Michael Phelps win five gold medals and one silver medal?

E 👤 **Make it personal** In pairs or small groups, sts prepare their own quizzes. Tell them to write five questions about well-known musicians, TV or movie stars, songs, albums, movies, characters, awards. Refer to the speech bubble as a model. (The answer to the speech bubble is Lewis Hamilton.) Make sure they include at least three subject questions. Monitor and prompt self-correction of mistakes. Have groups exchange quizzes to test each other. Sts answer the quizzes and see who got most answers right. Classcheck.

🎵 **Song line:** Turn to p. 333 for notes about this song and an accompanying task.

➔ **Workbook** p. 42

8.5 Can I use your phone?

ID Skills Understanding a story

Five common phone questions
1 I can't talk right now. Can I call you later?
2 Can I borrow your charger?
3 Can I use your phone? I left mine at home.
4 Is your phone working? I can't get a signal.
5 Can you tell me the Wi-Fi password, please?

A Do you remember the last time you asked 1–5?
I asked number 5 at a café last night.

B ▶8.15 Listen to the dialogue. Who's talking? Where are they? What's the problem?

C ▶8.15 Listen again and complete the dialogue. Predict what happens next.
Salesclerk: Hello, can I _help_ you?
Customer: Yes, I _____ so. There's a _____ with my new phone.
Salesclerk: OK. I'll try to help. What _____ is the problem?
Customer: Well, I _____ to transfer the data and all my _____, but only _____ of them are here.
Salesclerk: Hmm … OK, _____ you have a _____ in the Cloud?
Customer: Yes, I _____ so.
Salesclerk: OK, just a _____ please.

D ▶8.16 Listen to the end of the dialogue. What does the customer do?

E In pairs, role-play the dialogue.
A: You're the salesclerk. B: You're the customer.

F ▶8.17 Number the pictures 1–5 to make a story. Then listen to check.

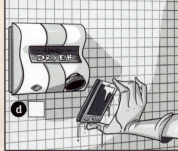

G ▶8.17 Listen again. What four questions does Mike ask Chris?

H 🔴 Make it personal Do you know any cell phone stories? Tell a story about something that happened to you or someone you know.
I left my cell phone in a taxi one day and …

8.5 Can I use your phone?

Lesson Aims: Sts learn more phone phrases to understand and tell an anecdote.

Function
Listening and telling stories about cell phone problems.
Speaking to customer services to talk about a problem.
Asking for and giving help.
Tell an anecdote.

Language
I can't get a signal. Can you?
Oh, no! My cell battery's dead. Could you see who it is?
What exactly is the problem?
The phone broke. There was no signal.

Vocabulary: Cell-phone related words (battery, signal, credit, recharge, make calls, etc.).
Grammar: Review simple past for telling anecdotes. *Can* and *could* for requests. *Will* for unplanned responses or decisions.

Warm-up Recycle routine verbs in the past. Write *What did you do yesterday?* on the board and have sts talk about what they did the day before class. Ask them to find three things in common. At the end, sts report similarities to the class, plus any surprises or special things they discovered about their partner.

ID Skills Understanding a story

A Ask: *How often do you use your cell phone? What do you use it for?* and see who in class is more addicted to phones.
Books open. Read common phone questions 1–5 with the whole class and have a conversation with all the sts. Use the example and give another of your own to help them get started, e.g. *Are you multitasking again? Stop it and listen to me! / Can I charge my phone off your computer?* As you read one at a time, check if they understand all the phrases and ask: *Do you remember the last time you said it? Where were you? What did you do?* etc. Have as many sts participate as possible. Respond positively (using impressed intonation as in the last lesson) to sts' contributions.

> **Language tip** In Portuguese and Spanish, there is only one word for *lend* and *borrow*, so this usually leads to confusion when learning the words in English. Clarify that when you **take** something from someone, you **borrow** it and when you **give** something to someone, you **lend** it.

B Books closed. Say: *You're going to hear two people talking. One of them has a problem with his cell phone. Who's talking? Where are they? What's the problem?* Play ▶8.15 and elicit the answers.

> customer and salesclerk, phone store, only some of the apps have transferred onto the customer's new phone

C Books open. Direct sts to the gap fill. Replay ▶8.15 again for sts to listen and fill in the blanks. Paircheck. Classcheck with answers on the board. Elicit predictions about what happens next in the story. Ask: *What do you think will happen next? How does the story end?*

> hope, problem, exactly, tried, apps, some, did, copy, think, minute

D Play ▶8.16 so sts can discover how the story ends. Ask: *How does he solve the problem?*

> leaves phone and password with salesclerk

> **Tip** Ask sts to turn to the AS on p. 166. Sts listen again and notice sentence stress.

E In pairs, sts role-play the complete dialogue. St A is the salesclerk and st B is the customer. Exchange roles afterwards.

F Pre-teach the words *drop*, *boss*, and *hand-dryer* from the pictures. Focus on the five pictures, and have sts put them in the correct order to make a story. They should write numbers 1–5 next to the letters a–e. Then, listen to ▶8.17 to check answers.

> 1 a   2 e   3 d   4 b   5 c

▶8.17 Turn to p. 320 for the complete audioscript.

G Play ▶8.17 again. Tell sts to listen to Mike and Chris again and remember which four questions Mike asks Chris. Paircheck. Classcheck. If time allows, go to the AS on p. 166.

> 1 What happened?
> 2 Then what happened?
> 3 Did you get it out?
> 4 What did you do?

H 🧑 **Make it personal** Ideally you would tell an anecdote of your own about losing or leaving your phone somewhere so they can ask questions and hear you respond. Ask: *Do you have any similar stories?* In groups sts tell their stories. Encourage other sts to ask for details, using some of Mike's questions and the expressions for responding, too. Ask sts to share any funny or interesting stories they heard.

225

8.5 Could you help me, please?

*Help! I need somebody,
Help! Not just anybody
Help! You know I need
someone, help!*

ID in Action Asking for favors

A ▶ 8.18 Match pictures 1–5 to favors a–e. Listen to five dialogues to check. Which favors did not happen?

B ▶ 8.18 Listen again and complete requests 1–7. Then match them to the responses.

Requests	Responses
1 Could you _____ who it _____?	☐ I'm really sorry. I have two parties to go to …
2 Could you _____ the _____ for me, please?	☐ Sure. There you go.
3 Can you please _____ the _____?	☐ Come on, I can do it tomorrow.
4 Could you please _____ the _____, Jim?	☐ Don't worry. I'll get it.
5 Could you _____ _____ this afternoon, please?	☐ Sorry, it's Brian's turn today.
6 Could I _____ you a _____?	☐ That depends. What do you want?
7 Can _____ _____ my son with you this weekend?	☐ OK, I'll do it now.

Common mistakes

Could you ~~to~~ help me?
Could you ~~make~~ *do* me a favor?

C Read the requests and responses in **B** again and complete the rules with the words.

| can   could   'll   will |

1 Use _____ or _____ to ask for favors. _____ is a little more polite.
2 Use _____ + verb for unplanned responses or decisions. The contraction is _____.

D 🎤 **Make it personal** Role-play. **A:** Ask a favor 1–4. **B:** Respond and ask questions. Then change roles.

1 You're having a party next week, but you don't have any good music.
2 You can't read French, and you got an email from a customer in French.
3 You bought a new dog, but you're going away for the weekend.
4 You have to go to the airport really early tomorrow morning.

> Hey, I'm having a party next week. Could you put some good music on my phone?

> Sure, I'll do that, no problem. What type of music do you want?

8.5 Could you help me, please?

Lesson Aims: Sts learn to use *can / could* to ask for favors.

Function
Listening to people request favors.
Asking for favors and offering help.

Language
Could you please wash the dishes? I'm really sorry, but I can't.
Don't worry. I'll get it.
Sure. There you go

Vocabulary: Vocabulary related to asking for a favor: *Do a favor, That depends.*
Grammar: Requests and favors. *Can* vs. *Could* for politeness. *Will* for unplanned responses or decisions.

🎵 **Song line:** Turn to p. 333 for notes about this song and an accompanying task.

Warm-up Books closed. Ask sts to try and remember the questions they used in ID Skills. Elicit the questions and write them on the board (Five common phone questions p. 106).

ID in Action Asking for favors

A Books open. Point to pictures 1–5 and elicit what they are doing / wearing / thinking, then say: *All the people need some help. They are asking other people to do them favors. Can you match the requests (point to 1–5) to the correct favors (a–e) below?* and sts try to guess the right combinations.

Play ▶ 8.18 for sts to check their answers. Classcheck. Ask: *Which actions a–e did not happen? Who didn't get any help?*

> 1 c 2 d 3 b 4 e 5 a
> Favors 1c and 5a did not happen.

▶ 8.18 Turn to p. 320 for the complete audioscript.

B Sts read questions 1–7 and try to remember the words in the gaps. Play ▶ 8.18 again for sts to complete the questions. Paircheck. Classcheck.

⚠️ **Common mistakes** Review the sentences and corrections. Write an additional Common mistake on the board *Can you borrow me your phone?* and elicit the correction (*lend me*).

Ask the sts to match the questions to the best responses in the right column. Paircheck. Classcheck. Elicit places and situations when sts usually make the requests in the list.

1	see, is	Don't worry, I'll get it.
2	open, door	Sure. There you go.
3	wash, dishes	Sorry, it's Brian's turn today.
4	cut, grass	Come on, I can do it tomorrow.
5	do it	OK, I'll do it now.
6	ask, favor	That depends. What do you want?
7	I leave	I'm really sorry, but I have two parties to go to …

C Sts work individually to complete the rules. Use the rules to explain the use of *will* in *OK, I'll do it now.* and *Don't worry. I'll get it.* Contrast with present continuous for arrangements, which are of course planned. Classcheck.

> 1 can, could, Could
> 2 will, 'll

D 👤 **Make it personal** Sts role-play situations 1–4 using *Could you …?* requests and the responses from **B**. Use the speech bubbles to illustrate what they have to do. Refer sts back to ordering in a restaurant (p. 81) for more examples of using *will*.

Weaker classes Sts might need more thinking time before they perform this activity. Give them time to write one or two dialogues together before they role-play the situations. Offer help whenever needed.

Tip If you want to continue to review phone language, have sts sit back-to-back with cell phones in hand and role-play that way. They could record their role-plays or even make real phonecalls to one another using their cell phones, with one of them stepping out of the room to make the call.

Have four different pairs of sts act out each situation for the whole group. For fun, at the end of the lesson, drop your pens / book on the floor, pretend your bag is too heavy to lift, your arm hurts so you can't open the door, turn off the light, etc. to spontaneously practice requests and get them to respond accordingly.

➡️ **Workbook** p. 43

➡️ **Richmond Learning Platform**

➡️ **Writing** p. 108

➡️ **Café** p. 109

Writing 8 A vacation message

*This is my message to you-ou-ou.
Singin' Don't worry about a thing.
'Cos every little thing gonna be alright.*

A Use the photos to guess where Tom went on vacation. Quickly read his email to check.

To: **Mom**
Subject: Hello!
Today at 16:03
All Mail

Hi Mom and Dad,

This is just a short email to tell you I'm OK. Monica and I are having a great time – there are so many things to do. The hotel is pretty basic, and there's no air-conditioning, but it's very cheap! The food's great, too – very hot and spicy! And the weather's excellent – it's much hotter than back home.

Last weekend, we visited a Buddhist temple in the jungle. We had to walk for two hours through the rainforest before we arrived. There were trees growing on the ruins and there were monkeys everywhere, too – it was beautiful. I took some fantastic photos – you can see them on my blog. After that, we rode an elephant – that was really cool.

Tomorrow, we plan to go kayaking in the bay – one of the most beautiful places in Vietnam … maybe the world! There are thousands of islands and secret beaches to explore – it's awesome and we're really excited!

Anyway, I have to go. Please say "Hi" to everyone, and don't forget to walk Toby!

Lots of love and see you soon,

Tom XXX

B Read again and answer 1–6.
1. Is their hotel comfortable?
2. What did Tom and Monica do last weekend?
3. Was it easy to get to the temple?
4. Did they see any animals?
5. How do Tom and Monica feel about kayaking tomorrow?
6. Who do you think Toby is?

C Which paragraphs answer 1–6? Complete the chart.
1. What are your plans for tomorrow?
2. What's the place / food / weather like?
3. Are you having fun?
4. What did you do before now? / How was it?
5. Where can we see your photos?
6. Do you have any other things to say?

Paragraph 1	Paragraph 2	Paragraph 3	Paragraph 4
		1	

D Read **Write it right!** How does Tom start and end his email? How does he start paragraphs 1 and 4? Underline five added comments.

> ✓ **Write it right!**
> Try to remember short phrases to start and end emails, or start paragraphs.
> Use — to add opinions or comments to a sentence.

E 🎧 **Make it personal** Write an email home in 150–180 words.

Before	Research a location for your vacation. Use the questions in C to help and imagine your answers.
While	Use starting and ending phrases, and write in paragraphs.
After	Check your email, then send it to a classmate to check again. Then send it to your teacher.

Writing 8 A vacation message

🎵 **Song line:** Turn to p. 333 for notes about this song and an accompanying task.

A Explore the photos and elicit what sts can see. Ask: *Where do you think this vacation is?* Sts quickly read the email to discover where Tom is spending his vacation. Classcheck.

Follow-up questions: Ask: *Who did he write to?* (His parents.) *Did Tom travel alone?* (No, he traveled with Monica.)

> Vietnam

B Point to questions 1–6 and have sts reread Tom's email in **A** to answer them. Paircheck. Classcheck.

> 1 No, it is basic and hot (there is no air-conditioning).
> 2 They visited a Buddhist temple in the jungle.
> 3 It wasn't easy. (They had to walk for two hours through rainforest.)
> 4 Yes, they saw monkeys and rode an elephant.
> 5 They're really excited.
> 6 Toby is probably Tom's dog.

C Point to the email again and ask: *How many paragraphs are there?* (Four.) Ask: *What does Tom talk about in paragraph 1?* (He says he's OK and talks about the hotel, food, and weather.) Point to the chart in **C** and to questions 1–6. Individually, sts match the questions to paragraphs 1–4 in the chart, according to the order in which the topics are mentioned in Tom's email. Paircheck. Classcheck with answers on the board.

Paragraph 1	Paragraph 2	Paragraph 3	Paragraph 4
2, 3	3, 4, 5	1	6

D Read **Write it right!** with the whole class. Ask: *How does Tom start and end his email? How does he start paragraphs 1 and 4?* Explain that the punctuation mark shown in the box is called a "dash" and is often used to add comments / opinions. Ask sts to also underline five added comments in **A**.

> Hi Mom and Dad,
> Lots of love and see you soon,
> Paragraph 1 – This is just a short email to …
> Paragraph 4 – Anyway, I have to go.
> – there are so many things to do
> – very hot and spicy
> – it's much hotter than back home
> – it was beautiful
> – that was really cool
> – one of the most beautiful places in Vietnam
> – it's awesome and we're really excited

E 🔊 **Make it personal** Say: *Imagine you're on vacation and need to send some news to your family.* Help sts plan their email to their family. Read the steps Before, While, and After with the whole class so as to better guide their writing. Suggest sts refer to Tom's email in **A** as a model. Tell them to keep their texts between 150 and 180 words.

As a follow-up activity, and before they hand in their texts, ask sts to exchange compositions / send each other their email, and ask each other questions to find out more details.

8 The favor

Café

1 Before watching

A 🔵 **Make it personal** In pairs. Do friends sometimes ask you for favors? Do you ask, too? Any good stories?

> My friend asked me to help him with his homework.

B What's August doing? Then watch to check.
- ☐ He's waiting to be connected.
- ☐ He's listening to music.
- ☐ He's checking his voicemail.
- ☐ He's working on his in**ven**tion.

2 While watching

A Complete with the simple past of the verbs.

Genevieve: Hi, Rory. What's up?
Rory: Oh, hey, Genevieve. It's Rory. Oh, but right. You just _____ (say) … Sorry, I _____ (not / know) you _____ my number. (have)
Genevieve: I'm a little busy here. Is there anything I can help you with?
Rory: August just _____ (call) me. He _____ (say) maybe you need help? With a music program or something?
Genevieve: Oh, I see. Yeah, I do need computer help.

B Order 1–7 to make sentences and questions. Some are two sentences / questions.
1. maybe / need / said / help / August / he / called / you / me / just
2. my / go / can't / I / day / there / it's / off
3. OK / anywhere / to / don't / you / need / go / it's
4. I / exercised / thanks / just / anyway / but
5. I / can / I / can / your / it / from / computer / here / fix / screen / and / see
6. weird / kind / of / sounds / safe / that / is / it
7. me / on / cup / and / your / first / coffee's / of

3 After watching

A Number the phrases in the order you hear them, 1–8.
- ☐ Call me back, OK?
- ☐ Could you do me a favor?
- ☐ Could you do something for me?
- ☐ He said maybe you need help?
- ☐ I need a favor.
- ☐ I really need your help.
- ☐ Is there anything I can help you with?
- ☐ What do you need me to do first?

B Who said it? August (A), Genevieve (G), or Rory (R)?

		A	G	R
1	Oh, sorry, yeah.			
2	Everything's fine.			
3	Tell her I'm sorry.			
4	Sounds simple!			
5	Put me on speaker phone.			
6	Oh, I see.			
7	What do you mean?			
8	That's all it was.			
9	Thank you so much.			
10	I really appreciate your help.			
11	You did me the favor!			

C Now check (✓) the things they did.

		A	G	R
1	asked for a favor			
2	called someone back			
3	fixed a computer			
4	listened to a voicemail message			
5	needed computer help			
6	thanked a friend			
7	didn't want to see Rory			

D In pairs, take turns asking and answering about what the characters did and said.

> Who said "…"?   Who asked …?

E 🔵 **Make it personal** Help! Choose a situation and call a friend for help.
1. You don't know how to use your new phone.
2. You need a babysitter for tonight.
3. You're in bed sick with no food at home.
4. You have a job interview today and your best suit is dirty.

> David? Help! I have a big problem. Could you do me a favor?
>
> What is it Marta? How can I help?

109

ID Café 8 The favor

1 Before watching

A 🔘 **Make it personal** Ask sts to think about the last time they asked someone a favor. Clarify the meaning of *favor*. Sts in pairs discuss the questions. Ask one or two sts to share examples with the class.

B Ask: *What's August doing?* Elicit some ideas and refer sts to the four sentences to discuss which they think is the correct answer. Play **Video 8** so sts can check answers. Classcheck.

> He's checking his voicemail

2 While watching

A Ask sts what they remember of the story. Put them into pairs to discuss this for one minute and then ask them to share ideas with the class. Ask sts to read the dialogue and complete the the past simple form of the verbs. Move on to **B** before you play **Video 8** again.

> said / didn't know / had
> called / said

B Elicit the correct order for number 1 (August just called me. He said maybe you need help.). Tell sts all sentences were taken from **Video 8**. Sts order sentences 2–7. Replay **Video 8** for sts to check their answers to **A** and **B**. Classcheck with answers on the board.

> 2 I can't go there. It's my day off.
> 3 It's OK. You don't need to go anywhere.
> 4 I just exercised, but thanks anyway.
> 5 I can see your computer screen from here and I can fix it.
> 6 That sounds kind of weird. Is it safe?
> 7 And your first cup of coffee's on me.

3 After watching

A Tell sts to number the phrases in the order they are said in the video. Paircheck. If time allows, play **Video 8** once more. Classcheck with answers on the board.

> 3 Call me back, OK?
> 1 Could you do me a favor?
> 5 Could you do something for me?
> 8 He said maybe you need help?
> 4 I need a favor.
> 2 I really need your help.
> 7 Is there anything I can help you with?
> 6 What do you need me to do first?

B In pairs, sts decide which character, August (A), Genevieve (G), or Rory (R), said sentences 1–11. Classcheck with answers on the board or, if possible, display the same page on the IWB with the *Digital Book for Teachers* and check answers in the chart.

		A	G	R
1	Oh, sorry, yeah.	✓		
2	Everything's fine.	✓		
3	Tell her I'm sorry.	✓		
4	Sounds simple!			✓
5	Put me on speaker phone.			✓
6	Oh, I see.		✓	
7	What do you mean?		✓	
8	That's all it was.			✓
9	Thank you so much.		✓	
10	I really appreciate your help.		✓	
11	You did me the favor!			✓

C In pairs, sts try to remember what each character did in the story. When they have finished, let sts perform **D** before you classcheck answers.

		A	G	R
1	asked for a favor	✓		
2	called someone back			✓
3	fixed a computer			✓
4	listened to a voicemail message	✓		
5	needed computer help		✓	
6	thanked a friend	✓		✓
7	didn't want to see Rory		✓	

D Change partners. In pairs, sts take turns asking: *What did August / Genevieve / Rory do?* and paircheck answers for **C**. Refer sts to the model dialogue in the speech bubbles. Classcheck **C** with answers on the board.

E Tell sts they are going to role-play a short phone call. Tell them to read through the options. Demonstrate the activity with a volunteer st if possible. Sts then work in new pairs and role-play a situation. If time allows, tell them to choose another situation and do a second role-play. If sts have access to phones, they could do this using their phones going to different parts of the classroom or school!

R4 Grammar and vocabulary

A Picture dictionary. Cover the words on these pages and use the pictures to remember:

page	
86	9 rooms and 19 furniture words
88	15 party items
91	13 prepositions of place
97	5 more *house* words
98	10 verb phrases
103	Ms. Riggs' story
107	5 favors
159	16 picture words for lines 3 and 4 of consonants

B Circle the correct alternative to complete 1–7.
1 Forty years ago, _____ no cell phones.
   a there were   b there was   c was
2 How many people _____ at the party?
   a were they   b there were   c were there
3 It _____ my sister's birthday yesterday.
   a is   b were   c was
4 _____ you at school last week?
   a Are   b Were   c Was
5 When was she _____?
   a born   b is born   c was born
6 Who _____ the Mona Lisa?
   a did paint   b painted   c was painted
7 What _____ Leonardo da Vinci paint?
   a did   b was   c is

C Complete stories 1 and 2 using the simple past of the verbs in parentheses. In pairs, compare. Do you know any similar stories?

1 I love Beyoncé, so when I _____ (**read**) about a writing competition to win tickets for her show I _____ (**be**) really excited. I _____ (**write**) about how her songs make me happy or sad and I sent the letter. I ____ (**not think**) about it anymore, but imagine my surprise when, two weeks later, a letter _____ (**arrive**). I couldn't believe it! I _____ (**win**) two tickets to the show. I _____ (**take**) my sister and we ____ (**have**) a really good time. She _____ (**give**) an unforgettable show.

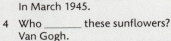

2 I _____ (**see**) BTS about two years ago when they _____ (**visit**) my city, and the best thing was – I _____ (**have**) a VIP pass! The band _____ (**come**) on and they _____ (**start**) with a song from their new album. Not everybody _____ (**know**) the words, but I _____ (**do**) and I _____ (**sing**) really loudly. They _____ (**finish**) with an old song. After the show, I _____ (**go**) backstage and _____ (**meet**) the band. They _____ (**be**) fantastic. I _____ (**get**) all their autographs.

D It's Monday morning. Put expressions 1–8 in the timeline.
1 the day before yesterday
2 tomorrow afternoon
3 Tuesday evening
4 last Friday
5 tonight
6 next Thursday
7 yesterday morning
8 last Thursday

Monday morning

E Complete the questions for the answers given.
1 Who _____ a famous second world war diary?
   Anne Frank.
2 Where and when _____ born?
   On June 12, 1929, in Frankfurt, Germany.
3 When _____ die?
   In March 1945.
4 Who _____ these sunflowers?
   Van Gogh.
5 When _____ this picture?
   He painted it in 1888.
6 How many sunflower pictures _____?
   He painted five of them.

F Play *Past tense tennis!* Take turns "serving" a verb for your partner to "return" in the simple past.

Agree.   Agreed.   Correct – well done!

G Correct the mistakes. Check your answers in units 7 and 8. What's your score, 1–10?
1 Some years ago, had two movie theaters in my town. (2 mistakes)
2 You was at school today? (2 mistakes)
3 A: Was your dad on vacation the last week? (1 mistake)
   B: No, wasn't. He was sick all the week. (2 mistakes)
4 Five years behind, there were a lot trees here. (2 mistakes)
5 I finished the school when I had eighteen years. (3 mistakes)
6 I no went to college. I get married and had children. (3 mistakes)
7 What did Ms. Riggs saw from her trip to Turkey? (2 mistakes)
8 What did happen to her there? (1 mistake)
9 With who did she traveled? (2 mistakes)
10 Could you to open the door for me? (1 mistake)

110

Review 4 Units 7-8

Grammar and vocabulary

A Picture dictionary. Pairwork. Sts test each other and review the main vocabulary items learned in units 7 and 8. There are some possible techniques mentioned on p. 9 of the introduction section on how to work with the Picture Dictionary in order to review vocabulary. You can select whichever of these best suit the needs of your class.

B Do the first one with the class. Sts do the rest individually or in pairs. Classcheck.

> 1 a   2 c   3 c   4 b   5 a   6 b   7 a

C If possible, show a photo of Beyonce and BTS and ask sts what they know about these artists and whether they like them. Individually, sts complete stories 1 and 2 with the past forms of the verbs given. Paircheck. Classcheck with answers on the board. Ask: *Do you know any similar stories?*

> 1 read, was, wrote, didn't think, arrived, had won, took, had, gave
> 2 saw, visited, had, came, started, knew, did, sang, finished, went, met, were, got

D Do the first one with the class. Sts then complete the time line in pairs. Classcheck.

> 4 8 1 7 5 2 3 6

E Refer sts to the images and ask what they know about Anne Frank and Vincent van Gogh. Sts complete the questions to match the answers given. Put sts into pairs and tell them to ask each other their questions.

> 1 wrote / kept
> 2 was she
> 3 did she
> 4 painted
> 5 did he paint
> 6 did he paint

F Sts play in pairs. One st "serves" a verb for his / her partner—i.e., picks a verb and says it out loud. The other st has to "return" the verb in the simple past—i.e., says the verb out loud in the simple past. Sts give each other one point for each correct simple past verb. Give them a time limit. If there's time, have a "play-off" between the two sts who scored the most points.

G Tell sts they are going to correct the mistakes. Draw sts' attention to the number of mistakes between parentheses.

In pairs, sts correct sentences 1–10. Whenever sts are uncertain, encourage them to flip back through units 7 and 8. Classcheck with answers on the board.

> 1 Some years ago, there were two movie theaters in my town.
> 2 Were you at school today?
> 3 A: Was your dad on vacation last week? B: No, he wasn't. He was sick all week.
> 4 Five years ago, there were a lot of trees here.
> 5 I finished school when I was eighteen years old.
> 6 I didn't go to college. I got married and had children.
> 7 What did Ms. Riggs see on her trip to Turkey?
> 8 What happened to her there.
> 9 Who did she travel with?
> 10 Could you open the door for me?

Skills practice

You're everything I need and more, It's written all over your face, Baby, I can feel your halo, Pray it won't fade away.

R4

A Read the fact files. True (T) or False (F)?

The Olympics
The first modern Olympics were in Athens, Greece, in 1896, but there are many differences between the early days of the games and the Olympics today. In the first games, there were 245 sportsmen from only 14 countries, only nine different sports, and 43 events. Nowadays, the whole world participates and there are approximately 17,000 competitors from 205 countries, and 306 events – that's an enormous change! Another big social change is in the number of women involved. In 1896, there were no women at all. Today, there are sportswomen in all the Olympic sports.

The soccer World Cup
The first World Cup was in 1930 in Uruguay. There were only 13 teams and all of the games were in Montevideo. There were four European countries, eight came from South America, plus the U.S. In the final, Uruguay beat Argentina 4-2. These days, over 200 teams try to qualify, but only 32 teams get through to the finals of the competition. There are other differences, too. Until 1970, there were no red or yellow cards. Nowadays, teams that don't get many cards can win the Fairplay award, and there are other awards, too. In 1930, there were only the winner's cup and the Golden Ball for the best player. Today, there are also the Golden Boot for the top goal-scorer and the Golden Glove for the top goalkeeper.

1. There weren't any women in the first Olympics. ____
2. There were more sports than countries in Athens, in 1896. ____
3. In 1930, there weren't World Cup games in different cities. ____
4. Argentina won the first World Cup. ____
5. The winner's cup is the only award teams can get in the World Cup. ____
6. There is the same number of countries in the World Cup finals as in the Olympics. ____

B ▶ R4.1 Read the blog about a visit to Amsterdam and number the paragraphs 1–5 in the correct order. Listen to check.

C Read again and complete 1-6. Which attraction would you like to visit most?

1. It *wasn't* cheap to rent a ____.
2. The bike tour ____ perfect because the bike ____.
3. They thought the Anne Frank museum ____.
4. They ____ to check out of the hotel before ____.
5. The journey to the airport was ____.
6. Their visit to Amsterdam ____ more positive than ____.

At last we were in Amsterdam! We were really excited to see everything the city has to offer, even though we were there for only a few days. We saw a lot! Here's what we did:

____
The next day, it rained all day and we got very wet in the morning! So, in the afternoon, we avoided the rain and went to some of the fabulous art galleries and museums in the city. My favorite was the Van Gogh Museum, where we saw hundreds of original Van Gogh paintings and learned a lot about his life. It was fantastic. After that, we ate in a tourist restaurant near the museum. It was a bad choice – the food was terrible, and it was very expensive, too.

____
First, we took a bike tour of the city. Amsterdam is famous for its bikes – people ride bikes everywhere, and it's definitely the best way to see the sights. It was more expensive to rent a bike than we expected, though. We had a great time riding around on the bike paths and narrow streets along the canals. But then I got a flat tire! We were a long way from the place where we rented the bikes, and we couldn't fix the tire, so we walked all the way back. It took ages and it wasn't the best way to end our first day.

____
We had to check out of our hotel at noon on our last day, so we left our bags there and found a cheap Vietnamese restaurant close to the hotel for lunch. It was great! There were lots of locals eating there, as well as tourists. Then we walked around and did some shopping for souvenirs, before collecting our bags and getting the train to the airport. It's a really easy journey by train.

____
I recommend Amsterdam for a visit. There were a couple of disappointments, but overall it was a really good experience.

____
On our second day, we got tickets for a canal cruise. This is a great way to see the city from the water. In the old part of the city, the canals are lined with amazing tall, narrow houses that are hundreds of years old. We stopped at different places and went to Anne Frank House, which is where she hid with her family in World War II and where she wrote her diary. The house is now a really interesting museum, but we all felt a little sad thinking about what she and her family suffered during the war.

D How many stars (from 1–5) do you think the blogger gave the visit? In pairs, compare and say why.

I think it was probably 3 stars because …

E 🔴 **Make it personal** **Question time**.
In pairs, practice asking and answering the 12 lesson titles in units 7 and 8. Use the book map on p. 2–3. Where possible, ask follow-up questions, too. Can you comfortably ask and answer all the questions?

Do you live in a house?   *No, I don't. I live in an apartment.*

How many bedrooms do you have?   *Just two, but there's an enormous terrace!*

111

Skills practice

🎵 **Song line:** Turn to p. 333 for notes about this song and an accompanying task.

A Sts read the text and answer the T / F questions. As an alternative, tell sts to cover the questions and give them 3 minutes to read the texts and remember as much as possible. Sts close their books and you read out questions 1–6. Sts work in pairs and write T or F. Classcheck to see who got the correct answers.

> 1 T 2 F 3 T 4 F 5 F 6 F

B If possible, display some images of Amsterdam and ask sts what they know about the city. Sts then read the blog quickly and order the paragraphs. Play ▶**R4.1** to check answers. Check pronunciation of the pink-stressed words.

> 3 1 4 5 2

C Individually sts read the text again to select the correct answers. Paircheck and classcheck.

> 1 wasn't, bike
> 2 wasn't, got a flat tire
> 3 was interesting
> 4 had, noon
> 5 (really) easy (by train)
> 6 was, negative

D Discuss how the blogger rated the city. After they discuss this in pairs, ask sts to give reasons for their answers. Ask sts if they would like to visit Amsterdam.

E 🔴 **Make it personal** **Question time.** Sts look at the book map on p. 2–3 and take turns asking and answering the lesson titles from units 7 and 8. Monitor closely for accuracy and encourage sts to ask follow-up questions when suitable. Sts can make use of recordings and the other suggestions made earlier in the TB notes for this exercise. At the end, ask them how they felt performing the task: *Do you feel comfortable with all of the questions? Which ones are easy? Which ones are difficult?*

9.1 How did you get here today?

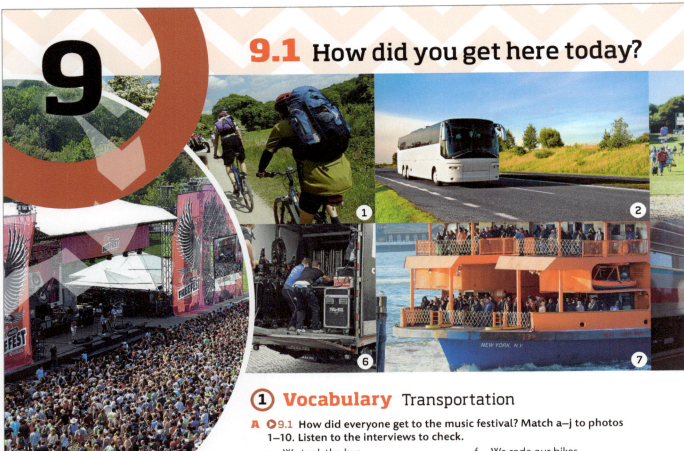

1 Vocabulary Transportation

A ▶9.1 **How did everyone get to the music festival? Match a–j to photos 1–10. Listen to the interviews to check.**
- a We took the bus.
- b We took the train.
- c We took the ferry.
- d They took a helicopter.
- e I rode my motorbike.
- f We rode our bikes.
- g I drove.
- h I drove the band's truck.
- i I flew.
- j We walked.

B In pairs, take turns asking and answering about the photos.
A: Point at a photo and ask "How did (they) get there?"
B: Answer.
A: Confirm and rephrase.

> He went by motorbike.   That's right, he rode his motorbike.

Common mistakes
did you get / come
How ~~you arrived~~ here?
on
I came ~~by~~ foot.

C Make it personal In pairs, ask and answer the questions.
1 What's the best way for you to get to:
   a the nearest shopping mall?
   b this English class?
   c your favorite restaurant?
   d your local airport?
   e a good beach?
   f a place with snow?
2 How did you get:
   a here today and how are you getting home?
   b to school when you were a child?
   c to your last vacation destination?

> What's the best way for you to get to the nearest shopping mall?
> By car. I live 20 kilometers away, so I always drive.

Unit overview: The main topics of unit 9 are means of transportation, more jobs, *be + going to* and present continuous for plans and future arrangements, as well as common requests (for permission). These are presented through the contexts of people talking about how they got / went to the music festival venue, how sts commute to and from places, listening / reading about plans and life changes, and about jobs which are likely to be in high demand in the future.

9.1 How did you get here today?

Lesson Aims: Sts learn to talk about how they get to places. Sts also talk about transportation problems.

Function
Listening / Talking about how people got to a music festival.
Talking about how you get / got to various places.

Language
By car. I drove.
How did she get there? By bike.
That's right. She rode.
How did you get here today?
What happened?

Vocabulary: Means of transportation. Occupations.
Grammar: *How do / did you get to ...?* By boat, by car, on foot, etc.

🎵 **Song line:** Turn to p. 334 for notes about this song and an accompanying task.

Warm-up Books closed. In pairs, sts take turns asking and answering the question *What did you do this morning / afternoon / last night?* to review simple past. Write different times on the board to prompt them. Ask one or two sts the questions to get the activity started.

1 Vocabulary Transportation

A Draw sts attention to the lesson title and use a variation of the explanation below to help with *get*:

> **Language tip** The verb *get* has many uses and meanings: *get an email* = receive, *get tired* = become, *get home* = arrive.
> To ask about transportation, we often use *get* in the question, but not in the answer: *How do you get to work?* (By car.) *How did you get here?* (I took the bus.)

Books open. Ask sts to look at the photos and describe what they can see. Ask: *Where are they? What are they doing?* Focus on the phrases and ask sts to read through them quickly. The words in the first column are cognates, the second are not. Have sts match them to photos 1–10. Paircheck. Play ▶9.1 for sts to check answers. Play again and ask sts to listen and repeat. Ask which verbs have similar vowel sounds (*drove / rode*).

🔑 1 f 2 a 3 j 4 e 5 g 6 h 7 c 8 b 9 d 10 i

▶9.1 Turn to p. 321 for the complete audioscript.

B Elicit or briefly drill *How did (they) get there?* questions by pointing to different photos on pp. 112–113.

⚠️ **Common mistakes** Point to photo 10 and elicit the question *How did they g_____ there?* Model the activity with a st:

T: (Point to photo 10) *How did they get there?*

St: *By plane.*

T: (Rephrase) *That's right, they flew.*

Refer to the speech bubbles and make sure sts understand they also need to rephrase their partner's answers by using either the means of transportation or verbs in **A**. In pairs, sts point to photos 1–10, follow the model, and test each other. Monitor closely for accuracy.

C 👤 **Make it personal** Change partners. In pairs, sts interview each other with questions 1 and 2. Check sts are clear on the meaning of *20 km away* before they start. Ask *How far away (from here) do you live?* Elicit some examples. To extend this activity, elicit some local places to add to question 1. Add extra questions, e.g. *How do you get home late at night?* to 2. Tell sts to include these in their discussion if they have time. Ask sts to report their partner's answers.

> **Tip** With a stronger class, put these phrases on the board: *It depends (on the weather). When I'm tired / in a hurry. It depends what day it is. On weekends, I _____.* and get sts to use them in their answers. This can be turned into a class survey, to find out the most popular ways to get to places.

9.1

🎵 *Oh, I want to get away, I want to fly away, Yeah, yeah, yeah.*

2 Listening

A ▶9.2 Guess which transportation problems a–f go with sentences 1–6. Listen to check. Were you right?

1 The train was late.
2 My plane was de<u>layed</u>.
3 My bus had a flat tire.
4 There was a traffic jam.
5 I made a wrong turn.
6 I had an accident.

B ▶9.3 Listen to two conversations at a party. Which problems in **A** does each person have? Which ones have you experienced?

Conversation 1 _____   Conversation 2 _____

C ▶9.3 Match the questions to the answers. Listen again to check.

1 Did you just get here?
2 Where do you live?
3 How did you get here?
4 How's it going?
5 What happened?

a Pretty good, thanks. How about you?
b I had an accident. Nothing serious.
c Yes, actually.
d Right now? In Chicago.
e I took the bus.

D 🗣 **Make it personal** Imagine you're at a party. Invent a character. In pairs, role-play a "problem" conversation. Then change partners. Who had the biggest problem?

Hi Bob! Great to see you! How's it going?   *Hi Jane! Sorry I'm late … I lost my car keys.*

> **Common mistakes**
>
> Where are you working these days?
> ~~Right now?~~
> ~~Actually?~~ In New York.

9.1

2 Listening

A Point to the photos and elicit the travel problems. Tell sts to read sentences 1–6 and match to the photos. Paircheck. Play ▶9.2 and ask sts to check their answers. Classcheck. Ask: *What words have the sound /ei/?* (train, plane, delayed, made). Check sts are clear on the meaning of key vocabulary in this activity. Ask: *Are there lots of traffic jams where you live? Do you remember the last time you were delayed? Are the trains often late?* etc.

> 1 e 2 f 3 d 4 c 5 a 6 b

Tip Sts learning English tend to produce every word and forget about connecting speech features. Remind them of the pronunciation of *do you* /dəjə/ and *did you* /dʒə/ in connected speech. Encourage sts to practice these sounds as they read the first three questions in **C** and try to pronounce correctly.

B Play ▶9.3 and ask sts to identify the problems. Paircheck. Classcheck. Ask sts if this kind of listening activity is useful. Encourage sts to talk about the most common problems they have from **A**, or problems they have / haven't yet had happen to them.

> Conversation 1: 2, 3, 4
> Conversation 2: 1, 5, 6

▶9.3 Turn to p. 321 for the complete audioscript.

C Sts read through the questions and try to match to the answers. Play ▶9.3 so they can check answers. Classcheck.

> 1 c 2 d 3 e 4 a 5 b

Draw sts' attention to the **Common mistakes** and tell them that *actually* is a false cognate, and is often a problem for Spanish and Portuguese speakers. Sts could Google other false cognates that are common mistakes for speakers of Romance languages, when translating from L1.

D Review the listening activities, ask: *How much did / didn't you understand? How much did you get right? What else did you pick up from listening?*

Make it personal Ask the class to imagine they are at a party. Allow some preparation time so sts can come up with an interesting, famous, or imaginary character (an occupation, a name, nationality, etc.). Sts work in pairs or stand up and mingle with as many classmates as possible. Sts role-play dialogues similar to the ones in ▶9.3. They could film short conversations on their phones, in the style of an Instagram story, and play the interactions for the class. Monitor and make a note of good language and errors (including pronunciation) and go over this afterwards. At the end, ask sts to tell you what they can remember about their partner / people they talked to, or share their videos.

Tip Play music in the background to create a party atmosphere.

➔ **Workbook** p. 44

9.2 What do you do?

1 Reading

A Guess the answers to questions 1–4. Then read the article quickly to check.
1. What's the man in the photo doing?
   a He's going to work.   b He's training for a marathon.
2. What's his job?
   a He teaches sports.   b He's a doctor.
3. How far is his commute to work and home?
   a eight miles   b two miles
4. Why does he commute like this?
   a He can't drive and is afraid to ride a bike.   b He wants to stay in shape.

An Unusual Commute

Most people commute by bus, or they drive, but not Ted Houk, from Towson, Maryland. For five years, Dr. Houk rode his bike to work, but then he decided to run, instead, because he wanted even more exercise. Then, for 15 years, Dr. Houk always ran to his internal medicine practice from his home in Lutherville, and back again every day. It's about four miles (around six and a half kilometers) there and four miles home, but he ran when it was sunny, when it was raining, and even when it was snowing. He ran if it was hot or cold, and if it was light or dark.

He always ran with a big bag in his hand. In the bag were his clothes, his stethoscope, his phone, and about two pounds of fruit and vegetables. His full bag weighed about ten pounds (around four and a half kilograms). When Houk got to work, he always rubbed alcohol on his body to remove perspiration. But sweat is not really a problem, he says, because "your sweat is clean."

Then, in 2013, Dr. Houk had a serious accident as he ran. He was seriously injured when a car hit him, and he was in the hospital for two months. Fortunately, he recovered and now works – and runs – again.

B ▶9.4 Listen and read again. True (T) or False (F)? Do you agree with Ted's ideas?
1. Dr. Houk lives next to his workplace.
2. He takes the bus to work if it rains or snows.
3. The bag he carried was empty.
4. He went by bike to work before he started running.
5. He thought the sweat on his body was a problem.
6. Dr. Houk started to run again after his accident.

C 🔴 **Make it personal** Do you know anyone with an unusual commute or way to exercise? What do your classmates do to keep in shape?

My aunt swims five kilometers every day.   *I never use elevators.*

9.2 What do you do?

Lesson Aims: Sts learn to talk in some depth about occupations and their good / bad points. Sts also learn to talk about distances and weight.

Function
Reading / Talking about ways to commute home and to work.
Talking about distances and weight.
Talking about unusual habits / ways to commute to work.
Talking about occupations.

Language
He never takes the bus to work. His bag weighs ten pounds.
He runs eight miles.
My father cycles two kilometers.
I never use elevators.
What does he do?
He's a computer programmer.
Doctors work long hours and make a lot of money.
What do you do?
What do / don't you like about your job?

Vocabulary: Commute to work. Jobs. Make money, work long hours, work alone.
Grammar: Countable and uncountable nouns. Quantifiers: *some* in + sentences and *any* in + and –.

♪ **Song line:** Turn to p. 334 for notes about this song and an accompanying task.

Warm-up Review simple present and past. Have these prompts written on the board and get sts first to ask you, and then to ask and answer the questions in pairs. Establish the model, e.g., *How often do you use elevators? Did you use one yesterday?* Classcheck by asking sts to report their partner's answers to the whole class.

1 *How often / use elevators? / use one yesterday?*
2 *How often / you ride a bike? / ride your bike yesterday?*
3 *How much exercise / you do? / exercise yesterday?*
4 *What / you do to stay in shape? What / do yesterday?*
5 *How / you get to work? How / get here today?*

1 Reading

A Ask sts to cover the text. In pairs, sts guess the answers to questions 1–4. Classcheck their predictions. For variation, sts can have fun reading the text in pairs, reading a few lines at a time then covering the text. Sts take turns to ask each other to recall the last few lines they read. Sts finish reading the text and check their answers. Classcheck with answers on the board.

🔑 1 a 2 b 3 a 4 b

B Sts listen to ▶9.4 and reread the text in **A** and in pairs decide whether sentences 1–6 are true (**T**) or false (**F**). Classcheck. Encourage sts to correct the false sentences.

Ask: *Do you agree with the doctor's ideas*? and put eight prompts on the board to help them answer:

running to / from work
running in all weather conditions
running with a bag in his hand
fruit is good for you
vegetables help with the memory
running is a good way to lose weight
use alcohol to remove perspiration
your sweat is clean

🔑 1 F 2 F 3 F 4 T 5 F 6 T

Tip Teach different measurements for weights and distances. Ask: *Does Dr. Houk carry a bag to work?* (Yes). *How much does Dr. Houk's bag weigh?* (Around 10 pounds). *Is it a heavy bag?* Ask: *How much is this in kilos?* Compare pounds (lb) vs. kilos (kg), and also miles (mi) vs. kilometers (km). Ask: *How far does he run?* (4 miles). Ask sts to convert distances.

Extra writing Sts write a paragraph giving their opinion about Dr. Houk's means of going to work. Sts can also mention if they know anyone like him.

C Encourage sts to think about the Reading text and consider if they found it easy / difficult / enjoyable / useful. Had they read it before the class? Did anything surprise them? Do they have any questions about Reading tasks in general?

🔴 **Make it personal** Ask the whole class: *Do you know any people, friends or relatives with unusual diets or ways to get exercise?* and encourage personal contributions. Use the two speech bubble examples plus some more of your own to set this up.

Extra activity Sts could prepare and carry out a class survey on how often / when / where people in the class exercise, and what they do. Sts present their findings to the class in pairs or small groups.

9.2

2 Vocabulary Jobs

♪ I'm too hot, Call the police and the fireman, I'm too hot.

A ▶9.5 Match photos a–j to the jobs. Which words are easy for you to recognize? Listen to students discussing the photos to check.

- a cab driver
- a computer programmer
- a cook
- a dentist
- a firefighter
- a flight attendant
- a hairdresser
- a personal assistant
- a photographer
- a police officer

B ▶9.6 Look at picture k. What job do you think each person has today? Listen to two of the friends talking about the group to check.

C In pairs, decide which sentences 1–7 apply to the jobs in **A**. Which are the best professions? Why?

1. You can / can't make a lot of money.
2. It's interesting / boring / dangerous work.
3. You work with other people / alone.
4. You work / don't work long hours.
5. You help / don't help a lot of people.
6. It's a job of the past / future.
7. It's a job I'd like / I wouldn't like to do.

> I think computer programmer is the best job because you can make a lot of money, and it's interesting.

D 🗣 **Make it personal** What's your occupation? What do you like about it? What don't you like? What's your dream job?

> What do you do?

> I'm a student. I enjoy it because my teachers are good, but I don't have any money!

⏱ **Common mistakes**

I'm student in City College.
    a   at

Doctors win a lot of money.
        earn / make

9.2

② Vocabulary Jobs

A Focus on photos a–j and elicit what some of the people do as a job.

> **Language tip** It's important to emphasize how much English and Romance languages have in common and how this can help sts learn faster. Ask sts to read the professions and count the number of cognates. They should be able to identify *taxi driver, computer programmer, photographer, police officer, dentist,* and *personal assistant* as a result.

> **Tip** To elicit more language, focus on actions rather than the occupations, e.g. Say: *I'm a teacher. I teach, prepare lessons, and correct tests.* Point to e and say: *She takes photos. What about d?* (*He drives a car.*)

Sts match the jobs to photos a–j. Play ▶9.5 so they can check. Paircheck. Replay if necessary. Classcheck with answers on the board. Drill the pronunciation of all jobs. Highlight that most jobs end in the unstressed suffix -*er*; e.g. *teacher, worker, manager, cleaner* .... but not *cook* (write *cooker* on the board and cross it out).

> **Tip** Get sts to quietly echo the pronunciation of each job as they hear it. Then, in pairs, sts remember and pronounce the words correctly together. Classcheck then have sts test each other. In pairs, sts cover the jobs and take turns pointing to photos a–h and asking *What does he / she do?*

> a a firefighter   b a flight attendant   c a police officer
> d a cab driver   e a photographer   f a computer programmer
> g a hairdresser   h a personal assistant   i a cook   j a dentist

▶9.5 Turn to p. 321 for the complete audioscript.

B Point to the picture in the center. Tell sts that it's an old picture and the teenagers in it are now the adults in photos a–j. In pairs, sts try to guess which job each person in the picture does today. Tell sts they will listen to Lisa and James talking about their old classmates. Play ▶9.6 to check their predictions.

> David a cook, Chris a flight attendant, Brian a computer programmer, Valerie a hairdresser, Amelia a dentist, Jane a photographer, James a cab driver, Martina a firefighter, Robert a personal assistant, Larry a police officer

▶9.6 Turn to p. 321 for the complete audioscript.

> **Tip** Ask sts to turn to the AS on p. 167. Sts listen again and notice /ə/ in articles and non-content words.

C In pairs, sts discuss the jobs which sentences 1–7 refer to and share opinions about which jobs they think are good / bad and why. Monitor and make a note of good language and errors in meaning and pronunciation and go over this afterwards. Ask some sts what jobs they think are the best / worst and why and encourage a class discussion.

> **Tip** Encourage sts to give examples and express as much as they can without over-correcting so they feel some degree of fluency.

At the end, they need to tell you / the whole class which job in **A** they think is the best one and why.

Common mistakes Read with the whole class (don't forget articles with jobs, use *at* + the name of the institution where you work).

D **Make it personal** Put sts with a different partner. In pairs, sts ask each other about their jobs. Sts report their partner's answers to the whole class.

> **Tip** With a young or unemployed class, get them to talk about the jobs of their family members.

Extra writing If time allows, sts can write their answer to **D**. Then collect and mix them up, read them to the class to see if they can guess who wrote them.

➔ **Workbook** p. 45

9.3 Where are you going to be in 2025?

1 Listening

A ▶9.7 Listen to Kelly and Michael discussing future plans and check (✓) the correct answers.

	Profession interested in?	Need to go to grad school?
Michael	☐ financial advisor ☐ pet psychologist	☐ yes ☐ no
Kelly	☐ financial advisor ☐ pet psychologist	☐ yes ☐ no

B ▶9.7 Listen again. Who says 1–8, Michael (M) or Kelly (K)?
1 That sounds boring. ____
2 You can make a lot of money. ____
3 You help people. ____
4 You can be your own boss. ____
5 Your parents are going to be happy. ____
6 I don't want to be a veterinarian. ____
7 It's going to be fun. ____
8 Tell me what that dog is thinking. ____

C 😊 **Make it personal** Which job do you prefer? Why?

> *I think I prefer the pet psychologist because I love animals, too.*

2 Grammar *going to* for future

A ▶9.8 Listen to these sentences from the conversation in **1A** and complete 1–7. Then complete the grammar box.
1 What are you _____ to do?
2 I'm _____ to _____ a financial advisor.
3 Your parents _____ going to _____ happy.
4 _____ going _____ be a pet psychologist.
5 It's _____ going to _____ easy, but it's what I want.
6 You can meet lots of people. _____ going _____ be fun.
7 I know I'm _____ going _____ be rich, but that's OK.

▶ **Common mistakes**
~~It isn't going be easy.~~ → *to*
~~Why you are going to do that?~~ → *are you*

Subject	A	⊖	going to	I	
I	'm			go	to grad school.
You	're	(not)	going to	like	it.
She / He / It	_____			make	a lot of money.
We / They	_____			study	psychology.

Q	A	S	going to	I		⊕⊖ Short answers
What	are	you	going to	do?		
	Are	you	going to	go	to grad school?	Yes, I am. No, I'm _____.

Use *going to* to talk about predictions and future intentions. In ⊖ sentences, use contractions.
1 I _____ not going to like the movie.
2 She _____ going to be late.
3 My parents _____ going to be happy.

➤ **Grammar 9B** p. 154

9.3 Where are you going to be in 2025?

Lesson Aims: Sts learn to use all forms of *going to* to talk about plans, intentions, and predictions.

Function
Listening / Talking about future plans and predictions.
Asking and answering questions about future plans.
Reading an online forum about future plans and predictions.

Language
I'm going to go to grad school.
We're going to be very rich.
What are you going to do this evening?
How are you going to celebrate your next birthday? We're all going to live on the moon.
I'm going to be a space pilot.

Vocabulary: Grad school, psychologist, veterinarian. Buildings, education, politics, space travel, population, business.
Grammar: Future with *going to*.

🎵 **Song line:** Turn to p. 334 for notes about this song and an accompanying task.

Warm-up Get sts to work in small groups and talk about their friends' and close relatives' professions. Write *What / your father do?* on the board and elicit the question (What does your father do?). Write prompts on the board for sts to ask and answer questions about (your *mother / father / brother / sister / best friend / husband / wife / boyfriend / girlfriend / son / daughter*). Tell them each st has to ask at least four questions and should remember their partners' answers. Classcheck.

> **Stronger classes** Encourage sts to ask follow-up questions *Does he like his job? Does he work long hours? Does he make a lot of money?*

1 Listening

A Introduce the Listening and explain that Kelly and Michael are talking about their future plans. Check that sts understand the vocabulary in the chart. Elicit what the work of a financial advisor and a psychologist might be. Then elicit for a pet psychologist. Play ▶9.7. Tell sts to listen and complete the chart. Paircheck. Classcheck.

> Michael: financial advisor, yes
> Kelly: pet psychologist, yes

▶9.1 Turn to p. 321 for the complete audioscript.

B Point to sentences 1–8 and ask sts to try to remember who said each line, Michael or Kelly. Replay ▶9.7 for sts to check their guesses. Classcheck with answers on the board or ask sts to turn to the AS on p. 167.

> 1 K 2 M 3 M 4 M 5 K 6 K 7 K 8 M

C 🔴 **Make it personal** In pairs, sts ask each other *Which job do you prefer? Why?* Have sts report their partner's opinions to the whole class

2 Grammar *going to* for future

A Ask sts to read the sentences and guess what goes in the blanks. Play ▶9.8 for sts to fill in the blanks in sentences 1–7. Paircheck. Classcheck with answers on the board.

> 🟠 **Common mistakes** Get sts to study the grammar box. Write *I'm going to be very rich.* on the board. Ask: *Is it about the present? Is it about the future?* and elicit the negative and interrogative forms of the same sentence. Write them on the board. *I'm not going to be very rich. Are you going to be very rich?* Elicit the short answers to the question. *Yes, I am. No, I'm not. I hope so!* Ask sts to complete the chart and rules.

> 1 going 2 going, be 3 are, be 4 I'm, to 5 not, be
> 6 It's, to 7 not, to
> 's, 're, not
> 1 'm 2 isn't 3 aren't

➡ **Grammar 9B** p. 154

Extra activity Ask sts to write their own true example sentences and prepare one *Are you going to (verb) …?* question to ask a partner. Sts work in pairs to read each other's sentences and answer questions. Encourage them to peer-correct any errors in grammar. Monitor closely for accuracy and help whenever needed.

Get sts to read out their sentences to the class. Sts should shout out *Bingo* if they have exactly the same one.

9.3

B Order these questions. Then find someone who has the same answers.

1 you / are / going / what / evening / do / this / to / ?
_____
2 you / going / tonight / are / TV / watch / to / ?
_____
3 year / going / you / to / go / vacation / are / on / next / ?
_____
4 are / where / celebrate / next / birthday / going / you / to / your / ?
_____

🎵 *I'm gonna swing from the chandelier, from the chandelier, I'm gonna live like tomorrow doesn't exist.*

C 🟢 **Make it personal** Where are you going to be in 2025? Discuss your answers in groups. Who has the most original answer?

I'm going to be in space. I want to be an astronaut. *Wow! How do you learn to do that?*

③ Reading

A ▶9.9 Read the article and write the name of the person who talks about these topics. There's one extra topic.

1 buildings _____
2 education _____
3 politics _____
4 space travel _____
5 conservation _____
6 transportation _____
7 shopping _____
8 technology _____

THE FUTURE?

What is work going to be like for young people? We asked some high school graduates for their plans and predictions for the world of work. This is what they told us.

"I'm not going to be like my parents. They have an online movie rental business. I want to open a physical store like in the old days!" **Saul, 17**

"We're all going to live on the moon, so I'm going to be a space pilot and fly people to the moon and back." **Mariana, 16**

"We're not going to educate our kids in the same way in the future. We're going to use video games to teach kids. I'm going to be an educational video-game designer." **Laisa, 18**

"Humans are not going to use cars forever. I think we're going to be able to teleport pretty soon." **Margarita, 17**

"I'm not going to work in an office. With technology, everyone can already telecommute, and more people are going to do it." **Chris, 19**

"Politics is a career that's not going to change. Even if you don't like politicians, this is an important job and it's what I'm going to do." **Javier, 16**

"Because we can print in 3D now, soon we're not going to need construction workers, and we'll be able to "print" new houses. I'm going to work in this business." **Marco, 18**

④ Pronunciation

A ▶9.10 Listen to the sentences. Check (✓) the ones that are pronounced "gonna" /ɡənə/ in rapid speech. Then listen again and repeat.

1 a ☐ b ☐   2 a ☐ b ☐   3 a ☐ b ☐   4 a ☐ b ☐

B 🟠 **Make it personal** Which predictions in 3A do you agree / disagree with? In pairs, compare answers.

I don't agree with Mariana. We're not gonna live on the moon in the future.

I'm not so sure. The future is a long time, and the population is growing fast!

> ⏰ **Common mistakes**
> I'm not going to be rich.
> Are you gonna to be famous?

9.3

B Elicit the correct order of the words for question 1. Individually, sts unscramble questions 2–4. Paircheck. Classcheck with answers on the board. Sts then ask and answer the questions in pairs or small groups. Ask some sts to report other sts' answers back to the class.

Stronger students / Fast finishers Sts can write more jumbled questions for their partner to order.

1 What are you going to do this evening?
2 Are you going to watch TV tonight?
3 Are you going to go on vacation next year?
4 Where are you going to celebrate your next birthday?

C **Make it personal** Sts work in new groups. Write *2025* on the board and ask: *Where are you going to be? What job are you going to have?* Don't get any answers, but tell sts to think quietly about their future dreams. Sts then discuss the question in groups. Ask sts to report back what their groups said and praise good examples of *going to*.

3 Reading

A Ask: *Are you optimistic or pessimistic about the future?* Encourage sts to exchange opinions with others in a short class discussion. Point to the online forum. Sts read about people and their plans and predictions for the future. Focus on words 1–8 and tell sts they need to identify who talks about each topic in the forum.

Tip To add variation for the Reading activity, divide the class into seven groups. You could copy the text and cut it up, giving each group one of the comments from the online forum. Sts close their books and have to work as a team to find the information that they need to complete the activity.

Play ▶9.9 for sts to complete the task. Paircheck. Classcheck with answers on the board. Now that sts have read the text and listened, you could listen again, this time pausing at certain points and asking sts to tell you if they can remember what comes next (without looking!). Elicit and drill pronunciation of the words with pink letters. Highlight the silent letter in buildings.

Extra activity Sts find six *going to* sentences in the text and mark them as P (predictions) or I (intentions). Paircheck. Classcheck.

1 Marco 2 Laisa 3 Javier 4 Mariana 5 Chris
6 Margarita 7 Saul 8 Chris

Stronger students could write a short text about conservation and the future, the topic not covered in the text from the list in **A**.

4 Pronunciation

A Ask sts to say one sentence from the text in **3A** with *going to* and write it on the board. Say it with careful pronunciation /ɡəʊɪŋtʊ/ and then with faster pronunciation /ɡənə/. Ask sts which sounds more natural and talk about how we often shorten words and phrases when speaking fast and informally. Play ▶9.10. Sts check what pronunciation they hear. Play it again for sts to listen and repeat.

Tip Try back-chaining and chunking to help sts produce the weak forms. Use the phrase *I'm going to live in space*:
space
in space
live in space
gonna live
gonna live in space
I'm gonna
I'm gonna live in space.

1 b 2 a 3 a 4 a

B **Make it personal** In pairs, sts take turns agreeing or disagreeing with the predictions in **A**. Read the speech bubbles to model language for the task. Monitor supportively and hear their ideas. Ask some sts to report their opinions to the whole class. Use a show of hands to find out the majority class opinion on each one, especially any more controversial ones.

Extra writing Sts can write up their opinions on the predictions for homework and post them on the class website.

→ **Workbook** p. 46

9.4 What are you going to do next year?

1 Vocabulary Life changes

A ▶9.11 Listen to Mr. James and complete phrases 1–11. Match six of the phrases to pictures a–f.

1 leave c<u>ollege</u>.
2 find a g_____.
3 get e_____.
4 get m_____.
5 leave h_____.
6 start a (new) j_____.
7 start a f_____.
8 get d_____.
9 m_____.
10 lose a j_____.
11 re<u>tire</u> (from a j_____).

B ▶9.11 Listen again to check. In pairs, what is one mistake that Mr. James made?

C 🗨 **Make it personal** In groups, discuss at what age people usually do these things in your country. Do you all agree?

learn to drive   leave home   go to college   get married   start a family

> We usually go to college when we're 17 or 18.   People usually start a family when they're about 30.

2 Reading

A Quickly read Alex's blog. What eight changes is he going to make?

New Year's Resolutions!

Well, I had a long talk with my dad the other day, and he con<u>vinced</u> me. We're very different, but I love him. So, I'm going to make a few changes in my life. And, anyway, today is a new year, so time for a new start!

First, I'm going to exercise more. I ate too much over the holidays! Then I'm going to get a new job. I'm a server in a restaurant, and I hate my boss. He makes me stay late and keeps my tips! I want to be a web designer, so I'm going to go back to school, get my ba<u>chelor's</u>, and show them all! I'm going to learn a new language, too. I want to learn to speak Manda<u>rin</u>.

I'm also going to move out of my mom's house and get an apartment with some friends. I think it's time, don't you? And I'm going to buy a new car. Then I'm going to find a new girlfriend – I'm so lonely! So … "How are you going to do all this?" I hear you asking.

Here's my plan: Well, after lunch, I'm playing basketball with my friend, Carl, and then tonight, I'm having dinner with my mom to tell her I'm leaving home. Next week, I'm talking to a career spe<u>cialist</u>, and I'm starting a class in Mandarin. And … I'm going on a date tomorrow night. Wow! Wish me luck! What do you think of my plan? Thanks for reading!

comment:
Hi Alex! I think this is a good plan. But why are you going to learn Mandarin? Why don't you learn Spanish or Portuguese?

B ▶9.12 Listen to and read the blog again and complete the chart.

⚠️ **Common mistakes**

~~are you doing~~
What ~~do you do~~ after class?
I'm going   I'm working
~~I go home.~~ ~~I work~~ tonight.

	Intention	Reason
1	do more exercise	he ate too much over the holidays
2	get a new job	
3	go back to school	
4	move from his mom's house	
5	get a new girlfriend	

C 🗨 **Make it personal** What do you think of Alex's plan? Follow the models above and below, and write a blog comment to encourage him.

> Hi Alex! I think your plan sounds great! I studied Mandarin, too, last year. It's not easy, but I really enjoyed it!

9.4 What are you going to do next year?

Lesson Aims: Sts continue to learn to talk about plans and intentions using *going to*, and also practice using the present continuous to talk about fixed plans.

Function
Listening and reading about life changes.
Talking about fixed plans and intentions.
Talking about New Year's resolutions.

Language
I'm going to get a new job soon.
I'm having dinner with a friend tonight.
I'm going to go on a diet on Monday.
Next year, I'm going to move.

Vocabulary: Verbs related to life changes. Leave college, find a partner, get engaged, start a family, move house, lose a job, retire (from a job).

Grammar: *Going to* vs. present continuous for plans.

 Song line: Turn to p. 334 for notes about this song and an accompanying task.

Warm-up Recycle *going to*. In pairs, sts play a miming game. Sts need to mime three things they plan to do this week for their partner to guess (by saying, e.g., *You're going to watch TV!*). Monitor closely for correct use. At the end, ask: *What are you going to do tomorrow?*

1 Vocabulary Life changes

A Sts listen to Mr. James talking to his son Alex. Explore the pictures a–f. Ask: *What's Mr. James doing / wearing / saying in each picture?* Focus on phrases 1–11. Sts need to complete them with one word. Play 9.11 for sts to do the task. Paircheck. Play the audio again if necessary. Classcheck with answers on the board. Ask which actions they can see in the pictures. Ask: *Did he enjoy his life? Do you think he's happy now he's retired?*

> 1 2 girlfriend 3 engaged 4 married 5 home 6 job
> 7 family 8 divorced 9 move 10 job 11 job
> a 2 b 4 c 5 d 7 e 9 f 11

▶ 9.11 Turn to p. 321 for the complete audioscript.

B Tell sts to listen again and identify the mistake Mr. James made. Paircheck. Classcheck.

C **Make it personal** Ask: *At what age do people usually leave college / get married in your country?* Elicit an answer and ask: *Do you agree?* Refer sts to the activities and ask them to think about when people do these things. In pairs, sts compare their ideas, e.g. *People in (my country / city) usually leave home when they're 25.* Ask one or two sts to report their opinion to the whole class.

2 Reading

A Tell sts the man in the photo is Mr. James's son, Alex. Ask sts to read the blog and notice eight changes he's going to make after having talked to his father. Classcheck.

> 1 Exercise more.
> 2 Get a new job.
> 3 Go back to school.
> 4 Get his bachelor's.
> 5 Learn a new language—Mandarin.
> 6 Move out of his mom's house and get an apartment with friends.
> 7 Buy a new car.
> 8 Find a new girlfriend.

B Ask: *Why is Alex going to do more exercise?* (He ate too much over the holidays.) Individually, sts listen to ▶9.12, reread the text and complete the chart with Alex's reasons. Paircheck. Classcheck. Help with any pronunciation questions.

> 2 he hates his boss
> 3 he wants to get his bachelor's
> 4 he wants to get an apartment with some friends
> 5 he's so lonely

C Write the example from the text *tonight, I'm having dinner with my mom* on the board. Elicit that Alex is talking about the future. Tell sts they have come across uses of present continuous for the future in the course already, and draw their attention to the following examples:

p. 39 *but I'm not the girl you're taking home*

p. 40 *I'm taking some exams in English*

Look at the **Common mistakes** together. More examples include:

Where ~~do you go~~ after class? (*are you going*)
~~You don't come~~ for a coffee? (*Aren't you coming*)
Sorry, ~~I go~~ home. ~~I work~~ tonight. (*I'm going / I'm working*)

Make it personal Focus on Alex's plan and elicit their opinions of him / his plan. Ask sts to write Alex a blog comment to encourage him. Walk around and read / help sts with their texts. In groups of four, sts read each other's comments and choose the best one to present to the whole class.

3 Grammar *going to* vs. present continuous

🎵 *Ooh, love, no one's ever gonna hurt you, love. I'm gonna give you all of my love. Nobody matters like you. So, rockabye baby, rockabye.*

A Are 1–4 in the present continuous (PC) or do they use *going to* (GT)?

	PC	GT
1 I'm going to leave this job when I find a better one.		
2 After lunch, he's meeting his teacher.		
3 Tonight, he and his mother are having dinner.		
4 I think we're going to win tonight.		

B Answer the question in the grammar box.

I'm going to do all my homework this weekend.	= an intention in the future
I'm starting a new job tomorrow.	= a fixed plan in the future

Use the present continuous to talk about a fixed plan in the future. For intentions or predictions, use *going to*.

Which sentences in **A** are intentions / predictions or fixed plans?

➡ Grammar 9C & 9D p.154

C In Alex's blog in **2A**, find four examples of intentions and four examples of fixed plans.

D Complete 1–5 with the present continuous or *going to*.
1 I'm _____ (travel) to Rio next week to see my mom. I got my ticket online yesterday.
2 They say it _____ (rain) tomorrow. I hate the rain!
3 My brother says he _____ (save) for a new car next year. He wants an electric one.
4 I think they _____ (win) the election.
5 Sofía _____ (not / go) to the movies with us on Saturday. She has a dance class.

> **Common mistakes**
> ~~going to go to sleep~~
> I'm ~~sleeping~~ early tonight.
> When *go* is the main verb or is part of an expression, always include it.

E 🟢 **Make it personal** In pairs, talk about:
1 your plans for the weekend.
2 things you intend to do next year.
3 predictions for your future (jobs, marriage, retirement).

💬 *I'm meeting my friends on Saturday. We're having a party at the beach.*

💬 *I'm taking my grandmother out for dinner. It's her birthday!*

4 Listening

A ▶ 9.13 Listen to four phone messages. What are these people going to do? Match 1–4 to the correct answers.
1 Carla's brother   move to a warm place ☐
2 John's parents   get engaged ☐
3 Julia   go back to school ☐
4 Martin   live in France ☐

B ▶ 9.13 Listen again and choose the main reason why each person is calling. Who do you think is going to be most surprised?
1 Carla wants Ronnie …   ☐ to cook dinner.   ☐ to help with packing.
2 John wants Melissa …   ☐ to give him information.   ☐ to move to Costa Rica.
3 Julia wants to tell her mom …   ☐ that she graduated.   ☐ some important news.
4 Martin wants Lucy …   ☐ to go to work.   ☐ to celebrate with him.

C 🟠 **Make it personal** Imagine it's New Year's Eve. Write a post about the changes you are going to make in your life next year.

💬 *Well, next year I'm going to …*

9.4

3 Grammar *going to* vs. *present continuous*

A Individually, sts mark if the sentences in the chart are in the present continuous (PC) or *going to* (GT). Paircheck. Classcheck with answers on the board.

> 1 GT   2 PC   3 PC   4 GT

B Refer sts to the grammar box and ask them to read it. Ask sts to complete the exercise and paircheck. Classcheck. If necessary, clarify using the following rule: Use the present continuous as future or *going to* to talk about the immediate future (*after school, tomorrow, this weekend*). When the future isn't immediate, use *going to* (*in a few years, in 2030, when I'm 25*).

Tell sts to refer to Alex's blog on p. 118 and underline one use of present continuous and one use of *going to* for future, and discuss in pairs whether the examples they have chosen are immediate actions or not.

> intentions / predictions: 1, 4
> fixed plans: 2, 3

→ **Grammar 9C & 9D** p. 154

C Sts find four more examples of present continuous and four more of *going to* in Alex's blog. Use one example they found in present continuous and rephrase it into *going to*. Write this on the board to help weaker sts. In pairs, sts rephrase to practice the form. Monitor and listen for accuracy.

> GT: I'm going to make a few changes, I'm going to exercise more, I'm going to get a new job, I'm going to go back to school, I'm going to learn a new language, I'm going to move out of my mom's house, I'm going to buy a new car, I'm going to find a new girlfriend, How are you going to do all this?
> PC: I'm playing basketball, I'm having dinner, I'm leaving home, I'm talking to a career specialist, I'm starting a class in Mandarin, I'm going on a date tomorrow night.

Language tip Portuguese speakers may have difficulty understanding future forms (*going to* / present continuous) in English as their two L1 equivalents can be the same without the altered meaning they have in English. Write two examples on the board and translate to the sts L1 to illustrate the differences between these languages. Explain that the different forms in English are the same in their L1.

D In pairs, sts complete 1–5.

> 1 travelling   2 's going to rain   3 's going to save   4 're going to win   5 isn't going

E 🔵 **Make it personal**   In pairs, sts discuss 1–3. Refer to the speech bubbles as a model.

4 Listening

A Elicit what is happening in photos 1–4. Ask: *What is / are he / she / they doing?* Sts will hear four phone messages and match 1–4 to the answers. Play ▶9.13. Paircheck. Classcheck. At the end, ask sts to identify who is who in the photos—ask: *Who's Carla's brother?* (photo 1) *Who are John's parents?* (photo 2) *Who's Julia?* (photo 3) and *Who's Martin?* (photo 4).

> 1 live in France   2 move to a warm place
> 3 get engaged   4 go back to school

▶9.13 Turn to p. 322 for the complete audioscript.

B Play ▶9.13. Sts listen again to notice the main reason why each person is calling / leaving a message. Ask them to notice who the most surprised person is and say why. Paircheck. Ask: *Did you enjoy the activity? Who was easier / harder to understand? Do the people from the audio remind you of anybody you know?* Classcheck. If it hasn't arisen already, highlight a common mistake with *help*: *I want ~~that you~~ help me.* (*I want **you to** help me*).

> 1 to help with packing
> 2 to give him information
> 3 some important news
> 4 to celebrate with him

Tip Ask sts to turn to the AS on p. 167. Sts listen again and notice the future verb forms.

C 🔵 **Make it personal**   Write *New Year's Eve* on the board and ask: *What do you usually do on this date? Do you make any promises / resolutions?* Tell them to imagine it is New Year's Eve and write a blog post (a paragraph) about the changes they are going to make in their lives in the new year. You might either collect their texts to mark at home or ask them to read their texts to the whole class.

Tip Do this orally with a stronger class or if time is short. Write prompts on the board to help sts: *exercise / health / study / love / home / family / job*

→ **Workbook** p. 47

9.5 Would you like to be a nurse?

ID Skills Making connections

Reading

A ▶9.14 Match jobs 1–6 to their area of work a–f. Listen to the talking dictionary to check.

1 a civil engineer
2 a dentist
3 a financial advisor
4 a market research analyst
5 a nurse
6 a software developer

a computers
b money and finance
c teeth
d health and medicine
e bridges and roads
f what people buy

B Read the article and match the jobs to the paragraphs 1–6.

| computer specialists | engineers | nurses |
| dentists | financial advisors | market research analysts |

THE BEST JOBS FOR THE FUTURE

What professionals are we going to need in the future? Here are predictions for the six jobs that are going to be in demand in the U.S. in 10 years.

1 _____
We will need more people to help the millions of workers who are going to retire in the next 10 years. Many people are going to ask experts to help them plan what to do with their money.

2 _____
People over the age of 65 are going to keep more of their own teeth, so there are going to be more professionals to show them how to keep their teeth healthy.

3 _____
What are we going to do about all the cars and buses? With more traffic, we need more roads and bridges, for example. We need more people who can build these large structures.

4 _____
Companies need people to help them understand what people want to buy. They want people who can analyze what customers want and tell them what products to make.

5 _____
People with IT (information technology) degrees and extensive computer experience are going to be in high demand, to make new software.

6 _____
There are going to be a lot more people over the age of 90 because of progress in medicine. This means we are going to need more people to help to look after them.

C ▶9.15 Listen and read again and circle the best answer.
1 When people retire they **don't need / need** help with their money.
2 People **always / don't always** know how to take good care of their teeth.
3 We need to build roads because of more **traffic / people.**
4 Companies want information about why people **buy / sell** things.
5 You will need a degree **or / and** experience to make software.
6 Medicine is going to be **good / bad** for people over 90.

D 🔴 **Make it personal** In pairs, do you agree with the six predictions? Which of the jobs would you most / least like to do?

I completely agree with number 1. People will need help to save money.   *I don't really agree with number …*

9.5 Would you like to be a nurse?

Lesson Aims: Sts practice looking for connections in an authentic text about the best jobs for the future.

Function
Reading and speaking about the best jobs in the future.

Language
People who know how to use a computer are going to be in high demand.

Vocabulary: Jobs. Areas of work. Bachelor's (degree), look after (old people), companies, in high demand, buy / sell, lend / borrow.
Grammar: Review: future tenses and *going to*.

Warm-up Books closed. Review jobs vocabulary. Ask sts to write down as many jobs as they can in one minute. Ask sts to work in groups of four and help count how many different jobs they have in total. Make sure they put their pens down and don't write more! Ask the groups to say how many they have and ask the group with the most to read them out. Correct any pronunciation errors with the whole class after they finish listing their jobs. Don't single out sts as they read their list.

ID Skills Making connections

A Books open. Refer sts to the photo and ask: *What's his job?* (engineer). In pairs, sts match jobs 1–6 to the area of work. Play ▶9.14 for sts to check their answers. Classcheck with answers on the board. Elicit / Drill the pronunciation of all jobs. Point to the photos on the page and ask: *Which jobs can you see in the photos?* Some photos are not obvious so elicit different possibilities.

> 1 e   2 c   3 b   4 f   5 d   6 a

B Focus on the text title, *The Best Jobs for the Future*, and elicit what jobs sts think are going to be really necessary or valued in the future. Sts read about six jobs which are going to be really important in ten years' time in the U.S. and match the jobs to the paragraphs. Elicit what job number 1 is about (a financial advisor). Classcheck. Elicit and drill the pronunciation of the words with pink letters. Ask: *What job would you like best?*

> 1 financial advisors   2 dentists   3 engineers
> 4 market research analysts   5 computer specialists
> 6 nurses

C Play ▶9.15 for sts to listen and reread the article and circle the best options in sentences 1–6. Classcheck. After sts have checked their answers, play ▶9.15 again, pausing after the pink highlighted words for sts to repeat them. Personalize, by asking sts to discuss in pairs if they agree or disagree with the statements, and to share their opinions.

> 1 need   2 don't always   3 traffic   4 buy   5 and   6 good

D Make it personal Write on the board:
Completely! Absolutely!
I agree / disagreee.
I'm not sure.
I hope so.
I hope not.
Maybe / Perhaps.

Drill the phrases, emphasizing intonation. Say the first sentence in **C** and elicit responses from sts using the phrases. Encourage them to sound convincing. Refer sts to the speech bubbles to clarify the task and check they understand what they have to do.

Sts then talk about the predictions and which jobs they would most / least like to do.

> **Stronger classes** Encourage them to make and discuss further predictions using *will* and *going to*, e.g. *Retired people are going to live longer and will need more money.*

9.5 Could I borrow your pen?

Lend me your ears and I'll sing you a song, and I'll try not to sing out of key. Oh, I get by with a little help from my friends.

ID in Action Asking for permission

A Guess what the people in photos a–d are asking for. Use these ideas.

to borrow the car
to borrow some money
to close a window
to leave work early
to take the day off
to turn on the air conditioning

I think in photo "a" the man is asking to …

B ▶9.16 Listen to dialogues 1–4 to check, and match them to photos a–d.
1 ☐ 2 ☐ 3 ☐ 4 ☐

C ▶9.16 Listen again. Complete the questions and circle the responses you hear.

Asking for permission	Giving permission	Saying no
Can I ask you something?	That's fine.	No, I'm busy.
Could _____ take the day off?	Sure. Go ahead.	Maybe next time.
Can I _____ the car?	Of course. No problem.	No, I'm sorry, you can't.
Could _____ lend me some _____?	Help yourself.	I'm sorry, but …
Do you mind if I turn _____ the _____ conditioning?	Not at all.	I'm sorry, but it's too cold.
		Sorry, I'm meeting a friend.

Common mistakes

Can I borrow ~~you~~ a pen? *from you*
Could you ~~borrow~~ me a pen? *lend*

D Role-play conversations for photos 1–4. Change roles. Be difficult sometimes!

Do you mind if I borrow your laptop? *I'm sorry, but I'm going home. And I'm working tonight.*

E Make it personal Choose something you could ask for permission to do. Go around the class and ask. How many positive responses did you get?

Could you lend me your phone for a minute? *I'm sorry. I left it at home.*

Can I borrow some money for a coffee? *Sorry, I only have my credit card with me.*

9.5 Could I borrow your pen?

Lesson Aims: Sts will ask for permission to do different things.

Function
Asking for, giving, and refusing permission.

Language
Could I take the day off?
Can I borrow some money?
Do you mind if I turn on the air-conditioning? Sure. Go ahead.
Help yourself.
I'd love to but …

Vocabulary: Asking for favors and help: borrow a car, borrow money, close a window.
Grammar: Asking for permission and responding to permission requests.

♪ **Song line:** Turn to p. 335 for notes about this song and an accompanying task.

ID in Action Asking for permission

A Point to photos a–d and say: *All the people in these photos are asking for permission (to do something)*. Point to the phrases and elicit what each person is asking permission to do (e.g. photo a shows a man who wants permission to turn on the air-conditioning). The easiest way for sts to express this is by following the example on the page.

B Play ▶9.16 and ask sts to write 1–4 next to four of the phrases in **A**. Paircheck. Classcheck. They then match photos a–d to conversations 1–4. Classcheck.

> 1 d   2 c   3 a   4 b

▶9.16 Turn to p. 322 for the complete audioscript.

C Give sts time to read the chart before you replay ▶9.16. Sts complete the questions and circle the responses they hear. Paircheck. Classcheck. Drill the pronunciation of some of the questions and all of the responses in the chart.

> **Tip** Vary your intonation and speed to add fun and energy to this repetition stage, e.g. *be happy, sad, angry, tired, in a hurry*, etc.

⚠ **Common mistakes** Explain the difference between *borrow* and *lend*. Associate *borrow* with taking and *lend* with giving. To quickly practice, get sts to ask for permission to use classroom objects with *Can I borrow …? / Can you lend me …?* first to you and then, in pairs, to each other.

> Can I ask you something?   That's fine.
> Could **I** take the day off?   Sure. Go ahead.
> Can I **borrow** the car?   No, I'm sorry, you can't.
> Could **you** lend me some **money**?   I'm sorry, but …
> Do you mind if I turn **on** the **air**-conditioning?   Not at all.

D In pairs, sts role-play conversations for photos 1–4 using the questions and responses from **C**. Monitor closely for accuracy. Ask some sts to act out their dialogues for the whole class. Refer weaker classes to the AS on p. 167 if necessary.

E 🔴 **Make it personal** Focus on the speech bubbles. Ask sts to think of something they could ask permission for in the class. Elicit or add these examples:

sit (here) / stand (there)
go (outside for a moment)
go and get (some water)
buy me (a cookie / some candy)
sing (a song)

Give them some time to plan their requests and then encourage them to stand up and ask different people for permission. Make sure sts give appropriate responses.

➔ **Workbook** p. 48

➔ 🆔 **Richmond Learning Platform**

➔ **Writing** p. 122

➔ 🆔 **Café** p. 123

Writing 9 A reply to a blog post

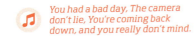 *You had a bad day, The camera don't lie, You're coming back down, and you really don't mind.*

A Read Michael's blog entry and answer 1–3.
1. Why did Michael have a bad day? (3 reasons)
2. What does he want people to do? (2 things)
3. What advice can you give him?

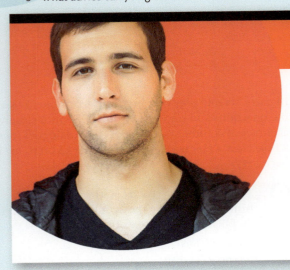

Michael's Blog

Today was terrible, seriously, one day to completely forget! I got to work a little late. OK, it wasn't the first time, so, of course, my boss didn't believe a word I said, and he fired me immediately. Yes, I actually lost my job! Can you believe it? Well, I hated that job anyway, but the thing is – what am I going to do now? I'm 25, I'm a smart guy (I graduated from college two years ago), I'm getting married next year, but I just don't know what to do. Come on blogosphere, give me some advice and tell me your plans! I need to make some money! Maybe I can get a few ideas from you guys.

B Read three replies. Which advice do you agree with?

 Hi, Michael. What a horrible day – are you OK? **I think you need to** find your *dream* and work hard for **it**! **That**'s what I'm doing. I want to go back to college to study medicine. I'm working as a personal assistant and living with my parents so I can save for it. When I graduate, my dream is to work as a doctor for a charity in Africa. Why not go back to college?
Megan, 20

 Sorry to hear about your job. I don't like **mine**, either. **Why don't you** take a course in your free time? I'm taking **one** in the evenings so I can get a promotion or do something different. You see, I work in a bank and I spend all day, every day **there**. But I want to work with customers in other countries, and for **this** I need to improve my English. **That**'s why I'm not going out until I pass this course! Go for it, Michael!
Jorge, 23

 Man, that is bad luck. I know how you feel, I really can't decide what I'm going to do, either. My teachers say I'm good at most school subjects. **They** say I'm ready to go to college, but I don't want to go right now. I'm going to Europe in the summer! I want to travel **there** and try lots of different jobs so I can see which **ones** I like, then … who knows? **Do you want my advice?** Take a break and go traveling, too.
Leon, 19

C Reread the replies. Circle the words or phrases that the **bold** words refer to.

D Complete the rules with the **bold** words in B.
1. *This*, *that*, and *it* all refer back to a thing or a situation.
2. _____ refers back to more than one person or thing.
3. _____ refers back to a place.
4. _____ or _____ replace countable singular or plural nouns.
5. _____ replaces *my* + noun.

✓ Write it right!
Use pronouns to avoid repetition.
I like red apples, but I don't like green ones.

E ✓ **Make it personal** Write a reply to Michael.

Before	Use your ideas from **A**. Include your own experience, what you're doing now, and your future plans.
While	Use the highlighted phrases to introduce your advice. Use pronouns to refer back to nouns and ideas.
After	Send your ideas to your classmates. Which is the best advice?

Writing 9 A reply to a blog post

🎵 **Song line:** Turn to p. 335 for notes about this song and an accompanying task.

A Point to Michael and tell sts that he had a terrible day and wrote a blog post about it. Elicit predictions about Michael's bad day.

Read questions 1–3 with the whole class. Sts read the blog entry and answer the questions. Paircheck. Classcheck.

> 1 He got to work late, his boss didn't believe him, and he lost his job.
> 2 He wants people to tell him their plans and give him advice.
> 3 Personal answer.

B Sts read the three replies and check if any of the people gave the same advice they talked about in **A** (question 3). Ask sts: *Which advice do you agree with?*

Integrated speaking Alternatively, split the class into groups of three and assign roles A, B and C. St A reads Megan's reply, st B reads Jorge's, st C reads Leon's. Within their groups, sts take turns telling one another about the reply they've just read and, at the end, decide which piece of advice is the most useful. Classcheck by asking sts to briefly summarize each blog reply and say which one they agree with the most.

C Point to the first word in bold in **B** (*it*). Ask: *What's **it** in this sentence? What does **it** refer to?* Show sts *dream* has been circled for them. Sts look at the other words in bold in the blog replies and circle the words or phrases they refer to.

Paircheck. Classcheck with answers on the board or, if possible, circle the answers on the *Digital Book for Teachers*.

Megan	Jorge	Leon
it = your dream	**mine** = job	**They** = my teachers
That = find your dream and work hard for it	**one** = a course	**there** = Europe
	there = a bank	**ones** = jobs
	this = to work with foreign customers	
	That = I need to improve my English	

D In pairs, sts complete rules 1–5 with the bold words in the replies in **B**. Classcheck. You could write the rules on the board.

> 2 **They** refer back to more than one person or thing.
> 3 **There** refers back to a place.
> 4 **One** or **ones** replace countable singular or plural nouns.
> 5 **Mine** replaces *my* + noun.

Read **Write it right!** with the whole class. Explain that pronouns are used to replace nouns and avoid repetition, particularly in written texts.

E 🔵 **Make it personal** Tell sts it's their turn now to give Michael some advice. Read the steps Before, While, and After with sts so as to better guide their writing. Tell them to refer to the blog replies in **B** as models to write their own. Don't forget to allow time for sts to share their ideas and choose the best reply in class.

9 The sky's the limit

 Café

1 Before watching

A Complete 1–4 with the words in the box.

| climatology | internship |
| meteorologist | tornado alley |

1 A _____ is a person who researches weather patterns.
2 In the Midwest of the U.S. they call the states of Iowa, Kansas, and Nebraska _____ because of all the strong wind storms.
3 He's applying for an _____ in a science department.
4 The study of the Earth's climate is called _____.

B In pairs, guess what Daniel is looking at, doing, and thinking in the photo. Write a thought bubble for him. Watch the start of the video to check.

> I think he's ...   I don't think so. I think he's ...

2 While watching

A Order the phrases 1–10 as you hear them. Complete the missing words.

☐ I think this is g_____ t_____ b_____ an important program for climatology.
☐ I wanna invent a m_____ or a p_____ that can tell people when a storm is coming.
☐ I'd like to go to grad school and then w_____ a _____ an environmental reporter.
☐ I'll s_____ y_____ the program as soon as I can. Express mail.
☐ So where do you s_____ y_____ in five years?
☐ Thank you for a_____ t_____ this interview.
☐ That's incredible. Could you let me k_____ h_____ that goes?
☐ Can you tell me a l_____ m_____ about your Storm Tracker?
☐ You a_____ n_____ a paid intern of the Foundation for Environmental Advancement.
☐ You'll be part of my r_____ s_____.

B Complete with the *going to* form of the verbs. Which ones would also be correct in the present continuous?

1 Daniel _____ (talk) on the phone in a few minutes.
2 Dr. DiChristina _____ (track) a tornado in Kansas.
3 His storm tracker _____ (be) useful for scientists.
4 Dr. DiChristina _____ (recommend) Daniel for a full, paid internship.
5 She _____ (email) him the address.
6 Daniel _____ (start) his internship after the semester ends.

C True (T) or False (F)? Correct the false sentences.

In the video ...
1 Daniel is waiting nervously to make a call.
2 Daniel and the doctor are meeting for the first time.
3 Only the doctor is asking questions.
4 Daniel is giving a video presentation of his Tracker.
5 Daniel talks about his past and his future dreams.
6 She asks him to send her his invention to test it.
7 She offers him a job.
8 He sends her his address.
9 He says he's going to contact her again soon.

3 After watching

A Cover the photo of Dr. DiChristina. In pairs, describe her office.

> On the left, there's a window and some ...   Is there a plant?

B Make five *Wh-* questions using the words in 1–5.

1 you / plan / after school
2 time / start / she / the interview
3 he / wait / for the phone call
4 they / do / after / their conversation
5 you / talk to / this evening

C ⬤ Make it personal In pairs, ask and answer the questions in **B**. Add some follow-up questions.

> Where are you planning on going after school?
> First, I'm going home, and then ...

D ⬤ Make it personal In groups, speculate about your lives in 10 years. Any big differences?

> In 10 years' time, I'm going to be married with a baby!
> Really? Who are you going to marry?

123

ID Café 9 The sky's the limit

1 Before watching

A Elicit / Drill pronunciation of all words in the box. Sts complete sentences 1–4 with the words. Paircheck. Classcheck.

> 1 meteorologist
> 2 tornado alley
> 3 internship
> 4 climatology

B Point to the photo showing Daniel. Ask: *What's Daniel doing? What's he looking at? What's he thinking?* and get sts to answer in pairs and write a thought bubble. Classcheck.

2 While watching

A Tell sts they are going to watch an interview with Daniel. Say: *Daniel was working on an invention, do you remember? So watch the video and tell me what he invented.* (A storm tracker.)

Tell sts to read through the sentences and predict what words go in the blanks. Play **Video 9**. Sts put the sentences in order and complete the blanks. Paircheck. Classcheck.

> 5 I think this is *going to be* an important program for climatology.
> 4 I wanna invent a *machine* or a *program* that can tell people when a storm is coming.
> 7 I'd like to go to grad school and then *work as* an environmental reporter.
> 10 I'll *send you* the program as soon as I can. Express mail.
> 6 So where do you *see yourself* in five years?
> 1 Thank you for *agreeing to* this interview.
> 2 That's incredible. Could you let me *know how* that goes?
> 3 Can you tell me a *little more* about your Storm Tracker?
> 9 You *are now* a paid intern of the Foundation for Environmental Advancement.
> 8 You'll be part of my *research study*.

B Ask sts to complete the gaps with the *going to* form of the verbs. Ask sts to discuss in pairs which can also go in the present continuous. Move on to **C** before you play the video again.

> 1 is going to talk
> 2 is going to track
> 3 is going to be
> 4 is going to recommend
> 5 is going to email
> 6 is going to start / is starting

C Sts work in pairs and read the sentences and try to remember if the sentences are true or false. Play the video again and ask sts to check answers. Classcheck and correct false sentences.

> 1 T
> 2 T
> 3 F Daniel also asks questions.
> 4 F Daniel is having a video conference call with Dr. DiChristina. (She has already seen his video presentation.)
> 5 T
> 6 T
> 7 T
> 8 F He's going to send her his program.
> 9 F Dr. DiChristina says they'll be in touch with Daniel.

3 After watching

A Tell sts to close their books. Ask sts what they remember about Dr. DiChristina's office.

Sts take turns to say sentences to their partner describing the office. Play the video again afterwards if there's time so they can check if they were correct. As an alternative, you could ask sts to write a description and then give it to another pair to correct while they watch the video again.

B Elicit *Wh-* words and keep a record of their contributions on the board. For prompts 1–5, sts make five *Wh-* questions. Point out that some of them may be both present continuous and *going to* questions.. Paircheck. Classcheck with answers on the board.

> 1 What are you planning to do after school?
> 2 What time is she starting / going to start the interview?
> 3 Why is he waiting for the phone call?
> 4 What are they going to do after their conversation?
> 5 Who are you talking / going to talk to this afternoon?

C ● **Make it personal** Drill pronunciation of all questions in **B**. Change partners. In pairs, sts take turns asking and answering the questions in **B**. Monitor closely for accuracy. Classcheck by asking sts about their partners' answers: *What is (partner's name) planning to do after school?*

D ● **Make it personal** In groups, sts talk about themselves in ten years' time. Round off by asking sts to report / tell the whole class what their partners think they are going to be doing five years from now.

10

10.1 Do you look like your mom?

1 Vocabulary The body and face

A ▶10.1 Label the photos with these words. Listen to a sports science class to check. Point to the part(s) of your body as you hear each word.

| arms | back | chest | fingers | foot / feet |
| hands | head | legs | stomach /k/ | toes |

B In pairs, say which parts of the body you use to do activities 1–8.

1 to think
2 to run
3 to swim
4 to ride a bicycle
5 to play soccer
6 to write
7 to do yoga
8 to learn English

You need your legs and your feet to run.   *And you need your arms, too.*

Common mistakes

I need warm socks because ~~the toes~~ are cold.
  my toes
      your
You need ~~the~~ legs ~~for~~ to run.

124

Unit overview: The main topics of unit 10 are parts of the body and face, appearance / personality adjectives, comparatives and superlatives, which are presented and practiced through the contexts of listening to part of a sports science class and a TV makeup artist, listening to the physical description of suspects given to a police officer, reading an article about an athlete, and listening to comparisons between two men. Sts also listen to / watch a video about "The New Seven Wonders of Nature". Sts read a quiz and practice making decisions by choosing a gig they'd like to go to.

10

10.1 Do you look like your mom?

Lesson Aims: Sts learn parts of the body and face to describe and talk about people's appearance and to describe suspects to a police officer.

Function
Talking about parts of the body and face.
Describing people's appearance.

Language
You need your legs and your feet to run.
I really like my ears and nose because they're not too big and they're not too small.
What does he look like?
He is short and slim.
He has long dark hair and brown eyes.

Vocabulary: The body and face (parts). Long dark hair, short fair hair, slim, overweight, average build, average height, short, tall. Wanted suspects.
Grammar: Irregular plural forms (feet, teeth). *What does he / she look like?*

Warm-up Have sts ask each other and answer as many question titles from units 1–9 as they can in about five minutes, plus a follow-up question to see what they can remember from the previous units. Ask some sts to say three answers they had in common or two things they found interesting about their partner's answers.

Tip If you are planning to use questions as the basis of an oral test at the end of this unit, remind sts that this is useful test rehearsal time out of class (e.g. on a cell phone) to prepare.

1 Vocabulary The body and face

A Books closed. Elicit names of some body parts: point to your own body (your head, hand, arm, stomach, back, etc.) and ask: *What's this in English?* When they don't know the answer, name it and ask sts to repeat after you.

Books open. Explore the photos. Ask: *Where are they? What's the relationship between them? What are they doing?* Point to number 1 in the photo and ask: *What's this in English?* (stomach). Check the pronunciation of the *ch* spelling in *stomach* /k/. Point to the numbered boxes 1–10 and tell sts to write the body parts in the correct boxes. Paircheck. Play ▶10.1 to classcheck answers. Ask sts to point to the body parts in the photos as they hear them. Encourage them to look at each other and compare answers as they do this.

Ask: *Have any of you attended a sports science class?* Elicit the plural form of *arm*. Say: *We say one* (gesture one with your finger) *arm and two … arms. What about hand? One hand and two …?* and let sts finish the sentence. Do the same for *finger, leg,* and *toe*. Focus on the box and make them aware of the two irregular plurals (both of which follow the same spelling pattern).

Tip Refer to the words in the Sounds and Usual Spellings chart on p. 158. Ask: *Do you remember any others?* (child / children, person / people, man / men, woman / women). These are the main irregular plural nouns.

Common mistakes Read with sts and explain that we use possessive adjectives (*my, your, his / her, our, their,* etc.) with parts of the body.

Give more examples:
*He's broken **his arm**.*
*She's washing **her hair**.*

| 1 stomach | 2 fingers | 3 legs | 4 toes | 5 arms | 6 chest |
| 7 head | 8 back | 9 hands | 10 foot / feet | | |

▶10.1 Turn to p. 322 for the complete audioscript.

Tip Add a "find the common sound" task. Write *write* on the board *Find two /k/ sounds in the ten body parts*. Sts work in pairs.

B Ask the class: *What body parts do you need to think?* (head). *What body parts do you need to run?* (legs, feet). Point to the prompts. Sts continue answering *What do you need to …?* questions 3–8. Classcheck. Expect a variety of answers.

1 head	3 every part of your body	4 legs, arms, hands, feet
5 head, legs, feet, toes	6 hands, fingers	
7 every part of your body	8 head (hands, fingers)	

261

10.1

C ▶10.2 Look at the photo and label these parts of the face. Listen to check.

ears	lips
eyes	mouth
eyebrows	nose
hair	teeth

D What part(s) of the face do you associate most with these verbs?

- ☐ eat
- ☐ listen
- ☐ look
- ☐ kiss
- ☐ read
- ☐ see
- ☐ smell
- ☐ speak
- ☐ watch

♪ *I feel it in my fingers, I feel it in my toes, Love is all around me, And so the feeling grows.* 10.1

E 🔴 Make it personal In pairs, think of more activities you can do with the parts of the body and face in **A** and **C**. Which pair has the most activities?

> You need your arms to get a taxi in the street.

> You have to have fingers to use a cell phone.

② Listening

A ▶10.3 Listen to descriptions of three suspects. Write the name, Adam, Charlie, or Mark, under the correct person.

B ▶10.3 Write the number of the suspect 1–3 for each item. There are four items for each suspect. Then listen again to check.

Weight
- ☐ average build
- ☐ overweight
- ☐ slim

Height
- ☐ average height
- ☐ short
- ☐ tall

Eyes
- ☐ blue eyes
- ☐ brown eyes
- ☐ green eyes

Hair
- ☐ long dark hair
- ☐ short dark hair
- ☐ short fair hair

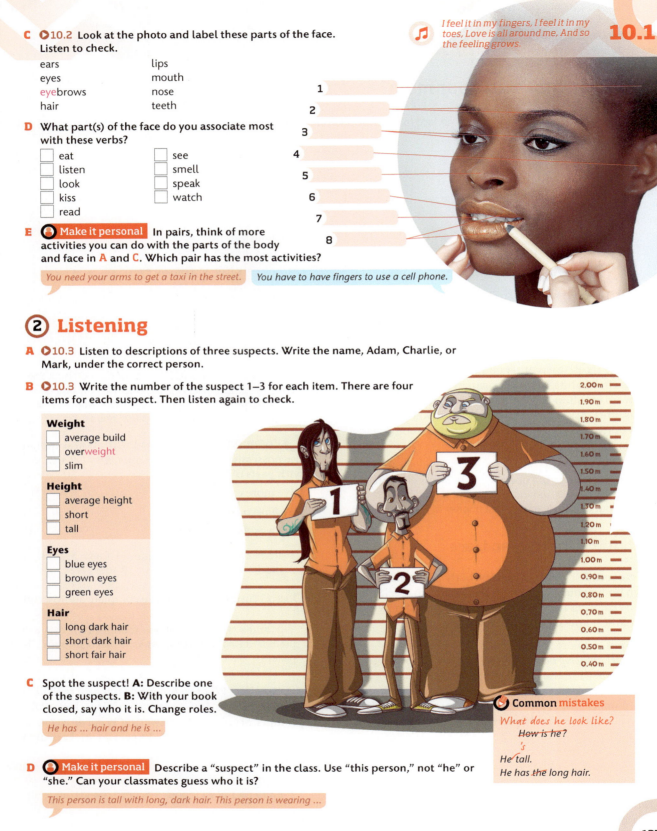

C Spot the suspect! **A:** Describe one of the suspects. **B:** With your book closed, say who it is. Change roles.

> He has ... hair and he is ...

⚠ **Common mistakes**

What does he look like?
~~How is he?~~

'𝑠
He ~~is~~ tall.
He has ~~the~~ long hair.

D 🔴 Make it personal Describe a "suspect" in the class. Use "this person," not "he" or "she." Can your classmates guess who it is?

> This person is tall with long, dark hair. This person is wearing ...

10.1

C Point to parts of your own face and elicit vocabulary sts already know and present items they don't. Have sts repeat parts of the face after you as you elicit / present them. Focus on the photo and ask *What's number 5?* (nose). Individually, sts match face parts 1–8 to the words. Play ▶10.2. Paircheck. Any spelling / pronunciation surprises? Sts check their answers. Classcheck.

> 1 hair 2 eyebrows 3 eyes 4 ears 5 nose 6 mouth
> 7 teeth 8 lips

▶ **10.2** Turn to p. 322 for the complete audioscript.

D Ask: *What part of our face do we use to eat?* (mouth / teeth). In pairs, sts match parts of the face 1–8 from **C** to the verbs. You could also add *taste*, which sts have seen before (p. 76) and elicit or teach *tongue* here, which is taught in 10.5. Classcheck. Note: that wat*ch* is similar to *see*. While we're not explicitly teaching this here, you could cover it here, if the class is strong enough. But it is fine if sts say, "see a movie / see my favorite TV program."

> 6, 7 eat   4 listen   3 look   8 kiss   3 read   3 see   5 smell
> 6, 8 speak   3 watch

E 🔑 **Make it personal** Change partners. Sts then think of other activities for different parts of the body. Set a time limit for this task to give sts motivation to do it quickly and make it more fun.

🎵 **Song line:** Turn to p. 335 for notes about this song and an accompanying task.

2 Listening

A Focus on the picture of the suspects. Sts hear the descriptions of Adam, Charlie, and Mark. Play ▶10.3 and tell sts to write the names of each suspect below the correct picture. Paircheck. Classcheck.

> 1 Adam   2 Charlie   3 Mark

▶ **10.3** Turn to p. 322 for the complete audioscript.

> **Tip** Ask sts to turn to the AS on p. 168. Sts listen again and notice the connections.

B Point to suspect 1 and say: *Look at his hair. Is it long or short?* (gesture "long" and "short"). Exemplify *dark* and *fair hair* with sts' hair or famous people's hair. Point to the 4th box of options (hair) and ask sts to write *1, 2,* or *3*, matching suspects to their description. Repeat procedures for the suspects' eye colors and physical shapes. Sts write *1, 2,* or *3* in all boxes. Paircheck. Play ▶10.3 again. Classcheck with answers on the board.

> **Tip** Search the Internet for images of celebrities as examples of *overweight / average build / slim* people. Make use of gestures to teach *tall / short / average height*. This will help to introduce comparatives in lesson 10.2.

> Weight: average build 1   overweight 3   slim 2
> Height: average height 1   short 2   tall 3
> Eyes: blue 1 and 3   brown 2
> Hair: long dark hair 1   short dark hair 2   short fair hair 3

C 🔑 **Common mistakes** Write on the board *1) What does he like? 2) What does he look like?* Elicit possible answers to both questions, e.g. *1) He likes chocolate. 2) He is tall and slim.* Drill the question *What does he look like?* with prompts *he / she / they / you*. Below question 2, write *He is ...* and *He has ...* and elicit possible sentences, e.g. *He is tall / short / average height*, etc. and *He has short dark hair and blue eyes*. Underline the words *hair* and *eyes* and for each of them ask: *Is it a noun or an adjective?* (noun). Make sure sts understand we use Subject + *have* + nouns and Subject + *be* + adjectives when describing people.

Sts play the game Spot the Suspect! Model the activity with the whole class. Get a st to ask you *What does he look like?* Describe one of the suspects, e.g. *He is tall and overweight. He has short fair hair and blue eyes* and ask the st to point / say which suspect you're talking about (Mark). In pairs, sts play the game. Use the example on the page to set this up and give a further example yourself. Monitor closely for accuracy. Sts might ask *How does he look?* or *How does he look like?* Refer back to 🔑 **Common mistakes** to correct sts.

D 🔑 **Make it personal** Sts play the same guessing game, but now describing "suspects" in the classroom. Make sure they start their descriptions with *This person* and not *he / she*. One st speaks at a time and the whole class tries to guess who the suspect / classmate is. Monitor closely for accuracy.

> **Tip** Split larger classes into two groups. Sts play the game and take turns describing people from their group or the other one. The other members of the group try to guess who is being described.

> **Tip** For extra practice of parts of the body, you can play Body Parts Bingo at any time. Sts write down six parts of the body, you call them out randomly until one st says *Bingo!*

Extra writing Sts can write a description of themselves, e.g. for an imaginary crime, and post it on the class website.

➡ **Workbook** p. 49

10.2 Are you like your dad?

1 Reading

A ▶10.4 Read the article and complete the information about Kelly. Listen and read again to check.

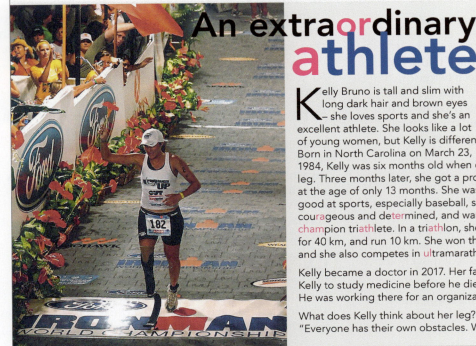

An extraordinary athlete

Kelly Bruno is tall and slim with long dark hair and brown eyes – she loves sports and she's an excellent athlete. She looks like a lot of young women, but Kelly is different. Born in North Carolina on March 23, 1984, Kelly was six months old when doctors amputated part of her leg. Three months later, she got a prosthetic leg and she began to walk at the age of only 13 months. She was very athletic in school and was good at sports, especially baseball, soccer, and running. She was also courageous and determined, and wanted to succeed. Now she is a champion triathlete. In a triathlon, she has to swim 1,500 m, ride a bike for 40 km, and run 10 km. She won the New York City Triathlon in 2008, and she also competes in ultramarathons – races of over 160 km.

Kelly became a doctor in 2017. Her father was a doctor, and he inspired Kelly to study medicine before he died in 2010 in an earthquake in Haiti. He was working there for an organization called "Food for the Poor."

What does Kelly think about her leg? "It's just an obstacle," she says. "Everyone has their own obstacles. Whatever yours is, just don't quit."

Full name: Kelly
Description:
Hobbies:
Occupation:

B ▶10.5 Read again and complete Kelly's timeline. Listen to a conversation to check.

6 months old	9 months old	13 months old	2008	2010	2017
doctors amputated part of her leg					

Is that thin? No, I know, slim!

C In pairs, match words 1–3 to definitions a–c. Then take turns miming a word from the article for your partner to say.

1 to quit
2 an earthquake
3 to succeed

a when the ground shakes
b stop, give up, abandon
c be successful

Common mistakes
~~is~~
What ~~does~~ she like?

D 🎯 **Make it personal** What do you think of Kelly's experiences and attitude? Choose three words to describe her. Compare your choices in groups. Do you know anyone like her?

| active | athletic | courageous | determined | extraordinary |
| energetic | heroic | ordinary | strong | |

Which words did you choose?

I think she's strong, determined, and heroic. My grandfather is like her.

10.2

10.2 Are you like your dad?

Lesson Aims: Sts learn to give better physical descriptions, to use comparative, and to describe / compare people's appearance and personality.

Function
Reading about an amazing athlete.
Expressing an opinion about an athlete.
Comparing people's appearance and personality.

Language
She was good at sports at school, especially baseball …
I think she's strong, determined, and heroic.
What about you?
Scott is taller than Jake.
Scott is more interesting than Jake.
Jake is happier than Scott.

Vocabulary: Recycling descriptions of people's appearance. Adjectives (active, athletic, courageous, determined, etc.).
Grammar: Comparatives (long and short adjectives).

1 Reading Recognizing cognates

A Point to the text title and ask: *Who's the extraordinary athlete?* Ask: *What's her name?* and have sts quickly find her name in the text. Individually, sts carry on reading and complete the chart. Set a time limit to encourage them to read quickly. Play ▶10.4 for them to listen and read the text. Paircheck. Classcheck with answers on the board.

> Full name: Kelly Bruno
> Description: tall, slim, long dark hair, brown eyes
> Hobbies: triathlons
> Occupation: doctor

Tip There are words / expressions in this lesson which would usually be considered too high-level for a Level 1 course. However, because of the monolingual context, many are cognates. Once sts have listened to the pronunciation and have stress clues for reference, they can use them immediately, which is motivating. Tell sts to revise all the cognates they have seen and to start a cognate dictionary and make sure they record the pronunciation.

B Ask: *What happened to Kelly when she was six months old?* and point to the first event in her timeline. In pairs, sts reread the text and complete Kelly's timeline with the other events from the text in **A**. Play ▶10.5 for sts to listen to two people talking about the article and check their answers. Classcheck. For a revision of past tense forms, make four columns with headings /t/, /d/, /ɪd/, and *irregular* on the board. Ask sts to categorize the past tense verb forms they hear according to how the endings are pronounced. (/d/ = *inspired, died*; /ɪd/ = *amputated, started*; irregular = *got, won, became*) As there are no examples of the /t/ pronunciation in the text, give some examples: *walked, wished, jumped, finished*.

> 9 months old: got a prosthetic leg
> 13 months old: began to walk
> 2008: won the New York City Triathlon
> 2010: father died
> 2017: became a doctor

▶10.5 Turn to p. 322 for the complete audioscript.

C Elicit pronunciation of the pink stressed words and ask *How many are recognizable from your language?* (*Earthquake* is possibly the most difficult word for Latin speakers to recognize but you can use the context of Mexico (2018), Ecuador (2016), and Haiti (2010) to help.) Elicit *shake*. Sts work in pairs to match the words to the definitions.

> 1 b 2 a 3 c

D 🔹 **Make it personal** Focus on the adjectives in the box and drill pronunciation for all of them. Again, most words will be cognates for Latin language speakers but check understanding. Sts ask each other in pairs *What do you think of Kelly?* Tell them they need to use three words from the box. Sts then discuss the second question.

Weaker classes Leave prompts on the board, as follows: *What / you think of Kelly? I think she's … . What about you?*

Round off the activity by asking sts to tell the class what their partners think of Kelly.

265

10.2

② Grammar Comparatives with *-er* and *more*

🎵 *What doesn't kill you makes you stronger, Stand a little taller, Doesn't mean I'm lonely when I'm alone.*

A ▶10.6 Listen to Maggie and Steve. Then match photos 1 and 2 to the adjectives.

☐ boring ☐ happy ☐ interesting ☐ sad ☐ short ☐ tall

B ▶10.6 Listen again and complete 1–4 with the word(s) you hear.

| happier | interesting | sadder | shorter | taller |

1 Scott is _____ than Jake.
2 Jake is _____ than Scott. Scott's _____.
3 It doesn't matter that he's _____ than Scott.
4 Scott is more _____ than Jake.

1 Jake   2 Scott

C Complete the grammar box.

> **Match 1–4 to a–d to make rules.**
> 1 Adjectives of one syllable:
> 2 Adjectives of two or more syllables:
> 3 Adjectives of two syllables (ending in *-y*):
> 4 Irregular comparatives:
>
> a *good → better; bad → worse*
> b use *more* plus adjective
> c change *-y* to *-i* and add *-er*
> d add *-er*.
>
> Spelling adjectives that end consonant + vowel + consonant (CVC), double the final consonant: "Russia is bigger than Canada." "It was hot yesterday, but today it's _____."
>
> ➜ **Grammar 10A** p.156

⏺ Common mistakes

My writing is ~~more bad~~ *worse* than my speaking.

Our apartment is ~~more big~~ *bigger* than Sheila's new house.

D Write eight comparative sentences with your opinions. Choose from the adjectives below or others of your own.

| bad | friendly | happy | interesting | relaxed |
| expensive | good | hard | nice | sad |

1 work / school   *School is more relaxed than work, I think!*
2 summer / winter
3 museums / movies
4 evenings / mornings
5 shoes / sandals
6 my mother / my father
7 the news in [country] / the news in [country]
8 rock music / hip hop music

E 🗣 **Make it personal** In groups, share your opinions in **D** and give reasons.

I think winter is nicer here because there aren't a lot of tourists.   *Yes, but it's cold!*

③ Listening

A ▶10.7 Listen and identify Brad's sisters Zoe and Rebecca in the pictures.

B ▶10.7 Listen again. Complete these sentences with Zoe (Z) or Rebecca (R). Are you more similar to Zoe or Rebecca?

1 _____ is friendlier than _____.
2 _____ is more generous than _____.
3 _____ is more timid than _____.
4 _____ is calmer than _____.
5 _____ is more intelligent than _____.
6 _____ is more organized than _____.

C 🗣 **Make it personal** Use adjectives from **2A**, **2D**, and **3B** (and others that you know) to compare yourself with someone in your family.

My dad is friendlier than me. He likes to go to parties and meet people. I'm a little shyer.

Do you look like him?   *Not really. He's a lot shorter.*

10.2

🎵 **Song line:** Turn to p. 335 for notes about this song and an accompanying task.

2 Grammar Comparatives with -er and more

Tip Books closed. For a fun presentation of comparatives, compare any pair of famous actors, musicians, etc. You can use the adjectives in **A**.

A Focus on the men in the photos. Elicit some physical descriptions, asking *What does he look like? What's he wearing? How's he feeling?* Focus on the six adjectives and ask: *What's the opposite of happy?* (sad). Gesture a person crying / make a sad face and teach them the word. Elicit the three pairs of opposites. Get sts to match them to the photos, 1 or 2. (*Boring* and *interesting* are subjective.) Play ▶10.6 and ask sts to compare with their ideas.

Tip Play ▶10.6. Pause after *what to do* and elicit the situation. Ask: *Who are they?* (friends). *Who has a problem?* (Maggie). *What is it?* (two people have invited her to two different parties on Saturday). Ask sts to guess who she chooses. Play the audio. Paircheck. Classcheck. Ask: *What did Maggie decide?* (She's going to go to both parties: the first with Jake from 7 to 10 p.m., and the second with Scott at 10 p.m.). Ask: *Do you think Maggie made the right decision?*

> 1 boring 1 happy 2 interesting 2 sad 1 short 2 tall

▶10.6 Turn to p. 322 for the complete audioscript.

B Focus on sentences 1–4. Play ▶10.6 again so sts can complete the sentences. Ask: *What's she doing?* (comparing them). Ask them to remember Steve's last line, too. Paircheck. Classcheck with answers on the board. Make sure sts notice the word *than* in all phrases. Pick up on the /ə/ in *than* and *-er* and drill example sentences from the activity, e.g. *Scott is taller than Jake.*

> 1 taller 2 happier, sadder 3 shorter 4 interesting

C **Common mistakes** Read with sts and ask: *Why can't you say **more stronger**?* Say: *You can say **more interesting*** (point to sentence 4). Write *tall, happy, short,* and *interesting* on the board. In pairs, ask them to notice what happened to the adjectives on the board in the sentences in **B**, and match the rules in the grammar box. Classcheck with answers on the board.

Tip For immediate practice, show some photos of locally famous pairs of people, places, cars, soccer teams, etc. for sts to compare in pairs, e.g. *(Robert de Niro) is younger / taller / richer / more famous / more interesting / better-looking than (Al Pacino).*

> 1 d 2 b 3 c 4 a
> hotter

Extra activity In pairs, sts say who would be the best guy for Maggie: Scott or Jake. Make sure they justify their choices with comparatives.

➡ **Grammar 10A** p. 156

D Write *school* and *work* on the board and elicit comparative sentences. Sts then write sentences 1–8, using the adjectives from the box. Monitor and check their grammar.

E 🔵 **Make it personal** Put sts into groups and ask them to compare their ideas. Tell them to ask *Why?* so they have to give reasons for their sentences.

3 Listening

A Play ▶10.7. Tell sts to listen to Brad and identify his sisters in the pictures. Classcheck.

> 1 Zoe 2 Rebecca

▶10.7 Turn to p. 323 for the complete audioscript.

Tip Write *What does he / she look like?* on the board. Ask sts to go to the AS on p. 168 and ask *Are they talking about Zoe's and Rebecca's appearance or personality?* (personality). Ask *What question do you use for personality?* and have sts find and underline two questions in the AS (*What's Zoe like? What's she like?*).

Write the prompts *friendly, shy, organized, calm, intelligent* on the board. In pairs, sts take turns asking and answering *What are you like? What's your (mother) like?* Monitor for accuracy.

B Sts listen to ▶10.7 again and complete sentences 1–6 with Z (Zoe) or R (Rebecca). Paircheck. Classcheck with answers on the board. **Books closed.** Do a quick repetition drill with sentences 1–6.

> 1 Z, R 2 Z, R 3 R, Z 4 R, Z 5 R, Z 6 R, Z

C 🔵 **Make it personal** Point to the lesson title question and ask: *Are you like your dad?* Have sts write down a few comparisons between them and someone in their family. Tell them to use adjectives from this lesson. In pairs, sts tell each other their sentences. Monitor closely for accuracy. Classcheck by asking sts to remember / tell the class their partner's comparisons.

Extra writing Sts can write several mini-comparisons about themselves and other members of their families, both physically (*What does he / she look like?*) and about their personalities (*What's he / she like*)?

➡ **Workbook** p. 50

10.3 Who's the most generous person in your family?

1 Reading

A ▶10.8 What is an enneagram, definition 1 or 2? Read the introduction to the website and choose the best answer. Then read and listen. Pause after each type and repeat the pink-stressed adjectives.
1 A new system to label positive and negative people.
2 A diagram that represents nine personality types.

Which type are you?

The en**nea**gram is an ancient **sym**bol used to de**scribe** person**al**ity types. It is a **cir**cle with nine points. Each of them repre**sents** a different personality type with both **neg**ative and positive characte**ris**tics. The enneagram says that we move between these negative and positive characteristics. All of us have one of nine basic personality types. Here is an example of each type:

 I'm **type 1**. I'm a per**fec**tionist and I'm idea**lis**tic. My negative side is that sometimes I'm very **crit**ical of other people.

 Type 4 people are romantic and want to understand other people. That's me! I like to understand how people feel, but sometimes I can be m**oo**dy.

 I love to have fun and be spon**ta**neous. I'm **type 7**, and I'm usually happy, but I can be dis**or**ganized when I'm trying to have fun!

 I love to help people and I'm very **gen**erous, but if you're my friend, I don't want to share you! I can be very po**sse**ssive. I'm **type 2**.

 I'm a **sol**itary person, and I want to try to understand what's happening in my world. That's **type 5**. Sometimes I feel depressed and that's my negative side.

 Type 8 people are strong, and they want to do important things for the world – that's me. My negative side is that I can get angry when you don't agree with me!

 Well, I'm **type 3**. I am am**bi**tious and good at things. If I do things well I can become more **arr**ogant – this is my negative side.

 I'm very **loy**al to my friends, and I'm very re**spon**sible. My negative side is that I can be sus**pi**cious. This is **type 6**.

 I'm **type 9** and I hate **con**flict, so I always try to be calm. The negative part of this is that I'm a little **pass**ive and accept things, just because I don't want any problems.

B Work in groups of three. Each student reads three personality types from **A** and completes their part of the chart with adjectives.

Student	Type	Positive side	Negative side
A	1	idealistic	
	2		
	3		

⚠ **Common mistakes**
Don't stress suffixes -ive, -al, -ous, or -ic.
po**sse**ssive, **pass**ive, **crit**ical, **loy**al, am**bi**tious, **gen**erous, idea**lis**tic, ro**man**tic

C ▶10.9 Listen to a conversation to check your answers. Which type(s) do you like best?

D 🎤 **Make it personal** What enneagram type are you? In groups, describe yourselves using adjectives from **A**. Similar or different?

> Well, I think I'm type 1. I'm idealistic, but I'm also critical.

> Me, too. I think I'm more critical than you.

10.3

2 Grammar Superlatives with -est and most

A Point to the photos and tell sts there's a corresponding question for each photo in the quiz. In pairs, sts match the questions to the photos. Ask: *What's the highest mountain in the world?* Gesture "tall / very high mountain" (sts should say Mount Everest). Ask: *What about the second highest?* (gesture "2nd"). Refer to the quiz title and introduction and make sure they understand the quiz is about second places, not first. In pairs, sts do the quiz. Play ▶10.10 for them to check their answers. If you need a tiebreaker to determine the winner, you could use this question: *Which is the second most populated city in the world? a) Shanghai b) Beijing c) Karachi.* (The correct answer in 2019 is Beijing, with 18.5 million people.) Ask: *Were there any surprises?* Pick up on and drill pronunciation of *-est* /ɪst/.

> **Tip** It is important to tell sts that the photos do not correspond to the answers of the quiz. The photos show the first in each category. The quiz is about the second in each category.

1 c   2 c   3 c   4 b   5 a

▶10.9 Turn to p. 323 for the complete audioscript.

> **Language tip** When talking about superlatives, Spanish and Portuguese speakers use the equivalent to the preposition *of* instead of *in*. So, when learning English, they may say *China is the most interesting country of the world*. Clarify the correct English usage with *in*.

B Read the three example sentences in the grammar box.

> **Tip** Give sts a visual example. Ask two average-height sts to stand up (not the tallest) and elicit the comparison, e.g. *(Julia) is taller than (Danielle)*. Then, ask all sts to stand up and ask *Who's the tallest in class?* The same demonstration would also work with adjectives *old* or *young*.

Then, have sts match a–d to the four rules. Sts study the quiz questions and decide the last question: *Which rule a–d do the superlative forms in the quiz follow?* Paircheck. Classcheck.

a add *-est*
b put *most* before the adjective
c change *-y* to *-i* and add *-est*
d good → the best, bad → the worst, more → the most
1 a   2 b   3 b   4 b   5 a   6 d   7 b   8 c

→ **Grammar 10B** p. 156

C Elicit the word order for question 1. Individually, sts order questions 2–7. Paircheck. Classcheck with answers on the board.

Common mistakes Read with sts and remind them of superlative forms of short and long adjectives. In pairs, sts take turns asking and answering questions 1–7. Monitor closely for accuracy. Encourage sts to give more complete answers. Classcheck. Elicit each pair's most interesting answers. Encourage sts to disagree if they want to, but make sure they use correct superlative forms.

1 What is the largest city in your country?
2 What are the most expensive restaurants in your town?
3 What is the highest building in your town?
4 What are the most popular beaches in your country?
5 What is the highest mountain in your country?
6 Who are the most famous people in the world?
7 Who is the youngest person in your class?

D **Make it personal** Sts work in new pairs. If they have access to the Internet, they can search for facts online. Refer them to the quiz and explain they have to write similar mulitple choice questions. Tell them to write their questions. Monitor and check grammar and make sure both sts write questions for the next stage. Put sts into new groups of four and tell them to ask their questions. You could make it a competition to see how many can answer most questions correctly in the groups. When they are finished, ask sts which questions were most difficult and to tell the class new things they learned.

→ **Workbook** p. 51

10.4 What's the best place in the world?

1 Reading

A Do you know the places in photos 1–9? Find examples of these things in the photos.

> a canyon   a cave   a forest   an island
> a lizard   a mountain   a river
> an underground river   a volcano   a waterfall

B ▶10.11 Quickly scan the article and match the places to photos 1–9. Then listen and read. Any pronunciation surprises?

C In pairs, try to answer 1–9. Then read again to check. Which place:
1 is in nine different countries?
2 has many different flowers?
3 has caves and lakes?
4 has an underground river?
5 is in two countries?
6 contains a volcano?
7 is a very deep canyon?
8 is home to a famous animal?
9 is a mountain over five kilometers high?

D 🟠 Make it personal   Do you agree with the choices? Which of the places do you most want to visit? Why?

> *I want to visit Table Mountain. I really want to go to South Africa, plus I love flowers.*

2 Pronunciation   Sentence stress

A ▶10.12 Watch the video and say which two of the nine places in the photos are not mentioned.

B ▶10.12 Watch again and number the places 1–7 in the order you hear them. Notice the most stressed words. Then read the pronunciation rules.

> We normally stress words that carry the message. Other words are often unstressed, reduced, and said faster. If you don't hear them, you can still understand the meaning.
>
> The <u>Pacific</u> is the <u>largest</u> <u>ocean</u> on <u>Earth</u>.

🟠 **Common mistakes**

the most common language in English is <s>the language most common</s> of the world.

C ▶10.13 In pairs, listen and underline the stressed words in each sentence.
1 The biggest lizard in the world is in Indo<u>ne</u>sia.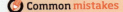
2 The Amazon rainforest is the largest in the world.
3 The River Nile is longer than the Amazon.
4 The <u>Arc</u>tic is the world's smallest ocean.
5 The Amazon River goes through six countries.

D 🟠 Make it personal   In pairs, search the Internet to find five surprising facts and say them, stressing the most important words. Then share the facts in groups. Which are the most interesting?

> *Look at this one! An astronaut wrote his daughter's initials on the moon!*
>
> *You're kidding!*

10.4 What's the best place in the world?

Lesson Aims: Sts contrast comparatives and superlatives, learn some stress rules and read / watch a video / talk about Wonders of Nature.

Function
Noticing and pronouncing sentence stress.
Writing comparative and superlative sentences.
Reading / Listening about The Wonders of Nature.
Talking about Wonders of Nature you'd like to visit.

Language
Everest is the highest mountain in the world.
São Paulo is the most populated city in the Americas.
Mexico City is more populated than New York.
The Amazon Forest is the largest rainforest in the world.
I want to visit Table Mountain.
I really want to go to South Africa and I love flowers.

Vocabulary: A canyon, a cave, flowers, an island, a lake, a lizard, a mountain top, a volcano, etc.
Grammar: Recycling comparatives and superlatives.

♪ **Song line:** Turn to p. 336 for notes about this song and an accompanying task.

Warm-up Turn to p. 158 and review the Sounds and Usual Spellings chart. Divide sts into groups of five. Give them time to cover the words and write down all 80 illustrated words, two per sound. Uncover the list at the bottom and check. They score one point for remembering the word and two points if they do so with the correct spelling.

Tip These picture words run throughout and are worth investing time in memorizing, for both form and spelling. Other common spellings for each sound are illustrated below the chart.

1 Reading

A Point to photos 1–9 on p. 131 and check if sts can recognize some of the places. Elicit vocabulary and introduce as many new, preferably cognate-friendly, words as possible. In pairs, sts find examples of each word in the photos 1–9. Classcheck. Elicit and drill pronunciation as necessary.

a canyon (8)   a cave (9)   a forest (7)   an island (1)
a lizard (5)   a mountain (3, 4)   a river (7, 8)
an underground river (9)   a volcano (6)   a waterfall (2)

B Elicit *Wonders of the World* (monuments) from sts, e.g. the Taj Mahal in India, Machu Picchu in Peru. Ask: *Which ones have you visited? Which ones have you heard of? Which would you most like to visit?* Tell sts to read about the New Seven Wonders of Nature and match the places to photos 1–9. Play ▶ ◯10.11 so sts can listen and read, and check answers. Paircheck. Classcheck.

Tip Get sts who haven't visited the places to ask questions like *When / go? Who / go with? How / get there? What / like?*, etc. for some genuine communicative practice.

1 Halong Bay   2 Iguazu Falls   3 Table Mountain
4 Mount Kilimanjaro   5 Komodo National Park   6 Jeju
7 Amazon rainforest   8 Grand Canyon
9 Puerto Princesa National Park

C Ask: *Which place is in nine different countries?* (the Amazon rainforest). Point to questions 1–9 and, in pairs, sts reread the text and answer them. Classcheck.

1 Amazon rainforest   2 Table Mountain   3 Halong Bay
4 Puerto Princesa National Park   5 Iguazu Falls   6 Jeju
7 Grand Canyon   8 Komodo National Park
9 Mount Kilimanjaro

D 👤 **Make it personal** In pairs, sts say if they agree with the selection of the New Seven Wonders of Nature in the text and ask which of those places they'd most like to visit and why. Classcheck by asking sts to report what their partner has said.

Extra writing Sts can research and write about the "seven wonders" of their country and post it on the class website or display it on the wall in the classroom.

2 Pronunciation Sentence stress

A Tell sts they're going to watch / listen to a video and at the end they need to say which two places were not mentioned. Play ▶ ◯10.12. Classcheck.

Grand Canyon, Mount Kilimanjaro

◯10.12 Turn to p. 323 for the complete audioscript.

B Play ▶ ◯10.12 again. Sts watch / listen and order the places 1–7. Classcheck. Point to the example sentence and focus on the four underlined words. Tell sts to read the information in the box. Check they are clear on the fact that the words that carry the meaning are also called content words and they are usually nouns, adjectives, and verbs (also adverbs). Drill the sentence in the box.

1 Amazon Rainforest   2 Halong Bay   3 Iguazu Falls
4 Jeju   5 Komodo National Park   6 Puerto Princesa National Park   7 Table Mountain

10.4

Tropical the island breeze, all of nature wild and free, This is where I long to be, La Isla Bonita.

The NEW Seven Wonders of Nature

In 2007, Bernard Weber started a project to find the seven most beautiful places in the world. People from all five continents voted for their favorite place. Here are nine of the finalists.

- [ ] **Komodo National Park** is in Indonesia. It opened in 1980 to protect the Komodo dragon, the largest lizard in the world. ___
- [ ] The **Amazon rainforest** is the largest in the world. It's located in nine different countries, and it's home to one of the world's longest rivers, the Amazon River. ___
- [ ] The **Grand Canyon** in the U.S. is more than 1.6 km deep. It has many canyons and caves. ___
- [ ] **Halong Bay** in Vietnam has thousands of rocks and islands in different sizes and shapes. It also has beautiful caves and lakes. ___
- [ ] **Table Mountain** in Cape Town, South Africa, got its name because it's flat on the top. More than 1,470 types of flowers grow there. ___
- [ ] The **Iguazú Falls** is one of the largest groups of waterfalls in the world. There are 275 different waterfalls there. The Falls are on the border between Brazil and Argentina. ___
- [ ] **Jeju** is the largest island in South Korea. It's home to Hallasan, a dormant volcano that's also the tallest mountain in South Korea. There are 360 other volcanoes around Hallasan. ___
- [ ] **Mount Kilimanjaro** in Tanzania is one of the highest mountains in the world. The top of Kilimanjaro is 5,895 m above sea level. ___
- [ ] The **Puerto Princesa National Park** in the Philippines has one of the world's longest underground rivers. ___

131

C In pairs, sts decide which words in sentences 1–5 are stressed. Play ▶10.13 for sts to check if their guesses were right. Classcheck with answers on the board. Play the audio again but pause after each sentence and ask for chorus repetition. Monitor closely for sentence stress.

1 biggest lizard, world, Indonesia
2 Amazon rainforest, largest, world
3 River Nile, longer, Amazon
4 Arctic, world's smallest, ocean
5 Amazon River, six countries

Tip Portuguese and Spanish also stress the words that carry meaning in a sentence. To help them understand word stress in English, write some superlative sentences in sts' L1 on the board and have them tell you where the stress is so you can mark it. Then, have sts identify the words that carry meaning. Guide them to notice that, in their L1, the stress is on the words that carry meaning.

Geographical note South America's Amazon River is the world's largest because it carries more water to the sea than any other river. The Amazon's discharge at its mouth is approximately 200,000 cubic meters per second.

Extracted from: http://geography.about.com/library/faq/blqzlargeriver.htm

Accessed on November 12, 2012

The Nile is the longest river in the world. The Amazon is the largest in volume of water.

The Nile is 6,650 km long. The Amazon is 6,400 km long.
Extracted from: www.unp.me/f8/top-9-longest-rivers-in-the-world-100757/

Accessed on November 12, 2012

D **Make it personal** This can be done online or at home. Sts need to have access to the Internet. To focus this task, ask them to search for facts related to nature, science, famous people, and events. Give some example superlatives to help them: *the longest / the richest / the tallest / the shortest / the biggest*, etc.

Sts work in pairs to write their sentences and practice pronunciation of the content words. Then, they work in groups of four or six and tell others in the group what facts they found. Ask the class afterwards: *What was the most interesting fact from your group?*

Workbook p. 52

10.5 What's your blood type?

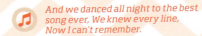
And we danced all night to the best song ever, We knew every line, Now I can't remember.

🆔 Skills Understanding facts

Vocabulary

A Match these words to pictures a–g. Which two words rhyme?

☐ a beard ☐ blood ☐ a brain ☐ a heart
☐ a lung ☐ fingernails ☐ a tongue

a

b

c

e

f

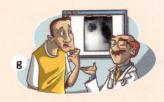
g

True or false? How much do you know about the human body?

1. The brain is more active at night than during the day.
2. Hair grows faster on your face than on other parts of your body.
3. Toenails grow faster than fingernails.
4. On average, women's hearts beat faster than men's.
5. Your right lung is smaller than your left lung.
6. Food is more important to humans than sleep.
7. The tongue is one of the strongest muscles in the human body.
8. The most common blood type in the world is Type A.

B ▶10.14 In pairs, take the quiz. Listen to check. Which fact is not illustrated?

C ▶10.14 Listen again and complete the words in 1–8. Which is the most interesting fact?

1. Your b_____ is very a_____ when you s_____.
2. It says that if m_____ don't shave, a b_____ can g_____ to more than 10 meters long!
3. Your t_____ grow slower than your f_____.
4. Women are s_____ than men, so their h_____ needs to move the blood f_____.
5. The h_____ needs a lot of s_____.
6. The l_____ time a person can go with no s_____ is 11 d_____.
7. When you eat or t_____, you are using your t_____.
8. The most c_____ blood type is _____.

For me, the most interesting fact is …

D 🔴 **Make it personal** *Memory test!* **A:** Ask a question from the quiz. **B:** Cover the quiz, answer, and give a reason. Google another fact of your own.

Is the brain more active at night than during the day?

Yes, it is. The brain is very active when we dream.

132

10.5 What's your blood type?

Lesson Aims: Sts practice understanding facts with comparatives and superlatives.

Function
Reading / Listening / Talking about human body facts.

Language
The most common blood type in the world is type A.
For me, fact 6 is the most interesting.

Vocabulary: Review parts of the body and face. More parts of the body and face (the beard, the brain, lungs, the heart, fingernails, toenails, blood, a tongue, blood type).
Grammar: Recycle comparatives and superlatives.

♪ **Song line:** Turn to p. 336 for notes about this song and an accompanying task.

Warm-up Ask sts to pair up with classmates they don't usually work with. In pairs, sts take turns asking and answering the question titles from unit 10. Get them to ask follow-up questions too. Monitor for use of grammar and vocabulary from these units. Go over good examples of both after sts finish speaking. At the end, ask sts to report one or two of their partner's answers to the whole class.

ID Skills Understanding facts

A Books closed. Review parts of the body and face. Point to some parts of your body / face and elicit the words from the class (e.g. your nose, your arm, your leg, your ears). In pairs, sts test each other for a minute. Monitor closely for vocabulary and pronunciation.

Books open. Point to pictures a–g and elicit vocabulary sts might already know, e.g. *heart*, *brain*, and *blood*. Help sts match the words to the correct picture. Classcheck. Drill pronunciation for all words (give extra help with *muscle*) and ask: *Which two words rhyme? Can you think of a word that rhymes with each word here?*

> a fingernails   b a brain   c a tongue   d a beard
> e blood   f a heart   g a lung
> rhyming words: a tongue, a lung

B Focus on the *True or false?* quiz heading in **A**. Ask sts: *How much do you know about the human body?* Point to facts 1–8 about the human body in the quiz and have sts decide in pairs whether each of them is true of false. Then, elicit some opinions about facts 1–8. Classcheck with ▶10.14. Ask: *Which fact is not illustrated? Who got the most answers correct? Who is the class expert on the human body?*

> 1 T 2 T 3 F 4 T 5 F 6 F 7 T 8 F
> Fact 6 is not illustrated.

▶10.14 Turn to p. 323 for the complete audioscript.

Tip Ask sts to turn to the AS on p. 168. Sts listen again and notice the sentence stress and the weak forms.

C Point to 1 and elicit the missing words. Make sure sts notice the first letter of each word has been given. Play ▶10.14 again. Sts listen to the conversation again and complete the facts. Paircheck. Classcheck. Ask: *Which is the most interesting fact, in your opinion?* Highlight the two example answers and get sts to give their opinions.

Tip Looking for pronunciation and spelling links between groups of new words is a great way to help sts process them intelligently and to notice aspects which may help them remember them more easily.

> 1 brain, active, sleep   2 men, beard, grow
> 3 toenails, fingernails   4 smaller, heart, faster
> 5 heart, space   6 longest, sleep, days   7 talk, tongue
> 8 common, O

D 🔴 **Make it personal** Refer sts to the speech bubbles and ask two sts to read them out. Ask: *What do you need to do in this activity?* Elicit instructions and check they are clear on the task. Sts then take turns answering questions. Monitor and make a note of good language and errors and go over this afterwards. Ask sts what questions they added and what they found most interesting about this lesson.

Tip Write the lesson title question on the board and ask: *How many different types are there?* Elicit answers. Say: *Who knows their blood type? If you know, please stand up.* Then ask standing sts: *What's your blood type?* getting them to sit down as they answer.

Biological note There are four blood types: A, B, AB, and O. Each blood type can be Rh+ or Rh– (rhesus positive or negative). Teach them how to say blood types in English (Type A+ (A positive), Type A– (A negative), Type B, Type AB, and Type O as in *phone*).

10.5 Is your English better than a year ago?

ID in Action Making choices

A ▶10.15 Listen and match conversations 1–3 to three of the photos a–d. Check (✓) the option they choose. Which of the three was the easiest to understand?

a
☐ Strawberry
☐ Chocolate
☐ Vanilla
☐ Coconut

b

c

d

B ▶10.15 Listen again and read AS 10.15 on p. 168 and try to remember all you can.

C In pairs, look only at the photos in **A** and practice the three conversations from memory. Create a similar one for the fourth picture.

So, which movie do you want to watch?

Hmm, the actors in the comedy are much better than in the others …

But the action movie looks so much more exciting!

D 🗣 **Make it personal** In pairs, discuss which of the three options in each of the situations below you'd like to do. Use any adjectives from this unit and make a decision.

Go and see Ed Sheeran, Taylor Swift, or Drake.
Continue studying English, start learning Chinese, or give up learning languages.
Go for a coffee, go home, or go out to dance.

Let's go see Ed Sheeran. He's the best.   *No, I prefer Taylor Swift. She's a better singer.*

10.5 Is your English better than a year ago?

Lesson Aims: Sts learn to express preferences and make suggestions.

Function
Listening to people making choices.
Making choices about restaurants, films, and gigs.

Language
I prefer the Chinese restaurant, but it's more expensive than the Italian.
Why don't we go to the Rolling Stones' gig?
I'm not sure. They're too old. Taylor Swift is more modern.

Vocabulary: Adjectives old, young, good, bad.
Grammar: Chunks for making decisions (*I prefer ...*, *Why don't we ...*, etc.).

ID in action Making choices

A Ask: *How many ice cream stores are there in this town? Which is your favorite store and flavor?* Focus on photos a–d and elicit what sts can see (a ice creams b movies c Italian / Chinese restaurants d beach / mountains). Sts listen to three conversations in which one photo is not mentioned. Ask them to match the three dialogues to the photos. Play ▶10.15. Paircheck. Classcheck.

> 1 c Chinese   2 a Vanilla   3 d beach

▶10.15 Turn to p. 323 for the complete audioscript.

B Say: *The people in the conversations were making decisions. Do you remember what they decided? Did they choose the Italian or the Chinese restaurant?* Play ▶10.15 for sts to notice the decisions made in each dialogue. Classcheck. *Can you remember any other interesting phrases they said?*

Ask sts to go to the AS on p. 168. For one minute, have sts read the conversations. Ask them to close the books and, in pairs, tell each other all they can remember. Classcheck.

Language tip A common mistake for Portuguese or Spanish speakers is the use of "that" / "than", instead of *to* when expressing preference, e.g. "I prefer pizza that" / "than sushi." Write *I prefer pizza to sushi* on the board and clarify that, in English, we use *to* when expressing preference between two nouns.

C In pairs, sts role-play one of the dialogues from the AS. Allow them to use the scripts at first. Encourage them to practice the dialogues without looking at the script and only at the photos.

Weaker classes Weaker sts may need to read, or at least refer to, the AS.

D 🔴 **Make it personal** Read the three options and ask sts to discuss their preferred option for each. If you prefer, give different situations that you know may be more relevant to your sts, or that refer to the local area. Encourage them to use the adjectives learned in unit 10.

Tip If sts struggle with language at this point, provide them with useful chunks / prompts on the board, e.g. *So what do you think?, Why don't we go to ...?, I prefer ..., He / She is more (fun / exciting / modern) than ...,* etc. Finally, ask sts to role-play their dialogues to the class.

Tip If you're working with a small group, you could have the whole class talk and decide the best option for each situation.

Round off the class by getting sts to ask each other the title question in pairs: *Is your English better than a year ago?* Ask sts to report what their partners said to the whole class. Hopefully they're all ending on a positive note!

➔ **Workbook** p. 53

➔ Ⓓ **Richmond Learning Platform**

➔ **Writing** p. 134

➔ Ⓓ **Café** p. 135

Writing 10 A family profile

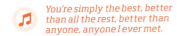
You're simply the best, better than all the rest, better than anyone, anyone I ever met.

A Read the family profile and complete Karina's family tree.

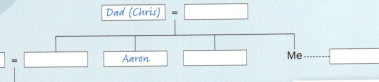

We're a close family. My dad, Chris, is an engineer. He's a big guy, a little taller than both my brothers. He's around 50, with gray hair and a beard, and he's strong and very calm. My mom, Kathy, works at the hospital as a nurse. She's quite short, with dark hair, and she's always busy – she's far more energetic than anyone I know.

My sister Rachel is the oldest. She's tall and slim with long dark hair, and she's the most athletic one in the family. She does triathlons – that's how she met her husband, Victor. He's a firefighter. They've been together for about five years and have a little girl, Salma. She's 15 months old and very cute.

My older brothers are twins. They look almost identical and are both very tall, approximately 1.95 m. In fact, Aaron is a little taller, and Ben is a bit heavier. Aaron is serious, ambitious, and idealistic; he can be moody and critical, but he's the most intelligent person I know. Ben is more spontaneous and very disorganized. He's less ambitious than Aaron, but a lot more fun.

Finally, there's Max the dog. He's 10 years old, which is around 70 in dog years! He has big brown eyes and long ears. He's very loyal and he's my best friend.

B Which member of the family:
1 is 10 years old?
2 is always busy?
3 is the most athletic?
4 is the tallest?
5 is fun to be with?
6 is the most intelligent?
7 is the youngest?
8 has the most energy?

C Read **Write it right!** and underline the connectors in the text in **A**.

> ✓ **Write it right!**
>
> To show approximation, you can use: *approximately, around*.
> To make a comparison more accurate, you can use: *a lot, much, a little*.

D Order these words to make sentences.
1 much / me / brother / heavier / my / than / is / .
2 know / I / he's / person / the / ambitious / most / .
3 romantic / think / boyfriend / far / is / more / than / her / people / her / .
4 a little / than / expected / exam / that / was / easier / I / .
5 her / than / Anya / much / is / ambitious / sister / less / .
6 men / stronger / is / a lot / some / than / she / .

E Answer the questions in **B** about your family, or a family you know.

F 🔘 **Make it personal** Write a family profile.

Before	Use your notes from **E**. Think of two more pieces of information about the family.
While	Use words / expressions to show approximation and more comparisons.
After	Check your writing carefully. Give it to your partner to check. Then email it to your teacher.

Writing 10 A family profile

♪ **Song line**: Turn to p. 336 for notes about this song and an accompanying task.

A Write *What's your family like?* on the board and remind sts of the meaning of *be* + *like*. Elicit a description from a student. Sts then ask each other about their families. Tell sts to look at the photo and read the profile to complete the family tree. Paircheck. Classcheck.

> Dad (Chris) = Mom (Kathy)
> Rachel = Victor   Aaron   Ben   Me   Max
> Salma

B Do question 1 with the class then sts answer questions 2–8. Paircheck. Classcheck.

> 1 Max the dog   2 Kathy   3 Rachel   4 Aaron   5 Ben
> 6 Aaron   7 Salma   8 Kathy

C Read **Write it right!** with the class and ask them to underline the connectors. You can do this on the board if you have an IWB and use the *Digital Book for Teachers*. There are a couple of extra connectors in the text which you could point out with a stronger class: *quite, a bit, about*.

> We're a close family. My dad, Chris, is an engineer. He's a big guy, <u>a little</u> taller than both my brothers. He's around 50, with gray hair and a beard, and he's strong and very calm. My mom, Kathy, works at the hospital as a nurse. She's quite short, with dark hair, and she's always busy—she's <u>far</u> more energetic than anyone I know.
>
> My sister Rachel is the oldest. She's tall and slim with long dark hair, and she's the most athletic one in the family. She does triathlons—that's how she met her husband, Victor. He's a firefighter. They've been together for <u>about</u> five years and have a little girl, Salma. She's 15 months old and very cute.
>
> My older brothers are twins. They look almost identical and are both very tall, <u>approximately</u> 1.95 m. In fact, Aaron is <u>a little</u> taller, and Ben is <u>a bit</u> heavier. Aaron is serious, ambitious, and idealistic; he can be moody and critical, but he's the most intelligent person I know. Ben is more spontaneous and very disorganized. He's less ambitious than Aaron, but <u>a lot</u> more fun.
>
> Finally, there's Max the dog. He's 10 years old, which is <u>around</u> 70 in dog years! He has big brown eyes and long ears. He's very loyal and he's my best friend.

D Sts order the words to make sentences. Classcheck.

> 1 My brother is much heavier than me.
> 2 He's the most ambitious person I know.
> 3 Her boyfriend is far more romantic than people think.
> 4 That exam was a little easier than I expected.
> 5 Anya is much less ambitious than her sister.
> 6 She is a lot stronger than some men.

E Sts can answer the questions in **B** individually, making notes of the answers, or in pairs, discussing the questions.

F **Make it personal** Read the steps Before, While, and After with sts so as to guide them to write their own family profile. Tell them to refer to Karina's profile in **A** as a model. As a follow-up activity and before they hand in their profiles, ask sts to exchange compositions and ask each other questions to find out more details about their families.

> **Tip** Ask sts to give feedback, identifying three things they think are good about the writing and one or two errors with the target language or other grammar / vocabulary.

10 Geminis

 Café

1 Before watching

A Complete 1–5 with these words.

attitude	genius	horoscope
tattoo	twins	zodiac sign

1 My sister has a bad _____. She thinks she doesn't have to work hard.
2 She has a _____ on each arm.
3 I read my _____ online every morning.
4 My _____ is Leo. My birthday is in August.
5 August is Gemini, and he thinks he's a _____.
6 I don't know any identical _____. Do you?

B 🔘 **Make it personal** In pairs, modify the sentences in A so they are true for you. Any similarities?

> My son has a positive attitude to school. He's never late.

C Complete the song lines with the comparative or superlative of the adjectives.

1 I'm your _____ (big) fan, I'll follow you until you love me, paparazzi. (Lady Gaga)
2 It seems to me, that sorry seems to be the _____ (hard) word. (Elton John)
3 Never mind, I'll find someone like you, I wish nothing but the _____ (good) for you. (Adele)
4 Just like a pill instead of making me _____ (good) you keep making me ill. (Pink)
5 Today this could be, the _____ (great) day of our lives. (Take That)

D Look at the photo. In pairs, predict four topics Lucy and Andrea will talk about. Watch to check.

> I think they'll talk about their plans for the weekend.

> Yes! Or … the celebrities in their magazines.

2 While watching

A Check (✓) the words you hear in the first part of the video.
- ☐ a beauty salon
- ☐ fashion and design
- ☐ your horoscope
- ☐ hair
- ☐ magazines
- ☐ pictures of celebrities
- ☐ outfit

B Complete with the comparative or superlative you hear.

Andrea: Can you believe her? That is _____ (ugly) outfit. No, no, this is _____ (ugly) outfit. And this is _____ (bad) nose job ever!
Lucy: Or, look at this one.
Andrea: No, no. That's ridiculous. She looked way _____ (good) before.
Lucy: I know. Her lips were already big and now she has _____ (big) lips in Hollywood.

C Watch the next part of the video. In pairs, remember what they say about:
1 the actress
2 the girl
3 Zoey
4 August

D Watch the final part of the video. True (T) or False (F)? Correct the false sentences.
1 Marlena was really nice to August at school.
2 She worked as an actress in scary movies.
3 She had the most wonderful voice and really positive attitude.
4 She wasn't mean to anyone.
5 The girls thought they saw Marlena in the salon.
6 Lucy's impressed by Andrea's love for her brother.
7 Andrea and August got their Gemini tattoos after the science fair.
8 August won the fair but then Marlena broke his experiment.

3 After watching

A In pairs, remember what these superlatives refer to.
1 the ugliest
2 the worst (x 2)
3 the biggest
4 the most annoying

B 🔘 **Make it personal** In pairs. Do you know anyone who has made changes to their physical appearance (cosmetic surgery, tattoos, piercings, etc.)? What do you think about them?

> Lady Gaga has lots of tattoos.

> Yes, you're right. My cousin has one of a dragon! I think it's cool.

ID Café 10 Geminis

1 Before watching

A Elicit / Drill pronunciation of all words. Sts complete sentences 1–6 with words from the box. Paircheck. Classcheck.

> 1 attitude   2 tattoo   3 horoscope   4 zodiac sign
> 5 genius   6 twins

B In pairs, sts make the sentences true for them. Give them your own examples to help demonstrate the task.

C Ask: *Are you good at remembering song lyrics?* Refer sts to the sentences and ask if they know the songs. Sts then complete the blanks with the correct form of the adjectives. Paircheck. Classcheck.

> 1 biggest   2 hardest   3 best   4 better   5 greatest

D Sts make predictions about the topics they will talk about. Ask them to make a note of these topics or write their ideas on the board. Play **Video 10** so sts can check their ideas. Classcheck answers.

2 While watching

A Point to the words and tell sts to check all they hear in **Video 10**. Paircheck. Classcheck. Move on to **B** before you replay the video.

> fashion and design, your horoscope, magazines, pictures of celebrities, outfit

B Read the dialogue with sts and tell them to complete it with a comparative or superlative according to what they remember from **Video 10**. Have them predict answers in pairs. Replay **Video 10**. Sts fill in the blanks. Paircheck. Classcheck with answers on the board.

> the ugliest   the ugliest   the worst   better   the biggest

C Ask sts to read the four options and then try to remember as many details as possible while they watch the next part

D Sts decide whether sentences 1–8 are true or false. Paircheck. If time allows, replay **Video 10** so sts can check their answers. Classcheck.

> 1 F Marlena was really mean to August in school.
> 2 F She was like someone in a really scary movie.
> 3 F She had the most annoying voice and really awful attitude.
> 4 F She was mean to everyone.
> 5 T
> 6 T
> 7 T
> 8 F August lost the fair because Marlena broke his experiment.

3 After watching

A Give sts a few minutes to think and remember what the adjectives referred to in the video. For weaker sts, ask them to make notes. Sts then discuss what they remember. After they finish, ask sts to share some of their ideas.

> 1 the ugliest: outfit
> 2 the worst: nose job, Marlena
> 3 the biggest: nose
> 4 the most annoying: voice

B **Make it personal** Change partners. In pairs, sts take turns asking and answering the questions. Encourage them to make comparisons, as shown in the model dialogue in the speech bubbles. Monitor closely for accuracy. Round up by having sts talk about their partners' answers.

R5 Grammar and Vocabulary

A **Picture dictionary.** Cover the words on these pages and use the pictures to remember:

page	
112	10 methods of transportation
115	10 jobs
118	6 life changes
121	4 short dialogues for photos a–d
124	10 parts of the body
125	8 parts of the face
125	descriptions of the 3 suspects
132	7 more parts of the body
159	16 picture words for lines 5 and 6 of consonants

B Read the chart and circle the correct alternatives in 1–5.

	Canada	China	Russia
Size in km²	9,984,670	9,598,086	17,098,242
Population	37 million	1,415 million	144 million
Life expectancy	82 years	76.5 years	71 years
Highest point	Mount Logan, 5,959 m	Mount Everest, 8,848 m	Mount Elbrus, 5,642 m

1 Russia is **smaller / larger** than China.
2 China has a **bigger / smaller** population than Russia.
3 Canada is **more / less** populated than Russia.
4 People live longer in China than in **Russia / Canada**.
5 Mount Logan is higher than **Everest / Elbrus**.

C **Make it personal** In pairs, ask and answer 1–4 with superlatives about your country.
1 Which country is the _____ (small / big)?
2 Which country has the _____ (large / small) population?
3 Where do people live the _____ (long / short)?
4 Which is the _____ (high) mountain?

D In pairs, ask and answer 1–6 about the picture.
1 What is Mark saying? And the chef's answer?
2 Are Fred and Rory honest? Why (not)?
3 What's Scott going to do? What's Laila going to say?
4 Is the floor going to get messy? Why?
5 Are Rachel and Owen happy? Why (not)?
6 Which character do you like best? Why?

E ▶R5.1 Order requests 1–6, adding a verb to each. Listen to check.
1 you / mind / / do / your / if / bike / I / ?
Do you mind if I borrow your bike?
2 a / / could / pen / me / you / ?
_____
3 door / I / / the / can / ?
_____
4 mind / I / / pizza / this / you / do / if / ?
_____
5 your / can / / laptop / I / ?
_____
6 earlier / home / / I / could / today / ?
_____

F In pairs, practice 1–6 in **E**. Vary your questions and answers.

Could I borrow your bike this afternoon?
No, sorry. I'm doing a triathlon next week. I need to train!

G Play **Describe it!** In groups of three, take turns describing an item from units 9 and 10 for your partners to guess. How many can you describe and guess in four minutes?

It's the opposite of (thin).
It's what you say when (you meet somebody).

H Correct the mistakes. Check your answers in units 9 and 10.
1 My mom is great cooker. (2 mistakes)
2 I'm student in UCLA and I'm an unemployed. (3 mistakes)
3 Sales assistants don't win a lot money. (2 mistakes)
4 I don't do anything special next weekend. (2 mistakes)
5 Are you gonna to go to the party? (1 mistake)
6 Could you borrow me your charger? (1 mistake)
7 We run the New York marathon the next week. (2 mistakes)
8 She looks like slim with the long curly hair. (2 mistakes)
9 I'm more big then my father. (2 mistakes)
10 It's the most old city of the country. (2 mistakes)

Review 5 Units 9-10

Grammar and vocabulary

A Picture Dictionary. Pairwork. Sts test each other and review the main vocabulary items learned in units 9 and 10. There are some possible techniques mentioned on p. 9 of the introduction section on how to work with the Picture Dictionary in order to review vocabulary. You can select whichever of these best suit the needs of your class.

B Individually, sts read the chart to choose the correct alternatives in sentences 1–5. Paircheck. Classcheck.

> 1 Canada is **larger** than China.
> 2 China has a **bigger** population than Russia.
> 3 Canada is **less** populated than Russia.
> 4 People live longer in China than in **Russia**.
> 5 Mount Logan is higher than **Elbrus**.

C 🔒 **Make it personal** Elicit the superlative form of *small* to complete question 1. Sts complete questions 2–4 with superlative adjectives. Paircheck. Classcheck with answers on the board.

At the end, have sts ask and answer the questions in pairs. Classcheck.

> 1 Which country is the smallest / biggest? China / Russia
> 2 Which country has the largest / smallest population? China / Canada
> 3 Where do people live the longest / shortest? Canada / Russia
> 4 Which is the highest mountain? Mount Everest

D Sts look at the picture and, in pairs, take turns asking and answering questions 1–6. Monitor closely for the use of *be going to*. Classcheck.

> Possible answers
> 1 Mark is going to take an order into the kitchen.
> 2 Fred and Rory are not honest. They are not going to pay.
> 3 Scott is going to ask Laila to marry him. She's going to say yes.
> 4 Yes, the wine is going to fall off the table.
> 5 They don't look happy or unhappy. They're not talking to each other.
> 6 Personal answers.

E Read sentence 1 with sts and tell them to order requests 2–6. Paircheck. In pairs, sts think of a verb for each blank. Play ▶R5.1 for sts to check their answers. Classcheck with answers on the board.

> 2 Could you lend me a pen?   3 Can I close the door?
> 4 Do you mind if I eat this pizza?   5 Can I use your laptop?
> 6 Could I go home earlier today?

▶R5.1 Turn to p. 323 for the complete audioscript.

F Change partners. In pairs, sts practice the dialogues in **E** as shown in the speech bubbles. Encourage them to vary the way they ask and answer. Tell sts to refer to p. 121, **ID in Action C**, for more options. Monitor closely for accuracy and appropriacy.

G Sts play **Describe it!** Have sts look back through units 9 and 10 and make a list of items to describe. Point out the examples and encourage sts to use the language given. Tell sts when you are starting the four-minute timer. The winner is the st who can describe the most items successfully in the four minutes.

H Tell sts to correct the sentences. Draw sts' attention to the number of mistakes between parentheses. In pairs, sts correct sentences 1–10. Whenever sts are uncertain, encourage them to flip back through units 9 and 10. Classcheck with answers on the board.

> 1 My mom is a great cook.
> 2 I'm a student at UCLA and I'm unemployed.
> 3 Sales assistants don't earn / make a lot of money.
> 4 I'm not doing anything special next weekend.
> 5 Are you gonna go to the party?
> 6 Could you lend me your charger?
> 7 We're running the New York marathon next week.
> 8 She's slim with long curly hair.
> 9 I'm bigger than my father.
> 10 It's the oldest city in the country.

Skills practice

Work it Harder, Make it Better, Do it Faster, Makes us Stronger, More than Ever.

R5

A In teams, play *Give us a clue!* **Team A:** cover card 2. **Team B:** cover card 1. Give one clue at a time. You score three points for a correct answer after clue a, two after clue b, or one after clue c. Write one extra question with three clues.

OK, number one. *The first clue is …*

Uh, we don't know. Give us the next clue.

CARD 1

1 People in this job:
  a studied a lot for their job.
  b usually wear a white coat to work.
  c work with animals.
2 People in this job:
  a wear a uniform.
  b have a dangerous profession.
  c look for criminals.
3 This type of transportation is:
  a common in big cities.
  b a kind of train.
  c under the streets.
4 This type of transportation is:
  a good for you.
  b free.
  c faster than walking.
5 a You have two of them.
  b They're part of your head.
  c You listen with them.

CARD 2

1 People in this job:
  a wear a mask.
  b are often unpopular with children.
  c care for our teeth.
2 People in this job:
  a serve people.
  b travel a lot.
  c work on a plane.
3 This type of transportation:
  a is large.
  b carries people.
  c travels on the road.
4 This type of transportation:
  a travels on the road.
  b is dangerous.
  c in heavy traffic, is faster than a car.
5 a You have lots of them.
  b They are part of your legs.
  c They are shorter than your fingers.

B **Make it personal** In pairs, ask and answer 1–3. Do you agree?
1 Which profession in **A** is the best paid / the most interesting / the most difficult / the most dangerous? Why?
2 Do you use the methods of transportation from the quiz? Which do you prefer? Why?
3 Which is more important to you: your eyes, ears, or hands?

C **Make it personal** In pairs, use the chart to ask and answer ten superlative questions. Do you agree?

Who / What is the	(bad) (delicious) (exciting) (famous) (funny) (good) (interesting) (young)	food restaurant singer actor writer student model cook politician	in the world? in this country? in this neighborhood? in our class?

D Read Laila's email. True (T), False (F), or Not mentioned (N)?

Hi Jenna!

All good with you? I hope so! Well, me, I'm finishing grad school soon and I have to start making plans now! I'm taking a vacation first. I'm going to Thailand with Scott for two weeks, I can't wait! But, before that, I'm moving out of my apartment, so right now I'm busy packing everything. I'm actually looking for a new apartment at the moment. Do you know anywhere I could stay? Fingers crossed! 🙂 Then when we get back from vacation, I'm going to find a job. Wish me luck!

Love, Laila

1 Laila left grad school recently. _____
2 Scott is Jenna's boyfriend. _____
3 After her vacation, she's leaving her apartment. _____
4 She's going to find a place to live alone. _____
5 She has a job to go to when she gets back. _____

E ▶ R5.2 Listen to Laila and Jenna and answer 1–3.
1 Which room does Jenna offer to Laila?
2 When is Laila going to fly to Thailand?
3 How long does she need the room for?

F **Make it personal** Question time.
In pairs, practice asking and answering the 12 lesson titles in units 9 and 10. Use the book map on p. 2–3. Where possible, ask follow-up questions, too. Can you comfortably ask and answer all the questions?

How did you get here today? *I came by car.*

Did you drive? *No, I came with a friend.*

137

Skills practice

A Sts play **Give us a clue!** Split the class into two groups, A and B, or, if working with very large classes, into larger groups comprised of A and B teams. Team A covers Card 2 and team B covers Card 1.

Refer sts to the model dialogue in the speech bubbles.

Team A starts: Sts give clues about number 1 from Card 1. Tell sts to give one clue at a time. Team B tries to guess the word being described. After number 1 is guessed, teams change roles: Team B gives clues to number 1 on Card 2.

Ensure that all sts have a turn reading the clues and trying to guess the words. For fun, make it a competition. Fast finishers can write one extra question with three clues.

> Card 1
> 1 a vet   2 a police officer   3 subway   4 bike   5 ears
> Card 2
> 1 a dentist   2 a flight attendant   3 a bus   4 a motorcycle
> 5 toes

B 🔘 **Make it personal**   In pairs, sts ask and answer questions 1–3. Encourage sts to agree / disagree with their partners' opinions. At the end, ask sts to report their discussion to the whole class.

C 🔘 **Make it personal**   Point to the list / column of adjectives in the chart and elicit the superlative forms for each of them. After that, elicit from sts a few combinations from the chart to form questions.

Try not to overcorrect as this is really intended to be a fluency activity. Praise all successful communicative responses at least as much as you intervene and "fix" errors. Sts, particularly in monolingual classes, need to see and feel themselves communicating successfully in English, no matter how few words they use or how many errors they make, in order to give them the courage to keep trying.

In pairs, sts take turns asking and answering questions from the table and agreeing / disagreeing with their partners' answers. Monitor closely for accuracy. At the end, ask some sts to report a few of their partners' answers.

D Ask: *Who is the email from?* (Laila.) *And who is it to?* (Jenna.) *What's the email about?* (Laila's finishing grad school and planning her vacation / making plans for the future.)

Sts read the email and decide if sentences 1–6 are T (true), F (false) or N (not mentioned.) Paircheck. Classcheck.

> 1 F   2 N   3 F   4 N   5 F

E Sts will hear Laila and Jenna talking on the phone. Allow sts some time to read questions 1–3 and play 🔘**R5.2**. Paircheck. Replay the track if necessary. Classcheck with answers on the board.

> 1 Her brother's room
> 2 On July 16
> 3 For about three and a half weeks

🔘 **R5.2**   Turn to p. 323 for the complete audioscript.

Tip Ask sts to turn to the AS on p. 168. Sts listen again and notice voiced *th* /ð/ and unvoiced *th* /θ/.

F 🔘 **Make it personal**   **Question time.** Sts look at the book map on p. 2–3 and take turns asking and answering the lesson title questions from units 9 and 10. Encourage them to ask the question titles from all ten units, and use this as the basis of an oral assessment. Monitor closely for accuracy and encourage sts to ask follow-up questions when suitable. At the end, ask them how they felt performing the task: *Do you feel comfortable with all of the questions? Which ones are easy? Which ones are difficult?*

Grammar Unit 1

1A Verb be ➕➖ and Yes / No ❓

The verb *be* only has three forms: *am, is, are*.
Use contractions when you speak or write informally.

➕		Contractions	
I *am*		I'm	a student.
You (singular) *are*		You're	Latin American.
He / She / It *is*		He's / She's / It's	Panamanian.
We *are*		We're	from Brazil.
You (plural) *are*		You're	students.
They *are*		They're	British.

➖	
I'm not	Colombian.
You're not or aren't	Asian.
He's / She's / It's not or isn't	Spanish.
We / You / They're not or aren't	Canadian.

		Short answers	
❓		Yes	No
Are you from the U.S.? Are you American?		Yes, I am. Yes, I'm Texan.	No, I'm not.
Is he a great player? Is she an OK actor? Is it a Chinese phone?		Yes, he is. Yes, she is. Yes, it is.	No, he's not. / isn't. No, she's not. / isn't. No, it is not. / isn't.
Are you students?		Yes, we are.	No, we're not. / aren't.
Are they actors?		Yes, they are.	No, they're not. / aren't.

We usually answer *Yes / No* questions with a short answer.
Are you Spanish? Yes, I am. NOT *Yes, I'm.*
Do not use contractions with ➕ short answers.

1B Adjectives and a / an + noun

a	an
She's **a** good person.	He's **an** interesting person.

Use *a* before a consonant sound / *an* before a vowel sound.

Adjectives

article adjective noun	article adjective noun
Neymar's a Brazilian soccer player.	Jennifer Lawrence is a fantastic actor.
Buenos Aires is a great city.	This is a green book. Those are green books.

In English, the adjective comes *before* a noun, and doesn't have a plural form.

1C Verb be: Wh- ❓

- What's your address?
- Where are you from?
- Why are they here?
- When's your birthday?
- Who's he?
- How are you?

Wh- question words come before the verb *be*.
Remember to invert in questions.
Where are you from? NOT *Where you are from?*

1D Demonstrative pronouns

Use *this / these* for things or people that are with you or near you (here).
- **This** is my pen. (It's with me.)
- **These** are my keys. (They're here.)

Use *that / those* for things or people that are with other people or distant from you (there).
- **That's** my pen. (It's on the table.)
- **Those** are my keys. (They're there.)

Remember to invert in questions.
Is this your book? NOT *This is your book?*
Use pronouns in answers.
Yes, it is. NOT *Yes, this is.*

1E Possessive adjectives

Subject pronoun	Possessive adjective
I	**My** car is blue.
You	**Your** green glasses are on the table.
He	**His** new laptop is fantastic.
She	That's **her** teacher.
It	This is my dog. Oh, what's **its** name?
We	**Our** friends are here.
You	Please turn off **your** cell phones.
They	**Their** city is really cool.

Possessive adjectives only have one form.
Possessive adjectives go before a noun or an adjective + noun.
My new shoes. NOT *Mys shoes news.*

Hi, I'm *your* teacher. **My** name's Bruno.

Unit 1

1A

1 Complete 1–5 with verb *be*. Use contractions when possible.

1. He _____ not from the U.S. He _____ Canadian.
2. We _____ not Hawaiian, we _____ Mexican.
3. It _____ not an Irish flag, it _____ an Italian flag.
4. They _____ from NY, but the statue _____ from France!
5. Her name _____ not Emma. It _____ Emily.

2 Complete 1–5 with verb *be*. In pairs, ask and answer. Remember to use short answers when possible.

1. _____ you Chilean?
2. _____ Christ the Redeemer statue in Spain?
3. _____ Justin Bieber American?
4. _____ you and Neymar friends?
5. _____ Idris Elba and Emily Blunt British?

1B

1 Correct the mistakes.

1. She's a girl cool.
2. They're not actors terrible.
3. Rio de Janeiro is a city excellent.
4. You're a player fantastic.
5. Is it a car Korean?

2 Order the words to make sentences.

1. interesting / is / San Francisco / an / city / .
2. actor / intelligent / an / Antonio Banderas / is / .
3. players / are / they / important / soccer / .
4. is / a / ridiculous / it / movie / .
5. excellent / I / student / an / am / .

1C

1 Order the words to make Wh- questions.

1. the name of / what / in Mexico / 's / that place / ?
2. are / when / home / you / ?
3. who / your / 's / friend / best / ?
4. you / why / are / here / ?
5. email / 's / what / address / your / ?

2 Correct the mistakes.

1. How's her name?
2. What's your favorite actor?
3. Is where his laptop?
4. Why you're in this class?
5. What's your favorite cities?

1D

1 Look at the examples and write questions and answers.

What are those?   Those are …
What's this?   This is …

2 Complete with the correct demonstrative pronoun.

1. _____ is a blue bookbag.
2. Is _____ your friend Tina?
3. _____ are my friends, Dan and Mary.
4. _____ is not my homework. _____ is my homework.
5. _____ is my email address.

1E

1 Correct two mistakes in each.

1. Her name is José and she's from Spain.
2. I think his name is Mary. She's american.
3. Is we in the same English class?
4. These is our teacher, Ms. Jones. We are in his class.
5. That not my phone. The my phone is black.

2 Complete with the correct possessive adjectives.

1. _____ name is Daniel and I'm from Mexico.
2. This is my friend. _____ name is Karina.
3. We are in English class together. _____ school is in California.
4. This is our new teacher. _____ name is Bruno.
5. These are my parents. _____ names are David and Marcia.

Grammar Unit 2

2A Simple present ➕ ➖

The simple present only has two forms:
1. The infinitive, used for *I / You / We / They*
2. The infinitive + *s* used for *He / She / It*

Use the simple present:
- for routines, habits, repeated actions
- for facts
- for scheduled events
- with time phrases (*every morning, sometimes*, etc.)

▸ *I wake up at 7 a.m. every day.* (routine)
▸ *You never study before tests.* (habit)
▸ *Banks don't open on weekends.* (fact)
▸ *We have a meeting today at 2 p.m.* (scheduled event)

Subject	➕	
I / You / We / They	live	in Paris.

Subject	➖	
I / You / We / They	do not / don't live	in Ecuador.

➕ Use *I, you, we,* and *they* + the infinitive. (I)
➖ Use *do* + *not* before the verb. Contraction = *don't*.
We don't have a car. NOT ~~We have no car.~~

Third person singular: *she, he,* and *it* + *s*

Subject	➕	
She / He	plays	volleyball.

Subject	➖	
She / He	doesn't play	golf.

Spelling rules:
Most verbs add -*s*: *knows, speaks, loves*.
Verbs ending in -*ch*, -*sh*, -*ss*, -*x*, or -*o*, add -*es*: *ch* – *watches*; *sh* – *finishes*; *ss* – *kisses*; *x* – *mixes*; *o* – *goes*.
Verbs ending in consonant + -*y*: change *y* to *i* and add -*es*: *study* – *studies*.

Notes:
do ends with *o*, so it is spelled -*es* (*does*) in the third person. When we use the auxiliary, the main verb is always an infinitive:
▸ *He works here. – He doesn't work here.*
▸ *She goes to school. – She doesn't go to school*

> Why does Superman have an ?
> Because he is the **third person**.
> He hate**s** kryptonite, he love**s** Lois, and he do**es**n't like bad guys!

2B Simple present ❓

A	S	I (O)	Short answers
Do	you	like sports?	Yes, I do. / No, I don't.
Does	he	live here?	Yes, he does. / No, he doesn't.
Does	she	play tennis?	Yes, she does. / No, she doesn't.
Do	they	work near here?	Yes, they do. / No, they don't.

To form a *Yes / No* question use:
Auxiliary (*do / does*) + Subject + Infinitive (+ object) = **A S I** (O).
Short answers use: *do / does* or *don't / doesn't*.

Q	A	S	I (O)
When	do	you	get up?
What	does	Joe	do in the evenings?
Why	does	Sue	work at night?
How	do	they	go to the beach?

To form a *Wh-* question use:
Question word + Auxiliary (*do / does*) + Subject + Infinitive (+ object) = **Q A S I** (O).

2C Frequency adverbs

100% → **always** → **usually** → **often** → **sometimes** → **occasionally** → **rarely** → **never** → 0%

▸ **How often** do you drink coffee?
  I **always** have two cups for breakfast.
▸ **How often** does he exercise?
  He **rarely** exercises.

Adverbs of frequency go before the main verb.

Use **time expressions** to say how many times something occurs.

▸ When do you go to the gym?
  I go to the gym at 7 a.m. on Mondays and Wednesdays.
  = I go to the gym **twice a week**.
▸ I go out every Saturday. = I go out **once a week**.

2D Prepositions of time

▸ *I sometimes go to work **at** around 5:15 p.m.*
▸ *We never go out **at** night.*
▸ *Dad usually visits me **at** Christmas.*

Use *at* with times, night, and holidays (without day).

▸ *Our vacation is always **in** January.*
▸ *See you **in** the morning / afternoon / evening.*

Use *in* with months and parts of a day (except *night*).

▸ *I do yoga **on** Tuesdays / Tuesday nights.*
▸ *I rarely work **on** Friday (evenings).*
▸ *We go shopping **on** weekends.*

Use *on* with days, day + part of a day, and *weekend*.

Unit 2

2A

1 Match the verbs to the people. Then complete 1–6.

drive exercise have breakfast
leave home live walk

1 Jane _____ at 8 a.m.
2 Mr. Jones _____ to work every day.
3 Andy _____ Jane to school by 8:30.
4 Mary and Jack _____ at 8 a.m.
5 Miguel _____ in the morning.
6 They all _____ in houses.

2 Make negative sentences about the people in 1.

1 Miguel _____ 8 a.m. (**not leave home**)
2 Jane _____ on weekdays. (**not exercise**)
3 Andy and Jane _____ at 8 a.m. (**not have breakfast**)
4 Mary and Jack _____ to work. (**not walk**)
5 Mr. Jones _____ to work every day. (**not drive**)
6 Mary _____ with Andy. (**not live**)

3 Circle the correct auxiliary.

1 What time **do** / **does** they usually get up?
2 When **do** / **does** he leave for work in the morning?
3 **Do** / **Does** you live with your parents?
4 Where **do** / **does** people go shopping in this neighborhood?
5 **Don't** / **Doesn't** we have school in December?
6 Where **do** / **does** their dog live?

2B

1 Order the words to make *Wh-* questions.

1 have / breakfast / you / do / when / ?
2 go / where / he / morning / does / every / ?
3 out / usually / time / what / she / does / go / ?
4 at / they / gym / often / exercise / the / how / do / ?
5 who / visit / when / go / you / do / you / Texas / to / ?

2 Complete the dialogue with auxiliaries.

A: Wow, you're here! _____ you always come to class this early?
B: No. I _____ always get here this early on Mondays.
A: I see. Well, _____ the class always start on time?
B: Hmm, sometimes it _____, but occasionally it _____. We never know.
A: Hey, _____ that girl always sit at the back of the class?
B: Yes, she _____. And she always listens to music before class.
A: I _____ that, too.

2C

1 Match the frequency adverbs to sentences 1–5.

1 They study on Mondays, Tuesdays, Fridays, and Sundays.
2 She goes to the office on Tuesdays and Thursdays.
3 He likes to relax and play video games every day.
4 They don't travel together.
5 We visit our parents twice a year.

☐ never   ☐ always   ☐ often
☐ rarely ☐ sometimes

2D

1 Circle the correct preposition.

1 We are always in class **at** / **in** / **on** 3 p.m.
2 Jackie is never **at** / **in** / **on** time for work.
3 You can complete this language course **at** / **in** / **on** 15 hours.
4 His birthday is **at** / **in** / **on** Monday. Let's have a party!
5 They start the semester **at** / **in** / **on** January.

291

Grammar Unit 3

3A Present continuous ➕ ➖

Subject	Present of *be*	Verb + *ing* + object	
I	am / am not 'm / 'm not	reading	this box.
You / We / They	are / are not 're not / aren't		
She / He / It	is / is not 's not / isn't	walking	right now.

Use the **present continuous** for actions in progress now.
Do not contract *am* + *not* (~~I amn't~~).

Spelling

Present participle (-*ing*)	Spelling rule
She's **listening** to a song. They're **playing** a game.	Most verbs, add -*ing*.
I'm **making** a cake. Our train's **arriving**.	Verbs ending in -*e*, change -*e* to -*ing*.
They're **running** a race. I'm **sitting** alone.	Verbs ending in consonant + vowel + consonant (CVC), double the final C + -*ing*.
Look! Mike's **boxing** now.	Don't double consonants *x* or *w*.

3B Present continuous ❓

Yes / No ❓

Present of *be*	Subject	Verb + *ing* + object	
Am	I		
Are / Aren't	you / we / they	listening	to the news?
Is / Isn't	she / he		
Is / Isn't	it	raining	now?

We usually answer Yes / No questions with a short answer.
▸ Aren't you coming with me? Yes, I am. / No, I'm not.

Wh- ❓

Wh-word	Present of *be*	Subject	Verb + *ing* + object	
Who	am	I	talking	to?
Why	are	you / we / they	driving	fast? that marathon?
When	is	she / he	running	
Where	is	it	raining	now?

We often use contractions in questions and responses.
▸ What's she doing?
  She's watching the weather report.

Present continuous for things happening around now

At the moment	Around now
I'm watching TV right now.	I'm watching TV a lot these days.
Look! He's taking her money!	I'm taking dance lessons this semester.

It is very common to use the **present continuous** to talk about things that are happening around now.

3C Simple present and present continuous

Use the **simple present** for a daily habit, routine, facts, or scheduled events.

Use the **present continuous** for:
▸ an action happening at the moment or a break in a routine.
▸ processes in progress but not necessarily happening right now.
  I'm doing a degree in Engineering (but I'm not studying today).
▸ for future plans/arrangements. (see Unit 9)
  What are you doing after class?
  I'm going home, then I'm working. NOT ~~I go home then I work.~~
  Are you coming out later?
  No, we're staying home all weekend.

Other future time expressions; *in a few minutes, this evening, tonight, tomorrow (morning), next week, this semester, in the summer,* etc. (See Unit 9)

Routine / Habit	Now, developing, or breaking routine
It never snows in March.	Look, it's snowing! (now)
I go to the salon every Saturday.	I'm driving to the salon. (now)

Adverbs of frequency and time phrases can help you decide when to use **simple present** or **present continuous**.

Simple present	Present continuous
always, sometimes, usually, often, every day, occasionally, never, first, next, then, rarely	at the moment, at this moment, just, right now, just now, now, still

Verbs for emotion, senses, or mental states

adore, appear, be, believe, dislike, hate, have, know, like, look, love, mean, prefer, remember, see, seem, smell, sound, surprise, understand, want.

Use the **simple present** not the present continuous with these verbs.

Correct	Incorrect
He believes you.	He's believing you.
She doesn't understand.	She's not understanding.
They like this party.	They're liking this party.
Do you remember it all?	Are you remembering it all?

Note: Phrases like "I'm loving it!" or "I'm liking this." are now used in informal conversation.

Unit 3

3A

1 Complete 1–6 with the present continuous.
1 Look, it _____ today. But it's really windy. (**not / rain**)
2 Why _____ her homework? (**not / do**)
3 Are you _____ a friend and _____ to me at the same time? (**text**) (**talk**)
4 Excuse me, I _____ the subway station. (**look for**)
5 Where _____ the other students _____ after class? (**go**)
6 I think they _____ for a coffee. (**meet**)

2 Look at the example and write sentences about the picture.
Victor is sleeping.

3B

1 Order 1–6 to form questions, then ask and answer in pairs.
1 right now / what / you / doing / are / ?
2 you / are / at the moment / with your family / living / ?
3 doing / much exercise / you / these days / are / ?
4 working / at the moment / where / are / you / ?
5 another / Chinese / are / or / studying / you / language / ?
6 learning / you / why / are / English / here / ?

2 Do 1–7 refer to right now (RN), around now (AN), or future (F)?
1 I'm watching a great show on TV, so I can't chat.
2 We're watching a lot of TV at the moment, usually around three hours a day!
3 I'm not coming on Monday, I'm going to the dentist's.
4 I'm working in Paris at the moment, lucky me!
5 I'm still working, so I can't come to the movies with you.
6 The sun is shining and we're sitting on the beach.
7 We're leaving early tonight to avoid the traffic.

3C

1 Correct the mistakes.

1 Hey. What do you do? Are you busy?
   No. I have lunch right now. What do you think of doing?

2 Where is she buying her clothes? I am wanting to go there, too!
   Yeah! She looking great. I think about buying the same dress!

3 Hey, where does he go? We having a meeting in a few minutes.
   I am not knowing. He talk on his cell phone in the hall.

4 I'm not believing you all finally here. Wow!
   Yeah, and we stay at a great hotel! We love New York in the summer.

5 I'm have a salad. Are you just eat a hamburger?
   No, I'm not. I'm always ordering French fries and a soda.

2 Circle the correct form of the verb.
1 I **'m talking** / **talk** to you on the phone and walking.
2 We often **are cooking** / **cook** dinner before watching TV.
3 I **'m hating** / **hate** talking about politics in class.
4 She **'s riding** / **rides** a bike to work, because her car is at the mechanic's.
5 He's not at the office, so he **emails** / **'s emailing** us from his smartphone.
6 I **'m not going** / **don't go** out tonight. I'm too tired.

Grammar Unit 4

4A Definite article *the*

English has only one definite article: *the*. The form never changes. Use *the*
- to refer to something already mentioned.
  I rent a place here. **The** *apartment's very nice.*
- when you imagine there's only one.
  Where's **the** *bathroom?*
- before superlatives and ordinal numbers.
  "Uptown Funk" is **the** *best Bruno Mars song.*
  These are **the** *first mangoes of the year.*

Do not use *the*
- with plural nouns.
  I love beans.
- with uncountable nouns.
  We often eat rice.
- to talk about things in general.
  I don't like politics, I enjoy watching detective movies.

4B Can

Can: ➕ ➖

Subject	Modal	Infinitive (+ object)
I / You He / She / It We / They	can can't / cannot	play the piano. drive a truck. speak English. dance well.

Can is a modal auxiliary verb with the same form for all persons. It is followed by infinitive without *to*.
We can swim. NOT *We can to swim.*
It means "be able to" or "know how to":
- *I* **can** *play tennis.* = *I'm able to play tennis.*
- *I* **can't** *drive* = *I don't know how to drive.*

Use *well, very well, (not) at all* to describe the level of ability.
- *He* **can't** *ride a bike* **very well***, but he* **can** *run.*
- *We* **can't** *play the piano* **at all***, but we* **can** *sing* **well***!*
- *She* **can't** *play golf, but she* **can** *play soccer* **very well***.*

Can: Yes / No ❓

Modal	Subject	Infinitive (+ object)	Short answers
Can / Can't	I / you / she / he / we / they	sing? come to the party? ski?	Yes, _____ can. / No, _____ can't.

- *I* **can** *speak English, but I* **can't** *speak Japanese.*

Can: Wh- ❓

Q	A modal (*can*)	S	I (+ object)
What	can	you	play on the piano?

Other meanings of *can*

Can has many different uses. Here are a few:
- **Possibility**: *You can read about the school on their website.*
- **Requests**: *Can I please see your passport and ID?*
- **Permission**: *You can use my car, but you have to come home by 10 p.m.*
- **Favors**: *Please can you pick me up at the airport?*

4C Possessive pronouns

Possessive adjective	Possessive pronoun
This is not **my** jacket.	**Mine**'s blue.
I think **your** keys are on the table.	These keys aren't **yours**.
Are those **his** glasses?	No, these green glasses are **his**.
Is that **her** phone?	No, this white phone is **hers**.
These are **our** sandwiches.	But those cookies aren't **ours**.
I think **your** coats are over there.	Are they **yours**?
Their house is beautiful.	Which house is **theirs**?

English only has six possessive pronouns. *Yours* is both singular and plural. A **possessive pronoun** substitutes a possessive adjective + noun.
Use *Whose* to ask about possession.
- *Whose book is that? Whose books are those?*
NOT *Of who is this book?*

4D Possessive *'s*

1. Add *'s* to names and nouns to indicate possession.
   That's the teacher's chair. NOT *That's the chair of the teacher.*
   - *That book is Jenna's.* → *It's hers.*
   - *Isn't that Nina's car?*
   - *This is someone's money, but not mine.*

2. Names ending in *-s*, use *'s* or just an apostrophe after the letter (*s'*).
   - *It's James's iPad.* = *It's James' iPad.*

3. Regular plurals add an apostrophe after the *s*.
   - *Isn't that your parents' house?*

4. Irregular plurals add *'s*.
   - *Which are your children's toys?*

Unit 4

4A

1 Circle the correct article in 1–10 (θ = no article).
1. I love **a / the / θ** dogs, but I hate **a / the / θ** cats.
2. We live in **a / the / θ** small house. My grandmother lives on **a / the / θ** same street.
3. Excuse me. Can you tell me where **an / the / θ** elevator is?
4. I need **a / the / θ** chocolate! Where's **a / the / θ** nearest grocery store?
5. My brother lives on **a / the / θ** first floor of that building. It's **a / the / θ** great apartment.
6. I never eat **a / the / θ** French fries at **a / the / θ** home.
7. **a / the / θ** Camila's sister has **a / the / θ** green eyes and **a / the / θ** beautiful dark hair.
8. I love **a / the / θ** sports and I'm really enjoying **a / the / θ** sports documentary series on Channel 5.
9. I never eat **a / the / θ** breakfast on **a / the / θ** weekends.
10. I hate **a / the / θ** messy people!

4B

1 Complete 1–5 with can / can't and the verbs.

drive   play   ride   swim   use

1. He loves American football. He _____ very well.
2. Is that your new bike? _____ you _____ it? It looks too big!
3. This hotel has an amazing pool. It's too bad I _____.
4. I don't know how she's a writer. She _____ a computer!
5. _____ you _____? I need to get home quickly!

2 What can / can't each person in the pictures do? Use your own ideas.
1. Lee can _____, but he can't _____.
2. Martin can't _____, but he can _____.
3. George can't _____, but he can _____.
4. Janice can _____, but she can't _____.
5. May can't _____, but she can _____.

3 Write Wh- questions for answers 1–5.
1. We can be at the train station by 6 o'clock.
   What time can you be at the train station?
2. You can take the train from Central Station.
3. He can't play soccer or baseball.
4. My mother can cook Italian food really well!
5. We can serve your breakfast from 7 to 10 a.m.

4 Are 1–5 ability (A), possibility (P), or request (R)?
1. Can you come to a party on Saturday night? _____
2. Can we open the window, please? _____
3. Can't we get tickets for the movie tonight? _____
4. Can I use your car this weekend? _____
5. Can she play the piano and sing? _____
6. Can you watch my bike for a moment, please? _____
7. Can you read that page without your glasses? _____
8. Can you help me with my homework, please? _____
9. Can you tell me how to get to Fifth Street? _____
10. Can you explain that word, please? _____

4C

1 Complete 1–5 with a possessive pronoun.
1. I'm a musician. That guitar is _____.
2. Marcy is always talking to somebody! I think that phone is _____.
3. Your sneakers are blue, not red. Are you sure these are _____?
4. It's really cold in here. Are those _____ sweaters?
5. It looks like Joe's wallet, but I don't think it's _____. He's traveling.

4D

1 Add the possessives ('s) or (').
1. Those are not my shoes, those are Marcus.
2. Where is your grandparent house?
3. My sisters new pants are yellow and blue.
4. That is Charles desk. His dad office is over there.
5. Her friends phone numbers are in her contact list.
6. My mom favorite album is *Queen Greatest Hits*.

295

Grammar Unit 5

5A There is / are ⊕ ⊖ ❓

There is / are ⊕ ⊖

	⊕	⊖	
Singular	There is a park near the river.	There's no / There isn't a	mall near here.
Plural	There are 20 people in the room.	There are no / There aren't any	animals in there.

Use *there is / are* to express "existence" in a physical space.
For negatives, use *there 's / is / are* + *no* or *there isn't / aren't* + *a / any*.

There is / are ❓

❓			Short answers
Is		a bank near here? an answer to the question?	Yes, there is. No, there isn't.
Are	there	any tourists here? any good restaurants in this area?	Yes, there are. No, there aren't.
Isn't		a swimming pool around here?	Yes, there is. No, there isn't.
Aren't		any cups on the table?	Yes, there are. No, there aren't.

Do not use contractions in ⊕ short answers.
Yes, there is. NOT ~~Yes, there's.~~

5B like / love / hate / enjoy / not mind + verb -ing

I	love	to swim / swimming
You	like	to camp / camping
Tom	likes	to read / reading novels.
Nina	doesn't mind	waking up early.
We	hate	cleaning the house.
You	enjoy	listening to music
My brothers	hate	playing baseball.

I don't mind going out on weekends. NOT ~~I don't mind to go out ...~~

Note: Use the gerund (verb + -ing which functions as a noun) as the subject of a sentence.
▸ Swimming is my favorite sport.
▸ Playing tennis is awesome.
▸ Studying on the weekend is boring!
Speaking English is important. NOT ~~To speak English is important.~~

5C Object pronouns

Subject		Object
I love animals, but I don't think they like		me.
You're always trying to help. But who's helping		you?
Martin says people don't understand		him.
Marta's not coming. But why don't you call		her?
Your bag's on the floor. Please put		it on a chair.
Don't worry, we're OK. Everything's fine with		us.
The windows are open, can you close		them, please?

English only has seven object pronouns. Use an **object pronoun** to substitute the **object** of the sentence.
It and *you* (singular and plural) have the same form for both subject and object pronouns.
The other five have different forms.
The object pronoun comes after the verb.
She loves him but he doesn't love her. NOT ~~She him loves but he doesn't her love.~~

Note: We usually refer to an animal with a name as **he / him** or **she / her**.
▸ Our dog, Bart, is great. He's really friendly! We all adore him.

5D Imperatives ⊕ and ⊖

⊕	⊖
Sit down.	Don't sit down.
Stand up.	Don't stand up.

Use **imperatives** to give orders or make requests.
▸ Go away! (order)
▸ Don't touch that! (order)
Imperatives only have one form for all persons.
Use *please* to make a request and sound polite.
▸ Please be quiet.
▸ Don't talk here, please.
There is no subject in an imperative sentence.
Don't go! NOT ~~Don't you go!~~

5E Comparatives and superlatives

To form comparatives and superlatives with long adjectives use **more / less + the most / the least** + adjective
▸ You're more adventurous than me.
▸ I'm less intelligent than you.
▸ Joao's the most adventurous in our class.
▸ Who's the least intelligent?
See p. 156 for more rules.

Unit 5

5A

1 Complete 1–5 with verb *be*. Contract when possible.
1. There _____ a racetrack in Belmont, Long Island.
2. There _____ very important horse races at the track.
3. We're happy because there _____ a new movie theater near us.
4. There _____ three nice hotels and two museums in this city.
5. In our city, there _____ a famous monument next to the station.

2 Order 1–6 to make sentences. Then change them so they're true for you.
1. city / is / football / there / an / enormous / stadium / my / in / .
2. this / restaurants / neighborhood / any / around / aren't / there / .
3. exhibition / is / good / our / local / museum / a / at / there / art / .
4. in / mall / no / there / is / neighborhood / this / .
5. street / my / there / swimming / a / on / isn't / pool / .
6. in / river / a / middle / city / of / our / clean / 's / the / there / capital / .

5B

1 Circle the correct alternative.
1. My son really loves **reading** / **read** comic books.
2. My little sister doesn't mind **to take** / **taking** piano lessons twice a week.
3. All our friends love **playing** / **play** and enjoy **watch** / **watching** international soccer.
4. I really like **go** / **going** to the movies, but it's expensive.
5. We hate **shop** / **shopping** and **to doing** / **doing** the laundry.

2 Correct two mistakes in each.
1. Anna loves wash dishes and to clean the bathroom.
2. I hate to reading novels. I like read biographies or true stories.
3. He doesn't mind to see a romantic movie sometimes, but he not enjoy horror movies.
4. We love to eating out on the weekend. We doesn't like cooking at home.
5. They hate to doing laundry, but don't mind to do dishes.
6. On vacation, I enjoy to hiking and snorkel, but I never go kayaking.

5C

1 Circle the correct object pronouns.
1. Ranger Juan works at this station. Please respect **him** / **her** / **it**.
2. There are bears in the park. Please don't feed **it** / **them** / **us**.
3. Cars are not allowed. Leave **their** / **they** / **them** in the parking lot.
4. Don't leave garbage at the campsite. Throw **him** / **her** / **it** in the trash.
5. We're here to help. Tell **us** / **we** / **me** what we can do for you.

2 Complete the dialogue with object pronouns.
A: I often come to this park. I really love _____.
B: Same here! Ranger Juan is so friendly. I like _____ a lot.
A: Yeah, and there are bears in the forest, but we never see _____.
B: Let's find someone who can help _____ see a bear.
A: Ranger Sarah gives bears medicine and food. Let's talk to _____.

5D

1 Which of 1–5 are orders (O) and which are requests (R)?
1. Please don't open the window. _____
2. Don't eat all the pizza! _____
3. Be quiet! _____
4. Open the door, please. _____
5. Listen to me! _____

2 Write the opposite instruction.
Come in. / *Go away.*
1. Sit down.
2. Listen to what I'm saying.
3. Please close your eyes.
4. Don't look at the board.
5. Please translate word for word.

Grammar Unit 6

6A Countable and uncountable nouns

Countable (C) nouns

Singular	Plural	Singular	Irregular plural
an apple	ten apples	a child	two children
a banana	three bananas	a foot	two feet
a bottle	two bottles	a man	five men
a box	eight boxes	a mouse	ten mice
a baby	four babies	a person	three people

C nouns can be singular or plural, regular, or irregular.
Most plurals are formed with -s, but also -es or -ies. There are a few irregular plurals.
Singular C nouns need an article (*a*, *an*, *the*), or quantifier (*some*, *any*, etc.)

Uncountable (U) nouns

U nouns have only one form.
Food-related: beer, bread, butter, cheese, chocolate, coffee, coke, ice, meat, milk, oil, pasta, pepper, rice, salad, salt, soup, sugar, tea, water, wine, yogurt.
Substances, materials: alcohol, deodorant, detergent, gasoline, gold, paper, perfume, plastic, metal, money, oil, wood.

1. To count U nouns use *a* / *an* / *number* + *portion* + *of*:
   a piece of bread; **two bottles** of water; **four spoons** of sugar.
2. Some U nouns have only a plural form and take a **plural verb**:
   glasses, gloves, jeans, pants, shoes, shorts, etc.
   ▸ My jeans **are** new. This is a new **pair of jeans**.

6B Quantifiers: *some* and *any*

Countable ⊕	Uncountable ⊕
We have **some** apples on our tree. (unspecified number)	I have **some** money for a tip. (enough to pay)
Countable ⊖	**Uncountable** ⊖
There aren't **any** children in the playground. (zero)	There isn't **any** water in the bottle. (zero)
Countable ❓	**Uncountable** ❓
Do you want **any** potatoes? (a portion)	Do you want **any** meat? (a portion)

Use **some** in questions when you expect the answer "yes":

Countable ❓	Uncountable ❓
Do you want **some** apples?	Do you want **some** cake?

Use **any** in questions when you expect the answer "no" or aren't sure:

Countable ❓	Uncountable ❓
Are there **any** tomatoes?	Is there **any** milk?

Use:
any with C nouns and the verb in the negative.
▸ There aren't **any** pens on the table.
no with C nouns and the verb in the affirmative.
▸ There are **no** pens or pencils on the table.
any with U nouns and the verb in the negative.
▸ There isn't **any** information on their website.
no with U nouns and the verb in the affirmative.
▸ There's **no** gas in the car.

6C Quantifiers: *a little, a few, a lot of*

Countable ⊕	Uncountable ⊕
I only eat **a few** fries on weekends.	There's **a little** cereal in the box.
There are **a lot of** donuts.	They eat **a lot of** pasta in Italy.
Countable ❓	**Uncountable** ❓
Do you eat **a few** cookies a day?	Can we eat **a little** ice cream?
Does he have **a lot of** tomatoes in his garden?	Does she eat **a lot of** bread for breakfast?
Countable ⊖	**Uncountable** ⊖
There aren't **a lot of** tickets available.	There isn't **a lot of** news online today.

6D *How much* and *how many* ❓

Question (*how much*)	Answer ⊕
How much **time** do you have?	There was **a lot of** information on the web.
How much **sugar** do you want?	Just **a little**, please.
How much **exercise** do you get?	I work out **a lot**.
Question (*how many*)	**Answer** ⊕
How many **dresses** does she have?	I know she has **a lot of** dresses. More than 20.
How many **eggs** do we need?	Only **a few**.
How many **people** are in the class?	**A lot**. Over 15!
Question (*how much* / *how many*)	**Answer** ⊖
How much **meat** do you want?	I don't want **any** meat. / I want **no** meat.
How much **homework** do you get?	Not much.
How many **apps** do you use?	I use **no** apps. / I don't have **any** apps.
How many **friends** do you have?	Not many.
How many **watches** do you have?	None. I use my phone.

Use:
how many to ask about **plural C nouns**.
how much to ask about **U nouns**.
any with a ⊖ verb, and **no** with a ⊕ verb in ⊖ answers.
any and **no** with the noun in the **plural** (**C nouns**).

Unit 6

6A

1 Circle the correct words in 1–5.
1. I'm buying some **cookies** / **cookie** for dessert.
2. I need some **information** / **informations** before I can go.
3. Remember to buy some **cheeses** / **cheese**, please.
4. Can you put some **breads** / **bread** in the toaster?
5. I'd like some **egg** / **eggs** for breakfast.

2 C or U? Cross out the odd word.
1. bread water ~~apples~~ milk
2. information books computers magazines
3. paper metal children rice
4. men women perfume bananas
5. eggs money dollars euros
6. news information paper ideas

6B

1 Complete 1–5 with *some* or *any*.
1. I'm looking for organic pasta, but I can't find _____.
2. There isn't _____ cheese for our sandwiches, so we're cooking _____ eggs instead.
3. There isn't _____ information about the restaurant online, so let's stay home and order _____ pizza.
4. I can't see _____ healthy dishes on the menu.
5. I don't eat meat, but I do eat _____ fish occasionally.

2 Complete questions 1–5 using *some* or *any*.
1. Is there _____ chocolate?
   No, of course not!
2. Do you want _____ of this delicious chicken?
   Yes!
3. Are there _____ tomatoes in this pie?
   No! It's a banana pie!
4. I know you don't like pasta, but do you want _____?
   No way, you can have it all.
5. It's your favorite cake, do you want _____?
   Yes, of course I do!

6C

1 Circle the correct quantifier.
1. I'm buying **a few** / **a little** sugar because I don't have **many** / **much** left.
2. Dad wants to cook **some** / **any** pasta, but he has **no** / **none**, so we're having potatoes instead.
3. There's **many** / **a lot of** meat, but not **much** / **many** milk in the refrigerator.
4. For breakfast, I like **a little** / **a few** eggs, but I don't drink **much** / **many** juice.
5. There's **no** / **any** fruit in the refrigerator for after dinner, just **a few** / **a little** chocolate.

2 Correct the mistakes. Are 1–5 true or false about you?
1. I don't eat a little meat, just once a week.
2. I drink a few juice for breakfast.
3. In my family, we eat a little bananas every week.
4. I don't drink a few coffee – about two cups a day.
5. I sometimes eat a few junk food, especially on weekends.

6D

1 Circle the correct words in 1–5.
1. How much **sugar** / **apples** do you want?
2. How many **pies** / **bread** is Mom cooking for dinner?
3. I don't know **how much** / **how many** coffee you drink, but I made a lot.
4. How much **money** / **dollars** did all this chocolate cost? You bought a lot!
5. He didn't know **how much** / **how many** eggs were in the refrigerator.

2 Complete 1–5 with *how much* or *how many* and match them to pictures a–e.
1. Please, tell the baker _____ cupcakes you'd like.
2. Let me know _____ people you're bringing to the party.
3. Look at this! _____ chocolate did you buy this time?
4. _____ slices of pie did they order?
5. _____ ice would you like in your drink?

Grammar Unit 7

7A There was / there were ⊕ ⊖

	⊕	⊖
Singular	There **was** a car in front of the house.	There was **no** gas in the tank. There **wasn't any** gas in the tank.
Plural	There **were** two cars on the street.	There were **no** parking spaces. There **weren't any** parking spaces.

Use: *there was / there were* for "existence" in a place in the past.
Form: *there* + past tense *be* + quantifier + noun phrase.
There was an accident in my street. NOT ~~It was an accident …~~
There weren't any police officers. NOT ~~Had no police officers.~~

There was / there were ❓

Past of *be* ⊕⊖		Object	Short answers ⊕⊖
Was / Wasn't	there	a gas station near here?	Yes, there was. / No, there wasn't.
Were / Weren't		a lot of people at the party?	Yes, there were. / No, there weren't.

Remember to invert in questions.
Were there any special offers? NOT ~~There were any special offers?~~
Note: Use *a lot of* + noun for large quantities.

7B Past of *be* ⊕⊖

Subject	Past of *be* ⊕	Past of *be* ⊖	Object phrase
I / She / He / It	was	was not / wasn't	at the party yesterday.
We / You / They	were	were not / weren't	

Be in the past tense has only two forms and two contractions.
Note: Be careful with *you* singular and plural.
▸ You were late. Yes, I was. Sorry.
▸ You were late. Yes, we were. The traffic was horrible.

Common past time expressions:
▸ She **was** here **a few minutes ago**.
▸ I **wasn't** at home **last night**.
▸ We **were** at the concert **last Saturday**.
▸ They **were** in Italy **in 2017**.

In time expressions, don't put *the* before *last* or *next*.
I was ill last night. NOT ~~the last night~~
See you next week. NOT ~~the next week~~

Yes / No ❓

Past of *be*	Subject	Phrase
Was / Wasn't Were / Weren't	I you	in your class? at the party?
Was / Wasn't	she he it	at the gym? in class? a good party?
Were / Weren't	we you they	in your class? in school? at work?

Short answers ⊕⊖

Yes, I was. / No, I wasn't.
Yes, you were. / No, you weren't.

Yes, she was. he it	No, she wasn't. he it

Yes, you were. / No, you weren't.
Yes, we were. / No, we weren't.
Yes, they were. / No, they weren't.

7C Prepositions of place

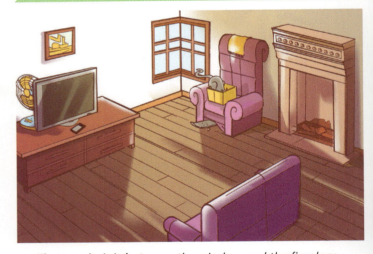

▸ The armchair is **between** the window and the fireplace.
▸ The box is **on** the armchair.
▸ The cat's **in / inside** the box.
▸ The picture's **above / over** the TV.
▸ The skateboard's **under** the armchair.
▸ The sofa's **across from / opposite** the TV.
▸ The phone's **in front of** the TV.
▸ The fireplace is **next to** the armchair.
▸ The fan's **behind** the TV.
▸ The TV's **below** the picture.

Unit 7

7A

1 Correct the mistakes in 1–5.
1 No had television when dad was a child.
2 In my last house, there wasn't any closets.
3 There no was food in that kitchen yesterday.
4 Were not there two bathrooms and a toilet downstairs?
5 No was there sofa or chair in that hotel room?

2 Order 1–5 to make sentences.
1 wasn't / furniture / any / her / in / apartment / there / .
2 balloons / there / no / at / party / his / birthday / were / .
3 snacks / table / the / on / were / there / .
4 was / kitchen / the / lemonade / there / in / .
5 napkins / any / there / on / table / the / weren't / .

7B

1 Order 1–5 to make questions and cross out the extra word in each.
1 were / at / park / on / you / last weekend / the / ?
2 yesterday / what / were / 6 p.m. / where / at / you / ?
3 there / who / with / you / where / was / ?
4 on / was / movies / there / any / were / last night / interesting / TV / ?
5 you / in / where / last Saturday / were / ?
6 in / your / country / family / this / were / last / the / summer / ?

2 Complete the dialogue with the past of verb be.
A: When _____ you in Seattle? I _____ there last year!
B: Wow! I _____ there in August. _____ you at the music festival?
A: No, I _____ . _____ there any good bands at the festival?
B: Yes, two local bands and one _____ from Australia.
A: Really? Cool. What _____ the name of the band?

7C

1 Look at the picture. True (T) or False (F)? Correct the false sentences.
1 The cell phone is under the desk.
2 The bed is opposite the desk.
3 There are shoes between the bed and the desk.
4 The night table is next to the desk.
5 There are books on the box.

2 Now circle the correct preposition.
1 The lamp is **in front of** / **behind** the alarm clock.
2 The poster is **above** / **on** the bed.
3 There are two boxes **under** / **behind** the desk.
4 The bed is **next to** / **opposite** the night table.
5 The socks are **on** / **under** the bed.
6 The light switch is **below** / **next to** the door.
7 The two shelves are **on** / **in** the wall, **over** / **below** the table.
8 There are lots of shoes **on** / **across from** the floor.

Grammar Unit 8

8A Simple past

Simple past ⊕ ⊖

⊕	⊖
Steve Jobs **lived** in California.	Jobs **didn't study** hard at school.
He **produced** the iPhone and iPad.	He **didn't finish** college.

Use the **simple past** to talk about completed past events. The simple past has only one form for all persons except *was / were*.
▸ I / You / She / He / It / We / You / They **lived** in Mexico City.
▸ I / She / He / It **was** born in Puebla.
▸ You / We / You / They **were** born in Cuernavaca.

Form the negative using *did not / didn't* + infinitive.
▸ Jobs **didn't live** with his parents. He **was** adopted.

Common past time expressions include:
▸ a few moments / minutes ago, an hour ago
▸ last night / Monday / week / month / year / century
▸ yesterday evening / afternoon / morning
▸ in 2017, in 1974

Simple past regular verbs – spelling rules

	Spelling rule
They **played** tennis yesterday.	Most verbs: verb + *-ed*.
She **danced** a lot at the party.	Verbs ending in *e*: + *-d*.
The car **stopped** at the traffic lights.	Verbs ending in consonant-vowel-consonant (**CVC**): double the final consonant + *-ed*.
They **tried** to talk to you last Monday.	Verbs ending in **consonant +** *y*: change *y* to *i* and add *-ed*.

8B Simple past irregular verbs

Irregular verbs don't end in *-ed*. They only have one form for all persons.

Most frequent irregular verbs

Infinitive	Past	Infinitive	Past	Infinitive	Past
become	became	hold	held	run	ran
bring	brought	keep	kept	say	said
buy	bought	know	knew	see	saw
do	did	leave	left	sit	sat
feel	felt	lose	lost	speak	spoke
forget	forgot	make	made	stand	stood
get	got	mean	meant	take	took
give	gave	meet	met	tell	told
go	went	pay	paid	think	thought
have	had	put	put	write	wrote
hear	heard	read	read		

Irregular verbs have no formation rules. For a complete list go to the Richmond Learning Platform.

8C Simple past ❓

Yes / No ❓

A	S	I	O
Did	she	go	to the concert?
Did	you	visit	your mom?
Did	they	call	him before the class?
Did	Fred	buy	a new laptop?

Did she call you this morning? NOT ~~She called you this morning?~~

To ask ⊖ questions, use the contracted form *didn't*:
▸ **Didn't he call** yesterday?

Short answers are the same for all persons.
▸ Yes, we did. / No, they didn't.
▸ Yes, she did. / No, he didn't.

Wh- ❓

Q	A	S	I	O
Where	did	you	go	last weekend?
What	did	she	do	last night?
When	did	they	get up	yesterday?
Why	did	he	stay	there?

8D Subject questions

Question word	Simple past	Object
What	happened was	yesterday? that noise?
Who	broke wrote went	the glass? the book? with you?

Subject questions ask for / about the **subject of the answer**.
Use **Wh-** words, but **don't** use the auxiliary *did*.
Who helped you? NOT ~~Who did help you?~~

Unit 8

8A

1 Complete with the verbs in parentheses.

Carmen Miranda was born in 1909, on February 9. She _____ (live) in Portugal until the age of one when she _____ (move) to Brazil with her parents in 1910.

In 1929, Carmen _____ (record) her first single and in 1932 she _____ (appear) in her first movie. She _____ (arrive) in the U.S. in May, 1939, and became a media sensation. She _____ (become) the most famous Latin American in the U.S. She _____ (die) at 46 of a heart attack on August 4, 1955.

2 Correct 1–5 by making them negative.
1 Carmen Miranda lived in Portugal all her life.
2 She moved to Brazil alone.
3 She recorded her first single in 1932.
4 She appeared in her first movie in 1939.
5 She arrived in the U.S. in 1955.

8B

1 Circle the correct forms in 1–5.
1 Bruce Lee **taught** / **teached** martial arts and **starred** / **stared** in movies in the 1970s.
2 His son Brandon Lee **didn't liked** / **didn't like** school and he didn't finish it.
3 Brandon **taked** / **took** a special test to get his high school diploma.
4 Brandon **studied** / **studied** acting and **makes** / **made** a few movies.
5 Brandon **get** / **got** engaged just before he **dead** / **died**.

2 Complete the story with these verbs.

be   not buy   dance   eat
get   go   have   look   love
see / not see   rain   walk

> I love London! On our first day it <u>rained</u> all day, and we _____ very wet! But, we _____ to the fabulous British Museum and _____ all types of amazing objects from around the world, including many from our country! I _____ the Egyptian mummies! It's huge, so we _____ more than 10% of what's there. After that, we _____ down Oxford Street and _____ in all the shops. I _____ anything as it was so expensive. That night, we _____ dinner in a pub. There _____ a cool band and we _____ for hours. A great day, even with the rain!

8C

1 Order 1–5 to make questions. Take turns asking and answering.
1 do / you / did / Saturday / last / what / ?
2 your / go / with / did / friends / you / ?
3 went / did / to sleep / what / do / you / before / you / ?
4 did / eat / last / what / you / night / ?
5 vacation / last / did / go / where / you / ?

2 Match answers 1–5 to questions a–e.
1 I went out of town last weekend for a few days.
2 I saw some old friends from college.
3 I really didn't spend any time in the city.
4 It rained all weekend, so we stayed in!
5 We watched TV and ate at the restaurant.

a What did you see downtown?
b What did you do at the hotel?
c Who did you meet up with?
d Where did you go for the holiday?
e What was the weather like?

8D

1 Complete dialogues 1–5 with the simple past of these verbs. Which are subject questions?

announce   give   go   happen   pay   tell

1 **A:** Hey, what _____? I heard they canceled your flight!
  B: Yes, they canceled it because of bad weather. Who _____ you that?
2 **A:** Sylvia saw it on TV. When _____ the airline _____ it?
  B: They didn't do it until 6:30 p.m. And my flight was at 7.
3 **A:** That's terrible. So, where _____ you _____ after that?
  B: I took a taxi back home with all my bags!
4 **A:** Gee … And who _____ for the taxi?
  B: Oh, at least the airline paid for it.
5 **A:** _____ they _____ you a new ticket?
  B: Yep, they gave me one for tomorrow morning.

2 Subject question (S) or object question (O)? Find the answers to the questions.
1 When did The Beatles start playing? _____
2 Who invented the name of the band? _____
3 What type of music did they play? _____
4 Why did the band finish? _____
5 Who composed the hit "Help!"? _____

Grammar Unit 9

9A Articles + jobs

Use an indefinite article in front of professions.
▸ *She's an engineer and he's a doctor.*

This becomes definite when we know who the person is.
▸ *The dentist I visit is very professional.*

Note: Don't use an article before adjectives with no nouns.
My father's retired. OR *My father's a retired firefighter.* NOT *My father's a retired.*

9B Future with *be + going to* ➕ ➖

Subject	➕	➖		Infinitive + object
I	'm	'm not		win this game tonight.
You	're	aren't		sing with the band tonight.
She / He	's	isn't	going to	get engaged when he finds a job.
We	're	aren't		visit you next week.
They	're	aren't		study English next year.

Going to is the most common future form in spoken English. Use *be* + (not) + *going to* + infinitive to talk about:
– general future plans: *I'm going to get married before I'm 30.*
– intentions: *We're going to study English next year, too.*
– predictions: *Look at those clouds. It's going to rain.*

Pronunciation of *going to* in informal speech is often *gonna*.

Be + going to – Yes / No ❓

Verb *be*	S		I + O	A
Am	I		finish my homework tonight?	Yes, I am. / No, I'm not.
Are	you		go out tonight?	Yes, I am. / No, I'm not.
Is	she	going to	find a job?	Yes, she is. / No, she isn't.
Are	we		travel to the U.S. next year?	Yes, we are. / No, we're not.
Are	they		work this weekend?	Yes, they are. / No, they're not.

Be + going to – Wh- ❓

Q	Verb *be*	S		I + O
What	are	you		do tonight?
When	is	she	going to	travel to Spain?
Why	are	they		study Mandarin?
How	are	you		get home?

9C Present continuous as future ➕ ➖ ❓

S	Verb *be* ➕ ➖	V + -ing + O
I	'm (not)	running the marathon next year.
You	're / aren't	leaving for Houston tomorrow.
She / He	's / isn't	taking a French class next semester.
We	're / aren't	having fish for dinner tonight.
They	're / aren't	visiting their grandparents in Europe in June.

Q	S	V + -ing + O	Short answers
Am	I	coming to your birthday party?	Yes, I am. / No, I'm not.
Are	you	watching the game tonight?	Yes, you are. / No you aren't.
Is	she / he	taking the bus to Mexico City?	Yes, she / he is. / No, she / he isn't.
Are	we	doing our homework at your house later?	Yes, we are. / No, we aren't.
Are	they	driving to the beach in the morning?	Yes, they are. / No, they aren't.

9D *Going to* and present continuous as future

Use both *going to* and **present continuous** to talk about future actions / events which are already decided or planned.
▸ *We are going to get a new car.*
▸ *We are getting a new car.*
There's only a subtle difference in meaning.

Going to

Use *be* + *going to* + **infinitive** for predictions and intentions.
▸ *I think they're going to win the election.* (prediction)
▸ *I'm going to do all my homework this weekend.* (intention)
▸ *Ted's going to try to take the day off on Friday.* (intention)

Present continuous for future

Use the **present continuous** (present of *be* + verb + *-ing*) for fixed plans, or personal arrangements with other people. (e.g., things you put in your calendar)
▸ *I'm leaving on the midnight train tomorrow.* (fixed plan = I have a ticket)
▸ *She's having dinner with her mom tomorrow!* (personal arrangement with other people)
▸ *We're buying Terry's car next week.* (personal arrangement with other people)

To differentiate from actions that are happening now, use a **future time expression**.
▸ *I'm leaving.* (**now**)
▸ *I'm leaving in half an hour.* (**future**)

Unit 9

9A

1 Complete the sentences with a / an / θ (θ = no article).

1. Tina's _____ actor.
2. Charlie's _____ flight attendant.
3. I'm _____ unemployed, so I'm going to look for a job.
4. Jack's going to be _____ cook.
5. You're not going to be _____ artist!

9B

1 Look at the picture. Are predictions 1–5 True (T) or False (F)? Look at the example and write sentences about the people in the picture.

1. Charlie's going to cook dinner. _____
2. The cat's going to eat the fish. _____
3. Tina's going to have dinner. _____
4. The kids are going to play games. _____
5. Jack and Jane are going to sleep. _____

Charlie's not going to cook dinner. He's going to wash the dishes first!

2 Circle the correct form in 1–5. Mark intention (I) or prediction (P).

1. People **is** / **are** going to buy flying cars in 10 years. _____
2. I **am going to** / **am going** be a pilot. _____
3. Food **is not** / **are not** going to be more expensive in five years. _____
4. Politicians **are not going** / **are not going to** have a salary. _____
5. I heard Walter and Jen **is** / **are** going to travel to Europe. _____

9C & 9D

1 Look at Rob's diary for next week. True (T) or False (F)? Correct the false ones. Look at the example and write some more sentences about Rob's week.

MONDAY	TUESDAY	WEDNESDAY	THURSDAY	FRIDAY	SATURDAY	SUNDAY
Dentist 9 a.m.	Coffee with Juan	Work	Work	Sofia's party 7 p.m.	Gym	Lunch with Mom and Dad.

1. He's seeing the dentist on Tuesday. _____
2. He isn't working on Monday. _____
3. He's working out at the gym on Saturday. _____
4. He's having dinner with his parents on Wednesday. _____
5. He isn't having coffee with Juan next week. _____

He isn't seeing the dentist on Tuesday. He's seeing her on Monday at 9 a.m.

2 Complete the dialogue with *be + going to* or the present continuous of the verbs.

Jake: Hey, Sam! How _____ ? (**do**)
Sam: Fine, and you? So, _____ to Lisa's party on Saturday? (**come**)
Jake: I don't know. Do you think she _____ me? (**invite**)
Sam: Sure! Check your email. Lisa _____ invitations tonight. (**send**)
Jake: Well, OK. I _____ my email later tonight. (**check**)
Sam: Um, do you need a ride? Pat and Sue _____ us there. (**drive**)
Jake: No, don't worry. I _____ the subway. (**take**)

3 Look at the examples and write sentences about:

1. your arrangements for this week / weekend;
2. your plans for this week / weekend (not arranged yet);
3. predictions for your future (jobs / marriage / retirement).

I'm visiting my parents this weekend.
I think they're going to have a barbecue.

Well, I'm going out with my girlfriend on Saturday. And maybe we're going to eat out on Sunday.

Grammar Unit 10

10A Comparatives with -er and *more*

Comparative adjectives usually go before *than*.
- Her husband is **stronger than** mine.
- Quito is **hotter than** Buenos Aires.

English is **easier than** Arabic. NOT ~~English is more easy than Arabic.~~

One syllable adjectives + -er

high	higher
long	longer
short	shorter

- Mike's **taller than** his brother.

One syllable CVC adjectives double the consonant + -er

big	bigger
hot	hotter
thin	thinner

- Belo Horizonte is **wetter** than Rio.

One / two syllable adjectives ending y change y to i + -er

friendly	friendlier
heavy	heavier
pretty	prettier

- My mom is **funnier than** my dad.

Use *more* before two-syllable adjectives ending -ed, -ing

bored	more bored
boring	more boring

Adjectives ending *-ing* describe things or people.
Adjectives ending *-ed* usually describe feelings.
- I feel **more tired** today than I did yesterday.
- Swimming is **more tiring** than walking.

Use *more* before adjectives with more than two syllables

dangerous	more dangerous
relaxing	more relaxing

- New York is much **more interesting** than Boston.

The opposite of *more … than* is *less … than*.
- Boston is **less interesting than** New York.

Irregular adjectives

good	better
bad	worse
far	farther / further

- I think Game of Thrones is **worse than** Modern Family.

10B Superlatives

Superlatives usually go after *the* and before a noun.
- Asia's **the largest** continent in the world.
- Raquel's **the most intelligent** person I know.

One-syllable → use *the* … + -est

high	the highest
long	the longest
short	the shortest

- Suriname is **the smallest** country in South America.

One-syllable CVC → double the final consonant + -est

big	the biggest
hot	the hottest
thin	the thinnest

- The Lion King is **the saddest** movie ever!

One / two syllable ending y → change y to i + -er

friendly	the friendliest
heavy	the heaviest
pretty	the prettiest

- Finland is officially **the happiest** country in the world.

Use *the most* before adjectives with two or more syllables

difficult	the most difficult
important	the most important

- My mom is **the most courageous** person in my family.

The opposite of *the most* is *the least*.
- He is **the least** interesting person in the room.

Irregular adjectives

good	the best
bad	the worst
far	the farthest / the furthest
less	the least

10C *Like*

Like has different meanings and uses.
It can be:
- a verb meaning *enjoy* or *want*.
  - I really like ice cream. I would like an ice cream right now.
- a preposition meaning *similar to*.
  - Your phone's like mine.
  - What's Stella like? Creative, just like her father.

Unit 10

10A

1 Complete 1–5 with a comparative and match to pictures a–e.

| dangerous | friendly | large | small | tall |

1 A whale's brain is about six times _____ than a human's brain.
2 Driving at night is _____ than during the day.
3 Dogs are usually _____ than cats.
4 Between the ages of 13 and 18, boys usually grow _____ than girls.
5 It's normal for one side of the body to be a bit _____ than the other.

2 Complete 1–5 with a comparative.
1 Sam is at math than other subjects. (**good**)
2 Carrie is than her classmates. (**organized**)
3 Their math teacher is than their science teacher. (**funny**)
4 Tomas thinks science is than English. (**inspiring**)
5 Marcus's mind is than his friend's. (**active**)

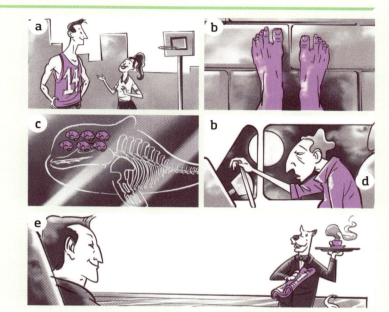

10B

1 Complete facts 1–5 with a superlative.

| far | friendly | high | long | populated |

1 Ojos del Salado, between Argentina and Chile, is _____ volcano on Earth.
2 Scientists believe Chimborazo in Ecuador is _____ place from the Earth's center.
3 The Andes Mountains in South America are _____ mountain range on the planet.
4 California is _____ state in the U.S.
5 The Abyssinian cat is _____ cat in the world.

2 In pairs, use *the most* or *the least* plus these adjectives to describe people a–d.

| annoying | bored | interested |
| talkative | tired | |

3 Find the answers to these questions. In pairs, compare your answers. Are they the same?
1 What's the tallest building in the world at the moment?
2 Who's the most popular singer in your country?
3 Who are the fastest male and female athletes in the world?
4 Where are the hottest / wettest / coldest places on Earth?
5 Which is the highest capital city in the world?

10C

1 Add *like* in the correct place in questions 1–5. Then write the answers.

I look more like my mom than my dad.
1 What's the weather today?
2 Do your look your dad?
3 Is your mom you?
4 Would you a coffee?
5 What's your best friend?

Sounds and Usual Spellings

S Difficult sounds for Spanish speakers
P Difficult sounds for Portuguese speakers

▶ To listen to these words and sounds, and to practice them, go to the pronunciation section on the Richmond Learning Platform.

Vowels

/iː/	three, tree, eat, receive, believe, key, B, C, D, E, G, P, T, V, Z	
/ɪ/	six, mix, it, fifty, fish, trip, lip, fix	
/ʊ/	book, cook, put, could, cook, woman	
/uː/	two, shoe, food, new, soup, true, suit, Q, U, W	
/ɛ/	pen, ten, heavy, then, again, men, F, L, M, N, S, X	
/ə/	bananas, pajamas, salad, minute	
/ɜr/	shirt, skirt, work, turn, learn, verb	
/ɔr/	four, door, north, fourth	
/ɔ/	walk, saw, water, talk, author, law	
/æ/	man, fan, bad, apple	
/ʌ/	sun, run, cut, umbrella, country, love	
/ɑ/	hot, not, on, clock, fall, tall	
/ɑr/	car, star, far, start, party, artist, R	

Diphthongs

/eɪ/ plane, train, made, stay, they, A, H, J, K
/aɪ/ nine, wine, night, my, pie, buy, eyes, I, Y
/aʊ/ house, mouse, town, cloud
/ɔɪ/ toys, boys, oil, coin
/oʊ/ nose, rose, home, know, toe, road, O

Sounds and Usual Spellings

Consonants

/p/	pig, pie, open, top, apple
/b/	bike, bird, describe, able, club, rabbit
/m/	medal, monster, name, summer
/w/	web, watch, where, square, one
/f/	fish, feet, off, phone, enough
/v/	vet, van, five, have, video
/θ/	teeth, thief, thank, nothing, mouth
/ð/	mother, father, the, other
/t/	truck, taxi, hot, stop, attractive
/d/	dog, dress, made, adore, sad, middle
/n/	net, nurse, tennis, one, sign, know
/l/	lion, lips, long, all, old
/s/	snake, skate, kiss, city, science
/z/	zoo, zebra, size, jazz, lose
/ʃ/	shark, shorts, action, special, session, chef
/ʒ/	television, treasure, usual
/k/	cat, cake, back, quick
/g/	goal, girl, leg, guess, exist
/ŋ/	king, ring, single, bank
/h/	hand, hat, unhappy, who
/tʃ/	chair, cheese, kitchen, future, question
/dʒ/	jeans, jump, generous, bridge
/r/	red, rock, ride, married, write
/j/	yellow, yacht, university

Audioscript

Unit 1

1.1
Hi! My name's Judy and I'm Brazilian. I'm from Brasilia. Nice to meet you.

1.2 Notice /ʌ/ and /uː/.
A OK. Let's check.
B Flag 1 is China.
A Yes, one point for you. And country 2?
B That's Spain.
A Yeah! Two points.
B Number 3 is Portugal.
A Right again!
B Flag 4 is the U.S.
A Yes! That's four points now!
B 5 is the UK.
A Correct!
B And 6 is Peru.
A Right! 6 points! And number 7?
B 7 is Canada and 8 is Argentina!
A Yes and yes! That's 8 points for you! Very good!

1.3
A Peruvian—that's flag 6, Peru.
B Argentinian—that's flag 8, Argentina.
A The next two are Spanish and British, flags 2 and 5.
B Then the North Americans, American and Canadian, flags 4 and 7.
A And finally, Chinese and Portuguese, flags 1 and 3.

1.4
A Am I Chinese?
B Yes, you are.
C No, you're not.
A Are you Argentinian?
B No, I'm not.
C Yes, I am.
A Is she Brazilian?
B No, she isn't.
C Yes, she is.
A Is he Colombian?
B No, he isn't.
C Yes, he is.
A Is it Indian?
B No, it isn't.
C Yes, it is.
A Are we Chilean?
B Yes, we are.
C No, we aren't.
A Are they Ecuadorian?
B Yes, they are.
C No, they aren't.

1.5
A Number 1 is Machu Picchu.
B Is it in Mexico?
A No, it isn't. It's in Peru.
B So photo 1 is Machu Picchu in Peru …

1.6 Notice *This_is* connects like one word.
This_is Machu Picchu, it's_in Peru. And number 2 is the Taj Mahal. It's_in India. Number 3 is the Alhambra. It's_in Granada, Spain. Photo 4 is Maroon 5. They're from the U.S. Photo 5 is Drake and Shawn Mendes. They're Canadian. And 6 is Salma Hayek. She's Mexican. Number 7 is Serena Williams. She's American. And this_is Neymar, in picture 8. He's Brazilian.

1.7 Notice the sentence stress.
1 **Mmmm!** This **pizza** is **amazing!**
2 This is cool. **Wheeeeeeeeee!**
3 I'm so **pleased!** The **teacher** says my **work** is **excellent.**
4 I **love** New **York.** It's a **fantastic city!**
5 **Yuck!** This **coffee** is **horrible!**
6 Here's an **important story** in the **newspaper.**
7 I think **Malala** is a **very intelligent person.**
8 **China** is an **interesting country!**
9 This **restaurant** is **OK.**
10 Bill **Gates** is a **very rich person!**
11 This **group** is **ridiculous!**
12 **No, no, no,** he's a **terrible actor! Terrible!**

1.8 Notice /z/.
1 Oh, yeah, I agree. Neymar's an amazing soccer player.
2 The Taj Mahal—it's a really cool monument.
3 Oh, yes, Serena Williams is a rich person. Very, very rich!
4 Malala's an intelligent person, in my opinion.
5 No, I don't want to go there on vacation! It's a horrible city!
6 I think Japan is an interesting country.
7 I really like him. He's an excellent teacher.
8 I love her movies. She's a fantastic actor.

1.9
1 a plane, a train
2 three, a tree
3 a pen, ten
4 nine, wine
5 a nose, a rose
6 a shoe, two
7 a car, a star

1.10
plane, train, A, H, J
three, tree, B, C, D, E
ten, pen, F, L, M
nine, wine, I
nose, rose, O
two, shoe, Q, U
car, star, R

1.11
G G K K N N P P S S T T V V W W X X
Y Y Z Z

1.12
eleven dollars, twelve cents, thirteen dollars, fourteen cents, fifteen euros, sixteen cents, seventeen dollars, eighteen euros, nineteen dollars, twenty cents

1.13 Notice the stress in these numbers is on the first syllable.
A A hundred dollars, please.
B OK, that's thirty, forty, fifty, sixty, seventy, eighty, ninety, a hundred. One hundred dollars.
A Thank you, sir. Have a great day.

1.14 Notice /θ/.
1 I'm eighty-five today. Happy birthday to me!
2 My address is seventy Blue Avenue.
3 I have eleven brothers and sisters!
4 This train ticket is ninety-nine dollars!
5 Hmm, I think it's fifteen miles to Los Angeles.
6 The number after thirty-nine is forty.
7 I have sixteen classmates in my English class.
8 Thirteen hours on a plane … I'm very tired!

1.15 Notice the stress in the questions.
A Name?
B Jack Moore.
A How do you spell that?
B J-A-C-K M-O-O-R-E.
2
A Good afternoon, I'm Dieter Quinn.
B How do you spell that?
A D-I-E-T-E-R Q-U-I-N-N.
3
A First and last name, please?
B Rochelle Johns.
A How do you spell that?
B R-O-C-H-E-L-L-E J-O-H-N-S.
4
A What's your name?
B George Wessex.
A Can you spell that, please?
B Sure. It's G-E-O-R-G-E W-E-S-S-E-X.
5
A Name, please?
B Joy Boscombe.
A How do you spell that?
B J-O-Y B-O-S-C-O-M-B-E.

1.16 Notice /m/ and /n/ endings and their spelling.
J = Jonathan K = Karin
J Welcome to Minerva reservations, Canada. This is Jonathan. How can I help you today?
K Hi, Jonathan. Can I make a reservation, please?
J Sure, no problem. I need a little information from you, OK? Uh, what's your name?
K Karin Spalding. That's K-A-R-I-N—Karin—S-P-A-L-D-I-N-G—Spalding.
J Where are you from? Are you Canadian?
K No, I'm not Canadian. I'm American, I'm from California.
J And what's your address, Ms. Spalding?
K 75 Kearny Drive, that's K-E-A-R-N-Y, San Francisco, CA 94133.
J Thank you. And what's your telephone number?
K Um, it isn't a Canadian number. It's American. OK? It's area code 415, then 675-8938.
J Thanks. And what's your email address?
K It's karinspalding@SPDG.com.
J Thanks. Now, what type of room …

1.17 Notice /k/ and /t/.
O = officer P = passenger
O Good morning. I'm sorry, ma'am, but we need to check your backpack, please.
P No problem. Here you are.
O OK, let's see. A wallet, a laptop, keys, hmm … a phone, a pencil, an umbrella, hmm … what's this?
P Oh, this is a lipstick. Look!
O I see … Are these glasses yours?
P Yes, they are.
O Right, and what are those?
P These are my earrings.
O OK … And what's that?
P Come on! That's a sandwich!
O Exactly! You can't enter this country with food, ma'am!!
P Uh-uh. Sorry, it's my first time here.
O I need to take that. Thank you.

1.18
1 lipsticks, laptops, wallets
2 earrings, pencils, keys, phones, shoes, umbrellas
3 sandwiches, glasses, boxes

1.19 Notice /i/ and /ɪ/.
R = Rosa J = Jake E = Ed L = Lara
1
R Is this your sandwich, Jake?
J Hmmm … Yes, it is. It's good!
R And are these your keys?
J Yes, they are, thanks.
2
E Is that your laptop, Rosa?
R No, it isn't. Is it your laptop, Lara?
L Yes, it is! That's my laptop!! It's new!
3
R & J Hey! Those are our potato chips!
L Come on, Ed! These are their chips! Stop eating them!
E Sorry.
4
E Where are my glasses?
R Er … Are these your glasses, Ed?
E Yes, they are. Thanks. How do they look?
5
J Are these your earrings, Rosa?
R No, they aren't my earrings. They're awful! Are they your earrings, Lara?
L Yes, they are. Hmpf! Thanks.

Audioscript

6
L That's someone's phone!
E I think it's her phone. Hey, Rosa! Is that your phone?
R No, it's isn't. My phone's new.
L I think it's his phone.
J Oh, yes, that's my phone ... Er ... Hi, Mom!

▶1.20
a Yellow is the color of bananas and the Simpson family. Yellow.
b White is the color of snow. White.
c Orange is a common fruit and also a color. Orange.
d The Pink Panther is a very thin cartoon animal. Pink.
e Charlie Brown is a small cartoon character with a dog called Snoopy. Brown.
f Blue Ivy Carter is Jay-Z and Beyonce's daughter. Blue.
g Red Riding Hood is a fictional character from a famous story. Red.
h Green Day are a Californian rock group who sing "American Idiot." Green.
i Black Friday is the day after Thanksgiving when everything is cheap. Black.
j "Purple Rain" is a popular Prince song. Purple.

▶1.21 Notice /b/, /g/ and /z/.
1 They're big and shiny ... The earrings.
2 They're big and blue. There are two in the picture ... The sofas.
3 They're small and gray ... The glasses.
4 It's not big or small, it's new, and it's on the table ... The laptop.
5 It's small and black, and it's on the sofa ... The phone.

▶1.22
1 I'm from Colombia, I'm Colombian.
2 I'm from Nigeria, I'm Nigerian.
3 I'm from France, I'm French.
4 I'm from Pakistan, I'm Pakistani.
5 I'm from the UK, I'm British.
6 I'm from Vietnam. I'm Vietnamese.

▶1.23 Notice /dʒ/ and the sentence stress.
M = Mark J = Justine
M Good evening! Welcome to Conference Registration. My name's Mark. How can I help you today?
J I need to register for the conference—your website isn't working.
M Certainly. I just need some information about you. First, what's your name?
J Justine Wallace.
M How do you spell that?
J J-U-S-T-I-N-E W-A-L-L-A-C-E.
M And what's your address, Ms. Wallace?
J 18 Jeffrey Drive, that's J-E-F-F-R-E-Y Drive, Denver, Colorado. Zip code 80202.
M Thank you, and what's your phone number?
J 720 is the area code and the number is 988-3405.
M Thanks. And what's your email address?
J It's jwallace26 at webmail dot com.
M Thanks, now, and can I ask about your nationality? Where are you from?
J I'm American.
M OK—so, you're all set—you're registered for the conference.

▶1.24 Notice /h/.
A Hi, Judy! How are you?
B Good, thanks. What about you? What's new?
A Not much. Things are good.
B So are you ready for the meeting? I hear ...

▶1.25
A How's it going?
B Fine, thanks!
A How are you doing?
B Not bad. And you?
C I'm well, thank you!
A What's up?
B Not much.

▶1.26 Notice the sentence stress.
1
A Here's your gift! Happy Birthday!
B Thank you!
A You're welcome.
2
A Excuse me.
B Oh, I'm sorry.
3
A Oops, I'm sorry.
B Don't worry about it.
4
A See you later!
B Bye for now!
5
A We have a great fish special today.
B Excuse me. Can you say that again, please?
A Sure ... I said we have a great fish special today.
6
A D'ya wanna order now?
B I don't understand.
C Oh, sorry. Are you ready to order?

Unit 2

▶2.1 Notice to /tə/ and to a /tu:wə/.
I = interviewer
I When do you go to these places?
A I go to a café every day before class for a coffee.
B I go to church on Sundays.
C I go to the gym after school.
D I usually go home after work.
E I go to a party on Saturdays.
F I go to school Monday through Friday, and Saturday morning, too!
G I go to the grocery store on Saturdays.
H I go to work at eight o'clock.

▶2.2 Notice stress on days of the week.
1 Sunday, lovely Sunday!
2 Oh, no! Tomorrow's Monday. School! Yuck!
3 Gee, it's only Tuesday—four more days of work.
4 I have an important meeting on Wednesday.
5 Only two more days of work—it's Thursday.
6 Today is Friday. Let's go to a bar after work!
7 Great! It's Saturday! My favorite day! No more work for the weekend!

▶2.3
1
A What time is it?
B It's midnight! Happy New Year!
2
A Time to get up!
B What time is it?
A It's six fifteen. Time to get ready for school.
3
A What time is it?
B It's six a.m. Come on, let's go and check in!

4
A Good evening. Welcome to "The Daily News." It's ten o'clock. I'm Katia Jones.
5
A What time is it?
B It's eight thirty. We're late!
6
A What time is it?
B It's six forty-five. We're right on time.

▶2.4 Notice /ɜr/.
I = interviewer W = woman M = man
I Hi, I'm doing a survey about sleeping habits. What time do you get up?
W Uh, um, at six in the morning. I go to school at six forty-five.
I Thanks. And what time do you go to bed?
W Hmm. At around ten p.m., during the week. Maybe at twelve midnight on Friday and Saturday.
I So you get about eight hours sleep a night?
W Yeah, that's it ... Bye!
I Thanks.
I Hello, we're doing a survey about working hours. What time do you go to work?
M Hmm ... I go to work at eight thirty a.m.
I Every day?
M No, no. From Monday to Friday. I don't work on Saturdays and Sundays.
I And when do you get home from work?
M Well, I usually get home at around six fifteen p.m. OK? Bye!

▶2.6 Notice /eɪ/ and word stress.
Well, I wake up at around six thirty a.m., but I don't get up immediately. I stay in bed for three or four minutes, then I get up and make my bed. Then I exercise for thirty minutes. After that, I take a shower, shave, get dressed and have breakfast—coffee, juice, and cereal.
Then I brush my teeth and, finally, leave home at around eight a.m.

▶2.7 Notice /s/ and /z/.
He wakes up at eight a.m., but he doesn't get up. He sleeps again and then he gets up at 8:50 a.m., but he doesn't wake up! After he wakes up he makes his bed. Then he exercises and he shaves. After that, he doesn't take a shower, he doesn't brush his teeth, and he doesn't get dressed!

▶2.9 Notice the intonation at the end of each question.
1
A What's your full name?↘
B I'm Miguel Hernandez. But please call me Mickey.
2
A OK. And ... are you Spanish?↗
B Yes, I am. I'm from Valencia.
3
A Where do you live?↘
B In Madrid, I work there. It's an amazing city!
4
A Do you live with your parents?↗
B No, I don't. I live with my girlfriend, Monica.
5
A Where exactly in the U.S. do you plan to travel to?↘
B Alaska. They say it's a beautiful place.
6
A Do you know anyone in Alaska?↗
B Yes, my sister lives there.

2.10 Notice the intonation at the end of each question.

M = Miguel W = woman
W Hm … Who's this?
M That's my brother, Juan.
W Uh-huh. Does he play soccer?
M Yes, he does! He loves soccer.
W And who's that?
M That's my sister, Martina.
W So you have a sister! Where does she live?
M In Alaska. And, those are my parents.
W Wow, Alaska! And, do your parents live there, too?
M No, they live in Barcelona.

2.11

R = Ruben J = Jan M = Maria G = Greg L = Lucia
Ge = Gerry Mi = Milton
R I never look at my phone when I eat. It's a really bad habit. Oh, except when I have lunch alone!
J I sometimes check my phone at breakfast. My dad gets really mad!
M My boyfriend occasionally checks his phone when we go out together. I think that's OK.
G My mom never checks her phone, so I have to call her!
L My friends send me WhatsApp messages all day, so I always check my phone every five minutes—when I'm not busy.
Ge My boss always sends me messages late at night, so I often need to check my phone at dinner.
Mi My son plays games and uses apps on his phone all the time, so he's always on it. I insist he stops at dinner!

2.12

I = interviewer G = Ginny
I What's your full name?
G Virginia Marie Lomond.
I Interesting! And how old are you?
G Umm … OK, I'm 23.
I Don't worry! Do you have a pet?
G Yes, I do. I have a dog called Boston. I love him!
I Where do you live?
G I live in Paris.
I And where does your family live?
G Well, my mom lives in Paris and my dad lives in L.A.
I Great! Do you have any brothers or sisters?
G No. I'm an only child.
I I see. And what do you do on the weekend?
G I sleep a lot and occasionally go for a walk. And I never work on Mondays so I often go to bed late on Sundays.
I OK, and what time do you go to bed on weekdays?
G I usually go to bed at 11 p.m. from Monday to Thursday, but I sometimes go to parties!
I And our final question! Do you exercise regularly?
G No, I don't exercise. Well, only occasionally (when I walk Boston). I'm a little lazy!

2.13

1
A Enjoy your meal!
B Thanks! You too!
2
A Merry Christmas!
B Merry Christmas!
3
A Have a good trip!
B Thanks!
4
A Congratulations!
B Thank you very much.
5
A Happy New Year!
B Happy New Year!
6
A Happy birthday!
B Thank you!

Review 1

R1.1

R = hotel receptionist S = Sandy
R What's your name?
S Sandy Clark.
R Are you American?
S No, I'm Canadian.
R Where in Canada are you from?
S Vancouver.
R That's a nice place. What's your address?
S 76, Burton Road.
R And what's your email address?
S saclark@hotmail.com
R Thank you. Here's your key. Room 89.

R1.2 Notice /ə/ in the articles and prepositions.

My name's Carla, I'm 17, and I live in La Floresta, a small town in Spain about 13 km from Barcelona. I live with my mom and dad and my six brothers and sisters, so, with me, that's a total of nine people in our house. It's a big family—I have over 40 cousins! I'm a student and I study at the University of Barcelona. I get up at 6 a.m. every day. It takes me 50 minutes to get to school, which starts at 8 a.m. In my free time, I like watching movies, and my favorite actors are Penelope Cruz and Jennifer Lawrence. I usually go to the movies on Monday night after school.

Unit 3

3.1 Notice /j/ and /dʒ/.

I = interviewer M = meteorologist
I You're a meteorologist, please tell us about the symbols that are used to represent weather.
M Well, when we use weather symbols we try to use symbols that everyone will understand. This yellow circle means the sun, or sunny weather. A cloud means cloudy, obviously, and this symbol means a wind or windy. The gray cloud is for fog or foggy weather. The cloud with these little lines means rain or rainy weather. And the white cloud with stars means snow or snowy conditions.
I So, it's easy to see what the weather is like just from the symbol?
M That's right.
I What about temperature?
M We usually use the words hot, warm, cool, or cold.

3.2 Notice /w/ and /v/.

A OK, in this photo, the weather is warm.
B Yes, it's hot and sunny.
A Maybe it's Cancún?
B And in this picture it's very, very hot!
A Yes, and it isn't raining. It's very dry.

3.3 Notice /d/ and /t/.

B = Bob M = Mary J = Joe
B Everywhere, the weather is … weird! Take the Amazon rainforest, for example. It's usually very rainy there, but now … no rain for three months! The Amazon river is down by 10 meters. It's weird! From the forest to the desert: the Atacama Desert is usually hot and sunny 350 days a year. This year, the days and nights are cool and cloudy. It's weird! And how's the weather in Chicago, the Windy City? Mary, tell us. What's the weather like in Chicago?
M Well, Bob, no wind for us! This month, every morning, it's cool and foggy. It's weird!
B Thanks, Mary. Let's go to the Alps. Those beautiful mountains. What's the weather usually like there? It's snowy, right? And what's it like this year? Tell us, Joe.
J Uh-huh. It's warm and there's absolutely no snow. Skiing is impossible. It's weird!
B How about Cancún, and the fantastic beaches? Well, tourists go to Cancún to enjoy the hot weather but this summer: it's cold. Really cold. It's weird! What's the weather like where you are? Any weird weather stories? Contact us to tell us …

3.4 Notice s = /s/ or /z/.

M = Maddie E = Eli S = Susan R = Rita
C = caller Mi = Michael
E Hello?
M Eli? This is Maddie. Are you busy?
E Actually, yes. I'm cooking dinner. What's up?
M Oh, no problem. Call you later.
E OK, bye.
S Susan.
M Hi, Susan. This is Maddie.
S Oh, hi, Maddie. Sorry, I'm running in the park. I can't hear you. Can I call you later?
M Sure, Susan. Talk to you later.
S Bye.
M OK, uh, bye. Not my day today, is it? Let me try Rita.
R Rita Rogers speaking.
M Hey, Rita!
R Maddie, darling. How are you doing?
M Great.
R Excuse me. Can you tell me where the butter is, please? Sorry, Maddie, I'm buying groceries. What's up?
M Well, I have …
R Oh, and the milk? Uh, sorry, Maddie.
M Oh, you're busy now. Don't worry. Bye.
R Bye, darling. Nice talking to you.
M So, Rita is busy, too. Maybe Michael? Let me try him. Uh … the line's busy …
M Ooh, someone's calling. Maybe one of my friends is finally free now. Hello?
C Gregory Hanes, please?
M Uh, I'm sorry, you have the wrong number.
C Oh, sorry. I'll dial again.
M Humph. Typical! Well, let me call Michael again.
Mi Hi, Maddie.
M Hi, Michael. Are you running?
Mi No, I'm not running! I'm riding a bike and my battery's dying. Call you later?
M Of course … Bye.

3.5 Notice the connections for similar sounds.

M = Maddie S = Sean
M I don't believe_this. One more call. That's it.
S Hey, Maddie. Long time_no see. How are things?
M Good! Uh, Sean, are you busy?
S Um, well, I'm doing_my homework.
M Oh, never min—
S … but I'm just finishing. What are your plans?
M I have two tickets to today's game. L.A. Lakers and Houston Rockets. It starts at three o'clock.
S So we have thirty minutes! Let's go!
M Are you saying yes?
S Of course! Why are you surprised?
M You have no idea … Meet you at the subway station. Let's go!

3.6

1
A Pass me the salt.
B OK—it needs more pepper, too.
2 Sound of someone singing and taking a shower.
3 Sound of someone humming while driving a car.
4 Sound of someone opening a can of soda and drinking.
A Ahhhh …
5 Sound of someone singing and vacuuming.

Audioscript

6
A This is really good!
B Yeah!

▶ 3.7
January, February, March, April, May, June, July, August, September, October, November, December

▶ 3.8
Four seasons or two?
Countries with a temperate climate, like the ones in Europe and North America, have four defined seasons: hot summers in June, July, and August; cold winters in December, January, and February, with heavy snow in some countries; cool, windy falls in September, October, and November, and warm springs in March, April, and May.
In contrast, tropical regions, especially around the equator, have only two seasons: the dry season and the rainy season. So, in places like India, West Africa, Central America, the north of South America, and the north coast of Australia, the rainy season is in their winter (June, July, and August), and it's accompanied by very high temperatures.

▶ 3.9 Notice /n/ and /ŋ/.
J = Jennifer   M = Marisa
J Hey, Marisa! Hi! It's great to see you.
M You too, Jennifer.
J What are you doing these days?
M I'm studying.
J Oh? Are you studying art? You're such a good painter.
M No, I'm studying biology.
J Really? And ... er ... where are you living?
M I'm living with my parents.
J Are you still dating Kevin?
M No, I'm not dating Kevin anymore. He's living in New York now. I'm dating a guy called Steve.
J Oh, that's nice. Well ... it was great to see you.
M You too. Bye.
J Bye, Marisa.

▶ 3.10 Notice /eɪ/ and /aɪ/.
S = Sammy   M = Marsha   L = Lucinda
K = KoolKat   D = Dadofthree   B = BBBaxter
S What do you think of technology?
M It's dangerous. Social media companies are changing the way we see privacy. Everyone is getting access to our personal information.
L I don't like a lot of the new video games. They're getting more violent and it makes people act more violently.
K People are going out less and spending more time alone with technology. We don't know our neighbors.
D People today are becoming obsessed with things! They want new clothes, new cars, new electronic devices, and they can buy it all online.
B My kids are spending more and more time on their devices and online, especially on social media. I don't know what to do. They panic when they don't have their phone with them. They just want to look at their phones.

▶ 3.11
I don't know if you've noticed, but celebrities are becoming more involved with activism. Some of their causes are cyberbullying, more education for girls, climate change, clean water, women's rights, animal rights, racism, to name but a few. Celebrities are bringing a lot of publicity to these causes and people are spending more money on the causes. But what do celebrities know about these problems? Please, George Clooney, stick to making movies; Emma Watson—you're a great actor, I don't want to see you talking about women's rights. Shakira, keep singing, and Oprah, keep on being a celebrity, not an activist.

▶ 3.12 Notice have to /f/ and kind of /v/.
M = Mark   L = Linda
M Hey, Linda, what are you doing? It's one a.m.!
L Oh it's you, Mark. Umm ... I'm working on this report. I have to turn it in tomorrow.
M Ah. Is it a big report?
L Yep, I still need to do three more pages.
M Ooosh. You tired?
L Yeah. Kind of.

▶ 3.13
M = Mark   L = Linda
M Wanna go home?
L No, I really have to finish this tonight.
M OK, so would you like a coffee?
L Are you having one?
M Yes.
L Yes, please, then. Black, no sugar, please.
M Do you want a sandwich, too?
L No, thanks.
M Cookie?
L Uh-uh, really. I'm not hungry.
M OK. One coffee, coming up.
L Thanks. You're great!

▶ 3.14
A Are you bored? Wanna go out for a coffee? Or a walk?
B Are you cold? Do you want a sweater? Do you want to use my jacket?
A Are you hot? Do you want a cold drink? Or some ice cream?
B Are you hungry? Do you want a sandwich? Wanna cookie?
A Are you thirsty? Would you like a drink?
B Are you tired? Would you like a coffee? Or would you like to go home?
A Are you stressed? Maybe you need a vacation? Or a new job?

Unit 4

▶ 4.1
T = Tasha
T Today's exciting events at the Olympic Games include basketball, soccer, tennis, volleyball, cycling, running, and swimming ... Wow!

▶ 4.2 Notice /i/ and /ɪ/.
T = Tasha   M = Mac
T Today's exciting events at the Olympic Games include basketball, soccer, tennis, volleyball, cycling, running, and swimming ... Wow! Tell us about it, Mac!
M Hi, Tasha! Yeah, it's July 2nd, and ... well, what a day of sports at the Olympics! A very exciting morning here at the Olympic complex. First we have basketball at the Olympic Arena. It's the semi-final between Cuba and Russia, at 9:00 a.m. Then, at 9:30, we have tennis, men's doubles, at the Central Courts. At 10:00 a.m. at the Olympic Stadium we have soccer, Uruguay versus Italy. What an interesting game! After that, at 10:30, it's time for cycling at the Igloo. The men's 5,000 meters final! And at 11:00 at North Park we have women's volleyball, the U.S. and Australia going for a bronze medal. And that's just this morning! Tasha, it's hard to decide what to watch!

▶ 4.3
1 airport – the airport
2 end – the end
3 Beatles – the Beatles
4 language – the language
5 English language – the English language
6 Internet – the Internet
7 office – the office
8 top ten – the top ten
9 umbrella – the umbrella
10 U.S. – the U.S.
11 universe – the Universe
12 answers – the answers

▶ 4.4 Notice intonation = speaker's emotion.
I = interviewer   W = woman
I Excuse me, miss? Can I ask you a question?
W Yes?
I What's your favorite sport?
W Skiing. I love↗ to ski.
I Nice↗! Thanks.
W You're welcome.
I = interviewer   B = boy
I Hi, uh, do you have a moment?
B Uh, OK.
I What's your favorite sport?
B It's golf↘. Absolutely, golf↗. To play and↘ to watch. Best↗ game in the world↘!
W Thanks.
I = interviewer   W = woman
W Uh, sorry. Excuse me!
I Sorry, er, hello! Do you have time to answer one question?
W Uh, what question?
I It's for a survey. What's your favorite sport?
W Let me think. It's definitely not↘ soccer. I hate↘ soccer.
I OK, but what sport do you like?
W Er ... is skateboarding a sport?
I Well, yes, I guess so.
W So it's skateboarding↘. I love↗ it.
I OK, thanks then!
W Is that all?
I Yes. Thanks very much!
W Oh, no problem!
I = interviewer   M = man
I Excuse me?
M Uh? What?
I Sorry, but, er ... Do you have time to answer one question?
M Uh, I guess↗. But only one↘!
I What's your favorite sport?
M To watch or to play?
I To watch and to play.
M Well, I like to watch baseball↘ on TV↘, but, you know, I don't play↘ baseball. I love to surf↘. I go surfing↗ every weekend.
I Watch baseball, and surf. Thanks a lot.
M You're welcome. Bye↗.

▶ 4.5 Notice the intonation in yes / no ❓ and Wh- ❓.
J = Janet   M = Mark
J Hi, Mark. My name is Janet and I'm your instructor.
M Oh hi, Janet. How's it going?↘
J Good. I need to ask you a few questions. Is that OK?↗
M Sure.
J What's your full name?↘
M Mark Swift. S-W-I-F-T.
J Swift, OK. How old are you, Mark?↘
M I'm 23.
J OK. Can you run two kilometers?↗
M Run? No, I can't. I don't think I can walk two kilometers! That's why I'm here.
J OK, great! How about swimming?↘ Can you swim?↗
M Er, yes, I can, but not very well. I need lessons.
J We can help you with that. Let's see ... Can you ride a bike?↗
M A bike? Yes, I can. But I don't like it.
J Hmm. OK. Can you play tennis?↗
M No, no, I can't play tennis at all. I hate tennis.

313

J I see. Well, so you can run in the gym every day, and our swimming lessons are...

4.6 Notice /aʊ/ and the connections.
Let_us pick_up our books_and our pens. They_are_our most powerful weapons. One child, one teacher, one book, and one pen can change the world. Education_is the_only solution. Education first. Thank_you.

4.7
action	corruption	motivation
combination	expression	opinion
conversation	information	organization
cooperation	isolation	question

4.8 Notice pronunciation of can in ? and can/can't in + − .
I = interviewer   M = man   W = woman

1
I Can you dance?
M I can't dance very well, but my wife can. She's a very good dancer.

2
I Who can cook well in your family?
W Not me! But my father can cook really well. His food is delicious.

3
I What about your friends? What sports can your best friend play?
M Hmmm, my best friend can't play baseball or volleyball. He doesn't like team sports.

4
I And winter sports? Can you skate?
W I can skate, but I can't ski at all. Skiing is too difficult!

5
I Can your friends play soccer?
M For sure! My friends can play soccer really well. They play every weekend.

6
I Can you do any martial arts?
W Yes, I can.
I What can you do?
W Tae kwondo.

4.10 Notice /æ/ and /ɛ/.
J = Joel   A = applicant
J Hello. I'm Joel Clinton. I have your curriculum vitae here and I want to ask you some questions.
A Sure.
J There is no information about your language abilities. How many languages can you speak?
A Er, apart from English, one. I speak a little Spanish.
J ¿Cómo estás?
A What?
J Yes, I can see you speak very little Spanish. Anyway, I'm also interested in your athletic abilities. Can you play any sports?
A Uh, a little, yes.
J What sports can you play?
A I can play volleyball and tennis, but not very well.
J Not perfect, but OK. One more question: can you text fast?
A Yes, I think so.
J How many words a minute can you text?
A I don't know—about 40, I think. But wait? Why are these questions relevant? Isn't this a job interview for a position as a babysitter?
J No, I want a nanny, and I want my son to have the best education.
A And how old is your son?
J Two!

4.11
Our first model is Justin. He's wearing a green T-shirt, orange shorts, gray sneakers, and beige socks. Ready for the gym or the park!
And here comes Sheila. She's wearing a brown blouse, a gold jacket, a pink skirt, and blue boots. Lots of colors on Sheila!
Next we have Dylan in a blue suit. To add more color, Dylan is wearing a purple shirt and a white tie. Blue shoes finalize the formal look. Formal and modern, that's Dylan.
Finally, here comes Marissa. Marissa is a picture of summer. She's wearing a yellow dress, and she guarantees glamour by wearing a silver belt and black sandals. She's ready for the night!
Now, please, welcome the man, the one and only ... Jacobelli Klein Karan!

4.12
V = Victoria   K = Kyle   T = Tanya
F Can organized and messy people live together?
V It's not impossible, but it's difficult. At home it's only me and my husband. My clothes and shoes are always organized, but his are not! Sometimes I get angry because he is messy and I'm neat, but usually it's OK.
K I confess: I don't like to share—it's too difficult! So my wife and I have separate closets. I have more things than she does, so my closet is enormous and hers is not. We are both clean and organized, but the problem is our kids! We clean our room, but we never look in theirs! Their rooms are messy and full of dirty sports equipment—balls, rackets, skis, etc. Horrible! It's hard for people who are very different to live together, but if you're family you can do it!
T In my house, we don't say "mine" or "yours." Everything is ours. Our house is small, and a little disorganized, but we like it like that. We share space and clothes. We occasionally have a conversation like this: "Whose sweater is this?" "It's yours!" "No, it's yours!" That's a big advantage of living with your twin sister! We are very similar. I can't live with people who are different from me.

4.13
my, mine, /ai/	his, his, /i/
your, yours, /o:/	our, ours, /au/
her, hers, /ɜr/	their, theirs, /e/

4.14
All Yours
Do you like healthy food and healthy living?
All Yours is the perfect place for you. There, in the same ultra-modern center you can find:
Super Salon with unisex hair stylists, manicurists, and pedicurists available from 8 a.m. to 10 p.m. seven days a week.
Natural Foods restaurant that serves high-quality, healthy foods, specially prepared by our expert chefs and nutritionists. Open from 7 a.m. to midnight daily.
World boutique with unique fashion designs from around the world for everybody, young or old.
Marvelous Me massage suite. Our fantastic therapists can eliminate all your stress.
Giant Gym. A great place to stay in shape and keep your heart and muscles healthy.

4.15
S = sales clerk   J = Jason
S Can I help you?
J Yes, please. Can I see the sweater in the window?
S Sure! What color? We have it in black, blue, or green.
J Uh, blue, please.
S All right. What size?
J Extra small.
S Extra small in blue? OK, just a moment, please. Here you are.
J Thanks. Can I try it on?
S Try it on? Uh, sure, no problem.

4.16 Notice the /t/ and silent t.
S = sales clerk   J = Jason
S The fitting rooms are over there.
J Thank you.
S Do you need any help, sir?
J No, no, it's perfect. What do you think? Blue is Jackson's favorite color. Isn't it, Jackson? Back in you go!
S And for you, sir? We have wonderful T-shirts, pants, jackets, suits ...

4.17
S = sales clerk   J = Jason
S Can I help you?
J Yes, please. Can I see the sweater in the window?
S Sure! What color? We have it in black, blue, or green.
J Uh, blue, please.
S All right. What size?
J Extra small.
S Extra small in blue? OK, just a moment, please. Here you are.
J Thanks. Can I try it on?
S Sure. The fitting rooms are over there.

4.18
S = sales clerk   J = Jason
J No, thanks. Just the sweater. How much is it?
S 49.99.
J Great! Here's my credit card.
S Thank you! Please, enter your PIN number.
J Here you go.
S Here's your receipt. Have a nice day! Bye Jackson!

Review 2

R2.1
T = Tyler   S = Shannon
T Hello?
S Hi, Tyler. This is Shannon. What are you doing?
T Oh, hi, Shannon. I'm watching the football game.
S Oh? Who's playing?
T You're kidding, right?
S Tyler, you know that I don't like sports.
T OK, OK ... the Cowboys and the Giants are playing right now.
S And who's winning?
T The Giants, 31–14. They always win.
S Sorry to hear that! Um ... do you want to go out later?

R2.2 Notice /r/ at beginning of words and /r/ at end of words.
G = Gale   R = Ricky
G And here with us today we have the Paralympic swimmer, Ricky Pietersen. Hello, Ricky.
R Hi, Gale. It's nice to be here.
G So, Ricky, what's your favorite sport?
R Well, I love swimming, of course!
G How about other sports? Do you like soccer?
R Yes, I love to watch my team play.
G Cool! What else do you like doing when you're not swimming or watching your team?
R Well, I like to help young kids with disabilities.
G That's great. And a final question: What is your next big challenge?
R I'm working hard to prepare for the next Paralympic Games. I want to beat my own record.
G Well, thank you for talking to us today, Ricky.
R Thank you, Gale!

Audioscript

◯ R2.3
My name is Cristina Valenzuela and I'm twenty-three years old. I live in Santa Monica, California. My parents are originally from Chile, so I can speak Spanish very well. I love sports. I go to the beach every day, and I surf and swim when the weather is good. It's usually very hot and sunny here! I love it! I'm a very casual person. I usually wear shorts and a T-shirt during the day, and jeans at night. When it's cold, I sometimes wear a sweater, but I don't like it very much. I prefer to wear summer clothes. Write me an email! Maybe we can go to the beach together next summer.

Unit 5

◯ 5.1 Notice /ə/ and /ʌ/.
A = adviser V = visitor
A Places to go out near here? Well, there's a bar, and a club, and a hotel. And there's a nice museum, and a park. And there's a very good restaurant. And a small stadium, oh, and an old theater.
V Great, thank you—that sounds good.

◯ 5.2
A = adviser V = visitor
A OK, let's check with the brochure where these different places are.
V Right. A is a mall, the Fourth Street mall, is that right?
A Uh-huh.
V B is a library, right?
A Yep.
V C is a movie theater, right?
A Right.
V D is a racetrack, isn't it?
A It is.
V E is a swimming pool, F is a bookstore, and G is the river. Is that right?
A Yes, that's right, you've got it. Enjoy your stay in Kentucky!

◯ 5.3 Notice the word stress.
Welcome to Louisville, the largest city in Kentucky! It's a great place to visit. Situated on the Ohio River with a population of about 750,000, it's the City of Parks. There are 122 parks in the city!
Downtown there are seven museums, and three theaters, plus the Louisville Ballet, Orchestra, and Opera.
Louisville is home to the famous Kentucky Derby horse race, sometimes called the Greatest Two Minutes in Sports! There's a famous racetrack and a museum at Churchill Downs. There's also a football stadium and a baseball stadium in the city. If you like shopping, there are three enormous shopping malls to choose from. And for readers, there's a fantastic public library with branches all over town.
Kentucky is the home of KFC (Kentucky Fried Chicken), but we don't only eat fried chicken! There are restaurants of all kinds here.
There aren't any public swimming pools in downtown Louisville, but there are six pools in the city, so everything is easy. And of course there are bars, clubs, and four multi-screen movie theaters. And seven world-class hotels, just in the downtown area. The only thing you won't find here? There are no unfriendly people—just friends you don't know yet!
So, come to Louisville—for relaxation and fun!

◯ 5.4
1 There are seven museums downtown.
2 There's a famous racetrack at Churchill Downs.
3 There aren't any swimming pools in downtown Louisville.
4 There are no unfriendly people.

◯ 5.5
Come to Markville! It's a great place to live. There are two museums and a great public library. There is also a movie theater, so you can see a movie if you want. There's no mall, but there are lots of cool shops and a historical bank. Markville has two hotels: there's an old traditional hotel and there is a new modern one, so you can choose where you stay. There are no clubs, but there is a bar inside one of the hotels. For food lovers, there are two delicious restaurants, one French, the other Mexican, and an interesting café, too. Downtown is for pedestrians, so there are no cars to ruin the peace. People are warm, the weather is too. The food is great, so see you soon!

◯ 5.6 Notice /ɪ/ and /aɪ/. Notice the position of also and too.
Well, I love playing video games. It's my favorite thing in the world. I also love going out with my friends. I like to shop and I like to eat out. And, um, I like blogging too. And I don't mind going to work. I also don't mind cooking—it's fun with a friend, but I don't like going to the gym very much. I don't like watching TV either, but the one thing I really hate is cleaning. I hate cleaning the house! What about you? Are you similar?

◯ 5.7
1 I love playing video games!
2 I also love going out with my friends!
3 I don't like going to the gym.
4 I don't mind cooking.
5 I hate cleaning the house!
6 I don't mind going to work.
7 I like to eat out, too!
8 I also like blogging!
9 I don't like watching TV.
10 I like to shop!

◯ 5.8
1 I don't mind cleaning the bathroom.
2 I love tidying my room.
3 I hate doing the laundry.
4 I like washing the dishes.

◯ 5.9 Notice main sentence stress on content words and at the end of phrases.
N = Natalie H = host
N I'm **Natalie** and I'm **ten** years old and I **love** to **sing**. I've been **singing** ever since I was **four**. I sing at **school**, I sing at **home**, I **sometimes** sing when I'm **eating** my **dinner**! I would **like** to be a **singer** and a **diva** and I **definitely want** to be like **Beyoncé**.
H Hello, darling.
N Hello.
H **What's** your **name** and how **old** are you?
N My name is **Natalie** and I'm **ten** years old.
H And **what** are you **doing today**?
N Well, I'm going to sing a **song** called **"No One"** from **Alicia Keys**.
H OK, yeah—I know that one. Good luck, **darling**.

◯ 5.10
camping, cooking, dancing, hiking, eating out, buying souvenirs, swimming

◯ 5.11
My favorite vacation activities are a) sightseeing, b) taking a class, c) sunbathing d) visiting museums, e) reading novels, f) snorkeling, and g) kayaking.

◯ 5.12 Notice the pronunciation of the -ing /ŋ/ form.
J = Josh E = Emily
J Let's go on vacation together, Emily. What do you like doing on vacation?
E Well, I love sunbathing and swimming. How about you?
J Hmmm, well, I don't really like swimming or sunbathing, but I love snorkeling and kayaking. I sometimes like to take a class or to visit the museums to discover more about where I am.
E Do you? I prefer reading novels and eating out and dancing, nothing cultural for me.
J What about sightseeing?
E I like sightseeing, but not too much.
J And camping? Do you like camping?
E Not really. I hate shopping, especially buying souvenirs, and cooking and hiking when I'm on vacation. I just want to relax.
J Those are the things I love doing on vacation! Hmm …

◯ 5.14
1 backpacker bus tour
2 camp in the jungle
3 fantastic rainforest
4 relaxing hammock
5 spectacular sunrise
6 yoga retreat
7 herbal tea
8 wonderful waterfalls
9 beautiful beaches

◯ 5.15
House sitting is when you exchange your services of taking care of a family's dog, cat, garden, pets, basically any house needs, and you exchange it in return for staying in the house for free. Some house sitters get paid and that's usually if they know the person or have been doing it a long time, but for travelers who house sit, it's mainly a free swap.

◯ 5.16
a) turn on the lights when I go in and turn them off when I go out
b) open and close the windows
c) don't let the cats out. Oh no!
d) feed the cats and the dog
e) give the cats and the dog some water
f) pick up the mail and put it on the table
g) walk the dog
h) water the plants

◯ 5.17 Notice the pronunciation of object pronouns in speech.
Hi, Lori! Thanks for house sitting for us during our vacation. Hope you don't have any problems.
Just a few things to remember. Er, when you come in, please pick up the mail↘ and put it on the table.↘
Um, yeah, please open the windows↘ and close them again every day↘ – oh, and water the plants every day↘. Also, don't forget the lights and air conditioning↘ – turn them off when you go out↘.
Feed Salt and Pepper (that's the cats!) and Chips (that's the dog!) in the morning and evening↘, but please don't give them too much food↘. Oh and, don't forget to give them some water.↘
Please, walk Chips in the morning and afternoon↘. But please don't take him near the road↘. He's nervous of cars. And please, please, don't let the cats out.↘
Call me if you have any questions↘ and please tell us if the cats or Chips escape↘. Thanks again! See you in two weeks. Have fun!↘ Bye.

◯ 5.18
1 boring
  fun / interesting
2 expensive
  cheap
3 safe
  dangerous
4 neat
  messy

◯ 5.20
1 Don´t be rude or messy.
2 Relax and don´t think about work.
3 Spend time at home.
4 Write a reference as soon as possible.

5 Invite friends to use your pool or have dinner.
6 Help with the household chores.

5.21
round the corner ... cross at the stoplight ... go straight ... turn left ... turn right ... Oh! a stop sign! Stop!

5.22 Notice st- at the beginning of a word.

1
M = man W = woman
M Excuse me.
W Hi! How're you doing?
M Oh, hi. Good, thanks, er, where's the mall?
W It's in front of you on Market Street. Cross here at the stoplight.
M Thanks.
W No problem. Have a nice day!

2
W = woman M = man
W Excuse me. Is there a movie theater around here?
M Yes, there is. Go straight on Market Street and turn right on Fourth Street. Go straight for one block and the movie theater's on the corner of Fourth and Mission Street.

3
M = man W = woman
M Excuse me. Do you know where the library is?
W Excuse me?
M The library?
W Ah, yes. Um, er, I know! Go straight on Market Street for four blocks. Turn right on Grove Street at the stop sign. Then, um, er, go straight for one block and the library is on the right.
M Thank you.

4
M1, M2, M3 = man 1, man 2, man 3
M1 Um, er, excuse me, are there any ...
M2 Sorry, my friend. No time, bye!
M1 Hmpf. Excuse me. Are there any bookstores near here?
M3 Yes, there are.
M1 Good, er, where are they?
M3 Oh yes, sorry. There's one on Market Street. Go straight for about four blocks. The bookstore's on your left. Before the stop sign.
M1 Sorry, can you say that again?
M3 I'm sorry. There's one on Market Street. Go straight for about four blocks. The bookstore's on your left. Before the stop sign. OK?
M1 Er, thank you.

Unit 6

6.1 Notice /ə/.
Let's see. We need bananas and chocolate ... oil and salt ... uh... maybe some spaghetti? Yes, definitely some spaghetti and some tea ... oh, and I have to get tomatoes and vinegar.

6.2 Notice s = /z/ and /s/.
We need some bread, milk, fish, and chicken ... oh, and some apples and carrots, Sandra loves carrots! Then some eggs and lettuce. Oh, and butter and onions. Oh, finally, some cheese, oranges, potatoes ... do we need sugar? Oh, yes, and some sugar.

6.3 Notice the silent letters and /sh/.
J = Jeff S = Sandra
S Jeff! I'm home.
J Hi, Sandra.
S What's all this food on the table?
J What do you mean, all this?
S Well, to be precise, some chocolate, tomatoes ... uh, some spaghetti ...
J Oh, that?
S I'm not finished! There's also some salt, some tea, oil, and vinegar here...
J I can explain ...
S ... and—eleven, twelve, no, thirteen bananas.
J There was a special offer on bananas. We can always freeze them!
S That's true—they make great smoothies! But, Jeff, we're leaving tomorrow. Why did you buy all this food for the refrigerator?
J Just some fruit: Apples and oranges.
S I don't like apples.
J But I like apples ... and you like oranges. And I got some onions and potatoes, too.
S Potatoes? I don't eat them.
J I also got some chicken and fish.
S Well, we can freeze those. But what do we do with the milk, cheese, and butter?
J Sorry, Sandra ... I got some lettuce and carrots for salad, too.
S Hm, I guess I can make a salad for dinner. And all those eggs!!
J Well, I can make an omelet!
S You do make delicious omelets—good idea. So we can use the lettuce, carrots, and some of the eggs for dinner. But, wait—what are these doing in the refrigerator?
J Er ...
S Here! Look! You put bread and sugar in the refrigerator! What are they doing there?
J Uh, I don't know.
S You don't know?
J I always put sugar and bread in the refrigerator, I don't know why. My parents and my grandparents did it.
S OK, but it seems weird!

6.4 Notice the stress in the phrases and /ə/.
1 a glass of juice
2 a cup of tea
3 some salad
4 a slice of bread
5 a piece of fruit
6 a bowl of rice
7 some meat
8 some fish
9 some eggs
10 some vegetables
11 a bottle of water
12 a piece of cake
13 some carrots or nuts

6.5 Notice the links.
So, today is day one_of eating more healthily. I eat too much junk food and sugar. For breakfast, I can have a cup_of tea, a slice_of wholewheat bread, and a piece_of fruit! For lunch, it's a bowl_of brown rice, some meat, some vegetables, and a bottle_of water. In the afternoon, for my snack I get some carrots or nuts! Hmm ... or maybe a piece_of cake. No, I don't think so. Carrots or nuts and that's it! Then for dinner, I get some salad, some protein again—some fish or eggs, and a glass_of juice.

6.6 Notice /ʌ/, /ʊ/ and /uː/.
M = Maria T = Tony
M Hi, Tony. Want some potato chips?
T No, thanks. I'm trying to cut down on junk food.
M Oh, OK—that's a good idea. How's it going?
T Great. I'm keeping a video diary. It really helps.
M So, what do you usually have for lunch?
T I have some brown rice for lunch—with vegetables and meat.
M That sounds pretty good.
T Uh huh, it is. And I can eat as much as I want. I'm never hungry!
M Now that's important!
T It's pretty easy, actually. I'm learning to cook, too.
M What about dessert?
T I never eat any sugar. But I eat a lot of fruit.
M Oh, come on. Never?!
T Well, OK, not at home. I sometimes have a piece of cake in restaurants.
M Do you ever eat bread?
T Of course! I have a slice of bread with my lunch.
M And what about cheese?
T Well, sometimes for dinner. But usually I eat fish or eggs. And a glass of juice. Natural juice!
M Wow! That sounds great—I think I might try it! Forget about these potato chips! Do you want this bottle of water?
T Um ... no, thanks. I think I'll have a glass of juice, instead!

6.7

1
A And what do you have with your fish?
B I usually have some brown rice.

2
A Do you like steak?
B I don't eat any red meat. I'm a vegetarian.

3
A Do you have dessert?
B No, I never eat any sugar. I just have fruit.

4
A I'm sure you don't eat bread.
B Yes, I do! I have some bread every day with meals.

5
A Do you want some water?
B No, I don't want any, thanks. I'm not thirsty.

6.8
J = Judy L = Lucas
J So Lucas, what do you usually have when you get up?
L I only have some water.
J Wow! You don't eat any food?!
L Well, I have some bread and some fruit two hours later.
J Two hours later? And do you have some coffee? You know, to stay awake?
L I don't need any coffee. I don't get up until noon!

6.9
B = Bill A = Amy
B So, Amy, how's it going?
A Great! I'm going to Tokyo next week ... for work! Can you believe it? First time!
B You'll love it. And the food ... it's so good. Even breakfast is special.
A Really? How?
B Well, there are two breakfasts in many hotels, a Western breakfast and a Japanese breakfast. The Western one is for tourists, you know, and people like us.
A And what about the Japanese breakfast? What is it?
B You can have fish, rice, and soup. It's called miso soup. And, of course, green tea. It's a nice way to start the morning. It's delicious, too!
A But I can't live without coffee!
B Don't worry, green tea has caffeine. Try it! You'll like it!
A OK. And the soup, is it healthy? What's in it?
B Tofu and many other things. It's good for you, but it has a lot of salt.
A I'm sure it's fine for just a week! I'm going to try the Japanese breakfast. Oh, and can you give me any information on transportation? I hear taxis are expensive!
B They sure are! Forget about taxis. Take the train or bus from the airport.
A But I don't speak Japanese.
B Don't worry, people will help you.
A "Don't worry." That's easy for you. You go to Japan a lot. I'm nervous!
B It's not hard, really. I always see tourists on the train. And you can buy coffee to take on the train ... in a can!

Audioscript

▶ 6.10
N = Nelly **W** = woman
- **N** Is chocolate really good for you? I have a confession to make: I love sugar. But I don't really eat a lot of candy. The secret to a "sweet" life is quality, not quantity. When I really want some candy or a dessert, I always go for the most delicious and the most attractive that I can find. And they even say chocolate is good for you!
- **W** Maybe you're smiling because Nelly's blog sounds familiar. That's not surprising. Chocolate tastes good! And some claim it has health benefits, too.
- If you have a lot of pressure and stress in your life, chocolate can make you feel better mentally and physically. Chocolate gives you energy!
- Chocolate will reduce your appetite. If you eat a small quantity of dark chocolate before a big lunch, your appetite might be 15% less!
- Chocolate can improve your heart! Some even say your cholesterol may improve, too.
- Chocolate keeps your skin hydrated, and it also has anti-aging properties that help you stay young.
- Chocolate has a little caffeine, but much less than coffee. And it has some sugar. Be sure to check the ingredients before you buy. And make sure your chocolate is at least 85% dark chocolate.
- So, is chocolate really good for you? No, not really! We usually eat it with a lot of fat and sugar, which aren't so good for you. But, the good news? A little chocolate now and again won't hurt you—and, of course, it tastes delicious!

▶ 6.11 Notice the dark *l* vs. normal *l*.
J = Joe **S** = Sandra
- **J** Hey, Sandra. Ready for lunch?
- **S** Sure. I'm so hungry!
- **J** Come on! Let's go to that Mexican restaurant on the corner. I'm dying for a burrito.
- **S** I don't think that's a good idea. I want to eat something healthy today.
- **J** Burritos are healthy! Look, I'm Googling the nutritional table. We can see what's in them.
- **S** Oh, I hate those lists! They're so out of date!
- **J** What do you mean?
- **S** My grandmother counts calories! The ingredients are important, not the number of calories.
- **J** Exactly! This chart doesn't even show calories. Let's look at the chicken burrito.
- **S** I can't see anything without my glasses.
- **J** Um, let's see. Well, it has five grams of fat.
- **S** Aw! That's a lot.
- **J** There's also a vegetarian burrito. It only has beans and cheese, and four grams of fat.
- **S** Ugh! Beans! But my doctor told me to watch my cholesterol. How much cholesterol does the vegetarian burrito have?
- **J** Only five milligrams.
- **S** And the others?
- **J** The chicken one has thirty milligrams and the meat one has thirty-five milligrams.
- **S** Hmm ... that's a lot. Another reason to be a vegetarian! What about sodium? It's not good to eat too much salt.
- **J** Well, let's see. The chicken one has 880 milligrams, the meat one 890 milligrams, and the vegetarian one only 730 milligrams. But they have a lot of protein! The chicken burrito has 18 grams and the meat burrito 19 grams. That's important, too. And they all have fiber, especially the vegetarian one: 14 grams.
- **S** You know what? I'm having the chicken burrito! I love chicken.
- **J** And I'm having the meat burrito. "Everything in moderation." And they're so delicious. We'll have the vegetarian burrito another day.
- **S** Great! Let's go. It's now one o'clock. I'm hungry!

▶ 6.12
R = Richie **G** = grandpa
- **R** OK, the chili's almost ready.
- **G** You can add some mushrooms, if you want.
- **R** How many mushrooms?
- **G** I don't know! A lot if you like them or a few if you don't.
- **R** OK—I get it. ... And how do I serve it?
- **G** With some rice.
- **R** How much rice?
- **G** A lot if you're hungry, a little if you're not.

▶ 6.14 Notice the the alliteration.
This is Wonderful Weekend at Fast and Fresh! Special savings on our fabulous favorites! Our special starter is the Chopped Chicken: a salad made with fresh lettuce and tomato and topped with grilled chicken. We offer you two choices from our marvelous main courses: Fish Fillet, our delicious grilled salmon in orange sauce. It comes with a baked potato. Or the Special Steak, a succulent half-pound barbecued steak topped with a light cream and pepper sauce. Finally, there's nothing like a light, refreshing dessert: our Seasonal Fruit Salad, which includes strawberry, mango, melon, and pear topped with fresh fruit juice. All for a great price! Come to Fast and Fresh and check it out!

▶ 6.15 Notice /ɪ/ and /iː/.
Me = Melissa **P** = Phil **Ma** = Marie
- **Me** Hi, my name's Melissa, and I'm your server today. Are you ready to order?
- **P** Yes, please.
- **Me** What would you like as a starter?
- **P** I'll have the tomato soup, please.
- **Me** OK. With croutons and parmesan cheese?
- **P** No cheese, please.
- **Me** OK. How about you, ma'am? What would you like?
- **Ma** What's in the chicken salad?
- **Me** The salad is lettuce, spinach, green peppers, red peppers, tomato, and onion. It comes with sliced grilled chicken.
- **Ma** That sounds good. I'd like that, please—but no onion. I don't like onion!
- **Me** Certainly. I'll be right back with your starters.

▶ 6.16
Me = Melissa **P** = Phil **Ma** = Marie
- **Me** OK. How are your starters?
- **Ma** Great, thanks.
- **Me** Would you like to order the main course now?
- **Ma** Yes, please. I'd like the Pasta Pomodoro, please.
- **Me** OK. And you, sir?
- **P** I'll have the Special Steak, please.
- **Me** Any drinks with your meal?
- **P** Can I have mineral water, please?
- **Ma** And I'll have lemonade, please.
- **Me** Sure. I'll be right back with those.

▶ 6.17 Notice /tʃ/ and the connecting sounds.
Me = Melissa **P** = Phil **Ma** = Marie
- **P** Excuse me?
- **Me** Yes, sir?
- **P** Can_I have some decaf coffee, please?
- **Me** Of course. And you, ma'am? What would_you like to drink?
- **Ma** I'd like some tea, please. What kind_of tea do_you have?
- **Me** Mint_or chamomile.
- **Ma** I'll have chamomile tea, please.
- **Me** Anything_else?
- **Ma** Uh, actually, I'd like some dessert. Can we have the Chocolate Chunk? It's to share.
- **Me** Certainly. It's very good.
- **P** Oh, and can you bring_us the check, too, please?

Review 3

▶ R3.1 Notice voiced th /ð/, and unvoiced th /θ/.
T = Tina **C** = Carl
- **T** I'm thirsty. Is there any juice in the fridge?
- **C** No, we didn't buy any juice this week. But, look, there are oranges. Do you want me to make you some juice?
- **T** Yes, thanks. Uh, and did we buy any cookies?
- **C** No, but there are still some cookies in the cabinet.
- **T** Great, thanks!

▶ R3.2
1. Hi, Mike, how are you?
2. This is Nick and this is Steve, I work with them.
3. Your coat is on the floor. Please put it on your chair.
4. That's Jessica. I go to school with her.
5. This is David's phone. Can you give it to him?

▶ R3.3
- **A** Hi. Is there a bookstore around here?
  Yes, there is. Go straight for two blocks. There's one on the left, opposite the theater.
- **B** Excuse me. How do I get to the movie theater?
  Turn left at the stoplight. It's on Brown Street, on the right, next to the library.
- **C** Do you know where the mall is?
  Sure. Turn right at the corner. Go straight for one block. The mall's on the corner of Brown and Liberty.
- **D** Excuse me. Is there a gym near here?
  Yes. Go straight for two blocks. Turn right. The gym is on Green Street between the grocery store and the French restaurant.

Unit 7

▶ 7.1
H = host **B** = boy contestant **G** = girl contestant
- **H** 1 Take a shower in ...
- **B** the bathroom!
- **H** 2 You can cook in...
- **G** the kitchen!
- **H** 3 You wash and dry clothes in ...
- **G** the laundry room!
- **H** 4 Store things you don't need in ...
- **B** the basement!
- **H** 5 You sleep in ...
- **B** the bedroom!
- **H** 6 People usually eat in ...
- **B** the dining room!
- **H** 7 People work in ...
- **G** the office!
- **H** 8 We watch TV in ...
- **G** the living room!
- **H** 9 We keep our car in ...
- **G** the garage!

▶ 7.2 Notice /eɪ/, and /æ/.
T = Tom **A** = Anna
- **T** This is the living room.
- **A** Hmm ... It's a little small.
- **T** There's a fireplace and a nice TV with cable ... and, er, armchairs, and er, what else, ah, we love this sofa—it's the center of the house.
- **A** Oh, but I never watch TV.
- **T** Oh. This is the kitchen—it has a gas stove and a microwave and you can wash the dishes in the sink here. Here's the refrigerator. It's new. And, er, there's a table and two chairs here if you want to eat in the kitchen.

A Well, it's not very light in here.
T Here in the dining room we have this big table with eight chairs. Good for dinner parties!
A I don't really like to cook very much, though.
T Now for the bathroom—just a toilet and shower, there's no bathtub, I'm afraid.
A Oh ... I really like to take a bath. Especially in the winter.
T This is your bedroom—you can see it's large and it has a large bed and a table and a big closet and plenty of storage space and there is a fan so you don't get hot at night.
A Hmm ... But what's that smell?
T Here's the laundry room—there's more storage space on these shelves here. So, what do you think? Do you like it?
A Well, I need to think about it.
T Sure. Give us a call tomorrow.

▶ 7.3 **Notice /ɔːr/ and the contractions.**
This is my tiny house. Come on in. Just inside the front door I've got these two puffy chairs flanking this little faux fireplace. It's a very tiny fireplace, but it's a tiny house. Closet storage and cabinet space below this desk. Computer storage space and there's a little table down here. When I pull this table out, believe it or not, as long as I have tiny plates, it seats four people. Like that.
Here in the kitchen I've got a bar sink, a double burner stove, a little refrigerator, and a toaster oven.
The bathroom is the shower, so when I want to take a shower the nozzle's on the ceiling and everything would get wet except for I've got these little sliding doors that keep things dry and I can put this plastic curtain in here over the toilet which is right down here.
Above the kitchen I've got access to the loft—that's where I sleep. So the loft is nothing more than storage and sleeping. I've got all the storage at this end and then at this end I've got the sleeping—with the bed. It sleeps two really comfortably. So this is my bed and I've got a window at this end and a fan vent behind the shelves at the other so that if it ever gets hot I can just turn this whole thing into a wind tunnel.

▶ 7.4
K = Katie L = Lenny
K Well?
L I don't think so, Katie! There weren't any closets.
K Yes, there were. I think there were two. There were closets in the bedrooms.
L OK. But what about the kitchen? It's so small! There was nothing in it!
K Well, there was no stove, I don't think. But there was a big window!
L And the bathroom is tiny, too. Was there a bathtub? I don't remember.
K I'm not sure.
L Katie, it's really tiny! We can't live there.
K Maybe you're right.

▶ 7.5 **Notice /ɛ/ and how /eɪ/ is usually stressed.**
Hello, my name's Liz Marshall and I'm a party planner. Today, I want to talk to you about how to give a great party. Well, it all starts with the invitation. Send the invitations early—three weeks before the party—and include all the important information. Where? When? What type of party? Now ... what do you need for the party? First, food and drinks: Well, for drinks you need some soft drinks, and always have water. I like to keep it simple: Just tea and coffee. You can have fresh juice, too.
For food, I recommend chips and one or two other snacks, perhaps a healthy option like carrots. Don't forget the plates, glasses, and napkins, too. If it's a birthday party, a cake is essential. And display your birthday cards! Next—decorations—again keep it simple with balloons. You can decorate the house with candles, too—this gives a nice atmosphere. And if it's a special occasion, you can even give each guest a small present to take home.
Now for entertainment—music is essential for a good party—make sure there's space for people to dance. OK, so it's time to start planning. Have fun!

▶ 7.6 **Notice the ↗ and ↘ intonation.**
M = Martha R = Rob
M I was at a great↗ party yesterday, Rob!↘
R Oh, that's nice, Martha. Where was it?↘
M It was at Jane Foster's home. It was her birthday.
R Oh! Were there a lot of people?↗
M Yep, there were about fifty.↘
R Wow!↗ Was there a lot of food?↗
M Oh yes, and there was an enormous↗ chocolate cake.↘
R Hmmm ... And ... was Jane's boyfriend there?↗
M Yes, he was. Rick and Jane make a perfect↗ couple↘!! He's so attractive↘, they were so beautiful↘ together, and the music was great↗ — everybody was dancing, you know.↘
R He sounds nice↗. Were Jane's parents there?↗
M No, they weren't↘. Do you know them? ↗
R Yes. Ummm ... I was Jane's boyfriend before Rick.↘
M Oh, I'm sorry↘ ... I didn't know that↘ ... in fact, the party wasn't that↘ great ... and her new boyfriend wasn't really that nice ...↘
R No problem. It's fine. Don't worry about it.↘
M Hey, there was a great show on TV last night. Did you see it?↗

▶ 7.8 **Notice /oʊ/ and /aʊ/.**
1 Is that ... Cheese? Mm. It is! Where is it? Is it in the box?
2 No ... Maybe under the table ... Hmmm. Where is it? ... People! Oh, no!
3 Now, quietly between the sofa and the table.
4 Slowly, next to the sofa ...
5 Where are the people? Where is the cheese?! OK, let's go! In the bed ...
6 Now on the bed ... and jump!
7 Ah! There they are! OK! I'm across from the people! I'm across from the people! Quick!
8 OK, concentrate, where IS that cheese? In front of the TV.
9 No. Behind the TV? No. Not here.
10 Ah, there it is! I see it. Now. How can I get above the TV? Hmmmm.

▶ 7.9 **Notice stress to emphasize change.**
M See that?
W What?
M There was a mouse **under** the **table**.
W Oh no! Where?
M Over there!
W Oh **now** I see it! It's **next to** the **sofa**. It's moving!
M Where did it go?
W Ahhhh! It was **in front of** the TV now it's **behind** the TV.
M Let me see if I can get it.
W Ahhhh! It's **on** the bed. It was **in** the bed and now it's **on** the bed!
M There it goes. It was **on** the **bed**, but now it's **in** that **box**.
W Quick, close the box and take it out to the garden.
M Good idea!

▶ 7.10
1 twenty seventeen
2 nineteen ninety-seven
3 two thousand
4 twenty ten
5 nineteen eighty-five
6 twenty twenty-three
7 nineteen eighty
8 two thousand and five
9 twenty thirteen

▶ 7.11
I was born in Barcelona in 1985. The city was very different then. In my neighborhood, there were a lot of old buildings and factories. Until 1997, there were only two coffee shops (we call them "bars"), and there were no other restaurants on my street. By 2005, the neighborhood was a little different, and by 2013, there were many new businesses. Now it's 2018, and there are families from all over the world. You can enjoy food from many countries, too!

▶ 7.12
San Diego, a changing city
by Bill Watson
As I arrive at my hotel in downtown San Diego in 2030, I am shocked. I was last here in 2018, and the city is very different. I almost think I'm in the wrong place!
Like many American cities, there has been urban renewal, and the downtown area has been renovated. It wasn't very nice when I was here in 1990, but, by 2018, visitors were able to enjoy good food, music, and theater, or even a baseball game at Petco Park. Now, in 2030, the neighborhood near my favorite hotel is completely transformed!
There are new roads, a park, and new traffic lights. There wasn't so much traffic in 2018, but now traffic lights on every corner are essential. There were some good grocery stores downtown before, but now there are three new ones on my block where you can send your robot to do the shopping. And there's more! When I was here in 2018, there was a movie theater next to the bank. I went there often. But now, there's an enormous movie complex with six large theaters! And there are security cameras everywhere, but there weren't any in 2018. Maybe that's because there's a new school across from the movie complex. In 2018, there weren't any schools in this area.
My recommendation: This is a great city! Beautiful weather, clean, too, and there are a lot more cars in Los Angeles!

▶ 7.13
M = man W = woman
M Shanghai is so different today!
W Really? How?
M Well, about 25 years ago, in the early 1990s, there were about 11 million people in Shanghai, but today there are about 24 million!
W Wow! That's a big change.
M It sure is. And in 1990, there wasn't much traffic downtown. Today the streets are full of cars. In 1990, the air was cleaner, too. Today there is smog.
W Mm. What else is different?
M There weren't many tall buildings in 1990, but, today, there are lots and they're building more all the time.
W Are there any famous sights in modern Shanghai?
M Oh yeah! There's the Oriental Pearl Tower, and the Shanghai Tower—which is one of the world's tallest buildings! There weren't any landmarks like this in 1990.
W Now you can't get lost, then!

▶ 7.15
Race the Beep!
36 tables
final score 4–1
1,200 guests at Windsor Castle
150 countries showed it on TV

Audioscript

270 guests
600 guests at the ceremony and reception
1.9 billion watched it
the first ceremony was in 1929
29 million watched it in the U.S.
100,000 went in Philadelphia
first one in North America
it lasted 15 minutes

7.16 Notice weak forms of to, at, for, and of.

1
Ma = Mara   Mo = Morgan
Ma Hello, Morgan!
Mo Hi, Mara!
Ma Scott and I are having a housewarming party on Sunday. Can you and Sandy come?
Mo Oh, I'm sorry. We already have plans for Sunday.
Ma Oh, well, that's OK.
Mo Thanks for inviting us and I hope the party goes well.
Ma Thanks, Morgan.
Mo See you.
Ma Bye.

2
W = woman   M = man
W Hi, Tony! How about going to the movies tonight?
M Sure. Sounds good. What time?
W The movie starts at 3 p.m.
M Great!

3
C = Carrie   T = Tommy
C Hi, Tommy! It's Carrie. We're having a barbecue tomorrow. Do you want to come?
T Thanks for the invitation, but sorry, I can't. I'm away all weekend, not back until Monday.
C Oh, well. Maybe next time, then.
T Yes, definitely.

4
W = woman   M = man
W Would you like to come to my sister's wedding with me?
M When is it?
W On March 28th.
M What time?
W It starts at 2 p.m.
M Great. I'd love to. Thanks.

5
M = man   R = Roz
M Hey, Roz! We're having a surprise party for Lucy's birthday. Are you free on Friday?
R What time?
M At about 7:30.
R Sounds great! What can I bring?
M Your favorite snack, maybe?
R OK—sure, see you there.

6
W = woman   K = Kit
W Hello, Kit! We're having a baby shower for Laura and Michael on Saturday. Do you think you can come?
K Of course we can! What time?
W 3 p.m. at Laura's.
K Great. See you there.

Unit 8

8.1 Notice the silent e of most -ed endings, and the /ɪd/ after t.

1 Maud was born in 1877.
2 She worked in the circus.
3 Gus wanted to go out with her.
4 She agreed to see him.
5 She married him.
6 She studied hard.
7 She learned how to tattoo.
8 She stopped work.
9 Lotteva started tattoo lessons at nine.
10 Maud died in 1961.

8.3 Notice -ed endings are /d/, /t/ or /ɪd/ (never /ɛd/).

Frida Kahlo was born on July 6, 1907, in an area of Mexico City called Coyoacán. Her full name was Magdalena Carmen Frida Kahlo y Calderón, something most people don't know. When Frida was a child, she lived in the famous Casa Azul, or blue house, with her family. It is now the Frida Kahlo museum and a fascinating place to visit! Frida painted her entire life, and was famous for her self-portraits. When she was young, she wanted to be a doctor, but in 1925, when she was only 18, she was in a bad bus accident. She then decided to be a painter, and in 1928, she married the world famous muralist Diego Rivera. Kahlo traveled to the U.S. with Rivera in the 1920s and 1930s, and she traveled in Mexico, too. She enjoyed her time in the U.S., but didn't like some aspects of American society. During this time, she developed her own unique style. Her first exhibition was in New York in 1938. In 1939, Kahlo went to live in Paris for a time. There, she exhibited some of her paintings, and met other artists, including Picasso. In 1943, she started teaching in Mexico City. Sadly, Frida was sick for most of her life. She died in 1954 at the age of 47 in her bed in the Casa Azul.

8.4

1
A How was your day off?
B Oh, perfect! I didn't do much. I took it easy and I read my book.

2
A How was your day yesterday?
B I slept late. Then I made brunch and had a good time with my friends.

3
A How was your Thanksgiving?
B Great! My sister and her family came over, and we ate a lot!

4
A How was your Sunday?
B Slow! I didn't get up until midday. Then I met some friends, and we saw a movie.

5
A How was your summer?
B Fantastic! We got up late every day and then we went to the beach.

6
A How was your weekend?
B Saturday, I went shopping and bought some new jeans. I did chores all day Sunday.

8.5

buy - bought
come - came
do - did
get - got
give - gave
go - went
have - had
know - knew
make - made
meet - met
say - said
see - saw
take - took
think - thought

8.6

June 1st, 1996
February 4th, 1988
September 7th, 1803
March 2nd, 2001
May 5th, 2016
January 8th, 1943
December 3rd, 2018
August 6th, 2005
July 9th, 1994

8.7

F = David's friend   D = David
F Hey, David! How was your vacation?
D Fantastic! My girlfriend and I traveled to Ilha Grande—that's Big Island in English!
F That's in Brazil, right? Off the coast of Rio?
D Yes. My friend Aidan recommended it. It was spectacular!
F How did you get there?
D We went by car and then took the ferry. There are no cars there, so we walked a lot!
F So, so what did you do on the island? Was it interesting?
D Yes! The island's incredible, the forest is really beautiful, and the smell of nature is absolutely fantastic. We mainly just walked around. We visited lots of beautiful beaches, too, and I saw three dolphins!
F And the food? What did you eat?
D Well, we ate fresh fish every day. It was very hot, so I drank a lot of cold soda, too!
F Can I ask ... was it expensive? Did you stay in a hotel?
D Yes, we did. We stayed in a tiny hotel right across from the beach, and met some cool tourists from Argentina there. And no, the price was really reasonable.
F It really sounds like the perfect vacation.
D It was. We had a wonderful time, and I can't wait to go back.

8.8 Notice sentence stress.

What did you **do** on your **last vacation**?
Where did you **go**?
Did you **meet anyone interesting**?
What did you **do** every **day**?

8.10

1 Where did you go?
2 Do you watch a lot of TV?
3 Did you relax?
4 Where did you stay?
5 Do you eat well?
6 When did you go on vacation?

8.11 Notice and imitate the connections.

I = interviewer   J = Jay
I So, what's your typical day like, Jay?
J Well, everyone thinks my life_is_exciting, but it can be pretty boring!
I Really? What did_you do yesterday?
J Yesterday? OK, I got_up_at_about 6 o'clock.
I Wow! So_early! That's amazing.
J That's when_I usually wake_up, you know.
I And then?
J I brushed my teeth, and then I made coffee. I absolutely can't start my day without_it.
I And did_you have breakfast?
J Yes, I had_a big breakfast. I love to cook, so then I made_an_omelet.
I That's great! And what did you do after that?
J After that, I turned_on the computer to check my email.
I Do you get_a_lot_of messages?
J I sure do! You have no_idea. I spent five hours_ on the computer yesterday. I answered 100 emails!
I You're kidding! That's_incredible.
J Well, not_all_at once. I_answered 30 messages, and then_around 10 a.m., I went out and ran_a mile. Then I came home and took_a shower. After that, it was time for lunch, so I had_a sandwich.
I And then?
J Well, I finished_answering all the emails. Then_at_about 2:30 p.m., I started to play the keyboard and_experiment with some ideas. I played for three hours ... and I wrote_a new song.
I That's fantastic! And what did you do after that?
J Well, then I went to visit some friends. My day_ended_at midnight. That's when went to sleep.
I You had_a full day!

319

◯ 8.12
1
A I got up at about 6 o'clock.
B Wow! That's amazing.
2
A I love to cook, so I made an omelet.
B That's great!
3
A I answered 100 emails!
B You're kidding! That's incredible.
4
A I practiced for three hours ... and I wrote a song.
B That's fantastic!

◯ 8.13
OK, is everybody ready? Let's start!
Question 1
Who sold more than 100 million records and recorded the most songs?
a) Elvis Presley   b) The Beatles
c) Michael Jackson
Question 2
Who became the first artist to surpass 50 billion streams worldwide in 2018?
a) Drake   b) Coldplay   c) Justin Bieber
Question 3
Which singer sang the film version of "Let it Go" in Disney's *Frozen*?
a) Celine Dion   b) Idina Menzel   c) Demi Lovato
Question 4
Who wrote the first rap song to win an Oscar?
a) Eminem with "Lose Yourself"
b) Kanye West with "Stronger"
c) Jay-Z with "Run this Town"
Question 5
Who made a massively popular music video in which the singer(s) walk and sing in the street, wearing colored suits?
a) Mark Ronson and Bruno Mars
b) Ed Sheeran   c) Maroon 5
Question 6
Who had the first song in Spanish to surpass a billion views on YouTube?
a) Ricky Martin ("Livin' la Vida Loca")
b) Luis Fonsi featuring Daddy Yankee and Justin Bieber ("Despacito")
c) Enrique Iglesias ("Bailando")
Question 7
Who was born when and where? Match the singer to their birthday and birth place. Here are the singers:
a) Ariana Grande   b) Justin Bieber
c) Rihanna   d) Shawn Mendes
And here are the dates and birth places:
March 1, 1994; London, Canada
February 20, 1988; St Michael, Barbados
August 8, 1998; Toronto, Canada
June 26, 1993; Florida, the U.S.
Question 8
Who didn't sing at President Barack Obama's inaugurations?
a) Beyonce   b) Kelly Clarkson   c) Lady Gaga
Question 9
Where did Reggaeton begin in the late 1990s?
a) Brazil   b) Colombia   c) Puerto Rico
And finally ...
Question 10
What did Bob Marley say to his son, Ziggy, just before he died?
a) "Love one another"
b) "No woman, no cry"
c) "Money can't buy life"

◯ 8.14 Notice spellings of /ɑ/ and /oʊ/.
Q = quiz host   M = man
Q So has everyone finished? Time for the answers. Number 1 was in fact the Beatles.
M Yes! We got that one!
Q OK, question 2. The first artist to surpass 50 billion streams in 2018 was Drake.
M Another one right!
Q Question 3. Idina Menzel sang "Let it Go" in *Frozen*.
M No!
Q OK, question 4. Eminem wrote the first rap song to win an Oscar.
M That is correct ...
Q A difficult one now. Question 5. Who made the video ...
M I know, I know, I've got it, I know the answer! It was Maroon 5!
Q Well, actually it wasn't ... it was Mark Ronson and Bruno Mars.
M I don't believe it. No. I'm sure it was Maroon 5 ...
Q Well I'm sorry. On to question 6. Enrique Iglesias sang the first song in Spanish to surpass a billion views.
M Hmm.
Q Now on to question 7. Ariana Grande was born on June 26 in Florida ...
M Oh.
Q ... Justin Bieber was born on March 1st in London, Canada; Rihanna was born on February 20 in Barbados and Shawn Mendes was born on August 8 in Toronto. Now, question 8. Lady Gaga didn't sing at President Obama's inaugurations.
M Really?
Q Yes, really. Question 9. Reggaeton began in Puerto Rico.
M I was sure it was Brazil.
Q And finally ... question 10. Bob Marley told his son, "Money can't buy life."
M Well, I got that one right ...

◯ 8.15
S = sales clerk   C = customer
S Hello, can I help you?
C Yes, I hope so. There's a problem with my new phone.
S OK. I'll try to help. What exactly is the problem?
C Well, I tried to transfer the data and all my apps, but only some of them are here.
S Hmm ... OK, did you have a copy on the Cloud?
C Yes, I think so.
S OK. Just a minute, please.

◯ 8.16 Notice sentence stress.
S = sales clerk   C = customer
S OK. So when did you buy this phone exactly?
C Er ... last week.
S And did you buy it in this store or another one?
C I bought it here.
S That's good! Well, did you keep the receipt?
C Yes, I think so ... Ah! Here it is!
S OK. Great. Can you leave your phone with me?
C Er ..., but, um ..., how long?
S You can come back in an hour. We just need to take a look.
C Phew! Thanks!
S Can you give me your password, please?
C Oh, well, OK. But the password is only for you!

◯ 8.17 Notice h.
M = Mike   C = Chris
M Hey, Chris! How's it going? I tried to call you.
C Hi, Mike, I'm not happy at all.
M Why? What happened?
C Well, I was at work at the hotel, right, and I had my phone in my jacket pocket. And my boss says, "Chris, can you clean the bathroom?" So OK, I went to clean the bathroom.
M Then what happened?
C I was cleaning the toilet when ... SPLASH! My cell phone fell in to the toilet!
M Oh no! Did you get it out?
C Yeah, but that phone cost $400!
M What did you do?
C Well, I put it under the hand-dryer, but it still doesn't work.
M Gee! That's bad luck. But at least the bathroom's clean now!

◯ 8.18 Notice the connections.
1
M = Mom   S = Sophie
M Oh no! Look at this mess. Sophie!
S Yes, Mom?
M Can_you please wash the dishes?
S Uh, sorry, it's Brian's turn today.
M OK, forget it. Brian!!!
2
M = man   W = woman
M Excuse me. Uh, could_you open the door for me, please?
W Oh, sure. There you go.
M Thank you so much.
3
W = woman   D = Dan
W Dan, there's someone at the door.
D Could_you see who it is? I'm busy.
W Don't worry, I'll get it.
4
W = woman   J = Jim
W Jim!
J Uh?
W Could_you please cut the grass, Jim?
J Er, but ... the game ... Come on, I can do it tomorrow.
W Could_you do it this afternoon, please? Your mother's coming to visit.
J Uh, OK, I'll do it now.
5
W = woman   M = man
W Could_I ask you a favor?
M Hmmm, that depends. What do you want?
W Can_I leave my son with you this weekend?
M Oh. I'm really sorry, but I can't. I have two parties to go this weekend, so I can't be with your son. Sorry.
W Oh, no problem. Thanks, anyway!

Review 4

◯ R4.1
At last we were in Amsterdam! We were really excited to see everything the city has to offer, even though we were there for only a few days. We saw a lot! Here's what we did.
Day 1
First, we took a bike tour of the city. Amsterdam is famous for its bikes—people ride bikes everywhere, and it's definitely the best way to see the sights. It was more expensive to rent a bike than we expected, though. We had a great time riding around on the bike paths and narrow streets along the canals. But then I got a puncture! We were a long way from the place where we rented the bikes, and we couldn't fix the puncture, so we walked all the way back. It took ages and it wasn't the best way to end our first day.
Day 2
On our second day, we got tickets for a canal cruise. This is a great way to see the city from the water. In the old part of the city, the canals are lined with amazing tall, narrow houses that are hundreds of years old. We stopped at different places and went to Anne Frank House, which is where she hid with her family in World War II and where she wrote her diary. The house is now a really interesting museum,

but we all felt a little sad thinking about what she and her family suffered during the war.

Day 3
The next day, it rained all day and we got very wet in the morning! So, in the afternoon, we avoided the rain and went to some of the fabulous art galleries and museums in the city. My favorite was the Van Gogh Museum, where we saw hundreds of original Van Gogh paintings and learned a lot about his life. It was fantastic. After that, we ate in a tourist restaurant near the museum. It was a bad choice—the food was terrible, and it was very expensive, too.

Day 4
We had to check out of our hotel at noon on our last day, so we left our bags there and found a cheap Vietnamese restaurant close to the hotel for lunch. It was great! There were lots of locals eating there, as well as tourists. Then we walked around and did some shopping for souvenirs, before collecting our bags and getting the train to the airport. It's a really easy journey by train.
I recommend Amsterdam for a visit. There were a couple of disappointments, but overall it was a really good experience.

Unit 9

▶9.1 Notice /oʊ/, /ʊ/ and /ʌ/.
Hello and welcome to the Woodbury Music Festival! So, how did you all get here?
1 We rode our bikes. 30 miles!
2 We took the bus.
3 We walked. We live nearby.
4 I rode my motorbike.
5 By car. I drove.
6 I drove the band's truck! The other roadies all came the same way.
7 We took the ferry.
8 We took the train.
9 Some of the bands took a helicopter, I think.
10 I flew. I'm from Canada and my airplane landed this morning.

▶9.2
a I made a wrong turn.
b I had an accident.
c There was a traffic jam.
d My bus had a flat tire.
e The train was late.
f My plane was delayed.

▶9.3
Jak = Jake Jan = Jane
Jak Hi, are you ...?
Jan Hi, I'm Jane. And you?
Jak I'm Jake, Marilyn's brother.
Jan Oh, nice to meet you. Er ... Did you just get here?
Jak Yes, actually, my plane was delayed.
Jan Oh, that's too bad. Where do you live?
Jak In Chicago. I came just for the party.
Jan That's great. How did you get here from the airport?
Jak Well, I took the bus, but then my bus had a flat tire.
Jan You're kidding!
Jak No, seriously. And then there was a big traffic jam. But here I am.
Jan I'm so glad you finally arrived!

K = Ken M = Marilyn
K Hi, Marilyn! Great to see you! How's it going?
M Pretty good, thanks. How about you? I'm so happy you're here, Ken.
K Cool party. And, wow, this is a beautiful house ... Now I can forget my problems!
M Problems?
K Well, first the train was really late, so I decided to drive a friend's car.
M Oh! What went wrong?
K First, I made a wrong turn ...
M Oh, I do that all the time, even with GPS! What happened then?
K Well ... I had an accident. Nothing serious.
M Oh, no! In your friend's car? What did you do?
K I called the police. But my friend doesn't know.
M He doesn't know? Here, you can use my phone.
K Oh, no, thanks. Not now. First, I want to enjoy the party!

▶9.4
An Unusual Commute
Most people commute by bus, or they drive, but not Ted Houk, from Towson, Maryland. For five years, Dr. Houk rode his bike to work, but then he decided to run, instead, because he wanted even more exercise. Then, for 15 years, Dr. Houk always ran to his internal medicine practice from his home in Lutherville, and back again every day. It's about four miles (around six and a half kilometers) there and four miles home, but he ran when it was sunny, when it was raining, and even when it was snowing. He ran if it was hot or cold, and if it was light or dark.
He always ran with a big bag in his hand. In the bag were his clothes, his stethoscope, his phone, and about two pounds of fruit and vegetables. His full bag weighed about ten pounds (around four and a half kilograms). When Houk got to work, he always rubbed alcohol on his body to remove perspiration. But sweat is not really a problem, he says, because "your sweat is clean."
Then in 2013, Dr. Houk had a serious accident as he ran. He was seriously injured when a car hit him, and he was in the hospital for two months. Fortunately, he recovered and now works—and runs—again.

▶9.5
OK. Picture A, she's a firefighter. The flight attendant is picture B. Next, picture C ... yes, he's a police officer. OK, picture D ... he's a cab driver. Now look at picture E. What does she do? She's a photographer. Next, the guy with the technology in picture F... he's a computer programmer. Picture G ... she's a hairdresser. The man in picture H is probably a personal assistant and the man in I is definitely a cook! Finally, the woman in picture J could be a doctor ... let me see ... oh no, actually she's a dentist!

▶9.6 Notice /ə/ in articles and non-content words.
B = Brian J = James
B Look at this old picture from school, James! What's everybody doing now?
J Well, you know I'm a cab driver, Brian.
B Yes, you always loved driving!
J And Valerie is a hairdresser. She cuts and styles hair, you know – she loves it.
B And Martina is a firefighter. She was brave in high school.
J I know. What about Chris? What does she do?
B She's a flight attendant. She loves to travel!
J And I hear that Jane is a photographer.
B That's great! She always took fantastic pictures.
J What about Larry? Do you know anything about him?
B Yes! He's a police officer!
J What about David and Amelia?
B David's a cook ... no surprises there. And Amelia's a dentist.
J Wow, and Robert?
B He's a personal assistant to a famous singer! You know how he loves to organize people!
J Yeah! That's Robert! Nice job!
B I know—and I'm a computer programmer.

▶9.7 Notice the sentence stress.
K = Kelly M = Michael
K What are you going to do when you finish school, Michael?
M Well, first I'm going to go to grad school and then I'm going to be a financial advisor.
K Really? Why? That sounds boring.
M Well, you can make a lot of money as a financial advisor.
K I see!
M But seriously, you help people and you can be your own boss.
K That's cool. Your parents are going to be happy. You can give them financial advice.
M What about you?
K Promise you won't laugh if I tell you?
M Of course not. C'mon, tell me. What are you going do?
K I'm going to be a pet psychologist!
M What? How?
K Stop laughing! You promised not to laugh!
M Sorry!
K Yeah, I'm going to go to grad school and study psychology and then get a certificate in animal behavior. I want to be a pet psychologist. It's not going to be easy, but it's what I want.
M That's great! But, er, why, why do you want to be a pet psychologist?
K Well, first because I love animals, but I don't want to be a veterinarian. I want to work with animals. You can meet lots of people and make them happy. It's going to be fun!
M Maybe ...
K Well, I know I'm not going to be rich, but that's OK.
M OK then ... tell me what that dog's thinking.
K Don't be ridiculous!

▶9.8
1 What are you going to do?
2 I'm going to be a financial advisor.
3 Your parents are going to be happy.
4 I'm going to be a pet psychologist.
5 It's not going to be easy, but it's what I want.
6 You can meet lots of people. It's going to be fun.
7 I know I'm not going to be rich, but that's OK.

▶9.10
1
A I'm going to read a book.
B I'm gonna read a book.
2
A She's gonna go to the library.
B She's going to go to the library.
3
A What are you gonna do next year?
B What are you going to do next year?
4
A Are you gonna be at home tonight?
B Are you going to be at home tonight?

▶9.11 Notice three pronunciations of o - /oʊ/, /ɑ/, and /ə/.
Well, Alex, maybe you can learn a few lessons from your dad. I left college in 1975, before graduating. I couldn't wait to get married, so I found a girlfriend immediately and got engaged after just three months! We got married only a month later, and I left home. At the same time, I started a new job as a photographer in a photography studio. And we started a family! But, as you know, things didn't work, and your mom and I got divorced when you were five. So I moved to a new house. Then I lost my job, because of digital photography, so I changed careers and became a computer programmer—boring, but it paid the bills. I finally retired from my job last week and now I think it's time for you to

make a few changes in your life—I don't want you to make the same mistakes I did.

🔊 **9.12**

Well, I had a long talk with my dad the other day, and he convinced me. We're very different, but I love him. So, I'm going to make a few changes in my life. And, anyway, today is a new year, so time for a new start!

First, I'm going to exercise more. I ate too much over the holidays! Then I'm going to get a new job. I'm a server in a restaurant, and I hate my boss. He makes me stay late and keeps my tips! I want to be a web designer, so I'm going to go back to school, get my bachelor's, and show them all! I'm going to learn a new language, too. I want to learn to speak Mandarin.

I'm also going to move out of my mom's house and get an apartment with some friends. I think it's time, don't you? And I'm going to buy a new car. Then I'm going to find a new girlfriend—I'm so lonely! So ... "How are you going to do all this?" I hear you asking. Here's my plan:

Well, after lunch, I'm playing basketball with my friend, Carl, and then tonight, I'm having dinner with my mom to tell her I'm leaving home. Next week, I'm talking to a career specialist, and I'm starting a class in Mandarin. And ... I'm going on a date tomorrow night. Wow! Wish me luck! What do you think of my plan? Thanks for reading!

🔊 **9.13 Notice the future verb forms.**

C = Carla J = John Ju = Julia M = Martin

1
C Hi, Ronnie! It's Carla. My brother's moving to Paris in July. He's going to fly there and he wants me to help him pack all his stuff. Can you help us too? it's going to take us weeks, but you're really good at packing. I hope you can! And I promise to buy you dinner! Thanks. Call me back.

2
J Hi, Melissa, it's John. Listen, you know I told you that my parents are going to retire in February. Well, they've decided that they're going to move to a warmer place—so they're going to travel through Central and South America, and I wonder if you could help ... I know you lived in Costa Rica with your parents for a long time. We really value your opinion!

3
Ju Hi, Mom! It's Julia. Uh ... Are you sitting down? We have some big news. Guess what! We're getting engaged! We're not going to get married until we finish school, so don't panic. So, uh, call me back when you get this message. Ciao!

4
M Hi, Lucy, it's Martin. I got in! It's official! Yeah! I'm changing careers at last. I'm going to study nursing, and I'm going to be a nurse. A nurse! Woohoooo! I just got the news—they accepted me at the nursing school. I'm so excited! Call me back, because we need to celebrate. I'm going to be at work all afternoon, but then I'm going home, so give me a call and let's go out! Love you! Yeah!

🔊 **9.14 Notice two pronunciations of e - /ɛ/, /iː/.**

M = man W = woman

M A civil engineer: an engineer who builds public works for example, bridges or roads.
W A dentist: a person who takes care of other people's teeth.
M A financial advisor: a person who helps people invest their money.
W A market research analyst: a person who studies the reasons people buy certain products.
M A nurse: a person who helps doctors to take care of sick people.
W A software developer: a person who writes new computer programs.

🔊 **9.15**

What professionals are we going to need in the future? Here are predictions for the six jobs that are going to be in demand in the U.S. in 10 years.

1
We will need more people to help the millions of workers who are going to retire in the next 10 years. Many people are going to ask experts to help them plan what to do with their money.

2
People over the age of 65 are going to keep more of their own teeth, so there are going to be more professionals to show them how to keep their teeth healthy.

3
What are we going to do about all the cars and buses? With more traffic, we need more roads and bridges, for example. We need more people who can build these large structures.

4
Companies need people to help them to understand what people want to buy. They want people who can analyze what customers want and tell them what products to make.

5
People with IT (information technology) degrees and extensive computer experience are going to be in high demand, to make new software.

6
There are going to be a lot more people over the age of 90 because of progress in medicine. This means we are going to need more people to help to look after them.

🔊 **9.16 Notice the connections.**

1
L = Len J = Jane
L Excuse me, Jane. Can I ask you something?
J That's fine, Len. What_is_it?
L Could_I take the day_off tomorrow? I need to take my son to the doctor.
J Sure. Go ahead!
L Thanks, Jane. Phew! That's great!

2
S = son M = Mom
S Can_I borrow the car, Mom?
M No, I'm sorry, you can't. I need_it this afternoon.
S Ooooooh! Why not? You never let me borrow the car ...

3
M = man W = woman
M Argh, do_you mind_if I turn_on the air-conditioning?
W Not_at_all. It's really warm_in here.
M Phew, thanks.

4
A I hate to ask this, but could_you lend me some money? I left my money_at home, and_I need to get something to eat.
B I'm sorry, but_I don't have_any money with me_at the moment.
A Oh, OK, I'll_ask Jeff. Thanks_anyway.

Unit 10

🔊 **10.1**

So, let's think about the important parts of the body we're going to study in this course. Any suggestions? OK, 1 the stomach ... 2 the fingers ... 3 the legs—very important in sports! ... 4 the toes—yes, good ... 5 the arms—of course! ... 6 the chest, 7 the head—mustn't forget that! ... 8 the back ... 9 the hands ... 10 the feet. Excellent. Now we're going to look at how each part of the body is important in sports ...

🔊 **10.2 Notice /aɪ/, /aʊ/ and /oʊ/.**

Well, my job is to get people ready for the camera. I have to think about all these things: first, the hair, then the eyebrows and the eyes, then I quickly check the ears and the nose. Finally, I work on the mouth, and this means checking the teeth and working on the lips. I want people to look absolutely perfect!

🔊 **10.3 Notice the connections.**

P = police officer A, B and C = witnesses

1
P So, the man who took your bag. What did he look like?
A Hmm ... he wasn't short or tall. He was, um_ average height. And he wasn't overweight_or slim, he was_average build_I think.
P And can you remember the color_of his hair?
A Yeah, He, er ... He had dark hair.
P Long_or short?
A Er, long dark hair_and he had blue eyes, I think.
P OK. I think_I know who you mean. That's_ Adam. We know where he lives. Thanks! Let's go!

2
P OK, and what does the suspect look like?
B Well, he's short_and slim. And he said his name was Charlie, but, well, who knows.
P Uh-huh? What else do_you remember?
B Hmm, er ... he has short dark hair_and brown_ eyes. Like you!
P OK, thank_you. Oh, and don't worry. I'm not Charlie.

3
P OK, can_you describe the suspect, please? You said his name was Mark, right? What does_he look like?
C Well, he's tall_and very_overweight.
P Hmm, OK, and what color_is his hair?
C Er, I think he has short fair hair_and blue eyes.
P OK – thank_you, ma'am.

🔊 **10.5**

A What are you reading?
B It's an article about a runner with a prosthetic leg.
A Really? What does it say?
B Well her leg was amputated when she was a baby—only six months old.
A Oh! That's terrible.
B I know! But she got a prosthetic leg at nine months old.
A Wow.
B ... and four months later she started to walk. She's incredible.
A You're kidding! At thirteen months? My niece is the same age and she can't even walk!
B But that's not all. In 2008, she actually won the New York Triathlon. Can you believe it?
A No way! She's really determined, isn't she?
B Well, yes, I guess so. And her father inspired her to be a doctor.
A Really?
B Yes. He died in 2010, but that didn't stop her. She became a doctor in 2017.
A Wow! She sounds incredible!

🔊 **10.6 Notice /ə/.**

M = Maggie S = Steve

M I need some help, Steve.
S What's up, Maggie?
M Two people have invited me to parties on Saturday.
S Well, which one do you like better?
M They're both nice. Well, Scott is taller than Jake and you know I usually like tall men.

Audioscript

S Yes, so go with Scott to the party!
M But Jake is **hap**pier than Scott. Scott's **sad**der.
S So, go with Jake! That's **more** important. It doesn't **mat**ter that he's **shor**ter than Scott.
M I know, but Scott is **more** interesting than Jake. Jake is a bit boring.
S Why don't you go to both parties? You can be friends with both of them.
M Good idea. I can go to the first party with Jake from seven to ten and then go to the second party with Scott at ten.
S **Pro**blem solved!

▶10.7 Notice word stress in the underlined words.

W What do your twin <u>sis</u>ters look like?
M Those are my twin <u>sis</u>ters, <u>Zoe</u> and Re<u>bec</u>ca over there.
W Wow, Brad! They look i<u>den</u>tical.
M Yes, but they're very <u>dif</u>ferent.
W What's Zoe like?
M She's <u>friend</u>lier than Rebecca and she's more <u>gen</u>erous. She likes to be with other <u>peo</u>ple and she's always giving <u>peo</u>ple <u>pres</u>ents.
W What about Rebecca? What's she like?
M She's more <u>tim</u>id than Zoe, and she's <u>cal</u>mer. She likes to be a<u>lone</u>, but she's more in<u>tel</u>ligent and more <u>or</u>ganized than Zoe.

▶10.9 Notice pronunciation of the suffixes.

A Type one is a per**fec**tionist. They're idea**lis**tic but sometimes they're **cri**tical of other people.
B And what about type 2? What are they like?
A They're **gen**erous people but they're also pos**ses**sive.
B And type 3?
A They're am**bi**tious but they can become **ar**rogant.
B Can you tell me about type 4? What are they like?
A Type 4. Umm, they're ro**man**tic, but sometimes they can be **moo**dy, too.
B What about types 5 and 6?
A Type 5 people are **sol**itary and they try to understand the world but sometimes they feel de**pres**sed. That's type 5. Type 6 people are **loy**al and re**spon**sible but also sus**pi**cious.
B OK, the last three?
A Type 7 people are spon**tan**eous, **hap**py and fun. But they are very dis**or**ganized. Type 8 people are strong and try to do important things. The bad side is that they get **an**gry. And the last one, type 9. They are calm and a**void con**flict. The negative side is that they are passive and ac**cept** things because they don't want any problems.

▶10.10

1 The highest mountain in the world is Mount Everest, but the second highest is K2, answer c.
2 The most spoken language in the world is Mandarin Chinese, and the second most spoken is Spanish, answer b.
3 The most populated city in the Americas is São Paulo, and the second most populated city is answer c, Mexico City.
4 The most successful movie of all time is *Gone with the Wind*, and the second most successful is *Avatar*, answer b.
5 The closest planet to the sun is Mercury, and the second closest is answer a, Venus.

▶10.11

In 2007, Bernard Weber started a project to find the seven most beautiful places in the world. People from all five continents voted for their favorite place. Here are nine of the finalists.
Komodo National Park is in Indonesia. It opened in 1980 to protect the Komodo dragon, the largest lizard in the world.
The Amazon Rainforest is the largest rainforest in the world. It's located in nine different countries, and it's home to the world's longest river, the Amazon River.
The Grand Canyon in the U.S. is more than 1.6 kilometers deep. It has many canyons and caves.
Halong Bay in Vietnam has thousands of rocks and islands in different sizes and shapes. It also has beautiful caves and lakes.
Table Mountain in Cape Town, South Africa, got its name because it's flat on the top. More than 1,470 types of flowers grow there.
The Iguazu Falls is one of the largest groups of waterfalls in the world. There are 275 different waterfalls there. The Falls are on the border between Brazil and Argentina.
Jeju is the largest island in South Korea. It's the home to Hallasan, a dormant volcano that's also the tallest mountain in South Korea. There are 360 other volcanos around Hallasan.
Mount Kilimanjaro in Tanzania is one of the highest mountains in the world. The top of Kilimanjaro is 5,895 meters above sea level.
The Puerto Princesa National Park in the Philippines has one of the world's longest underground rivers.

▶10.12

Ladies and gentlemen, adults and children, citizens of the world, welcome to the announcement of the first count and provisional results of the global vote to elect the new seven wonders of nature.
The moment has come and I now proceed to announce the provisional new seven wonders of nature in alphabetic order.
Amazon – South America
Halong Bay in Vietnam
Iguazu Falls in Argentina and Brazil
Jeju Island in South Korea
Komodo in Indonesia
Puerto Princesa Underground River in the Philippines and Table Mountain in South Africa.

▶10.13

1 The biggest lizard in the world is in Indonesia.
2 The Amazon rainforest is the largest in the world.
3 The River Nile is longer than the Amazon.
4 The Arctic is the world's smallest ocean.
5 The Amazon River goes through six countries.

▶10.14 Notice the sentence stress and the weak forms.

W = woman M = man
W OK, so let's **see** how we **did**. Number **1** is **true**. **Scientists** don't know **why**, but your **brain** is very **ac**tive when you **sleep**.
M OK—I **knew that** one.—Number **2**?
W **True**. It says that **if** men don't **shave**, a **beard** can grow to **more** than **10 me**ters long!
M **Wow! What** about number **3**?
W That's **false**. Your **toe**nails grow **slow**er than your **fin**gernails because they get **less** sun.
M Hmm. **In**teresting. And number **4**?
W This is **true**, because **wo**men are **small**er than **men**, so the **heart** needs to **move** the **blood fas**ter to the **dif**ferent parts of the **bo**dy.
M Oh! I **didn't** know that. **What** about number **5**?
W **False**. The **heart** needs a **lot** of space, so the **left** lung is **small**er.
M **Real**ly? **OK**, what about number **6**?
W That's **false**. We can **live** for a **month** or even two months without **food**, but the **long**est time a person can go with **no** sleep is **11** days. **Sleep** is **more im**portant than **food**.
M **Wow**, this is **real**ly **in**teresting! And number **7**?
W This is **true**. When you **eat** or **talk**, you are **us**ing your **tongue** so it gets a **lot** of **ex**ercise.
M I sup**pose** so. Blablabla! What about **8**?
W This is **false** – the **most com**mon **blood** type is **O**.
M I think **I'm** type **O**. How about **you**?

▶10.15 Notice the connections.

1
A So, what do you think?
B I'm not sure, Chinese or Italian?
A Hmm, I pre**fer** the Chinese res**t**aurant, but it's more expensive than the Italian.
B Yes, but the service is faster in the Italian restaurant than in the Chinese.
A I can't de**cide**.
B Well, we're not in a hurry, so let's go to the Chinese restaurant.
A OK. Sounds good!
2
C Hmm, which one is best?
D Well, the **straw**berry is the **sweet**est and the **co**conut is more **in**teresting. **Cho**colate is very **pop**ular!
C What do you recommend?
D I like the va**nil**la best.
C OK. I'll have the vanilla.
3
E So, where do you want to go? To the beach or to the **moun**tains?
F Well, the beach is **warm**er than the mountains.
E Yes, but it's more **peace**ful in the mountains.
F Well, I don't know. I can't de**cide**.
E OK, why don't we go to the beach? We need to have some fun!
F That sounds great!

Review 5

▶R5.1

1
A Do you mind if I borrow your bike?
B No, sorry. I need it.
2
A Could you lend me a pen?
B Sure. Here.
3
A Can I close the door?
B Of course. Go ahead.
4
A Do you mind if I eat this pizza?
B No, not at all. That's fine.
5
A Can I use your laptop?
B Sorry, but I'm leaving now.
6
A Could I go home earlier today?
B Sure. That's fine.

▶R5.2 Notice voiced *th* /ð/ and unvoiced *th* /θ/.

L = Laila J = Jenna
L Hi, Jenna, how are you?
J Hi, Laila. I'm great, **th**anks. Hey, I got your email. Great news about your trip.
L I know! I'm so excited!
J Listen, Laila. My bro**th**er went to work in Los Angeles and his room is empty. You can stay **th**ere until you go to Thailand.
L Your brother's room! Really? Oh, **th**at's very kind of you. Are you sure he doesn't mind?
J No problem at all. But when exactly are you going on vacation?
L Well, I finish school on June 20**th** and I'm going to fly to Bangkok on July 16**th**.
J So you need a room for about two weeks, right?
L Umm, let me check ... No, about **th**ree and a half weeks actually.
J **Th**ree and a half weeks. No problem.
L **Th**anks so much, Jenna. OK, now tell me about you ... how are you?

323

Songs

1.1

🎵 **Song line:** When I see your face, There's not a thing that I would change, 'Cause you're amazing, Just the way you are.
Song: *Just the Way You Are*, released in 2010
Artist: Bruno Mars (American)
Lesson link: verb *be* – present
Notes: This was Bruno Mars's debut single, and it topped the charts in 5 countries. It was also the best-selling digital single of 2011. He reportedly wanted to write a simple song which came straight from the heart.

After **2A**, read the song line to sts without singing it, and ask them if they recognize which song it's from. If they do, encourage them to sing it together, and help them with any pronunciation difficulties. Next, have sts work in pairs, and ask them to find examples of the verb *be* in the song line (they will probably be able to find the three uses (*there's, you're, you are*)). Explain that, here, the fixed expression *there's* refers to existence, and despite the fact that it also uses the verb *be*, it is not the focus of this lesson. Then have sts observe that in the two other uses in the song line; one is contracted and the other is not. Ask: *Why isn't the second **are** contracted?* Encourage them to guess and explain that, besides the song's rhythm requiring the full form of the verb, we can only contract the subject and *be* when there's a complement (noun, adjective, adverb). Finally, ask sts to search the web for more examples of song lines containing the verb *be* in the simple present and encourage them to share them with the whole class.

1.2

🎵 **Song line:** It's fun to stay at the **Y.M.C.A**.
Song: *Y.M.C.A*, released in 1978
Artist: Village People (American)
Lesson link: pronunciation of letters
Notes: This upbeat dance track was the Village People's most successful song, reaching number 1 in countries all over the world. It is often sung at sporting events, with the crowd spelling out the letters of the title with their arms.

After **1C**, have sts read the song line silently, and ask: *Can you identify the song?* Encourage them to answer. They will probably be able to because they have just learned how to spell the letters of the alphabet and should recognize the pronunciation of these letters in the song. To practice spelling with a few more song lines, write the lyrics below on the board, and ask sts to read them out loud and identify the songs. If possible, search for videos or audio clips of the songs so you can play the song lines to sts after they try to identify them.

1) Girl, before I met you, I was F.I.N.E, fine (Aerosmith / What It takes - 1989)
2) So give me more L-O-V-E, love (Al Green / L-O-V-E [Love] - 1975)
3) R.O.C.K in the U.S.A., R.O.C.K in the U.S.A., R.O.C.K in the U.S.A., yeah, yeah, Rocking in the U.S.A. (John Cougar Mellencamp / R.O.C.K in the U.S.A. - 1985)
4) M-O-V-E, I love it when you, love it when you feel the beat, C-O-M-E, Come on, I wanna see you (Luke / Move - 2015)

1.3

🎵 **Song line:** You can stand under my **umbrella**, ella, ella.
Song: *Umbrella*, released in 2007
Artist: Rihanna (Barbadian) feat. Jay-Z (American)
Lesson link: personal objects
Notes: Having been named one of the best songs of 2007, this song was extremely successful. Ironically, the day after *Umbrella's* release, the UK was hit with torrential rain and flooding, leading to the storms being labelled "Rihanna's curse".

After **3A**, read the song line to sts, and have them identify which song it's from. Encourage them to remember the lyrics right before the line in the book (*you can stand under my umbrella ...*) and immediately after it (*... under my umbrella, ella, ella eh eh eh, under my umbrella, ella, ella eh eh eh, under my umbrella, ella, ella eh eh eh*). Encourage sts to sing the whole chunk in order to practice. Then, have them work in pairs and search the web for lyrics of three different songs containing different personal objects from **3A**. When they have completed their search, have the pairs share their findings. Take note on the board of the different songs sts mention, and finally, have them vote for their favorite Personal Objects song.

1.4

🎵 **Song line:** **Purple** rain, **purple** rain, I only want to see you bathing in the **purple** rain.
Song: *Purple Rain*, released in 1984
Artist: Prince and The Revolution (American)
Lesson link: colors and adjectives
Notes: *Purple Rain* is considered to be one of Prince's most well-known songs. After his death in 2016, it rose to its all-time peak position of number one in the UK and U.S. iTunes charts.

After **3A**, have sts read the song line and identify which song it's from. Have them sing the line aloud, and ask: *Do you like the color purple?* Encourage them to answer. Next, have sts work in pairs or threes, and ask them to write down as many songs as they can remember with colors in the title. Explain that they should not search the web for this because it must be a song that they can sing or hum a part of for the other sts to guess. When they're ready with their lists, have the pairs take turns singing or humming parts of their songs containing colors in the title for the others to guess. Some possible well-known songs with colors in the title are:

Back in Black (AC/DC), Baby's in Black (Beatles), Black or White (Michael Jackson), Blue Suede Shoes (Elvis Presley), Brown Eyed Girl (Van Morisson), Brown Sugar (Rolling Stones), Green Eyes (Coldplay), Lady in Red (Chris De Burgh), Men in Black (Will Smith), Pink (Aerosmith), Red (Taylor Swift), Red Light (U2), Red Red Wine (UB 40), White Wedding (Billy Idol), Yellow Raincoat (Justin Bieber), Yellow Submarine (Beatles)

1.5

🎵 **Song line:** Hey, I just met you, And this is crazy, But **here's my number**, So **call me**, maybe?
Song: *Call Me Maybe*, released in 2012
Artist: Carly Rae Jepson (Canadian)
Lesson link: meeting people and social interaction
Notes: This song was a success worldwide and the best digitally sold song of 2012. It is primarily about love at first sight, and the video features Carly Rae Jepson falling for a neighbor. The idea behind the video was that it was to be about a girl liking a boy, rather than the more typical boy-meets-girl story.

After **ID Skills** activity **D**, have sts read the song line silently and identify which song it's from. Once they do, have them sing it aloud. Then ask: *What is the situation described in this song line?* Encourage them to answer, and make sure they understand that the girl in the lyrics just met a boy and she is giving him her phone number (probably without being asked) so he can call her later if he wants to. Next, ask: *Is this common for someone to do when they first meet in your city / country? What do you think?* Have sts share their opinions about it. Then encourage them to read the complete song line again and ask: *What about for the character in the song, do you think this is common for her?* Make sure sts realize that the fact that she says *"and this is crazy"* before giving her number probably indicates that this is not very common for her, even though she did it.

Songs

Writing 1

🎵 **Song line:** Tell me, **where are you now** that I need you? **Where are you** now?
Song: *Where Are U Now*, released in 2015
Artist: Jack Ü (American) feat. Justin Bieber (Canadian)
Lesson link: questions with verb *be*
Notes: This song was produced by Skrillex and Diplo (who together make up Jack Ü), and the vocals were performed by Justin Bieber. The original demo track was a piano ballad by Bieber, but his collaboration with Jack Ü made it into a globally successful electronic dance track.

Before **ID in Action**, have sts read the song line aloud and ask: *Can you identify the song?* Encourage them to answer and sing it if they know it. Then ask: *What is the connection between this song line and the lesson?* Encourage sts to quickly look at the content on p. 15 and find the lesson link with the song line. Make sure they know that the link is "questions with the verb *be*." Then write four or five answers on the board (see suggestions below) and explain that only one of them properly answers the question in the song line. Have sts work in pairs to choose the correct answer.

1) I'm OK now.
2) I am happy now.
3) **I'm right here.**
4) I'm your friend now.
5) I am Peruvian.

2.1

🎵 **Song line:** I don't care if **Monday**'s blue, **Tuesday**'s gray and **Wednesday** too. Thursday, I don't care about you.
Song: *Friday I'm In Love*, released in 1992
Artist: The Cure (British)
Lesson link: days of the week
Notes: Featured in several recent films, including *About Time* and *He's Just Not That Into You*, this song is still fairly popular over 25 years since its release. It was written with an aim to be a happy, naïve pop song.

Before **1D**, have sts read the song line and ask: *What is the next line in the song?* Encourage them to answer (… It's Friday I'm in love), and have them sing the whole chunk. Next, ask: *What is this song about?* and have sts answer (the days of the week). Help them notice that there are only five days mentioned in this part of the lyrics and ask: *What are the two missing days?* (Saturday and Sunday). Then ask: *Do these days appear in the rest of the lyrics?* (yes), and have sts search the web for the complete lyrics to find out. Finally, ask: *Based on the lyrics, what's the composer's favorite day of the week?* (Friday), and encourage sts to answer.

2.2

🎵 **Song line:** Don't forget me, I beg, I remember you said, "Sometimes it **lasts** in love but sometimes it **hurts** instead."
Song: *Someone Like You*, released in 2011
Artist: Adele (British)
Lesson link: simple present
Notes: Adele's most successful song is the 4th most downloaded song of the 21st century. It was inspired by a break-up Adele had been through, after she found out her ex-boyfriend had gotten married. She says that writing this song was the one thing that made her feel more at peace with the break-up.

Before starting section **2** (**Grammar**), have sts close their books, and write the second part of the song line on the board, but without the third person *s* in verbs *last* and *hurt* ("*Sometimes it **last** in love but sometimes it **hurt** instead*"). First, have students try to identify the song with just this part and encourage them to sing it. As they do so, ask: *What's missing on the board?* Have sts work in pairs to spot the mistakes. They probably won't be able to explain why these verbs need the *s* in this line, but if they know the song, they will be able to spot the mistakes anyway. If necessary, you can find a video of the song online and play this part for sts to compare with what's written on the board. Finally, explain that they'll learn more about the third person *s* in this lesson.

2.3

🎵 **Song line:** We are **family**, I got all my **sisters** with me, We are **family**, get up everybody and sing!
Song: *We Are Family*, released in 1979
Artist: Sister Sledge (American)
Lesson link: family members
Notes: This song ended up becoming Sister Sledge's signature song, after its success in Europe and the United States. In 2007, a cover version of the song was released which showed over 100 characters from children's television performing it, including Barney the dinosaur, Spongebob Squarepants, and Winnie the Pooh.

After section 1 (Reading and Vocabulary), have sts read the song line and identify the song. Encourage them to sing it aloud. As they do, write the word *family* on the board and mark the stress on it. Next, have sts look at the word you wrote on the board and ask them to say it aloud. Since they have just heard the word *family* on the audio in activities **1A** and **5**, they will probably be able to stress the first syllable correctly. Then have sts sing the song line again and ask: *What's different? Where is the stress in the word family in the song?* Help them notice that, in the song, the stress is on the last syllable of *family*, because they need it to rhyme with *me* and *sing*. Finally, ask sts to find other examples of words that are stressed differently in songs and bring videos of them next class.

2.4

🎵 **Song line:** I will **never** say never! (I will fight), I will fight till forever! (make it right)
Song: *Never Say Never*, released in 2010
Artist: Justin Bieber (Canadian) feat. Jaden Smith (American)
Lesson link: frequency adverbs
Notes: This song, Bieber's second top-ten hit, was used as the theme song for the remake of *Karate Kid* (2010), which stars Jaden Smith, who was also involved in the recording of the song. The video shows clips of Bieber and Smith recording the song, interspersed with clips of Smith learning karate.

Before sts arrive, write "*I will **always** say never! (I will fight) I will fight till forever! (make it right)*" on the board. As sts arrive, have them read what you wrote on the board. When all sts are in the classroom ask: *Do you recognize this?* Encourage them to answer, and, if they don't recognize it, explain that this is a song line but with one wrong word in it. Have sts work in pairs to find out the wrong word and correct the song line. When they're ready, encourage them to sing the corrected song line aloud. Finally, explain to sts that the word that they have corrected in the song line is a frequency adverb (*always*), and it was corrected to another frequency adverb (*never*), which is the opposite of *always*. Tell sts that they'll learn more about frequency adverbs in this lesson.

Songs

2.5

🎵 **Song line:** Music's got me feeling so free, We're gonna **celebrate**.
Song: *One More Time*, released in 2001
Artist: Daft Punk (French)
Lesson link: celebrating
Notes: This is an electronic song, featuring heavily auto-tuned vocals, which were performed by Romanthony. The music video is part of the film *Interstellar 5555: The 5tory of the Secret 5tar System*.

Before **ID in Action**, have sts close their books and explain that they will play *Telephone* with a song line. Start the game by whispering the complete song line very clearly to the first student and have them whisper it to the classmate on their left, and so on. Remind sts that it is a song line—knowing this might help them make any corrections during the game—but explain that even if they recognize the song they shouldn't hum or sing it, they must just whisper the line to the classmate on their left. When it gets to the last student in the sequence, have them say it aloud. Finally, have sts open their books to check the actual song line and spot the differences.

Writing 2

🎵 **Song line:** You are not alone, I am here with you, Though we're far apart, You're always in my heart.
Song: *You Are Not Alone*, released in 1995
Artist: Michael Jackson (American)
Lesson link: review of verb *be*
Notes: Although this is not Jackson's most popular song, it reached number 1 in both the U.S. and the UK charts.

Before the class, search for a clip of the song, with just the lyrics that are in the song line. As sts arrive at class, ask them not to open their books. When all sts have arrived, play the clip once and have sts write down what they hear. Play the video once or twice more, as necessary, for sts to catch any words that they didn't hear the first time that they heard it. When you believe sts are ready, have a volunteer write what they heard on the board. Then encourage volunteers to come to the board and correct anything they think is a mistake in the song line that's on the board. Allow them to discuss and make any changes they think are necessary. Remind sts not to open their books or check the web for the lyrics. Finally, have sts read the song line at the top of p. 28 to compare, and ask: *What were the most difficult words?* Encourage sts to share their opinions.

Review 1

🎵 **Song line:** But just because it **burns**, **doesn't** mean you're gonna die, You gotta get up and try.
Song: *Try*, released in 2012
Artist: Pink (American)
Lesson link: simple present
Notes: This song is about holding on to your dreams and aspirations despite the risks that are involved. It was co-written by Ben West, who has written a few hits for singers like Kelly Clarkson and Katy Perry among others.

Before sts arrive, write the song line from p. 31 on the board, but with the following mistakes: "But just because it **burn**, **don't** mean you're gonna die. You gotta get up and try." As sts arrive at class, ask them not to open their books. When all sts arrive, have them look at the song line that you wrote on the board and ask: *Do you know this song?* Encourage sts to answer and sing it if they want to. Then ask: *What's wrong with the song line that I wrote on the board?* and have sts work in pairs to spot the mistakes. When the pairs are ready, have volunteers point out the mistakes in the song line. Check and correct as necessary.

3.1

🎵 **Song line:** I wanna know, Have you ever seen **the rain**, Comin' down on **a sunny day**?
Song: *Have You Ever Seen the Rain*, released in 1970
Artist: Creedence Clearwater Revival (American)
Lesson link: weather nouns and adjectives
Notes: Creedence Clearwater Revival was a rock group in the 1960s and 70s. They often included lyrics commenting on socio-political issues of the time, such as the Vietnam War. However, according to the writer, this song is about developing tensions in the band, who were not happy even though they had achieved fame and fortune.

After section **3** (Vocabulary), have sts look at the song line at the top of p. 33 and ask: *Do you know this song? Can you sing this part?* Encourage them to recognize the song and sing that part of the song. Clarify meaning by asking *What happens when it's sunny and it suddenly starts to rain?* (A rainbow is formed.) Make sure sts understand what a rainbow is. If necessary, find a picture of a rainbow on the Internet and show it to them. Next, write the song line on the board, leaving two blanks where the weather words (*rain* and *sunny*) are: *I wanna know, have you ever seen the ____, Coming down on a ____ day.* Then have sts work in pairs, and explain that they must complete the blanks using other weather-related words with the same functions as the ones in the original song line (noun and adjective, respectively). Finally, have them share their ideas with the class singing their new lines. **Note:** If a pair chooses the word *wind* for the first blank, explain that this would also require a change in the expression *coming down*, as this expression can be used for *rain*, *fog*, *cloud*, *snow*, and even *sun*, but the expression for *wind* would use the word *blowing*.

3.2

🎵 **Song line:** Winter, spring, summer or fall, All you got to do is call and I'll be there, yeah, yeah, yeah, You've got a friend.
Song: *You've Got a Friend*, released in 1971
Artist: James Taylor (American)
Lesson link: seasons
Notes: Originally written by Carole King, James Taylor's version of this song reached the top of the charts in the United States.

Before starting section **3** (Reading), have sts close their books and write on the board: "**Summer**, **winter**, **spring** or **fall**, *all you got to is call and I'll be there, yeah, yeah, yeah. You've got a friend.*" Have sts read it aloud, and ask: *Do you know this song?* Encourage them to identify the song and sing it. Then ask: *Is there anything wrong with this line?* (The inverted order of the seasons.) Have students work in pairs to find the mistakes in the line you wrote and put the seasons in the correct order according to the actual song. Explain that, in order to make it more challenging, they should not use their devices to search the web for the lyrics. Finally, have sts open their books at p. 35 and compare the actual song line with the order they suggested. Make sure they realize that the original song line starts with winter and the other seasons appear in the order they occur: winter, spring, summer, fall.

3.3

🎵 **Song line:** Don't stop me now, **I'm having** such a good time, **I'm having** a ball.
Song: *Don't Stop Me Now*, released in 1979
Artist: Queen (British)
Lesson link: present continuous
Notes: Although this song didn't chart very highly anywhere but the UK and Ireland on its release, it has since become one of Queen's most well-known songs. This is due to heavy airplay and use in the advertisements as well as cover versions by popular artists, including McFly.

Songs

Before starting lesson 3.3, have sts read the song line at the top of p. 37 and ask: *Do you know this song?* Have students try to identify it and sing it if they can. Then ask: *What is the link between the song line and the lesson?* (present continuous). Encourage sts to take a quick look at the lesson to find the link and present it to the class. Next, have them work in pairs and ask them to use their devices to search the web for two or three other famous song lines that use the present continuous. When the pairs are ready, have them present their song lines to the whole class. Encourage sts to sing them instead of writing them on the board. Monitor and help as necessary. Some possible famous songs with the present continuous are: *I'm with You* (Avril Lavigne), *Don't Speak* (No Doubt), *Mr. Jones* (Counting Crows), *Spending My Time* (Roxette), *Stairway to Heaven* (Led Zeppelin), *On Bended Knees* (Boyz Two Men), *This Is What You Came For* (Calvin Harris feat. Rhianna), *Sailing* (Rod Stewart), *Tom's Diner* (Susan Vega), *Singing in the Rain* (Gene Kelly).

3.4

Song line: I'm **giving** it my all, but I'm not the girl **you're taking** home, oh, **I keep dancing** on my own.
Song: *Dancing on My Own*, released in 2010
Artist: Robyn (Swedish)
Lesson link: present continuous
Notes: Inspired by the disco genre, this song is a dance pop ballad. It is about a girl alone in a club seeing her ex-partner dancing with someone else. The music video echoes this, switching between Robyn performing the song, and her alone on a crowded dance floor.

Before sts arrive, write the song line from p. 39 on the board, with the verb tenses that are in the present continuous changed to the present simple. It should look like this: *I give it my all, but I'm not the girl you take home, oh, I keep dance on my own.* As sts arrive, tell them not to open their books yet so they don't read the correct version of the song line. When all sts have arrived, explain that this is a song line, but it has three mistakes in it. Have them work in pairs or threes to find out what the three mistakes are. In order to make it more challenging, do not tell sts where the mistakes are and do not allow them to search the web for the lyrics. Go around the classroom to monitor and help where necessary. Finally, have sts share their corrected versions of the song line. If they know the actual song, ask them to sing it with the corrections they've made. Make sure sts realize that the three mistakes on the board are in the verbs *give*, *take* and *dance*, which should be in the present continuous but were put into the present simple.

3.5

Song line: So one last time, I **need** to be the one who takes you home, One more time, I promise after that, I'll let you go.
Song: *One Last Time*, released in 2014
Artist: Ariana Grande (American)
Lesson link: needs
Notes: This was the last song performed by Ariana Grande at her Manchester concert on May 22, 2017, just a few minutes before the terrorist attack that killed 22 fans. Right after the tragedy, a campaign led by fans took the song to its peak in the UK chart, at the 11th position in the week following the event.

After **ID Skills**, have sts read the song line and ask: *Do you know this song? Can you identify the link between the song line and the lesson?* (needs). Encourage sts to answer and allow them to sing the song line if they want to. Then ask: *What do you think this song is about? What does the singer really need?* Encourage them to discuss in pairs. When sts are ready, have them share their opinions with the whole class. In case they haven't figured it out, explain that the song is about a girl who feels guilty for having cheated on her boyfriend and is asking to be with him one last time before letting him go. So, what she needs is one last time with her boyfriend. Finally, ask: *Do you know someone like this?* and encourage sts to answer and share their opinions/experiences.

Writing 3

Song line: Louder, louder, And we'll run for our lives, I can hardly speak I understand.
Song: *Run*, released in 2004
Artist: Snow Patrol (Irish / Scottish)
Lesson link: practice of *louder*; speaking skills
Notes: This song was Snow Patrol's first hit in the UK. Gary Lightbody, the band's lead singer, said in an interview that he wrote the song while he was recovering in his small room near Hillhead after he had fallen down the stairs.

As sts arrive at class, ask them not to open their books. When all sts arrive, put them into teams of four or five and explain that they will play *Telephone* with a sentence that you will whisper to the teams. Do not tell sts that the sentence you are going to whisper is a song line, or this can make the task much easier for sts who know the song. Then start whispering the song line to the teams clearly and slowly, but at a natural pace. Do not repeat it. Encourage all sts to quickly write down what they hear on a piece of paper before whispering it to the next, so that you can track the miscommunication points later on. When the sentence gets to the final student in each team, they must write what they heard on the board for comparison. Finally, ask: *Do you know this sentence? Where have you seen or heard it?* Encourage sts to answer, and if they know the song line, allow them to sing it if they want to.

4.1

Song line: No time for losers, 'Cause we are the **champions of the world**.
Song: *We Are the Champions*, released in 1977
Artist: Queen (British)
Lesson link: sports
Notes: While this song did not reach number 1 in any major market on its release, it was voted the world's favorite song in 2005, and after scientific research in 2011, it was concluded that *We Are the Champions* was the catchiest pop song in history. It is used as an anthem at sports matches and was the 1994 FIFA world cup theme song.

Before sts arrive, write the song line from p. 43 on the board with all the vowels missing. Leave enough space between letters and words so sts can take turns coming to the board in order to complete it. The song line should look like this: *N_ t_m_ f_r l_s_rs, c_ _s_ w_ _r_ th_ ch_mp_ _ns _f th_ w_rld*. Before sts open their books, explain that this is a famous song line that has a link with the topic of the lesson they will work on today, sports. But make sure they realize that the version you wrote on the board has all the vowels missing and they will have to complete it. Then have sts work in pairs and give them a few minutes to complete it. Don't allow them to check their books. When they're ready, have volunteers come to the board to complete one or two words at a time. Finally, ask: *Do you know this song?* and encourage them to sing that part aloud.

4.2

Song line: Heal the world, Make it a better place, For you and for me, And the entire human race.
Song: *Heal the World*, released in 1991
Artist: Michael Jackson (American)
Lesson link: making the world a better place
Notes: This song was written and produced by Michael Jackson. It was criticized at the time, because it was considered too similar to the USA for Africa single, *We Are the World*, which Michael Jackson co-wrote. In 2001, Michael said in an interview that this song, which was about man's inhumanity to his fellow man, was the song he was most proud of having written.

Songs

After **2E** (**Make it personal**), have sts read the song line at the top of p. 47 and ask: *Do you know this song?* Encourage sts to answer and sing the song line if they want to. Next, ask: *Can you identify the link between the song line and the lesson?* and have sts work in pairs to scan the lesson and identify the link. When they are ready, have them share their ideas. Hopefully, if they manage to understand the song line, they will be able to link Nobel Peace Prize winner Malala Yousafzai, the videos and the **Make it personal** activity to the idea of healing the world and making it a better place for all of us, as the song line puts it.

4.3

Song line: Filled with all the strength I found, There's nothing I **can't** do! I need to know now, know now, **Can** you love me again?
Song: *Love Me Again*, released in 2013
Artist: John Newman (British)
Lesson link: can ⊖, ⊕, ❓
Notes: This song was written by John Newman in attempt to get back with his girlfriend after cheating on her, but according to the singer, the attempt didn't go as well as planned. One thing that makes Newman very proud is the fact that the song features on the FIFA 14 video game soundtrack, as he's a massive soccer and FIFA video game fan himself.

Before the class, write the song line on the board, exchanging *can't* and *can*. It should look like this: *Filled with all the strength I found, There's nothing I **can** do! I need to know now, know now, **Can't** you love me again?* As sts arrive, do not let them open their books. Start the class by having sts read the song line on the board and ask: *Do you know this song?* Encourage them to sing it if they do. Next, ask: *Is there anything different between the song line that's on the board and the song you know?* Have sts discuss in pairs to find the two differences. Explain that these two mistakes are not really language mistakes, because you can say what's written on the board, but they are not what the actual lyrics say. Since the differences are subtle for sts at this level, if they have difficulty finding the two differences from the original song, allow them to open their books to p. 49 to compare.

4.4

Song line: Oh, oh, oh, Sweet child o' mine, Oh, oh, oh, Sweet love o' mine.
Song: *Sweet Child o' Mine*, released in 1988
Artist: Guns N' Roses (American)
Lesson link: possessive pronouns
Notes: This song was Guns N' Roses' only number one hit in the U.S. This was partly thanks to the success of the video, which depicts the band rehearsing with their girlfriends and one member's dog on set. The video was a success on the MTV channel, which helped its airplay on mainstream radio.

After section **3** (**Grammar**) have sts look at the song line and ask: *Can you identify the link between the song line and the lesson?* At this point, expect sts to notice the possessive pronoun *mine* in the song line. Then write *o'* on the board and ask: *Do you know what this means?* Encourage sts to guess and explain that this is an informally abbreviated form of the preposition *of*. Next, write a few more examples of the same structure that's in the song line, using *of + possessive pronoun*, such as: *She's a friend of mine.* (meaning one of my friends) and *He's a student of hers.* (meaning one of her students) and explain that, although this is a structure they don't use in their L1, in English it is commonly used.

4.5

Song line: You **can't** always get what you want. But if you try sometimes, yeah, you might find you get what you need.
Song: *You Can't Always Get What You Want*, released in 1969
Artist: The Rolling Stones (British)
Lesson link: can't
Notes: This song was first recorded by the Rolling Stones in 1968, in the sessions for *Beggars Banquet*, but it didn't make the cut to that album. It was then released one year later in *Let It Bleed*. The voices of the 60 kids from the London Bach Choir were double-tracked, so there seems to be even more than 60 children singing in the recording. When the choir found out the name of the album, and that there was a song about a serial killer in it (*Midnight Rambler*), they tried removing their name from it.

Before **ID in Action**, have sts read the song line and ask: *Do you know this song? Can you sing this part?* Encourage sts to answer and sing it if they know it. Then ask: *What do you think this song is about?* (It's about always wanting more, no matter what you get.) Have sts work in pairs to discuss their ideas about the song. Allow them to use their devices to search the web for more information about the song and its lyrics. Monitor and help where necessary. When the pairs are ready, have them share the information they found about the song with the class.

Writing 4

Song line: Sweet **home** Alabama, Where the skies are so blue. Sweet home Alabama, Lord, I'm coming home to you.
Song: *Sweet Home Alabama*, released in 1974
Artist: Lynyrd Skynyrd (American)
Lesson link: homes
Notes: This song is about the state of Alabama and was written in response to two Neil Young songs, *Alabama* and *Southern Man*, which accuse people in the southern U.S. states of racism and slavery. It has since been used in tourism campaigns for the state and as a slogan on license plates.

Before students arrive at class, write the song line from the top of p. 87 on the board with the vowels missing. It should look like this: *Sw__t h_m_ _l_b_m_, Wh_r_ th_ sk__s _r_ s_ bl__.* When all sts are in class, have them work in pairs to complete the song line with the missing vowels. Explain that this is a line of a very well-known song that has a link with the lesson they are about to study. Ask them not to open their books while they complete the song line. Finally, have volunteers come to the board to complete the missing vowels and ask: *What is the link between the song line and the lesson? Do you know this song? Can you sing it?* Encourage sts to answer and sing the song line a little (or more) if they want to.

Review 2

Song line: California girls, we're undeniable, Fine, fresh, fierce, we got it on lock, West Coast represent, now put your hands up.
Song: *California Gurls*, released in 2010
Artist: Katy Perry (American) feat. Snoop Dogg (American)
Lesson link: Californian girls' lifestyle
Notes: Katy Perry says this song is an ode to fun in the sun, and it is perfect for summertime. The singer says she wrote this song about California after she was inspired by Jay-Z's song *Empire State of Mind*, where he sings about his home city, New York.

When you finish the **Review** lesson, have sts read the song line at the top of p. 57 and ask: *What is this song about?* (the perceived way of life in California). Encourage them to answer. Then ask: *What is the link between this song line and this lesson?* Have sts scan the lesson for a link with the song line. Hopefully they will be able to match the theme of the song line with the text about Cristina Valenzuela, a surfer in

Songs

California, in **Skills practice** activity **E**. Finally, ask: *Do you like the Californian lifestyle? Would you like to have a lifestyle like this? Why (not)?* and encourage sts to share their opinions.

5.1

🎵 **Song line:** **There's** nothing you can't do, Now you're in New York, These streets will make you feel brand new, Big lights will inspire you.
Song: *Empire State of Mind (Part II) Broken Down*, released in 2009
Artist: Alicia Keys (American)
Lesson link: *there's / are*, public places
Notes: This song was a second version of the original track, performed by Jay-Z and featuring Alicia Keys, named *Empire State of Mind*. Keys recorded it because she wanted to see how the song would sound if it was just sung by her, showing how she personally felt about New York City.

Before sts arrive, write the song line on the board with a few mistakes for sts to spot. It could be something like this: **There** nothing you **can** do, Now **you** in New York. Depending on the level of the class, you may choose to highlight where the mistakes are, like in the example, but it gets more challenging if you don't. When all sts are in class, have them read the song line on the board and ask: *Do you know what this is?* Encourage them to answer and explain that this is a song line of a famous song that has a link to the lesson they're about to study, but there are three mistakes in it that they need to spot (*There's*, *can't*, *you're*). Have sts work in pairs to spot and correct the mistakes. Monitor and help where necessary. When they are ready, have them present their corrected versions. Finally, encourage them to sing it aloud if they know it. **Note:** It could be interesting to revisit the song line after they have studied section **2** (**Grammar**) in order to ask which of the three mistakes they corrected has a link to the lesson. At this stage they should be able to identify that the mistake that was related to the lesson was *There's*.

5.2

🎵 **Song line:** **I don't mind spending every day**, Out on your corner in the pouring rain, Look for the girl with the broken smile.
Song: *She Will Be Loved*, released in 2002
Artist: Maroon 5 (American)
Lesson link: *love / like / not mind / hate* + verb *-ing*
Notes: This song is most well known for its music video, which is about a love triangle between a girl, her boyfriend, and her mother. It parallels the girl's relationship with her mother's unhappy one, and the girl's boyfriend falls in love with the mother.

Right after section **2** (**Grammar**), have sts read the song line and ask: *Do you know this song line? Can you sing it?* Encourage sts to answer and sing the song line if they know it. Next, ask: *How many words ending in -ing can you identify in the song line?* (two). Encourage sts to answer. Then have them work in pairs and ask: *Do these two words have the same linguistic function in this song line?* (No, the first one is used as a verb with infinitive meaning, the other is used as an adjective.) Finally, ask: *Which one has direct link to what we have just studied in this lesson?* Expect sts to identify a lesson link with "… don't mind spending …"

5.3

🎵 **Song line:** Dance the night away, Live your life and stay young one the floor.
Song: *On the Floor*, released in 2011
Artist: Jennifer Lopez (American) feat. Pitbull (American)
Lesson link: vacation activities, dancing
Notes: A global success and one of the best-selling singles of all time, this song was inspired by Lopez' Latin roots. It brought together two sides of her career—dancing and singing.

Before the class, search the Internet for a clip of the song where you can get just the song line to play to sts. When sts arrive, do not let them open their books just yet and explain that you will play a clip of a song (just the part with the song line), and they will have to write what they hear on a piece of paper. Play the song line clip two or three times for sts to write it down. When they're ready, have them exchange their piece of paper with a partner and correct their partner's work, as they believe it should be. Next, have sts present their versions of the song line and correct the activity with the whole class. Finally, ask: *Do you like dancing when you're on vacation? What other fun activities do you like doing on vacation?* Encourage sts to share their opinions and ideas with the whole class.

5.4

🎵 **Song line:** Hey Jude, **don't take it bad**, **take** a sad song, and **make** it better. **Remember** to let it into your heart, then you can start to make it better.
Song: *Hey Jude*, released in 1968
Artist: The Beatles (British)
Lesson link: imperatives
Notes: This song was originally written by Paul McCartney as *Hey Jules*, as a way of comforting John Lennon's son, Julian Lennon because of his parents' divorce. But Julian only learned about this from Paul in 1987, when he ran into the former Beatle at the hotel both were staying in New York.

When you finish Lesson **5.4**, have sts read the song line and ask: *Do you know this song? Can you sing this bit?* Encourage them to answer and sing the song line if they want to. Next, ask: *Can you identify the link of the song with the lesson?* (imperatives) and have sts work in pairs to scan the lesson pages and find out the link of the song line with the lesson. Then, ask: *How many imperative structures can you find in this song line?* (four). Finally, encourage sts to use their devices to search the web for more famous lyrics containing imperatives/commands/orders, and have them share their findings with the whole class.

5.5

🎵 **Song line:** In my **place**, in my **place**. Were lines that I couldn't change, And I was **lost**, oh yeah, I was **lost**.
Song: *In My Place*, released in 2002
Artist: Coldplay (British)
Lesson link: directions
Notes: This song was written collaboratively by all members of Coldplay, and because of this they found it hard to agree on how the song should sound when recording it. The video is very simple, showing the band performing the song in a large empty room.

Before **ID in Action**, have sts read the song line at the top of p. 67, and ask: *Is the verb lost used in this song line in a figurative or literal meaning?* Encourage sts to analyze the song line and help them notice that it is safe to assume that the composer is probably using the word *lost* in a figurative meaning, as opposed to geographically lost, because of the first part (*In my place, in my place*). Next, ask: *Can you tell us about a situation where you have been actually lost? Where were you? How did you find the way?* Have sts work in pairs or threes and describe any situations where they were lost. Then, have them report their situations back to the class and ask: *Which is the most interesting one?* Finally, explain that they will now learn about giving and following directions in English, which might prevent them from getting lost in future situations.

Songs

Writing 5

🎵 **Song line:** Round my hometown, Memories are fresh, Round my hometown, Ooh the people I've met, Are the wonders of my world.
Song: *Hometown Glory*, released in 2007
Artist: Adele (British)
Lesson link: cities
Notes: Adele says that this song was written when she was 18, in about 10 minutes, right after her mother tried to convince her to move out of London for university. The singer says that she sang the song to her mother as a protest and said, "This is why I'm staying." The fact that this song was featured on the 2008 season finale of the *Gray's Anatomy* TV series helped Adele take her hits to the U.S.

Before starting **Writing 5**, have sts read the song line at the top of p. 68 and ask: *Do you know this song?* Encourage sts to answer and sing it if they want to. Next, ask: *Can you identify the link between the song line and the lesson?* (cities). Encourage sts to scan the lesson and answer. Then explain that this song was written when Adele was 18 and her mother tried to convince her to move out of London to study. She wanted to let her mother know how important it was for her was to live in London, so she wrote the song. Next, have sts work in pairs to search the web for more songs that talk about good things in a city. When they're ready, have the pairs share their findings. Finally, ask: *What we can learn about the cities in these songs? What is your favorite city?* and encourage sts to share their opinions and engage in the discussion.

6.1

🎵 **Song line:** Your sugar, Yes, please, Won't you come and put it down on me?
Song: *Sugar*, released in 2014
Artist: Maroon 5 (American)
Lesson link: countable and uncountable nouns
Notes: The video for this song was inspired by the 2005 film *Wedding Crashers*. The band contacted grooms ahead of their weddings asking if they could perform their new song as their first dance song, which would be a surprise to the bride and other guests. These performances were filmed and make up the music video.

Search the web in advance for a video / audio clip of the song line on p. 73. When sts arrive, do not let them open their books. Before starting lesson **6.1**, explain to sts that you will play a clip of the song line and they have to write down what they hear. Next, play the song line clip and have sts write it down. Play twice or three times if necessary. When they are ready, have volunteers read the song line they wrote down, and allow them to open their books and read the song line at the top of p. 73 to compare with what they wrote. Finally, have sts quickly browse the picture of the food items on p. 72 to find the link between the song line and the picture. They should be able to identify the sugar cubes in the fridge.

6.2

🎵 **Song line:** You want **a piece of** me, I'm Mrs. Lifestyles of the rich and famous, You want **a piece of** me.
Song: *Piece of Me*, released in 2007
Artist: Britney Spears (American)
Lesson link: *a piece of*
Notes: Britney used this song as a response to the media's portrayal and scrutiny of her private life. In this song she claims that she's still famous and successful even with the constant media harassment and the challenge of raising kids.

After section **1** (Vocabulary), have sts read the song line at the top of p. 75 and ask: *Do you know this song?* Encourage them to share their background knowledge about the song and sing it if they want to. Next, ask: *What portion expression is used in the lyrics?* Expect sts to identify the expression *a piece of*, and ask: *Is she talking about food? What is she talking about?* (She's talking about herself using the expression with a figurative meaning.) Then ask: *Which items of food can take the same portion expression as the lyrics?* Have sts work in pairs to discuss some items of food that can be fractioned using *a piece of*. Lead students to notice that we can use *a piece of* with most solid food items, even if the most common expression for some might not be this one. For example, we can break *a slice of* bread into small *pieces of* bread and refer to each of them as *a piece of* bread.

6.3

🎵 **Song line:** All I'm askin', (ooh) Is for **a little** respect when you come home (just a little bit).
Song: *Respect*, released in 1967
Artist: Aretha Franklin (American)
Lesson link: quantifiers
Notes: This R&B classic demands respect towards women. Coming at a time where women in America were taking part in the Civil Rights Movement but not receiving any recognition, this song became an anthem for feminism and black rights.

Before section **2** (**Grammar**), have sts close their books. Write the following examples on the board (or others you may prefer) using the word *little* with different meanings: 1) I have **a little** kid. 2) She just needs **a little** time. 3) They have just **a little** money. 4) We live in **a little** house by the lake. 5) Is that the sport we play with **a little** ball? 6) There's just **a little** milk left on the fridge. Then ask: *Does the expression* **a little** *mean the same in all these examples?* Have sts work in pairs to analyze the examples you wrote on the board, compare the uses of *a little* in them, and then have them share their answers with the class. They should be able to identify that examples 1, 4, and 5 use *a little* referring to size, whereas examples 2, 3, and 6 use it referring to quantity. Next, have sts read the song line at the top of p. 77, and ask: *What about the song line, does* **a little respect** *refer to size or quantity?* Help sts notice that, the way it is used in the song line, *a little* refers to quantity, not size. Finally, explain that in the Grammar section of this lesson they will learn that, when combined with uncountable nouns, *a little* refers to a small quantity.

6.4

🎵 **Song line:** But she said where d'you wanna go? **How much** you wanna risk? I'm not looking for somebody, With some superhuman gifts.
Song: *Something Just Like This*, released in 2017
Artist: The Chainsmokers (American) and Coldplay (British)
Lesson link: *how much* vs. *how many*
Notes: The lyric video for this song has over 1 billion views on YouTube and has an outer-space theme to it. This song was used as the theme song for the 2017 NCAA basketball tournament in the United States.

Before sts arrive, write the song line from p. 79 on the board, but instead of *how much*, use *how many* to see if sts can spot that mistake. The song line on the board should look like this: *But she said where d'you wanna go? How many you wanna risk? I'm not looking for somebody, With some superhuman gifts*. When sts arrive, ask: *Do you know this song? Can you sing this bit?* Encourage them to sing it if they know it. Then ask: *Can you spot any mistakes in the lyrics?* If sts know the song, they might be able to identify the mistake, even if they cannot explain why it has to be *how much* and not *how many*. Finally, explain to sts that, in this lesson, they will learn that we use *how much* to ask about the quantity of uncountable nouns and *how many* to ask about the quantity of countable nouns. **Note:** Even though this is not directly connected to the lesson, since the structure appears twice in the song line, you could ask students *What does* **wanna** *mean?* to check if they know that *wanna* is the informal combination of *want to*.

Songs

6.5

Song line: I am sitting in the morning, At the diner on the corner, I am waiting at the counter, For the man to pour the coffee.
Song: *Tom's Diner*, released in 1987
Artist: Suzanne Vega (American)
Lesson link: placing an order
Notes: The titular diner of this song is Tom's Restaurant in New York City, where Vega spent time. The song was written in this restaurant and is based on the idea of someone seeing their life through a pane of glass.

Before starting **ID in Action**, have sts close their books, and explain that you will play *Telephone* with them using a song line. Depending on sts' level, you may have to break the song line up into four pieces—1) *I am sitting in the morning*, 2) *At the diner on the corner*, 3) *I am waiting at the counter*, 4) *For the man to pour the coffee*—so sts can understand and memorize the chunks better than they would if you whispered the whole song line in one go. After playing *Telephone* with each part of the song line, write them on the board. When you have the four pieces together, have sts read it aloud and allow them to open their books to check and compare with the actual song line at the top of p. 81. Then ask: *Which part of the song line (1–4) was the most difficult for you to understand?* Encourage sts to share their opinions. Finally, ask: *Can you identify the link of the song line with the lesson?* (ordering at a restaurant) and have them answer.

Writing 6

Song line: Have some more chicken, have some more pie, It doesn't matter if it's broiled or fried, Just eat it.
Song: *Eat It*, released in 1984
Artist: Weird Al Yankovic (American)
Lesson link: food
Notes: This song was Al Yankovic's first big hit. It is a parody of Michael Jackson's *Beat It*, and it talks about an eater that has to work on his table manners. The singer said in a later interview that he was surprised to have received Michael Jackson's permission, because in 1984 Jackson was the King of Pop.

Before the class, search for two video clips: one of Yankovic's song (*Eat It*) containing the song line, and one of Jackson's original version (*Beat It*) containing the equivalent part. After activity A in Writing 6, have sts read the song line at the top of p. 82 and ask: *Do you know this song?* Encourage them to answer. Most sts probably won't associate the song line to the parody of Michael Jackson's *Beat It*, so play the clip and ask: *What about now?* Encourage sts to answer, and make sure they understand that Weird Al's song is a food related parody of *Beat It*. Next, ask: *Can you remember the lyrics for the original song line?* and have sts work in pairs or threes to try and come up with the original version. When they're ready, have them share their versions with the whole class and write them on the board. Finally, play Jackson's original version (just the part of the song line which is: "*Showing how funky and strong is your fight, It doesn't matter who's wrong or right, Just beat it.*"), twice or three times if necessary for sts to check.

Review 3

Song line: There's a mountain top that I'm dreaming of, If you need me you know where I'll be, I'll be riding shotgun underneath the hot sun.
Song: *Shotgun*, released in 2018
Artist: George Ezra (British)
Lesson link: there is
Notes: This song was one of the first songs written for the album *Staying at Tamara's*. He wrote this song after spending some time in a hotel garden halfway up the Montjuïc hill in Barcelona, looking at the people around doing their own thing. The name of the album comes from the fact that, while in Barcelona, George stayed at an apartment owned by a woman called Tamara.

Before starting **Review 3**, have sts read the song line at the top of p. 85 and ask: *Do you know this song?* Encourage sts to answer and sing the song line if they want to. Next, ask: *Can you identify the link between the song line and the lesson?* and have sts work in pairs to scan the review pages and identify the link (*There is*). When the pairs are ready, have volunteers share their answers. Make sure sts understand what the link is, and ask the pairs to search the web for more songs with *There is* or *There are*, preferably with videos where they can hear the expressions. Allow sts a few minutes to search, and have them share their findings with the whole class. If they're playing videos, remind them to play just the part of the video where the requested chunk of language can be heard.

7.1

Song line: We're going home, If we make it or we don't, we won't be alone, When I see your light shine, I know I'm home.
Song: *We're Goin Home*, released in 2018
Artist: Vance Joy (Australian)
Lesson link: homes
Notes: This song was written in 2015 while the singer was on tour in the U.S., opening shows for Taylor Swift. Vance Joy says the song is about "stepping into the unknown and finding out what you're made of." He explains that this is kind of how he felt when opening shows for Taylor Swift during that tour, which according to him was a bit scary.

Before sts arrive, write the song line from the top of p. 87 on the board with all vowels missing. It should look like this: W_'_ _ g_ _ng h_m_, _f w_ m_k_ _t _r n_t, w_ w_n't b_ _l_n_, Wh_n _ s_ _ y_ _r l_ght sh_n_, _ kn_w _'m h_m_ As sts arrive, ask them not to open their books. When all sts are in class, have them read the sentence that you wrote on the board, and explain that this is the song line that's on p. 87 of their books but with all the vowels missing. Have sts work in pairs to complete all the missing vowels in the song line. Remind them not to open their books or use their devices to search the web for the lyrics. When the pairs are ready, have volunteers come to the board to complete the song line. Finally, read it aloud and ask: *Do you know this song?* Encourage sts to answer and sing the song line if they want to.

7.2

Song line: 'Cause we were just kids when we fell in love, Not knowing what it **was**, I will not give you up this time.
Song: *Perfect*, released in 2017
Artist: Ed Sheeran (British)
Lesson link: past of verb *be*
Notes: This is a waltz-time love song that Ed Sheeran wrote to his girlfriend, who happens to be an old friend from school, when she was living in New York. In September 2017, he recorded a new version of the song in a duet with Beyoncé. The new version was renamed *Perfect Duet*.

Songs

When you finish lesson **7.2**, have sts read the song line at the top of p. 89 in pairs and ask: *Do you know this song? What is the link between this song line and the lesson?* Encourage sts to discuss and find out that the link is the past of verb *be* (*were/was*) and allow them to sing the song line if they know it and want to. Next, ask: *Were you in love when you were a kid?* Have sts discuss their experiences in pairs. Monitor and help as necessary. When they're ready, have them share their stories with the whole class. Then, ask: *Do you still have any kind of connection/relationship with that person today?* and encourage sts to answer.

7.3

♪ **Song line:** But here I am, **Next to** you, The sky's more blue, **in** Malibu.
Song: *Malibu*, released in 2017
Artist: Miley Cyrus (American)
Lesson link: prepositions of place
Notes: *Malibu* marks Miley Cyrus' move away from her more controversial material towards a more acceptable image. It is about the renewal of her relationship with Liam Hemsworth, and the cover artwork is of Miley with her engagement ring on.

Search the web in advance for a video / audio clip of the song line so you can play it to sts in class. Before starting section **3** (**Grammar**), have sts close their books and explain that you will dictate the song line at the top of p. 91. Do not tell them that you will make mistakes on purpose while dictating the song line. Use the following line, instead of the actual song line: "*But here I am, **Close** to you, The sky's more blue **on Honolulu**.*" When you finish dictating it, have a volunteer write on the board what they understood. Next, play the video/audio clip of the song line and have sts compare what they hear with what they have just written on the board. Encourage them to notice that you have made three intentional mistakes while dictating it. Have them identify the three mistakes, and ask: *Which one is not just a mistake in the lyrics, but also a grammatical one?* (The preposition *on* used with a place/city/country, when it should be *in*.) Finally, explain to sts that, in this next Grammar section, they will learn more about prepositions of place.

7.4

♪ **Song line:** Was it all in my fantasy? **Where are** you now? Were you only imaginary? Where are you now?
Song: *Faded*, released 2015
Artist: Alan Walker (British/Norwegian)
Lesson link: verb *be* questions
Notes: Alan Walker describes this song as a "happy yet emotional song, appropriate for both sad and/or uplifting occasions." According to the DJ, the song is about searching for someone, something or somewhere lost, or just about feeling lost.

Before the class, search the web for a clip of the song *Faded* by Alan Walker in which we can hear the song line. As sts arrive at class, ask them not to open their books. When all sts are in class, explain that you will play a clip of song line and they should write down what they hear. Play the audio or video twice or three times, if necessary, so sts can write down what they hear. Next, have volunteers come to the board to write parts of the song line. Have each volunteer write one of the questions that make up the song line. Then have sts open their books and read the song line at the top of p. 93 to compare with what they wrote on the board. Finally, ask: *What were the most difficult words to understand?* and encourage sts to answer.

7.5

♪ **Song line:** This is an **invitation** across the nation, A chance for folks to meet, There'll be laughing and singing, And music swinging, Dancing in the streets.
Song: *Dancing in the Street*, released in 1964
Artist: Martha and the Vandellas
Lesson link: making an invitation
Notes: This song, which was originally produced as a dance song, was inspired by people in the streets playing in the water from fire hydrants in Detroit. It was later used in civil rights demonstrations, although the writers maintained that it had not been intended for those purposes.

At any stage during the lesson, have sts read the song line at the top of p. 95 and ask: *What do you think is happening? What kind of event is the invitation in the song line for?* (Probably a huge music festival in the streets of a city.) Have sts work in pairs to discuss what they believe the song is about. Encourage them to imagine and describe the event to which the song line is "inviting the whole nation." When sts are ready, have them share their ideas with the whole class, and ask: *Would you like to go to any of the described imaginary events?* Encourage them to share their opinions.

Writing 7

♪ **Song line:** If we took a holiday yeah, Took some time to celebrate, Just one day out of life, It would be so nice.
Song: *Holiday*, released in 1983
Artist: Madonna (American)
Lesson link: vacations
Notes: This song was Madonna's first hit. It was written by Curtis Hudson and Lisa Stevens, who were part of a pop group called Pure Energy. An interesting fact about the song is that before being offered to Madonna, it was first offered to Mary Wilson, a former member of The Supremes, but she refused it.

Before starting **Writing 7**, have sts read the song line at the top of p. 96 and ask: *Do you know this song?* Encourage sts to answer and sing the song line if they want to. Next, ask: *What is the song about?* and have sts answer. Make sure they understand that the song line is about taking some time to escape from everyday life and celebrate. Then have sts work in pairs or threes and discuss their ideal way of escaping from everyday life. Go around the classroom to engage in sts' discussions and help where necessary. When the groups are ready, encourage sts to share their thoughts with the whole class. Next, ask: *Do you look at online reviews to choose what to do and where to stay when you travel?* and encourage sts to share their experiences and opinions. Explain that in this lesson they will learn how to write an online review.

8.1

♪ **Song line:** So wake me up when it's all over, when I'm wiser and I'm older. All this time I was finding myself and I didn't know I was lost.
Song: *Wake Me Up*, released in 2013
Artist: Avicii (Swedish)
Lesson link: simple past
Notes: This is a folktronica genre song, blending together aspects of EDM, soul, and country music. Aloe Blacc wrote the lyrics for this song, but he wasn't credited on the track as an artist. Blacc released a separate acoustic version of it later.

After section **2** (**Grammar**), have sts read the song line at the top of p. 99 and ask: *Do you know this song line? Can you sing it?* Encourage sts to answer and sing the song line if they want to. Next, ask: *What link can you find between the song line and the lesson?* Expect sts to notice that the structure *didn't know* in the song line is in the simple past negative. Then ask: *Can you identify the other verb that's in the simple past in this*

Songs

song line? (*was*). However, make sure sts notice that *was* is first used as part of a past continuous structure (verb *be* in the past + main verb -*ing*) (*was finding*).

8.2

🎵 **Song line:** I **knew** it when I **met** him, I loved him when I **left** him, Got me feelin' like, Ooh, and then I **had** to tell him, I **had** to go, Havana.
Song: *Havana*, released in 2017
Artist: Camila Cabello (Cuban)
Lesson link: irregular past verbs
Notes: Cabello co-wrote this song with Pharell Williams. The song is a tribute to Havana, the capital city of the singer's home country, Cuba. Cabello says that this song is more upbeat than most of her songs, which, according to her, are more emotional.

Before sts arrive, write on the board "*I* **knowed** *it when I* **meeted** *him, I loved him when I* **leaved** *him, Got me feelin' like, Ooh, and then I* **haved** *to tell him, I* **haved** *to go, Havana*". As sts arrive, ask them not to open their books. When all sts are in class, ask: *Can you recognize this song line?* Encourage sts to answer and sing if they want to. Next, explain that there are five mistakes in it and ask: *Can you spot the mistakes?* Have sts work in pairs to try and find out what the mistakes are. Explain that they should not open their books or use their devices to check the web for the actual lyrics. When they're ready, have volunteers come to the board to correct the song line. Check and correct where necessary. Since they haven't yet worked with the simple past of irregular verbs, explain that these five verbs are irregular, so they don't take the –*ed* ending like the regular ones. Finally, tell sts that, in this lesson, they will learn about irregular verbs in the simple past.

8.3

🎵 **Song line:** Oops!... **I did it** again, I **played** with your heart, **got lost** in the game, Oh baby, baby.
Song: *Oops!... I Did It Again*, released in 2000
Artist: Britney Spears (American)
Lesson link: simple past
Notes: This is a pop song about someone seeing love as a game, leading people on to make them think she loves them when she doesn't. The music video is set on Mars, where an astronaut falls in love with Britney spears, who goes on to reject him.

At any time during lesson **8.3**, have sts read the song line at the top of p. 103 and ask: *Do you know this song line? What is it about?* Have sts work in pairs to discuss it for a while. When they're ready, have them share their opinions. Help sts notice that the person in the song line is probably used to playing with people's hearts and getting lost in the game because she says that she did it again. Then ask: *Are you, or do you know anyone, like her?* Encourage sts to share answers and engage in the discussion. Finally, allow them to sing the song line if they want to.

8.4

🎵 **Song line:** Right now, I'm in a state of mind, I wanna be in like all the time, Ain't got no tears left to cry.
Song: *no tears left to cry*, released in 2018
Artist: Ariana Grande (American)
Lesson link: music quiz on p. 105
Notes: This was the first track released by Ariana since the attack that killed 22 of her fans in May 2017, just outside one of her shows at the Manchester Arena in the UK. The song won Best Pop Video at the 2018 MTV Video Music Awards.

Search the web in advance for a video / audio clip of the song line so you can play it to sts in class. Before sts open their books explain that you will play a clip of the song line from this lesson and they will have to write down what they hear. Play it twice or three times if necessary, so sts can write it down. When they're ready, have volunteers write what they understood on the board. Check and correct where necessary. Finally, ask: *What activities can put you in a state of mind you wanna be in all the time?* and encourage them to answer. If necessary, help sts understand the meaning of this part of the song line by miming "a positive state of mind" and giving them your own examples of activities that usually put you in a good state of mind.

8.5

🎵 **Song line:** Help! I need somebody, Help! Not just anybody, Help! You know I need someone, Help!
Song: *Help!*, released in 1965
Artist: The Beatles (British)
Lesson link: asking for help
Notes: Lyrically, this song represents writer John Lennon's stress after the Beatles' rapid rise to fame. The song was also used for the band's film of the same name, in which they fight against an evil cult.

Before starting **ID in Action**, have sts read and sing the song line at the top of p. 107. Next, ask: *Do you think the singer/composer is desperate for help? Why? What do you think he needs help for?* Have sts discuss their ideas in pairs, before sharing them with the whole class. Encourage them to be as creative as possible, thinking of fun situations related to the song and the way the singer screams for help. After sts have shared their ideas, ask: *What about you? When do you usually ask for help?* Allow the pairs to discuss the question for a while, and, when they're ready, have them share their answers with the whole class. Finally, explain that in this lesson they will learn different ways of asking for help / favors.

Writing 8

🎵 **Song line:** This is my message to you - ou - ou, Singin': "don't worry about a thing, 'cause every little thing gonna be alright."
Song: *Three Little Birds*, released in 1977
Artist: Bob Marley and the Wailers (Jamaican)
Lesson link: *going to* vs. present continuous
Notes: This is one of Bob Marley's best-known songs. It is reportedly about three birds that used to sit next to his house. It calls for people to stop worrying about everything.

Before the class, search the web for a clip of the song, *Three Little Birds*, in which you have just the song line, so you can play it for the activity. As sts arrive at class, ask them not to open their books. When all sts are in class, explain that you will play a clip of a very famous song line and they should write down what they hear. Play the the song line twice or three times, if necessary, so sts can write it down. When they're ready, invite volunteers to come to the board to write what they heard. Next, have sts open their books to p. 108 to compare. As they do, ask: *How close did you get to the actual song line? What were the most difficult words to understand?* and encourage sts to answer.

Review 4

🎵 **Song line:** You're everything I need and more, It's written all over your face, Baby, I can feel your halo, Pray it won't fade away.
Song: *Halo*, released in 2008
Artist: Beyoncé (American)
Lesson link: Beyoncé
Notes: This song is about a love that is so strong and special that it is heavenly. It won the best song award at the 2009 MTV Europe Music Award and the 2009 Grammy for Best Female Pop Vocal Performance.

After the **Grammar and vocabulary** section in **Review 4**, have sts read the song line at the top of p. 111, and ask: *Do you know this song? Encourage them to answer and sing the song line bit if they want to.

Songs

Next, ask: *Can you identify the link between the song line and this review lesson?* (Beyoncé). Have sts work in pairs or trios to scan the review pages and find the link. **Note:** Finding the link this time might be a bit trickier for sts who don't know that this is a Beyoncé song, so maybe threes would work better than pairs. Once sts find the link between the song line and the lesson, have them share their answers, and ask: *Do you have an artist you're a big fan of, like the people in activity C? Do you go to many of this artist's concerts?* Encourage sts to share their preferences and experiences with the whole class.

9.1

♪ **Song line:** Oh, I want to get away, I wanna **fly** away, Yeah, yeah, yeah.
Song: *Fly Away*, released in 1998
Artist: Lenny Kravitz (American)
Lesson link: transportation
Notes: One of Kravitz's most successful songs, *Fly Away* earned him a Grammy. It has been used in several commercials, including ones for Peugeot, Nissan, and MSN.

As sts arrive at class, ask them not to open their books. When all sts are in class, put them into four groups and explain that you are going to whisper a song line to each of the groups for them to mime and the rest of the class to guess. You can use the following lines, or any others you wish to (note that the first one is the same as the one at the top of p. 113):

"*Oh, I want to get away, I wanna fly away …*"

"*Oh Lord, won't you buy me a Mercedes Benz? My friends all drive Porsches …*"

"*Take a backseat, Hitch-hike, And take a long ride on my motorbike*"

"*You got a fast car, I got a plan to get us out of here*"

Allow the groups to use their devices to search the web for the meaning of any unknown words and help them if necessary. Explain to sts that they can draw on the board, too, or else it could be too hard for them to mime, for example, Mercedes or Porsche. But make sure sts understand that they cannot write any letters. They can either mime or draw. Allow sts a few minutes to plan and rehearse their mime. When all groups are ready, have them take turns miming their song lines for the others to guess. Meanwhile, write the song lines on the board and ask: *Do you know these songs?* Encourage them to answer and sing the song lines if they want to. Finally, have students open their books and ask: *What's the link between the song lines on the board and the lesson?*

9.2

♪ **Song line:** I'm too hot, Call the **police** and the **fireman**, I'm too hot.
Song: *Uptown Funk*, released in 2014
Artist: Mark Ronson (British) feat. Bruno Mars (American)
Lesson link: jobs
Notes: This song is one of the bestselling singles of all time, the 5th most viewed music video on YouTube, and it won two Grammy Awards. It was heavily influenced by funk music and topped the American charts for a consecutive 14 weeks.

As sts arrive in class, ask them not to open their books. Start the class by playing *Telephone* with the song line. Explain to sts that you will whisper a sentence into one st's ear and they will then have to whisper it to the st on their right until it gets to the last student in the class. Do not tell them that this is a song line, as this will make the task a little easier for those who know the song. Next, whisper the song line at the top of p. 115 to the first st in the sequence, and let the whole process run until the song line gets to the last st in the sequence. When it does, have that st come to the board to write down what they heard, and ask the first st in the sequence: *Was that what I told you?* Have him or her answer, then have sts open their books to p. 115 and ask them to compare the actual lyrics to what they wrote on the board. Ask: *What were the most difficult words to understand and repeat?* and have them share their opinions with the whole class. Finally, ask sts: *Do you know this song? What is the link between the song line and the lesson?* (jobs), and encourage them to answer.

9.3

♪ **Song line:** **I'm gonna** swing from the chandelier, from the chandelier, **I'm gonna** live like tomorrow doesn't exist.
Song: *Chandelier*, released in 2014
Artist: Sia (Australian)
Lesson link: *going to / gonna*
Notes: This is an electropop song about the ups and downs of the life of a "party girl." The music video shows Maddie Ziegler from Dance Moms performing an interpretative dance routine.

Before the class, write the song line from the top of p. 117 on the board, but instead of writing it completely, leave the vowels out for sts to complete. It should look like this: _'m g_nn_ sw_ng fr_m th_ ch_nd_l_ _r, fr_m th_ ch_nd_l_ _r, _'m g_nn_ l_v_ l_k_ t_m_rr_w d_ _sn't _x_st. As sts arrive in class, ask them not to open their books. When all sts are in class, have them work in pairs to try and complete the song line on the board with the missing vowels. Allow them some time to do this, without opening their books. When they're ready, have volunteers come to the board to complete the missing vowels in the song line. Check and correct where necessary. Next, ask: *Do you know this song? Can you sing this bit?* and encourage sts to sing the song line if they want to. Finally, focus on the two occurrences of *gonna* + verb in the song line, and tell sts that this is an informal version of the verb tense they are about to learn in this lesson.

9.4

♪ **Song line:** Ooh, love, no **one's** ever **gonna** hurt you, love. **I'm gonna** give you all of my love. Nobody matters like you. So, rockabye baby, rockabye.
Song: *Rockabye*, released in 2016
Artist: Clean Bandit (British)
Lesson link: *going to / gonna*
Notes: This song tells the story of a single mother who tries to give her son a better life. It is about doing anything that you can to give your child a decent life, even if that means sacrificing things and going through bad times to do so.

Before the class, write the song line from the top of p. 119 on the board, with mistakes in both occurrences of future with *gonna* and another one in the verb *matter*, where it should be *matters*. The song line on the board should look like this: *Ooh, love, no one ever gonna hurt you, love. I gonna give you all of my love. Nobody matter like you. So, rockabye baby, rockabye.* As sts arrive at class, ask them not to open their books. When all sts are in class, have them read the song line that you wrote on the board and ask: *Do you know this song?* Encourage sts to answer and sing the song line if they want to. Next, ask: *Can you identify the three grammatical mistakes in it?* and have sts work in pairs to find the mistakes. When they're ready, have volunteers come to the board to correct the mistakes, one at a time. Then, have sts open their books and read the song line at the top of p. 119 to compare.

Finally, have sts flick back to p. 108 and read the song line that's at the top of that page. Encourage them to focus on the final bit (*… every little thing gonna be all right*) and ask: *Grammatically speaking, what's missing here?* Encourage sts to answer, and explain that even though Marley doesn't sing the verb *be* (is), we should always use it before *going to* or *gonna* when we use this future tense.

Songs

9.5

Song line: Lend me your ears and I'll sing a song, and I'll try not to sing out of key. Oh, I get by with a little help from my friends.
Song: *With a Little Help from My Friends*, released in 1977
Artist: Joe Cocker (British)
Lesson link: lend / borrow
Notes: Originally written by The Beatles, Cocker changed the arrangement of the song a fair amount, using different chords and a longer introduction. Both versions were included in the film *Across the Universe* (2007).

After **ID in Action**, have sts read the song line at the top of p. 121, and ask: *Do you know this song?* Encourage sts to answer and sing the song line if they want to. Next, ask: *What's the link of the song line with the lesson we have just finished?* (lend / borrow). Have sts read the song line again and scan the lesson to try and find the link. When they're ready, have volunteers share their answers. Then ask: *How can we rewrite the initial part of this song line using* **borrow** *instead of* **lend** *but keeping the same meaning?* Have students work in pairs to come up with their versions using *borrow* instead of *lend*. When they're ready, have volunteers come to the board to write their version. Check and correct where necessary. Finally, explain that in order to use *borrow*, they'd have to either use a question format (*Can I borrow your ears?*) or a future form with *will*, which they haven't seen yet (*I'll borrow your ears ...*).

Writing 9

Song line: You had a bad day, The camera don't lie, You're coming back down and you really don't mind.
Song: *Bad Day*, released in 2009
Artist: Daniel Powter (Canadian)
Lesson link: having a bad day
Notes: This song is a pop power ballad about someone having a bad day, although the lyrics have been criticized for lacking any depth. It was used a lot in the media, for example it was performed by Alvin and the Chipmunks in their movie.

At any time during **Writing 9**, have sts read the song line at the top of p. 122, and ask: *Do you know this song?* Encourage them to answer and sing the song line if they want to. Next, ask: *Can you identify the link between the song line and the lesson?* (*Having a bad day.*), and have sts scan the **Writing** lesson page to find the link. Make sure sts can identify the link between the song line and the lesson. Then, have sts read the song line again and ask: *Which grammar mistake can you identify in this song line?* Encourage sts to share their answers and make sure they understand that some artists actually use incorrect grammar structures in their lyrics, either for better rhythm—as is the case in this song—or just for style. This is what artists call *poetic license*. Finally, have sts work in pairs and use their devices to search the web for more songs with structural mistakes. When they're ready, have them share their findings with the whole class.

10.1

Song line: I feel it in my **fingers**, I feel it in my **toes**, Love is all around me, And so the feeling grows.
Song: *Love Is All Around*, released in 1995
Artist: Wet Wet Wet (British)
Lesson link: body parts
Notes: Originally performed by The Troggs, the best-known version of this song was performed by Wet Wet Wet. It features extensively in popular media, most notably in Richard Curtis' films *Four Weddings and a Funeral* and *Love Actually*.

After section **1** (**Vocabulary**), have sts read the song line at the top of p. 125, and ask: *Do you know this song?* Encourage sts to answer and allow them to sing the song line if they want to. Next, ask: *What's the link between the song line and the lesson?* (parts of the body). Allow sts to scan the lesson pages to find out and answer. Then ask: *What are the two rhyming words in this song line?* (*toes, grows*). Next, explain that they should change the word *toes* in the song line for another body part and choose a word that rhymes with it to substitute the word *grows*. Have sts work in pairs to do so and allow them to change the word *feeling*, too, if it is necessary for sense. Monitor and help when needed. When they're ready, have them read or sing their new versions of the song line. Finally, ask: *What's the most interesting new combination?* and have the class vote for the funniest / most interesting new version.

10.2

Song line: What doesn't kill you makes you **stronger**, Stand a little **taller**, Doesn't mean I'm lonely when I'm alone.
Song: *Stronger (What Doesn't Make You)*, released in 2011
Artist: Kelly Clarkson (American)
Lesson link: comparatives
Notes: The chorus for this song was inspired by a quotation from Friedrich Nietzsche and suggests that anything that you survive can be used to your advantage. It was written to promote self-empowerment.

Avoid the song line until after section **2** (**Grammar**). When you finish teaching this section, have sts close their books and explain that you will dictate a song line for them to write down. Next, dictate the song line from the top of p. 127 with mistakes in the two comparative adjectives. You should dictate *more strong* instead of *stronger* and *more tall* instead of *taller*. It should look like this: *What doesn't kill you makes you more strong, Stand a little more tall, Doesn't mean I'm lonely when I'm alone*. Don't tell sts that you are dictating the song line with mistakes. If necessary, say it twice for sts to get all of the words. When they're ready, have volunteers come to the board and write what they heard. Check to see if they've got it exactly as you dictated it. Then ask: *Based on what we've just learned, is the song line on the board grammatically correct?* Have sts analyze it and point out what's wrong with it. Finally, have them open their books again to check the correct version at the top of p. 127 and ask: *Do you know this song?* Encourage them to answer and allow them to sing it if they want to.

10.3

Song line: Don't give up, I won't give up, Don't give up, no no no, I'm free to be the greatest, I'm alive, I'm free to be the greatest here tonight, the greatest.
Song: *The Greatest*, released in 2016
Artist: Sia (Australian)
Lesson link: superlatives
Notes: Part of the album *This Is Acting* (2016), this song is Sia's anthem about refusing to give up. The Australian singer likes singing about perseverance and resilience and has used the same theme in other songs, too, including *Unstoppable*, from the same album.

Before starting lesson **10.3**, have sts read the song line at the top of p. 129, and ask: *Do you know this song?* Encourage sts to answer and sing it if they want to. Next, have sts work in pairs, and ask: *What's the link between this song line and the lesson we are about to study?* (superlatives). Allow the pairs a few minutes to read the song line again and scan the lesson pages to find the link. They should be able to identify the structure *the greatest* in the song line and then identify similar structures in the grammar box and other places around lesson **10.3**. Then teach the lesson, and right after completing the grammar box in section **2** (**Grammar**), have sts read the song line again, and ask: *Which of the rules from the grammar box (a, b, c, d) explain the formation of the superlative in this song line?* At this stage sts should be able to identify rule a as the explanation for the formation of *the greatest*.

Songs

10.4

🎵 **Song line:** Tropical the **island** breeze, all of **nature wild and free**, This is where I long to be, La Isla Bonita.
Song: *La Isla Bonita*, released in 1986
Artist: Madonna (American)
Lesson link: nature
Notes: This song was Madonna's first Latino pop song; in the music video, she plays two different characters—a pious Catholic and a flamenco dancer. The song is about a beautiful island, and according to Madonna, the beauty of Latino people.

After section **1** (**Reading**), have sts read the song line and ask: *Can you sing this song line?* Encourage sts to sing it if they want to. Next, ask: *What is the kind of place that the singer probably prefers going to?* (beaches, islands, tropical places with a lot of nature). Have sts answer and ask: *What about you? Are you like the singer? What kind of places do you most like to visit?* Have sts work in pairs and allow them a few minutes to discuss their opinions and preferences. When sts are ready, have them share their preferences with the whole class. **Note:** If time allows, you can also ask sts to use their devices to search the web for a song line that mentions the kind of place that they most like to visit.

10.5

🎵 **Song line:** And we danced all night to **the best song** ever, We knew every line, Now I can't remember.
Song: *Best Song Ever*, released in 2013
Artist: One Direction (British)
Lesson link: superlatives
Notes: In the video for this song, One Direction play the role of a team of people trying to make the new music video, when the real One Direction hate every idea they come up with and start dancing around the office. This is mixed with shots from their movie *This Is Us*. This video won a Brit award in 2014.

Before the class, write the song line from the top of p. 132 on the board with the following five mistakes: *And weird danced on nine to the blessed song ever, We new every line, Now I can't remember.* As sts arrive at class, ask them not to open their books. When all sts are in class, point to the song line on the board and ask: *Can you identify this song?* Encourage sts to answer and allow them to sing the song line if they want to. Since the wrong words in the song line have almost the same pronunciation as the original words, sts will probably be able to sing it without even noticing the words are wrong, unless they know the song really well. Next, ask: *Is there anything wrong with this song line? Can you spot any mistakes? How many?* Have sts work in pairs to find out. Do not let them open their book or use their devices to search the web for the lyrics. When they're ready, have volunteers come to the board to correct the mistakes on the song line. Finally, have sts open their books to p. 132 to check the actual song line, and ask: *Did you manage to spot and correct all of the five mistakes?*

Writing 10

🎵 **Song line:** You're simply **the best**, **better** than all the rest, **better** than anyone I ever met.
Song: *The Best*, released in 1989
Artist: Tina Turner (American)
Lesson link: superlatives and comparatives
Notes: This song was first recorded by Bonnie Tyler in 1988, but it only became a tremendous hit with Tina Turner's version. During Turner's show celebrating the end of the 1993 F1 season, in Adelaide, the singer called F1 driver Ayrton Senna to the stage and dedicated this song to him.

Before starting **Writing 10**, have sts read the song line at the top of p. 134 and ask: *Do you know this song?* Encourage sts to answer and sing the song line if they want to. Next, ask: *What is the song line about?* and have sts answer. Make sure they understand that the song line is about someone special for the composer, someone the person who wrote the song believes to be the best person in the world. Then have sts work in pairs and encourage them to think about someone that would fit the description of the song line in their own lives. When the pairs are ready, have sts share the information they learned about their partner's best person with the whole class. Ask: *Anything curious or interesting?* Finally, have sts flick back to p. 129 and ask: *Which rule (a, b, c, d) from the grammar box explains the formation of the superlative in the song line from Writing 10?* Expect sts to identify rule d as the explanation for the formation of *the best*.

Review 5

🎵 **Song line:** Work it Harder, Make it Better, Do it Faster, Makes us Stronger, More than Ever.
Song: *Harder, Better, Faster, Stronger* released in 2001
Artist: Daft Punk (French)
Lesson link: comparatives
Notes: On this song, Daft Punk samples a 1979 song called *Cola Bottle Baby*, by Edwin Birdsong. The band also appropriated and adapted the famous line from the 70's TV show The Six Million Dollar Man: "We can rebuild him better, stronger, faster."

After the **Grammar and vocabulary** section in **Review 5**, have sts read the song line at the top of p. 137 and ask: *Do you know this song?* Encourage sts to answer and sing the song line if they want to. Next, ask: *Can you identify the link between the song line and the review lesson?* and have sts work in pairs to scan the lesson pages and find the link. Make sure students understand that the song line is filled with comparative adjectives and that this is the link. Finally, have sts flick back to p. 127 and ask: *Which rule (1, 2, 3, 4) from the Grammar box explains the formation of the comparatives in the song line from Review 5?* Make sure sts realize that rule number 1 explains the formation of *harder*, *faster*, and *stronger*, whereas rule number 4 explains the formation of *better*.